One Step from Murder

the friendly burglar

RAPIST

UPDATED EDITION
8/8/2023

the true story of the FBR

Robert J. Sadler

with foreword by

Thomas H. Covington Jr.

ONE STEP FROM MURDER: THE FRIENDLY BURGLAR-RAPIST

ISBN-10:1477432388

ISBN -13 - 978-1477432389

Website: robertjsadler.com

wordscupltorpress

Printed in the United States of America 8765432109

Book Cover Design by Robert J Sadler

Author's Photograph by
Bill Crump
billcrumpphotography.com

Bingo Jack![1]

for
my intrepid partner, Tom
and his wife, Janie

for
those who wear the badge
and never give up

to
the stalwart men and women
of the DPD Sex Crimes Unit
most particularly
Det. Lori Long Tittle & Det. Reed Dilbeck

and to
the women of Dallas
who were the prey of the FBR
(those who worried about being raped
and specifically those who were)
Tom and I never forgot you!

in
memoriam
to
Sr. Cpl Thomas Harvey Covington Jr (Ret.)
Det. John R. Landers (Ret.)
Det. Truly M. Holmes (Ret.)

and

Deputy Chief Robert O. Dixon (Ret.)
for letting us do our job
when it wasn't ours to do

THANK YOU

---

[1] **Bingo Jack!** is a congratulatory exaltation, see page 77

Author's Beginning Note:[2]

We know the exact number of rapes, attempt rapes and burglaries, etc. 'we' attributed to the FBR. After reading this book you will know what the FBR said regarding his 'frequency' and you can judge for yourself how many rapes this man committed.

The rapes detailed herein are based on what we knew; actual reported[3] rapes (and other offenses). This is a true story, however, to protect the identities of the women involved rather than including their full names—only their initials, capitalized in italics, are used, e.g.: if the complainant's name were Agatha Christie, I used *AC* or if Agatha British Christie, I used *ABC*.

Also documented is the genesis of our quest and how that beginning allowed us to reach the 'happy ending'.

Thus *One Step from Murder: the Friendly Burglar-Rapist* is *our* story of *1 Rapist, 82 Victims and 2 Cops* on a three year and three month saga of tenacity and perseverance, in defense of the citizens of Dallas Texas, to capture The Friendly Burglar-Rapist.

---

[2] I was police officer when my first wife, Susan Willsey (Sadler) Scott, and I met. She had some idea what life, living with a cop, would be like. That does not mean it was easy. I was often obdurate and focused on being a cop. Though our work schedules fit while I was a Division Analyst, that was not always the case, and even when my hours were supposed to be 'regular' they were not. I do not recall her ever complaining. She was supportive throughout my 39 month hunt for the Friendly Burglar-Rapist. And though I tried not to bring my 'work' home with me, I'm sure living with me was not easy. So, in this small space here, please allow me to thank her and remind her she was loved and appreciated. Thank you, Susan, for your love, support, encouragement and for blessing me with our wonderful son during our marriage.

[3] Quotes from actual offense reports are entered in upper and lower case lettering if that was how the Reporting Officer (RO) wrote his/her report. Where the RO used all uppercase printing, the quoted report is also included herein as all capital letters.

Foreword:
Thomas H. Covington, Jr.

Guy Marble began a series of rape offenses on November 15, 1973 and continued until Valentine's Day 1977.

The Dallas Police Department was working with the best methods of the day; follow-up, developing suspects, comparing fingerprints, and looking at prior sex offenders. This was not working. Then two men in the Central Patrol Division, Robert Sadler and I, Tom Covington, began to sort information.

Two officers, a Crime Analyst and a Crime Prevention Officer started sifting through information and stayed interested for the entire three years, tracking this rapist. Eventually we developed a method of graphs to track the rapist using only information in the offense reports.

This book will relate these offenses, these heartbreaking incidents plus some memories of the humorous events which occurred.

[Note: Excluding offense reports and offense supplements, we reviewed over 17,000 documents of various types to gain insight into preparing our method of prediction, which will be referred to at various points in the text as a "date, time and day survey". These same techniques would prove successful on numerous occasions in the future.]

Professional jealousies were not dominant, but did occur under the surface and were noticeable by these two, who were not "detectives". The idea seemed to be for the 'real' investigators: *We are the detectives. We wear suits and we solve crimes better, quicker and more completely than Perry Mason. Uniformed cops do little more than write tickets and thump heads.*

Publicity given to the Friendly Burglar Rapist (FBR) over his three-year spree opened a multitude of doors for Crime Prevention. Many thanks should go to the City of Dallas, Parkland Hospital and the Dallas County Rape Crisis Center. My wife Janie, who was a volunteer with the Dallas County Rape Crisis Center, and I, working through these organizations, gave numerous educational speeches and presentations about *rape prevention* and *what to do if*. All of this, the publicity and our efforts (both police and private), helped change the attitude of the public about the crime of rape in the 1970s.

Many, many thanks are not enough for our Division Commander, Chief Robert O. Dixon who allowed us to spend so much time working on this crime spree. He continually wanted briefings and eventually recommended our prediction system be used to deploy twenty-two officers for sixty days. Chief Dixon took us to the Patrol Bureau Commander, Chief Jim Souter, who gave us the men and time to carry out the capture. We used less than one week of that two months.

Special thanks should also go to Dr. David Paul, a London Police Surgeon, came to Dallas on a lecture tour. His presentation about the crime of rape and its effects on the perpetrator, victims and society as a whole was eye-opening. Using Dr. Paul's theory on an offender's progression from rape to murder in five steps, we demonstrated *the Friendly Burglar Rapist* was *One Step from Murder.*

Author Note: In fact, though Tom is too humble to admit it, long after I left the DPD he continued on with and improved on our prediction methodology. For example, Tom successfully plotted and predicted the movements of a burglar of video and computer equipment valued at over 3.5 million dollars and when captured, thanks to Tom, his arrest cleared over 200 offenses. Another time, a rash of safe burglaries in NE Division caught Tom's attention. Connecting them by MO and other factors he was able to predict likely targets which resulted in the arrest of a suspect who cleared 23 of those safe burglaries. These are just a few of the cases in which Tom made use of our now tried and true method of prediction; work that brought him well deserved recognition with recommendations for Officer of the Month and Officer of the Year. Oh, and Tom garnered over forty personal commendations for his actions during his career... any one of which would make one hell of a story.

Foreword:

Janie Covington

What are my memories of the three years covered in this book? I was the wife of a police officer obsessed, well, that may be too strong a word, but sometimes he was close to that. In the Seventies, as a volunteer with the Dallas Rape Crisis Center, I felt as strongly as Tom did that this guy should be caught.

I spent nights at Parkland Hospital with victims who didn't understand what had happened to them. I spent hours on the phone with husbands, brothers, fathers and other family members who wanted revenge. It was my job to listen first, advise very little – perhaps question a lot.

Eighty-two (82) FBR offenses; that is unbelievable! Not only did I believe with Tom and Robert that there was a connection between these crimes, it really did appear that one man was committing them and continuing to elude DPD detectives and seemingly get away with this crime again and again... again and again.

Tom and Robert agreed that the detectives were doing everything in the book to catch this guy, but it wasn't working so they continued to chart the crime reports by day, time and date. Some nights Tom and Robert would meet in North Dallas—just to check out the scene of the latest FBR reported offense. Sometimes to see if their prediction was right. Sometimes to see why not. Then they continued to look for patterns... and found them. Finally, they made two predictions in a row that were correct and the division commander said: "let's deploy on your next prediction." It took some time to get the manpower available when and where they wanted them. That night Tom left me home alone and went to work at midnight; it was Valentines Day.

Tom always liked code-words and nicknames, so when my phone rang in the middle of the night and Tom said, "BINGO JACK," I knew this meant that they had arrested the Friendly Burglar Rapist. For many reasons, I can tell you I was as pleased as Tom was to see an end come to the crime spree of the rapist identified as Guy Marble, Jr.

Many times since that night, over thirty years ago, a book has been discussed and now that one of the original officers has become an author, I sense the story will be told—with the good times and the bad times. The good and the bad parts of what police officers do with their time. The good and the bad relationships between departments and the men and women of the Force. The good and the bad reasons the Dallas Police Department is one of the best in the nation. Most of all, I believe Robert has captured that realism in a good story about one really bad guy and how he was finally caught.

As an adjunct to this police story; back then in our society, people more often blamed the rape victim rather than the perpetrator. Tom and I saw it as our job try to change public opinion. From the mid-70's on Tom and I did a lot of public education on the subject of rape; that rape is about violence or power, not about sex. I believe we helped, as public opinion is not so harsh today.

Epigraph

Dallas Morning News 9-13-1897
Quotes from article: **Criminal Assault Problem**[4]

"I confidently assert that right here is the school that develops the rapist. I do not believe a man becomes a full graduate in crime in a day."

"We must not remain deaf to the outcries of the one being injured nor let her oppressor escape. If we invariably punish the man who in any manner inflicts blows upon a woman severely we would have no cause to hang rapists. Let it be known that any man was sure to suffer that had in any manner struck or beaten a woman, and that day would see the end of raping and outrage."

Jas. B. Seargent

Dallas Morning News 5-24-1998[5]

Quotes from article: **Rapist to leave prison...**

"Sexual abnormalities and obsessions are hidden in a dark corner of the mind, an emotional cancer that sprouts in childhood and seldom gets treated in our society," he wrote. "The rehearsals for my crimes began in grade school, and nobody ever took enough interest to notice, to help me understand. Acting out those fantasies as a young adult was inevitable."

the **Friendly Burglar-Rapist**

---

[4] Appendix A - Newspaper Article # 36 **CRIMINAL ASSAULT PROBLEM**. [full text] *Dallas Morning News* page 3 September 13, 1897 from article dateline Orange, Texas September 9, 1897 [see website: robertjsadler.com]

[5] Appendix A- Newspaper Article #34 *Dallas Morning News* 05.24.98 (text) "**Friendly Rapist to leave...**" [see website: robertjsadler.com]

Preface

Dallas, Central Patrol Division, Beat 127
2:30 pm Thursday, November 15, 1973
Offense Number 0 (R-1)

THE RAPIST WAITED in the shadows that were growing on the east side of the Oak Lawn area's Toll House Apartments, a complex of buildings at 4316 Brown Street in Dallas, Texas. The warm winter afternoon had not quite hit the high for the day which would be 77 degrees. *PJT*, a twenty-three year-old white female who lived in #223, left her apartment, to go down to the laundry room, without locking her front door. Five minutes later she returned only to confront a "fully clothed" man in her bedroom, wearing a red ski mask over his head. *PJT* screamed and ran for the door.

The ski-masked man caught her and clamped his hands over her eyes and mouth saying, as he walked her back into the bedroom, "Everything's going to be all right, you just caught a burglar in the act." He pushed her down on the bed, gently tied her wrists to the bed with one of her belts and a bra saying, "I didn't hurt you, did I?" He shook out one of the bed pillows from its case and slipped the pillowcase over her head.

Having secured and effectively blinded his victim, he pushed himself up off the bed and pulled off his ski-mask.

She could hear him rummaging around, opening closet doors and drawers, moving items around on top of the chest and nearby tables. A few minutes later she realized he was standing over her, next to the bed, when he spoke.

"You don't have much worth stealing."

She felt him begin to unbutton her pants and she began to struggle. In a quiet voice he said, "This won't hurt one bit, there's a jar of Vaseline in the bathroom."

Three years and three months later...
Dallas, Northeast Patrol Division, Beat 256
1:00 am Monday, February 14, 1977

HIS NEXT VICTIM would be number 83 and she was somewhere up ahead. It was now Valentine's Day and the hooded figure had already been in several apartments since midnight but, as yet, had not made a choice. He was three-quarters of a mile east of Park Lane at Central Expressway (U.S. 75) and one quarter mile east of what locals called "Five-Points," the intersection created by the crossing of Park Lane and Ridgecrest Road at Fair Oaks Avenue.

He darted across Ridgecrest and jogged through the 6200 block in the apartment-rich environs of North Dallas; a location since the middle sixties that had become known as a 'single's haven'. It was 'the' apartment location of choice for bachelors attracted to its high concentration of females: stewardesses, nurses, school teachers, secretaries, waitresses, store clerks and students.

The waning sliver of the fingernail moon hung low in the clear, dark sky. It was still five and three quarter hours till the eastern sky would begin to brighten around 6:46am. Sunrise would be at 7:11am CST. With the dew point at 33 degrees and the light breeze out of the North northwest, the night's temperature was hovering around a 'comfortable' 48 degrees. Perfect weather for the inveterate jogger wearing his, now trademark, grey cotton hooded sweatshirt.

LATER WHEN THE sun did come up, and those who worked nights had gone to bed, it would be another prototypical Valentine's Day for the women of Dallas, Texas. It was Monday, so young school girls would be getting cards from shy grade school boys just discovering the opposite sex. High school boys would be working to impress their girlfriends and would-be girlfriends with cards and candy. Moms would be receiving handmade cards from their children and more adult remembrances from husbands.

Single women, not in relationships, would be longing to have a Valentine to call their own while those 'fortunate sisters' having a suitor relished their specialness, while basking in the gifts from their paramours of cards, candy, flowers, jewelry, and dinners out.

Local radio juggernaut, KVIL's morning-drive host Ron Chapman, would likely riff on what a banner day it would be for Hallmark cards—and might have segued into his next tune, with electric guitar notes in the background—saying, *for all of Cupid's captives to the naïveté's of love, Tonight's The Night* as the gravely voiced Rod Stewart sang: *stay away from my window*

/ stay away from my back door too / disconnect the telephone line / relax baby and draw that blind...

IN A MATTER of moments, if the hooded figure (the man the media referred to as *The Friendly Burglar-Rapist*) and later *The Friendly Rapist*, had his way, at least one woman in North Dallas would have a very different memory of Valentine's Day 1977.

Author's Introduction

...Present Day
Dallas, Texas
1:10 am February 14, 2009

I BEGAN WRITING this book, chronicling three years and three months of events, on the anniversary, thirty-two years ago, of the capture of Dallas' Friendly Burglar-Rapist (FBR)[6].

I had been wanting to write this story since at least April Fool's Day 1975 when I reviewed the Offense/Incident Report (O/IR) which detailed a rape suspect claiming to be a Dallas Police Officer. I knew there would be a 'story' there. I even sketched an idea for the book's cover.[7]

The most riveting parts of this book are unquestionably the statements of the victims of the FBR as detailed by the Reporting Officer's interviews with each complainant.

However just relating those events would do a disservice to the citizens of Dallas and the police officers severing them who had to endure three-plus years of uncertainty in the Friendly Burglar Rapist's reign of terror. Each deserves to know the genesis and the behind the scenes story of what led to our ability to track and predict the movements of The Friendly Burglar Rapist that led to his capture.

NOTE: Hereafter you will see **events noted in bold print** on the right margin with a **location, time, day & date** and the **offense number** attributed to the event. If the offense reported was a rape it will be noted in parenthesis i.e. **(R-1)** indicates the first rape offense. If prints were lifted at the scene that will be so noted. **BTW, footnotes are important! Yellow highlighting is added for emphasis by the author**.

---

[6] [**NB**: According to THC, I was the first to use the phrase "friendly burglar-rapist".]

[7] Appendix C, FBR Book Cover Illustration - Evolution
[see website: robertjsadler.com]

1973

the FBR: The Beginning - Only We didn't know it

Dallas, Central Division Analyst's Office
9:00 am Friday, November 16, 1973
Offense Number 1 (R-1)

THE RAPE OFFENSE[8] on beat 127, the previous day, was unusual as to MO and time of day. The suspect wore a ski mask and said he was *"just a burglar..."* I put out a BOLO (Be On the Look Out) bulletin to the squads working the 120s. It would be a while before CAPERS (Crimes Against Persons) would have anything to go on—if at all.

I stuck a dot on my map to mark the location of the crime. It was the only daytime 'rape-dot' on the map at the time.

I picked up the remainder of the O/I R's and methodically worked through them.

Dallas
Evening, Tuesday, November 27, 1973

CRY RAPE, A made for TV movie directed by Corey Allen and staring Andrea Marcovicci, aired on prime-time TV. It is one of the initial TV films to feature rape as its subject, although the storyline is more about the wrongly accused look-alike suspect than the victim. It did raise the public's awareness about rape, something seldom broached on TV. However it aired as 'movie of the week fare' at the beginning of the week following the Thanksgiving holiday weekend. ABC was airing its *Tuesday Movie of the Week* against CBS's #1 rated *Hawaii Five-O* followed by *The New CBS Tuesday Night Movies*. Both movies were up against also-ran NBC's *Chase, The Magician* and *Police Story*. The movie *Cry Rape*, received little attention.

Did the "just a burglar" rapist I had just 'mapped' eleven days earlier watch this movie? Did his victim? I wondered?

---

[8] See Offense Number 0 in the Prologue, page 8 (both '0' & '1' are same offense)

A Chronicle - How We Got from 1966 to 1974

A series of seemingly disparate events would transpire during this period that would have a profound, lingering and positive effect on me and the hunt for the FBR. The connective mental tissue between serial murders in California and the terror they induced would persist in my mind particularly when the FBR would send Dallas spiraling toward a similar fate. And, a career criminal by the name of J.C. Shannon Jr., would be the proving ground for my and Tom's analysis and system for catching the FBR. Certainly, J.C. Shannon Jr. would never imagine that his future criminal activities would ultimately set forces in motion that would result in the arrest of the most prolific serial rapist in the history of the Dallas Police Department.

1966

Chapter 1

Bingo, Jack! Prelude

**Riverside, California
Sunday evening, October 30, 1966**

"ON A WARM Sunday night in 1966, the day before Halloween, an eighteen-year-old former Ramona High school cheerleader named Cheri Jo Bates climbed into her lime-green Volkswagen Bug and drove to the Riverside City College Library."[9]

The subsequent brutal murder of Ms. Bates that night found its way two days later onto the pages of *The Dallas Morning News* on November 1, 1966. In section A, page 11, amidst other headlines and beside a seven column advert for a huge carpet sale was the headline "California Cheerleader Found Dead on Campus" It was broken over two columns and fitted around ads for 'backyard' cabins and 5% annual interest rate on savings accounts at a local bank, Exchange Savings.

---

[9] *Most Evil*, page 110, ©2009 Steve Hodel, Dutton 375 Hudson Street, New York, NY 10014. Also see: www.stevehodel.com

It was not a big item, but its placement and its sensationalism (college cheerleader found dead) caught the eye.

I was at the time a student at Oklahoma State University in Stillwater. I had gone to our campus library to read my hometown newspaper. I read the article mostly out of general curiosity as the young woman's death had nothing to do with crime in Stillwater, Oklahoma or Dallas, Texas. The *DMN* article read:

California Cheerleader Found Dead on Campus

RIVERSIDE, Calif. (AP)

The body of a pretty young coed, marked with stab wounds and a slit throat, was found early Monday on the Riverside City College campus, police reported.

Miss Cheri Jo Bates, 18, an attractive blonde cheerleader, was found on a driveway between two buildings at 6 a.m. by a school custodian, officers said. She had been reported missing earlier by her father, Joseph C. Bates.

The girl's body was fully clothed except for shoes.

Her body was discovered about 100 yards from her compact car, on which the distributor and condenser coil had been yanked loose. Police said the killer may have attacked her as she tried to start her car.

Police said they found a man's wristwatch about 10 feet from the body, but said they had no other clues.

Ms. Bates lived with her father. She has a brother in the Navy, and her mother is in a rest home.

Carrollton, Texas
November 22, 1966

GOOD LUCK FOR J.C. Shannon, Jr., "a Negro male age 22," (per the case report) who had been caught in a stolen car, a 1966 Chevelle; perhaps, as a neophyte, his burgeoning life of crime would end here. He was arrested in the northern Dallas suburb of Carrollton by Carrollton police officers and fingerprinted. The fingerprint card was sent to the Dallas Police Department, I.D. Bureau, where they positively matched the prints in and on the stolen car with Shannon's DPD fingerprint card. It was an open and shut case. His two accomplices V.T. Hull, Jr., and Robert Odell Allen were also charged in the offense. For his part, Shannon was convicted of Theft/Over $50 (Auto) and sentenced to two years in the Texas State Penitentiary; luckily, he received probation.

If ever there was to be a time in the life of J.C. Shannon, Jr. for introspection, to find the straight and narrow path, now was that moment.

Dallas, Texas
November 22, 1966

DOWNTOWN, KENNEDY MEMORIAL SERVICE
– 3 YEAR ANNIVERSARY –

On the morning of Tuesday, November 22, 1966, three years after the assassination of President John Fitzgerald Kennedy the following article appeared:

IMAGE AS MARTYR CITED
AS MAIN REASON FOR CHOICE

WASHINGTON (UPI) – Americans believe by a 5-1 margin that John F. Kennedy will be recorded as a greater president than Lyndon B. Johnson, a public opinion survey reported Monday.

On the eve of the third anniversary of Kennedy's assassination in Dallas, the copyrighted Louis Harris Poll published in the Washington Post showed that the Kennedy legend still carries influence, particularly in politics.

Of those polled, 44 percent or 5 percent more than in September said they would prefer Sen. Robert F. Kennedy over President Johnson as the Democratic presidential nominee in 1968. Mr. Johnson's rating in November was 37 per cent, same as in September.

"The main reason people cite JFK as the greater president is that 'he was a martyr,'" Harris reported. "The main reason for preferring Sen. Kennedy is that he reminds voters of his brother."

NO SPECIAL CEREMONIES or change of routine was planned Tuesday at the Kennedy gravesite in Arlington National Cemetery. The Democratic senator from New York and other members of the Kennedy family were expected to make quiet visits to the cemetery, where the permanent, $2 million memorial gravesite is nearly completed.

Controversy continued to swirl around the circumstance of the assassination three years after the tragic event in Dallas.

The Texas White House said President Johnson would have no comment on the Life magazine article, published Monday, which called for a new investigation. The magazine said a "reasonable and disturbing doubt remains" about the Warren Commission's primary conclusion that Lee Harvey Oswald acted alone as the assassin.

WHITE HOUSE Press Secretary Bill Moyers referred reporters to Mr. Johnson's news conference remarks Nov. 4, when he said, "I know of no evidence that would in any way cause any reasonable person to have a doubt about the Warren Commission. But if there is any evidence and it is brought forth, I am sure that the commission and the appropriate authorities will take action that may be justified."

Moyers said he knew of no Johnson plans to attend any memorial services Tuesday.

Malcolm M. Kilduff, a former assistant press secretary to the late president and who was in Dallas Nov. 22, 1963, dismissed as "pure garbage" the rash of books and articles critical of the Warren Report.

Kilduff, now a Washington public relations man, said in a taped radio-TV interview that the Warren Commission "did as thorough a job as possible."

But he acknowledged he disagreed with one of the commission's findings—that the bullet which passed through Kennedy's neck also struck Texas Gov. John Connally, who was sitting in front of the president in the limousine.

Kilduff said he and Connally both believe a second bullet struck the governor. The former press aide said, "This is a result not only of my own feeling, my own investigation, but also as a direct feeling of Gov. Connally."

[NB: Now, forty-three years later, there are still conspiracy theories abounding as to what exactly happened. From my own questions to various members of the Dallas Police Department (in particular then homicide detective 'Davis' who interrogated both Oswald and Ruby) there was/were no conspirator/s, or other gunmen, etc. Based on my trust in these men, I find myself on the non-conspiratorial side.]

1967

Dallas Criminal District Court #2:
Docket C67-1521JI
May 26, 1967

CHARGED WITH BREAKING & Entering a Motor Vehicle and stealing a .22 caliber Winchester leaver-action rifle and a box of shells, J.C. Shannon, Jr., age 23, along with his three accomplices, had his day in court.

Back in February, while still on probation for his November 22nd conviction for the Carrollton, Texas auto theft three months earlier, J.C. Shannon and three other men had visited a nearby used car lot on the pretext of buying a car and needing to 'test-drive' the vehicle.

A citizen saw Shannon get out of the auto-lot car, enter a pickup truck, steal a rifle and drive off. Another witness copied down the license number. Police traced the getaway car back to the auto dealer who gave them Shannon's name. Witnesses observing a police lineup identified Shannon and his accomplices.

Now in court and faced with the witness testimony, stacked against him, Shannon pled guilty before the court and was sentenced to six months in the state penitentiary.

Dallas Police & Courts Building
Downtown Dallas, Texas
July 21, 1967

RIGHT HAND RAISED, I swore, in part, to uphold the Constitution of the United States, the State of Texas and the laws thereof as well as those of the City of Dallas. Taking this oath, I was sworn in as a Dallas Police Officer. And as others have noted, it is an oath from which (along with the one I made upon entering The United States Army) I have never been relieved

1968

Dallas, Texas: U.S. Army Recruiting Station
February 2, 1968

We are in a war. It seemed logical that police and firemen were 'fighting' the war on the home-front and as such would be deferred, but that was not the case. I had recently relinquished my gun and badge and joined the Army. I had received my draft notice, but rather than be 'drafted' I preferred to enlist. I boarded a bus in downtown Dallas for Fort Polk, Louisiana where I would take my basic training. Vietnam was a good possibility, but I would leave that up to God and the United States Army. I didn't know if they were in cahoots, but the Army got its way.

Fort Polk, Louisiana
April 4, 1968

The night before our graduation, there was considerable tension in the barracks. The levity had gone out of our pending 'release' from bootcamp the next morning. We learned Dr. Martin Luther King, Jr, had been shot and killed while standing on a the balcony of the Lorraine Motel in Memphis, Tennessee. At the time, he was not a figure I had taken much notice of beyond his speeches reported on TV. That was not the case with our black brothers in uniform. We had no access to news except word of mouth—the word was not good.

Fort Hood, Texas
June 5, 1968

Settling in at the 518th Military Police Battalion on Fort Hood, I watched the TV news in the 'dayroom' that night. The news was Robert F. Kennedy had won the California Democrat Party primary. Moments later we were all stunned to 'see' and 'hear' the aftermath of his murder by a man later identified as Sirhan Sirhan.

Chicago, Illinois
August 1968

As the summer heated up, with riots in a number of cities and the Democrat National Convention convening in Chicago, part of our Military Police battalion was put on alert and sent to Chicago. On the night of August 28, 1968, all-hell-broke-loose.

Dallas County Grand Jury
November 11, 1968

AT AGE TWENTY-FOUR, J.C. Shannon, Jr. had broken the left front vent window of a 1968 Chrysler bearing Louisiana license plates at 3:30pm on October 3, 1968. Shannon opened the car door and rummaged through the clothing in the car before leaving the scene empty-handed.

Shannon did not realize a witness not only saw him break into the car, saw him leave the scene in a black 1954 four-door Chevrolet sedan, splotched with grey primer paint and noting that the front of the hood was dented, but also called the police and told them what he saw.

Later arrested, Shannon's case was presented to the Dallas County Grand Jury on November 11, 1968, which, after a hearing, declined prosecution. In the police department case report, on the blank after the word "Disposition" remains the hand-stamped notice: "NO BILLED BY G.J.". The ex-con dodged another bullet and once again had the chance to turn his life around.

1969

San Francisco, California
Dallas, Texas
Sunday, October 19, 1969 & November 4, 1969

On October 19th, page 4A of that Sunday's *Dallas Morning News* really caught my attention, as I finished my first cup of coffee, when I read: "'Zodiac Killer' Terrorizes California." It was my last few days in Dallas. I was on my thirty day leave before deploying to Vietnam on November 5th.

I would soon visit my father in Hanford, California before his driving me to San Francisco on November 4th.

Staying in a Holiday Inn near the airport, I bussed into SF for an afternoon of sightseeing. Among other more hospitable places, I found myself down on the docks alone, walking where I shouldn't have been—wondering if the Zodiac Killer was lurking beside the next warehouse.

November 5th I flew to Sea-Tac and Fort Lewis Washington to process-out for Vietnam and a year in-country.

1970

Dallas, Southwest Patrol Division
10:30 pm Tuesday, June 9, 1970

MINDING THEIR BUSINESS, patrolmen C.S. Tull and C.E. Plumlee were doing 'cop-stuff' as they sat in the driveway of a closed business in the mostly commercial/residential mean streets of West Dallas, west of downtown and west of the Trinity River. A passerby, either pissed that the officers (writing up a report from their last call) didn't seem to be doing anything or had a grudge to settle with the men in a nearby alley, told the officers that two guys were stripping a car around the corner. "They's be strippin' it rat-now."

"We'll check it out." Tull, the driver and senior partner, said as he rolled up the window again not wanting too much of the AC-cooled air in the patrol car to escape. Turning to his partner he said, "Hold you're shit, Plumlee." Lights-out, the squad car shot across the street and down Akron as the junior partner tried to stow his clipboard with its half-completed offense/incident report and stab at his uniform pocket with his ballpoint pen trying to secure it in the bouncing car.

With the sun having set at 9:03 pm CST it was just now full-dark under a waning quarter moon and, across the Continental Street Viaduct, the red neon lights of the Flying Red Horse atop the Magnolia Building were clearly visible. Tull turned their squad car down the alleyway in the 1900 block of Akron Street. The wind, though out of the South, had cooled the night air to seventy-nine degrees from the day's high of eighty-nine. Here and there you could smell the fragrance of Mimosa blossoms in the air.

There in the glare, as Tull and Plumlee simultaneously snapped on the squad car's headlights and red lights, was a beige over black, two door 1970 Pontiac. Frozen in the twin beams of light intermittently punctuated with red, were twenty-six year-old J.C. Shannon, Jr. and his accomplice, twenty-nine year-old J.C. Walker. Both were in the process of removing parts from the vehicle. The two men, whose race according to the custom at the time, was later marked on the arrest report as 'colored', fabricated six stories as the officers approached them. A check of the vehicle's license number against their 'hot-sheet' told the officers the car was stolen. The dispatcher ran the number again and reconfirmed they had a stolen car. Tull and Plumlee would soon be marking their activity sheet with an on-view felony jail arrest, which would also 'clear' at least one offense; the kind of 'mark' that makes supervisors happy.

To make matters worse, not only did Tull and Plumlee not believe Shannon and Walker's stories, Shannon had no comeback when he was found with two chrome lug-nuts in his right front pocket; lug-nuts that had only recently been removed from the stolen vehicle in front of them.

Dallas, Police & Courts Bldg., courtroom
11:01 pm Wednesday, June 10, 1970

RIVERSIDE EIGHT, NINETY-seven eleven, extension 556 was the phone number of Auto Theft Detective F.G. Phillips of Crimes Against Property. It was his job to fill out the case report and have the two seminal citizens, J.C. Shannon and J.C. Walker, arraigned before a judge. This Phillips accomplished with his usual professional aplomb. Attached to his notes was a copy of the DPD fingerprint card of J.C. Shannon, Jr., listing: AGE: 26;

SEX: MALE; RACE NEGRO; DPD# 58459; FBI# 939765 F; DPS# 1341212. Other pertinent demographics listed his, height 5'8½", weight 155, hair Black, eyes Maroon, complexion Dark and occupation, Carpenter. It stated he was born 1-22-1944 in Melvin Arkansas. It listed one brother as his nearest relative and noted he was married.

Dallas, Kennedy Memorial
Wednesday, June 24, 1970

THE LONG AWAITED JFK Memorial is dedicated in the City of Dallas today. Not quite seven years after President Kennedy's assassination which rocked the city, the country and the world, Dallas had erected and dedicated a memorial to his memory located approximately one block east of the place where he was fatally shot.

Dallas County District Court 2:
Docket #C70-5003I
Friday, October 23, 1970

IT WAS NOT a good day for J.C. Shannon; the jury had returned its "Guilty" verdict and the judge assessed his punishment as four years imprisonment at the Texas Department of Corrections—TDC. His stay that morning outside his county jail cell had been short lived and the fact that it had been an Indian Summer seventy-two degrees overnight and the rain at noon was going to cause the temps to drop into the sixties never entered his mind as he was escorted back upstairs to his jail cell.

It would likely be a few days before he would be riding the State Trooper-guarded, taxpayer's bus down to Huntsville to begin completing his sentence.

Kings County, Hanford, California
Monday, November 16, 1970

RETURNING FROM A year in Phu Bai, Vietnam, as rear-echelon support staff, on November 5, 1970, I again met my father (William [Bill] Henry Sadler, Jr.) in San Francisco where we spent the day as he made business calls. As co-owner,

President and General Manager of KLAN[10] radio in Hanford, he made regular trips to larger market cities to acquire regional and national advertisers.

That afternoon was particularly interesting. We came out of a tall San Francisco building onto the street to walk to a nearby restaurant. The old Civil Defense/Air Raid/Weather Warning sirens went off. So incongruous was the sound, I reverted to in-country instincts of the past year and dove for the nearest bunker, expecting incoming mortars or rockets to begin impacting around me. All I could do was grab onto, and flatten myself against, the building's wall. The strange looks I got from San Francisco pedestrians soon reminded me I was no longer in Vietnam. Dad thinking I looked strange trying to mate with the building, simply said, "We're okay, Son."

Later we had a great "I'm-back-in-the-world" dinner and went to a nearby comedy club and saw an improv group called The Ace Trucking Company. They were considered one of the most innovative comedy troupes of the 60s and 70s. They "consisted of four guys and one woman: George Memmioli, Michael Mislove, Bill Saluga Patti Deutsch and Fred Willard. They were doing "sketch comedy" long before shows such as "Saturday Night Live" (1975), "Friday" or "MADtv" (1995) ever came long."[11]

Eleven days later the Monday morning *Los Angeles Times* headlines read: "Zodiac Linked to Riverside Slaying." The morning newsman on KLAN radio detailed the story of the murdered cheerleader, Cheri Jo Bates, from October 30, 1966.

I remember thinking about the Cheri Jo Bates murder in Riverside and the Zodiac murders in San Francisco and surrounds and saying to myself, "I'm glad we don't have that kind of thing going on back in Dallas."

That night, from my father's home in Hanford, California we watched the Monday Night Football broadcast (only its ninth). In the famed Cotton Bowl Stadium the Dallas Cowboys were blanked by the St. Louis Cardinals 38-0.

---

[10] When my father bought the station the DJs all had Scottish names: Sandy McTavish, etc and they 'played' on the theme of a Scot's 'clan', even had a tartan clad figure on their plaid-filled logo of KLAN letters. See robertjsadler.com for the graphic.

[11] See: http://www.imdb.com/name/nm1674443/bio

In a matter of days, I would return from military leave and rejoin the Dallas Police Department.

Apple not falling far from the tree...

As you see below my father, Bill Sadler, founded a civilian program to help police catch criminals and prosecutors make their cases via a Secret Witness program. I used his model to promote, behind the scenes, the creation of a similar program within the DPD.

Honored by J.K. Sweeney, the chairman of Board of Supervisors who said: "(f)or four years Bill Sadler has worked countless hours and given real leadership to this program." Hanford Police Chief Curtis Henderson said, "There are quite a few criminals serving prison terms, a danger removed from our streets because of the job that Bill Sadler has done."

Bill Sadler founding president
of
"Secret Witness"
Kings County California

Two Years Later

1972

Preparation & Preparedness

Dualities and dichotomies abound in life. One such enigma is the difference between preparation and preparedness. Both words have the same root from the French préparer and Latin præprāre to make ready beforehand. Preparation is then the action of putting in order, equipping, or in general getting ready beforehand. Having thus gone through the process of preparation one can then be in a state of readiness called preparedness. Of preparation and preparedness my partner Tom, the long-time Scoutmaster, would simply say, "Oh, you mean, 'Be Prepared'."

Dallas, August 1972

THE DIXIE MAFIA, a loose knit confederation of thieves, burglars and contract murderers whose reputed headquarters was on The Strip in Biloxi, Mississippi, had various tentacles gripping the Dallas underworld in the 1970s.

One of the tools street cops and detectives carried with them BC (before computers) was a book of known criminals, who we called "hooks". A standard hook-book contained the 'hook's' mug-shot, name, DOB, physical description, list of aliases, last known address, associates, and list of arrests. In addition a hook-book would include what we would later call BOLO's (Be On the Look Out) and Wanted Persons Bulletins. I was aware of the Dixie Mafia's reputation and knew that some of their members were working in Dallas. I even had Stanley Lee Cook, aka "The Creeper" in my hook book.

But I never thought I would meet him, like I did.

Early Wednesday morning, August 30, 1972, I was working a one-man squad in the Oak Lawn area. My beat was an enclave of apartments and older residences whose younger residents were still trying to live the Sixties life-style and were heavily influenced by a wannabe Haight-Ashbury vibe; pot and other drugs were readily available to them. I was in patrol, working "deep nights," the 11pm to 7am shift out of Central Patrol Division. Beat 127, one of the two northern most beats in our sector (the 120s), was a triangle slice of geography generally bounded on the west by the Dallas North Tollway (DNT) to a point where the DNT met Lemmon Avenue, a divided boulevard that ran from northwest to southeast through the area. The third leg of this triangle was Oak Lawn Avenue.

I had just made a swing through the homes north of Oak Lawn and Cedars Springs. As I recall, it was just before two o'clock. The bars would be closing soon and I wanted to check my neighborhoods before I started watching for the drunks. Drunks who were just now having their one-more-for-the-road would soon be heading to their cars.

Soon the after-hours, parking lot, bar fights would start. And these altercations would often be followed by the DWI's and later the spousal abuse calls when the drunks got home.

Beat 127 contained a number of bars and restaurants. The businesses had closed hours ago and as soon as the bars closed, and if the drunks dispersed without incident, I would usually concentrate on watching for both business and residence burglars as well as looking for stolen cars. I was on Rawlins Street headed *northwest* at about twenty minutes after two, one block *west* of Lemmon Avenue when I got a "man down" call in the parking lot in front of 4305A Lemmon Avenue. I turned right (*northeast*) on Wycliff and turned left (*northwest*) through the corner gas station before I reached Lemmon Avenue.

I pulled up in front of 4305A Lemmon Avenue, the location of a nightclub/bar called the Lemon Twist (if memory serves, part of its logo signage contained a yellow twist of lemon). I had been in there only once or twice, checking their liquor license, but I had never had trouble there, unlike the bars off Cedar

Springs and Oak Lawn at the other end of my beat. At that moment the parking lot was nearly devoid of cars, and no one was standing around.

I saw him before I stepped out of my squad car, there *was* a "man down". He was still lying in the parking lot. As I bent over the man I could see he had a single gunshot wound to his chest; what we called in the Army a 'sucking-chest wound'. CPR was not going to help. The red bubbles surrounding the hole in his chest meant his lung was most probably perforated. Any compressions would likely only pour more blood into his lungs. In my hopeful imagination he managed a couple of ragged breaths as I crouched over him to apply pressure to the wound.

This man's body had already lost it normal warmth, even on a late summer's night with temperatures in the low 80s. I checked for a pulse at his wrist and neck, nothing. I flicked my light over his open, staring eyes. His pupils were fixed and dilated; I realized he was dead.

The body lay face up in the parking lot. His head toward the strip of shops behind him and his feet pointed toward Lemmon Avenue. The green and yellow light from the Lemon Twist's sign threw its jaundiced glow over the scene mixing with the overhead street lights and the other neon signs. His face was lit by this surreal lighting. The man's body reminded me of the body discovered by the David Hemmings' character in the 1966 British film, *Blow Up*. Like the movie's character, I wondered where the shot or shots had come from?

But this was not the movies. As I looked up from the body my eyes strained to see into the shadows in the adjacent parking lots and the vacant lot across the street wgere elevated billboards looming over the cityscape from which a sniper could take the perfect shot. Was it over, would more shots ring out of the dark?

Although I was the first cop on the scene and had been just around the corner when the call went out, the man had obviously been dead for some minutes; there was nothing I could do to help him. I waited on the ambulance and homicide detectives as I corralled the gathering looky-lous that had seemingly appeared out of nowhere.

Trying to elicit a statement or expose a witness from those gathered I asked, "Anyone know this man?"

"Stanley Cook," one man said.

I looked again at the dead man and nodded. I recognized him too. It was Stanley Lee Cook, aka "The Creeper".

Dixie Mafia Leader Slain

Single Bullet Kills Cook Outside Oak Lawn Nightclub

By JAMES EWELL

Stanley Lee Cook, an alleged Dallas gangster who had successfully outmaneuvered authorities' efforts to put him in prison, was killed outside an Oak Lawn nightclub early Wednesday by an unseen assailant who picked him off with a single rifle shot.

The bullet apparently was fired across a parking lot and struck the 31-year-old Cook as he was about to enter a late mod.' automobile. Cook had emerged from the Lemmon Twist, at Rawlins and Lemmon, accompanied by a man and a woman he had met hours earlier at Dallas Love Field on their arrival from Houston.

Cook was believed to be the latest member of a gang of traveling criminals known to police across Texas and the southeastern states as the "Dixie Mafia" to die violently, leaving the gang's reputed leader, Kirksey McCord Nix Jr., now imprisoned in Louisiana on a murder conviction, as the lone survivor of the inner organization.

Curiously, police found no weapon on the slain underworld figure although Cook reportedly went well armed at all times.

COOK HAD a reputation of being deadly and authorities, although never with the evidence to prove it, nonetheless credited Cook with a number of killings in his reputed role as the Dixie Mafia's enforcer.

One Dallas detective said Cook's friends feared him as much as his foes.

The couple with Cook when he was slain, the only known witnesses, were permitted to return to Houston Wednesday afternoon after convincing police they could add very little to the investigation.

Police identified the couple as Willie Eugene Courson, 38, a jewelry salesman, and Cynthia Marie Webb, 29.

The couple told police that Cook took them to dinner after meeting them at the airport about 6:30 p.m. Tuesday.

Their next stop after dinner was the Lemmon Twist, where Miss Webb said they stayed for only one drink each.

IN APPROACHING the car, police said the couple had gone around to the right side while Cook walked to the driver's side.

Miss Webb told police she heard a noise she thought was an exploding firecracker. She said Courson pushed her down beside the car where they both waited for three to four minutes. As other persons began gathering, Miss Webb went back inside the club, telling police later that she still did not know it was Cook who had been shot.

Detective George Thomasson of the homicide unit said the bullet passed through Cook's chest and dropped on the sidewalk after striking the plate glass window of a beauty salon in front of which Cook had parked the car, about 100 feet from the night club. The salon is in a cluster of shops fronting a parking lot on Lemmon.

The detective said the angle of the bullet lines up with vacant lots on the opposite side of Lemmon. A large billboard sits on one lot and Thomasson said the assailant could have stood behind it.

POLICE RECEIVED but tended to discount a report by the night manager of a nearby service station of seeing two "well-dressed, clean-shaven" men driving south on Lemmon in a black over dark green 1969 Ford moments after the manager heard the shot.

Police shifted two members of the intelligence division which keeps up on gang activities to assist five homicide detectives assigned to the case.

Cook was linked with former Texas

Insurance Commissioner John Osorio in a lawsuit filed here 10 days ago in an alleged conspiracy with others to seize control of Century Development Corp. of Dallas last June.

Cook's arrest record included two assault to murder charges, the latest filed last summer after he was arrested for shooting another police character near NorthPark Shopping Center. In both cases, however, Cook was no-billed when witnesses refused to testify.

Cook was scheduled to go on trial here Sept. 18 for possession of cocaine. Police alleged that 29 packets of cocaine were found in Cook's motel room the last time he was arrested on an assault to murder charge.

Cook survived a shooting on a North Dallas street two years ago which reportedly involved a former FBI agent on the trail of stolen jewelry.

Stanley Lee Cook ... was to have faced trial Sept. 18 for cocaine possession.

***Dallas Morning News*
Dixie Mafia Leader Slain
by JAMES EWELL**

THE ONLY THING my friend Jim Ewell, longtime police beat reporter for the *Dallas Morning News* (*DMN*), had incorrect were the location and the spelling of the nightclub's name, The Lemon Twist only has one 'm' and was located closest to the corner of Lemmon Avenue and Wycliff, not Rawlins which runs parallel to Lemmon Avenue, one block to the West. In the article, I had been one of the 'police-saids'.

At the time in Dallas, we had two home-town newspapers *The Dallas Morning News* and *The Dallas Times Herald* (the evening paper). Not to be outdone in local gangland murder reporting the *DTH* police-beat man was also present and quoted me by name.

DTH Wed. Evening, August 30, 1972
Gangland figure slain in ambush - no byline

Stanley Lee Cook, reputed leader of the Dixie Mafia, was "executed" in gangland fashion Wednesday as he and two companions stood by a car in the parking lot of a Dallas nightspot.

The 31-year-old Cook, known as "The Creeper" to the Dallas underworld and police, was struck in the chest by one of three bullets fired by unseen snipers. He was dead on arrival at Parkland Hospital minutes later. Police said the predawn shooting occurred at 2:30 a.m. outside the Lemon Twist Lounge, 4305 Lemmon Ave.

"It was impossible to tell if the shots were fired from a pistol or a rifle," one witness told The Times Herald. "It appeared to be a deliberate, planned execution. The sniper -- or snipers -- apparently had waited for some time and caught him just as he and the others reached the car.

"As far as I know, no one actually saw the sniper as the shots were fired."

Police identified Cook's companions as Willis Eugene Courson, 36 and Cynthia Marie Webb, 20, both of Houston. Neither was struck by the gunfire.

"They were standing on the passenger side of the car," reported Patrolman R. J. Sadler. "Cook had driven them to the club and they were just returning to the car when the shooting occurred.

Cook was on the drivers' side. The one shot caught him just under the right arm."

Other officers said the two remaining shots went wild, one apparently ricocheting off the surface of the parking lot and the second shattering the window of the nearby beauty shop.

A fourth person, believed to have been with Cook just prior to the shooting, was not immediately identified.

Police said the attendant at a nearby service station heard the shots, then saw two men drive rapidly from the vicinity of the nightclub. The officers said the attendant described the pair as clean-cut and neatly dressed and were driving a late model black or dark green car.

Homicide Capt. Jack Davis said the shooting had all the earmarks of a gangland slaying.

"In any killing like this there are lots of suspects, but we have no one person in mind at the present time." Davis said, "In fact, right now we still don't know definitely which direction the bullets came from."

He said two detectives, Joe Poe and George Thomason, had witnesses recreating the shooting.

Detectives said the usually well-armed Cook was not carrying a weapon when the shooting occurred. They said they found $260 in cash and personal jewelry in his pockets but did not locate a wallet.

An autopsy performed at midmorning disclosed Cook died of a gunshot wound through the right and left lungs and liver.

The medical examiner said the bullet exited from the body, indicating it was fired from a high-powered weapon -- probably a carbine or rifle.

Cook only last week was named in three civil suits field in Dallas district courts.

The suits, filed Aug. 21 by Dallas businessman C.A. Hamby, name six other persons including former Texas Insurance Commissioner John Osorio and allege they conspired to gain control of Century Development Corp.

Cook surfaced in the Dallas underworld more that five years ago when detectives began hearing his name crop up during the course of investigations concerning underworld shootings and killings.

Even then he was know as "The Creeper."

Cook reportedly took over the "Dixie Mafia"--a band of roaming criminals--last year in the wake of the conviction of gangland leader Kirksey McCord Nix Jr. in Louisiana.

Two years ago Cook was shot and seriously wounded in a gunfight near NorthPark.

A few months before the shooting Cook was taken into custody by federal agents for alleged violation of the Omnibus Crime Act. Agents seized a number of weapons in his apartment at that time.

"WHO SHOT 'THE Creeper' on my beat?" I wanted to know. It was mysteries like these that propelled the nagging questions for which unresolved answers were often the outcome. This is the frustration of the beat cop; often there when something happens, rarely at the conclusion when answers are found.

WHAT, YOU ASK, do the Cheri Jo Bates, Zodiac murders and the Creeper's murder have to do with the capture of the Friendly Burglar-Rapist? Only that they all helped form the subliminal mindset I still had a year later in October of 1973; wanting the answers to questions I knew being in patrol was not going to provide. It was preparation.

1973

Dallas, October 1973—a mid afternoon

THE RAPIST WEARING business-casual attire went into his afternoon meeting with his fellow workers, who joked about the day's weather and discussed their mutual projects.

THE OFFICER WEARING the department issued dark navy-blue, long-sleeved winter uniform with green epaulette bands, indicating he worked patrol, entered the building. He had taken the Main Street entrance ramp down as he done thousands of times and parked his squad car in the basement of Police & Courts Bldg. at 106 South Harwood between Main and Commerce. He walked across the tire-worn concrete driveway at the bottom of the ramp where eleven years earlier Lee Harvey Oswald had been gunned down by Jack Ruby on national television.

That description fit almost every uniformed officer on the department. That day, I was that Officer.

I was working the Central Patrol Division of the Dallas Police Department, the three to eleven shift, with Sunday's and Monday's off. I had been called to the watch commander's office by my sector sergeant. While working my beat, I had received the dreaded radio call, 'report to five-eleven'.

Five-Eleven (511) was the telephone extension for our division's patrol headquarters: detail room, line-up stage and the Watch Commander's office. Five-Eleven was, among other duties, the place where administrative infractions were brought to the light of day, and ass-chewin's or more severe punishments if required, were meted out.

A call to go to Five-Eleven was only trumped by a call to go to Internal Affairs or the jack-pot-of-dread, report to the Chief's office.

I was about to face the unknown of a command visit to Five-Eleven.

Sgt. Tom R. Gregory was sitting in the chair in front of our Watch Commander, Lieutenant Wayne Posey, who was sitting behind his desk. I walked up and knocked on the frame of the open door. Standing in the doorway I wondered, as I had the entire drive in from North Dallas, *what have I done now?*

Sergeant Gregory, an almost always affable character whose most often repeated phrase (if you asked him for time off) was *if yu're waitin' on me yu're backin' up*, smiled.

Sergeant Gregory said, "The department's created a new position called Division Crime Analyst. He'll be responsible for analyzing the crime in the Central Division; like Lieutenant Macsas' group does in the Operations Analysis Section of Planning and Research for the city.

"Ours will be the first one in the city and if it goes well, the department will put a Division Analyst program at the other four patrol division headquarters." Lieutenant Posey silently nodded.

"Sounds like a good idea," I said.

Author Note: *I was familiar with Lt. Cliff (Arab) Macsas' group and their work. While working out of the Chief's office in the Public Information Office (PIO) I often had coffee in their 'map room' discussing crime, and had taken photos of the unit and their 'map room' for the PD's 1971 annual report. I had developed good rapport with Lt. Macsas, whose nickname was "Arab", usually pronounced with a long "a" as in A-rab, Lt. Sanders, as well as Officer Billy Hamby, non-sworn programmer Carl Makres and two non-sworn assistants, Kathryn Bonham and Margret McGee.*[12]

Planning & Research - Crime Analysis Group
Standing l-r: Lt. C.J. Macsas, Officer B.J. Hamby, Lt. H.E. Sanders
Sitting l-r: C.M. Makres, M.S. McGee & Kathryn A. Bonham
wall maps for "Residence Burglary", "Auto Theft", & "Business Burglary" can be seen

---

[12] Two years earlier, in 1971, I don't remember anyone in the group, at the time, being referred to as an 'analyst' or having the job title: 'Crime Analyst' nor was it, as I have captioned above: 'Crime Analysis Group', they were the: Operations Analysis Section of Planning and Research.

THE SERGEANT SAID, "Glad you think so, Sadler, you're gonna to be our new analyst!"

Posey nodded his agreement.

"I don't know," I said, "I'm just getting my feet back on the ground in patrol..."

Author Note: *Since coming back from Vietnam and rejoining the police department in November 1970 I had done a brief stint in patrol getting reacquainted with cop-work before being cajoled and assigned to the Community Services Division, a public relations job that morphed into the Public Information Office (PIO) which reported directly to the Chief of Police.*

But now back 'in harness' and back on the streets, I was just beginning to feel I was back where I belonged, "fightin' crime". The idea of sitting behind a desk again had no appeal. It was what had happened to me in the Army; I had been pulled from the line to take over administrative duties because of my aptitude scores and typing ability. I had silently cursed my high school counselor, James Darland, for pushing me into an elective typing class—though I realized later that that skill had likely saved my life in Vietnam.

THE INTENTIONALLY NON-LOQUACIOUS lieutenant Posey said helpfully, "You'll have the office across from mine, but you'll report directly to Chief Dixon."

Then came the sergeant's sales pitch with the closing line, "You'll be working 'days' with Saturdays and Sundays off!"

I had a young wife, Susan, who worked 'normal hours', so my going to work at three in the afternoon and coming home near midnight every night, sometimes later if a late-shift jail arrest took longer to write up and book-in, was not conducive to good relations. Even my days off, Sunday's and Mondays were disruptive.

I didn't ask and never learned whether my selection was due to my observed or perceived abilities to get the job done, or if the sergeant was forced and had to pick someone from his squad and I was perhaps, in Sgt. T.R. Gregory's mind, the man he hated to lose the least.

Both the lieutenant and sergeant nodded their heads knowingly when I agreed to take the job.

Division Crime Analyst
Central Patrol Division
Dallas Police Department

PILES OF REPORTS came into the newly created Division Crime Analyst's office every day covering the six major crimes groups reported to the FBI for statistical UCR tracking. The six categories of the Uniformed Crime Report were: Assault, Burglary, Murder, Rape, Robbery, and Theft. Burglary had two subcategories: of a Business, and of a Residence. Burglary of a Motor Vehicle (which was originally charged as Breaking and Entering a Motor Vehicle or BEMV, later becoming Burglary of a Motor Vehicle or BMV), was actually classified and reported under the Theft category.

Hundreds of these crimes were reported daily in Central Patrol Division (CPD). Each written up by the patrol officers taking the reports in the field on the department's Offense/ Incident Report Form 70-31-R; reports that generally contained multiple pages. This was 1973 which meant that this Offense/ Incident Report Form (O/I R) version had been promulgated in 1970 and had been revised thirty-one times.

"My" office, across from the watch commander, had been the sector sergeants' office where they had done their paperwork, so they were not real happy about being ousted from their office (by a patrolman).

It was obvious to me, from my time with Macsas' group, that the visual component of maps with pins or dots on them was critical to relaying the crime picture. I had been supplied with a desk and a filing cabinet, as I recall. Everything else I 'procured'. There was no 'Division Crime Analyst' budget. So if I wanted maps, I had to be creative.

Early on, that first weekend, after trying to work for a week without maps and having finagled to have printed six, four-foot by four-foot street maps of the Central Patrol Division, I got busy. On Saturday I went to the hardware store bought three 4'x8' sheets of quarter-inch plywood and ninety-six feet of 3/8 inch, angle-aluminum for framing. In my garage I cut the plywood in half, pasted on the maps, cut, bent and framed the edges with the angle-aluminum. On Sunday I took 'my' framed maps to the office and hung them on the walls.

Here I am, apparently posing, holding an Offense/Incident Report
with two of my six, 4'x4' crime maps on the walls behind.

I then affixed clear plastic overlays on each of the maps. I had
also procured rolls of stick-on red-colored dots. I figured dots
would be more efficient with overlays (I'd be able to project 3
months activity at one time, rather than sicking different colored
pins in a map; pins that would have to be removed.) The monthly
plastic overlays could be stored for later use, or thrown away.

I also began making and distributing smaller beat maps with
crime-dots on them for the sector sergeants and beat officers.

Every morning I came into my office and began sorting the
Offense/Incident Reports that had been 'written up' during the
previous twenty-four hours in the CPD. I divided those reports
into the various groups and subgroups. Next I posted the new
O/I R's on one of my six, four foot square, map blowups of the
Central Patrol Division.

The patrol beats and their corresponding radio call numbers
for the CPD were the '100s'. The maps showed the boundary of
the CPD inclusive of its four sectors, the 110s, 120s, 130s and
140s. Each sector generally had eight individual beats, such as
121 through 128.

For each offense a colored stick-on dot was placed on the clear plastic sheet overlaying the map at the incident location. Each dot was marked with the shift number: one for deep-nights (11pm-7am) , two for days (7am-3pm), and three for evenings (3pm-11pm) .

At the end of the month a new sheet was applied over the previous two, with three months in view at a time. A different color dot was used for each month.

Covering my office walls were the individual maps for each of the UCR crimes, a graphic and visual representation of crime trends was easily observed and understood. For example a handful of paper reports of residential burglaries in a sector took on a completely different context when viewed as a menacing cluster of dots on your beat.

That was state-of-the-art crime analysis in Dallas. There was no departmental handbook on Crime Analysis and I received no detailed instruction in the specifics of what a Crime Analyst was to do, other than a few days observation with Lt. Macsas' Operations Analysis Section of the department's Planning and Research Division.

I applied, for the CPD, what P&R had been doing for several years on a city-wide basis; collating Offense/Incident Reports, dotting maps, and looking for trends. Where Lt. Macsas' group reported to *the* Chief and his staff, I would be responsible for the analysis of crime in the Central Patrol Division reporting my findings to Deputy Chief Robert O. Dixon, Central Patrol Division Commander.

On a city-wide basis, as often as possible, when the P&R crime analysis group developed information that could be tactically acted upon, a problem area might receive saturation patrols from the Tactical Unit, or convenience stores might be staked out by an undercover shotgun squad, laying in wait behind one-way mirrors, to stop what we called "hijackings" or armed robberies. The sheer volume of city-wide O/I R's made it more and more difficult for this information to filter down to the patrol officer who might be able to interdict the crime on his beat, if he only knew it was happening.

Beat officers were obviously aware of the crimes that occurred on their beats, especially when they took the actual O/I R, but the crimes that occurred on their days off or on the other two shifts often didn't make it onto their radar.

There were the exceptions; the great street cops who seemed to have the knack for catching bad guys regardless of when they worked. A day shift officer, coming on duty, working a residential area would often cruise his neighborhoods looking for the appearance of residential burglars and parked stolen cars as the citizenry left their homes to go to work.

A great street cop like Truly Holmes who would be doing just that might also, either on a hunch or on the tip of some informant he had developed, stop some guy in the neighborhood for ostensibly good reasons. Thus Truly would discover the fruits of the previous night's burglary in the guy's car as the beleaguered burglar came home from 'work'. An arrest would ensue allowing Truly to clear one or a handful of nighttime business burglaries.

My analysis put sector and beat crimes on the radar of the beat officers and their supervisors. The visualizing of crimes by beat and by sector got everyone's attention and projected a way for supervisors to hold officers accountable for the crime on their beats. Everyone became more conscious of what was happening on their beats and how what happened on one beat might, and frequently did, affect crime on a neighboring beat or sector.

I realized I didn't have to be an accountant or actuary to be a decent crime analyst. "Primarily you have to be able to count and know the difference between apples and oranges," I would satirically tell my wife's friends. "Next you have to know what 'normal' is and when you've got more apples in the barrel than were normal, you have to ask the question "why?", and then find the answer. If you can't find the answer, you at least can notify the watch commanders, sector sergeants and beat officers to be on the lookout for those guys and arrest'm for A.B.W.O.P!" The friends would always ask, "What's ABWOP?" I would laugh and say, "Adding to the Barrel WithOut Permission."

This was a grand oversimplification of what I did, but again, crime analysis was exceedingly rudimentary in 1973. Everything was 'hand-cranked' with pencil, paper, some graph paper, wall maps and a small Texas Instrument's calculator.

The police department and the City of Dallas did have computers, sequestered in large air-conditioned rooms, attended by people who knew (in my then opinion) very little about police work or how the two could intersect; but they *were* learning.

The department was working diligently to convert reports from handwritten to computerized data entry. Several of the department's information systems could be searched via a smattering of terminals in various offices. Some State and Federal databases could be accessed for items such as warrants, DMV driver's licenses or vehicle registrations, etc.

Unfortunately commercial and particularly the forensic use of computers in the police department was nonexistent. For example data on arrest reports could not be compared with data on Offense/Incident Reports , etc. If you had an officer write up an O/I R with a suspect driving a 1973 Olds Cutlass, license number so-n-so and another officer arrested a man driving that car the next day unfortunately the two pieces of data never crossed paths. In fact, information on two separate O/I R's could not be compared, except by hand.

When tasked to aid law enforcement in some meaningful way, say analyzing a crime trend using numbers in areas not defined by a reporting area or finding correlating information, the city programmers struggled to write programs that might accomplish the task. Often the data proved to be of less value than the time it took to create it; therefore such requests were not pursued with relish.

The more O/I R's I reviewed and posted the more familiar I became with the number of apples going into the barrel. The increasing or decreasing trends were relatively easy to track. Tying individual bad guys to the numbers was a much harder job. To assist with that task I also began reviewing arrest reports (AR's) and the investigator's Supplemental Offense/Incident Reports or SO/I R's to try to correlate offenses with known offenders: 'hooks'.

In the end, crime analysis in the Seventies amounted to amassing a concentrated understanding of what crimes were occurring; knowing the when and where; determining all the data points involved: times, dates, victims and victim types, perpetrator MO (Method of Operation), suspect physical and vehicle information, etc.; and putting all this information in the only computer then capable of doing the job, a human brain.

Though I rarely worked only 8-5 and my routine varied day by day, depending on the volume of any one task or groups of tasks, this is pretty much how my day would shake out:

Hour	Task
8:15 AM	Sort all new O/IR's (beefs or beef sheets)
	Post all new beefs to their appropriate map
	While reading beefs - analyze re correspondence with previous beefs on maps - current to last 3 mo; note for intel to pass fwd; noting trends, susp info, veh info, arrest info or other FYI
	Read Murder beefs
	Read Rape beefs
	Read Robbery beefs
	Read Assault beefs
	Read Burglary (business) beefs
	Read Burglary (residence) beefs
	Read Thefts (general) beefs
	Read Thefts (Auto) beefs
	Read Thefts (BMV) beefs
	Sort all new Supplement Reports (SR)
Noon	Retrieve original O/IRs and add new SRs
	Analyze each SR-O/IR for intel to pass forward - make notes
	Analyze all new O/IRs for intel to pass forward - make notes
	Review all crime stats: Central, NE, NW, SE, SW & city-wide & compare - run numbers, percentages, trends: plus & minus
	Create patrol intel form (when pertinent) and forward to watch commander
	Log patrol intel form
	Create Division Crime Analyst Information Bulletin (when pertinent); make copies and distribute
	File all new O/IRs and their attached SRs
	Collate and file all other relevant documents
	Post relevant data to various FBR charts and graphs
	Make follow-up phone calls
	Order fingerprint comparisons
	Order arrest reports
	Order SRs
	Write interdepartmental memos to inform or request info, or write letters to outside sources to inform or request info
5:15 PM	Write end of day activity memo
Varied hours	Conduct field work: recon & surveillance, interviews

Author Note: *with the exception that later when we were working together Tom and I were in constant contact—particularly after my office moved from 511. Tom and I moved into Apple Jack Brown's old office on the second floor of the Police & Courts Bldg. facing west, overlooking the 100 block of South Harwood and the Bar-B-Q joint across the street...*

Once the information was stuffed into my brain it was my job to makes sense of it, to synthesize and apply this comprehensive knowledge to the function of creating one of two ends. First, effectively insulating the bad guys from their target (with targeted or saturation patrol, for example) which often only moved bad guys from one place to another, or second, and preferably, catching the bad guys. Whether 'moved' or 'caught' their dots stopped cluttering up my crime maps.

To get some of this 'intel' out, rather than read it out loud in detail, (which I did) I promulgated the *Patrol Division Analyst Information Bulletin* (and later other forms) to relay crime patterns, offense clusters, and suspect information to CPD officers.

Chief Dixon was a constant visitor in my office, I think he liked seeing the maps fill up with dots. Not because he wanted to see crime increase, but rather he was fascinated by seeing it materialize in a visually graphic form. He also liked to ask me questions about what was going on.

Not intentionally, I became somewhat indispensable to my chief which later became the basis for his letting Tom and I do as we wished.

At the end of my first month as Division Crime Analyst, a fact sheet was laying in my in box. Attached was a memo routing sheet, a 'buck slip', from Chief Dixon with a simple "FYI" marked in the comment area. I lifted up the buck slip and found the crime stats for the city broken down by UCR (Uniform Crime Report) crime categories and giving the raw totals for each of the five patrol divisions. I made a file folder for the info and filed it away—I knew these data points were important, but had no idea what they would mean to my future.

One of my jobs, when I was in PIO, was attending and helping manage the media at the Chief's monthly PC, (press conference). The PC was always preceded by the Chief's staff meeting attended by senior department heads including the chief's of the five patrol divisions.

At those senior staff meetings the month's crime figures always came up. With the raw totals it was easy to see which patrol division had had the highest numbers in each of the crime categories. Each of the chiefs would get to talk about their part of the city and their crime numbers. So woe be it unto the chief whose area of the city was experiencing the biggest numbers.

It seemed at the time that last month's numbers were the only concern. If you had lower numbers than somebody else you were not likely to be on the hot seat. Chief Dixon did not like being on the hot seat, but the numbers were the numbers. I changed all that.

Starting with the end of my second month and with receipt of the second FYI crime numbers fact sheet, from Dixon, I got to work. I started doing some statistical analysis. Nothing fancy, but I was able to give Dixon percentages of increase and decrease within our own patrol division and compare our percentage of change, etc., with the other patrol divisions.

The next time Dixon went to a staff meeting he was armed with statistics that no one else had. He started spouting how Central Patrol Division had reduced thefts by such-and-such percentage over last month, last year and was able to do that with each of the six UCR crime categories. Dixon was now able to compare and contrast Central's crime stats against each of the other patrol divisions as well as the city as a whole. He could just recite our numbers or, if he wanted to, he could pick and choose where our numbers were better than someone else's. This information pleased Chief of Police Frank Dyson, and seriously irked the other four patrol division chiefs.

It was several months later that Dixon called me into his office, all smiles, to thank me for my monthly crime stats and told me about the furor he and they had caused among the other chiefs. He said he had finally been forced to admit where he had gotten his figures. I became the most despised patrol officer in the city by four disgruntled patrol chiefs!

Although there is no question my actions facilitated the expansion of the DCA program to the other patrol divisions almost immediately, it was not expanded specifically because I had done my job so well or just because my excellent crime analysis skills had made the Patrol Division Crime Analyst program a complete success. It was expanded in part because the other four patrol division chiefs, who didn't have a Division Analyst, were having their crime states thrown in their face every month by Chief Dixon and *his* Analyst! The other four patrol chiefs were carping, wincing and moaning about it and demanded their own Division Crime Analyst.

In the midst of all this political theater, I had placed a red sticky-dot on my 'pin' map to mark a November 15, 1973 rape offense. This would later be the first offense attributed to the Friendly Burglar-Rapist, FBR, as (R1) then came R2, R3 and R4 of which I was not yet aware.

Dallas, Northwest Patrol Division
Thursday, December 13, 1973
Officer Donald Paul Tucker, Sr. ~ Murdered[13]

---

[13] Officer Donald Paul Tucker, Sr., badge #1181, 18 year veteran police of DPD was gunned down answering a disturbance call on Thursday night, December 13, 1973.

1974

Not Yet On the Radar
Offenses Marked R2 through R7 are interspersed in chronological order, but remember they have not yet been "discovered" or "attributed" to the FBR!

A One Off?

Dallas, Northeast Patrol Division, Beat 236 4:17 pm
Wednesday, February 6, 1974 Offense Number R-1?
NOT ORIGINALLY ATTRIBUTED to FBR[14]

No Prints Lifted

After 4:00pm on this Wednesday afternoon in early February, when the average daytime temperature was 48 degrees, this day, February 6th, was described as "a very cold day" and "very windy". That afternoon, suffice it to say, it was cold enough for a heavy coat. With sunset two hours away at 6:03pm, the temperature was already trending downward. And, regardless, whether clouds would be present or not, in three hours a full moon was scheduled to rise at 7:19pm.

On her day off *GDSB*, a white female, twenty-five years of age, and a flight attendant with American Airlines, returned home from the grocery store to her apartment #2080 at 12884 Noel Road at five or ten minutes to four. After carrying up a load of groceries *GDSB* left her apartment door open while she went back downstairs to get a another load of groceries. She returned to her upstairs apartment. Inside *GDSB* was confronted and raped.

---

[14] This offense (not included in previous editions of OSfM) was brought to my attention in 2014 by Mr. J Patrick Rick. Now in January 2016, I am considering that this offense may have been committed by the FBR. Regardless, the information is illuminating.

Offense/Incident Report

According to their Offense/Incident Report (O/IR) it would appear that Officers Brown and Bradshaw were working patrol element 236 together out of the Northwest Patrol Division and were dispatched at 4:17pm on February 6, 1974 to 12884 Noel Road, apartment #2080 on a Signal 40.

DPD O/IR, Service #38546-F, lists Officer Roy Brown #1937 as the "reporting officer" (RO) and W.D. Bradshaw #2065 as the "other officer" (OO). It was customary for the junior or less senior officer, (by badge #) especially if the junior officer was "in training", to write up the O/IR as the RO. Some partners switch off report writing duties just as they would take turns driving; the report writing falling to the officer not driving. Regardless, for this O/IR, the senior officer was the RO.

Generally a call dispatched as a "Signal 40" or "Other" is so designated when the dispatcher is not sure of the type of call, perhaps because of a lack of information, or he/she wishes to disguise the nature of the call to anyone who might be listening to police broadcasts. In any case, being dispatched on a Signal 40, Brown and Bradshaw would not know that their complainant would be reporting a rape, which was usually dispatched as a Signal 25, Criminal Assault.

It is unknown how long it was between the time the officers were dispatched at 4:17pm and the time they arrived (their Code 6 time) at the complainant's apartment and then took the Complainant's statement. The O/IR shows that the officers cleared the call and were back "in service" and available for other calls at 7:38pm.

In the O/IR's areas designated: "Location of Offense", "Day(s)", "Date(s)", "Hour(s)" the RO filled them in as: Wednesday 2/6/74 at 4:00pm.

The "M/O" was listed as: "Stocking on face - showed gun and made Comp disrobe"

The "Narrative" section of the O/IR
filled-in (handwritten) by Officer Brown
is as follows: (shaded areas are the author's)

Comp. stated that she had been shopping for Gro. and was carrying sacks up stairs, leaving her front door open. She stated after she got Gro. in apt. she walked into her bed room and Suspect stepped out of her bathroom with a stocking over his head. He then pulled a gun on Comp and told her not to scream that "He was a Burg. that just got caught, and that he makes his living by Burg." She states she began to scream so he put her in the closet and closed door. She stated she could hear him going thru drawers then he came back and let her out of closet and made her disrobe then he placed a pillow case, from the bed, over her head then rape her. He then pulled phone out of wall and left apt. She stated she grabbed her husbands gun and ran down hall to catch him When her husband walked into apt. He stated he met suspect just outside his apt. and spoke to him. Comp's Husband witness #1 ran next door and told witness #2 that his wife and been raped and that Suspect was a white male 25 5' 8" to 5' 10". 155-160 lbs (arrow) Bushy headed and large mustache, wearing a brown suede (unknown word) car coat with a fur collar, black colored gloves and was carrying a large gun. Witness #2[15] stated he saw arrested suspect walk to Dumpster trash container and throw something in it then got back in a 1969 Ply 1973 Texas (license # blacked out) take something out of it then go into apt. We went to the trash container and found two stockings laying in it. comp. stated that they were like the ones that she had hanging in the bedroom. We the(n) checked Reg on the car and got name of Suspect then called apt mgr. and was advised that suspect lived there (12838 Noel Rd. #1037). We went to location and knocked on door. Suspect answered door and we ask if we could come in and talk to him, he states no but that he would come outside and talk to us. We talked to him and (word scratch-out) he told us that he had a pistol in (scratch-out) trunk and a pair of leather gloves in front

---

[15] Rather than the neighbor/witness finding "the suspect" walking around in the complex or running in or from the complex, he finds a man driving into the complex who the neighbor/witness thinks looks like description given him (second-hand) by the husband/witness. The neighbor/witness follows this man, watches him park, sees him go to a dumpster, takes down his license number and reports the man the neighbor/witness says matches the suspect description to RO. The RO leaves out the part where "the suspect" was driving into the complex not just "walk to Dumpster trash container and throw something in it then got back in a 1969 Ply 1973 Texas (license # blacked out) take something out of it then go into apt.".

seat of his car. he then went to car unlocked it and handed us both gloves & Gun. He was advised of his (words scratched-out) writes* by officer Brown. [*should be "rights", as in Miranda Warning, no time listed]

Comp. stated Suspect taped her hands together with surgical tape, I asked her how see (sp) knew it was surgical tape and she said because she was (word scratched-out) allergic (to) it Surgical tape and that her hands were (word scratched-out) beginning to break out.

Stockings, gun, & Gloves placed in prop room under tag number 148971.

This three page O/IR, in the section marked "Offense As Reported and Date" was filled in as: "Agg. Rape (21:03) and in the report section, "Date of this Report" was filled in with "2/6/74". It was signed by Roy G. Brown #1937 as RO and the box indicating the "Status Recommendations was X'd as "Open".

Although the section of the O/IR for "Suspect/s" lists: "James Patrick Rick w/m/ (Arrested)" the later narrative section (shown above) did not indicate before or after the Suspect "was advised of his writes" that the Subject was arrested.

After reading the above, this would be the usual ending point of most O/IR reviews; having ended with nothing other than a vague suspect description, and perhaps later, a few latent prints. However, for this offense there was an actual arrest. The vague description of the Complainant was turned into an ID of a possible suspect by a third party witness. What follows is an arrest of a rape suspect that could have ended the criminal career of the FBR... had the Arrested Person *been* the FBR.

Arrest Report

Indeed the Suspect, for O/IR #38546-F, one Rick, James Patrick, was arrested. He is listed on Arrest Report (AR) No. 74-8100, as a: w/m/25 or 26 (numbers are blurry), height 5-8, weight 140, hair Brn. The "Date and Time of Arrest" was filled-in as: 2-6-74 5:00 P.M. He was charged with "Inv. Agg. Rape 21.03, 1st Degree Felony".

According to the AR the arrest was made on "Call", which means the arresting officer/s made the arrest in conjunction with or subsequent to "the call" for service as opposed to an "on-view" arrest where the offense took place in their presence of the arresting officer/s.

Per this AR the Arrested Person (AP) was sober, not observed drinking, did not resist. The APs drug use was marked Unk." Box "22 Weapon (Describe)" is blank, box 23 "Armed" is marked "No". The "Date - Time Booked" is marked "2-6-74 ?:?? PM. (The time is either marked out or blacked out on Mr. Rick's redacted copy.) The AR lists the complainant along with her husband as a "Witness" and a Mr. "Gayland Wardell" of 12884 Noel Road #2018 as "Witness".

The jail booking sergeant relies upon the arresting officers' written narrative in their Arrest Report for the probable cause elements with which to either approve or disapprove the the APs arrest. Here is that Arrest Report's

"Narrative (Elements of Offense)":

Officers received a call on a rape above location. On arrival victim's husband stated that he had just arrived home and observed a white male fitting the Suspect's description walking down hallway from direction of his apartment appx. five feet away. Victim's husband then went to his friend's apartment next (*door?*) and told him what happened and asked Mr. Wardell if he would drive around apt. complex and see if he could spot a possible suspect. Mr. Wardell began driving thru complex and spotted suspect get out of a 1969 Ply, color green, Tex 73 Lic (number blacked out) and walk over to large dumpster trash receptacle and (word scratched through) throw something into it. Mr. Wardell went back to victim's apartment (words scratched through) and told (word scratched through) victim's husband what he saw and described suspect to them. The victim stated at that time that description of suspect and the man that Mr. Wardell saw were the same. Victim told officer that suspect was in her apartment when she returned home and pulled a gun on her that looked like a 45-automatic and that suspect had one or two ladies stockings over his head but that she could see that he had busy hair and a mustache. Suspect made her take her clothes off and taped her hands together with surgical tape and put a pillow case over her head and then raped her. Officers went to trash receptacle and recovered a pair of ladies stockings laying on top of trash. Officers went to suspects apartment and suspect came to door and walked outside to talk to officers. Officers placed suspect under arrest and read rights to suspect. Suspect gave permission to officers to search his car and suspect opened his trunk where officer Brown found a 22 cal. pistol in a sock[16] and a pair of brown leather gloves. Victim told officers that suspect was wearing a pair of black gloves. Evidence was placed in central jail property room on tag #148971.

Note 1:

Graphic shows actual sizes of [1] a ".45 Automatic" as described (with help) by DGSB and reported in O/IR Service #38546-F and [2] the similar type of .22 caliber revolver found in a sack, under the spare tire in the trunk of J. Patrick Rick's car. (See top of page: 47 →)

Note 2:

On the AR in section "29 Property Placed in Property Room / Tag Numbers", it was filled in with: "22 pistol, pair ladies stockings, pair of gloves." Tag number not listed here. Then below the section for the Narrative is section "50: Scars, Tattoo, Hair Style, and Mustache". Given the suspect description supplied by the Complainant (and witnesses?) as "Bushy headed" with a "large mustache", one would think these boxes/areas in AR would be filled in with the relevant information as to the Arrested Person's hair style and mustache. They were not.

Note 3:

Graphic shows actual and presumed events occurring on 2/6/74. The times and order of each occurrence, are unconfirmed. **Time notations are approximate as indicated. (See bottom of page: 47 →)**

---

[16] Officer Brown's hand-written AR uses the word "sock" (SOCK). In January 2016 Mr. *f* clarified and explained that the "Saturday Night Special was in a paper sack (SACK) that was stapled together and laying under the spare tire for over a year..." While true the gun was found "in the trunk", it was not, according to Mr. Rick (testimony) laying there in plain view... he had to tell the officers where the gun was... under the tire in a sack. A reasonable inference, reading Brown's AR, would be that when Mr. Rick opened the trunk the gun and gloves were laying right there, as if they had just been tossed in recently. However, it was Mr. Rick that dug through the miscellaneous detritus, moved the spare and retrieved the sack with the gun which was handed over to the officers. And Mr. Rick's brown driving gloves with holes on the back, knuckles and fingers were in the front seat of the car.

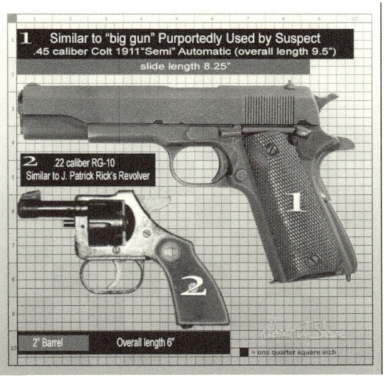

Activity	EVENT TIME		ELAPSED TIME	
	Begin	End		
Comp Said Criminal Assualt Occurred	3:50p	4:15p	25 minutes	
Call Dispated	4:17p	NA		
Call Duration	4:17p	7:38p		
Officer on Scene (Code 6)	Unk	Unk		
Interview Comp.	Unk	Unk		
Observed Crime Scene	Unk	Unk	43mins	
Interview Witness/s	Unk	Unk		
Gather Intel on Susp.	Unk	Unk		
Interview Suspect	Unk	Unk		
Search Veh.	Unk	Unk		
Arrest Suspect	5:00p	NA		
Suspect Read "Rights"	Unk	NA		3hrs 21mins
Transport Suspect to City Hall	appox 30min	approx 30min		
Comp.(w Husband) Goes to PHM	6:00p*	6:30p*		
Comp. Examined by Dr # PMH ER	7:00p*	7:30*		
Comp. (w Husband) taken to DPD	7:30p*	8:00p*		
Susp Taken to CAPERS	Unk	Unk		
Polaroid Pix taken of Susp.	Unk	Unk	2hrs 38mins	
Write Up O/IR	Unk	Unk		
Write Up Arrest Report	Unk	Unk		
Comp Arrives @ PD - CAPERS	8-8:30p*	9:30-10pm*		
Comp Shown PhotoArray w Susp	Unk	Unk		
Husband Shown PhotoArray w Susp	8:30-9:30p*	NA		
Suspect Booked-In	Unk	Unk		
Officers Return to Service	7:38p	NA		
Inv Hudson Writes up PR	Unk	Unk	Unk	

From Call to Arrest to Jailing of JPR re O/IR #38546-F & AR #74-8100 & (*per Exam. Trial)

* times are approximate and or thought to be accurate as of available information - 3.1.2016

Supplemental Report/s
(form used to add pages to or continue an O/IR or add investigative follow-up)

SUPPLEMENT REPORT of Physical Evidence Section (PES) regarding "Rape 2-6-74". "Date of This Report: 2-7-74"

Narrative section:

"Pes. #29417
Invs R. A Pettie and R. T. Hunter went to the residence of (blacked out) Rape Services #38546-F. Photos taken. Collected piece of tape used to bind compl.'s hands."
RO (typed in): R.A. Pettie & R.T. Hunter, however, none of the "Status" boxes appear to have been checked or X'd to indicate status.

SUPPLEMENT REPORT re Investigator's Supplement "Offense As Reported and Date: Agg. Rape 21.03 (A-2)", "Date of This Report: 2-7-74"

Narrative section:

Code 02112
"Below listed susp. arrested and filed on this date."
"CBA"
"Full Name of Arrested Person: James Patrick Rick wm26 12838 Noel Rd #1037"
Reporting Officer Name ID and Status Recommendation: "C W Hudson 2533" Status box "Closed" was marked with an "X". "Supervisor Approving: Sgt. F.O. Mote 868"

THE NEXT DOCUMENT I read was the eighty-seven page, typed, double-spaced, transcript of Mr. Rick's examining trail.

City of Dallas
Dallas County Texas
Tuesday, February 19, 1974

Examining Trail - Partial Transcript of Proceedings

NO. 15186
STATE OF TEXAS
VS.
JAMES PATRICK RICK

APPEARANCES:

MR. MIKE GILLETTE, Dallas, Texas
  For the State of Texas
MR. JAMES A GANDY, Dallas, Texas
  and
MR. JEFFREY H. KILGORE, Dallas, Texas
  For the Defendant

* * *

Be it remembered that on the 19th day of February, A.D. 1974 the above styled and number cause came on for hearing before the honorable Joe B. Brown, Jr., Judge of the Justice of the Peace Court of Dallas County Texas, Precinct 7, Place 2 and the following proceedings were had:

THE COURT: Number 15186, the State of Texas versus James Patrick Rick, charged with rape.

MR. GILLETTE: Your Honor, at this time the State of Texas is ready..

MR. KILGORE: Your Honor, the Defendant is ready.

THE COURT: Does the Defendant know of his right to make a statement?

MR. KILGORE: Yes, sir.

THE COURT: Does he wish to make one?

MR. KILGORE: Yes, he does, Your Honor.

THE COURT: He knows of his right, but does he wish to make a statement?

MR. KILGORE: Yes, he does.

THE COURT: Does he wish to testify in his on defense as a witness, or does he wish to make an unsworn statement at the beginning of his testimony--I mean at the beginning of the examining trail?

MR. KILGORE: He will testify as a witness in his own behalf.

THE COURT: As I understand it, and correct me if I am wrong, he would then be subject to cross examination just like any other witness.

MR. KILGORE: Yes.

THE COURT: Very good. Would all the witnesses in the case against James Patrick Rick please stand to be sworn?

(The witnesses were sworn.)

THE COURT: Is the rule to be invoked by either--

MR. GILLETTE: The rule will be invoked by the State, Your Honor.

THE COURT: The rule has been invoked, and everyone, other than the Defendant, must remain outside the Courtroom until they are called to testify, and let me direct all of the witnesses before you finally step outside--let me direct all of the witnesses to refrain from discussing the case among yourselves. You are not to discuss this case among yourselves. Thank you very much. You may remain outside.

I will spare the reader, at this point, the intervening eighty pages, however I would like, in summary, to point out twenty-one (21) details revealed in the transcript of the examining trail:

1. GDSB said attack occurred between 3:50 and 4:15pm
2. GDSB said time passed between Susp leaving and husband arriving, not more that five minutes
3. GDSB said husband came in apartment at 4:15pm
4. Husband says he sees Susp on landing at 4:10pm
5. GDSB and husband leave apartment at approx 6pm for Parkland Hospital (PMH) with police
6. Trip time to PHM approx 15-20 minutes
7. GDSB examined by Dr. at PMH ER
8. GDSB left PMH with police at approx 7:30p to 8pm to ride downtown to police headquarters
9. Unknown if GDSB and Husband were shown photo array separately or together... I am assuming separately.

10.GDSB when asked at ET if she could ID Rick from pictures:

    a. Q Where you shown pictures of anybody after this happened?

    b. A Yes, I was.

    c. Q Were you able to tell anything from the pictures

    d. A No

11.Husband shown pictures at approx 8:30 or 9:30

12.Husband said he was shown photo array but couldn't ID Rick because photos so dark, had to make a second pass

13.GDSB and husband arrived home at approx 10-10:30pm

14.Husband ID's Rick at ET as man he saw at 4:10pm

15.Rick testifies to being at work (PMH) from approx. 7:30a-7:45a on date of attack and was in the company of other workers the majority of the day

16.Rick testifies that at approx. 3:45p he and 3 others were in the intensive care burn unit with a patient, having just administering a life-saving treatment

17.Rick testifies to being with his boss (Dr. Willerson) by the elevator at 4:05pm about to leave PMH for the day

18.Rick testifies it took him about 8 minutes to walk to his car

19.Rick testifies it takes approx 30 min to drive home

20.Rick arrives at apartment complex at approximately 4:30pm

21.Prosecutor contends[17] that (per Rick's testimony: he left work at 4:05pm, arrived at his car 8 minutes later at 4:13pm and adding 30 minutes for the drive home) Rick would have arrived at 4:43pm, not 4:30pm

I will conclude the examining trial information with the Judge's statement on page 83 of the court reporter's transcript:

THE COURT: All right. Let's -- I believe it would be best if we wound it up at this point. As you all know, the Court is not called upon to decide the guilt or innocence of the accused to determine whether he might have committed an offense, and while some serious doubt has been raised concerning this, I do feel that there is sufficient evidence to bind the case over to the Grand

---

[17] A time frame that makes it even less likely Mr. Rick could have been at the Comp's apartment between 3:50pm and 4:15pm

Jury and do find that there is probably cause, and we'll consider at this point the bond the Defendant should be released upon. I understand the Defendant is out on bail at the present time.

More: Back To The Future

On April 17, 2014 I received and email from Mr. Pat Rick containing, as attachments, several Dallas Police Department documents: 1) Offense/Incident Report (O/IR) #83546-F, dated February 6, 1974 regarding the criminal assault of *GDSB* on the same date; 2) the Supplement Report/s for O/IR #38546-F; 3) Arrest Report #74-8100; 4) the transcript from the above mentioned Examining Trail of 2/19/74 which bound the case over to the Dallas County Grand Jury; and 5) the PD's Prosecution Report showing the Grand Jury's disposition of the case: "NO BILLED BY G.J."

My first reaction after reading the O/IR from February 6, 1974 was to immediately exclude this offense as being attributable to the FBR and his method/s of operation. (Bare in mind I was reading this O/IR and evaluating it with the knowledge available to me in 2014, not as I would have had I seen it in February 1974.)

However, in trying to understand how I might have included or excluded this O/IR at the time of its occurrence, several things come to mind as I read and reread these documents.

In February of 1974 I was only aware of the one rape offense from November 1973 that would later in 1975 be designated as the first Dallas rape offense attributed to the suspect who would be known as the Friendly Burglar Rapist, or Friendly Rapist. In February of 1974 there had been no patterning or definitive 50+ MO Markers (developed later based on multiple offenses). The only MO known was that provided by that "first" rape offense occurring at 2:30pm on the afternoon of November 15, 1973.

The biggest differences the 11/15/73 rape and the rape in this "new unknown" O/IR from 2/6/74 was that in the first case no implement of intimidation and compliance was displayed or spoken of and in the second case the Suspect displayed a gun. A significant MO Marker of The FBR was that he would often use/display/or say he had a knife. A gun was never used/displayed or spoken of as tool of intimidation or compliance during any of the offenses attributed to the FBR. Was this a one-off?

However, had I seen this O/IR in February of 1974, I might very well have included it because the suspect is quoted in the O/IR by the RO that suspect: *He then pulled a gun on Comp and told her not to scream that "He was a Burg. that just got caught, and that he makes his living by Burg."*[18]

Given the run-on nature of the Reporting Officer's narrative style, use of grammar and spelling and lack of time markers and other specificity, I have to question if the RO got this quote wrong. Did Complainant actually use the third person "He" which the RO then quoted? Was it more of a characterization of Comp's words or her actual quoted words? Or if RO had asked Comp to specifically use the same words as suspect, would she have said her attacker actually said: "You just caught a burglar in the act... I make a living doing this... or I make a living burglarizing... rather than "he makes a living by Burg(lary)?"

The transposition of a first-person statement repeated as a third-person "he said" does not clarify the statement.

Police Department, City of Dallas, Prosecution Report

The final document provided by Mr. Rick[19] was the "Police Department, City of Dallas, Prosecution Report referencing DPD O/IR Service No. 38546-F. This is a referral document prepared by the investigator assigned to the case (C.W. Hudson #2533) subsequent to his/her investigation. It provides a summary to the District Attorney of the case elements, showing probable cause.

Inv. Hudson's Supplement Report, dated 2.7.74 (the day after the alleged assault) states: "Below listed susp. arrested and filed on this date. CBA" The status is X'd "Closed". CBA stands for Closed By Arrest or as sometimes said, Cleared By Arrest.

No mention is made in Inv. Hudson's Supplemental Report of his interviewing or interrogating Mr. Rick. No mention is made of polaroid photos being taken of Mr. Rick. Inv. Hudson makes no mention of interviews with Comp (DGSB) or her husband or that a photo line-up which included a photo of Mr. Rick (wearing

---

[18] See pages 433-442 for further explanation

[19] These documents were provided to Mr. Rick in response to his "Open Records" request of the Dallas Police Department which they received on October 31, 2012.

his coat[20]). was shown to either. No mention was made of the results of those photo line ups which were: Comp was unable to ID Mr. Rick from the photos and Comp's husband was unable to ID Mr. Rick on first look and had to take "a second pass".

Likewise no mention was made of interviews or discussions with the reporting/investigating/arresting officers to confirm how they obtained their "evidence," the search of Mr. Rick's vehicle and the recovery of an old, rusty .22 caliber pistol that comes no where close to matching the Comp's statement: the Suspect had "big gun," "an automatic," "a .45." or how the ROs apparently helped the Comp understand the difference between a revolver and an "automatic." There is no mention of an examination of the "evidence": "one pair of gloves, one cal. pistol, one sock[21], one pair ladies hose much less the items being shown to Comp for her identification.

Lastly there is no mention that Inv. Hudson inquired as to Mr. Rick's whereabout prior to, during, and or after the alleged assault.

The reader may want to go back and re-read the narratives from the O/IR and AR to refresh their memories so as to identify any differences in them with the narrative of this Prosecution Report. This section of the PR is the "Summary of Case":

> Complainant was taking some groceries from her car to apartment. Upon completion, she went into the bedroom when defendant stepped out of bathroom with ladies nylon stocking pulled over his head to conceal his identity, pulled a pistol[22] on complainant. Defendant then told complainant that he was a burglar and that he just got caught. That he (def) made his living (*repeated*: his living) that way and not to scream and he wouldn't hurt her. Complainant began to scream, so defendant put comp in closet and closed the door. Defendant then ramsacked the apartment and came back to the closet where comp was. Defendant then took comp out of the closet, made

---

[20] It would be unusual to have on hand photos of white males with a similar look as Mr. Rick *and* wearing a winter coat.

[21] Note the use of the word "sock" rather than "sack".

[22] In the 70s the generic term "gun" (handgun) would likely be interpreted as either revolver or an 'automatic;' i.e. a semi-automatic, (like a .45 cal. 1911) unless you specifically qualified the term pistol as 'semi-automatic pistol'. Whereas the term "pistol" was most often a generic term for a revolver, rather than an 'automatic'.

her take her cloths off, then put a pillow case over head and had intercourse with her. Defendant then left apartment. Defendant was seen leaving the apartment by complainant's husband.

On the right side the Prosecution Report (PR) is the "Filing Information" which shows it was filed with Brotherton by D.A. Unit on 2/7/74. In the center, is box-stamp to be filled-in which shows the PR was "Approved for Filing" by "Sgt. W.M. Parker #2055" as "Supervisor" with a squiggle of initials.

Dallas
Evening, Wednesday, February 20, 1974

A Case of Rape made a big splash as a made for TV movie starring, TV's Bewitched, Elizabeth Montgomery. This was a more realistic portrayal of rape and its aftermath: dealing with the victim's treatment by police, hospital staff, and the courts. The movie garnered a lot of water-cooler buzz and awards... generating sympathy for the victim. It's about time.

Valentines Day had been on the previous Thursday. *A Case of Rape* aired in prime time.

I wondered what affect this movie would have on the citizens of Dallas, the cops I worked with and around, as well as the attitudes of doctors and prosecutors. I considered it was not going to have much impact on defense attorneys.

Dallas
Police Department
Friday, February 22, 1974

On the left side of the aforementioned Prosecution Report (PR) referencing DPD O/IR Service No. 38546-F are the blanks for the case "Disposition". This report shows a date-stamp of "FEB 22 1974", and in specific the case brought against RICK, James Patrick, shows the "Disposition" blank is filled by an ink stamp noting, in thick bold black-inked capital letters: "NO BILLED BY G.J."

READING THESE FOUR documents (in 2016) and given the points below, it is understandable that the G.J. returned a bill of no indictment, i.e.: a No Bill:

1. the lack of specificity and discontinuity between the three narratives (O/IR, AR, & PR)
2. the disparity between suspect descriptions
3. failure of Comp to ID Mr. Rick as attacker either by photo line-up or face-to-face in court
4. coupled with the examining trail transcript revelations, among them: Mr. Rick's time-line precludes his participation in the assault of GSDB.
5. the unknown/secret testimony provided the G.J. [23] [24]

Had I read, at the time, the February 6, 1974 O/IR, and the AR, I might have included this rape as the second rape in what would become the offenses attributed to the FBR. Also, I might note, that as this would then be FBR offense number two, the gun would not be an MO anomaly, rather it would be a new factor. The fact or supposition would remain that the suspect in the first rape could have had a gun but never displayed or spoke of it and or the complainant was never aware of a gun.

One final point of interest, the tape. The adhesive tape, said to be wide surgical tape, used to bind Comp.'s wrists was never found anywhere but on the Complainant. Where did the rest of the tape go? The officers found ladies hose, but no tape, no gun. It would be difficult to assume that the tape used to bind the Comp. was somehow all the suspect brought with him. If the tape had belonged to either the Comp. or her husband, it was not mentioned or ruled out other than to say the Comp was allergic to surgical tape which is how she 'knew/knows' hands were bound with surgical tape. There was no roll of tape found on Mr.

---

[23] Mr. Rick, as he did in his examining trail, revealed that he did testify before the Grand Jury. As Mr. and Mrs. Rick observed GSDB in the hallway outside the Grand Jury room it is assumed that she testified. Neither GSDB's husband nor Mr. Wardell were seen that day by Mr. Rick. It is unknown if they, the reporting/arresting officers, the investigator assigned to the case or the P.E.S. investigator testified. However I am now (2016) aware that Mr. Rick's attorney provided to the Grand Jury five (5) statements of alibi witnesses for Mr. Rick that corroborated his whereabouts at the time of the 'assault', as well as a polygraph examiner's report which bolstered Mr. Rick's claim of no involvement.

[24] On February 8, 1974 Mr. Rick submitted to a polygraph examination conducted by state licensed polygraph examiner Kenneth H. Brettman who reported the following result. "EXAMINER'S OPINION: Evaluation of the polygrams resulting from this examination fail to reveal to this examiner significant criteria that would indicate deception on the part of this subject's statement that he did not have sexual relations with, nor did he rape *DSGB.*"" In layman's terms, Mr. Rick is telling the truth, he did not assault *DSGB*. *NOTE the examiner used DSGB's name, I have replace her name with initials.

Rick or in his car. Apparently there was no subsequent search of Mr. Rick's apartment for any potential evidence such as a large gun or tape matching that recovered by P.E.S.

Additionally, on or after February 22, had I been aware of the G.J.'s No Bill, Mr. Rick might have remained, subliminally, a person of interest for a time, even if I believed the G.J. No Billed Mr. Rick for all the right reasons. However I would soon know the real FBR was still out there. In fact the suspect in the next rape would also use tape to bind his victim.

And as the FBR cases began to mount, Mr. Rick would be eliminated, if scrutinized, by dint of lack of opportunity.

Mourning The Loss of a Fellow Officer

Dallas, Central Patrol Division, Sector 110
Saturday, March 2, 1974
Officer Leslie G. Lane, Jr. ~ Murdered

One of my friends on my old patrol detail, was mercilessly killed not long after 11pm by a fleeing felon. The parolee assaulted a police woman, she managed to escape, but left in her now stolen car was her service revolver. After a high speed chase the felon wrecked out and Officer Leslie G. Lane Jr. pursued him on foot into the dark where this scum of a felon killed Lane with the police woman's service revolver.

The sadness over Les' killing is profound; never to be forgotten.

Dallas, Northwest Patrol Division, Beat 521
4:30 am Thursday, July 30, 1974
Offense Number 2 (R-2)

THE RAPIST HAD been there before, inside apartment #133 of the Arroyo Place Apartments at 2600 Arroyo in Dallas. That previous Thursday, while rummaging through the apartment he had found *JP*'s spare key from the kitchen. She was gone. He unscrewed the ear and mouth pieces of the phone's handset before leaving.

JP, a white female 33, had reported the broken window, phone problem and lost spare key to the apartment manager, who fixed the lock.

This morning he stood beside her as she lay in bed asleep. She woke to the shock of a rubber-gloved hand over her mouth. He put a knife to her throat, made her roll over and pushed her face down into the pillow and said, "Don't move, I'm a burglar. I won't hurt you, but I have to tape your hands and mouth."

The rapist put a pillow case over her head, then taped her hands and her feet together. He talked constantly, saying things like, "This won't take but a second…" then, "I'll get in my truck and leave."

He raised her nightgown to her waist and fondled her. He tried unsuccessfully to penetrate her before applying a lubricant to complete the rape of *JP*. The rapist told her, "you should be more careful, this could happen to you again."

JP heard him unscrew the mouthpiece from the phone and leave her apartment.

Dallas, Northeast Patrol Division, Beat 222
5:30 am Saturday, August 3, 1974
Offense Number 3 (R-3)
Partial Print

THE RAPIST PUSHED open the sliding glass door to unit #104 in the Hill Top House Apartments at 10454 E. Northwest Highway. Inside he roamed through the apartment before heading into the bedroom.

RG, a white female 29, nestled under the bedcovers, was asleep until she felt the covers being lifted off of her-in her sleep-state; she laid still, telling herself she was dreaming. Then the rapist's elbow hit her on the side of the head as he tried to put a pillowcase over her head. He raised her gown and removed her panties.

When *RG* regained consciousness she realized there was a something covering her head and felt the man fondling her. The rapist told her, "If you hold still I won't have to hurt you." Unable to penetrate her he slid down between her legs and performed oral sex, asking, "Do you like that?" His next attempt at penetration was successful.

Startled at 5:45am by *RG*'s bedside alarm clock going off, the rapist quickly got up and left her apartment.

Fifteen months later on 11-30-1976 Tom would make a "Request For Latent Print Check" for this offense. P.E.S.

Thompson compared the partial prints lifted at the scene with those of the FBR. Results, per Thompson: "Yes—it's him, positively identified by finger prints."

Dallas, Northeast Patrol Division, Beat 235
9:45 pm Thursday, August 8, 1974
Offense Number 4 (R-4)

IT WAS A quarter to ten in the evening when *SL*, a white female 24, who had been in her back bedroom, walked into the living room and was grabbed by the rapist.

Her ground floor apartment, number 118, was located in the Emerald Forest Apartments at 13626 Maham Road.

He put a knife to her stomach and said, **"Don't' say anything, I will kill you,"** then asked, "Where is your roommate?"

When *SL* didn't reply he pushed her down the hall and into her bedroom, keeping a knife to her back, and then threw her onto the floor.

Scared for her life, *SL* stayed face down as the rapist walked around the apartment. When he asked if she had any money SL replied, "Seventeen dollars in my purse, in the living room."

After pocketing her money he returned to the bedroom and tied SL's hands with leather straps he'd found there in the bedroom then left her alone again. When he came back he turned her over and cut the leather straps and put a bath towel over her face. He pulled up her blouse, took off her bra and fondled her breasts before pulling off her jeans and panties.

During the rape he asked her, "Do you like this?" After his orgasm he told her, "Don't move for five minutes." He left and she lay on the floor counting the minutes.

The rapist jogged across the courtyard.

Issuing from someone's open window, the sounds of Maria Muldaur's *Midnight At the Oasis* floated on the air.

Chapter 2

Before *the FBR* there was

Operation Bi-GatorSmooth

READING, ANALYZING & PLOTTING crimes on my maps I realized crime trends were predictive only based on what had happened before. So it made sense that before you could find out why a trend was happening today you had to look into the past; track it from its beginning.

Though this made sense, after several months I recognized crime trends were generally short-lived with not many numbers to substantiate them. As such, it was not efficacious to spend much time ordering old O/I R's to review when I had all the new ones I could handle coming in day after day.

Everyday new dots were put on my wall maps and analysis reports were given to the Chief and watch commanders. The only 'crime dots' of note were from what I began observing back in early April 1974.

The theft map had become heavily dotted with motor vehicle break-ins. Particularly, a continuing problem with burglary of motor vehicles (BMV's) at the Holiday Inn located downtown at 1015 Elm Street. A preliminary pattern was observed and defined.

In mid-May, with the assistance of DPD Investigator James (Jim) E. Bryan of Intelligence Liaison, I set up a lengthy surveillance. This surveillance did not produce any arrests but it did seem to have the desired effect as the BMV's virtually stopped through June, July, and August.

IN SEPTEMBER 1974, Officer Thomas Harvey Covington Jr., working out of the Community Services Division, was assigned to a Special Project to review Central Division Thefts. Covington found that not all Theft O/I R's were coming to the Office of Central Division Analyst. And surprise, surprise, among the reports that had not been received were numerous BMV offenses at 1015 Elm Street.

Tom Covington, Jim Bryan and I formed an immediate alliance. It was "us against the crooks". Without official sanction and on our own initiative, Investigator Bryan and Officers'

Covington and Sadler re-launched our own investigative operation.

THE RAPIST[25] GOT out of bed and began pulling on his sweatpants.
"Where are you going?"
"Can't sleep, I'm going for a run, go back to sleep."
"How long will you be gone?"
"Till I get tired, I guess."
"Be careful," his wife said.
"I always am."

JIM, TOM, AND I were each at home, possibly dreaming of ways to catch the culprits breaking into the cars at the downtown Holiday Inn.

BMV was not as serious a crime as assault or murder, obviously. BMV wasn't particularly high in the priority of property crimes since the dollar amounts were relatively low. But the number of citizens whose cars had been burglarized was growing, not to mention the number of dots on my Theft map.

These cars, belonging to the hotel guests and employees, were being burglarized of everything from stuffed toys to audio equipment—really, anything left behind by citizens thinking their vehicle was secure. With their ignition key and separate trunk/glove box key in their possession, their car and contents should be secure, right?

In the not too distant past a locked trunk, less so a locked 'glove compartment', presented problems to car burglars: time, noise and exposure. The more time, the more noise, the more exposure meant possible witnesses or even 'on-view' capture by the cops. This is just one reason car burglars were often car thieves, taking the victim's car elsewhere to burglarize it without scrutiny.

Now, in 1974, most new car models, particularly those in the General Motors line, had this great new idea: the inside trunk-latch leaver, usually just inside the driver's side door, under the dash; the next innovation was the remote trunk-button usually located inside the glove box. Each of these labor saving devices

---

[25] My speculative conversation between the FBR and his wife. What did she know? What did she suspect, on the nights he was gone, over the next three years, if anything?

allowed the trunk to be unlocked from inside the car without ever having to put the separate trunk key in the trunk lock and giving it a turn.

Therefore the BMV burglar of the 1970s did not need to resort to breaking car windows or prying open trunks with a crowbar or screwdriver. The accomplished BMV burglar carried a single tool of the trade, a "Slim-Jim," a two-foot long thin strip of metal with cutouts on one end. It would be silently slipped between the glass and the door to reach and then to catch the control rods in the door panel to unlock the door. The less prepared, but no less professional burglar, might have with him or might depend on finding, right there in the parking lot, the ubiquitous and often abandoned coat-hanger. Both items allowed burglars to enter cars without the breaking windows or jamming screw drivers into the lock-holes to gain access. Thus the term or crime of 'breaking and entering a motor vehicle' or BEMV became simply 'burglary of a motor vehicle or BMV.

COPS GET JAZZED about catching bad guys and with the number of BMV's at the Holiday Inn growing; the desire to catch the bad guy or guys was growing exponentially. Like the hangman and his 'gallows humor', the doctor and his 'O.R. vulgarity', cops have their own special brand of 'police or cop humor'. This behavior, according to some psychologists, is a coping mechanism used by those faced with the sometimes all-consuming tension of life and death decisions.

These inside jokes and irreverent fun were not meant for public consumption—many a hangman, doctor and cop have suffered, uttering indiscrete lampoons within the public earshot.

This irreverence was only one of the reasons Jim, Tom and I got on so well, but it was one of the main releases we had for the tedium, boredom and frustrations of long hours of records research, analysis, surveillance and the sustained failure to catch the bad guy.

We each knew the longer the bad guy or bad guys went uncaught, more citizens and officers would be affected and potentially placed in danger if the untoward BMV turned into a physical attack on a vehicle owner, a hotel security guard, or police officer on patrol.

Our 'humor' became our constant surface level of discourse as we approached 'the cop work' we each did with professionalism and pride.

Nicknames are ubiquitous in groups like the military and paramilitary organizations like police departments. In patrol you get stuck with a 'handle' often for strange reasons not always indicative of the name. Jim Bryan, when he was in patrol used to wear to and from work in winter a big white coat with white sheared wool lining and collar. Officer Frank L. Hearron (later Deputy Chief Frank Hearron) nicknamed Jim the 'White Buffalo'. It stuck. Lt. Macsas was 'the Arab'. One of our sector sergeants always seemed to precede his sentences with "Say Dad," or alternately "Hey-Dad," and became know as "Say-Dad" or "Hey-Dad" to his troops and by extension all who worked around them. Another sergeant had the unfortunate habit of starting his sentences with 'Err-ah' and became known as "Sergeant Err-ah".

The southern drawl of the slow-talking Sergeant Err-ah, sector sergeant for the 140s, amplified his unfortunate knack for creating moments of laughter for the troops.

Case in point. The city and county had been on a manhunt for days. All law enforcement resources were searching high and low, night and day for the men who had recently murdered five sheriff's deputies.

The last murderer had been identified, but not yet caught. It was believed that he was 'holed' up in an apartment somewhere in the 110s (East Dallas). The SWAT team was out in force, the tactical unit had been deployed, all available beat officers were combing the East Dallas neighborhoods. And in the night sky, the DPD helicopter had been illuminating the ground search for the last couple of hours.

Sergeant Err-ah was apparently the go-to patrol supervisor at that moment in time.

The intensity of that kind of manhunt has all your faculties focused on the sober job at hand. The radio had been very quiet with few interruptions by the dispatcher for calls for service. In the midst of this quiet intensity the radio crackled with the voice of the helicopter pilot. He was notifying the ground supervisor that he was running out of gas and was returning to base to refuel. The irony and hilarity of the moment went something like this:

"Helicopter to one-forty."

"Err-ah, this is err-ah one-farrty... go ahead."

"One-forty, we'll be returning to base to refuel."

"Err-ah, one-farrty to th' helicopter... err-ah... stand by."

Everyone else listening to the radio had understood the import of the helicopter pilot's notification and is thinking... *duh, the man didn't ask your permission, he just told you he's running out of fuel and is returning base so he doesn't run out of gas and fall out of the sky... and you tell him to "stand by".*

Though not sanctioned radio protocol, pressing the button on your radio mike to talk produces a single click, pressing the button several times was equivalent to clapping for or laughing at something just said on the radio.

The moment after Sergeant Err-ah said, "err-ah, stand by," the previous radio silence erupted with a cacophony of clicks that sounded like thousands of castanets.

Later that night a tip had led beat officer Ed Duncan to the suspected criminal's lair, where Ed made the arrest.

I got tagged with the nickname: 'Cocky-Bob'. I think Officer Fred Overstreet was the first to call me that. On its own it sounds derogatory, but I never heard anyone use it that way. I never bothered to find out the genesis of the name. Was I 'cocky'? Did someone perceive me that way? It didn't matter, once you get a nickname, it just sticks...

Tom didn't come into our threesome with a nickname and Jim just called me 'Bob', but started calling Tom, 'Tom-Bob', a stereotypical double naming used in the south where the first and middle names are fused phonetically as one.

Jim Bryan became 'Jim-Bob' and apparently 'Bob-Bob' was too much trouble so I became Billy-Bob. Thus we three amigos were, Tom-Bob, Jim-Bob and Billy-Bob. 'Nicknamery' was organizationally in our blood.

Another case in point: The coining of a new catch-phrase seemed a necessity after we had become tagged "the wino-cops."

Our undercover assignment was to catch and stop a rapist who was assaulting women in various downtown parking lots. A lone woman in the middle of parking lot was easy to isolate and attack with little notice. This undercover job was our first foray into what became our 'wino' personas. The second time was using these 'costumes' to stop ongoing burglary of motor vehicles in some of the same parking lots.

We had our moments. While on our operation *'stop downtown parking lot rapes'* we got into a little trouble. As cops do from time to time; we got 'caught'. We had briefed Chief Dixon on our plan to interdict the parking lot rapist. I had made sure he was aware of the offenses, where they were happening, our concern that winos or indigents could be involved... If he heard the rest of my spiel his reactions later would indicate he had not.

Chief Dixon, an inveterate runner, had gone for his daily run a the Y and thought while driving back to the cop-shop he would loop through some of the downtown parking lots. Once a street cop, always a street cop, Dixon cruised one of the lots and saw three suspicious 'winos' prowling between the cars. He crept up on Jim, Tom and me in his smooth car and jumped out to surround us. We of course recognized him and didn't try to escape. So he thought he had just caught three desperados!

He looked us up and down, took in our unclean, disheveled appearance and called for back up. We did appear to be three 'drunks'. Public drunkenness was, after all, a jail offense. When he finally recognized us he said, "What the hell are you guys doing?"

I started to explain and to remind him he had authorized what we were doing... Thankfully Tom jumped in, cutting to the chase, and said with a grin, "Catchin' bad guys, Chief!"

Dixon just harrumphed, bit down on his pipe, got back in his car and drove off shaking his head.

Being called "the wino-cops" didn't hurt our reputations within the Department, but it was easily misinterpreted by the public—as in the press. Not that the new phrase was particularly better or more funny, but when we told other officers we were working undercover on "Operation Bi-GatorSmooth" the words were esoteric sounding enough to garner lots of 'What's' from the inquisitive and simple 'Harrumphs' from those who immediately couldn't be bothered with what they knew would be a trap of an explanation, as if it was the answer to a bad knock-knock joke.

Jim, Tom and I had, over several weeks, already put in long hours of surveillance working to interdict BMV's in the parking lots of downtown. It was not hard to understand why these parking lots were such good targets. The majority of the city's banks, insurance companies and businesses had offices downtown. Each drew workers from all corners of the city and county by car—cars which out of necessity, sat in open unguarded and unattended parking lots for eight hours a day.

As any hunter knows, blending into the surroundings is a key to observing while not being observed. We three amigos contacted various businesses in the area and arranged to have access to roofs and offices that overlooked several acres of the most heavily attacked parking lots. We three clean-cut cops stood out like an exotic dancer at a Baptist convention.

Observing the transit of pedestrians across these lots during the day it was surmised that the wandering indigent, the winos, were some of the likely BMV suspects; breaking into cars for the money they could find, knowing spare change equals cheap wine. Though less likely the winos/indigents were also prime suspects for the rapes; they at least had "opportunity."

Therefore it was not long until we three amigos skipped shaving, starting wearing our oldest clothes and visiting the Goodwill to find other appropriate costume.

Our cop's 'uniforms' became dirty clothes, faces, and hands. The true wino, unless he's on his way to buy a bottle of wine, has in one hand or pocket a bottle of wine in a brown paper sack.

Now transformed into three winos, Bryan, Covington and Sadler carried in-hand, like winos, the same ubiquitous rumpled, stained brown paper sacks; only ours contained heavy portable police radios.

With one man of the team (taking turns) up high in a building or on a roof 'observing', the other two (out in the weather) would be sitting in doorways, alleyways or holding up the sides of buildings sitting, like human buttresses against, the walls adjacent to our target parking lots or drunkenly stumbling through them on re-recon. Activities which one would expect to go unnoticed, given all the real winos in the area.

Up in an office building scanning the parking lots through a window with binoculars Jim said, "You've got a squad[26] coming your way, Elm Street side."

The two apparently inebriated winos, listening to their brown paper sacks, got up and ambled in the opposite direction. Moments later, in the warmth of his thirty-fifth floor office, Jim Bob was laughing hilariously as his partners Tom Bob and Billy Bob were put in the back of a squad car and driven away.

Tom said to the officer driving, "I thought you guys got the info we'd be working the parking lots today... dressed like this! Didn't you see us in detail this morning?"

"Yeah we saw you," the officer in the passenger seat said with a smile."

----

[26] Unfortunately I don't remember the officers' names who 'captured' us that morning.

"So?" I said, "What are you doing—you're blowing our stake-out!"

"So? So what are we supposed to do," the driver said as he pulled over a couple of blocks away.

"Yeah," his partner said, "we get the call—there's drunks at Elm & Pacific. We gotta talk to the complainant, right? And try to keep your cover, right? But the complainant says 'you gotta do something, those guys aren't just drunks, their crazy!' 'How so,' my partner asks. The complainant says, 'we get drunks here all the time, they drink their wine from their paper sack and fall asleep in the sun, they don't hurt nobody—but these guys gotta be crazy—"

The driver was doubled over laughing as his partner gave Tom and I, the two cop-winos, sitting in the back seat of their squad car, the punch line, "these guys gotta be crazy b'cause—I haven't seen'm take a drink all day, they just keep talking into their sacks!"

So much for occupational camouflage and blending into the neighborhood, but our presence and the arrests we made did help stem the parking lot rapes and thefts. Of course the winos were pissed as police awareness regarding the winos in the parking lots caused the beat officers to remove them more quickly.

Another, humorous to us, event occurred with our 'chase-cover'. The watch commander had acceded to our request and gave us Officer Guadalupe (Lupe) Alvarez as our patrol back up. He was on loan to us each day. He would park in a nearby parking garage and wait for one of us to call him if we spotted someone leaving the lot, either on foot or in a car, that we wanted followed and stopped and or arrested. Since lunch was always a requisite we would task Lupe with procuring same.

On this particular day we radioed him to contact us, so he could go to Henderson's Chicken and bring us several bags of their wonderful fried chicken, fries, jalapeño peppers, and drinks. The call was made to Lupe, he "Ten-four'd". Then a few minutes later he said he couldn't. Lupe's English was heavily accented making understanding him over the radio problematic at best. He tried his best to make us understand without actually saying what his problem was over the radio. We ended up going on foot to find Lupe, to make sure 'he' wasn't in trouble.

We get there and he explains that he had to go to the bathroom, left his squad car and when he came back, just as we could then plainly see, he found his car blocked-in by another parked car! We left Lupe to extricate himself and we called on another squad as needed back-up to acquire our chicken dinners.

ANOTHER EVENT THAT happened during our *'stop-the-downtown-parking-lot-rapes'—op* that probably had some carry over to events later in this story, though we thought nothing of it at the time. While we were watching the parking lots next to the Bryan Tower a woman was abducted nearby (fortunately for our psyche's that lot was not then under our surveillance) and we felt somewhat responsible. We knew we shouldn't feel that way, but we did.

We heard the call come in over the radio that a woman had been abducted in her own car, driven to a location south of downtown and criminally assaulted. Not knowing what else to do once her attacker left her, she drove to the nearest police station at 106 South Harwood.

She pulled into the basement of the downtown cop-shop. The dispatcher needed someone to meet the complainant in the basement, adding she was the woman abducted from the downtown parking lot.

The three wino-cops hot footed it over to the basement of Police & Courts Bldg. a couple of blocks away. By the time we arrived, Investigator Evelyn Reba Crowder is with the female complainant. During a lull in their conversation, as Reba sort of steps away, we 'badge' and introduce ourselves to the woman, to let her know a) we're cops and b) we're working the parking lots trying to stop what happened to her.

We start asking her questions, in hopes of her helping us to catch the bad guy, see if her description describes anyone we might have seen in the lots we were watching, questions of that nature. Evelyn turns, sees us and becomes incensed, wanting to know who the hell we are and why we are questioning her complainant. We try to explain that this offense happened on us and that we were on stake-out trying to stop this exact thing from happening.

Investigator Crowder didn't want our 'interference' and tells us, in no uncertain terms, to back off and that this is her case.

Looking back, this may be the reason Reba seemed to still have her nose out of joint when Tom Bob and I went to her in 1975 regarding the Friendly Burglar-Rapist. On the other hand, some investigators are very territorial about 'their cases'

FOR OUR PARKING lot 'op' Jim, Tom and I had needed old dirty clothes, unshaved faces and handie-talkie radios for communications while on foot. This operational experience was modified, on an equipment allocation basis, for the Holiday Inn surveillance to stop their hotel BMV's. We would still be undercover on this operation but, would need to be more mobile.

The answer was to use what officers in the department called 'smooth cars'; police vehicles having radios but no outward police markings and with red lights and sirens hidden under the hood and behind the grill. Of course the 'hooks', bad guys, knew smooth cars on sight and ran from them just as fast as they did marked squad cars.

So we checked-out three smooth cars from the police motor pool and converged with our binoculars on the Holiday Inn to stake-out the building. The thirst of our long hours of surveillance was mitigated by a new and popular electrolyte replacement drink called Gatorade. And, given the necessity to remain in-place, the empty Gatorade bottle also served a necessary, if somewhat indelicate, purpose.

One day, the three amigos were sitting in our command center (The Division Crime Analyst's Office) on the second floor of the police department. Jim and I watched as a light went on in Tom's head, "Ya know on this deal…" Tom swung his arm and aimed a finger at the BMV map with it's heavy cluster of dots where the Holiday Inn sat, "…we've got binoculars, smooth cars and Gatorade… well what we have here, pure and simple, is a sure enough, by God, Operation… ah… Operation Bi-GatorSmooth!"

The moniker immediately stuck much to our delight.

Chapter 3

Back To The Future: Bingo, Jack! One

Dallas, Police & Courts Bldg.
Office of the Division Crime Analyst
August 30, 1974

NO ONE LIKES forms... more paperwork, more things to fill-in or fill-out, least of all me. But often we were losing information that needed to be communicated to and from the guys who were out on the street.

To help keep from losing these bits of intelligence, often scribbled on "scraps of paper", I promulgated a new form to be used by each of the five Division Analysts and patrol officers to record and disseminate information. The form contained an area for pertinent info, then a larger narrative section for more detail, a place to identify the source, a distribution block and a control number for tracking. This "will allow the information to be read out in detail for three consecutive days, insuring officers on days-off do not miss the intel."

Dallas, Central Patrol Division, Beat 127
11:20 pm Thursday, September 5, 1974
Offense Number 5 (R-5)
Glove Marks Found

THE GIRLS' SECOND floor patio sliding glass door was unlocked making access easy for the rapist.

BG, a white female 20, lived with her roommate *PD*, a white female 19, in apartment number 268 in the Toll House Apartments at 4327 Congress in the Oak Lawn section of Dallas.

Inside he found *PD* in her bedroom. He put the knife to her throat and shook her awake. "Turn your face to the wall," he said, "I'm just an ordinary burglar and I haven't hurt anyone yet. Don't make me mad and I won't have to start."

He lifted her T-shirt and just stared at her for a few moments. When he started touching her, *PD* started to sob and said, "Please don't touch me, don't hurt me, please leave me alone."

"Shut up," the rapist said and continued to grope her. He was quiet for several minutes, then said, "You got any guns?" With her "no," he got up and left the room.

In the other bedroom he roused *BG*, putting the knife to her throat. The rapist said, "Be quiet and you won't get hurt." After pulling a pillowcase over *BG*'s head he took her to PD's bedroom, tied up BG and left the two scared young women lying together. Before leaving the room he said, "This is just a burglary and if you keep quiet you won't be hurt."

They heard him ransacking their apartment. About ten minutes later, in the bedroom again, he said, "There is nothing worth stealing here, do you have any guns in the house, guns are selling good now." They mumbled "no".

BG felt him grab her. He cut her loose and took her back to her bedroom where he retied her. He pushed her down on the bed, pulled up her gown and pulled down her panties. After the rape, he repeated what he had said several times, "I'm going to get in my truck and leave."

BG heard him leave the apartment and listened in vain for the sound a truck starting.

Dallas Police Department
Intelligence Unit
Afternoon, Tuesday, September 8, 1974

IT WAS A day, internationally, nationally and locally of consequence. Over the Ionian Sea, eighteen minutes into TWA Flight 841's voyage from Athens a bomb explodes in the cargo hold killing eighty-eight souls. Nationally, thirty days after succeeding Richard Nixon on August 9th, President Gerald Ford today pardons Richard Milhous Nixon. Locally, our buddy, DPD Intelligence Officer James E. Bryan #1935 (aka: Jim Bob) was feted on his birthday!

Thank goodness for our protective, care-taker secretaries; otherwise the ol' boys would do nothing in the way of remembrance of one another, other than maybe a clap on the back and a muted "Happy Birthday"... certainly there would be no birthday cards, much less cake!

Intelligence Officer James E. Bryan #1935 (aka: Jim Bob)

Dallas, Police & Courts Bldg.
Office of the Division Crime Analyst
Late September 1974

I HAD SPENT countless hours, by this time, plotting the BMV's at the Holiday Inn. Little did I know there were holes in my developing pattern theory. Tom, looking at my maps saw what he thought was a discrepancy. Tom and I began comparing data. Tom, who had been on Special Assignment to review all theft reports, found that I had not been receiving all my reports, particularly on the BMV's. We began working as a team to interdict these thefts, reviewing O/I R's and looking for clues. Again a pattern became more evident when 'all' the offenses were combined and was growing more significant with each new offense.

Was it one suspect or several, who was committing these car break-ins and thefts? We considered the hotel employees (such as a desk clerk, bellman, cook, room service personnel, housekeeper, parking attendant or maintenance engineer), considered whether the culprit or culprits had accomplices such as an efficient operating fence; a place to unload the stolen items. We considered non-employees, or someone with nearby outside employment such as at the Lowe's Theater across the street (perhaps a ticket taker, custodian or other employee), or perhaps other outside hotel maintenance or contract people. Even friends of hotel employees were considered.

It seemed obvious that the suspect either walked in or drove in. If the suspect walked in or worked at the hotel then maybe he or she was taking loot to a vacant room, since no property had been observed leaving. Or, of course, if the suspect drove in, the loot would most likely leave the parking garage hidden in the suspect's vehicle.

The pile of O/I R's of BMV's at the Holiday Inn, both those before and after I began noticing the trend, now amounted to nearly ninety offenses. Using a crude handmade graph, I was plotting fourteen indices on a yellow pad: date of offense, floor parked on, car left locked/unlocked by owner, items taken from interior, items taken from trunk, does vehicle have 'trunk button' in glove box, was car locked when offense discovered, signs/no signs of forced entry, used key, day of week, watch, time reported, offense type, year and make of car attacked.

A third of the victims lived in town, two-third out of town, with two-thirds having in-state license plates and one-third with out of state plates. Roughly 35% of the cars attacked were Oldsmobiles, Pontiacs. "Others" came in at 23% each, 17% were Chevrolets and Ford made the statistical list at something less than .5%.

The BMV's were occurring with the highest frequency on Friday's, Saturday's and Sundays; Saturday being the number one day. The highest probability for 'time of occurrence' was after 5am and before 11am. The times were predicated primarily on the time the victim reported the offenses.

Our friend and fellow Central Patrol officer Jim Bryan had been part of our friendly anticrime cabal, since May. We had explained what were doing and again enlisted his help—or he volunteered, I can't remember which.

Jim, or Jim-Bob, was our patrol officer liaison with Intelligence and performed all manner of investigative and undercover assignments for the intelligence unit. All with the purpose of supporting the CPD with actionable intel. Given the times, wearing long hair and hippy-style clothing pretty well tagged you as 'not a cop'; a helpful public presumption if you worked undercover. Jim was and is a big man. Thus, with moderately long hair and Seventies mod clothes, Investigator Jim Bryan did not look like he was a cop, he looked like a hippie.

Tom and I surmised and Jim concurred, our BMV suspect was not too lazy to get up early, as the majority were being hit between 5am and 7am on Saturday's.

With our minds set, as to what we wanted to do, I invited Chief Dixon to come up from his basement office to my and Tom's office on the second floor of Police & Courts Bldg., since all the maps, offense reports and plotting materials were there.

With Investigator Bryan present, I made a serious presentation to Chief Dixon with some hilarious assistance of Tom and Jim. As a result Central Patrol Division Chief, R.O. Dixon assigned Investigator J. E. Bryan #1939, T.H. Covington #2273 and R.J. Sadler #2441 to make an investigation of the problem occurring at the parking garage, which of course, we had already been doing.

Bi-GatorSmooth was now officially sanctioned. The three of us took the bit between our teeth and ran with it.

In order to catch our thief in-the-act, an active surveillance, a stake-out, would be the key. We also knew that no one in the department was going to be supplying us with manpower; we would have to do on our own. That suited us just fine.

[NB: Most of you have heard the term, but here is the derivation. From the OED: Stake-out [f. vbl. phr *to stake out* see stake *v.*] An act or period of surveillance of a place by police or investigative agents. Also *transf.* and *attrib.* First appearing in English: 1942 Berrey & Van den Bark *Amer. Thes. Slang* §499/2 *Stake-out*, a surrounding of a criminal to spy upon or prevent the escape of criminals. 1943 R. Chandler *Lady in the Lake* (1944) xl. 208 Somebody stood behind that green curtain, as silently as only a cop on a stake-out knows how to stand.]

Dallas, Northwest Patrol Division, Beat 524
9:00 pm Friday, September 20, 1974
Offense Number 6 (R-6)
Prints Lifted

HE SAW HER through the sliding glass door lying on the floor watching TV.

The new Darren McGavin series *The Night Stalker* had debuted the previous Friday night at 9pm with an episode titled *The Ripper* in which a serial killer preying on women haunts Chicago, and Kolchak comes to believe that the killer is the original Jack the Ripper, a seemingly immortal killer who has slain women in many cities over the last century. In tonight's episode *The Zombie*, according to TV Guide, Kolchak deals with a voodoo priestess who animates her dead son to take revenge on the gangsters that killed him.

BB lived in a ground floor apartment, unit 110 in an apartment complex called The Tuileries at 9633 Starlight.

The man noticed the slider was open about two inches and decided to make his move onto her patio. Quickly pushing the sliding glass door open he jumped on *BB*, a white female 22. He rolled her over on her stomach, took her glasses off and told her, even though he was wearing a stocking-mask, "Don't look at me."

BB started screaming.

The rapist told her, "I'm just a burglar and won't hurt you if you won't scream; I've got a knife!"

He left her silently cowering on the floor and prowled around the apartment, lifted the telephone receiver and left it off the hook. *BB* could hear him opening and closing drawers and moving in an out of rooms as he kept telling her to "be quiet," "don't look at me," "I'm a burglar... I'm not going to hurt you... I hope I don't have to use this knife on you... I've got a pick-up truck... I make my living by burglarizing..."

BB told the rapist, "I don't have anything, I've only been here a week." He looked around and replied, "You sure don't have anything!"

He turned off the TV and called her into the bedroom and had her sit on the foot of the bed. He pulled off her pants and panties, tied her wrists with some of her own nylons and a headband and then pulled her shirt off over her head. He pushed her down on the bed and put a pillow over her face.

As he rubbed his hands over *BB*'s body she said, "I'm in my period."

"Aw shit!" The rapist said. He took out her Tampax and threw it on the floor, used a Kleenex to wipe her off, then raped her. *BB* could smell her lime and peach scented face cream as well as her almond scented suntan lotion on him.

After his orgasm he said, "I've got to go outside for something to wipe my fingerprints off everything" so "no one will know I was here... now don't leave."

According to Inv. J.J. Shubzda #3357's supplement report of 9.24.74 he "lifted prints off front door where susp. exited."

At the time there were no other prints to compare—offense to offense, as would happen later—and to my knowledge this print was not determined to be the Complainant's. It belonged as far as we could tell, to our FBR suspect. Also, on several previous occasions, though fingerprints were not found 'glove' prints were!

Dallas, Central Patrol Division
12:54am Thursday, September 26, 1974

OUR FIRST BREAK in the BMV thefts came when we interviewed the attendant, who usually worked the hotel parking garage on weekends and was available now on a weekday. Cops are always amazed when citizens demonstrate how aware they really are, in jobs where they are often seen to be inattentive. Not Mrs. B of Garland, Texas.

Tom and I had noted that she was a witness listed on some of the BMV reports and had, indeed, provided a suspect description and given the reporting officers a vehicle license number.

She told us that on several occasions, on weekends, she had noticed a car leaving the parking garage early in the morning. Why did she notice, we asked? "Because invariably someone would report that their car had been broken into..." Putting two and two together she began watching for the vehicle.

Not expecting much from the next question, I said, "Can you describe the car," she said, "sure, it's a '73 brown Pontiac Gran Prix.

"You didn't happen to copy down the license number," Tom said. Again she surprised us. She flipped open a note pad and said, "It's a Texas plate, NMK-257—and the driver is a black male. I told all this to the officers when the cars were broken into."

"Yes, Ma'am," I nodded, "we just needed to confirm what you told the reporting officers."

Beyond pleased, Tom and I headed back to the Police & Courts Bldg. to run registration on the vehicle. "It's probably stolen," Tom said. That thought dampened our spirits somewhat. "Surely," I said, "the crook was smart enough not to use his own car and if it's a stolen car, he wouldn't keep using it—would he?"

In the basement we stopped by the patrol office to use their computer terminal and input the Texas license number NMK-257 to access the Texas Crime Information Center (TCIC).

The TCIC provides immediate access 24 hours a day, 7 days a week to law enforcement agencies throughout Texas to information regarding the status of stolen property and wanted persons. It also provides a direct link to it's "National" sibling, NCIC, where instantly knowledge about whether a vehicle, a boat, or other property under investigation is stolen, or a person in question is wanted anywhere in the country.

The TCIC report came back a few minutes later. The printer spindle clicked and the dot-matrix nozzle buzzed as it scanned from left to right pecking dots on the manifold computer paper. I tore off the report and Tom, reading over my shoulder said, "No Wants, that's good."

Tom smiled and exclaimed, for the first time, "Bingo, Jack! We have a suspect!"

A new sitcom had just debuted called "Good Times", promo'd as: "A poor Afro-American family makes the best of things in the Chicago housing projects." The tall, skinny comedian Jimmy Walker played the loud, ego-driven, James 'J.J.' Evans, Jr. His catch phrases were dynamite, which he pronounced: "die-no-MITE", and "Bingo Jack!" Walker's "die-no-MITE" was the phrase that caught on and was immediately heard everywhere. It was Tom who first used **"Bingo Jack!"** It became literally *our* "catch" phrase. An acknowledgement of our *Eureka Moment*.

"Bingo, Jack!" then morphed into our exclamation *du jour*, anytime we ID'd a suspect, made a great connection on a case or an arrest; we'd smile and, adopting "J.J.'s" word accents, say "Bingo, Jack" to one another. It was our personal exaltation: a sign of congratulations, a verbal high-five!

According to the TCIC the license number the parking attendant gave us, NMK-257, came back on a 1973 Pontiac two-door hard top; just like Mrs. B. said. The registered owner was one Hugh M. Hodges, Jr. with a listed address in Dallas of 5610 Forney. It listed the date of the lien on the vehicle as 12/13/1973 and designated Southwest Bank & Trust in Irving, Texas as the lien holder.

A surveillance of our presumed suspect Hodges' residence would have to be set up. In the meantime we began to make inquiries. We found that Hugh M. Hodges, Jr. was an attorney. The ever-inventive Tom suggested we needed an edge for our surveillance of the Forney residence. Tom talked to Jerry Huckaby, a Civil Engineer Tom had worked with in scouting. Tom asked for the loan of some surveyor equipment. When Tom told Jerry what we were intending to do, Jerry said, "You'll never make it," and suggested he'd give us a hand, but he wouldn't be available for the next few days.

Of course, Jim was an old hand. In college he had been a civil engineer major and already knew how to set up and level a transit, how to take measurements and the hand signals used to move the "sticks". Over the next days we made periodic checks of house at 5610 Forney. What we found at this location was a somewhat dilapidated residence, not what we expected for the home of a 'successful' criminal attorney.

We thought, perhaps it was a rental property.

With our now borrowed surveyor's sticks (surveying rods), transit instrument and tripod, using Jim's Toyota and with clipboards, chalk and hand signals Jim-Bob, Tom-Bob and Billy-Bob spent a day in front of 5610 Forney Rd., making a very accurate survey of his street, waiting for the 1973 Pontiac to show up.

During our surveillance/surveying of 5610 Forney we observed a black male driving two different cars. One was the '73 Pontiac 'suspect vehicle' registered to Hodges and the second vehicle was registered to a J.C. Shannon.

In a continuing review of the offenses at the Holiday Inn Tom and I found a James Roland Brown, DPD ID 48839 had been arrested on October 3, 1974, and charged with a burglary of a motor vehicle which had been committed at 'our' Holiday Inn. Further we found that Brown had been apprehended while driving a vehicle which was registered to J.C. Shannon, Jr. and

Brown was subsequently represented in court by Mr. Hugh M. Hodges, Jr.

Now we had connections between the Holiday Inn, the 1973 Pontiac, J.C. Shannon, 5610 Forney, and attorney Hugh M. Hodges, Jr. We knew where our BMV suspect Shannon was staying, what he was driving. What remained was locating the 'real' Hodges domicile, surveil it to see if Shannon showed up there and to stake out the Holiday Inn to catch Shannon 'red-handed'.

We kept scratching our heads trying to figure out why a criminal defense attorney would be registering his car to the 5610 Forney address, clearly not his permanent residence, and why he was allowing Shannon, an ex-con and client, drive 'his' car. We could think of several perfectly legal reasons, but being cynical cops we could also think of a number of nefarious reasons as well.

One of the nefarious scenarios we conjured, was that Shannon was in debt to his attorney and was using his ill-gotten gains to pay his bill. Perhaps even 'fencing' some of these stolen good through the attorney. If we caught Shannon burglarizing vehicles and followed him... would he go home, to a fence, to his attorney's or where—we wanted to know.

We found the attorney's 'real' residence and decided to "survey" his street as we had done at 5610 Forney where we'd found J.C. Shannon. For this round of surveillance nothing would do but for Jerry to take off a couple of days from work to school us in the fine points of surveying. Jim and Tom (I was laid-off from the survey crew duty for a family obligation) again Jim's Toyota Land Cruiser truck was used as their surveyor's vehicle. Jerry even stood up for Jim and Tom when the anxious and inquiring mind of Hugh Hodges decided to come out to the street to see who we were and what the **** we were doing in front of his house. Blithely Jerry told him we were conducting a flood plane survey to determine drainage in the area...

Later Jerry told Tom, "Those were the two most exciting days I can remember."

Dallas, Northeast Patrol Division, Beat 233
11:05 pm Thursday, September 26, 1974
Offense Number 7 (R-7)

THE MOON WAS three-quarters full and the temperature was hovering just above sixty degrees at the Willow Creek Apartments located at 7915 Rock Willow. It was warm inside apartment number 150. Having come in through an unlocked ground floor front bedroom window of the 33 year-old white female's apartment, the rapist stood in the dark listening to *NF*'s side of her telephone conversation. She lay on the sofa. When she put down the phone he rushed into the living room and pushed her head into the sofa, "Don't look at me," he said—not that it mattered; he was wearing a stocking over his head.

Now, "shut up and let me see what you have." He tied *NF* to a chair in the dining area and filched through her things.

"I'm going to have to take your TV and put it in my pickup."

Outside he could see someone standing around, "I'll have to wait—guess I'll have to watch Johnny Carson." He looked at *NF* and reconsidered, "No, the only thing left is you." The rapist took *NF* into her bedroom tied her hands to the bedpost, put a pillowcase over her head and raped her.

Dallas, Central Patrol Division
Texas-OU Weekend
October 11-12, 1974

In the midst of trying to capture our downtown car burglar, Tom and I were tasked by Chief Dixon to assist him in his planning for the upcoming bad weather. Each year in October, the second week, the local weather turned frightful and often unruly. A hot moist cloud of burnt orange and white would surge up from Austin as a crimson and cream mass of hot air would blow down from Oklahoma. In 1900 when these two volatile air masses mixed over downtown Dallas, a phenomenon, known as Texas-OU Weekend, was born.

Almost every year since, the University of Oklahoma Sooners and the University of Texas Longhorns have played football in Dallas (a 'neutral' and essentially equidistant location from Norman, Oklahoma and Austin, Texas). The wins and losses seem to come in bunches. To this point Oklahoma had won 24 games and Texas had won 42, with only two ties. Much to the delight of the Sooner fans they were coming to Dallas after winning the game for the last three years. They were cocky, and with good reason. This cockiness did not go over well with the Longhorn faithful.

For years this annual rite of passage, called Texas-OU Weekend by Longhorn fans and OU-Texas Weekend by the Sooner fans, began late on Friday afternoon with a parade of cars wagon-training into and through downtown Dallas. There were three main 'east-west' streets: Elm, Main and Commerce. Main Street, between Elm and Commerce, was appropriately enough the main strip of concrete in downtown. Each of these streets carried four lanes of traffic, two in each direction. Commerce had the old Hotels, the bars, and was the usual route from downtown to Fair Park, home of the State Fair of Texas, the Cotton Bowl and the annual Red River Rivalry.

Commerce became the *de facto* 'cruising strip'. Imagine, if you will, car loads of kids hanging out of the windows of sedans and stuffed into open convertibles drinking, wearing their school colors, shouting their individual school battle cries, coming at each other like jousters galloping in cars instead of on horseback. The hurling of insults along with all manner of projectiles; fights and drunkenness were *de rigueur*.

While the jousting took place on the street, the sidewalks on either side were a wall-to-wall free-for-all of pedestrians headed east and west in constant battle for taking a step in their intended direction. Drunks and near drunks walking, drink-in-hand, being jostled and running into one another kept the pedestrians in a constant state of frenzy, where fights erupted like a steady stream of little red and orange volcanoes.

For years, literally 600, 700, 800 really drunk and really rowdy folks ended up spending the night in the city jail, hopefully sobering up and getting bailed out in time to make the next day's noon kickoff.

Tactics were beginning to change. Vehicular traffic was no longer allowed to go both ways on Commerce, it became all one way. So making the circuit took considerably longer and there was no oncoming car jousting, just the harangue with the cars going the same way you were. Additionally the decision was made to barricade the streets and sidewalks. Now the pedestrians could no longer step out into the traffic as they had done for decades and they were forced to walk one way as well. The south sidewalk went east and the north sidewalk went west. And you had to walk ten or fifteen blocks before you could cross to the other side. These two tactics tended to take the wind out of the sails of many.

Alongside the barricades on each side of Commerce stretched a row of hundreds of cops: Dallas officers, Dallas Sheriff's deputies, State Highway Patrol troopers and a company of Rangers. These were the uniformed protectors and line of demarcation between the curb-edge barricades and the street's passing motorists.

Between working their regular patrol shifts and this special assignment most of the officers in Dallas Police Department would be on duty.

Even so, many of the businesses along the route hired off-duty officers to stand guard at the entrance to their closed and/or open businesses to keep out the drunk and disorderly.

In the 70's there were two hotels in downtown that got the bulk of the business, the Statler-Hilton at 1914 Commerce and the Adolphus Hotel at the 1315 Commerce. Neither wanted their patron's-only bathrooms used by the horde.

Since I did not get assigned to 'the line', I 'hired-out', with three other officers, to the Statler-Hilton to man their front entrance, (a series of large plate glass windows and doors). If you were a guest of the hotel and had your room key in your hand you would be allowed to enter.

There were so many drunks that one's level of inebriation was tolerated until you became a danger to yourself or another.

It had been a pretty good night. The crowd noise and revelry were dwindling, even as the alcohol consumption went up, due to the length of time it took to walk from one end of the barricades to the other where you could cross the street and start back the other way. Just after midnight four drunks, plastic cups of beer in hand, two guys and their 'dates' came sloshing toward me and tried to pass. I asked politely if any of the four was a guest of the hotel. One of the guys slurred, "The girls gotta pee." I explained where the only public restrooms where, which were not close. They argued for a few minutes trying to claim to be guests who'd forgotten their keys, etc. The guys and gals were getting belligerent and called me and the hotel management rude and unflattering names.

Their public drunkenness and verbal abuse, under other circumstances, would have landed them in jail. But on this night, once a year, we graded on a curve. The girls realized when they were not going to be let in that they no longer wanted to argue the point, finding the 'ladies' room was a more pressing matter.

The moment had almost passed into a nonevent as the four moved off several paces. Then, inexplicably, one of the men turns around and throws a nearly full cup of beer on me. That crossed the line. As he turned and ran deeper into the crowd, my long arm of the law (and how I and it got there so quickly I'll never be able to explain) reached out and grabbed the man by the shoulder. He tried to pull away as I wrestled him toward me to detain him. Off balance the man ran at me as I gathered him in. Now both of us off balance go flying back into a six foot wide by eight foot tall plate glass window. The glass gives way and shatters into thousands of pieces that come raining down on us as we unexpectedly tumble into the lobby, the drunk on top of me. I do a quick reverse and pin him on his stomach and grab for my cuffs. While I'm putting bracelets on my drunk the other officers had to take the rest of his crew into custody.

Plate glass is expensive; I don't know how this guy settled-up with the hotel after getting out of jail on his charges: public intoxication, assaulting a police officer, resisting arrest and destruction of private property.

By contrast, if memory serves, that year's arrests were down below 200, an all time-low. The tally would continue to go down in future years till there was apparently not much desire on the part of locals, much less Texas or Oklahoma students to cruise or walk the line on the Friday night before the big game.

Two years later in 1976 the famed Tina Turner was scheduled to perform at the Statler with her husband Ike Turner. Reportedly, Tina left her abusive husband asleep in their suite, snuck down the back stairs, walked to another nearby hotel "with a Mobil credit card and thirty-six cents." And the rest is history. Times were changing, the Statler-Hilton would eventually lose its *raison d'être*.

Oh yes, the game. It was 79 degrees at kick-off which was observed by 72,032 fans filling the Cotton Bowl. The OU crowd went home happy for the fourth year in a row. Tex 13 - OU 16.

Dallas, Texas
October 20, 1974
The J.C. Shannon Case Arrest
The Good Part

JUMPING *FORWARD*, AFTER months of our analysis, investigation, and stake-outs Tom and Jim arrested J.C. Shannon. DPD Investigator Kavanaugh was the beneficiary of our arrest and did a super job of summarizing the case for presentation to the DA's office. Here is his summary:

The Holiday Inn Central Motel, located at 1015 Elm Street, Dallas, Texas has an attached elevated multi-story enclosed parking garage. The parking garage is attended by one person who is stationed at the entrance/exit at street level. This attendant simply collects the designated parking fee from customers as they leave the garage.

In the time period of January 1st, 1974 up to October 20th, 1974 there have been ninety (90) separate burglaries of motor vehicle offenses made at this location. As a result Central Patrol Division Chief of Police, R.O. Dixon assigned Patrolmen J. E. Bryan #1939, T.H. Covington #2273 and R.J. Sadler #2441 to make an investigation of the problem occurring at the parking garage.

Subsequently the patrol-investigators were able to catalog the ninety offenses which occurred at the location. They were able to establish:

1) That the offender probably utilized a wire (coat hanger) to open cars.

2) Usually committed the offenses on a weekend.

3) They found that on two of the reported offenses, a vehicle registered to Hugh M. Hodges Jr. (an attorney) was the registered owner of the suspect vehicle and that it had been driven by a black male.

4) They found on two other offenses reported there, that a vehicle (listed as a probable suspect vehicle) was registered to J.C. Shannon Jr.

The patrol-investigators made periodic checks of J.C. Shannon Jr.'s residence, located at 1819 Duluth Street[27], Dallas. They found that Shannon not only had possession of the singular vehicle registered to him, but that he had possession of the vehicle registered to the attorney, Hugh M. Hodges Jr. In further review of the offenses reported at the Holiday Inn, the patrol-investigators found that a James Roland Brown DPD ID 48839 had been arrested on October 3, 1974 and charged with a burglary of a motor vehicle which he had committed at the location under investigation. Further they found that Brown had been apprehended while driving a vehicle which was registered to J.C. Shannon, Jr. and Brown was subsequently represented in court by Mr. Hugh M. Hodges, Jr.

The patrol-investigators interviewed the attendant who usually worked at the parking garage on weekends. They found this attendant to be a Mrs. Mary B. of Garland Texas.

In their interview of Mrs. B., she made the statement that on several occasions, on weekends, she had noticed that a 1973 brown Pontiac Grand Prix bearing 1974 Texas license plates NMK-257, driven by a black male adult, would depart the parking garage and invariably someone would report that their car had just been broken into. This is the vehicle registered to the attorney, Mr. Hugh M. Hodges, Jr. and from the patrol-investigator's surveillance, they recognized that J.C. Shannon, Jr. possessed the vehicle.

The patrol-investigators checked with the DPD ID Bureau and found that J.C. Shannon, Jr. had been, since 1967, filed on three separate times for BEMV and had served two separate sentences at the Texas Department of Corrections in 1967 and again in 1970.

The patrol-investigators reached the conclusion that the most probable suspect, relative to the unusually large number of burglary of motor vehicle offenses occurring at 1015 Elm Street, would be J.C. Shannon, Jr. They began

---

[27] Somehow, we didn't notice at the time, Kavanaugh substituted Shannon's 'other real address' on Deluth in West Dallas for the address of our surveillance on Shannon at 5610 Forney Road in Southeast Dallas.

to establish periodic covert surveillance inside the parking garage on weekends in an attempt to apprehend the offender.

On Sunday, October 20, 1974, at 5am, Officers J.E. Bryan and T.H. Covington set up such a surveillance at the parking garage. At approximately 6:05am, they observed a man they recognized as J.C. Shannon, Jr. driving the vehicle previously motioned and registered to Mr. Hodges, drive into the garage. Officer Covington entered the garage, attempting to keep Shannon in sight but keeping from being seen. He, Covington, followed Shannon to the fourth level where Shannon parked his car. Officer Covington, from a place of concealment, watched as Shannon immediately walked to a 1974 Oldsmobile parked in the garage and utilizing a wire he opened the right rear door and took two stuffed toy dogs out of the car. Shannon re-locked the car and placed the toys in the rear of his own car.

Officer Covington continued watching as Shannon then approached a 1973 Oldsmobile parked on that level and again using a wire unlocked that car too. Covington watched as Shannon laid down in the front seat of the car he had just entered. Shannon reappeared carrying a tape deck player and numerous tapes. The officer watched, from a place of concealment, as Shannon placed this merchandise into the trunk of his own car.

Officer Covington continued to watch Shannon, as he walked toward Covington's place of concealment. Covington and Bryan had previously agreed not to attempt to apprehend the offender at the parking garage but rather they would attempt to follow him after the offenses in an attempt to determine where he was taking the stolen property. Since Covington was reasonably assured of being seen by Shannon if he stayed on the level, Covington decided to return to Officer Bryan's position outside the parking facility and await Shannon's departure.

Several more minutes passed while the officers waited outside the building and they agreed among themselves that Shannon was probably burglarizing even more cars. Shannon finally reappeared, driving this car out of the parking garage. The two officers had alerted one of the DPD helicopters and the two units began attempting to covertly follow Shannon to his destination. After several minutes of following Shannon, the officers began to realize that he had probably become suspicious of them and finally they watched as Shannon pulled his car into a parking lot at the 111 Continental Building, off the 100 block of Parkhouse Street. They observed Shannon pull his car into a parking space and watched as he shut off his lights and motor and lay down in the front seat.

They were forced to assume that Shannon had discovered them following him and they made the decision to effect his apprehension immediately. They called for patrol assistance and Patrolmen R.H. Cawthon and G. Alvarez arrived to assist them. The four officers confronted Shannon and placed him under arrest.

Officers Bryan and Covington began removing the property from Shannon's vehicle to impound it. They found the property taken form the 1973 Olds and impounded it on tag#161394. They later found that the property belonging to Mr. L.S. Melton and his offices is reported on service number 335626F. They also found the toys taken from the 1974 Olds and impounded them on tag number 1613939. They later found that these belong to a Mr. K. J. Kepke and his offense was reported on service number 335618F.

Additionally the officers found a great deal more property which they were not immediately able to identify but they assumed that some if not all of it had been taken from other cars after Officer Covington had to leave his place of concealment where he had been observing the offenses.

While officers were booking Shannon on the two vehicle burglaries which Officers Covington had observed, a Mr. John Smith called to report that his car, parked at 1015 Elm Street, had been broken into and a large number of specific name eight-track tapes taken. Covington and Bryan checked the property they had just seized minutes earlier from Shannon's car and found that they had the same name and number of tapes that Mr. Smith was missing. His offense report was prepared on service number 335723F and the tapes impounded on tag number 161518.

As they continued booking Shannon, a Mr. Larry Deatherage called in to report that his car, parked at the same location as the other three offenses just committed by Shannon, had been broken into and some clothing and eight-track tapes had been taken. Again they checked the seized property and found that they also had Mr. Deatherage's property. They prepared an offense report on service number 3335773F and impounded his recovered property on tag number 161396.

Since, in the search of Shannon's vehicle, Officer Covington found a vial of fourteen (14) Ionamin capsules in the center console, the officers also booked Shannon for Investigation of V.C.S.A (Violation of the Controlled Substances Act) Section 4.04 Class A Misdemeanor as well as the four counts of Investigation of Burglary of a Motor Vehicle Section 30.04.

Officer Bryan and Covington prepared a set of arraignment forms and at 1:54pm, they did have Shannon arraigned before Municipal Judge George Orndoff.

Subsequent to Shannon's arraignment, Mr. Hugh M. Hodges, Jr., attorney at law, arrived at the Police and Courts Bldg. and presented himself as Shannon's attorney. Despite an attempt to discuss the offenses with Mr. Hodges and Shannon, Mr. Hodges left the impression that he did not care to discuss the matter with the officers.

Later Investigator R.L. Kavanaugh of the Crimes Against Property Section prepared the investigative summary and prepared the cases for filing.

Dallas, Texas
October 20, 1974
The J.C. Shannon Case Arrest
The Funny Part

JUMPING *BACK* IN time, we had already run one targeted weekend surveillance. Unfortunately our suspect disrespected us by being a no-show. But we got no respect from our own either.

Tom recalled, "Remember when you called the helicopter?"

"Right!" I had contacted the helicopter unit's commander and informed him of our stake-out and he said, "Well, just let the pilot know you are there, so he can help if necessary."

Thus, it was assumed that the chopper unit commander had let his duty pilot know our situation and possible request for assistance. There was no need on first contact to alert anyone who might be monitoring the police bands what our stake-out location was. Standard protocol was to identify yourself by your call number and request assistance when it was required.

"So we get set up on our stake out. We're in separate cars, at different points around the hotel. My call number was 1325—"

"Right," Tom said. "I'm in my car and I hear Billy Bob break squelch, '1325 to the helicopter.' And the chopper pilot says, 'Who are you?' Sadler sort of ignores him because the helicopter pilot is supposed to know who we are and says, '1325 to the helicopter, we might need you—' and the pilot said again, 'Well... who are you?'"

Things went downhill from there as we sat from midnight to six in the morning without seeing our suspect.

Based on our analysis and predictions, we again decided that we'd deploy for a surveillance of the Holiday Inn the next weekend of October 20th. We had a lot of data and we thought our prediction was good, not great. We knew we could cover the obvious window of opportunity, but the window of probability was still hit and miss.

Typically, Saturdays and Sundays were our days off. I had already pulled so much overtime, with family coming into town, I was going to be *persona non grata* at home if I didn't beg off from this surveillance. So the three amigos were minus one.

Tom and his Boy Scout troop were set to go on an in-town camping trip that same weekend. They set up camp down off of Dogo Road, right there by the Trinity River, not far from where Lone Star Park racetrack sits today, in Grand Prairie.

Jim accompanied Tom and once they got the boys all set up they left the scout encampment in the care of scoutmaster Charlie Wilkins.

Tom and Jim drove into downtown Dallas to set up for another night of mind-numbing surveillance; smoking cigarettes and drinking Gatorade.

As Tom said later, "No way did we think we were gonna catch that ol' boy, this was our second time. The system we used to predict the next hit wasn't all that great, if it had been great we wouldn't have to be sittin' up on'm a second time, well, we did."

Our suspect, J.C. Shannon Jr., lived, we thought, southeast of downtown at the 5610 Forney address; our current surveillance location was the 1000 block of Elm Street on the far western side of 'downtown'. So after Tom and Jim spotted Shannon entering the hotel and Tom saw him break into and steal from several vehicles, Tom radioed Jim and returned to his car.

When Shannon exited onto Elm Street, which ran one way, west, Tom and Jim expected him to turn south on Lamar or head to IH 35 East and then head southeast toward his place at 5610 Forney Road. (We didn't know at the time that Shannon also 'stayed' at 1819 Duluth Street in West Dallas, just a 2.2 miles and 6 minutes west of the Holiday Inn across the viaduct.) Instead Shannon, in the 1973 brown Pontiac Grand Prix with Texas plates NMK-257 turned north on Lamar.

Jim was in the lead car. It was still dark, Shannon had his lights on, so did Jim and Tom who both killed their lights. "That's when he snapped on us," Jim said later, "I think that's when he burned us, when we went dark."

Spotted or not, Jim and Tom continued following Shannon till they lost him going under the Continental Street viaduct. On the other side of the underpass he had disappeared. Fortunately the helicopter, alerted by Jim and Tom, and who this time 'knew who we were', found Shannon's car parked in a small apartment building parking lot in the 100 block of Parkhouse Street only a few blocks away.

The helicopter vectored their cars in for the arrest, if that was Shannon's car. The pilot had not seen any activity in or around the car.

Most likely you have seen a helicopter circle in the sky above your city, with its beam of light cutting through the darkness. If you had ever been in that blanketing circle of that light, you would know what real 'brightness' is. Outside the circle you can see, sometimes more clearly, things it illuminates than perhaps you would in the middle of the day. Inside that circle of light is surreal like watching a 3D movie without the 3D glasses. Everything in the circle of light is visible but disorienting because the angle of the shadows keeps changing as the helicopter hovers and circles.

Caught in the 50,000,000 candle power of the "Nightsun" J.C. Shannon Jr., curled up on the floorboard of his Grand Prix, trying to hide from the light and the law.

Jim and Tom checked its license as they zeroed in on the Pontiac; it was Shannon's car.

Shannon was holding on for dear life as Jim and Tom attempted to lay hands on him to extricate him from the car. There were arms, and legs, and feet, and hands flying every-which way.

The perception is that two guys can handle one guy easier than a one-on-one confrontation. Although you have a force-multiplayer on your side it does not compute to easier, quicker control of your arrestee, especially if all you are trying to do is take the suspect into custody without harming him or her. But to the bystander it can appear abusive even excessive, in terms of use-of-force.

Crimes or criminal events often seemingly go unnoticed. Cops are constantly rolling up on the scene of some complaint, trying to find out what happened by interviewing bystanders, or canvassing a neighborhood, only to be told: "I didn't see a thing!" However, when cops are involved, someone almost always 'sees'!

The dispatcher's voice crackled over the radio calling, "134, meet the complainant, 100 Parkhouse." "134, Ten-four," the beat officer responded.

In this out of the way and seedy, low-rent and no-rent (wino-squatting in vacant units) apartment building in an enclave of warehouses a 'good citizen' called the police! When asked the nature of the emergency the complainant breathlessly explained, "There's a black guy being mugged by two white guys, out in the parking lot." "Can you describe the suspects," the dispatcher asked. "Yeah," the man responded, then gave the dispatcher the men's description.

Having dispatched 134 to the location and gotten the beat officer's acknowledgement the dispatcher, trying to keep the smile out of his voice said, "134, complainant reports a black male being robbed by two white male suspects, 'a big hippie and a Boy Scout'!" The radio-air began to fill with officers breaking squelch on their radios. The 'click-clacking' sound was the equivalent of uproarious laughter by all who were listening to the radio.

Funny as it sounded, the 'good citizen's' description was dead-on-accurate.

The big, long-haired "hippie" was Central Patrol Division Intelligence Liaison Officer, Jim Bryan and the "Boy Scout", (in his Scout Master's uniform) was Community Service Officer, Tom Covington (on Special Assignment to Central Patrol Division Crime Analysis) effecting the arrest of J.C. Shannon, Jr.

Shannon was escorted to 106 South Harwood, taken directly to Burglary and Theft and presented to the duty sergeant. Shannon was immediately interrogated. Jim and Tom then booked Shannon on the offenses Tom had seen him commit.

One J.C. Shannon Jr. mystery we never solved was the missing bearer bonds. These financial instruments are just like cash, whoever possesses them has the right to cash them in.

We couldn't get Shannon to cop to stealing them, much less ever seeing them.

However in one of the BMV reports we scrutinized over and over, was the fact that this particular complainant listed as stolen, during the burglary of his vehicle, bearer bonds—sixty-thousand dollars worth of bearer bonds! We thought it possible that Shannon had found them and possibly surrendered them to his attorney. We were never able to make the connection or determine what happened to the bearer bonds.

It also crossed our minds that this was a good way for an individual or institution to cover a loss. At the time, as best as we could determine, the bonds had not been redeemed.

Chapter 4

Back to the Friendly Burglar Rapist

The Chase Begins

Dallas, Northeast Patrol Division, Beat 236
5:00 am Saturday, October 25, 1974
Offense Number 8 (R-8)
Prints Lifted

A FLIGHT ATTENDANT, 24 year-old *GT* was asleep in her second floor Buttonwood Tree apartment at 5557 Alpha Road. At 5:00am it was sixty-one degrees and mostly cloudy. The window of unit 2061 was accessible. The rapist climbed onto the wooden patio fence and then onto the ledge beneath the window. He removed the window's screen, raised the window and slipped inside. He stood beside her for several minutes watching the sleeping woman in the darkened bedroom. What light there was did not come from the almost full moon; it had set an hour and a half before.

The rapist put his hand over *GT*'s mouth and as she awoke told her, "I'm a burglar... I won't hurt you if you don't make trouble." She felt the poke of something sharp, she assumed it was a knife. He threatened her again and pulled *GT*'s nightgown over her head. He continued threatening her as he went through the apartment, taking eight dollars from *GT*'s purse but leaving behind several pieces of jewelry.

He roamed the apartment then went back into the bedroom and tied *GT*'s hands with a pair of her panty hose. With her dark colored nightgown still pulled up over her head, he forced her out of bed and pushed her into the living room and onto the couch. Though he penetrated her, the indignity of his assault lasted only a moment before he had climaxed and was ready to leave.

He guided her into the kitchen and tied her to the refrigerator. "Don't tell anyone," he said, "or I'll be back... in a minute I'll get in my truck and be gone."

GT later described her attacker to reporting officer J.T. Carey #2448, saying he was a "white male, maybe 18-24 years old, maybe five-foot-eight, a hundred-fifty pounds." She said he wore "plastic gloves, had on crepe sole shoes and had short straight black hair." In a follow-up interview with the investigator *GT* said, "I doubt very seriously if I could identify him. With the gown over my head it was pretty dark."

Dallas, Northwest Patrol Division, Beat 521
5:00 am Thursday, November 7, 1974
Offense Number 9 (R-9)

SHE FELT THE gloved hand on her mouth and a knife on her neck. "Don't make a sound—or I will kill you. Shhh, shh, I'm a friendly burglar, I'm just a friendly burglar; I won't hurt you, if you keep quiet."

He tied her hands to the bed post with her panty hose. The rapist opened the door of unit 210 of the Pueblo Square Apartments at 4503 Lake Avenue and stood out on the second floor landing overlooking a courtyard. Everything was glazed with drizzle making the fifty-one degree temperature feel more uncomfortable.

CN a white 21 year-old student struggled against her bonds and finally got herself untied. Unfortunately for *CN*. the rapist returned before she could call or escape. He grabbed her from behind put, his arm around her neck in a choke-hold and put his knife to her throat. "Gotta get you out of here, away from your neighbors so they won't hear you."

He pushed *CN* out the door, down the steps and over to another building and into the ground floor laundry room. Once in the laundry room he pushed her into a closet and took off her clothes, keeping the knife pressed against her skin. He shoved her into the wall. "When I'm finished, I'll get in my truck and leave." Facing away from him she could feel his erection against the small of her back, felt him inserting his fingers in her vagina before shoving her to the floor. He forced himself inside her and copulated until he ejaculated.

He stood up and said, "Now, don't move until I leave." He turned and threw her clothes out into the laundry room.

I'll never forget that voice, CN thought.

[NB: This offense was one of the strangest in that it was throwing off 'the pattern' because the rapist took his victim out of her apartment exposing himself to be observed by witnesses. The why of this MO anomaly was never answered.]

Dallas, Southeast Patrol Division, Beat 321
4:30pm Monday, November 18, 1974

AT FIFTY-SEVEN degrees the light breeze out of the South, gusts up to twelve miles an hour, gave the afternoon the appropriate winter feel.

I finally get to get in on the action. Additional cases were filed and two Felony Warrants of Arrest were issued. Arresting Officer's (Sadler, Bryan & Covington) went to Shannon's residence address, and found the now 30 year-old, mustachioed J.C. Shannon, Jr. in his front yard where the warrants were served and Shannon was again brought to jail for the last time by the Bi-GatorSmooth squad.

Dallas, Northeast Patrol Division, Beat 231
12:30am Wednesday, December 18, 1974
Offense Number 10 (R-10)
Palm Prints Lifted

BB[28], a thirty year-old white female clerical engineer at Braniff Airlines, had gone to bed early the night before and had thus been asleep for three hours when she was awakened by a rubber-gloved hand over her mouth. She had felt safe in her third floor apartment. Unfortunately the complex, called the Corners, located at 6059 Village Glenn, was now a hunting ground for a rapist.

At 9:30pm when *BB* went to bed it was forty-five degrees and the mostly cloudy skies obscured the edges of the first-quartering moon. Three hours later, when the rapist had come through the window of unit 3208, the South winds had pushed away the cloud cover and raised the temperature to fifty-one degrees. The sky was dark as the little slice of moon had already set.

Startled awake, a hand harshly covering her mouth, *BB* heard the intruder say, "Don't move," and she began to struggle. He

---

[28] Same initials, different woman from *BB* in Offense #6 (R-6) on pages 75

said, "Calm down or I'll hurt you... I've got a knife, if you give me any trouble I'll use it!"

Her mind raced, *this is a joke... Sister's boyfriend...* then she got her only look at him. In the dark her mind took it all in, in an instant: white man; thirties; 150-170 pounds' dark blond or light brown hair-thick, below the ears; medium build; broad shoulders; light colored jacket, possibly...

"Quiet and I won't hurt you. Put your hands out." He took out a roll of adhesive tape from his pocket and taped her hands in front of her. "Roll over—on your stomach and don't move." He pulled the bed sheets over her head, "Now face the wall. Do you have a TV? All I want is your TV, now keep facing the wall."

BB heard him take the phone off the hook and punch several numbers and heard the flick of the light switch and saw the brightness through the sheets. She heard the faint click of the thermostat as he pushed the leaver over to fan and heard the blower come on and stay on.

He looked around the room, "Where's your jewelry and purse," he asked. The light went out again. "Is your TV black & white or color?"

She heard him going through drawers and told him, "My jewelry is only costume, everything I have I've worked for!"

He said, "I thought you're one of those rich kids from SMU."

She could hear him moving around the apartment, his voice constantly asking "Are you lying still?"

In the bathroom he found her hand cream and took it with him.

Back in the bedroom the intruder pulled *BB* out of bed and faced her toward the bathroom. "I'm going to tape you to the shower stall so I can get away fast." He skipped a few beats then said, "All I wanted was your TV, but I think I'll take you instead —get back in bed."

No longer wearing his rubber gloves the intruder pulled her nightshirt over her face and made her lie on her back. He rubbed his hands over *BB*'s body and said, "I'll really make you relax." She began to cry. "Don't scream," he said, "I have a knife, but I've never hurt anyone."

Between sobs *BB* said, "Please don't hurt me—take what you want; this isn't the way to do it. Please leave me alone." She told him she couldn't breathe and he told her, "Relax."

She heard him taking off his pants. He squeezed out some of the cold viscous hand lotion on his erection. Lying vulnerable on the bed, her nightshirt over her head she felt him get on top of her and felt the coldness of his erection penetrate her, felt him violating her, felt him climax.

As the rapist dressed he kept telling her, "Don't look at me." After he dressed he said, "I'm going to tape your feet. I have to tape you up so I'll have time to get away with your TV, I'm going to put it in my truck."

She pleaded with him not to, when he told her he was going to tape her to the shower stall. Instead he threw the covers over his victim's head, "Lie still and don't make any noise. After I leave if you want to call someone you can, but why would you want to do that?"

BB heard the TV cart being moved and could hear him fishing around with its electrical cord. Then she heard the door open and close. *BB* lay there for a while before gnawing off the tape from her hands with her teeth. As she went to the phone to call for help she saw the TV had not been taken.

Investigator G.E. Thompson #2185 of the Physical Evidence Section, went to 6059 Village Glenn, Apt 3028 on 12/18/74. He lifted two partial palm prints along with collecting a pillow case, tape used to bind complainant, sheets, and hair from sheet.

The right palm print would be comparable, if there were someone to compare it to.

1975

Dallas, Crimes Against Persons
January ?? 1975
Inv. (Reba) Evelyn Crowder Put In Charge

According to a compilation article that appeared in *The Dallas Morning News* on Sunday, February 20th, *after* the FBR had been captured the previous Monday, Valentines Day, February 14, 1977, the following was reported:

> Before the end of 1974, six[29] other rapes of a similar nature were reported, most of them in North Dallas. After his last assault of Dec. 18 of that year, the rapist took a rest.
> The Police, at the time, were moving toward a more systematic approach to the case. Rather than assign the cases to various investigators, Capt. Jack Davis, who was in charge of the police division that investigates crimes against person, decided early in January of 1975[30] to put one investigator on the rapes full-time.[31]
>
> The job went to Evelyn Crowders, a former airline stewardess who had married a policeman and joined the forcer herself nine years ago, after her third child was out of infancy. She went from the dispatch office to personnel to the tactical division. Within five years, she was a detective.

---

[29] By the end of 1974, the rapes I attributed to the FBR were 10 not 6.

[30] This statement appears at odds with Deputy Chief Fannin's November 7 1975 memo "further correlating" offenses under Crowder. (see page 161)

[31] I cannot definitively confirm Crowder's assignment and the consolidation of "similar rapes", as the rapes I attributed to the FBR were still being assigned to different investigators until late spring of 1975.

By this time, the label "friendly"[32] was routinely being applied to the rapist by the press and the police, but Mrs. Crowder was not given many clues.

"There was almost nothing to go on," she says. "We had no fingerprints and none of the victims could describe him."

In the weeks before the "friendly rapist" turned up again on March 15, Mrs. Crowder went through the police department's list of former sex offenders and known burglars and questioned dozens of them. Nothing.

She went through names of employees at apartment buildings where rapes had occurred, looking for a common denominator. Nothing.

She held group meetings with victims, probing their backgrounds for any point, however minute, where their paths might have crossed. Nothing.

She checked companies that did business with the apartment complex--carpet cleaners, gardeners, telephone installers, maid services, security patrols-- looking for a name to appear more than once. Nothing.

~

Throughout the spring of 1975, the investigation went nowhere.

"Then we got a fingerprint," says Mrs. Crowder, who was beginning to weary of the chase. "I thought we had him for sure."

She fed the print through computers from the courthouse to the FBI office in Washington and waited for the name of the suspect to land on her desk. Nothing.

Her conclusion: the man she sought had never been arrested.

[the article continues... *end of this excerpt*]

---

[32] To my knowledge there had been no mention in the press of one or multiple rapes of with similarities and do not recall any press or media using the the term "friendly" or "friendly rapist" in late 1974 or early 1975. Quite the contrary it appeared that neither CAPERS nor Planning & Research were focused on a serial rapist. Even after Crowder began to collect the North Dallas rape cases, she still maintained they were not committed by a single suspect. Moreover I have not been able to find a single article or press/media mention of a serial rapist, particularly a "friendly" rapist until after he was caught.

NOTE 1: the first latent print was a right palm printed lifted from the scene of the 10th attributed FBR rape on December 18, 1974 and the first fingerprint lifted was from a rape that occurred on May 9, 1975.

NOTE 2: it must have been in the early spring of 1975 when Inv. Crowder came across the rape offense from February 6, 1974. The year-old offense not only listed a suspect, that suspect had been arrested. Unfortunately, for Crowder, the man, Mr. James Patrick Rick, had been No Billed by the Grand Jury. Apparently undeterred by the G.J. action, according to Mrs. Rick, investigators went to the school where she taught. Though, today, she is unable to identify these investigators, she remembers vividly their statement: "Just because he was No Billed, doesn't mean he's not guilty."

NOTE 3: Crowder was correct when she told the newspapers that when she took on the FBR rapes there had been no suspects and no fingerprints. And although her seemingly only suspect, Mr. Rick had a full set of his fingerprints taken at the time of his arrest. It is easy to assume that Crowder was anxious for any rape scene lift that she could then have compared to Mr. Rick's digits. At some point she became aware of the latent right palm print that was lifted from the rape on December 18, 1974. And, like a dog with a bone, Crowder contacted Mr. Rick's attorney to see if Mr. Rick would allow DPD to print his right palm. Mr. Rick readily agreed, had a print made of his right palm, which was then dutifully compared by one of the Identification Section experts. Mr. Rick's right palm print did not match the right palm print lifted from the December 18, 1974 rape of *BB*.

Dallas, Central Division Crime Analyst
5:00pm Wednesday, January 15, 1975

It was gratifying to receive the performance evaluation below from my boss and to be appreciated for the work I had been doing as Division Analyst.

DALLAS POLICE DEPARTMENT
Performance Evaluation Report
PATROL BUREAU

Employee Name (Last)	(First)	(Initial)	I. D. Number	Rank or Title
Sadler,	Robert	J.	2441	Police Officer

Rating Period	Assignment(s)	Division
From 7/1/74 To 12/31/74	Division Analyst	Patrol/Central

IF CATEGORY DOES NOT APPLY—MARK BOX
DO NOT LEAVE BLANK
Rater Mark With Check Mark (✓)

Reviewer Mark With (X)
If Not in Agreement.
Second Reviewer Mark With (O)
If Not in Agreement With Originator.

INITIATIVE — Initiation of Action By an Employee
1. Offers suggestions and constructive criticism.
2. Develops and utilizes methods to solve crime and crime trends.
3. Works without close supervision.

PUBLIC CONTACT
Officer's Contacts With the Public
1. Exercises patience in citizen contacts
2. Treats each citizen contact with interest and concern

COOPERATION — Ability to Work With Others
1. Willingness to share information.
2. Willingness to share recognition for work jointly done.
3. Completes his share of group work assignments.
4. Fellow officers and other divisions, bureaus, and agencies.

SAFETY PRACTICES — Awareness and Concern For the Safety of Herself/Himself and Others in:
1. Operation and care of vehicles.
2. Handling of firearms.
3. Handling of prisoners.
4. Potentially hazardous situations.
5. Others — Specify

DEPENDABILITY — Accepts and Fulfills Responsibilities
1. Observes rules regarding duty hours.
2. Proper use of sick and/or injury time.
3. Remains on assigned beat.
4. Observes rules regarding markouts.
5. Makes all assignments
6. Keeps supervisor informed.

VOLUME OF ACCEPTABLE WORK*
1. Arrest activity in relation to offenses.
2. Traffic enforcement in relation to motor vehicle accidents and traffic problems.
3. Calls for service answered.
4. Felony in-the-act arrests.
5. Offenses cleared by arrest.
6. Stolen property recovered.

*Delete on supervisor rating

WORK ATTITUDE — Interest and Enthusiasm for the Job.
1. Willingly adapts to new procedures and surroundings.
2. Accepts direction (training, supervision, instruction).

APPEARANCE AND DEMEANOR
1. Correctness and condition of uniform and personal equipment.
2. Physical appearance (weight, posture, hair trimmed and combed, etc.)
3. Presents an alert and professional manner while performing his duties or dealing with the public.

FIELD PROFICIENCY AND EFFECTIVENESS — Quality of Work
1. Interrogation and interviews.
2. Written reports (makes proper reports in a correct manner).
3. Knowledge and proper utilization of procedures, policies, and regulations.
4. Radio procedures.
5. Oral communication.
6. Development of information sources.
7. Field notebook.
8. Practices aggressive patrol techniques.
9. Ability to improve through field experience.

JUDGMENT — Evaluate situations, Consider Alternatives, and Arrive at Effective Solution
1. Reliability under stress.
2. Consistency.
3. Unbiased and impartial.
4. Ability to control emotions.

SUPERVISORY EFFECTIVENESS — For those who supervise others.
1. Training
2. Leadership
3. Evaluation of Subordinates
4. Scheduling and Coordinating
5. Decision Making
6. Maintains Discipline

DALLAS POLICE DEPARTMENT

Rater Interview Summary

PATROL BUREAU

Officer___Sadler, Robert J.___ I. D. # _2441___ Rating Period From 7/1/74 to 12/31/74

1. STRENGTHS (Define—Do Not List—Use Extra Sheet if Necessary)

This is one of the most efficient and dedicated officers that I have had the opportunity
to supervise. It is only necessary for me to "suggest" that he accomplish a task and he
performs this task in an outstanding manner without any detailed instructions. His
contact with the many members of this Department in an effort to accomplish Divisional
goals always receives favorable comments. He is constantly aware of the crime problem
in the Central Patrol Division and constantly offers constructive suggestions to combat
the problem. He is genuinely interested in his assignment, Goals of the Central Patrol
Division and this Department.

2. IMPROVEMENTS NEEDED to meet or exceed standards—(Outline Specific Steps For Ratee to Follow)

NONE

3. IMPROVEMENTS ACCOMPLISHED Since Last Rating Period.

During this rating period he has become involved in the operational aspect of this
Division, and has had more inner action with field personnel. This effort on his part
has earned him recognition from other officers which will assist him in his assignment.
He has developed more meaningful methods for disseminating information to field personnel.
He has also made progress in his current assignment.

4. OVERALL RATING for This Period. ☒ Exceeds Standards ☐ Meets Standards
☐ Improvement Needed ☐ Not Satisfactory

RATER: I certify this report represents my best judgment.

Rater's Signature _Robert O. Crofr_

Title _Dep Chief_ Date _1-15-75_

REVIEWER: (If None, So Indicate)

Reviewer's Signature_____

Title_____ Date_____

Reviewer's Signature_____

Title_____ Date_____

EMPLOYEE: I certify that this report has been discussed
with me. I understand my signature does not necessarily
indicate agreement.

☐ I wish to discuss this report with the reviewer.

Comment:_____

Employee's Signature_____

Date_____

Dallas, Central Division Crime Analyst
5:00pm Tuesday, February 18, 1975

SINCE THE FBR's second attributed rape, on July 30, 1974 (212 days after the first on November 15, 1973), I felt this burglar-rapist would hit again—until he was caught. Tom agreed.

'Caught' usually meant two or three rapes. Even in the 1970s we knew that most rapes were by persons who knew their victims, had some type of relationship or one with some minimum degree of separation. Thus multiple rapes by the same suspect were rare.

[NB: *Jim Bryan remembered being in on the manhunt for "The Oak Lawn Rapist" of the 1960s, who was responsible for a half dozen rapes before being caught. Also back in the late 40s a man was arrested for the rape of Vickery area woman and sentenced to death. Though capital letters were not used he was referred to as "the phantom rapist" who "had terrorized Dallas women for the better part of a year before his arrest on Thanksgiving Day, 1949"* [33]

His arrest "cleared at least fifty burglaries and a number of rapes. This violator, like the FBR, was essentially a rapist who burgled.]

Various 'cat burglars' in the past had taken advantage of the presence of a female in a residence they were burglarizing at night to commit rape. Generally the 'cat burglar' mentality was all about the thrill of getting into someone's residence undetected and stealing from them while they slept and sneaking out again, undetected, with their loot. Not being detected during the commission of their theft was a point of pride with these offenders. They considered committing a rape as being fraught with possibilities of identification.

I had painstakingly gone back to 1970, reviewing criminal assault beefs, looking for the same or similar M.O. November 15, 1973, appeared to be ground zero for the Friendly Burglar-Rapist. I wasn't so sure. I'm still not sure that I didn't miss something before Case 0! It appeared that the FBR had struck a total of ten times since.

Now, by the end of 1974, the number of days between offenses had gone from 212 days between his first and second rape to an irregular sequence of: 4; 5; 28; 15; 6; 30; 12; and 41 days respectively. How could there not be other offenses during those 212 days?

---

[33] DMN Article : Adair Declared Insane, Escapes Death in Chair [see robertjsadler.com]

Author Note: *I was only tracking rape offenses with this unusual MO at this time, not the potentially related offenses like prowlers, trespass, and burglaries per se. Before the end of 1974 I had ordered copies of all these prowler, trespass, burglary reports for the previous two years. Tom and I combed through these offenses looking for any similarity to the MO-Markers we had observed with the FBR rapes.*

It was clear to me and Tom that we had a suspect responsible for multiple rapes, just like J.C. Shannon had been responsible for multiple BMV's.

Catching the FBR seemed the only way to stop him. We had been working on that for months. To help, we solicited every asset we could think of including (Tom's idea) the police department's consulting shrink, S.A. Somodevilla, PhD. Tom had run into Dr. Somodevilla and discussed the FBR case with him, asked him if we provided the O/IR's could he look at what he was doing and saying and give us some idea of who he is. Dr. Somodevilla said he probably could and would give it a try. Though we didn't ask for a "profile" or "psychological profile", per se, that was what Dr. Somodevilla called his result.

The FBR's first ten rapes were used as the baseline data for a psychological profile of the suspect in the Friendly Burglar-Rapist case.

Dr. Somodevilla and Officer C.F. Baker, M.A. provided their psychological profile (see below) to Investigator Evelyn Reba Crowder, CID, Crimes Against Persons. We had hoped that this profile being sent to Crowder would galvanize her efforts in what we (Tom and I) knew to be multiple, one suspect, connected rapes. We were wrong.

Multiple crimes committed by the same person [such as J.C. Shannon's 90 some BMV's] were not rare. Though multiple murders or rapes by the same person were statistically rare and were the bane of law enforcement everywhere. The term 'serial', as in 'serial murder' or 'serial murderer' had not yet come into vogue.

Case in point, see 'chain killer' below. My friend, retired LAPD Homicide Detective and author of *Black Dahlia Avenger*, and *Most Evil*, Steve Hodel, recounts the following about the 1940s Lone Woman Murders in the Los Angeles area in his book *Black Dahlia Avenger II*[34]:

---

[34] *Black Dahlia Avenger II*, by Steve Hodel, (Thoughtprint Press), page 232

"Cornell's 1943 radio drama, *The White Rose Murders* told the story of a 'homicidal Maniac' who frequented the city's downtown dancehalls, where he met, danced with and picked up lone women. The killer then lured them out into the night where he strangled them to death. As a signature of his kills the madman carefully places a 'white rose' next to the body of each of his victims.

In the vernacular of the day, the police detective described him as 'a chain killer' and as the story begins we find the city is gripped in terror as the unidentified suspect has just slain his fourth victim, and is about to kill his fifth."

Regarding the word 'serial' and its application to a criminal as in 'serial murder', 'serial murder', 'serial killer', 'serial killing' or 'serial rapist' the Oxford English Dictionary did not include its reference (a "Draft partial entry June 2001") on this use of the word 'serial' until 2001. Note first use is 1961 in another dictionary. Next we have the OED's "Draft partial entry June 2001" for 'serial killer' (first use 1981) and 'serial killing' (first use 1984).

OED Draft partial entry June 2001

> Of a person: that repeatedly or regularly performs a specified activity; inveterate, persistent; *spec.* (of a criminal) repeatedly committing the same offence and typically following a similar characteristic behaviour pattern. Of an action or practice: performed by the same person on a regular or sequential basis; habitual, recurrent. Later uses in this sense are probably influenced by the frequency of the compounds serial killer and serial killing (treated separately below).

a **1961** S. Kracauer in *Webster's 3rd New Internat. Dict. Eng. Lang.* (1961) 2072/3 [He} denies that he is the pursued serial murderer. **1968** *Etc.* June 235 Yet we must also admit that this revolution has created serious problems which express themselves among adults as an increase in serial polygamy, neighborhood 'key clubs', partner-swap parties, [etc.]. **1980** *Washington Post* 29 NOV. D4/5 The program focused..on sexual homicides, mass murders and 'serial' murder--murders spaced out over a period of time. **1993** *Independent on Sunday* 22 Aug. (Weekend) 9 In Leisure World, everyone is old. Behind the barbed-wire in Southern California, 'active retirees' become serial golfers, swimmers, gymnasts. **1997** *Scotl. on Sunday* (Electronic ed.) 2 Nov. According to both Bunkhanovsky and Tkachenko serial killing with the spin-off of serial cannibalism happens most in heavily militarised countries where the individual is relatively impotent. **2001** Guardian 26 May (Saturday Rev.) 2/6 A serial espouser of every reactionary cause.

Next we have the OED's "Draft partial entry June 2001" for 'serial killer' (first use 1981) and 'serial killing' (first use 1984).

OED Draft partial entry June 2001

> **serial killer** *n.* a person who commits a series of murders, often with no apparent motive and usually following a similar, characteristic pattern of behavior.

1981 *N.Y. Times Mag.* 3 May 66/1 Some Atlantans fear racial violence if a '*serial' killer is discovered to be white. **1994** *Time* 4 Apr. 66/1 Birnes and Norris have divided the serial-killer life into seven phases of activity, a repeating cycle that begins with desire and ends with morose feelings-- aura, trolling, wooing, capture, murder, totem and depression. **2001** *Evening Chron. (Newcastle)* (Electronic ed.) 24 Jan. A gruesome serial killer was running amok in the streets.

OED Draft partial entry June 2001

> **serial killing** *n.* and *adj. (a) n.* (any of) a series of murders with similar characteristics committed b y the same person; the committing of such murders (also in extended use); *(b) adj.* that is a serial killer.

1984 *U.S. News & World Rep.* 30 Apr. 53/1 The phenomenon of *serial killings has been recognized since a man dubbed Jack the Ripper murdered seven London prostitutes in 1888. **1990** *Entertainm. Weekly* (Electronic ed.) 28 Dec. A serial-killing investment banker who skins women alive. **1997** *Sporting Life* (Electronic ed.) 3 Mar. In the early hours of Friday morning, during a serial killing of claret bottles, he was to be heard whingeing quietly. **2000** *Daily Record (Glasgow)* (Electronic ed.) 6 July The FBI have already admitted that serial killing has reached an 'almost epidemic proportion' in the United States, with between 35 and 50 killers currently on the loose. **2000** *Bath Chron.* (Electronic ed.) 27 Sept. Christian Bale..caused controversy in America with his role as a serial killing Wall Street trader in American Psycho.

It an article (Interview by Jane Goldman, *The book of the Unexplained II*[35], Robert Ressler, the father of FBI's BAU, said *the mind of a murderer is a dangerous place to be* and that *getting into the mind of a murderer is as essential and effective a part of crime-solving as collecting forensic evidence.* He completed his thought: *grasping a murderer's motivation is often the only way his/her next move can be anticipated*[36].

---

[35] Provides fans of the X-Files TV series with background information about the real events, phenomena, and folklore that inspire actual X-Files shows... etc.

[36] From internet article re: BSU, retrieved on 1/18/10 from http://hem.passagen.se/blenda1/page2.html [see article on website: robertjsadler.com]

When going into the mind of the bad guy provides no insight into his capture, you are left with pattern recognition, statistical analysis, and the E.G.; educated guess.

Tom and I were never able, in spite of the Dr. Somodevilla's profile, to get into the mind of The Friendly Burglar-Rapist. We understood his potential psychological intentions, his target; women (approximately half the population), and his primary prey-territory (generally North Dallas). We understood that the burglary aspect of his M.O. was not about burglary and we understood that the criminal assault aspect of his M.O. was not *per se* about sexual gratification or sexual conquests. Regardless, his aberrant behavior was positively reinforced with each new burglary and rape. We understood he had a 'hunger' and was either addicted to the chronic repetition of his hunger-quest because of the perceived benefit it afforded him or his hunger remained somehow unsatisfied in spite of the recurring positive reinforcement.

In the case of the Dallas' Friendly Burglar-Rapist, the most prolific serial rapist in America at the time, it was not enough to understand his motivation. By example, if I knew a man's motivation was hunger, that he was likely to be hungry approximately three times a day, that he liked hamburgers for either lunch or dinner, that he particularly liked Whataburger hamburgers, that he was likely to satisfy his hunger at the Whataburger nearest to his home or place of business... I could perhaps anticipate some of his moves. But if I don't know where he works or lives, I would need to stake-out thousands of Whataburger's in order to include the suspect in that search sphere. Even so, if I don't know who the suspect is then I must use whatever description there is to narrow my search parameters, beyond a profiler's categorization of sex and age. Such was the case in trying to identify and anticipate the moves of the FBR.

The variables were almost inexhaustible. In 1973, '74, '75, & '76 there were none of the future Dr. Russmo's Geoprofiling algorithms to employ[37]. There was no FBI Behavioral Analysis Unit to enlist for help. In fact, to the best of our knowledge, Dr. Somodevilla's and Officer C.F. Baker's psychological profile of

---

[37] Kim Russmo, PhD: Former Vancouver Police Detective Inspector and developer of the 'Russmo formula' a geoprofiling algorithms and founder of ECRI employing it's Rigel™ geoprofiling analytics. (See Pages 580-588)

the FBR (dated Feb 18, 1975) preceded FBI profilers by two years.

It is often said of the terrorist and preventing terrorist attacks that military, civilian, law enforcement authorities have to be 'right' one-hundred percent of the time in their assessment and preventive deployments to foil attacks, whereas the terrorist only has to be lucky once, to negate all prevention efforts. Conversely the criminal has to be successful in his M.O. one hundred percent of the time and law enforcement only has to get lucky once[38], in order to arrest a suspect. Sadly, this fact contains the uneasy knowledge that, in the case of this serial offender, more women would be raped in the meantime. They were his 'successes' and our 'failures'.

The institutionalized hesitancy to believe two street cops could do what their specialized investigators had not done was very frustrating, but understandable. Institutional 'turf' is highly protected. More than once we were told our jobs were on the line —if we were wrong. Tom and I didn't question the incongruity of 'wrongness' of not focusing on a 'serial rapist' by departmental brass; we focused on the fact that every offense that came through our hands meant a citizen of Dallas had had her life changed forever.

Were others looking for a rapist responsible for individual rapes in Dallas? Yes, absolutely. Beat patrolmen, tactical officers and various investigators were 'on it'. Physical Evidence Section investigators Ron Pettie and Bobby Brown, for example spend many a night, in between crime scene calls, printing joggers in the area in hopes of stopping 'the one'. Even Capt. Milliken who took over Crimes Against Persons after Capt. Davis, had spent hours at night walking the area, looking for the FBR.

But that was just it. They were on 'it', the individual rape offenses perpetrated by the unknown suspect—not an unknown suspect responsible for all the similar rapes and other offenses in three different sectors of the city: Central, Northwest and Northeast. The department's efforts were fragmented at best.

In our opinion, for a long period of time the hope of catching the FBR lay solely in our hands and we worked untold hours to arrange a meeting between the FBR and his arresting officer. In

---

[38] See Appendix A Article 14b3: Captain Don Milliken on 2.14.1976 made a similar observation: 'We only have to trick you once,' suspect told. [see website: robertjsadler.com]

the end Tom and I had marshaled enough actionable knowledge to put someone in a position *to get lucky*.

Though DPD Investigator Crowder had 'caught' several of these cases, those that preceded her had yet to be lumped together, as Tom and I had done, and when she was assigned as the investigative lead on these "similar "rapes" she was still of the opinion that multiple suspects were involved, not a single perpetrator as we insisted.

The following memo was dated February 18, 1975, and listed as its subject: A Psychological Profile of the "Friendly Rapist". Somodevilla and Baker wrote:

> This is a single white male, approximately 24-28 years of age and weighing about 160 lbs. He has long, styled, brown hair and is very neat and clean. He has some college and his IQ is about 115, making him of above average.
>
> Socioeconomically he is middle class, but his parents are probably upper middle class. His excellent use of English, lack of profanity, and even gentlemanly behavior, as well as his compulsive need for order and meticulousness suggest that this man probably works in a professional or semiprofessional setting in occupations such as lab technician, nursing, or other medically related fields. The statement of several victims to the effect of his hands being soft rather than callous tends to verify his job as not involving heavy manual labor.
>
> He is probably known as a nice guy, slightly introverted, and someone who doesn't make a strong impression either way, positive or negative. He can be polite and a gentleman with women but seldom has meaningful relationships (sexual or emotional) with them.
>
> The "truck" statement can be seen as a way of giving a false lead, however, at a deeper psychological level the reference to a truck, a masculine symbol, can be see(n) as an unconscious attempt to convey a sense of masculinity.
>
> Psychodynamically this man is not psychotic. He is in touch with reality and knows the difference between right and wrong. However, he is suffering from severe personality conflict to the point of sexually acting out. He is an inadequate, pensive, masochistic male who identifies with his victims due to his own repressed homosexuality which he has never acted out. Thus the rape itself is a reaction formation against his fear of homosexuality.
>
> The breaking and entering and ritualistic searching around provides him with an excitement (here he gets the erection) which he finalizes through intercourse. This is really more of a masturbatory activity since coitus itself lasts on the average of two minutes. Thus he has already been quite excited by the time he penetrates his victims. Thus the rummaging around is a preparation (or foreplay) for intercourse.
>
> His ambivalence towards females is manifested in his gentleness and kindness, almost apologetic, on the one hand (when he covers

them up, etc) and his forcing himself on his victims and threatening them with a knife on the other. The victims are not sexual objects, per se, but instruments to fulfill his ritualistic need to feel potent and masculine. This is due to the repressed homosexuality referred to above.

He is, within his pathology, quite stable and does not appear to have become worse since the first reported offense. If, however, he finds himself in a situation where he panics due to an uncooperative, screaming, fighting, victim, he may lash out violently. This would be a slash-and-run fashion rather than a premeditated one. His first choice would be to run away.

Submitted by: Officer C.F. Baker, M.A.
                S.A. Somodevilla, PhD.

[**NB**: Somodevilla/Baker profile was later placed in the Patrol Officer's Handbook Tom and I created to educate our officers on the Friendly Burglar-Rapist.]

[**NB**: A white male, GWM Jr., 2/25/47 was one week from his 28th birthday when the Somodevilla/Baker profile was issued.]

[**NB**: According to a 2004 article, by Lea Winerman of the Monitor, titled *Criminal profiling: the reality behind the myth*, the impetus for law enforcement consults with psychologists by American law enforcement began with the New York City police in 1956 when "the frustrated investigators asked psychiatrist James Brussel, New York State's assistant commissioner of mental hygiene, to study crime scene photos and notes from the (Con Edison) bomber. Brussel came up with a detailed description of the suspect: He would be unmarried, foreign, self-educated, in his 50s, living in Connecticut, paranoid and with a vendetta against Con Edison--the first bomb had targeted the power company's 67th street headquarters." Additionally Winerman states: "In 1974, the FBI formed its Behavioral Science Unit to investigate serial rape and homicide cases. From 1976 to 1979, several FBI agents--most famously John Douglas and Robert Ressler--interviewed 36 serial murderers to develop theories and categories of different types of offenders." Other sources indicate the BSU opened in 1972 and that Douglas transferred to BSU in 1977 where he taught hostage negotiation and applied criminal psychology at the FBI Academy in Quantico. Va.]

Author Note: *To the best of my knowledge Guy William Marble Jr., (in prison in 1977, 1978 & 1979) was not included in their interview of serial offenders; murders or rapists.*

Dallas, Central Division Crime Analyst
5:00pm Tuesday, February 28, 1975

We received our copy of the *Dallas Police News* [39] today with the front page story (*to catch a thief...*) about the new Real-time Tactical Deployment (RTD). The DPN reports:

RTD "... proving to be one of the most successful Impact-funded projects in the country as well as the only one of its type for municipal police departments. 'And it works,' Lt. C. J. Macsas, project director, recently told city officials in a packed briefing session. 'We now have a tool with almost unlimited potential.' Coupled with DPD's sophisticated reporting system, RTD goes to work at 6 a.m. daily. Keyed at present on residential burglaries, all computer banks are quickly scanned for reports on such offenses and the situation is sized up by beat--descending from the 'hottest'. A portrait of each is given with how many offenses were committed that day and what time, 14 and 30 day histories and averages, what has been taken, manner of entry into what sort of structure, whether there is a suspect, whether a vehicle is known to have been used... 'Looking at this page, you can see your problem immediately,' said Officer Bill Hamby of Planning and Research.' 'We're able now to attack problems in its early stages rather than during or after its peak,' said Tactical Sgt. Johnny Corum. RTD has cut days, weeks and months out of locating and defining problem areas--a job where time is of the essence.

'Before,' Hamby said, 'we could only spot them (on pin maps) as they built up.' The project, designed by a Systems Development Corporation team led by Sam McMillan, 'has applications that haven't been thought of,' said Carl Makres, operations research analyst. 'We can utilize its capabilities to deal with any sort of crime problem from most any approach.'"

Author Note: *To my knowledge, the RTD was never employed to deal with the "sort of crime problem" known as the on-going rapes committed by the FBR.*

---

[39] See website: robertjsadler.com for graphic & text

Dallas, Northeast Patrol Division, Beat 213
5:00am Saturday, March 15, 1975
Offense Number 11 (R-11)

THE IDES OF March was marked by Shakespeare in his play *Julius Caesar* as the fateful day of Caesar's death, it had held no other significance in *TH*'s life until today. In the first floor apartment, number 1042, of the Willowick Apartments located at 4692 Amesbury, *TH*, a twenty-six year-old white female sociologist lay sleeping.

"Don't be afraid," he said as she woke to the pressure of a hand over her mouth. She became very afraid. "I have a knife, don't move." That became the mantra she heard him repeat over and over: "Don't move…"

He put a pillowcase over her head, "Don't move." He tied her hands with an electrical cord, "Don't move." He made her lay face down and tied her hands to the bed post, "Don't move." He stood up, "Don't worry, after I leave you'll be able to get loose very easy—but you shouldn't call the police. Don't move—you have any money? Where?" She told him she had twenty dollars in her purse. She heard him looking through her purse and saying "don't move," then heard him leave the bedroom.

When he returned he told her, "Turn over on your back." "I can't—", she said, "my hands are tied to the bed post." He untied her hands from the bedpost, but her hands were still bound as he turned her over on her back. He pulled the covers away from her body and pulled off her panties. She felt him crawl on top of her and commit his rape.

Afterwards he cut the cord from her bedroom phone and asked if there was another one, which he also cut. He asked where she kept her jewelry and told her, "I'm going to take your stereo and put it in my truck." A few minutes later *TH* heard a door shut. Outside the rapist jogged away into the overcast, forty-eight degree, morning. The eastern sky, high above the clouds, was just beginning to pink with dawn, though sunrise was more than an hour away.

TH lay in bed in shock and disbelief for twenty or thirty minutes before realizing he was really gone. She ran next door to a neighbor's to call the police. Returning to her apartment she realized the rapist hadn't taken a thing, only talked about it.

In the Supplement Report, dated 3/22/75 Investigator Reba Crowder #2894 wrote: "Compl. contacted 3-18-75 by phone and by personal interview at her home 3-22-75. This offense is similar to other offenses committed by "the Friendly Burglar Rapist." Compl. did not see susps face & no prints were collected. Susp did use compls hand lotion to lubricate himself and one of her butcher knives to threaten her."

Author Note: *Wonder where Reba picked up that name? To my knowledge this was the first instance of a CID investigator using this 'moniker' in a police report.*

First 12 FBR Attributed Offenses & Inv.'s Assigned

O/IR #	FBR #	FBR Bk Page	Complainant Name	Comp. Initials	Offense Date	Inv. Assigned/Reporting
340698-E	O/R-1	7 & 10		PJT	11/15/73	Inv James E Ozment #1818
237116-F	R-2	53		JP	7/30/74	Inv D.H. Fitzgerald #2978
242158-F	R-3	54		RG	8/3/74	Inv Eugene N. Stansell
248973-F	R-4	55		SL	8/8/74	Inv James E Ozment #1818
283127-F	R-5	66		BG	9/5/74	Inv N.W. Agee #2553
300572-F	R-6	71		BB	9/20/74	Inv Debra A. Gardenier #3321
307548-F	R-7	75		NF	9/25/74	Inv Unk (no Inv follow up in file)
342398-F	R-8	89		GT	10/26/74	Inv R.M. Wagoner #709
356401-F	R-9	90		CN	11/7/74	Inv C.W. Hudson #2533
401910-F	R-10	91		BB	12/18/74	Inv J.W. Murdock #1534
83737-G	R-11	108		TH	3/15/75	Inv Reba Crowder #289
103880-G	R-12	110		EH	4/1/75	Inv Linda T. Fulghum #2937

I was never able to discern exactly what cases (offenses) that CAPERS had put Inv. Crowder in charge of as of early January 1975. Clearly the first ten (10) rape offenses I would attribute to the FBR were being assigned to various different investigators. It was not until March of 1975 before Crowder 'caught' her first FBR offense (R-11). And, if she was assigned to all 'similar' (a term that was never defined) rapes, then why did Inv. Fulghum 'catch' R-12, arguably the most important and incendiary FBR offense before or after.

Chapter 5

On the Radar

Dallas, Central Patrol Division, Beat 126
1:30am Tuesday, April 1, 1975
Offense Number 12 (R-12)

APRIL FOOLS' DAY another rape in the City of Dallas
occurred; one of the dozens and dozens that had already changed
the lives of their victims that year. But this one was different and
this one would change everything.

Dallas, Central Division Crime Analyst's Office
8:30am Tuesday, April 1, 1975

I HAD BEEN in my office for fifteen minutes, had just
started drinking a cup of coffee. Most of the other officers and
staff were wandering back and forth from the detail room to their
offices and passing by would wave, a cigarette in one hand their
cup of coffee in the other. I had the weird habit of only smoking
at night. A quirk I'd inherited from observing my father's
smoking regime.

My inbox was stacked with the usual pile of O/I R's. My first
task was to take the pile and make smaller ones. I took the stack
of reports and started dealing them across my desk into seven
piles: assaults, murders, rapes, robberies, burglaries, thefts and
others.

I didn't plot the 'others' but they often made for good reading,
like the one in which officers met a complainant in her home
where she reported a goat was standing in her kitchen sink, its
foot caught in the disposal. In answer to the officer's innocuous
and understandable question, the complainant said, "No, I don't
own a fuckin' goat!" The situation deteriorated from there.
Afterwards, as the story circulated, wherever officers gathered—
everyone would break up laughing as someone in the group
would, cup his hand to his mouth, as if he was talking into a
microphone, like a dispatcher, and would say, "113, see the
woman about an indisposed goat—handle code two."

Somehow the priority of looking at the worst offenses first,
the crimes against persons, then running through the rest down to

property crimes and ending with the 'others' had seemed a good methodology from Day One. I was still following the same method over a year later. The more numerous thefts demanded the greatest part of my time between reviewing, reading the O/I R's, posting the latest offense locations on my maps and then analyzing the results for various reports and after action follow-ups.

In my seven stacks were the O/I R's from the 2nd and 3rd watch for Monday, March 31 and 1st watch for Tuesday, April 1, 1975.

There were the usual number of assaults which ran the gamut from fisticuffs in a bar, to domestic battery; husband on wife, wife on husband or the social equivalent.

Where assaults take place in public, some police pressure can be brought to bear. However when the behavior occurs 'inside' a private residence or business, overt police response is always after the fact and if suspect information is available, investigative work can commence and officers on patrol will start looking for the suspect/s in their area.

Nothing of note caught my eye as I read each report, put the corresponding location dots on my 'assault' map, and filed the O/I R's in a file cabinet drawer marked: Assaults.

Murder in 1975 in Dallas, Texas was most often a 'friend on friend' rather than a 'stranger on stranger' crime; crimes of passion between those who knew each other. A smaller category of homicides would be as a result of the commission of another crime, such as an armed robbery of a convenience store where the robber shoots the clerk. Homicides were aggressively followed up by homicide investigators and were, though not the easiest to solve, often cleared through arrests.

Fortunately homicides were low in Dallas, less than one a day; there had been 226 the year before, although the trend seemed to be going up in the first quarter of 1975. What everyone knew, at that moment in time, was that murder occurred one or two (rarely) at a time and the killer almost never had the opportunity to do it again. The word serial killer or serial rapist, for that matter, had not yet entered the vernacular of police, the press, or the public. With that 'one' Dallas murder statistically divided up between the five patrol divisions, there might be days or weeks that went by without a murder beef crossing my desk. Today was a no-murder day.

Rapes were another matter, they were often committed by 'friends', known acquaintances, and relatives. When the victim names the suspect, his apprehension was pretty much guaranteed. Cops and psychologists, counselors, and social workers often found out about rapes months or years later in unrelated conversations with victims that had chosen, for one reason or another, not to report their rape when it occurred. Things would emerge such as, "Uncle So-n-so died," "I was too embarrassed to…"; "my husband won't understand…"; "I'm so ashamed…", "he said it was my fault for teasing him…". So the conventional wisdom was that rapes were under-reported by anywhere from twenty to eighty percent.

This morning I had one criminal assault O/I R on my desk. I let my eyes scan the upper left hand corner of the report: Element 126, Beat 126. A kind of *déjà vu* struck me, this was one of the old beats I used to work. The offense-incident line was printed in big bold capitol letters with: AGGRAVATED RAPE 21.03 (the Texas Penal Code Section). I thought, *that hand writing looks familiar.* It was. It belonged to one of my patrol partners, Max Countryman. *Well, if anything, I know this report will be thorough,* I said to myself.

Author Note: *it would not be until months later that I connected the dots regarding the name of the second reporting officer on this offense (P. A. Crawford #3644). Pat Crawford was new to the force and she was already one of the top pistol shots on the DPD pistol team, along with Max. She would later become Mrs. Max Countryman.*

The offense, Service number 103880-G, had occurred at 2800 Douglas Avenue, in apartment 114. I made a mental note: *ground floor apartment.* I looked at the address again and looked at the 3-D map of my old beat that I kept filed in my head. *That's the Stepping Stone Apartments… corner of Douglas and Congress! Number 114 would front on Douglas…damn… I searched a moment longer and said #6 or was it #7.*

I flashed back a couple of summers when we had worked beat 126 and how we had numbered all the apartment complex swimming pools, which out of necessity we would be required to pass by while on routine patrol for bad guys. Given the number of young pretty women, particularly stewardesses, in the area it was not unusual to see one or several out sunbathing on a weekday.

When a particular lovely vision deserved more protection than one officer was capable of supplying, and since the sector sergeant would not approve of the officer just parking his squad car for idle chitchat, we would key the radio and give out the pool number. It didn't take long for the other guys in the sector to learn the system. Soon, those that could would slowly cruise pool number six and the sector sergeant would be none the wiser and the pretty young woman by the pool would feel very 'protected'.

No, number six was across the street... I don't think Stepping Stone had a pool...

My eyes came back to the report and I shook my head. I knew the complainant was going to be raped as I read. I knew there would be suspect information later as Max wrote in the Suspect/s box: SEE BACK of REPORT. Max had also listed under 'Stolen Property' Various Change from Purse $6.00. I began reading Max's report in the Narrative box. It started out routinely.

> Compl. advised she went to sleep about 11:00pm (3/31/75) & had been asleep for approximately two hours when she was awakened by Suspect. Compl. was lying on her stomach when Suspect put his hand over her mouth & put a knife to the back of her neck & said, "don't move, or I'll Kill you." Suspect then placed a Pillow Case over Compl's head & tied her hands to the bed post with a halter top. Suspect then wandered around her Apt. talking to Compl. Advised her not to be afraid because he was just a Burglar. **Suspect** also **advised he was a Dallas Police Officer...**

My heart pounded as my eyes jumped back to the sentence to reread it; to make sure I read what I thought I had—*Damn—he's a cop? A Dallas Cop! Jesus!*

I took a yellow marker from my desk drawer and marked the sentence from "Suspect also advised..." to "trained in Houston." I backed up and read it a third time and kept going:

Advised her not to be afraid because he was just a Burglar. Suspect also advised he was a Dallas Police Officer for about one year & was trained in Houston. Suspect asked if Compl. had any Diamond Rings & when Suspect got the six dollars from her purse he stated, "Your job must not pay well either, That's why I do this. The Police Dept. don't pay enough. He told Compl. he had already Burglarized three houses earlier.

Suspect then untied Compl's hands & walked her into the Living Room & back into the bedroom & again tied her hands. Suspect then took Compl's nightgown off & wrapped it around the Pillow Case on her head. Compl. attempted to scream & Suspect pushed a Pillow down on her face & stated "the Bedroom window is Open & I'll cut your throat or suffocate you & be out the window & gone because my truck is Parked out back. Suspect fondled Compl's body, then pulled his pants down & had intercourse with Compl.

After intercourse Suspect told Compl. if she called the Police he would know about it since he was a Policeman & he would come back and fix her for good.

When Suspect Left he advised Compl not to move for an hour & that he would tap on her window to let her know when he was outside the Apt.

Compl. untied herself & ran to a neighbors Apt. The Time was about 2:45 am (4/1/75). Compl was afraid to call the Police because she had seen what happened to girls on TV.

> Suspect had opened all windows in Compl's
> Apt. & cut the phone cords on Compl's two
> phones. MO is the Same as Suspect on
> Previous Assaults in North Dallas Area.
> Suspect was very talkative & told Compl he
> had met her at Love Field.
>
> Suspect--w/m 20-30. Suspect told Compl he
> was 20, but Compl thought he would be closer
> to 30.

My first thought, *un-fucking-believable*...and my second, *good on-ya Max, this is like the BOLO... God, when was that?*

I got up from my desk and went to the file cabinets and pulled the rape files. It took some digging. I found it, almost sixteen months back. A criminal assault in the 4300 block of Brown on beat 127—less than two football fields away, as the crow files, from Douglas and Congress on the adjacent beat 126, where the latest rape occurred. *Damn that's a hell of a flimsy pattern, over a year apart and a block away... coincidence or pattern?*

Looking at the service numbers on the two O/I R's I did a rough calculation. Over a half a million O/I R's had been generated between the first rape I noticed in November of 1973 and this new one on April 1, 1975. If each of the five divisions had a somewhat equal share of offenses, that would mean I had read, analyzed and posted something over 100,000 O/I R's.

I was amazed at how much of the November 15th offense came back to me, but I kept thinking, *this is only number two?... but the similarities?...read it again Sadler, read it again!*

The rape occurred on a Thursday, the fifteenth of November 1973... *in the afternoon?* Between 2:30 and 3:00 pm. The reporting officer filled in the Suspect box with "w/m/24-26 5'11", 185-190 lbs, white T-shirt, red ski mask, stocky next to fat, light complexion, hairy arms, dark brown or black gloves (heavy). *Hmm, maybe the guy's slimmed down in the last year?*

I reread the reporting officer's Narrative:

> Compl left Apt. to go to wash room. She was gone
> approx. 5 min. She left door unlocked. When she
> returned she confronted the above Susp. standing in the

doorway of bedroom. She screamed and attempted to run for front door. Susp. grabbed Compl. and covered her eyes & mouth with his hand & stated "Everything's going to be all right, you just caught a Burglar in the act." Susp. then tied Compl. wrist's with a belt & bra to the bed & placed a pillow case over her head. Susp. then rummaged around the Apt. in drawers , etc. He stated "you don't have much worth stealing." Susp. then began to undress Compl. & said, "This won't hurt one bit, there's a jar of Vaseline in the bathroom." Officer found a med. size jar Vaseline with only one application of the contents missing. (new jar). Compl. stated Susp. seemed extremely nice & (asked) if he hurt her when he tied her up. She stated that intercourse lasted only a very short time & then Susp. got dressed & left and advised her not to call Police because if he should get caught he would say that she invited him to her Apt. Compl. waited to call Police because she felt that it wouldn't do any good because she could not identify a Susp. She & her husband also felt that it was humiliating to retell the story. Compl. declined the examination at PMH. Both she & husband concurred. Compl. also stated the Susp. told her he would be watching her.

I thought, *so he's progressed from using cop jargon like, 'caught in the act' and 'don't call the police because I'll just say you invited me... to don't call the police, because I am the Police!' Jeeeze. If this gets out...every man on the department will be a suspect.* I laughed, *well, hell, I guess we are...*

I put the two O/I R's side by side... shaking my head, *what the hell kind of cop would tell somebody he's rapin' that he's a cop— a moron, bad enough to claim to be "just a burglar," then say you're a cop; trying to make ends meet. Nobody's gonna believe that... but it would make juicy headlines.* My eyes jumped from line to line, page to page.

My pencil point was tapping my desk pad as I thought about this rapist's MO, and I scribbled out a *nom de guerre*, which seemed ironic and caused me to laugh... not at the name I had coined for the rapist, it was the place my 'brain' went...

I flashed on the Mel Brooks film *Young Frankenstein* that my wife and I had seen back in December. In the movie the character Igor (played by Marty Feldman) brings back the wrong brain, the one marked abnormal. The cross-eyed Igor's attempt to steal the brain of a revered scientist from the local "brain depository" goes awry when he takes one labeled, "Do Not Use This Brain! Abnormal". Upon Igor's return, doctor Frankenstein asks about the brain. Igor confesses that he brought A.B. Normal's brain which he pronounces "Abby Normal"! This snafu causes Frankenstein to attempt to strangle Igor.

I was still laughing at Igor when one of the sergeants looked in on me, disdainfully. Composing myself, I looked at what I had doodled and saw in the middle the name I had scribbled for this burglar and rapist with a seemingly courteous manner: Friendly Burglar-Rapist. That thought immediately sobered me.

I knew I needed to think more deeply about this suspect. Was he or could he be a cop, even a Dallas cop? At that moment the only people who knew about this aspect of this offense was the complainant, Max, his partner Pat, and now me. Who else might have read this report? Someone in the Report Division? It was possible that the offense had not yet been assigned to a CAPERS investigator. Given the volume of work Lt. Macsas' group had (looking at offenses for the entire city), it was also possible they had not yet tumbled to this MO.

After diligently reviewing the two offenses that I now believed were connected, I gathered up my papers and went to Chief Dixon's office. I briefed him about the possibility we had someone responsible for at least two rapes in the 120s and he could be a policeman, a Dallas policeman.

The Chief's demeanor visibly shifted. He took his briar pipe out of his mouth, tapped its bowl on his ashtray. "Good work."

I said, "Chief, I don't like this length of time between offenses. Eighteen months just doesn't make any sense. I think maybe there is more to this."

I knew what I had in mind was stepping outside my bailiwick. I was responsible for crime analysis for Central Division, P&R was still looking at the other four patrol Divisions (Northeast, Northwest, Southwest and Southeast), as well as Central. Asking for permission, at least obliquely, was the smart thing to do.

I said, "If you don't mind, I'm going to be looking into past offenses and order rape offenses during this period from the other four divisions to look for similar MO's."

Chief Dixon gave me a single nod and said, "Do what you need to do. Keep me informed."

Dallas, Central Division Crime Analyst's Office
5:30 pm Thursday, April 10, 1975

Given the incredible revelation reported by the complainant EH, I ordered the Supplement Report for this office. Investigator L.T. Fulghum #2937 stated in her report, dated 4-9-75:

"Investigator made personal contact with compl on 4-1-75 at 10:15am at PMH. Compl verified facts of assault as originally reported. compl further stated that suspect used some moisture lotion on himself before the assault. Compl stated she never saw suspect at all during the entire time he was in her apartment (1-2 hours). Compl stated suspect had a rather high pitched voice and was very talkative, also that he prowled around her apt, taking six dollars from compl's purse. **Suspect stated he was a Dallas Police officer and had trained in Houston.** A check of personnel records revealed that we have no officers with this Department at the present time who have worked for the Houston Police Department prior to coming to DPD. One poor print was lifted from the telephone in compl's apt. The suspect had cut phone cords on both telephones. Also, the suspect mentioned seeing compl at the "airport", however compl had left canceled plane ticket stubs laying around the apartment when she returned on a flight on 3-31-75, so suspect possibly saw tickets while he was prowling the apt. The medical report showed positive evidence seminal fluid and sperm. This offense will be suspended pending development of new workable leads.

Author Note: *Bold font, emphasis added - mine.*

[**NB:** Remember the complainant's statement, taken by the reporting officer reads:

Suspect also advised he was a Dallas Police Officer for about one year & was trained in Houston. (see page 117-118)]

Chapter 6

Lucky Thirteen

Dallas, Northeast Patrol Division, Beat 231
3:30 am Wednesday, April 23, 1975
Offense Number 13

THE FALLS APARTMENTS lay in the rapist's crosshairs. The convenience of a ladder left out by maintenance personnel made easy his entry into the second floor apartment, #229, of *SM*, a white female 25, at 6525 Melody Lane. Fortunately, for *SM*, she was not at home.

The mostly full moon was covered by the mostly overcast skies, so no one saw him enter or leave. Slipping through deeper shadows the strong breeze chilled the sweat on the rapist's skin; a combination of the 72 degree temperature, the adrenaline of breaking and entering apartments and not knowing what he might find.

He made his way two buildings north in the Falls complex and chose another second floor apartment, number 250, because of two factors. First it had an open window. Though the rapist did not know its resident, *MN*, was a 29 year-old white female nurse, the plants in the window, the second factor, generally said the resident was a girl, not a guy. He carefully removed the window screen, reached above and laid it on the rooftop then moved the potted plants aside and entered the apartment.

The 30 year-old male friend of *MN* was asleep on the couch and awoke to see the rapist, an unknown male of medium build, come through the window. "Who is it!" *MN*'s friend asked.

If the unknown male of medium build was stunned or shocked, there was no fight and his flight response was to nonchalantly walk to the front door of the apartment, remove the chain and leave. In moments the rapist was like smoke in the wind.

So many woman being abused and assaulted. Always a devastating experience for the complainant, realizing they have been violated; that neither society or anyone around them had protected them from this predator. Not a pleasant thought for someone charged with keeping the public safe. An even more uncomfortable thought, realizing that as a police officer, much less as a brother or son, it was almost impossible to keep safe even one's own wife, sister or mother. Even if it is your mother's birthday; fortunately she was safe and unmolested. The unspoken and most uncomfortable thought was, what if *I* had a daughter? How would I feel? What would I do?

Dallas, Northwest Patrol Division, Beat 523
11:42 pm Tuesday, April 29, 1975
Offense Number 14 (R-13)

SITTING ON HER bed, the rapist reached over and gently shook the 25 year-old white female lab tech.

He had gained entry through her unlocked patio door and he had already roamed through *JAR*'s apartment, number 145 at 4619 Lake Avenue. With the cord jerked from the telephone and the cord from her hair dryer, the rapist tied the wrist of the now awake *JAR*.

All *JAR* could make out, before he placed a pillow case over her head, was that her assailant was wearing a ski mask and gloves. He told her he was a burglar and wanted her TV and credit cards. When she started to speak, he shook her and said, "Don't you dare make a sound or I'll kill you!"

Sightless, bound and in fear of her life, *JAR* did not resist as she felt his rubber-gloved hands rubbing and probing her body, felt him jerk her down to the foot of the bed, felt him spread her legs and felt him penetrate her repeatedly until he climaxed. She noted he smelled of her Vaseline Intensive Care lotion.

When he finished he said, "Stay in bed, I'm coming back after I take everything I want." *JAR* waited for five minutes before freeing herself, but her rapist didn't come back.

Dallas, Northeast Patrol Division, Beat 213
5:45 am Tuesday, May 9, 1975
Offense Number 15 (R-14)

PERFECT MORNING FOR his 'run'. At 5am it was only 68 degrees, the winds were calm, the sky was clear and although moonrise was twenty minutes away, it was phasing toward a new moon; only a haze of the moon's edge would be visible. First light was an hour away with sunrise at 6:33am.

His first few forays were fruitless, then he found the partially open living room window of 26 year-old white female *SH*, a bank clerk, who lived in apartment 145 at 4620 Amesbury in the Willowick II apartments.

He removed the screen and entered. Quietly moving around the apartment he passed *SH*'s roommate's bedroom, looked in, but left her unmolested as he continued down the hall past her bathroom, its light on. He opened *SH*'s closed bedroom door and stepped inside and closed the door behind him.

In a start of fright and confusion *SH* woke to feel the rapist's rough-gloved hands over her mouth.

"I'm your friendly burglar, don't say anything. I've got a knife in my back pocket and that's what I used to get in"

Frozen in panic, her heart thundering she heard him say, "I'm going to remove my hand, don't say anything and put your face in the pillow."

SH did as she was told. He took the pillow case off one of her other pillows and pulled it over her head. He continued in a whisper, "I'm only going to look around and see what I can find…"

In the bathroom the rapist found the two items he was looking for, the tube from his victim's douche bag and Baby Magic hand lotion.

She heard him in her bathroom and heard his footsteps coming back toward her. He told her, "You'd better cooperate if you don't want to see your roommate hurt." He tied her hands to the bedpost with the tubing. Next she heard him go to her roommate's bathroom and when he came back he turned on *SH*'s bedroom light. He went through her drawers and jewelry box before coming back to the bed. He stood there for several seconds then pulled down her bed covers.

SH began to hyperventilate, "Can't breathe, I can't breathe!"

He raised the pillow case up over her mouth, then pulled up her nightgown. He put his hands on her belly and hooked his fingers under the waist band of her panties and pulled them off.

She heard him unbuckle his belt and pull his pants down, heard him say in whisper, "Spread your legs." *SH* cried, "Don't hurt me!"

After he climaxed she heard him pulling up his pants. He said, "I'll come back and tell you when I am leaving, don't say anything."

For some time *SH* heard him moving about the apartment. She waited in fear of his return, straining to hear movement, dreading it when she did; dreading it even more when she did not. When it got light, *SH* united herself from the bedpost and ran to her roommate to check on her. *SH*'s roommate then untied *SH*'s hands as *SH* recounted to her roommate what happened. Together they pushed a dresser against the door and called the police.

A couple of days after this offense was reported, I saw the FBR moniker coming back at me for the second time[40] from the same investigator. In Reba Crowder's supplemental investigative report, dated 5-15-75, on this offense she wrote: "The MO of susp. fits MO used by Friendly Burglar Rapist."

One of the tools Tom came up with was a questionnaire we sent out to FBR complainants requesting a battery of information. We felt this might help pinpoint similarities, oddities or produce outright leads not yet in hand from the initial OI/R or the investigator's supplemental reports. Question 58 asked: "Is there anything that you can add that hasn't been asked?" *SH*, the complainant in Offense Number 15, responded: "PLEASE CATCH HIM!!"

Dallas, Northeast Patrol Division, Beat 232
3:15 am Monday, May 26, 1975
Offense Number 16 (R-15)

OUR SECOND WEDDING anniversary (mine and Susan's) would be today, but at the moment we were sound asleep, while the rapist was absent from his matrimonial bed in search of a new victim.

The Friendly Burglar-Rapist stepped quietly through the unlocked sliding glass door, leaving it slightly open.

Today would also be the Memorial Day holiday for *RG*, a 28 year-old white female 'saleslady' who was looking forward to the time off. She had gone to bed at the normal time and was soon fast asleep.

---

[40] See pages 112-113 see; "the Friendly Burglar Rapist."

The Shadybrook Apartments were located at 6306 Shadybrook Lane in North Dallas. Apartment 1204, on the ground floor, was occupied by the sleeping *RG*... that is until the rapist woke her, his gloved-hand over her mouth saying, "Don't make a sound, I have a knife, I'm robbing you." He immediately put a pillow case over *RG*'s head then pushed her over onto her right side.

He kept talking to her in his low, confident voice as he rummaged through her apartment. A short time later he returned with a white vinyl belt with which he tied her hands in front of her. Leaving again, he returned the next time with an electrical cord and tied her hands to the bed post.

Then it began. At first she had felt the rough unevenness of his gloves, then he took them off. He lifted her gown and continued to fondle her. She felt the bed move, heard him take off his pants and then felt the bed move again as he mounted and raped her.

Afterwards he went to the living room, got a pair of scissors and came back to the bedroom and cut her loose from the bedpost. "Keep your eyes closed for ten or fifteen minutes," he said. Keeping the scissors, he grabbed a cold Coors beer from the fridge on his way out. In his pocket he carried the 14 karat yellow gold and one carat diamond ring *RG* had won in a beauty contest four years before.

She kept listening for the truck he constantly said was "outside", but she never heard it.

The rapist jogged toward his car and into the 15 mile an hour head wind, the full moon intermittently peaking between the mostly cloudy skies of the warm 86 degree summer night.

Dallas, Northwest Patrol Division, Beat 532
7:25 am Tuesday, May 27, 1975
Offense Number 17

"HE DIDN'T RAPE me" *ML*, the thirty year-old bank clerk, told the officer.

The veteran patrol officer had asked her when she first opened the door for him, "Are you okay, Ma'am?"

"Yes," she said as she rushed through her story which she concluded with, "he didn't rape me."

Trying not to show any disbelief the officer said, "He came in, cut your panties, took your money... and left; he didn't—"

"No."

"When did this happen?"

"About 5:25-5:30 this morning."

The officer looked at his watch and thought *I got the signal 20 at 7:17 an' Code 6'd at 7:25.* "So he's been gone about two hours?"

The complainant who was dressed for work replied, "Yes."

"Okay, tell me what happened, in order."

ML sighed. "I had taken a sleeping pill before I went to bed... I guess that's why I didn't wake up immediately. When I woke, I rose up and saw a man standing by my bed. I realized he had cut completely across the crotch of my panties. He told me to lie back down, cover my head and he wouldn't hurt me. He asked me where my purse was and when I pointed to the small chair he went over opened it removed some money, all I had was four dollars and change; and then he dumped the rest on the floor." *ML* paused.

"Then what," the officer prompted.

"A short time later he left out the back door." *ML* said.

"Did you see a weapon?"

"No, he kept his right hand behind him... so he could have had something..."

"How much money did he take?"

"Like I said, about four dollars and maybe fifteen cents."

After his interview of the complainant the officer sat waiting for the Physical Evidence Section guy to arrive and wrote up his O/I R. In the M/O section he wrote, "Removed Window Screen – Crawled through Unlocked Raised Window." Outside on *ML*'s porch he found a lounge chair pulled up under her bedroom window where the suspect had gained entry. The missing window screen was found around the corner underneath a parked car in the Kings Trace Apartment complex at 4917 Lahoma Street.

Back inside, the officer observed *ML*'s bedroom. He noticed the bed's sheets and spread in disarray with the pillows on the floor. To the officer it didn't look like a bed occupied by only a woman who had taken a sleeping pill. He found two mismatched men's socks by the bed and wrote in his report: "one was black and one brown".

The P.E.S. investigator collected evidence, took pictures and lifted partial prints. In his supplemental report he wrote:

"collected one brown and one green sock used over suspect's hands during robbery."

[NB: Since I did not see this evidence, I don't know if the statement of either the RO or P.E.S. officer misstated the color of the second sock, got it wrong, or someone was color blind. They both reported one sock was brown and the second sock was different. Bottom line, this discrepancy never needed to be explained.]

Regarding whether or not the complainant was actually raped and just didn't want to report it, "Who can say," the P.E.S. investigator said to the officer as they walked to their cars. "If they don't want to make a rape complaint, we can't force'm."

"No but it doesn't add up... why would he cut her panties, only take four bucks and leave? Why would she wait two hours to make the call to report a robbery of four bucks?"

"She was scared?"

"She was scared all right, but more embarrassed than scared... if she was scared she would have called right away, and if she did call right away then the suspect was there longer than she said—b'sides she was dressed for work when I got there... so she must have taken a shower."

"We may never know." The P.E.S. investigator shrugged and headed to his car.

Author Note: *Question—did the FBR use the scissors[41] he had 'lifted' from his rape on May 26 to cut this complainant's panties?*

---

[41] See page 127 "scissors"

Chapter 7

1975
Summer Movie Shoot - Hollywood Comes to Town

"Logan's Run" to be filmed in Dallas will be directed by Michael Anderson and starring: Michael York, Jenny Agutter and Farrah Fawcett-Majors."

I got the call that officers were needed for security on an upcoming movie to be shot in Dallas. I had worked on several movies before and found that security for a movie was usually, as an extra, off-duty-job, a 'good gig', so I said, "sign me up".

The casting call had gone out for men and women over 18 and under 30 wanted for extras on "Logan's Run" a sci-fi flick where citizens are euthanized when they turn 30. As it happened, I was not yet 29, I fit in with upper end of the extras age-range and was not likely to be euthanized for three more months.

Here's the storyline from IMDB (Internet Movie Data Base):

> "It's 2274 and on the surface, it all seems to be an idyllic society. Living in a city within an enclosed dome, there is little or no work for humans to perform and inhabitants are free to pursue all of the pleasures of life. There is one catch however: your life is limited and when you reach 30, it is terminated in a quasi-religious ceremony known as Carousel. Some, known as runners, do try to escape their fate when the time comes and it's the job of a Sandman to track them down and kill them. Logan is such a man and with several years before his own termination date, thinks nothing of the job he does. Soon after meeting a young woman, Jessica-6, he is ordered to become a runner himself and infiltrate a community outside the dome known as Sanctuary and to destroy it. Pursued by his friend Francis, also a Sandman, Logan and Jessica find their way to the outside. There they discover a beautiful..."
> *Written by garykmcd http://www.imdb.com/title/tt0074812/*

Principal shooting in Dallas took place at the Dallas Apparel Mart. Other Dallas locations were: RCA Building; Stern Health Center; 1st National Bldg; Zale Building; Oz Restaurant; Hall of Nations, World Trade Center; and in Fort Worth at the Ft. Worth Water Gardens.

On my first day (on what would be the set where the Carousel sequences would be shot in the main atrium of the Dallas

Apparel Mart) thousands of would-be extras lined up for their shot at being in a Hollywood film.

I never got a count on the number of males that where hired, but the number of female 'extras' appeared to top five-hundred.

(Shooting schedule[42] for Mon. June 30 - see dotted area.)

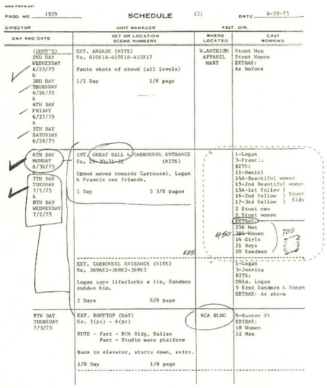

I didn't see the casting so I have to rely on what I was told. I have only the empirical data of personal observation. The result seemed to bear out the story. The guys, were an almost a cursory afterthought. It was the women who received all the scrutiny.

I was told the assistant directors (AD's) went through the women in groups and the women were individually assigned

42 web.archive.org/web/20110607184348://http://www.snowcrest.net/fox/loganmovie/logmov2/_06.html

numbers one, through three. I was not privy to what criteria constituted the handing out of the One, Two, or Three cards. But if you held one of those numbers at the end of the day, you were invited back.

There were other rounds where some of the Threes were 'dismissed' and occasionally a Two was upgraded to a One or a One or a Two might be downgraded.

Apparently in 2274 all women wore short diaphanous ponchos, a hole in the middle for your head and then it was pulled in on the side with a belt. Perhaps, the 'costume' was more 'tailored' than I describe, but that's what it looked like to me. The material was some type of silky see-through material. The result of the number system shook out this way... the better looking, the better your body (assumedly according to the Director and AD's agreed-upon tastes) the lower your number. So a One was considered very, very attractive. I didn't disagree with any of the director's choices. You might quibble about some of the Two's and Three's as 'should have been One's or Two's', but I wasn't choosing.

Also your number appeared to coincide with the number of layers your diaphanous 'costume' contained. Three's had three layers, Two's two layers and yes, One's had one layer of the material. So, the younger you were, the better your body, the more attractive you were, according to the directors, the less you had covering your body.

A number of the One's were picked by the various AD's to grace their scenes, closest to the camera. And it was rumored that a select few of the One's were promised speaking parts (a word, or a line) by the director.

Regardless of one or three layers, the women were virtually exposed, there were apparently no undergarments. Of course none of us were told this was what was happening, but that is what "we" observed. "We" being all the males on the set: security, crew, actors, and extras.

The first few days on the set were harrowing. There were five hundred women scantily clad doing all manner of 'extra' things like, running here and there, standing and sitting. It was very distracting work!

Imagine seeing a thousand breasts every day, one literally could not look away for seeing someone in the next direction you looked. The old Mae West line, "Is that a gun in your pocket, or are you just glad to see me?" was an often asked question from the female extras.

We did, after about a week, begin to get used to seeing all these women almost naked.

After ogling, even without specific intent, a thousand breasts and the other female attributes on display day after day, it became old-hat. Things began to calm down. Then an amusing phenomenon occurred.

All the men, instead of watching the girls come out of the dressing rooms in their scant costumes every morning, began to gather at the dressing room door in the evening. The men all began to admire and comment on the girls dressed in their street clothes. That became even more provocative than the seeing them 'in costume'. The male psyche, go figure.

The FBR was never far from my mind, he was continuing to rape and burglarize. Tom and I still had no clue who this guy was. Looking at all these beautiful women, I couldn't help wonder how the FBR would fare one-on-one with any of these One, Two, or Three beauties. Several paragraphs of Dr. Somodevilla's February 1975 report titled *A Psychological Profile of the "Rapist"* came to mind:

> He is probably known as a nice guy, slightly introverted, and someone who doesn't make a strong impression either way, positive or negative. He can be polite and a gentleman with women but seldom has meaningful relationships (sexual or emotional) with them.
>
> ...he is suffering from severe personality conflict to the point of sexually acting out. He is an inadequate, pensive, masochistic male who identifies with his victims due to his own repressed homosexuality which he has never acted out. Thus the rape itself is a reaction formation against his fear of homosexuality.
>
> The breaking and entering and ritualistic searching around provides him with an excitement (here he gets the erection) which he finalizes through intercourse. This is really more of a masturbatory activity since coitus itself lasts on the average of two minutes. Thus he has already been quite excited by the time he penetrates his victims. Thus the rummaging around is a preparation (or foreplay) for intercourse.

I concluded that the Friendly Burglar-Rapist most likely would not be able to 'score' with any of these women. But what was more disturbing to me, was the fact that any of these women could or might become one of his victims if they just happened to live in one of the areas he terrorized.

Thinking of his favorite entry target, an unlocked or open window or sliding glass door, many a female extra was counseled on the need to keep their windows and doors closed and locked.

Elvis Has Left The Building

Dallas, Memorial Auditorium
8:30 pm Friday, June 6, 1975

Cops get to do lots of dirty jobs, but additionally some cool jobs come our way that are fun and entertaining like the movie set I had just worked. We also are tasked with security/protection for various VIPs, such as politicians, heads of state and rock stars. I worked security details for President Richard Nixon, Governor George Wallace (when he was running for president & before he was shot), movie/TV actors Robert Preston, Kris Kristofferson, Burt Reynolds, JR himself: Larry Hagman; singers like Englebert Humperdinck, Frank Sinatra and "The King", Elvis Presley (twice).

At a then undisclosed location, The King and his entourage arrived late on the evening of Thursday, June 5th. Our security team of off-duty Dallas officers had already secured the floor which would serve as the encampment for Elvis and the TCB (Taking Care of Business) staff for the next twenty-four hours. Our job was simple, as we were told, "don't bother Elvis, and make sure no one, not on the list, walks this floor."

When Elvis arrived he was escorted by his closest associates and his 'nurse'. He warmly smiled, shook hands and greeted the uniformed officers there to protect him. Elvis loved cops. He went into his room and did not reappear till an hour before showtime the next night.

When he disappeared into the elevator; we were told, he would not be returning. But our job was just beginning. Not only did we have to secure the location for the twenty-four hours before his arrival, we were to keep the location secure until his show concluded at the concert venue and we were notified, with the now iconic phrase, that "Elvis has left the building".

TCB staff told us that fans would, if given the chance, enter the rooms and 'take' anything thinking The King might have touched it... even used Kleenex! We were to hold the fort until the hotel cleaning crew had refreshed all the rooms and Elvis really had, "left the building."

Of course the word got out where Elvis was staying. We had a steady stream of fans, male and female, trying to breach our 'security desk'. And some of his fans were *fan-natical*.

I was a smoker at the time. While manning my post, a table placed across one end of the hallway that led to Elvis's suite of rooms, I was supplied with a folding chair, a list of the TCB 'who's-who', some styrofoam cups of coffee, an ashtray and a book of hotel matches.

One young woman had beguiled her way past the security perimeter and wanted me to let her see Elvis. She did not want to take no for an answer and offered several kinds of personal inducements, to let her pass. When this did not work she appeared to settle for conversation, which seemed harmless enough. At some point she asked me had I seen Elvis, did I shake hands with him? Without giving anything away, I answered yes to both questions. She then wanted to shake my hand. I declined, as that might have put me in a compromising situation. She noticed that I had been smoking and asked, pointing to my book of matches next to the ashtray, "did you light your cigarettes with those matches?" I said yes. Her eyes lit up, and with a magician's quickness, she reached out and grabbed the matches, knocking over my coffee, then ran off shouting, "Elvis touched these, Elvis touched these!"

I guess the fact that my hand had touched Elvis' hand and then my hand had held the matches, was close enough for her.

Here, for the Friends of Elvis, out there, is a scan of the TCB who's who, with coffee stain. I'm sure some of these names will be familiar to fans. Elvis's name was not on the room list (it was handwritten off to the side, his room number 221, his nurse supposedly in (217) then someone thought better of it and scribbled over Elvis' name. There were a number of 'nurses' (names penciled in) accompanying various staff.

Dallas, Northeast Patrol Division, Beat 234
12:45 am Thursday, June 26, 1975
Offense Number 18

SHE SCREAMED INTO the rough gloved-hand over her mouth. He was straddling her in bed. "Shut up and roll over," he said. He held her hands down till she rolled over then he tied her hands. "Be quiet and I won't hurt you."

He got up from the bed and roamed the apartment, cut the telephone cords and then returned to the bedroom; put a pillow case over the head of 23 year-old *PS*, a white female, DISD teacher.

He had entered through the unlocked front window of *PS*'s ground floor apartment, number 112, in the Horizon East Apartments at 8224 Meadow Road.

At the foot of the bed he pulled the top sheet off the bed. Holding her driver's license he said, "What's your name?"

"P******a."

"Is that the name on your driver's license?"

"Yes."

"I don't want to hurt you. You have too beautiful a bod to hurt."

PS said, "You want to be charged with murder too?

"Don't try to reason with a crazy person, I'm crazy. He took his knife and cut *PS* hands loose and told her to stand up.

PS stood up holding the sheet against her body.

"Drop the sheet!"

"No!"

The rapist shoved her across the bed and ripped her underwear off. *PS* curled up into a ball and refused his commands to 'spread your legs.'

He retied her hands to the headboard and asked, "Is anyone coming to see you?"

"My boyfriend is coming over; he's at a soccer game he will be here any minute!"

Given that it was almost one o'clock the rapist doubted her story, but it could be true.

Though not fully explained, the reporting officer R.B. Bounds #2184 wrote, "Comp states that susp was unsuccessful in his rape attempt."[43]

The FBR went to the window and looked out. "There's some people outside in the parking lot beside my truck, I can't leave yet."

"Just take my stereo and money and leave!"

"I already took'm."

She pleaded with him to go and not hurt her.

---

[43] On 7-5-75 Investigator G.E. Luther #2354 wrote in his Supplement Report that he "contacted Comp in person on 6-26-75 at 10:30am. Comp verified facts originally reported except that she stated Susp had short hair." **NB**: Comp did not go to hospital, no rape kit was collected.

"I haven't hurt anyone before, but I'm not afraid to start!" Be quiet, "I'm going to check to see if I can leave."

PS waited but when he didn't return in a little while she freed herself and while running over to her sister's apartment she saw a man that fit the description of her attacker in the parking lot next to a 1960s model gold or copper colored station wagon.

He simply watched her beating on another apartment door, got in and drove away.

Author Note: *What was the reason for the one month lay-off? We constantly speculated on reasons for the intervals between FBR offenses. In this case (June 26-July 27), we asked ourselves, 'was he laying low because his last victim may have seen him in the parking lot? We only had a general physical description to go on... and of course officers were told about the station wagon. If you drove a gold or copper station wagon and rolled through North Dallas you most likely got stopped and questioned.*

Dallas, Northeast Patrol Division, Beat 213
3:40 am Sunday, July 27, 1975
Offense Number 19 (R-16)

IN THE PARKING lot of the Willowick Apartments in the 4600 block of Amesbury Drive he scanned the complex. The full moon had been up for almost four hours, it lit up the night producing shadows. It also made it easier to spot open windows on eighty degree summer nights. The wind in the cloudless sky was blowing out of the south-southwest at twenty miles an hour. A good thing for those who liked to leave two windows open to pull in the breeze.

He felt aroused as he jogged toward the center of the complex. Walking toward a breezeway he noticed the living room window to apartment 1070 was unlocked, gave it a lift and slipped inside. He stood there in the dim light furnished by the moon and let himself calm down before beginning his prowl. It was a two bedroom apartment. Telephone cord and butcher knife in hand, he went into the first bedroom and faced the sleeping woman, *BDD*.

In the second bedroom he found *KSW*, a white female 25, asleep in her bed.

He pressed his gloved-hand over her mouth and felt her stir. "Don't scream," he whispered, "and I won't have to hurt you or your roommate." He tied her hands to the bedpost. "Don't look at me," he said as he roamed around her bedroom. She heard him moving in the other part of the apartment then return to her bed. He pulled her nightgown over her head, pulled off her pink panties, raped her and left.

In shock, *KSW* freed herself, woke her still sleeping roommate (*BDD*)[44] and called the police.

Dallas, Northeast Patrol Division, Beat 233
4:45 am Wednesday, August 20, 1975
Offense Number 20 (R-17)
Comparable Prints Lifted

POLITELY HE ASKED, "Can you breathe?" He had just slipped a pillow case over the head of MFT, a sixty-three year-old white teacher. As he tied her hands with the cord he cut from the wall telephone, "Don't try to look at me and I won't hurt you."

The full moon shone low in the clear sky; it would set in about an hour. He had unscrewed the outside light and pulled a patio chair up to the window. When he lifted the unlocked window he felt the cool air-conditioned air rush past his face into the eighty degree heat of the morning. *Guess I'll have to take these with me.* He had to move three silver pieces, a pitcher, a goblet and a salt cellar before he could climb in the window.

He rummaged through his victim's apartment, found her purse, wallet, driver's license, noticing her age, and pocketed sixty dollars in cash.

After he had her hands tied, he raised her gown as he said, "Let's see what an old lady looks like." He lubricated his erection with the Jergens® Lotion he found in her bathroom and raped her. Though not included in the report, by the R.O., we later learned *MFT* said the FBR really made her mad when he said, "Not bad for an old woman."

Afterwards he took her watch from her arm, but intentionally dropped it on the floor as he left, saying, "Stay on the bed," as he headed into the living room.

---

[44] See Offense Numbers 56 (page 234) & Offense Number 62 (page 271-273)

She heard the front door open and close. *MFT* waited for five minutes before untying herself and going to neighbors to call the police.

In connection with this case, two men were arrested for this offense; a Rodney Dale O------d w/m 24 and a Huston Collier McA----y. According to Inv. Crowder's Supplement Report dated 8-22-75, both men were "cleared by prints & polygraph". Additionally in Crowders report she wrote: "Compl. states reporting officers told her this sounds like the 'friendly burglar rapist' & everyone in the apts. was afraid."

Author Note: *I do not want the reader to presume that the only things our P.E.S. folks did was dust for prints. The forensic lab we used could perform a number of comparative tests if the case warranted the expenditure. DNA testing was in its infancy, very expensive, and was nowhere near or indicative of the results now available to the modern day CSI-type lab. The following Supplement Report for this offense (284374-G), dated 8-21-75, was representative of the work done at the scene of one of a criminal assaul*t:

P.E.S. 39761
Inv. J. M. Maberry of the Physical Evidence Section, went to 7700 block Meadow Rd, apt 134, rape, complainant, MFT, service #284374-G. Took color photos, collected bed spread, compl. night gown, and telephone cord used to tie up compl. Also collected Jergens® lotion bottle,and carpet fiber sample. Lifted partial latents from inside window at point of entry, phone, and Jergens® lotion bottle, prints are comparable. Suspects Rodney Dale O------d, w/m and a Huston Collier McA----y w/m, check with latent prints lifted, prints lifted do not belong to suspects.-- check by Sgt. Hankins. Suspected this offense connected with 7756 Willow Wind Ct. apt 125, on service #284367-G:

11	01	1	Photo/scene
7A	02	1	bed spread
80	03	1	night gown
7A	04	1	telephone cord
76	05	1	lotion bottle
78	06	1	carpet fiber sample
26	07	1	Prints/window
26	08	1	Prints/phone

23 09 1 Prints/lotion bottle
/s/ Pat. J. M. Maberry # 3121

The above Supplement Report by Officer Maberry was not the end of the fruits of his discoveries from 8-21-75. Two months later, on 10-31-75 Lt. Day of P.E.S. would write up a very significant Supplement Report[45] for O/IR 2843734-G.

Dallas, Northwest Patrol Division
Thursday, August 21, 1975
Officer Alvin Duane Hallum ~ Murdered[46]

Dallas, Northeast Patrol Division, Beat 213
3:30 am Sunday, August 31, 1975
Offense Number 21 (R-18)

THE DALLAS COWBOYS' 28 to 24 pre-season win over the Vikings on Thursday night was still the buzz on all of Saturday night's training camp TV sports reports at 6 and 10pm. Everyone was reporting on the "Dirty Dozen": Randy White, Hollywood Henderson, Burton Lawless, Bob Breunig, Pat Donovan, Randy Hughes, Herb Scott, Scott Laidlaw, Mike Hegman, Mitch Hoopes and the rest of the twelve rookies picked to make the team as camp came to a close.

At the end of the broadcast, as a promo for that network's Sunday Morning 'news show', the local TV anchor listed the show's guests and that they were sure to debate the fact that hundreds of delegates to the American Legion national convention in Seattle, Washington shouted "No" when Presidential hopeful Jimmy Carter said he would pardon all Vietnam draft resisters his first week in office and then booed him for three minutes. KI and her roommate JW switched the channel to catch the late late movie.

The other TV hullabaloo that week had been the water-cooler conversations started after the airing of NBC's made for TV

---

[45] See pages 148 (Offense Number 25) and page 155

[46] Officer Alvin Duane Hallum, badge #3660, who had been an officer for 9 months, and his partner stopped a car used in an extortion offense. The driver came out shooting, wounding Hallum's partner. Hallum emptied his weapon. He took cover behind a car to reload. The suspect ran up and shot Al in the head. The suspect fled, was chased, firing at pursuing officers. He was killed by return gunfire.

movie "Who is the Black Dahlia?" It starred Efrem Zimbalist Jr. as an LAPD cop and Lucie Arnez as the beautiful and tragic heroine Elizabeth 'Betty' Short, whose brutal murder in 1947 remains unsolved[47]. Not a movie to set a single woman's mind at ease.

At 1:30am on Sunday morning the roommates headed to their respective bedrooms.

Around 2:30am something broke through her fog of sleep… a light flashing in the bathroom… *a flashlight? No, I'm probably dreaming KI* thought, as she fell back asleep, her stomach virus had sapped her strength.

He had become a proficient burglar, getting in and out of apartments with ease; so many windows left open or unlocked summer and winter. Sometimes a window screen needed to be pulled off or cut, such as this time at the Willowick Apartments at 6006 Sandhurst Lane, #2012… *second floor apartments are just as easy*. He ducked under the window frame, stood up and pressed down on the top of the window till he had it closed. He had found that doors were always a better place to exit than back through a window. People are expected to come out of doors; windows, not so much.

He took a knife from the kitchen and cut the phone cords. When he found two purses he went through them looking for money, driver's licenses and credit cards. The money he would keep, the driver's license just provided information on his victim, and credit cards and other things he found further verified the identification.

This wasn't the first time he had two women to choose from, the license picture and height-weight helped, but what the hell, *I just did a woman 63…*

In the bathroom he flashed the light around and settled on a jar of Vaseline and headed toward his bedroom of choice. He picked *KI* a white female age 22, and pretty according to her driver's license picture, a church secretary.

He lifted the covers on her bed and lowered himself down beside her. Startled awake, she gasped. He grabbed her head, turned and pushed it into her pillow.

"How did you get in?" It was all she could think to say.

---

[47] The murder of Elizabeth Short (aka: The Black Dahlia) has been solved by Steve Hodel, LAPD Homicide Detective III (ret.). See Steve Hodel's four books: *Black Dahlia Avenger*, *Black Dahlia Avenger II*, *Most Evil* and *Most Evil II*.

"Shhh," he whispered, as he tied her hands over her head with telephone cord; "I don't want to hurt you so be quiet and do what I say. Got any guns?"

"No."

"All I want is your cash and credit cards. How about knives, where are your knives?

"In the kitchen."

"Do you have any guns?"

"No."

"Is anyone else in the apartment?

"Yes, in the other bedroom, my roommate."

"What's your roommate's name?"

"*JW*."

"That's right; remember I know where you work. Are you alone?"

"Yes," *KI* said.

He told her to lay still and be quiet or he would have to hurt her roommate. *KI* lay in bed and heard him in the kitchen, heard him come back and cut the telephone cord in the bedroom.

She felt something go over her head and heard him say, "I know who you are. Shhh, I know your name, *KI*, and where you work!"

He pulled her nightgown up and over her head and began to fondle her till he felt what he realized were Band-Aids on her nipples. He whispered, "Are you hurt?"

"No."

"Why the—"

Too embarrassed not to answer, *KI* said, "I wear these when I don't wear a bra."

KI struggled and said, please no, "I've never had sex before…"

He smiled to himself, "You're a virgin?"

"Yes."

"Be quiet and do what I say, if you don't want me to hurt your roommate."

He removed the Band-Aids and continued fondling *KI*… he took his time. When he was ready, unbuttoned his pants and pulled them down then lubricated himself with her Vaseline.

She indeed, had been a virgin.

Hours later, at 6:30am, The Friendly Burglar-Rapist said something about getting to his truck, went to the patio door then returned to *KI*'s bedroom and whispered, "I can't leave there's kids out by the pool."

After another ten minutes had passed *KI* heard the patio door slide open then close. When she felt it was safe *KI* got herself free and woke her roommate.

It was 7:42am when Officers Townsend and Wren, working Element 214 were dispatched to take a criminal assault complaint on beat 213; they were told that the suspect was no longer at the scene.

Dallas, Northeast Patrol Division, Beat 232
4:15 am Friday, September 12, 1975
Offense Number 22 (R-19) & 23

A WORKING MAN, either coming home from the late shift or headed in early, was the look the rapist was going for, long sleeve shirt and corduroy slacks; clean shaven. Perhaps that's what he had told his wife the night before: "I've got go to in early in the morning, big presentation to work on."

After almost two years of terrorizing the "Village" and "Five-Corners" or "Five-Points" area apartments in North Dallas, the Friendly Burglar-Rapist was right at home. He knew every nook and cranny, knew his escape routes. His close calls had been few and far between. But he hadn't taken too many chances.

He was in the Hill II Apartment complex at 6455 Shadybrook where he found three unlocked windows this morning. In the first apartment he cut a grey telephone cord from one of the phones, found a purse took some cash, looked at the driver's license in the wallet. He shook his head and left.

Through the second unlocked window he found himself in a cluttered apartment, dishes in the sink and no one at home.

At the third apartment, number 55, he found a downstairs kitchen window unlocked, pushed it up. Once inside he realized he had hit the jackpot a two bedroom, three roommate apartment. He found the purses of two of the roommates, the sisters: *PE* and *EE*, dumped the contents on the table, taking the cash and perusing their driver's license pictures and information.

He didn't know which was which, but as was his custom, he went into every room; it was part of the thrill, part of the excitement. He found two girls in one bedroom and left them sleeping.

He went into the third girl's bedroom and closed the door. He roamed around and was standing by *JEC*'s bed when his movement must have awakened her. She did a double-take and gasped.

He wasn't wearing a glove, but put his hand over her mouth, "Turn your head, don't look at me... I've got a knife. She felt something cold, liked the blade of a knife touch her hand. "Be quiet," he whispered, "and no one will get hurt," so "don't wake up your roommates."

Besides, "I'm a burglar, I do this for a living... I'm sorry that I woke you up." He picked up one of the pillows from the bed, removed its pillowcase and handed to *JEC*. "Put this over your head."

When she had complied, he grabbed the grey phone cord he'd cut earlier at another apartment and tied her hands in front of her. "Don't move," he'd said, his voice trailing. She heard him open her purse which had been on her dresser, heard him digging around in it. She was trembling as she heard his footsteps moving back toward the bed.

He grabbed her tied hands, "Get up, get up... walk to the window." The half-moon had been up for several hours but it was occluded by the overcast skies. The only light coming in the windows was from the various walkway lamps and parking lot lights. It was enough to see by. Once by the window he commanded, "Close your eyes, I want to see your face."

She felt the pillowcase move and she shut her eyes tightly. She could feel his eyes on her, and then he lowered the pillowcase. Standing in the half-light she felt him grab the hem of her knee-length gown; felt it being pulled up and over her head then down her arms till it hung between and around her tied hands. Next she felt him grasping the waistband of her panties and slowly pulled them down till they were around her ankles. He looked at her for what seemed like forever.

"Let's go back to bed." He guided her to the bed and told her to lie down and then tied her hands to the upper righthand bedpost. She heard him move away, heard him in the bathroom and heard him return to her bed. "Are you Peggy," he asked.

"No." *My God,* she thought, *he thinks I'm Peggy?*

"What's your name?"

"*J*", *JEC* said as she heard him unzip his pants.

The Friendly Burglar-Rapist stroked his erection, then leaned over and picked up the bottle of hand lotion he found in her bathroom and lubricated himself.

He told her to do as he said; to be quiet and no one would get hurt. "I haven't had to hurt any one yet." He reminded her to not wake her roommates then told her to spread her legs.

She felt his weight move onto the bed; she could feel the rough material of his trousers, *probably corduroy,* she thought, against her thighs as he penetrated her. He kept talking as he raped her, saying, "You probably have a boyfriend and get screwed all the time." She didn't admit that it had been at least two weeks since she'd last had intercourse.

After his orgasm, after he was satiated, he got up and pulled the sheet up to cover her. She heard him go into the bathroom, heard water running, heard a towel being pulled off the towel rack… *he's cleaning himself off?*

Standing next to the bed again, he whispered, "I suggest you go on back to sleep and wake up and find you have been burglarized. He walked across the room, turned on the light, then a moment later tuned it back off. "I'm going downstairs and look and see if it is all clear for me to get to my truck and tell you when I'm leaving…. I think you can get your hands untied, but I would wait until you are sure I am gone."

The FBR opened the bedroom door. She could feel the change in the air, could sense he was standing in the doorway watching her or listening.

"I'm going down now."

JEC heard his footsteps on the stairs till they got faint. He slipped soundlessly out the patio door.

She continued to listen, hoping to hear a door open or close. In the dread of shock over what had happened and the dread of his possible return, *JEC* lay there imagining sounds, tensing at every creak. She lay in her bed, her hands still tied over her head to the bed post till her alarm when off, an hour and a half to two hours later, at 6:50am. After she freed herself *JEC* went into the two sister's bedroom and woke them.

The three of them jumped, first, at the ten mile an hour north wind blowing the branches of a tree up against a window, and second when they heard the heater kick on, trying to counter the sixty-nine degrees outside temperature. They all ran to the phone so *JEC* could call the police.

Dallas, Office of Central Division Analyst's Office
9:15 am Monday, September 15, 1975
Offense Number 24

I had just finished the reading and posting of the murder and rape O/I R's from over the weekend. I shook my head and put another dot on the 6400 block of Shadybrook on beat 233. The MO sounded like the FBR, I could not be absolutely sure at this point, given the publicity, that it was not a copycat.[48] *It's him!* I assured myself as I checked our chart. If Tom and I were correct, this was number eighteen by our then-current count.

I put my hand-drawn chart under the desk pad and plopped the stack of thefts, BEMV's, residential and business burglaries down in front of me.

An hour and a half later I was rereading a residential burglary report at 5927 Milton, NE Patrol Division, beat 213 with Complainant *BAS* (our Offense Number 24). I got up and went to the wall maps, *Yep, The Citadel Apartments, nowhere close.* Doing some rough figuring *...going the long way, Lover's to Greenville then north to Park Lane then south on Shadybrook... that's just over two miles; maybe five minutes by car...joggin maybe fifteen to twenty minutes, and walking...*

I looked at the offense times. The Milton burglary occurred between 1:15 and 2:15am Friday morning and the Shadybrook rape happened around 5:15am, *could be connected... but man, if so this guy is really moving around.*

Author Note: *At this point we had no idea that his MO included multiple burglaries in the same area much less in different areas.*

The reporting officer RR Horan #3041 wrote:

COMP: *BAS*, W/F/21; OCC: Hostess; M/O: Removed bedroom screen and raised unlocked window.
NARRATIVE: Compl stated that at approx. 2:15am she got out of bed to let her roommate in the front door. Compl was sure that a chain lock on the front door was

---

[48] Except that the media had never known or published all of the FBR's M/O Markers... further it was extremely unlikely that any one victim, telling her story, would have experience all the FBR's M/O Markers.

left off in order for her roommate to enter without awakening her. At this time the Compl noticed the back door, which had been locked previously, was unlocked. At 8am 9/12/75 Compl noticed the telephone cord in her bedroom had been cut. She went downstairs and noticed that the telephone cords in the kitchen and downstairs bedroom also had been cut and the screen had been removed off the downstairs bedroom window. Several items in the Apt had been disarranged but Compl can find nothing missing at this time. Compl stated that as she was getting ready for bed a W/M/ 25-30 was looking up at the bedroom window. Approx. 10 minutes later she saw the same white male walking away from the scene. This W/M had brown hair neatly cut and was wearing a blue denim shirt and blue jeans. Compl feels that someone was in her Apt when her roommate knocked to get in the door and was scared off. Compl can find nothing missing at this time but will call later if she does. P.E.S. was at the location. This matches the MO of previous rape offenses that have been occurring in this area.

I picked up my desk phone. "Hey, Tom-Bob, come down here, I've got something you've gotta see."

Tom came down to my office. As Tom put down the two reports, I said, "You think it's our guy?

"Gotta be."

"I agree."

"Wow that's a ways to go… you think he's going into multiple places…" Tom said.

I nodded, "Sounds that way… who woulda thunk it. Bet he used the phone cord he cut on Milton in the rape on Shadybrook, she didn't have any phone's cut but she was tied up with a phone cord….

"Right!" Tom said.

"Plus, now we got a pretty good description…" I added.

Chapter 8

Bingo, Jack, it's our guy!

Dallas, Northeast Patrol Division, Beat 231
1:40 am Monday, September 22, 1975
Offense Number 25

A NOISE WOKE him!

AT 6467 Melody Lane, apartment number 1044, *GF* a twenty-one year-old white male and a waiter who worked the five to midnight shift at a local watering hole at Central and Caruth Haven blinked his eyes in the dark. He had not been in bed long when heard a noise in the living room and went to investigate. He saw someone outside prying on the patio door. *GF* pounded on the wall and scared the guy off. *GF* later described the suspect to police as a white male, with light brown hair, light blue shirt and blue jeans.

The next day, a Tactical Unit went to the scene and lifted prints.

[NB: With P.E.S. short-handed and the department needing to stretch resources, Tactical Officers were doing double-duty at crime scenes collecting evidence, etc., then turning over the evidence collected for P.E.S. to process.]

Later that day the nighttime supervisor of the Identification Section, Lieutenant J.C. Day #391, made the following Supplement Report (SR):

> Inv. R.P. Burke #2948 lifted some prints off a light bulb apparently unscrewed by the prowler at 6467 Melody Lane, Apt. 1044. Det. B. G. Brown of P.E.S. has determined the prints (#6 finger) was made by the same person whose prints were found at the following rape offenses:
>
> 7000 Meadow Rd., Apt. 134, 8/20/75
> 6006 Sandhurst, Apt. 2012, 8/31/75

When I read Lt. Day's SR, I immediately called Tom and said, "Bingo, Jack, it's our guy... just like we thought!" Tom and I yelled, "Bingo, Jack," at each other for the rest of the day.

Now, *all* we had to do was find and arrest the FBR!

Dallas, Central Division Analyst's Office
8:15 pm Tuesday, September 23, 1975

Looking through today's stack of reports I found the Supplement Report of Inv. C.F. Royal #2692 regarding Offense Number 22 that had occurred on Friday, September 21st. Royal's short report was attached to the other related documents for this offense. Royal had interviewed the complainant, and noted, "no other additional or new information has been gathered". His last paragraph was: "A C------n C-----s wm, suggested as possible suspect by Captain Milliken has been checked. His fingerprints do not match nor is his blood type correct. Recommend this report remain suspended at this time, until other leads develop."

Dallas, Northeast Patrol Division, Beat 233
3:30 am Saturday, October 4, 1975
Offense Number 26

CLEAR AND COLD, a perfect night for a fire in the fireplace, it was fifty-one degrees, not a cloud in the moonless sky. *JT* a 37 year-old white female manager of a local business, had spent her Friday night on the couch watching TV and had fallen asleep.

Apartment #170 in the Willow Creek Apartments located at 7919 Shinning Willow Lane was the FBR's next choice. The bedroom window on the east side looked appealing so he removed the screen and slipped the lock. He was wearing a dark sweater, dark pants, a ski mask and gloves. He stood inside the bedroom letting his eyes adjust; no one was in bed. Stepping quietly into the living room he cut the cord of the telephone as he watched the woman asleep on the couch.

As he put his hand over her mouth she immediately came awake. He put more pressure on her mouth and told her to be quiet. "I'm a burglar, I don't want to hurt you. You've got a television and I want that." He told her to put her hands together and he tied her hands.

As soon as he turned his back to roam the apartment, *JT* began untying herself. He managed to find her purse before he realized she was getting loose; he retied her hands. When she untied them a second time he said, "You aren't giving me enough time to get to the truck, you're being unreasonable, this is how I make my living and I used a knife to get in..." He let the inference of using the knife on her hang in the air.

The FBR took his victim to a spare bedroom and tied her up but she managed to untie herself, again. He then took her into her bedroom and tied her to the bed. He left and went through her purse pocketing twenty dollars and found a couple of bottles of Vaseline Intensive Care in her bathroom.

Back in her bedroom, he started to raise *JT*'s nightgown. *JT* tensed and said, "I'll scream!"

"I won't hesitate to use my knife, I haven't hurt anybody yet, but I will if I have to—" He raised his fist.

JT screamed... and kept screaming!

The Friendly Burglar-Rapist kept his word; he still hadn't hurt anyone, at least not with a knife. He ran for the bedroom window he'd left open and disappeared into the inky night.

An enraged *JT* untied herself for the fourth and last time, then ran next door to her neighbor's and called police.

Subsequently, another potential suspect went on 'the list' of persons who had been 'looked' at and eliminated. Such was the case with Mr. J---y T----s M----r w/m, who has an office and runs a cleaning service nearby his Amesbury apartment. He cleaned the apartment of the complainant in this offense. He was eliminated by fingerprints. Tom Covington and Bobby Smoot were constantly trading names of persons contacted by investigators, ourselves, and patrol officers for potential elimination as suspects in the FBR case.

Dallas, Northeast Patrol Division, Beat 232
5:30 am Monday, October 6, 1975
Offense Number 27
See Appendix A - Newspaper Article # 29a

I'M GETTING GOOD at this he thought as he lifted the sliding glass door out of its running track and entered the living room of apartment number 5162 in the Corners III Apartments at 8459 Southwestern. The Friendly Burglar-Rapist would have been surprised if he had known his next victim was in advertising, an assistant media director. *LH*, the 23 year-old white female was asleep in her bedroom, with the door closed.

The heater's thermostat was set at a comfortable 70 degrees and would have kicked in, on its own, when enough of the fifty-three degree outside air had streamed into the apartment along the floor displacing the hotter air that had rushed outside through the open patio door. The FBR turned the fan on the HVAC control from 'Auto' to 'On', to drown out the noise.

LH, not particularly a light sleeper, woke as the door to her bedroom opened. Maybe it was the sound made by the HVAC fan, maybe it was the change in temperature, or maybe it was her guardian angel.

Lying on her back, facing the door, *LH* saw a man standing in the doorway looking at her. He was wearing a nylon stocking over his head with a long slit for his eyes. He looked to be a white male, middle twenties of medium height and build. In the moment this took to register the man stepped to the bed and put his hand over her mouth. "I'm just a burglar," he said. "I'm not going hurt you, if you'll be quiet." *The last one screamed her head off;* he said to himself, *show her you mean business… let her feel the blade.* He stroked her arm with a knife and told her to turn over. She did.

After he taped her hands to the headboard with some two-inch wide adhesive tape, he asked, "Where is the purse?"

"I don't know," *LH* responded.

He cut the cord to the phone on *LH*'s nightstand, and asked about her and her roommate. He left her room, pocketing a few dollars from a purse, and returned a few minutes later with a pillowcase which he slipped over *LH*'s head. In a low whisper he warned, "If you don't be quiet, I'll slit your throat." To emphasize his words he again ran the blade of the knife along *LH*'s arm.

He quickly pulled down the covers, lifted *LH*'s nightgown and then pulled down her panties. "I just want to look at you and touch you." He rolled her over onto her back then left the room.

When he came back into the room and she could make out his movements, he had what looked like a white sheet he was holding over his head. He walked around the room for several minutes not saying anything.

When he tried to spread her legs, *LH* started to say she was in her period, but instead stammered, "I, I have an infection."

"Oh," he replied sarcastically, "you get that from fooling around?"

He turned her over and began stroking himself till he ejaculated on *LH* and her bed. When he was finished he left the room and went to the roommate's bedroom but her door was locked.

LH heard him come back into her bedroom. "Why is your roommate's door locked?"

"I don't know, she just locks it sometimes."

He whispered, "I'll leave when it is clear to get in my truck. Don't make any noise." He left for a moment then came back and told her it wasn't clear yet. "Someone's out there, so don't make any noise... I'm still here." He left again, but this time did not return. When *LH* thought it was safe she yelled out for her roommate, who came and untied her and called the police.

Dallas, Northeast Patrol Division, Beat 232
6:00 am Tuesday, October 14, 1975
Offense Number 28

NO NOISES WOKE her. The twenty-one year-old white female student woke up when he reached across her and put his hand over her mouth. "Don't move, I'm just a burglar. If you scream I'll slit your throat!" He quickly bound her hands with two-inch white cloth surgical tape. He went through his usual motions: find some lotion; a jar of Vaseline, find the victim's purse, money, ID. He noted how filthy the apartment was, looked again at the driver's license picture of his intended victim and changed his mind. He told her he had to hurry and leave.

He went to the sliding glass door to the patio and looked out. A witness, about seventy-five yards away, looking out his own window, later described a man looking out the victim's sliding door as a white male, 20's, brown medium hair, fair skinned wearing a faded-out blue work shirt, maybe 5'10", 160 lbs.

The 'picky' Friendly Burglar-Rapist unlocked the front door and left: no cash, no rape. Even so, he left his fingerprints.

Dallas, Northeast Patrol Division, Beat 231
2:00 am Friday, October 17, 1975
Offense Number 29 (R-20)
See Appendix A - Newspaper Article # 29a

CHANGE TACTICS, HE wondered? He had been less than successful his last few attempts, *a run of bad luck*, he surmised. He didn't know his next victim might cost him his life.

LB was a white female only nineteen and the daughter of a police officer, a Dallas Police Sergeant. *LB*, a young secretary, fresh out of high school, lived in a second floor apartment at 5951 Melody Lane.

Bathed in the light of the full moon, The Friendly Burglar-Rapist found the kitchen window unlocked around 1:45am in the morning. The winds were calm but at fifty-three degrees it felt good to be inside. He quickly found a knife and began to explore the multilevel apartment.

As usual, his victim was asleep. He moved quickly to subdue her. He put his hand over her mouth and whispered, "Don't yell, do as I say, I have a knife, but I won't hurt you unless I have to." He immediately ripped off a strip of two-inch adhesive tape and put it over her mouth, then turned her over and taped her hands behind her back. *No more untying telephone cords too quickly...*

"I'm not going to hurt you; I'm just here to burglarize your apartment." He told her, "this is my profession". *LB* asked if he enjoyed his profession and the FBR responded: "It's great, but the hours are terrible!"

She heard him go into her bathroom, heard him rummaging through her purse that she had left there.

"Get up, stand up," he demanded as he returned to the bed. He pitched the bottle of Avon Veto-Mist Body Lotion he'd brought from the bathroom on the bed.

She could feel he was naked as he rubbed and fondled her body. He ordered her back onto the bed, spread her legs and quickly entered her, climaxing immediately.

She felt him move off the bed, heard him putting his clothes back on. Then he said, "I'm going outside to look around, be quiet and don't yell."

He had not covered her head. She later told police her assailant was a white male, 5'10", of medium build, with a soft voice, wearing a light-colored shirt with red plaid slacks. She said he had a stocking over his head, but had on glasses.

As soon as he was out the balcony door, *LB* rushed to the door and closed it, ran downstairs to wake her male roommate who was asleep with his girlfriend. He got up and rushed outside but did not see his roommate's rapist.

Fortunately for the police, and unfortunately for the FBR, he once again left an identifiable fingerprint.

Dallas, Northeast Patrol Division, Beat 213
1:45 am Thursday, October 23, 1975
Offense Number 30 (R-21)

HIS MASKED FACE loomed over her face as he put his hand on her mouth. His soft voice said, "Don't be afraid, I'm only here to burglarize your apartment. Now, I do have a knife," she remembered his telling her and that he had no wish to hurt her.

PAM, a twenty-six year-old white female bank secretary, had heard of the rapes in the area. She lived at 5928 Sandhurst in apartment #129. She and friends had talked about the Friendly Burglar-Rapist on more than one occasion. She told herself; *maybe I can talk him out of it.*

"This is my profession," he said.

"Do you enjoy your profession?"

"It's great… but the hours are terrible."

The roll of tape came out quickly. He taped her hands in front and put a piece of tape over her mouth.

She realized now, *there would be no talking him out of anything…*

He walked around the bedroom, "You got any valuables or large sums of money on hand?"

Her mouth taped, *PAM* shook her no.

She watched her attacker and later told the RO that the man, looked white, was maybe 5' 8" with a medium build and was probably in his early twenties wearing a stocking with slits holes for his eyes and mouth.

PAM saw him clip the phone lines with some kind of pliers or wire dikes. He scavenged through her purse taking her cash. Then he left the bedroom. She could hear faint snips like she had heard when he cut her bedroom phone cord.

He came back and stood beside the bed, "Don't make any noise, I'm not going to hurt you." She had on a pajama top which he began to unbutton, "Remember, I've got a knife."

It was rape, "short and to the point;" he did climax, but she later told the reporting officer J.T. Carey #2448, "He was very gentle and expressed concern for not harming me. He told me not to get up, that he was going to see if it was clear to leave."

Moments later the FBR came back to *PAM* and told her, "There are some people outside standing next to my pick up... I can't leave right now."

This always seemed to buy him some extra time. He had lied, there was no one standing by his truck in the full-moon light of the rain-wet parking lot. He didn't drive a truck and his car, though it was near, was not close. He left the bedroom for the last time and went to the unlocked sliding glass door where he had entered and exited his latest victim's apartment. He shivered in the fifteen mile an hour sixty-two degree wind, out of the SSE, filled with the moisture of recent light rain showers.

Dallas, Central Division Analyst's Office
8:15 am Monday, November 3, 1975

Received in today's inner-office mail were the reports and supplements from Friday, Saturday & Sunday. Lt. Day wrote a Supplement Report, dated 10-31-75 for O/IR 2843734-G.[49]

His report provided some very welcome revelations:

Examination of the latent prints from rape offenses in North Dallas indicate the same person was responsible for the following rapes:

1. 8459 Southwestern on 10-6-75, service # 344796-G *[Off. Number 27]*
2. 6334 Shadybrook on 10-14-75, service # 354830-G *[Off. Number 28]*
3. 6006 Sandhurst on 8-31-75, service # 299194-G   *[Off. Number 21]*
4. 7700 Meadow # 134, on 8-20-75, service # 284374-G *[Off. Number 20]*

The latent prints have been searched as completely as possible through Dallas P.D. and Sheriff's office files, and the fingerprint files as well as miracode file at DPS in Austin.

We have not been able to identify the suspect.

/s/ Lt. J. C. Day 391

---

[49] See page 140

Dallas, Northwest Patrol Division, Beat 534
3:00 am Thursday, November 6, 1975
Offense Number 31 (R-22)
See Appendix A - Newspaper Article # 29a

THE POTATO PEELER was pressed against her neck."

PA and her sister *NA* lived in a two bedroom, two bath apartment, #118, at 3104 Oradell. PA was the younger of the two white females. *PA*, twenty-two, was a secretary as was her older sister *NA* who was twenty-four.

PA had retired to her bedroom and left her sister *NA* in the living room where she had fallen asleep on the couch.

Inside their apartment he found the potato peeler on the counter. It looked like a knife; he picked it up. He found the girls purses, their ID's and money. The cash, about forty dollars, went into his pocket. He looked at the ID's saw the girls had the same last name; one was two years older, both in their early twenties. *Maybe tonight's the night I have a double...*

The girl on the couch was laying face down; he couldn't tell which sister she was. He went into the bedroom and found sister number two asleep.

He jumped atop *PA* and held her down, pressing the 'sharp object' to her throat. In his soft voice he ordered, "Keep quiet if you don't want your roommate to get hurt!" *Should've brought the tape tonight...* He got off *PA*, reminding her to keep quiet, he was just a burglar, and went to her closet. He retrieved two belts and used one to tie her hands to the bed post.

"You have any guns... or know where I can get one?"

PA shook her head no. As she looked down at herself a pillowcase came down over her face. She had only worn panties to bed and now he was pulling those off. She felt sick at her stomach.

He told her again, "Keep quiet if you don't want your roommate to get hurt!"

He held her legs apart and gently entered her, moving slowly till he climaxed.

Afterwards *PA* could hear him walking around in her bedroom, hearing him zip and unzip something... she couldn't figure it out. "Remember I have a knife, be quiet."

The FBR was trying to decide if he had enough stamina to go again. He walked into the living room and pounced on the sister sleeping face down on the couch. He immediately covered her mouth and said, "If you don't want your roommate to get hurt keep quiet." Then he began his mantra: "I am not going to hurt you; I am just a plain ol' burglar." He put a pillow case over her head.

His hands on her shoulders, he guided her into the unoccupied bedroom and tied her hands to the bedpost with the other belt he'd gotten in the first bedroom.

NA could see his outline in the security lights shining in from outside as he walked toward the patio door and looked out.

"Are you leaving?" *NA* asked.

"Can't leave yet, there is someone in the parking lot." He continued to walk around the apartment, helped himself to can of Coke, opened drawers and bathroom cabinets as well as the girls' purses... again.

While he was out of the room *NA* managed to get one hand free and was working on the other when he came back into the room.

In an angry but low voice he threatened, "Don't forget I have a knife!" He tugged on her pillowcase. "If you see me I couldn't leave you here." He retied her hands and went back into the living room and cut both phone cords.

As sufficient time had elapsed and he felt himself becoming aroused again, he went back into *NA*'s bedroom and starting pulling up her high gown.

Angry and defiant *NA* said, "I've got cancer," Isn't that enough? "I don't want to be raped too..."

The Friendly Burglar-Rapist pulled her nightgown back down, put a pillow under her head and left the room.

He went back into PA's bedroom where she was still tied to the bedpost. "I'm going out to my truck and I'll be back."

When they realized he probably wasn't coming back the two sisters called out to each other and managed to simultaneously get loose. At a neighbor's the two sisters called the police.

I imagine, several blocks away in his car, the FBR shivered, started his car, turned on the heater and pulled out of another apartment complex parking lot and headed home. He patted the money in his pocket, *lunch-money... it wasn't much,* he smiled, *it's like I'm getting paid for...* then he frowned, *I almost had a double tonight... I wonder if she really has cancer?* He wondered again about fingerprints, he heard his newspaper buddies talk about cops and fingerprints. *But,* he smiled again, *they don't have mine on file!*

Not So, Jack!

From their Supplement Report (re Offense Number 31), "Inv. R.A. Pettie & R.A. Furr of P.E.S. went to 3104 Oradell Lane, Rape, *NA*, w/f/22 & PA, w/f/22, complainant's, Service #382904-G. Photos were taken. Prints lifted from Coke can, milk carton. Unknown point of entry. Suspect tied complainants with dress belts and cut telephone wires. Note: One of the prints off the Coke can is the same print (number 6) found at 8459 Southwestern 10-6-75 on Service $344796-G. Also found 10-14-75 at 6334 Shadybrook, Service #354830-G."

CAPERS Inv. Reba Crowder #2894 wrote in her Supplement Report: "Compl. contacted at her apt on several occasions ie.: 11-7-75; 11-8-75; & 11-12-75. This offense was committed by the same unk susp. that committed the following offense #284374-G; #344796-G; #354830-G; & 382904-G. Several susps were checked & cleared by fingerprints. This offense will be suspended & investigation continues."

Chapter 9

Little Richard

Dallas, Office of Central Division Analyst
5:00 pm Friday, November 7, 1975

THROUGH CHIEF DIXON'S office I was routed the memo below from CID's Deputy Chief W.C. Fannin. It did three things: first it began to aggregate the rape offenses of the 'so-called "friendly burglar" under Investigator Reba Crowder who would, we assumed, be assigned all future FBR rape offenses. Second, it finally put CID and Planning & Research on the same page with Tom and me. What the assignment of Investigator Crowder to the FBR rapes and attempt rapes did not do was account for the other FBR related offenses: the burglaries, criminal mischiefs, suspicious persons, and prowler calls). No one was accountable for connecting these dots. But then, Tom and I already knew that. We had it handled.

This memo was the beginning of the short-lived[50] (just under a year) and contentious (in our opinion) involvement of Inv. Crowder in the FBR case.

Later John Landers, an academy classmate of mine, and then Truly Holmes, who I knew from 'the streets' would take over the FBR assignment in CID, each becoming staunch supporters of Tom and my methods and information.

As a side note, we never questioned Crowder's capability as an investigator. Our problem with Crowder, (which we also had with others during the FBR's activities), was her failure to take seriously the information and knowledge that we had amassed. We offered what we had learned freely and sought no aggrandizement, only the capture of the suspect.

The third thing the memo did was to foster what I believed was a manufactured concern that Reporting Officers were suggesting 'erroneous or misleading information' to complainants rather than just taking down their story. This sounded to Tom and me like the kinds of things we were hearing

---

[50] To my knowledge DPD, up until this time, had not had any Crimes Against Persons cases of this duration in which the suspect was still at large, still committing crimes. Remember the first FBR offense had occurred two years before in November 1973.

from Crowder, as reasons why an individual offense really wasn't, or couldn't be *the* FBR.

It is certainly plausible on occasion that RO's may have suggested the complainant's rape suspect might be the FBR, after all, he had been out there raping for over two years. But patrol officers know not to lead witnesses or complainants, and did an excellent job of getting us "just the facts, Ma'am", as Sgt. Joe Friday used to say on Dragnet.

To draw the conclusion RO's were doing else-wise, when so much public knowledge was available on the FBR's activities, was doing them an injustice.

> NB: In the eighty-plus offenses I had extensively reviewed and which Tom and I attributed to the FBR, I saw less than handful in which the narrative written by the reporting officer *might* have contained suggestive elements not initially volunteered by the complainant. And those that did actually suggest that the suspect on the O/I R might be or was the FBR occurred long after the FBR's M/O had been well established in various media reports. One example could be (see pages 139-141) Inv. Crowder's Supplement Report dated 8-22-75, where she wrote: "Compl. states reporting officers told her this sounds like the 'friendly burglar rapist' & everyone in the apts. was afraid." It is not logical that the RO would make such a statement to the complainant *before* she told the officer what had happened. Even Crowder's words belie her and Chief Fannin's assumption. Crowder states the officer *told* the Compl. "*this sounds like...*" He would have no reason to make the statement until *after* he had *heard* the complainant's account.
>
> Further, as mentioned in Chief Fannin's memo (Subject: "Friendly Burglar" Rapes), I have no idea where the term "Little Richard," came from; it was not contained in any of the eighty O/I R's or supplements I read, reviewed and analyzed. Parenthetically, I never heard any scuttlebutt or saw any note or statement by any investigator, RO or complainant that made mention of the size or lack thereof of the FBR's 'equipment'.
>
> It is entirely possible that Complainants were telling the CAPERS (Crimes Against Persons) investigators things spoken of by the reporting officers, which would be concurrent or subsequent to the RO's obtaining the complaining witness' statement; before makes no sense. And it was no secret what the FBR was doing 'in the neighborhood'. I thought it disingenuous to put the "making a difficult investigation more difficult" on the guys in the trenches who were busting their asses every night trying to find and stop this, heretofore, ghost of a suspect from continuing to pile up victims on their beats.
>
> When this memo came out, Reba Crowder was the 'go-to' investigator on the offenses CAPERS had decided were the responsibility of the Friendly Burglar-Rapist. And note that the copy that went into our Patrol Officers Handbook on the FBR had Reba's name crossed out when she was later replaced by Truly M. Holmes.

The following memo became part of the Patrol Officers Handbook[51] on the FBR:

Memorandum

DATE November 7, 1975

CITY OF DALLAS

TO Deputy Chief J. L. Davis, Northeast Division
Deputy Chief R. O. Dixon, Central Division
Deputy Chief G. H. Reed, Northwest Division

SUBJECT "Friendly Burglar" Rapes

In an effort to further correlate rape offenses committed by the so-called "friendly burglar" Investigator Reba *T.M. Holmes* Crowder will be made available to respond to any of these calls day or night. If one of your officers believes that it would be helpful for Investigator Crowder to come to the scene during the time that the Crimes Against Persons Section is closed, the request should be made through the supervisor in Communications. During the hours that the Crimes Against Persons Section is open, the request should be made to the supervisor of that section.

We are continuing to have offenses of this type (or similar) where the Patrol officer who answers the original call is "leading" the complainant by suggesting that "this looks like the FBR--or Little Richard." One complainant stated that the officer showed her a list of locations of other "friendly rapes." Our follow-up investigators are often determining that erroneous or misleading information is being given by the complainant and/or being included in the report due to unnecessary verbal input and suggestion from the officer answering the call. This only succeeds in making a very difficult investigation more difficult.

Please ask your officers not to suggest clues, etc., to these complainants but to let the complainants tell their story so that we can conduct the most efficient follow up possible.

Thank you for your help in this matter.

W. C. Fannin
Deputy Chief of Police
Criminal Investigation Division

WCF/as

With the circulation of this memo, Tom and I again went to see Investigator Crowder. We called and made an appointment. We carried our notebooks stuffed full of case information with

---

[51] Copy of this memo (which had be re-circulated later with Reba Crowder's name marked out and T.M. Holmes' name written in) was placed on page 6 of our Patrol Officers Handbook on the FBR.

us. We tried to give her the benefit of our knowledge. However our information was met with much the same attitude as when we first met her in the basement when the Bi-GatorSmooth crew 'tried' to interview her rape complainant from the downtown parking lot rapes that our three-man surveillance had been attempting to interdict.

Reba had been in charge of the FBR cases since January 1975, when we first met with her and were rebuffed. And, as kindly as I can put it, she did not appear to want our help and quite possibly was annoyed by, from her perspective, our having insinuated ourselves into her domain. And, unlike Investigators Lander's and Holmes, Reba did not work with us, did not engage us for our help or ever share any of her notes on what she had done investigatively in her diligent follow-up.

Though we certainly had no clue what all she was up to with the FBR case, there was no question in our minds that she did not have or see the whole picture. Additionally we were not on the same page with her regarding the number of offenses attributable to the FBR suspect to date. Nor was she even convinced that the cases 'she' aggregated as *possibly* being attributable to the FBR suspect were all committed by the same person. Reba, it seemed, felt copycats were at work. Such as the FBR case she dubbed "The Tongue Twister" six months later.

Dallas, Northeast Patrol Division, Beat 233
3:20 am Saturday, November 8, 1975
Offense Number 32 (R-23)
See Appendix A - Newspaper Article # 29a

WILLOW CREEK APARTMENTS, were close to Presbyterian Hospital where *PSS*, a 43 year-old white female, worked as a Labor and Delivery RN. *PSS*'s apartment, number 102 was located at 7706 Willowstream.

On the patio, he could see the window was unlocked so he moved the white plastic table out of the way. He raised the window and slipped inside.

In the kitchen he picked up a butcher knife, cut the telephone cords and walked back to the bedroom. He stood beside her bed for a moment, and then he lay down on top of the sleeping woman. In a coarse tight whisper he said, "Don't' holler, don't scream, I am a burglar, all I want is your money. If you are real still and don't move or make a sound you won't get hurt." He put the knife to her throat, "I mean business!"

She thought she caught a glimpse of her alarm clock, it was 3:23am.

He pulled a pillowcase from one of the pillows and put it over PSS's head. He tied her hands over her head and then tied them to the headboard with the telephone cord.

"Where do you keep your money?"

"There is some in a silver teapot in the living room."

The FBR got up from the bed and went from room to room, briefly turning on and off the lights. In the living room he found the teapot and took the seventy-two dollars it contained.

When he came back into *PSS*'s bedroom she asked, "How did you get in?"

They always want to know that… like they always keep all their windows and doors locked. "I got in by jimmying the back door with a knife," he lied.

"Why do you do this?" She asked.

"This is my first time," he lied again. "I don't have a job and I need the money." As he finished his sentence he jerked the covers off *PSS* and sat on the bed looking at her. "I'm not going to hurt you; I'm just a look-and-touch man." He then spent the next few minutes running his hands up and down *PSS*'s body, exclaiming, "Terrific."

He kept reassuring her, "Hold still, be quiet and I wouldn't hurt you," He continued fondling her. "Terrific," he kept repeating.

He got up from the bed and paced up and down by the bed with a butcher knife in his hand saying, "You'll know me, you'll remember this, you'll know me, you'll know me, you'll know me…

Do you have any guns here? Do you have any credit cards?

Don't make me hurt you… don't call the police or anyone when I leave or you'll get hurt.

He took his time, letting the excitement build.

"Are you by yourself?"

He kept running commentary going about why he was a burglar, couldn't find a job and this was not what he intended to do. Then as he rolled her over on he back, "If you move or scream I'll hurt you."

He climbed between her legs, pulled down his slacks and picked up the bottle of Xanadu hand and body lotion he brought from her bathroom and applied the lotion to his erection. He entered her and for the next two minutes as he pushed and pulled himself to orgasm he kept whispering to her in different sequences, "You'll know me, you'll remember me," and "you'll remember this."

When he had finished he got up and stood by the bed, "I'm going to leave now. Don't call anyone, give me five minutes because I don't want to come back here and hide."

PSS heard him leave the room, heard the rear door open and close. When she figured he was really gone she worked her hands free, and when she could see a clock again she realized he had been there almost an hour. As quickly as she could she went to a neighbors and called police.

The RO's reported continued: "P.E.S. #48 and Crowder of C.A. Persons were at the scene. Compl. was taken to P.M.H. and examined by Dr. Cunningham. Compl. state to officers that susp appeared very nervous during the rape but was very gentleman like and tried to be very reassuring to compl. Compl. stated susp had very soft hands and appeared to be very clean. Compl feels sups is probably not over 25 because his speech seemed to be very immature.

Dallas, Office of Central Division Analyst
9:00 am Tuesday, November 11, 1975

RECEIVED IN TODAY'S inner-office mail reports and supplements from Monday, November 10th. Lt. Day of P.E.S. wrote a new Supplement Report, dated 11-10-75 for O/IR 327607-G.[52] (see next page) This report links the FBR's #6 fingerprint on this Attempt Burglary with five FBR rapes!

Why was this good news? It reinforced our belief that other crimes: burglaries, criminal trespasses, etc. are the FBR just not finding a suitable victim to rape.

Eleven days later on 11-21-76 Inv. Reba Crowder penned a Supplement Report (to Offense Number 32) in which she wrote: "Compl. contacted 11-8-75 at offense scene & later that same day at her residence & several times by phone. This offense is similar to a number of others in the N. Central Dallas area. Prints

---

[52] See pages 140-148

of susp. were lifted at the scene. Neighbors of compl. contacted. No one saw sups. or could offer further info on sups. Susp. used the phrase "Terrific" several times. Suspend. Investigation will continue."

Why did Investigator Crowder use more ambiguous language regarding her take on the suspect and MO? Was she suggesting she thought this might not be an FBR rape? Was she having second thoughts about 'this single suspect'? In any regard, she was not apparently aware of Lt. Day's 11-10-75 Supplement tying this offense to five others committed by the same suspect.

P.E.S. Supplement linking this offense to five (5) others:

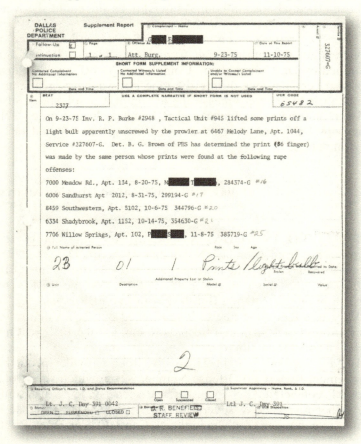

[NB: also see page 155]

Dallas, Northeast Patrol Division, Beat 231
6:45 am Wednesday, November 26, 1975
Offense Number 33

OVERCAST AND FREEZING—it felt good to be inside. In the kitchen he pulled a knife from the drawer and cut the line to the phone, then set it on the floor. Apartment 119 at 5929 Melody Lane had been easy to get into. The residents were two white females in their early twenties. He was aroused, but there was no money in either of their purses...

It was overcast, the wind blowing out of the NW at twenty-five miles an hour and gusting into the mid thirties. Even without the wind-chill, twenty-eight degrees is too cold to be outside for long. Behind the overcast skies the half-moon had set six hours ago and it was getting late; it was already dawn, with sunrise in less than fifteen minutes.

It was the growing light outside that made him think twice when he heard movement in one of the bedrooms, heard a toilet flush.

JDM, a local waitress had the seven-to-three shift and she was running late. She was about to turn on the water in the sink when she heard what sounded like a key in the front door, then heard a noise in living room.

Curious she walked into the living room and shivered in the cold draft coming through the open patio door. She noticed her phone on the floor, then discovered the cord was cut when she went to pick it up.

At work she was talking with the other waitresses who agreed it sounded like she had luckily only been *visited* by the Friendly Burglar-Rapist.

Dallas, Office of Central Division Analyst
9:00 am Monday, December 8, 1975

BEING IN THE MIDST of the long-enjoyed baseball comedy routine of Abbott & Costello, about "Who's on first" was how you felt when you were asked or tried to explain which of the two lieutenants, commanded which of the two shifts of the ID section; days and nights. The answer was: Lt. Day worked nights and Lt. Knight worked days.

Today a memo arrived at our office with a buck slip on it from Lt. Day for Tom. The memo dated 12-5-75 was *to* Evelyn

Crowder - Crimes Against Person, T.H. Covington - Central Division, and B.B. Smoot - Central Division. Bobby Buck worked NE, I worked Central... so I don't know if I was supposed to have been on the distribution or they got Bobby Buck's division wrong. What mattered was, we had the memo!

Lt. Day's memo, subject: Rapist Fingerprints, contained one sentence: **"The FBI has been unable to identify the prints submitted on the friendly burglar."**[53]

On more lead run down to its dead end. Of all the millions of prints available for comparison by the FBI, none of the prints collected at the scene of various FBR offenses to date were found to have a match in their system.

About this time Tom and I lost the third member of the BiGatorSmooth crew! Without fanfare, such as when one retires, Jim Bryan resigned from the Dallas Police Department and became an "oilman". Or as we say in Texas, he went into the *o'l biddness*. Though we kept in touch, Tom and I missed his friendship, input and help.

Author Note: *Jim rejoined the DPD in early 1990 and then later retired in 2008 with 30 years of service, but the clock is still ticking as he is now a DPD Reserve Officer and regularly teaches at the police academy.*

Dallas, Northwest Patrol Division, Beat 534
2:00 am Thursday, December 11, 1975
Offense Number 34 (R-24)

A WARM DECEMBER night, it was 60 degrees with a gulf breeze out of the south blowing through clear skies at 13mph.

The Walden Place Apartments was new territory for the Friendly Burglar-Rapist. But it was the same story, unlocked windows and doors; in spite of the weather and despite the danger.

The kitchen window to apartment #218 at 2850 Clydedale was unlocked. He removed the screen, stepped back and threw it like a Frisbee onto the roof. He raised the window and crawled into the kitchen, shutting the window behind him. He went to the front door and unlocked it. He retrieved a knife from the kitchen

---

[53] Copy placed in FBR - Patrol Officers Handbook on the FBR

and cut the phone cords and began rummaging through the apartment, opening the cabinet doors, drawers, and then headed for the bedroom.

CB, the twenty-six year-old white female claims adjuster, was lying on her back, asleep in her bed. She awoke with a start to a knife pressed against her throat and a whisper-voiced man saying, "Turn over, don't scream!"

He pulled a pillow case over her head and tied a knot in a corner of the pillowcase so it wouldn't come off easily. He poked her again with the knife, "I'll cut your throat with the same knife I used to open your front door."

He then tied her hands with the kitchen phone cord and left her on her stomach. "Don't move, don't make any noise," he told her as he went back into the living room, kitchen and bathroom.

When he came back he stood beside the bed and made her stand up. When she did, he pulled down her panties, made her step out of them and then told her to lie back down. She could hear him pull his pants down and could feel his bare chest moments later when he was on top of her.

He lubricated himself with Baby Oil from her bathroom before he raped his bound-up prey.

After his climax he got up and got dressed. He reminded her of the knife and to not scream or get up. "I'm going to see if I can get to my truck without being seen." He told her he'd be right back. He opened the front door, carrying something that would cause any witness to immediately believe he was a resident.

CB heard the front door close and waited several minutes then freed herself before going to a friend's to call police.

When the police arrived she was able to tell her story with two interesting additions; "the bastard" took two dollars from her purse and her green plastic garbage can from the kitchen, full of trash.

On December 11th, the same day as this offense, Lt. J.C. Day #391 of P.E.S. analyzed and compared the prints taken at this scene by Inv. J.M. Maberry and wrote they "have been identified as being made by the same person responsible for other rapes in the North Dallas area:

Right index finger on outside window molding-right side.
Left middle off outside window molding-left side.
Left middle off the door knob to dining room closet."

Investigator Crowder's Supplement Report on this offense was written-up five days later on 12-16-75. Her report, in part, reflects Lt. Day's. She wrote: "Prints picked up at the scene are the same as those found at several other North Dallas Rapes."

As of December 11, 1975, Tom and I had identified thirty-four (34) offenses that we had attributed to the FBR. There were twenty-four (24) rapes; one (1) attempt rape; two (2) robberies; three (3) burglaries; one (1) attempt burglary; two (2) criminal trespasses; and one (1) criminal mischief. Of these thirty-four cases, all but five had investigators assigned. So twenty-nine of these offense were assigned for follow-up by fifteen (15) different investigators. Investigator Evelyn Reba Crowder caught five (5) of the FBR offenses prior to Chief Fannin's 'correlation' memo of November 7, 1975. Thus far, three of the five FBR cases Crowder caught had latent fingerprints lifted that matched to a single suspect. The man Tom and I called the FBR.

With the case (also having FBR prints) Inv. Crowder caught on 12-11-75 she was now investigating six FBR cases.

Tom and I would have thought she was on board for a single suspect who was the 'so-called' Friendly Burglar-Rapist.

1976

Dallas, Central Division Analyst's Office
6:00 am, Thursday January 1, 1976
New Year's Day

IT HAD BEEN twenty days since the last FBR offense. I was captured by the same annual nagging question. Had the FBR finally gotten tired of not being caught and just stopped his criminal activity? Or was he on his end-of-the-year hiatus? I went into my office to see if there was an answer in my "in" box.

For the past three years there was an extended, unexplained, interruption in his activities usually spanning the time period from mid December to mid March.

I tried again to fathom why the FBR seemed to take off for sixty to ninety days this time of the year. I was drawing the same ol' blank.

Coming out of my office, I would say everyone was surprised to see me at 6am, but no one else was around the office, it was after all a holiday. After I had checked my interdepartmental mail and left my office, I went to the downtown crowd control post I was 'working' for the Cotton Bowl Parade.

For once the weather was reasonable. The wind was blowing at a reasonable twelve miles per hour and the temperature under a clear blue sky was in the upper fifties. After the parade left downtown, I headed to the Cotton Bowl at Fair Park where I was also 'working' the game.

At game time it was in the middle sixties—perfect football weather. There were over seventy-seven thousand on hand to watch the Arkansas Razorbacks put up thirty-one points to the Georgia Bulldogs' ten.

Life would move forward for many people in ways that they were used to except this year was a big birthday for our country, our Bicentennial! Many things would be the same. People would go about their daily lives, would buy cars, go to school, the doctor, pay their taxes and among other things, go to the movies. Here is list of what some would say were the Top Ten Most Popular Films of 1976:

1. Taxi Driver
2. Rock
3. Carrie
4. Network
5. The Outlaw Josey Wales
6. The Omen
7. **Logan's Run**[54]
8. All the President's Men
9. In the Realm of the Senses
10. The Last Tycoon

Not to be out-done, television would host an incredible number of feature films both the theatrical releases and made-for-TV varieties. One of the top, most watched, films of the decade would air in April over two nights. Such was *Helter-Skelter* TV viewership in April 1976 that the network decided it could go full circle and re-air the movie about Charles Manson and the Tate-LaBianca murders in January 1977.

For some 1976 would be a good year. For others, the FBR's victims... not so good. I would do a brief stint back in patrol and have a negative epiphany.

---

[54] See page 130 for location filming in Dallas

chapter 10

Month-At-A-Glance
If you were in Dallas then, what were you doing on theses 'Marble' days?

[NB: Though it may be for the reader to determine the actual significance of these entries, lean as the are. They are included to provide context and insight into the 'notated' days from the FBR's own work calendar for 1976. From this point on they will appear throughout the book in chronological order as brief inclusions, as below. The script font is not indicative of the FBR's writing, only to set it apart. Tom and I did not have access to this information during the investigation. A copy of it came into our possession after the FBR's arrest.] (See Appx A - Article # 23, robertjsadler.com)

FBR's *Month-At-A-Glance 1976*
January 1-3:   Holidays

FBR's *Month-At-A-Glance 1976*
Monday, January 5:   9:00 Bruce

FBR's *Month-At-A-Glance 1976*
Tuesday, January 6:   Pero 7:30

FBR's *Month-At-A-Glance 1976*
Thursday, January 8:   8:30 Gary

FBR's *Month-At-A-Glance 1976*
Monday, January 12:   Note

FBR's *Month-At-A-Glance 1976*
Tuesday, January 13:   1:30 w (indecipherable)
                              4:00 IABC

FBR's *Month-At-A-Glance 1976*
Wednesday, January 14:   Payday

FBR's *Month-At-A-Glance 1976*
Thursday, January 15: 10:00 Bruce

FBR's *Month-At-A-Glance 1976*
Thursday, January 22: 10:00 Bruce

FBR's *Month-At-A-Glance 1976*
Monday, January 26:   Credit mail
mike?
10:15 Harry|Cindy

FBR's *Month-At-A-Glance 1976*
Tuesday, January 27:   → 11:30
1:30 NT

FBR's *Month-At-A-Glance 1976*
Wednesday, January 28:   Payday

FBR's *Month-At-A-Glance 1976*
Thursday, January 29: 1:30 Bruce

FBR's *Month-At-A-Glance 1976*
February 1-4:   ← SF →

FBR's *Month-At-A-Glance 1976*
Monday, February 9:   IABC 4:00
Big Spring ?

FBR's *Month-At-A-Glance 1976*
Tuesday, February 10: IABC Lunch
11:30

FBR's *Month-At-A-Glance 1976*
Wednesday, February 11:   Payday

FBR's *Month-At-A-Glance 1976*
Thursday, February 13:   Note

Dallas, Northeast Patrol Division, Beat 242
1:50 am Tuesday, February 17, 1976
Offense Number 35 (R-25)
Glove Marks - No Prints of Value Found

THE FULL MOON was occluded by the overcast skies, its light defused into darkness. The Friendly Burglar-Rapist was not uncomfortable in the sixty-six degree air, fed by an almost 14 mile an hour southerly wind.

He mentally counted the number of times he had walked, jogged or driven through the Willow Creek Apartments; it had been three months ago, a different street address on Willowstream, tonight the address was 7731, and a different apartment number. Whose would it be tonight?

The cotton gloves felt good even though it wasn't that cold. His eyes scanned windows and sliding glass doors. He walked close to the ground floor patio fences to peer over them and looked above him at the second floor patio doors for points of entry. He walked through breezeways to check the windows facing them.

He found what he thought was probably a living room window unlocked, he removed the screen; it was locked. The number on the apartment door was 125. He removed a second screen; it's window was unlocked. He raised it and slipped inside. In the kitchen he picked up a knife and cut the telephone cord, walked down the hall turned the fan lever on the HVAC thermostat from 'Auto' to 'On'. The sibilant noise of the fan became constant.

He stood in the bedroom doorway staring at his victim; she was asleep, on her stomach. He took three strides forward and jumped on her back.

LR, the office manager at an ancient downtown Dallas business association, was a 29 year-old divorcee and a five foot three, one-hundred-ten pound, blue-eyed blond who, like many other unattached women her age, was home alone that night. But Monday nights were usually the only night in the week she was at home and alone. She frequented the local clubs: Prime Time, Key Note, Grady's and Landmark with her Push Club friends who, like her, enjoyed dancing and socializing. She also liked to go to The Point and Reflections. Monday had seemed like a long day at work and she had gone to bed at 9:30pm. She shopped at all the usual places, the Tom Thumb, in Meadow Creek Mall,

Sanger-Harris in Preston Center and the stores of North Park Mall.

It was 2:00am on Tuesday morning when the FBR had pulled the plug on the electric clock and now he was straddling *LR*'s back. With his hand clasped around her mouth he said, "I am a burglar, shsss, be quiet. I'm a burglar, I got in with a knife, so keep your mouth shut and I won't hurt you." As he said this he was shaking loose a pillow from its case and slipped over *LR*'s head.

She could hear him cutting something then felt her hands pulled together and tied. Next he tied her hands to the bedpost. At the foot of the bed he stood facing the headboard and repeated, "I'm a burglar, so be quiet and I won't hurt you. She could hear him walking around her room and apartment.

He returned to the bed and cut her hands loose with a pair of scissors. *LR* thought, *where'd he get those… I can't even find my scissors…* He pulled her down on the bed and pulled her nightgown down over her body, removed it and positioned himself between her legs. She could hear him unbutton and then unzip his pants. They felt to her rough like denim.

As he lubricated himself with some of her hand lotion he said, "Don't scream and you will be alright."

LR could feel his hands now, he'd taken off his gloves, but he didn't fondle her, just positioned himself to rape her. She could tell he had only lowered his pants and had kept his shirt on.

After his orgasm, he got off the bed and threw the sheets back over *LR*, covering her completely. She heard him in the bathroom, heard the water running, washing his hands or genitals. He came out of the bathroom and continued to roam around *LR*'s apartment. He returned the A/C fan setting to 'Automatic' and unlocked the deadbolt on the front door. He walked very quietly, the only thing she could hear was the fabric on his thighs rubbing together as he walked. From her purse in the living room he pocketed fifteen dollars and some business cards.

Back in the bedroom he asked *LR* if there were any other phones. She told him there was one in the living room, but didn't mention the one in the kitchen. "I'll tell you when I am going to leave… don't move until I tell you I am gone."

He went to the kitchen and opened the refrigerator. The R.O. wrote: "Upon leaving susp took 1 qt. of Dr. Pepper and threw the cap on the living room floor." It appears he left through the patio sliding glass door where he also dropped the calling cards (business cards taken from the Complainant's purse) before hopping the redwood fence that surrounded the patio.

FBR's *Month-At-A-Glance 1976*
Tuesday, February 17: Hair cut → 11:30
(arrow may be an indication haircut moved to Wed 18ᵗʰ)

FBR's *Month-At-A-Glance 1976*
Thursday, February 19: ← 3:00 →
(arrow indicates Tulsa IABC 19-21)

FBR's *Month-At-A-Glance 1976*
Friday, February 20: ← Tulsa IABC →
(arrow indicates Tulsa IABC 19-21)

FBR's *Month-At-A-Glance 1976*
Saturday, February 21: →
(arrow indicates Tulsa IABC 19-21)

FBR's *Month-At-A-Glance 1976*
Wednesday, February 25: Payday

FBR's *Month-At-A-Glance 1976*
Thursday, March 4: Bd Mtg 4:30
Tobin 10:00

Dallas, Central Division Analyst's Office
5:00 pm, Thursday March 4, 1976

Received Investigator Crowder's Supplement Report, dated 3-2-76, for Offense Number 35 occurring on 2-17-76. Crowder notes the similarities, but does not mention the FBR:

"This offense is similar to a number of other Rapes in the North Dallas area. Susp wore gloves, had a knife, stated he was a burglar & tied compl. with phone cord. Money was taken from Compls. purse & hand lotion was used for a lubricant. Compl. did not see susp. Compl. & neighbors were interviewed. No workable leads at this time. Investigation will continue.
Glove prints only!"

[NB: When Inv. John Landers reinterviewed *LR* on 6-30-76, he noted: "Comp. is sure suspect brought this own scissors -"]

Dallas, Northeast Patrol Division, Beat 212
3:15 am Friday, March 5, 1976
Offense Number 36 (R-26)

"IN MY PERIOD! I'm in my period," she told him again, hoping to rebuff her assailant.

It had been a nice beginning to a weekend. It was chilly outside, in the fifties and overcast. *BHB*, her roommate and her roommate's boyfriend had watched TV together. They had gone to bed first. *BHB* had stayed up and only turned off the TV and gone to bed when her cramps had finally subsided.

It wasn't unusual, he'd seen it before; windows that were actually locked. He didn't know it when he pried off the screen, it looked unlocked, but it wasn't. However it did not take much force to push the locking tab beyond its catch; voilà, it was open.

The routine he had perfected rarely changed. He opened drawers in the kitchen until he found a butcher knife to cut the telephone cords in the kitchen and living room. This time he just jerked the phone's cord out of the wall in the living room. As he went down the hall he pushed the A/C fan lever to "On" and waited while the fan kicked on. There were no purses in the kitchen or living room… *must be in their bedrooms or baths.*

He quietly opened the first bedroom door he came to, there were two bodies in bed. As his eyes adjusted he saw it was a man and a woman. He pulled the door to. *Quietly,* he told himself as he felt his excitement grow.

He opened *BHB*'s bedroom door and closed it behind him. He wasted no time. She woke to his trademark M/O.

With a gloved-hand over her mouth he whispered, "Don't move or I will kill you!" He put the butcher knife to her neck for emphasis. "Lie on your stomach." As she did so, he tied her hands with telephone cord. He pushed her. "Lie on your left side," he said, "facing the wall and don't turn over."

As she turned over, the last thing she saw before he pulled a pillowcase over her head was her clock; it was 3:15.

With a man and woman asleep in the adjacent bedroom he didn't feel he had the time to play his, *I'm just a burglar,* deception game.

From her bed he took the few steps into *BHB*'s bathroom, turned on the light, located a bottle of lotion and turned off the light. As his eyes readjusted he stood beside the bed and told his victim to roll over on her back. He reminded her he still had the knife as he pulled her nightgown over her head.

When she felt the knife between her skin and her panties, felt it sawing through the fabric, felt him pull the pieces away, she knew what was going to happen next. The first "I'm" wasn't audible as she told him she was in her period which she repeated, hoping that would turn him off.

He wasn't fazed; he reached between her legs and pulled on the Tampax string till he removed it. Then, as if he'd done it a thousand times, he squeezed some Vaseline Intensive Care lotion in his hand and rubbed it into her vagina, then raped her.

After his climax he got out of bed and pulled up his pants saying, "No one would ever find me... because I have on gloves."

He came out of the bathroom with the towel he'd used to wipe himself off, "You have any money?"

"On the dresser, in my purse."

He'd already found her purse and taken the five dollar bill in her wallet. The told her he had to go see if he could get to his truck." Moments later he said, "Don't move, I'll be right back...

In the kitchen he took a bottle of Orange juice with him. She heard the fridge door close, she waited what she thought was five more minutes and realized he must have left...

Time often seems to stretch. From the time *BHB* saw the clock at 3:15am till the time she called the police and the dispatcher dispatched Officers D.P Winterbauer #1356 and D.W. Brown #1977 at 3:23am, only eight minutes had elapsed. Eight minutes that BHB would never forget. As usual the P.E.S. guys took all the evidence, including a knotted phone cord, for analysis.

A week later Crowder's Supplement Report (dated 3-13-76) crossed my desk. Crowder was non-committal: "The method used by susp. is similar to other rapes in the area."

Dallas, Northeast Patrol Division, Beat 215
1:10 am Friday, March 12, 1976
Offense Number 37

THE ALMOST FULL moon peaked out from the partly cloudy skies. With the 65 degree wind blowing out of the SSW at 14mph, it was almost as if the scent of spring was in the air.

The Friendly Burglar-Rapist, his ski mask in his pocket, loped through the Willow Creek Apartments, settling on 7911 Rockwillow and a ground floor apartment. With a gloved hand he unscrewed the light bulb on the patio. In seconds he had forced the lock and opened the window into the living room of apartment 110. He took sixteen dollars from the woman's purse on the table and left her driver's license; he just glanced at the picture in the dark. In the kitchen he obtained a knife and cut the phone cord, which he carried with him toward the bathroom. He searched the cabinets and found several bottles of hand lotions and creams, which he tossed on the bed before attacking his victim.

Following his S.O.P. he put his hand over her mouth and told her, "don't move, I have a knife" and, "I only want your money." As he put a pillowcase over her head he asked, "Where's your money."

RH, instead of answering his question, asked her own. "How did you get in?"

"I told you earlier," he said, "I have a knife. Now, turn your head to the wall, I'm going to turn on the light." He left the room and returned a few moments later, with more phone cord. "Stand up, I'm going to tie your wrists, stand up, I'm want to tie you to something." He tied her hands then tied them to the headboard.

Everything had gone according to plan. The A/C fan was blowing, the phone lines had all been cut, he had his victim's money and he had her own lubricant to facilitate her own rape.

As he had done dozens of times before, he lifted his victim's nightgown. *RH* was standing with her back to him. When she felt the gown uncovering her, she became very indignant and shouted, "Quit, I'm an old lady!"

He hadn't really looked at his victim or paid attention till she shouted. His immediate reaction was, "Oh, my God!" He sat her down on the edge of the bed and left the room.

She listened, but didn't hear any sounds and a few minutes later *RH*, a retired 65 year-old white woman, managed to free herself and found she was indeed alone in her apartment.

DPD Officers J.F. Martin 3236 and B.J. Wapner 3577 were dispatched on an aggravated robbery call at 2:26am. At the scene P.E.S. collected evidence, such as the ubiquitous cut telephone cord, only to find one with a knot which 'appears identical to knot in cord used on offense #76996H' the week before. Wapner wrote, in part, "This MO seems to follow that of the friendly rapist. No further info at this time."

Dallas, Northeast Patrol Division, Beat 212
1:30 am Friday, March 12, 1976
Offense Number 38

UNDETERRED BY CIRCUMSTANCES, the FBR left the Willow Creek Apartments and drove three miles north on Central Expressway to the Willowick Apartments at 6002 Sandhurst. This would be his fifth time there and his first time going into apartment number 1003.

The sheer number of apartments he entered on a given night no longer had any impact; it was just what he did.

He didn't know *JT* was a white female student of 23 or that her roommate *JL* was also 23; but he could have guessed and he would have bet they were both asleep. He squatted down in the flower bed and removed the window screen, raised the window and crawled in. He went to the front door and unlocked it, preparing his escape, per usual. Just because he'd had bad luck on his last 'in', he was still careful.

JT was in bed with her boyfriend *SC*. *JL* was in her bedroom alone when she woke and saw her bedroom door open, and a man looking in. *JL* thought it was *JT*'s boyfriend. *JL* was trying to get back to sleep when she heard the front door open a short time later.

The Friendly Burglar-Rapist had once again slipped away.

In the morning *JL* asked *SC* about his looking in her bedroom and he said he hadn't been out of bed. On hearing this *JT* immediately checked the apartment and found the front door ajar, mud on the carpet and by the window in the living room.

They called police.

Remembering a prior event in the apartment of *JT*, Reporting Officer L.L. Barbee 2945, in his Offense/Incident Report, wrote

"Resident in Apt. 2003 was victim of Crim. Assault in Dec 1975. Susp. "The Friendly Burglar".

FBR's *Month-At-A-Glance 1976*
Friday, March 12:   Note

Dallas, Office of Central Division Analyst
5:00 pm Friday, March 12, 1976

Reducing my handwritten chart to the typewritten (scanned) version below, we had been tracking prints and comparing the victim and the suspect's blood type from early on.

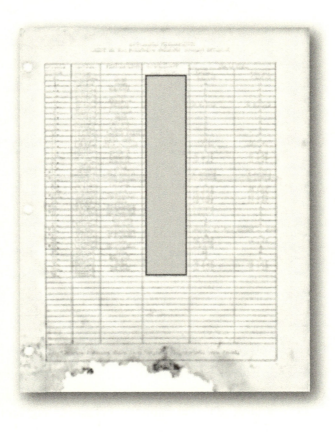

Here is the same info using 'modern' technology. Please note 1) the list was created before the Friendly Burglar-Rapist moniker was applied, and 2) that as time passed, the sequencing of Attributed FBR Offenses changed when one previously not located or attributed needed to be fit chronologically into the list.

The 'list' would not be completed until the FBR was caught!

Offense Number	Service Number	Fingerprints	Complainant Last Name	BLOOD TYPE VICTIM	SUSPECT
		COMPARABLE FINGERPRINTS EXIST ON THE FOLLOWING FRIENDLY BURGLAR OFFENSES			
0	340698E	NONE	P	Unknown	Unknown
1	237116F	NONE	J	A	A
2	248973F	Unknown	S	A	A
3	283127F	NONE	B	O	A
4	300572F	POSSIBLE	B	O	A
5	307548F	Unknown	N	No Record	No Record
6	342398F	POSSIBLE	G	O	A
7	356401F	NONE	c	O	A
8	401910F	PARTIAL	B	O	A
9	83737G	Unknown	T	O	A
10	103880G	1-Poor PRINT	E	O	A
11	139028G	GLOVE MARKS	J	O	A
12	150346G	POOR PARTIAL	S	Negative	Negative
13	172369G	Unknown	R	O	A
13A	173655G	PARTIAL	M	No Test	No Test
14	211573G	Unknown	P	No Test	No Test
15	252691G	NONE	K		A
*16	284374G	COMPARABLE	M	No Record	No Record
*17	299194G	COMPARABLE	K	No Record	No Record
18	314966G	PARTIAL	J	A	A
18A	314810G	NONE	B	No Test	No Test
*18B	327607G	COMPARABLE	G	No Test	No Test
19	342302G	NONE	J	No Test	No Test
*20	344796G	COMPARABLE	L	Unknown	A
*21	354830G	COMPARABLE	M	Unknown	A
22	358213G	PARTIAL	L	O	A
23	365250G	Unknown	P	O	A
*24	382904G	COMPARABLE	P	Can't Be Done	Can't Be Done
*25	385719G	COMPARABLE	P	A	A
26	407009G	NONE	J	No Test	No Test
*27	424823G	COMPARABLE	c	Unknown	A
28	56459H	NONE	L	AB	A
29	76996H	Unknown	B	O	A
30	84982H	NONE	R	No Test	No Test
30A	85087H	Unknown	J	No Test	No Test
31	89702H		S		

* Denotes Offenses Where Same Suspect's Fingerprints were found.

As you can see we were making progress: comparable prints, same suspect thus ID's on multiple offenses, augmented by serology results—or *so we thought*.

Dallas,, Northeast Patrol Division, Beat 213
11:30 pm Wednesday, March 24, 1976
Offense Number 39 (R-27)
Glove Prints Found

"HEY, WAKE UP!" he demanded, with his knee pinning her leg to the bed. "Don't scream or give me any trouble. I have a knife!"

Crossroads III Apartments were just north and east of Old Town in the Village, the hottest single's spot in Dallas and the curvy Southwestern Boulevard was the vehicular river that ran through it. From 8463 Southwestern you could look south across the football field and ball diamonds to the Village Club House, the heart of the 'village' and its surrounding acres of apartment complexes. Apartment number 6174 was easy to access on the complex's private road off Southwestern. Easy in, easy out; it was a prime location. In spite of its number it was an upstairs apartment, number 5174 was the downstairs unit.

It was still early for the Friendly Burglar-Rapist, in fact he had been out 'scouting' for several hours. Experience had taught him he didn't always find his victim on the first or second try. It was mostly cloudy with moonrise not for three more hours. The air temperature was a comfortable 58 degrees, due to the mild south breeze, when he pulled into a parking space.

The target he had already observed was only minutes away. He unscrewed the bulb in the downstairs light fixture, hurried his pace as he climbed the stairs then stopped at a beckoning window. To be honest, he no longer cared if this window wasn't open, unlocked, or wouldn't budge; he would go on to the next.

Before attacking the window he unscrewed the upstairs light as well. A little jimmying and he was in, and in mere moments had a knife and something with which to tie his victim.

Perhaps it was the difficulties he'd recently encountered with uncooperative victims, but tonight he took no chances. Feeling the pressure of his knee on the back of her leg she heard his command: "Turn your head on the pillow; I'm going to put this pillowcase over your head... Don't scream!"

Holding a length of telephone cord he said, "Put your hands in front of you."

KS, a 23 year-old white female who worked in sales for a local television station, did as she was told which included not moving.

He spent the next five to seven minutes in burglar-rapist foreplay, skulking around the apartment opening drawers, cabinets; looking into anything that caught his attention, like a cold bottle of Coke in the fridge; he helped himself. It was part of the arousal process; thinking about his helpless victim who had already submitted to his mental rape and was about to receive his physical assault.

He tripped on the end of the bed coming back into the bedroom, lubricant in hand. Irritated he grabbed the covers and gave them a yank. *KS* was cowering in bed her nightgown her only protection. She heard him coming closer and said firmly, "Don't touch me!"

He almost laughed. "Everything will be okay, be quiet, I won't hurt you. Don't forget, I have a knife."

He reached for her nightgown and she tried to hold it down with her tied hands. "No, I have my period."

She couldn't see him shake his head as if to say, *so what's new... been there before...* he was married, he knew most women used Tampax, intra-vaginally, rather than the older & bulky Kotex pads usually worn with the aid of an elastic belt.

"Slide over to the edge of the bed," he prompted. When she had her feet on the floor he asked, "Do you want to take it out or do you want me to?"

After *KS* had complied he told her to "stand up and turn around." He pulled up her gown and fondled her breasts and vaginal area. When he was ready he had her lie down on the bed and spread her legs. He stood at the end of the bed spreading Vaseline Intensive Care lotion on himself. Then he crawled up from the end of the bed and got on top of his victim. As he penetrated her he told her to pull her legs up. He kissed her breasts and sucked her nipples then began kissing *KS*'s mouth, something he had never done to one of his victims, or at least never reported. He continued kissing her, pushing his tongue into her mouth and sucking her tongue into his.

After he had climaxed he got off the bed and threw the sheets over *KS*, then headed to her bathroom where he used a towel to wipe himself off. "Where is your purse?" he asked in an off-handed way. "I'll be gone in a few minutes, you've been real good and I didn't hurt you."

He walked into the bedroom, "I'm going to take your TV."

"I have some jewelry," *KS* offered.

"Do you have any diamonds?"

"No."

"If you don't have diamonds I can't pawn them."

She heard him leave out the front door and head down the stairs… then heard him come back up the stairs and into the apartment again. Her heart sunk.

"I can't leave right now…"

KS heard him say something about a truck, and tried to remember that so she could tell the police… what he said about the truck, she couldn't remember.

"I'll come back and tell you when I leave."

Ten minutes later, having heard no more noises in her apartment she pulled off the pillowcase and started untying the knotted phone cord. She noticed lights on that she had not left on when she went to bed. In the living room the front door was ajar; she ran to it and immediately locked it behind her. Five or ten minutes later she saw some neighbors and had them call police.

Officer R.J. Catona # 2942 responded to the rape call. As he was interviewing his complainant she physically shied away. *KS* asked, "What kind of cologne are you wearing?"

"Aramis," he replied."

"That's what he was wearing," she said.

KS also told Officer Catona that around 9:30pm that evening she had seen a w/m/25-28, 5'11" to 6', 170lbs, light brown curly hair, white T-shirt and dark pants and possible mustache watching her as she unloaded a punchbowl from her car and carried it upstairs. "It was kind of strange, he just kept starring, but he was gone when I came back down to the car."

Once again P.E.S. commented that the phone cord had 'an unusual knot'.

This was now the tenth FBR case assigned to Inv. Crowder. Her Supplement Report for this offenses was dated and filed on 4-6-76.

FBR's *Month-At-A-Glance 1976*
Friday, March 26:   **TACT Prog. Pro. Serv.**

April 1, 1976
Made for TV Movie
Helter Skelter, Part 1 Airs
Tied for 13th most watched movie* of the decade (Seventies).

I wondered if the televising of this bloody, grisly series of murders in California would have any impact on the FBR and his behaviors here in Dallas.

FBR's *Month-At-A-Glance 1976*
Friday, April 2:   **Photo's & copy from B.S.**
                          8:00 Game fields

April 2, 1976
Helter Skelter, Part 2 Airs
Tied for 9th most watched movie* of the decade (Seventies)
http://www.superseventies.com/telecasts.html
* network prime-time feature films,
both those made specifically for TV

FBR's *Month-At-A-Glance 1976*
Monday, April 5:   **TACT Photo's**

Dallas, Northeast Patrol Division, Beat 242
11:15 pm Monday, April 5, 1976
Offense Number 40 (R-28)
Comparable Prints Found

THE MAGIC PAN waitress, *PCA*, a white female 23, had gotten off at 4:00pm and was out running errands. She arrived back at her apartment #101 in the Willow Creek Apartment complex, 7885 Willowfalls, between 10:00 and 10:30pm with a girlfriend who stayed and visited for a few minutes and then left. *PCA* was in bed by 11:00pm and glad to be out of the smoke.

The day's overcast skies had been filled with smoke from an outbreak of grass fires that began about the time *PCA* got off work. The calm winds had allowed the smoke to linger.

After moving the flower pots and climbing in the kitchen window he stood there in the dark a few moments trying not to cough. He found a kitchen knife, a phone; cutting its cord, turned the A/C fan lever to 'On' and headed into the *PCA*'s darkened bedroom.

She woke with a man bending over her, on his hands and knees. He reached out and covered her mouth, "Don't move around or I'll hurt you with this knife." She felt something sharp against her arm and remained still.

"Take your arms out from under the covers one at a time." When she had both her arms free he tied her hands to the bedpost. He straightened up, grabbed one of her pillows stripping off its pillowcase.

As he slipped it over *PCA*'s head, she noticed a strong fishy smell to the man, like he had been working around or handling a lot of fish. In the darkness of the bedroom she had tried to make out his face before he covered hers. It seemed to *PCA* that his features were all mashed together, like he was wearing a stocking over his head and face.

He got up and said, "Don't scream, be a good girl. I'm going to look around.... how much money do you have in your wallet?" In the apartment he found her wallet and pocketed her ten dollars.

When she started crying he came back into the bedroom, "Be quiet," he told her, "don't make any noise or you'll attract attention."

He had already removed her panties, the only thing she had had on, and she realized what was next when she heard him unzip his pants.

During the rape he fondled her breasts and raised the pillow case to French kiss her, but she moved her head and said, "Wouldn't it be better if you did it with someone who wanted you?"

"Just think of me as Sicko... some people just do it for the kicks. Now, be quiet."

Afterwards he told her, "I'm going to leave now as soon as people leave the parking lot and you will hear the sliding glass door close."

She never heard the sliding glass door open or close. After a short wait *PCA* freed her wrists and walked into the living room. The sliding glass door was locked, but the kitchen window was open and ten bucks had been taken from her wallet.

Could the "sicko" reference, something the FBR had never said before, be a result of *Helter Skelter*?

Dallas, Office of Central Division Analyst
8:15 am Wednesday, April 7, 1976

This morning in the inter-office mail I received the Supplement Report for the FBR Offense Number 39 (with complainant KS) which occurred back on March 24th. This is the tenth FBR case (of the 40 Tom and I had attributed to the FBR) to have been directly assigned to Inv. Crowder. Her Supplement Report for this offenses was dated 4-6-76 and contained the following: "Compl. contacted on the scene the evening of offense. The MO of this offense is similar to others in the area. Neighbors contacted -- saw nothing. Apt. mgr. contacted --- also a friend of compl; Gary F----l w/m/7-7-47 of 8545 Southwestern #190 contacted. Compl. states she did not see susp & he whispered -- but during the assault he 'frenched [*sic*] Kissed' her, almost pulling he tounge [*sic*] out of her mouth ---- & she remembered above friend tried to French kiss her once. No further leads at this time. Unusual knot. Suspend! Investigation Continues."

What is interesting about the statements in this SR is that it was written on the same day that Crowder interviewed *PCA* regarding her rape that occurred on April 5th, although it most likely had been April 6th when the interview occurred, since the RO was only dispatched on the call at 23:56 on April 5th. The point is, that both the March 24th (Offense Number 39) and the April 5th (Offense Number 40) rapes involved the FBR kissing the complainants. Crowder's SR for Offense Number 40 (with complainant *PCA*) would not be filed until April 16, 1976 and would contain, in my and Tom's opinion, a very strange notation regarding her conclusion from these two complainant's kissing comments.

FBR's *Month-At-A-Glance 1976*
Wednesday, April 7:   Payday

FBR's *Month-At-A-Glance 1976*
Thursday, April 8:   Thurs Bd mtg !
                     9:30 **Wayne**
                     Lunch Wayne

FBR's *Month-At-A-Glance 1976*
Friday, April 9:   10:00 NewZ

Dallas, Northwest Patrol Division, Beat 553
10:45 pm Sunday, April 11, 1976
Offense Number 41 (R-29)
Glove Prints Found

ONCE AGAIN AN almost full moon blazed white in the clear sky. Spring was in full bloom, the temperature was hovering at 70 degrees in the light southerly breeze.

BJ, a 24 year-old secretary who worked downtown, was already in bed at 10:45 on a Sunday evening. She was lying on her stomach reading next to a small lamp when a man came running into her bedroom and jumped on her. He pushed her face away from him.

"Be quiet, I have a knife! I haven't hurt anybody yet, so you'd better stay quiet." He kept a running commentary going as he tried to calm her and get something to tie her hands. "I used a knife to get into through the door." Don't worry, "I'm just a burglar." He told her he'd just get her stuff and take it to his "truck."

He tried to put a pillowcase over her head but she resisted and kept struggling. "Keep your head turned away, if you don't want to get hurt." With her kitchen knife he cut the cord to her telephone and tied her wrists together then to the bedpost. Feeling she was sufficiently cowed he got up and wandered the apartment.

When he came back into the bedroom he put the pillowcase over her head.

He unbuttoned her gown and with gloved hands stroked her breasts and genitals.

"Leave me alone, please, I have a Herpes infection and you can catch it!"

He continued touching *BJ*, saying, "I don't believe you." He unzipped his pants and lubricated himself before raping *BJ*. During the rape and before he reached a climax he pulled the pillowcase up and began kissing *BJ*.

Afterwards he smiled at his hooded victim and he told he her heard something out by his "truck" and went to the window and stood for a while. He then went into the bath, turned on the water and washed himself.

When he had gone through her purse and only found change he asked her were her money was, when she didn't answer his rhetorical question, he threw the change on the floor. You know, "I'm a neighbor of yours... I've been watching you!"

Leaving the bedroom he said, "I'm going out on the patio to see if it is safe to leave." He turned off the A/C fan on his way down the hall.

When *BJ* didn't hear any more noise she pulled off the pillowcase, untied her hands and got out of bed. In the living room the floor was cold on her feet. She found the front door still locked, then noticed the cold air was coming from the kitchen, the kitchen window was still open. The screen was no longer in place so she closed and locked the window, put her flower pots back on the window sill, then left her apartment to call police to her Willow Creek Apartment.

[NB: Complainant did have a Herpes infection. Did the FBR contract it, did he then expose his next thirteen rape victims to this communicable disease?][55]

FBR's *Month-At-A-Glance 1976*
Friday, April 16: Houston
(Good Friday is circled)

The Dallas Morning News
Sunday, April 18, 1976

Since my April Fool's Day meeting with Chief Dixon the year before, I had only used the term Friendly Burglar-Rapist around Tom Covington, Jim Bryan and the P&R Crew and Investigator Crowder, as I recall.

While the first page of an O/I R was considered publicly accessible information, neither the public nor the newspaper's police-beat reporters were privy to supplemental police reports.

---

[55] In retrospect, it should have been protocol that all officers and investigators be made aware of this potential health hazard and mandatory that any criminal assault complainant (particularly those believed to be victims of the FBR) be advised that they may have been exposed to the Herpes virus and any 'rape kit' include examination for and lab tests for the primary sexually transmitted diseases.

It is my opinion someone other than 'the three amigos' had talked to a reporter with *The Dallas Morning News*. I had my suspicions who that might be.

It is also possible, by this time, that a reporter 'got hold of', 'saw' or was 'told' about Deputy Chief Fannin's, memo (Subject: "Friendly Burglar" Rapes) of November 7, 1975. (See page 139.)

Thereafter my *nom de guerre* for this guy (The Friendly Burglar-Rapist) became his supernumerary moniker in the Dallas papers, on TV and Radio, along with "Friendly Rapist" and "Friendly Burglar".

Dallas, Office of Central Division Analyst
8:15 am Monday, April 19, 1976

When I got in that Monday morning, the previous days' O/IRs and SRs from Friday the 16th, Saturday the 17th and Sunday the 18th were filling my inbox. When I got to the SR for *PCA*'s rape, I just shook my head. Crowder's SR for the *PCA*'s offense that occurred on April 5th was dated April 16, 1976. The fact that the SR was written ten days after her interview of 4-6-76 did not bother me. I had no way of knowing all that she was doing in terms of follow-up on all the cases she had been assigned or how backed up her paperwork might be. And, it did seem that Reba was making several contacts with the complainants before summarizing those contacts in an SR. What did bother me was the juxtaposition of this SR with the two 'kissing' anomalies in Offenses Number 39 and 40. I say anomalies, because no one had mentioned or reported the FBR suspect *per se* 'kissing' them before. It may have happened and like other sensitive issues regarding being violated, the complainant may not have wanted to admit to having been kissed.

Even faced with previous cases where MO markers pointed to a single suspect, the man Tom and I called the FBR, Crowder had become rather couched, we thought, in her avoidance of the FBR moniker.

This SR started off, couched, like others. Inv. Crowder wrote:

"Compl contacted at scene of offense shortly after it occurred & also several times since. There are similarities between this & other area rapes, probably committed by several susp -- lumped together and collectively called friendly Burglar Rapes. This offense committed by the susp that likes to french kiss his victims, whom I have dubbed "The Tongue Twister". Blood Type A. $10 taken from purse. No beard or mustache. Hands smelled of fish. Compl. lives with her boyfriend at apt. [*sic*] but he was out of town. His name and hers are on the mail box with first initial only, there [*sic*] last name. Several susps. checked out with negative results - No ID by compl. Suspend! Investigation will continue.

As I reread Investigator Crowder's words: *"There are similarities between this and other area rapes, probably committed by several suspects lumped together and collectively called Friendly Burglar Rapes. This offense committed by the susp that likes to french kiss his victims, whom I have dubbed "The Tongue Twister"*, I could not stop shaking my head.

When Tom came in, I handed him the supplement and said, "Tom, you won't believe this, Reba's dubbed him 'The Tongue Twister'."

Tom read it and harrumphed, grabbed a red pen, circled the words "The Tongue Twister" and scrawled on the report: *"Dummy -- he's still the FBR"*.

It was obvious to us, that Investigator Crowder still did not believe our information... even after we had almost forty cases we had identified involving the FBR. In our minds Reba had 'jumped the shark'.

Just because *the Suspect* kissed and was told on, and was reported to have no mustache there were too many MO markers in this offense to have concluded this was not the FBR who just happened to have kissed two of his victims and may (possibly) have shaved off his mustache. As for the 'fish smell' who knows what that means!

Equally obvious to me was that Inv. Crowder was entitled to her own opinions and conclusions, even if they varied from mine or Tom's. In fact, neither of us knew exactly what Reba's opinions and conclusion were. She would not discuss the case or share her thoughts with us. All we had to go on were her investigative supplemental reports and the words she used to describe her efforts and conclusions. Still, we thought she had 'jumped the shark'.

Author Note: *Looking back, though I didn't specifically make note of it at the time... and though I entertained the thought early-on (as a possibility) we never had one case that Tom or I really thought belonged to or could be substantiated as a 'copy-cat'. Even with all the media reports about these rapes and break-ins no-one was out there perpetrating rapes by copying the MO of the FBR. More importantly, after the arrest of Guy William Marble Jr there were no more rapes attributable to FBR MO markers.*

Chapter 11

Close Calls Happen

FBR's *Month-At-A-Glance 1976*
Wednesday, April 21:   Payday

Dallas, Northeast Patrol Division, Beat 242
11:45 pm Wednesday, April 21, 1976
Offense Number 42

MB, A WHITE female forty-nine, living at #127, 7723 Willowvine in the Willow Creek Apartments, was lucky and called police immediately. Within six minutes of the event Officer G.J. Fernandez #3282, working beat 214, was dispatched on a Criminal Trespass complaint on an adjacent beat.

Arriving within minutes, Fernandez was told by *MB*, that she was a homemaker, sitting at home alone in her living room typing. Hearing a noise, like someone was on her patio removing a window screen, she got up and saw a white male approximately twenty-five, five-ten, 180lbs, with blond curly hair wearing a white shirt standing on her patio. As soon as he saw her, he ran.

FBR's *Month-At-A-Glance 1976*
Thursday, April 22:   skatebds 11:00

FBR's *Month-At-A-Glance 1976*
Friday, April 23:   10:00 Crohn
                          1:30 Bruce
                          3:00 Bailey

FBR's *Month-At-A-Glance 1976*
Monday, April 26:   TACT Program

FBR's *Month-At-A-Glance 1976*
Thursday, April 29:   Tact

Dallas, Northeast Patrol Division, Beat 243
4:50 am Friday, May 7, 1976
Offense Number 43

ANOTHER CLOSE CALL—almost. Two stewardesses, one twenty-four *SLD* and one twenty-nine *GLI* were roommates living at the Woodscape Apartments, number 1041 at 8209 Meadow Road. Fortunately for *GLI*, she was not at home.

SLD was in the front bedroom getting ready for work when her bedroom door opened and she saw a white male, 24-28 years old, six-foot, 190 lbs. and clean shaven standing in the doorway. *SLD* let out a blood-curdler. Her scream scared off the FBR who escaped through the open front window he'd come in.

Counting her blessings that nothing was taken, she thanked Officer G.H. Wren for getting there so quickly. Officer Wren, badge #3618, wrote up this O/I R as a Criminal Trespass (30.05).

The next day *SLD* had to call the police again. That morning, again preparing to go to work, she realized she was missing something: a one carat brilliant-cut diamond in a Tiffany setting on an eleven millimeter wide, Florentine yellow-gold band, valued at $1,000.00.

It was the Friendly Burglar-Rapist's first 'big' haul?

Dallas, Northeast Patrol Division, Beat 256
2:00 am Monday, May 10, 1976
Offense Number 44 (R-30)
FBR Print #7

THE BAVARIAN STEAKHOUSE on Southwestern and Central Expressway was only minutes away from the Settlement III Apartment complex at 5951 Melody Lane. The five-foot-seven, green-eyed and redheaded *MJH*, a hostess at the steakhouse, arrived home from work at 11:00pm, climbed the stairs to her apartment and opened the door to number 210.

MJH quickly changed out of her work clothes, put on a caftan robe, popped into bed to watch TV and promptly fell asleep.

Once inside, the Friendly Burglar-Rapist retrieved a knife from the kitchen and set about cutting all the phone cords. In the hallway he turned the A/C fan to 'On' and headed into his victim's bedroom. A little lamp next to the bed was on. She was asleep on her side, the TV was not off. He stepped over to the lamp and turned it off then climbed on top of *MJH*.

She awakened immediately to the soft-sounding man's voice; "Don't make any noise. I won't hurt you; I never hurt anybody." But, to literally get his point across he added, "I have a knife, don't make any noise."

She could feel the knife sticking her in the back as she lay on her side facing the window. To add to her frustration the lamp she had left on was off and she could not see her attacker as it was. He held his hand over the side of her face and said, "Don't look at me till the pillowcase is in place," then he put a pillowcase over her head and tied her hands. "Now be quiet," he reminded.

"Where's your purse?" With her answer in hand he left the bedroom and scoured the apartment. He took the twenty-two dollars he found in her purse before returning to the bedroom via the bathroom.

"Stand up," he commanded as he stood beside the bed. As she stood up he took the hem of her caftan and pulled it over her head, leaving her naked. He fondled her breasts and body and then told her lie back on the bed. "Keep your hands over your head," he instructed.

Sitting at the end of the bed he took off his clothes as he talked about her continuing to be quiet and then used some of her body lotion to lubricate his erection.

In spite of his warnings to keep her hands over her head, she brought them to her face and covered her eyes while he raped her. After his climax he got up and went to the bathroom where she could hear the water running. The water shut off and he came back into her bedroom. *MJH* could hear him putting on his clothes.

Tentatively *MJH* asked, "Let me know when you are ready to leave?"

"You'll know when I am gone." He got up and came toward her and grasped her wrists and unloosened the phone cords he tied her with.

[NB: This behavior not reported during any prior assaults.]

When she heard the door slam she got up and gave a tug on the cords and they come loose. In the living room she found the door ajar. She went to the phone in the kitchen; its cord had been cut. She went to the bathroom and found the cord to that phone had also been cut, as well as the one in the bedroom where now, with the light on, she found on the end of her bed her bottle of hand lotion.

It had been twenty minutes since her rapist had awakened her. He was gone and *MJH*, at a neighbor's, called the police who dispatched Officer N. Abney #3222 at 2:21am.

P.E.S. Investigator's (RA Pettie 2514 / RA Furr 2377), in their SR dated 5-10-75, examined the latent prints they lifted from the scene and wrote: "Latent print lifted from telephone belongs to FRB (FBR) - suspect. Latent print is #7 of suspect's print."

In his SR, dated 5-16-76, Investigator E.N. Stansell #1089 wrote: "This comp left town after the offense occurred and did not return until 5-12-76 when she was contacted at her apt. at 9:20pm. She cannot identify the suspect and advised he spoke very little during the attack. P.E.S. lifted prints and classified the suspect as the now famous "FBR". Sally Williams advised the blood type of Suspect is "A." The offense will remain pending as there are no present workable leads."

FBR's *Month-At-A-Glance 1976*
Tuesday, May 11:   3:00 IABC
                         ~~4:00~~

FBR's *Month-At-A-Glance 1976*
Wednesday, May 12:   Programs →

FBR's *Month-At-A-Glance 1976*
Thursday, May 13:   B.s.

Chapter 12

Reba's On Board?

Dallas, Northeast Patrol Division, Beat 242
5:45 am Friday, May 14, 1976
Offense Number 45 (R-31)
FBR Prints #7 & #8
See Appendix A - Newspaper Article # 29a

C.E. MAXWELL #2768 and L.L. Barbee #2945 were patrolling beat 214, located several miles south of beat 242. It was just over an hour till their change-of-shift when they got the call at 6:20am; an aggravated rape at 10806 Stone Canyon Road, apartment 2118.

Neither officer said it out loud, but they both thought, *Guess we won't be getting off on time today, partner.*

The Cobblestone Apartments were bathed in the full moon's light, though it was edging toward the horizon. Cool for a morning in the middle of May, the fifty-three degree temperature combined with the eleven mile an hour northwest wind felt good to the officers. Their eyes were heavy with the fatigue of the constant vigilance of the last seven hours of night patrol; straining to read license plates at a distance or see house numbers in the dark while on-coming car lights extinguished their night vision if they didn't close an eye or turn their heads quickly enough.

Aware of the Friendly Burglar-Rapist and his general description, they both, without prompting, scouted every car, (moving or parked), every nook and cranny for a possible suspect leaving the area as they approached the complainant's address.

They met the very distraught complainant *CML*, a white female twenty-four who stated that she worked as a secretary at Xerox on Stemmons Expressway. Officers Maxwell and Barbee gently coaxed her to tell her story. Officer Maxwell wrote:

COMP STATES THAT AT APPROX THE ABOVE TIME SHE WAS AWAKENED BY A MAN PUTTING HIS HANDS OVER HER FACE. SUSP STATED, "DON'T MOVE. ALL I

WANT IS YOUR PURSE & SOME MONEY. BE QUIET & I WON'T HURT YOU." SUSPS THEN PLACED A PILLOW CASE OVER COMP'S HEAD & TIED HER TO THE BED WITH AN ELECTRICAL CORD. COMP STATED THE SUSP THEN RUMMAGED THRU THE APT, RETURNED TO THE BEDROOM & RAPED HER. FURTHER DETAILS NOT AVAILABLE AT THIS TIME AS COMP IS EMOTIONALLY UPSET. COMP STATES THAT SHE WOULD PREFER TO GIVE FULL DETAILS TO A FEMALE OFFICER. SUPPLEMENT WILL NEED TO BE MADE AT A LATER DATE. EVELYN CROWDER, CRIMES AGAINST PERSON, WAS NOTIFIED BY OFFICER MAXWELL AT 6:30AM.

P.E.S. Inv. B.T. Beddingfield 1513 was at the scene on 5-14-76 and completed his SR on the same date. His report, in part, states: "Print from window screen and telephone in Comp's bedroom same as (# 7 & 8) prints lifted from other rapes in the NE Dallas area."

Investigator R.E. Crowder #2894 from Crimes Against Persons met *CML* at Parkland Memorial Hospital to follow up on the complaint regarding the call from Officer Maxwell:

"Compl. contacted 5-14-76 at PMH & again 5-15-76 at a friends apt. Compl. states that at approx 2am she heard 3 distinct taps on a window. That they woke her up but she again fell asleep & did not awaken again until susps placed his hands on her face. She doesn't remember a knife. Compl states he had a calm, soothing voice, his body smelled stale & at one point he turned on the lights & Compl believes he was inspecting her vagina. Susp rummaged the apt & Compls purse, raped her & said he wouldn't leave right away because someone was out there. Compl states susps also had bad breath & cold hands. Compl. did <u>not</u> see susps face or body. Prints have been rapped[56] as same as susp who has committed a number of other North Dallas Rapes. Suspend. Investigation will continue."

Author Note: *This was Investigator Evelyn Reba Crowder's last FBR rape case... The above quoted SR was written up on May 25, 1976 and as she notes, the FBR's prints (#7 & #8) were identified. It would appear that Inv. Crowder was still not convinced. I do not know if she ever believed or looked at all the other cases (Attempt Rapes, Prowlers, Burglaries & etc.) Tom and I attributed to the FBR.*

It appeared Investigator Crowder was only acquainted with the Criminal Assault cases she had been assigned or for which she was responsible as the lead investigator. Even then, for example, when the FBR's prints had been 'rapped', as on this her last FBR case, she would not 'aver' to using his nom de guerre... Instead she relinquished her hunt for the suspect Tom and I knew to be the FBR.

This letting go is understandable. Being on call 24-7 is much tougher than it sounds. For starters it means missing sleep, days off, family and other obligations; that alone is stressful, then add to it an ever increasing caseload with seemingly no break either by the perpetrator or in your attempts to stop the perpetrator's criminal acts, much less catch him... and Investigator Crowder had been working this case for 18 months.

---

[56] **Rap** or **rapped**, a term used in the criminal justice system and law enforcement to indicate a person's legal associations with 'the system'. Though I have found no definitive early use re: it's etymology other than as a 'charge' or 'rebuke', particularly a criminal charge: "he got the rap for the robbery," "he got a bum rap," (a false charge), "he beat the rap," (was acquitted of the charge). That is what I have always known "rap" to mean: an allegation or charge. A rap sheet (a police record) then was a list of the charges, i.e. arrests and if convicted, convictions tied to an individual. When the term "rapped" is used, it is meant that something or someone has been identified with or tied to a crime. Used as above by Inv. Crowder, "Prints have been rapped," means the FBR's fingerprints found at the scene of the crime matched other FBR prints previously identified. Whether "rap" is an acronym for "Record of Arrest and Prosecution" is unknown. I find no credible source, such as OED, to confirm this, although this use is found in Wikipedia and in general terms elsewhere on the internet.

Later, in a police department Division Crime Analyst survey (sent by Officer B.B. Smoot) that *CML* filled out regarding the offense, she clarified that she was a 'color analyst' at Xerox. She described herself: blond hair, blue eyes, Caucasian, one-hundred-fifteen pounds, five-foot-five. Also she amplified what her assailant said to her: "I'm just a burglar; I'm not going to hurt you, just tell me where your purse is. Do you have a dog or cat or guns in the apartment? If you make any noise I'll hurt your roommate." He also told her, "There's a pick-up out front, I'll let you know when I'm leaving."

He did eventually leave, having stolen *CML*'s sense of security and the money he found in her purse.

We also learned that he made entry through her kitchen window, that he used one of their kitchen knives to cut the various telephone cords and one of those cords was used to bind *CML*'s wrists and tie her to the bed.

Her roommate at their Cobblestone Apartments, number 1117, was *CP*, a white female twenty-five, who also worked at Xerox as a sales rep. *CP* described herself: blond hair-short, five-foot-five, one hundred-twenty pounds. Luckily for *CP* she slept through the rape of her roommate; undisturbed and did not see or hear a thing.

Dallas, Northeast Patrol Division, Beat 214
1:30 am Monday, May 17, 1976
Offense Number 46

SIXTY YEAR-OLD, *GS* of Gainesville, Texas was in Dallas visiting her twenty-four year-old granddaughter, *BMS*, who lived in the Corners East Apartments at 6071 Village Glenn, number 3225.

Enjoying the sixty-five degree cool summer night as the Friendly Burglar-Rapist stepped between moon-shadows, he found the window of number 3225 unlocked and went in.

Alone and astonished Grandma *GS* had been asleep on the floor behind the table in the dinning area when she saw a white male that she guessed was thirty, with full but not long blonde hair, who was of medium build and wearing blue jeans. The man came out of her granddaughter's bedroom, down the hall and crossed the living room to the patio's sliding glass door and unlocked it. He slid it open a bit. *GS* watched him walking through the apartment, being very careful not to make any noise. She could see he was carrying something in his mouth that looked dark, but she could not make it out. She was barely breathing and, like the intruder, trying not to make a sound.

She watched him go into the bathroom. She took a breath, he hadn't seen her! Again she watched him come into the main part of the apartment and finally he saw her lying on the floor.

A quizzical thought passed briefly through the intruder's mind before he quickly walked down the hallway, into the bedroom and closed the door.

Seconds later he was safe. As he headed to another apartment complex to try his luck he wondered about the jewelry box, what it contained. He had opened it but had no time to see if it contained anything he wanted.

> [**NB**: The previously unobserved witness (*GS*) gave us insight that we had not had before; specific confirmation of what we were sure was happening (regardless whether a criminal assault occurred) when the FBR entered an apartment: 1) he was stealthy and quiet, 2) he set up his escape route, 3) he pilfered or rummaged through the apt before cutting phone cords or waking his victim and 4) given the chance, flight was his option, not fight! I just hopped none of his victims ever cornered him, I felt, Tom felt he would be dangerous, even deadly.]

FBR's *Month-At-A-Glance 1976*
Monday, May 17:   Denise / out

Dallas, Northeast Patrol Division, Beat 212
2:10 am Tuesday, May 18, 1976
Offense Number 47
FBR Prints #1, #2, #3

THE RAPIST ENTERED the living room window of apartment 1004 in the Willowick Apartments at 6010 Sandhurst Lane. On the apartment's south side after removing the screen and prying up the window, he entered and then unlocked the front door. It hadn't been all that easy. He had to move potted plants used as a hedge in front of the window. He had already secured a little darkness by unscrewing several lights in the area, but he'd had to hide in the lee of shadows from the hunchback moon as several residents walked by in what was an unusually cool clear night for mid-May.

It was a two bedroom apartment occupied by three white females: *CLM* a twenty-three year-old, five-foot-one, ninety pound, blonde-haired, blue-eyed clerk in a downtown engineering firm; *SKM* a twenty-one year-old, five-foot-six, one hundred-fifteen pound, blonde-haired, gray-eyed Southern Methodist University student; and *MJM* a twenty-one year-old, five-foot-eight, one hundred-forty pound, brown-haired, green-eyed paralegal at a law firm on Main street.

SKM was out of town, leaving *CLM* and *MJM* to face the Friendly Burglar-Rapist.

He was in the apartment ratting around, looking in drawers and cabinets, opening the refrigerator and pilfering their purses, pocketing the cash he found and scoping-out their driver's licenses.

The first bedroom he went into was empty, but he found another telephone and a pair of chrome scissors. He used the scissors to cut the phone cord, taking both with him.

He was in a quandary as he approached the closed door of the second bedroom. He'd found two driver's licenses, but three names. Were there two roommates or three? If one bedroom was empty who was behind the closed door? In the hallway he tripped the A/C fan lever to 'On' then cautiously opened the bedroom door. No lights were on, it was dark but he could hear breathing, the slight stirring of movement didn't faze him.

Then the lights flashed on. *CLM* who had turned on her nightstand light was staring right at him and the woman in the other bed was stirring.

He did not hesitate, he ran. He was out the now unlocked front door before *MJM* was fully awake. The perspiration and fright that was popping out of Friendly Burglar-Rapist was cooled by the fifty-seven degree outside air as he ran to safety.

P.E.S. Inv.'s B.E. Barnes 1552 and B.G. Brown 1057 were called to the scene by the reporting officer M.J. Harrison #3317 who felt this Burglary offense had the MO of the FBR. Their SR, dated 5-18-76, proved Harrison's instinct correct, in part it read: "Partial prints lifted from screen that was removed. Partial print from outside light shade. Prints lifted same as Friendly Rapist at other locations. Collected phone wire ends."

Dallas, Northeast Patrol Division, Beat 214
2:00 am Wednesday, May 19, 1976
Meet Complainant

THREE MONTHS EARLIER, almost to the day and at the same time of the morning, *LR* had been the victim of the Friendly Burglar-Rapist. She still lived in the Willow Creek Apartments, same apartment, 126, at 7731 Willowstream. This morning she would not be a victim, but a witness and hopefully a spoiler.

The last three months had not been easy. The memories of her ordeal were still fresh. She knew now that they would never go away, but understood, as friends had persuaded her, time would precede recovery and a new perspective. She hadn't yet achieved a new perspective and was having trouble sleeping, especially between the hours before and after the time, three months before, when the clocks had stopped.

This morning she was again watching the clock move toward 2:00am and decided to get up to check the windows and doors. She walked toward her bedroom window, focused on the locks. In the living room she pulled on the sliding glass door to her patio; it was locked. She unlocked it and tugged it open and then looked out into the courtyard. She was dumfounded and shocked to see an approximately 6' foot tall white male in his twenties with blond, curly, shoulder length hair, wearing a sweatsuit & tennis shoes jump out of the bushes beside her neighbor's window.

LR shouted, "STOP!" But the man ran away.

LR called police and she gave officers M.R. Scoggins #3601 and L.T. Page #2710 the description of the man she had seen, but regretfully told them, "I never saw his face."

Dallas, Northeast Patrol Division, Beat 256
3:00 am Wednesday, May 19, 1976
Offense Number 48
FBR Prints #2, #3 & Right Palm

HIGH SCHOOL TEACHER, *BIB*, aged twenty-eight who
described herself as five-foot-six, one hundred-thirty pounds
with blond hair and blue eyes, was asleep in the bedroom with
her boyfriend who had been staying at *BIB*'s apartment (number
1536) every night since the first of February.

The Season's Apartments located at 6257 Melody Lane were
part of his regular loop when in this area; so many open
windows. He moved the cat's bowls from the windowsill and set
them down outside. In *BIB*'s kitchen The Friendly Burglar-
Rapist made himself at home, unlocking the front door then
checking out the contents of the refrigerator. He saw *BIB*'s
brown leather shoulder strap purse, picked it up and carried it
down the hallway.

In *BIB*'s bedroom he saw two figures in bed, one a man. The
FBR turned on his heels and left the apartment.

Outside it was clear and cool, sixty degrees with a mild
breeze out of the east southeast. In a shadow cast by the waxing
moon he stopped and opened *BIB*'s purse, lifted the wallet and
grabbed the cash he saw, fifteen dollars. He dropped her purse in
the grass and walked away. He didn't realize there was another
thirty-seven dollars elsewhere in the purse, not to mention a half-
dozen credit cards, her Social Security card, driver's license, two
sets of keys and her check book.

P.E.S. Inv. J.J. Shubzda 3357 reported in his SR, dated
5-19-76, in part: "Partial Palms & F.P.'s off window sill. One F.P.
identified as #2 finger of friendly rapist."

BIB's purse and its contents, a haul any modern day ID thief,
or any unscrupulous person, would have made a fortune with.
was gone. Three days later a neighbor would return her purse
minus only the fifteen dollars from her wallet. *BIB* called Inv.
J.R. Raef #3080 to inform him that her purse had been returned
intact and asking him to cancel the stolen report on all her credit
cards and other property.

Dallas, Northeast Patrol Division, Beat 256
4:00 am Wednesday, May 19, 1976
Offense Number 49

THE TEMPERATURE HAD dropped almost three degrees in the last hour to the fifty-seven degree range, but the east southeast wind in the clear moonlit sky had only strengthened to eight miles per hour.

Three roommates, all females, shared apartment #161 at 6219 Shady Brook Lane in the 250 unit Village Hill Apartments.

DG had come home at 2am, one of her other two roommates was away; PT was asleep in her room. *DG* changed clothes and sat in the living room watching TV till at least three when she fell asleep on the couch.

Apparently, the Friendly Burglar-Rapist had come into *DG*'s apartment while she was still awake. He took a pillow from the bed and stepped into a closet where he removed the pillow from its case and waited.

When all was quiet he came out of the closet and ransacked *PT*'s purse, while she slept, but found nothing worth taking. He cut her phone line before going into the adjoining bath and into the other bedroom, which was unoccupied, where he cut that phone line and rummaged through the drawers. He repeated these actions in the third bedroom.

In the living room/den area he found *DG* asleep on the couch. In preparation he dropped the blue pillow case on the back of the couch; it slipped off and fell to the floor as he headed to the front door. He unlocked the door and pulled it part-way open. In her purse he discovered thirty-five dollars that immediately went into his pocket.

In the kitchen he cut the phone line and made a loop with it for his couch-sleeping soon-to-be rape victim. He opened the fridge, closed it and began opening and closing the cabinets.

Roused by the minor clicks and clacks of sound in the kitchen *DG* raised up on the couch and saw what she told Officers M.R. Scoggins #3601 and L.T. Page #2710 was a white male, 25 to 26, five-foot-ten to six foot and of medium build wearing a sheer type mask on his face standing in her kitchen going through the cabinets.

He heard her sharp intake of breath and turned and headed toward the couch and *DG*. He tried to cover her mouth with his hands and she started screaming… and kept screaming.

In three long strides he was at the partially opened front door, then gone into the moonlit night.

Inv. M.L. Kidd 3094 wrote in his SR, dated 5-25-76: "Investigating officer contacted complainant and after talking with her it appears that this is another case of the friendly rapist. She stated that when CSS arrived they asked if the telephone cord had been cut. They checked and it had been cut. She further stated that she found her pillow in the closet of her roommate who was not home that night and the pillowcase was by the couch where she had been sleeping. A screen was missing from the bedroom of the roommate (who) was not home that night and it has not been found. It appears that is how he gained entry to the apartment. The fact that the pillow was found in that bedroom closet makes it appear that he might have been inside the apartment waiting prior to the time the complainant came home. She came home at 2AM and she stated that she was still awake at 3AM and never did hear any noise such as someone breaking in. Recommend this offense be suspended at this time due to lack of workable leads. However, investigation is still continuing because of the large number of cases which point to this one suspect."

FBR's *Month-At-A-Glance 1976*
Thursday, May 20:   DENVER ___
(Line/arrow indicates Denver TABC May 20-26)

FBR's *Month-At-A-Glance 1976*
Wednesday, May 26:   DENVER ___
(Line/arrow indicates Denver TABC May 20-26)

Chapter 13

Stage Five?

Dallas, Northeast Patrol Division, Beat 212
5:45 am Sunday, May 30, 1976
Offense Number 50

THE SIX-FOOT FENCE was not an obstacle once he had noticed the sliding glass door open behind its screen door. On the patio he tested the screen, it was locked. He sliced through the thin metal screening next to the lock and then slipped the lock; he was in. Stepping gingerly he made it to the front door, unlocked it and left it almost ajar. He quietly found the nearest phone, cut the cord and carried it to the bathroom where he found a bottle of body lotion. There were two bedrooms, two sleeping women; which to choose?

Once in the bedroom of choice, he encountered the sleeping *SB* a white twenty-three year-old accountant for a downtown firm. He approached her bed then dove on top of *SB* who was sleeping on her back.

Immediately awake, *SB* felt the weight of her assailant pressing into her body. They were eyeball to eyeball. Her shaken partial description was given to Officer R.L. Newell #3476 as a white male five-foot-nine or ten, light complexion, twenties to thirties with a muscular build... and he had something like a nylon stocking over his head.

"Roll over; I don't want to hurt you. Don't look at me!"

SB **refused to obey** his commands **and struggled with him** in bed, **trying to get him off of her. Then she felt the right side of her mouth explode with pain as his elbow busted her lip.**

SB immediately began screaming for her roommate who was asleep in the next bedroom. Foiled again, The Friendly Burglar-Rapist dropped the wooden handled steak knife in his panic and ran for the front door of apartment 114 of the Spanish Keys Apartments at 5932 Sandhurst.

The apartment, on the north side of the complex, was only steps away from Sandhurst but the escaping FBR ran east toward Amesbury under a moonless canopy of scattered to mostly cloudy skies into the eighty-five percent humidity of a south southeast, seventeen mile an hour wind. This Sunday morning was heating up quickly, it was nearing seventy-four degrees and in the quickly lightening skies, with sunrise still thirty minutes away, jogging became easier for those running to keep in shape and those running to keep out of jail.

This was an FBR first. The 'busted lip' the complainant received in her struggle with the FBR, whether it was intentional or unintentional on his part was, his first act of violence, in terms of 'battery"; striking of blows. On Dr. David Paul's six-step scale of criminal escalation from rape to murder, the FBR had just reached step five. Only time and circumstances would dictate, but the **FBR was now only one misstep from murder.**

Dallas, Northwest Patrol Division, Beat 553
3:00 am Thursday, June 4, 1976
Offense Number 51

WAS IT, OR wasn't it the Friendly Burglar-Rapist? Officer W.M. Manson #3506 didn't speculate, he just took the statement of the complainant, ML a white female, age 25 who lived in apartment 1135 in the Trails Apartments at 3147 Chapel Creek. He left the speculation to others.

Overhead the moon was either half-full or half-empty, it was a balmy night with calm winds, smoke hanging in the seventy-one degree air that was holding onto a humidity of eighty-four percent. The suspect description given by *ML* was that of a w/m/ 20's, 5'9" to 5'10", slender build, 160 lbs, light brown medium length hair, wearing a long sleeve blue shirt (denim material) and white jeans. The M/O was listed as "pried open screen of dinning room window, which was open, used kitchen knife & exit same."

In section 64 of Mason's O/I R, which was listed as: 29.03 Aggravated Robbery, with a loss of twenty dollars in cash. His narrative provided the following:

> Comp stated that she was asleep in bed at above time and when above listed suspect jumped on her (and) brought a knife against her side. Suspect told Comp not to yell or he would kill her. Suspect told Comp to keep her eyes closed he then took a pillow case and placed it over her head. Suspect told Comp that he was going to screw her and that he had watched her for sometime and

that he wanted her body. Suspect then began running his hand over Comp's body, Comp in the meantime continued speaking to the Suspect trying to persuade him not to go thru with the act. Suspect spoke with a soft voice and he didn't appear nervous, he appeared quite calm and sure of himself. Comp stated that Suspect's hands were soft that Suspect had no body odor and was clean shaven. The Suspect apparently knew his way around the apartment, was able to locate light switches without any difficulty. Comp was able to get a make on the Suspect (description listed above) when Suspect entered the bathroom. Suspect came back with a container of Vaseline Intensive Care Lotion, his intentions were apparently to use it in the rape. Comp continued to talk to Suspect all through this. Suspect did not rape Comp, instead he masturbated while seated along side of the Comp on the bed. Suspect then told Comp not to look or move from the bed. He then went to the Comp's roommate's bedroom and took a purse and brought it out to the dinning [*sic*] room. There along with the Comp's purse he emptied the contents and took the above listed money. Suspect returned and told Comp he was leaving and that he was going to do so by the front door. Suspect told Comp not to move. Comp heard the dinning [*sic*] room table and chairs knock together, no further noises. Comp after a few minutes got up and called the police. Entry was apparently made thru the dinning [*sic*] room window, they had been unlocked and left up, screens on them only. Suspect had pried off the screen and carried it away from the location about thirty feet. Suspect then entered apartment went to kitchen and took a knife from a drawer then jumped Comp. Front door was found unlocked but closed. Comp believes the Suspect left by the window. Suspect took knife with him.

Was it, or wasn't it the Friendly Burglar-Rapist? Tom and I didn't speculate either. We read Officer Mason's report and counted enough of the FBR's M/O markers to conclude yes, it is more likely this is the FBR than not.

Dallas, Northeast Patrol Division, Beat 242
1:30 am Tuesday, June 8, 1976
Offense Number 52

GUESS, GUESS AGAIN. The waxing moon was getting fatter and lower on the horizon. The cicadas were noisy in the trees and were competing with the whirring of June bugs in the grass. The high humidity made the seventy-one degrees feel warmer.

It was forty-three minutes after one in the morning when Officer J.M. Hunter #2874, working element 214 got the burglary of a residence call on beat 242. He met the complainant, a white female, twenty-seven, at unit 105 in the Willow Creek Apartments at 7714 Willowvine and learned the offense had happened only fifteen minutes before he arrived.

Hunter was painfully aware of Friendly Burglar-Rapist offenses on his beat and the more than half-dozen similar incidents at the Willow Creek Apartments. When the complainant, JG, gave him the suspect's description, he was not surprised. He listed the suspect's M/O: PRIED SCREEN FR WEST SIDE WINDOW & CRAWLED THROUGH TO LIVING ROOM.

In the narrative section Officer Hunter wrote:

COMP WAS IN HER BEDROM WATCHING TV & HEARD A NOISE IN HALLWAY. AS SHE GOT OUT OF BED THE DR HANDLE TURNED. THEN SHE PULLED ON THE DR & SUSP RAN FR THE HALL INTO THE LIVING RM. COMP CHASED SUSPS INTO LIVING ROOM & OBSERVED SUSP EXIT WEST SIDE WINDOW. SUSP HAD CUT TELEPHONE CORD IN THE KITCHEN & HAD RANSACKED THROUGHOUT HOUSE. COMP CALLED A GIRLFRIEND WHO PICKED HER UP & TOOK HER TO ANOTHER LOC BEFORE POLICE WERE CALLED. OFFS WERE UNABLE TO FIND SCREEN SUSP REMOVED FR WINDOW. CID 1144 CAME TO SCENE. DESCRIPTION OF SUSP: WM/ 20'S 511, 180 LBS, MED LENGTH BRN OR BLN HAIR COMBED OVER TO RGT SIDE, SHT SLEEVE WHITE SHIRT & LIGHT PANTS.

Listed in the stolen property section of his report was: Quan/ Description: TOP OF 2 PIECE BATHING SUIT; Where located: LOC DEN; Age: 6MOS; Value New: NEW $10; Value now: $2.

Author Note:
This was Investigator John Landers'
first FBR offense to 'catch'.

Dallas, Northeast Patrol Division, Beat 256
4:15 am Tuesday, June 8, 1976
Offense Number 53 (R-32)
FBR Prints #2, #3 & #6

TWO HOURS AND forty-five minutes later and two and a half miles to the southeast, the Friendly Burglar-Rapist was entering unit 2415 of The Seasons Apartments at 6232 Ridgecrest.

The white female (*JM*) in bed asleep was a twenty-five year-old registered nurse who worked at Methodist Hospital and described herself as being a half-inch over five feet tall, 115 lbs, short dark brown hair with hazel eyes and measurements of: "36"-"28"- "34½"; a figure she kept in check by belly dancing at Meara's school on Abrams Road.

In the presence of the Reporting Officers: D.D. Melacon #3760 and L.L. Barbee #2945 and Investigator John Landers #2445 Crimes Against Persons/CID, who arrived only minutes after the call went out, the complainant told her story.

The Friendly Burglar-Rapist mounted the fence surrounding the downstairs patio, looked around the patio and decided to forego the ground floor. He pulled himself up and over the balcony fencing of unit 2415. He slipped the lock on the sliding glass door and went into the living room. He froze as he knocked over some potted plants just inside the door.

Only momentarily roused, the complaint fell back asleep.

The FBR stepped over to the front door which he unlocked. In the kitchen he turned on the stove light, found some scissors and cut the cord from complainant's iron. In the hall, before entering the bathroom, he turned the A/C fan lever to 'On'. Closing the bathroom door he turned on the light and searched.

Having what he needed, lubricant, scissors, and something to tie his victim, he re-entered the complainant's bedroom.

This time his movements woke her, "Who's there?" *JM* asked.

He turned his head away, "I am a burglar, I have a knife, If you don't want to get hurt, don't look at me; turn your head away. Keep your eyes closed, turn over."

The complainant complied and turned over on her back. When he started to slip a pillowcase over her head, she protested, pleading and begging him not to cover her head, "I have claustrophobia."

He tied her hands with a cord he'd cut from her iron and told her, "you'll be able to get loose by yourself; I'm not going to tie you up tight."

With eyes squeezed shut she could hear the sound of scissor cutting and then felt them as he cut off her nightgown. She felt what she described as "large shears type scissors" slicing through her underwear.

He spent considerable time caressing her, running his hands up and down the complainant's sides but focused mainly on the fondling of her breasts.

When he was ready he squeezed the lotion out of its tube and rubbed it on the complainant's vulva. He put the tube on the bedside table then pushed down his pants and forced himself inside his victim. During the rape, that according to the complainant, lasted about two minutes, he told her "wrap your legs around me." When she did, he told her to squeeze, "that's good," he replied.

According to the complainant after he climaxed he got up, told her to "lay still" and roamed her apartment.

He went back to her bedside and again told her to be still, "I'm going to go quietly, I'm going to check the parking lot see if it's okay for me to leave."

She heard him open the refrigerator. (His half-drunk Coke was left on the counter.) She did not hear him leave.

After freeing herself, she said she found the front door had been left open, that all of her telephones had their wires cut, but that a bowl of change and a five dollar bill on the coffee table were left behind. Also two pairs of surgical scissors in the bathroom and a pair of large scissors lying in the living room appeared not to have been disturbed.

Some days later, after being referred to, and in the presence of, a female rape crisis counselor, the complainant (*JM*) reported that her assailant had not only raped her vaginally, but also anally. [See Dr. Paul's: Stage 3, pages 278-279, & 411.]

For Investigator John R. Landers 2445, this was his first FBR assignment and he hit the jackpot with three of the FBR's fingerprints being identified with this crime scene. John, an academy classmate of mine, was now in charge of the FBR investigation, taking over from Reba Crowder. There had been no FBR rape since her last FBR call-out May 14, 1976, although Tom and I had attributed seven (7) other (non-rape) offenses to the FBR in the 24-day interim. John would now inherit all the knowledge Tom and I possessed regarding FBR offenses.

Whether he chose to make use of it or us remained to be seen.

FBR's *Month-At-A-Glance 1976*
Wednesday, June 9:　　　BZ.
(unk info before BZ.)

FBR's *Month-At-A-Glance 1976*
Friday, Jun 11:　　Zale Foundation
　　　　　　(indecipherable comment)
　　　　　　Xerox

Dallas, Northeast Patrol Division, Beat 214
A Street Cop Perspective

COPS, EVERYDAY AND night, are working to protect the citizens of the city. In particular, as a patrol officer you develop a visceral relationship with your area of responsibility, your beat. You meet citizens in friendly and unfriendly circumstances that go from the ridiculous to the sublime, from literally the 'high' of rescuing a cat up a tree (not the sole purview of firemen) to witnessing the aftermath of a senseless murder.

I recently heard from retired Dallas officer **L.T. Page #2710.** His story is an example of the point above as well as an illustration of the idea of 'copy-cats' and helps debunk the idea that patrol officers were 'prompting' complainants that their rape was or might have been committed by the FBR.

Page said, every night, when I worked deep nights, at Northeast I believed that I was going to be the officer that captured the Friendly Rapist. Numerous bulletins had been distributed dealing with the suspect's MO and at the old forth-floor City jail there was a poster of the suspect's prints.

When he was not answering calls for service Page spent his time checking apartment complexes; rolling through with his vehicle's lights out or walking on-foot trying to catch the FBR. One such night a rape-in-progress-call was broadcast on the radio at the Willowcreek Apartments at Walnut Hill and Central. As luck and personal diligence would have it Lester Page "was in the complex when the call came out" and he "observed a suspect jump off a balcony and apprehended him."

The complainant told Lester the Friendly Rapist had tried to rape her and that he fled before he complete the act. "I was on such an adrenaline high," Lester said, "as I believed that I had caught the Friendly Rapist... and could not wait to get downtown with the suspect, who was not saying anything." Lester admitted his attention was split when the complainant went through her story which was a replay of the MO "used by the Friendly Rapist... in the local media." In addition Page said, "the complainant pointed out the suspect had written in lipstick on her bathroom mirror that he would return..." It didn't dawn on him (Page) at the time, Lester said, that "the suspect had never used lipstick on a mirror that he would return."

From a great 'high' to disappointment, Page found "on arrival at the forth-floor jail my suspect was quickly eliminated as the Friendly Rapist, as his prints did not match."

"The detective interviewing my silent suspect told him that he was being handled as a rape suspect. The suspect immediately opened up that he *was not* a rapist but *he was* stealing potted plants to resell. I returned to the scene and found the suspect's vehicle filled with potted plants!"

The suspect on the balcony was in the wrong place at the wrong time... fortunately, a thief was caught in-the-act. It could have been the FBR, unfortunately for the City of Dallas, its citizens and Officer Page it was not. Was the "Friendly Burglar-Rapist" having a detrimental affect on the women of Dallas, even those not personally assaulted? Yes! In the case of this complainant, a rather server affect; this very lonely woman, a DISD administrator, had made up her story to get attention and did not even know the suspect was on her balcony when she called police." Unfortunately, Page related, she "was later admitted to Terrell State Hospital for mental evaluation."

Chapter 14

The Disillusionment

Dallas, Central Patrol Division, Sector 110's
Sunday, June 13, 1976

AFTER ALMOST THREE years of stalking the FBR, working long hours, racking up more comp-time than I would be allowed to take, being frustrated by our constant head-bumping with investigators and supervisors, I was shunted off the FBR investigation. It was suggested that I rotate back to patrol. I took a transfer back to the streets for a short time.

Although I was back in patrol, I stayed in contact with Tom who continued our work on the FBR.

SUNRISE HAD BEEN at 6:18am. At 7:00am it was seventy-five degrees under mostly cloudy skies. It would reach ninety degrees by late afternoon. Though a southerly breeze was blowing at fifteen miles an hour, I kept the squad cars windows up and the AC on. It was a fine summer morning. It was Sunday. Working a one-man squad, I had been rolling through my beat in the sleepy neighborhoods of near East Dallas.

I was watching for things out of place, like abandoned stolen cars, as I patrolled the streets while most of the residents were still asleep. I checked all the Sunday-closed businesses on my beat, looking for open doors, signs of break-ins or persons loitering near; business-burglars like Sunday mornings.

Traffic was predictably light and after a couple of hours I decided to take a break for breakfast before preparing for 'church activities'. Sunday morning was often the time we received calls from church officials to report they had been broken into the night before; so far, no such calls had come in. Additionally cars parking in church parking lots were vulnerable to car-burglars while their owners were attending services, likewise residential-burglars like to do home break-ins while the residents went to church.

After breakfast, I would be cruising church parking lots and the residential neighborhoods.

I was working the 110's and hungry, I went to my favorite little breakfast spot on Greenville Avenue for a Signal 50. I had scrambled eggs, hash browns, bacon, toast and coffee. When I walked back out to my car, it was nearing eighty degrees. I mentally remarked on what a great day it was and how good I felt. I cleared off my Signal 50 with the dispatcher and headed south on Greenville Avenue.

As I approached the Ross Avenue intersection there was one car in front of me when the light turned red. There was a sign on the stanchion ahead that read: No Turn on Red. (The city had only recently begun to allow a right-turn-on red.) This intersection was an exception. It was not a typical 'square' four-way intersection. On the left Ross Avenue approached Greenville Avenue from the east, but as it crossed Greenville, it turned to the southwest.

The car in front of me, a sedan, didn't even pause, it just turned right and headed southwest on Ross Avenue.

I had been having a great morning, it was quiet. The bad guys were sleeping-off their weekend and the good guys were futzing around their houses or getting ready for church. I was not mentally prepared for what happened next. I should have been. I knew better, but the tranquility of the spring-like Sunday morning had lulled me to sleep—so to speak.

I could see the driver up ahead was male, a female was in the front passenger seat and an unknown passenger, maybe a young girl, in the back seat. I checked my watch as I reached down, without looking, to flip on the squad car's red lights.

A number of things had occurred almost simultaneously. I saw the light on the intersection stanchion turn from yellow to red before the car reached the intersection. I saw the car fail to stop and continue making a right turn against the light. I thought, *church, a family going to church, probably comes this way every Sunday morning and just didn't realize he couldn't make a right on red here, that he's gotta wait for the green arrow to turn right... he's just not paying attention.*

I made the decision that I would just stop the man, bring it to his attention, that he needed to stop at the light, and let him go with a verbal warning.

This is a psychological no-no for a police officer and I knew better. If you aren't going to write a ticket you shouldn't make the stop; I knew that.

As I approached the man's car it was clear to me that the family was dressed to go to church. I had already formulated my approach, I would ask the man for his driver's license and then say, "Sir you probably didn't realize that you can't make a right turn on red at the intersection," check his license and let him go.

I asked for his driver's license and he immediately got defensive. Rather than give me his driver's license which he was required to do by state law, regardless of the reason why I had stopped him, he shot back… "What are you stopping *me* for?"

Still in mind to cut the guy slack for his oversight which at that moment had not caused or presented any danger to anyone, I said, "Sir you probably didn't realize that you can't make a right turn on red back there at the intersection."

In my generosity, I realized this guy probably had been coming this way to church for years, had probably turned right at the corner thousands of times and just didn't realize he had run the light. Perhaps he was in a hurry, perhaps he was talking to his wife and was distracted, perhaps his wife was talking to him and he was distracted, perhaps he'd looked in the rear view mirror and saw me and missed the light changing… or his daughter was a reason for his being distracted.

All those possibilities flashed through my mind… this church-going family-man had inadvertently run the red light on his way to church… and really, in the grand scheme of things, no harm no foul. But he had done it right in front of a police officer and I could not ignore the breach I had just witnessed.

But rather than 'turn-the-other-cheek', rather than being 'meek' or 'charitable' for what I was doing on behalf of the citizenry as a whole, rather than saying, "I'm sorry officer, I don't believe I did, or I come this way all the time and I sure thought I stopped," Mr. W copped an attitude and vehemently denied running the red light. "I did not!"

Faced with an angry citizen who had just accused me of stopping him for no reason, I had to change my tack. I was forced to consider that this man, who appeared to be on his way to church, had something to hide.

I required of him his driver's license as he continued to berate me. I had to explain to him that if he did not tender his license I would have to take him to jail. He finally complied.

I went to my squad car literally shaken, by the actions of a man whom I had taken for a 'square-john-citizen'. I ran his license plate for stolen and him, via the information on his driver's license, for wants and warrants. Both came back clear. I was now faced with the fact that I either had to write this guy a ticket or let him go, my original intent.

It was clear this was not going to turn out well, from a public relations point of view. Logically and obviously from what he had already said, if I had returned his license and said, 'have a nice day' he was going to claim I had harassed him (the lack of issuing a ticket would have tended to support his claim), he'd already demanded my name and badge number. I had only one option; write him the ticket for the traffic violation I had observed. I wrote out the ticket and took it up to his window.

I explained the nature of the ticket that, his signature was his promise to appear at the appointed court date. He refused to sign. I again tried to get him to understand that if he didn't sign the ticket I had no option other than to place him under arrest and take him to jail.

Things, in the general sense, had gotten way out of hand; he had blown this whole thing out of proportion. He continued to lambast me, how I was keeping him from doing the Lord's work, he was a deacon in the church, his wife was the organist, I was keeping them from exercising their right to worship... and used derogatory and defamatory language to me. All the while calling himself a Christian and that I had no right to do what I was doing; I was violating his constitutional rights, that I was the Devil, doing the Devil's bidding. He quoted some scripture about hindering the work of the Lord.

After he asked me if I was a Christian and I had answered yes I am... and he continued to belittle me saying that I couldn't be because a Christian "wouldn't treat me this way,"

I had finally had enough. I said, in a very even tone, "I don't think *your* attitude is very Christian." I pulled from memory the Lord's warrant for police officers. I said, "Are you familiar with Romans 13-4." The fuming man only looked puzzled, if he even heard me. I could have given him the King James version which sounds even more menacing but I quoted from the The Living New Testament version of the Bible, saying, "Romans 13-4, 'The policeman is sent by God to help you. But if you are doing something wrong, of course you should be afraid, for he will have you punished. He is sent by God for that very purpose.'"

It had no effect on the man, other than to anger him more. "Don't lecture me on my attitude, you are the one out of line," he blustered. He felt wronged and nothing I could do was going to change that. I tried several more times to get him to sign the ticket, he continued to refuse. Even so, I did not want to take the man to jail.

My next step would have been to call a squad to meet me to transport this man to jail. I was totally shocked by this man's behavior. I racked my brain for another solution short of hauling this recalcitrant idiot to jail.

I got back in my squad car and called for a Supervisor. When one of the adjacent beat officers heard me call for a supervisor and already knew I had checked out on traffic, he came by to assist. When asked if I needed any help, I told him to go ahead and stay, as I might have to take this guy to jail.

In nearly ten years of policing I had never called a Supervisor to assist me. When Sgt. Tommy R. Gregory arrived, he said in his usual affable manner... "Well what have we got..." only it sounded like, "Whale whutawegot?"

I explained the situation to TR and said I've written the ticket, I'm not going to tear it up or void it... he ran the red light (Violation of a traffic control device – turning on red without the arrow), I can't get through to this guy... I don't want to take him to jail, but either he signs the ticket or I take him to jail.

Sgt. Gregory went through ten more minutes of harangue with the driver, who wanted TR to arrest me and take me to jail. Finally the man agreed to sign the ticket. He signed, I gave him his copy showing him where my name and badge number was on the ticket and the date for him to appear in court if he wanted to contest the ticket and then I let him go.

[NB: Standard procedure when issuing a ticket was to cite the violator to court on your next court date, three weeks out. – that would have put Mr. W's court appearance date at about the week of July 5th through 9th but it could have been set for the week July 12-16.]

The whole event could have taken thirty minutes or fifty, I don't remember. What I do know is if he had just followed my lead, he would have given me his driver's license, I would have checked to see that it was not expired, checked the photo with the driver's face, would have been politely advised him of what I had observed, warned him to be more vigilant and sent on his way; actions that would have taken less than thirty seconds to accomplish.

I was taken aback by the ugliness this self-proclaimed "Christian" man had dumped on his fellow "child and servant of

God". I was still shaking as I came down from the adrenaline pump.

I had a few worried-moments in Vietnam. I had attended a Dixie-Mafia lieutenant, gunned down on my beat; shot with a rifle from a distance, at night. He died just before I got to his side... his sucking chest wound making CPR problematic. I had chased burglars and robbers down dark alleys, and encountered drug freaks in blacked-out warehouses, had disarmed a knife wielding attacker in a restaurant filled with diners, worked major accidents where teens had beheaded themselves going through windshields... I had seen many horrific and scary things in my years on the street; just like lots of other officers... but nothing had upset me like this incident had.

I knew it was time for me to do something else. I was also angry with myself for not being prepared for a good-guy to really be a bad-guy.

I knew I was right, that I was the good-guy in this and I wouldn't stand for being painted as the bad-guy. I was not jaded enough to say, "Fuck you, you silly ol' fart, run a red light on my beat an' yore ass is gonna be mine every time and I don't care if you are late to church; shouldn't have broke the law." I knew guys that demonstrated that attitude.

I realized I made the cardinal mistake of thinking I could just warn someone, I should not have stopped the guy if I was not going to write-him-up from the git-go. (Thanks to Mr. W. no other citizen ever got that break again.) As a cop you should never do something you haven't thought through before hand, if at all possible.

That Sunday morning, for that traffic stop, I had not held up that protective psychological shield. I was disarmed by the unprovoked aggression of a citizen; I would never make that mistake again.

Still shocky from the adrenaline rush, I went to the nearest firehouse and called my wife, told her what had happened and said, "That's it, I'm outta here." She was very supportive... she had been ready for me to leave police work, for sometime.

I did not try to imagine what this guy was telling his friends and congregation about his pre-church encounter with one Dallas' Finest, because it would never have occurred to me to tell others how I had acted, if I were him. Particularly when the man's ugly behavior had been witnessed by his wife and daughter. But this man was righteous in his own eyes and I was the Devil and he was not a forgiver. He was, as I would soon find out, the personification of the woman scorned.

FBR's *Month-At-A-Glance 1976*
Wednesday, June 16:   Printer
(unk info before Printer)

FBR's *Month-At-A-Glance 1976*
Friday, June 18:   Complete Update

Dallas, Northeast Patrol Division, Beat 256
1:58 am Tuesday, June 22, 1976
Offense Number 54 (R-33)

SEVENTEEN YEAR-OLD white female, *DN*, a sales clerk at Sanger-Harris department store in Big Town shopping mall was asleep. She had made love to her boyfriend, around 11:00pm, who afterwards had gone home. She was now alone in her bed. In the bedroom down the hall was her roommate *JB*, also seventeen, who was sleeping with her boyfriend, twenty-year-old MS.

What would be a fingernail moon had not yet risen under the scattered clouds tossed by a twenty-three mile per hour southeast wind. The A/C in apartment 1060 had cooled the place down to a very comfortable seventy-one degrees, while in the parking lot of the Melody Terrace Apartments, the tarmac was still dissipating the day's heat at something higher than the surrounding air temperature of seventy-five degrees.

How long the man had been in unit 1060 was not known. *DN* caught a glimpse of the clock on the nightstand: 1:58am. What is known is that Officer J.M. Hunter #2874 working element 245 received his second aggravated rape call in as many weeks, not in his sector but in another North Dallas beat: 256 at 6131 Melody Lane.

CAPERS/CID Investigator John Landers #2445 had put himself 'on-call' for the duration. He had taken this series of rapes, which he was now in charge of investigating, seriously. He knew that talking to complainants to glean current, fresh information might make the difference. Landers was in a smooth-car, cruising the area of previous North Dallas rapes. Landers arrived at the complainant's residence only minutes after the call to Element 245 had been dispatched at 3:20am.

Hunter's O/I R read like most of the forty some-odd FBR offenses. The suspect was described as W/M 5-9 to 5-11, 170 to 180 lbs, wearing blue jeans. One additional description was different. The complainant described to Hunter that the suspect's voice was a "high-pitch feminine voice." The suspect reportedly made off with twenty dollars in assorted currency, that he had "entered the south side dining room window, exited south side patio door." In his narrative Hunter wrote:

COMP WAS ASLEEP IN HER BEDROOM AND WAS AWAKEN BY SUSP LEANING OVER HER BREATHING HEAVY. COMP WAS NUDE AND SUSP TOLD HER THAT HE HAD A KNIFE & NOT TO MAKE ANY NOISE. COMP AT THIS TIME WAS LYING ON HER STOMACH, SUSP MADE HER KEEP HER FACE IN THE PILLOW SO SHE COULD NOT SEE HIM. SUSP TIED COMPS HANDS W/ TELEPHONE CORD AND ATTACHED THE CORD TO THE BED POST. SUSP WAS INTERRUPTED BY WIT#2 (MS) WHO WALKED INTO THE KITCHEN AREA OF THE APT. SUSP TOLD COMP TO LIE STILL AND DO NOT MAKE ANY NOISE OR HE WOULD SLIT HER THROAT. WIT#2 (MS) RETD TO THE SECOND BEDROOM. SUSP WAITED APPROX 5 TO 10 MINS AND TURNED COMP OVER ON HER BACK IN THE BED AND SUSP THEN CRIMINALLY ASSAULTED COMP. COMP STATED THAT HE HAD A SHARP OBJ. THAT SHE BELIEVED TO BE A KNIFE TOUCHING HER NECK MOST OF THE TIME HE WAS IN THE ROOM. SUSP FINISHED RAPING COMP. HE ASKED HER WHERE HER PURSE WAS. SHE REPLIED: IN THE LIVING ROOM AND TEHN SUSP SAID: I AM GOING OUT THERE TO SEE IF I CAN FIND SOMETHING WORTH TAKING. SUSP THEN ROLLED COMP OVER ON HER SIDE AND SLIPPED A PILLOW CASE OVER HER HEAD AND TOLD HER IF SHE MADE ANY NOISE, HE WOULD COME BACK IN AND CUT HER THROAT. SUSP MADE NUMEROUS COMMENTS TO COMP TELLING HER TO CALM DOWN, BE QUIET

AND THAT HE WOULD NOT HURT HER. COMP DID NOT HEAR SUSP LEAVE THE APT, BUT APPROX 5 MIN LATER, SHE HEARD A CAR START AND LEAVE THE PK LOT DIRECTLY OUTSIDE HER BEDROOM WINDOW. SHE SAID THE CAR SOUNDED LIKE A HOT ROD, BUT LEFT THE PK LOT AS QUIETLY AS POSSIBLE. COMP WAITED A FEW MORE MINS THEN CALLED TO ROOMMATE, NEITHER WIT#1 (JB) AND WIT#2 (MS) SAW SUSP AT ANY TIME. COMP FOUND ABOVE STOLEN PROP MISSING FROM HER PURSE WHICH HAD BEEN LEFT IN THE DINNING ROOM BY SUSP. SUSP APPARENTLY USED COMP'S BOTTLE OF ALOE HAND LOTION WHICH COMP HAD LEFT ON DRESSER. SUSP USED LOTION TO LUBRICATE HIMSELF. THE CAP TO THE BOTTLE WAS FOUND IN THE BATHROOM AND THE BOTTLE WAS FOUND UNDER THE BED IN COMP'S BEDROOM. SUSP CUT TWO TELEPHONE CORDS IN THE APT, BUT HE DID NOT ENTER THE SECOND BEDROOM WHICH REPORTEE (WIT#1 JB) AND HER BOYFRIEND OCCUPIED. SUSP APPARENTLY WIPED HIMSELF CLEAN WITH A TERRY CLOTH TOWEL AND LEFT IT IN THE HALL. P.E.S. WAS ABLE TO LIFT SEVERAL PRINTS FROM THE LOC. ALSO THERE WAS A PIECE OF A MAN'S SHOE HEEL FOUND IN THE LIVING ROOM.

P.E.S. also found a small leaf and a couple of pieces of grass cuttings on the floor inside the dining room window, leading them to speculate that this window was his POE, point of entry.

Investigator Landers wrote in his supplemental report, "I talked with Complainant just minutes after offense occurred.-Suspect committed oral sodomy on Comp which wasn't mentioned in offense report.[57] Comp had just had sexual intercourse with her boyfriend approximately two hours before suspect arrived. Comp cannot identify suspect and the prints

----

[57]This 'previously unreported' information was not the first such incident. Another comes to mind (see page 214). The point being that although we 'think' we know 'everything' that the FBR 'was doing/saying' via the Complaints' statements, as reported by the ROs at the scene, there were things complainants hesitated to tell us or intentionally withheld.

lifted at scene by CSS did not match those of "Friendly Burglar-Rapist."

It remained unknown to whom the 'lifted' prints might belong. Of course, this was not the first offense where the FBR left no recovered prints.

Hollywood
June 23, 1976
Theatrical release of Logan's Run
filmed in Dallas in the summer of 1975

FBR's *Month-At-A-Glance 1976*
Thursday, June 24:   Billy & Baggerly
10:00 Security
(this item is circled, an arrow indicates appt moved to 6/25/76)

Chapter 15

Dear Chief

Dallas Police Department, Chief's Office
10:00 am Thursday, June 24, 1976

The following letter (attachment #1) was received by the Chief of Police; Donald A. Byrd, logged in and forwarded, along with two other letters of complaint; attachment #2 (logged in the previous day) and attachment #3, to Chief Souter for disposition. That meant that once read they would be forwarded to Internal Affairs where citizen's complaints would be investigated.

Author Note: *Though the individuals below chose to make their pronouncements public, calling my credibility into question and besmirching my character and I have every legal right to publish their names, I have blacked-out their full names out of a sense of charity. On the other hand, as the individuals in Attachments #2 & #3 chose to name their church as a badge of their own righteousness and veracity, that name is not blacked-out. It is unknown to what extent the members of Gaston Avenue Baptist Church have had their view of the Dallas Police Department tainted, over the years, by the perception of the one-sided account of this event. Likewise it is unknown if the church sanctioned the use of it's name by members of its congregation in the making of a public complaint against an officer of the law, someone who swore an oath before God to protect, defend and serve the citizens of Dallas. It is hoped that many more of the members have had good experiences with members of the department. It is further hoped that the members will and have since equally applied and borne witness to the fidelity of their members so far as their knowledge of said behavior warrants and have refrained from bearing witness to that which they were not a party while permitting the possibility of the fidelity and veracity of the officer involved instead of dismissing that possibility out of hand... as in "judge not, lest ye be judged".*

You've already read my account of what happened on June 13th, now you can read Mr. W's account, along with the 'well-meaning' I'll-vouch-for-Mr. W letters.

███ Richard Ave.
Dallas, Texas 75206

June 22, 1976

Mr. Don Byrd,
Chief of Police
Dallas, Texas

Dear Mr. Byrd,   Re: Municipal Court Citation # 41833

With regard to the Municipal Court Citation # 41833 issued to me Sunday, June 13, 1976, I wish to make a formal complaint against Officer # 2441.

I charge the Officer with the following:

- Ignorance of the particular traffic signal he charged me with violating.

- Not having witnesses to back up his charges against me.

- Highhanded tactics bordering on brutality.

- Deliberately depriving me and my family of our civil liberty.

- Making a public spectacle of the matter by calling other Officers to the scene.

- Causing embarrassment and mental anguish to me and my family by hindering us in the Lord's work without just cause.

- Not having a valid case against me and provoking me into a situation where he could charge me with offenses which had nothing to do with the violation for which he stopped me.

- Painful harrassment by falsely accusing me of a traffic violation, lecturing me on my Christian attitude, attempting to suppress my freedom of speech, needlessly detaining me and my family and thereby causing us to be late in our Church appointments and issuing a citation making it necessary for us to take additional time to defend our Constitutional Rights in Municipal Court.

- Immature judgement and professional incompetence.

Sent to *Chief Byrd*
Log No ⑤ 6-04-76
Answer 27 _____
Return To Chief's Office _____

ATTACHMENT # /

Please understand that I do not consider the mere fact that we were on our way to church a justifiable reason for breaking the law, if indeed we did break the law.

I accord the arresting Officer the full right to stop me and issue me a citation if he believed he saw a violation of the law. On the other hand, I have constitutional rights as a citizen which cannot be violated.

I protest his brusque way of handling the matter. I do not recommend severe discipline such as demotion, et cetera, but I do recommend reprimand and proper training in the handling of such cases. I think he should be trained sufficiently before being allowed to practice on law abiding citizens. The authority he had should not be in the hands of a novice.

A personal apology from the Officer to me and my family would be appropriate and the dropping of the charges against me immediately would be appreciated.

,, I shall appreciate a prompt reply.

Very truly yours,

C. [redacted]

ATTACHMENT # 1

It was apparently not enough that the 'driver' sent *the* Chief a letter; here is the two page letter hand-written from his sister, LDW. I have transcribed it so you can more easily read his complaint based solely on… well you will see. [Note: Both Capt. Prince and Investigator Ford referred to LDW as 'his brother' and "Mr." my reading of LDW's signature is that the first name is a female name, thus I refer to LDW as 'his sister'.

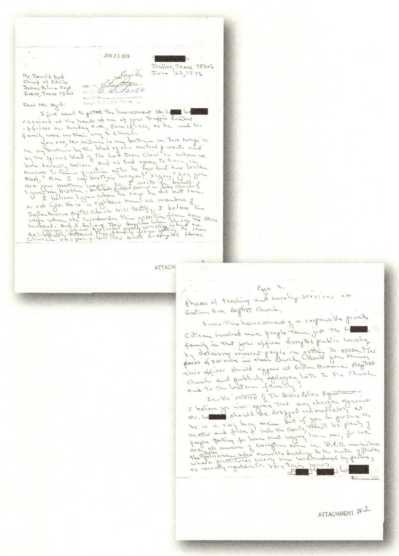

As you can make out the above heading information, I will start the letter's transcription after "Dear Mr. Byrd:"

I just want to protest the harassment Mr. L. W. received at the hands of one of your traffic control officers on Sunday A.M., June 13, 1976, as he and his family were on their way to church.

You see, Mr. W. is my brother – in two ways is he my brother – by the blood of our mutual parents and by the spilled blood of the Lord Jesus Christ in whom we both devoutly believe. And as God spoke to Cain in answer to Cain's question after he murdered his brother Abel, "Am I my brother's keeper?" Saying "Yes, you are your brother's keeper." So I write in behalf of L. my brother. He is God's faithful servant in God's church.

I believe L. when he says he did not run a red light. He is a righteous man as members of Gaston Avenue Baptist Church will testify. I believe his wife when she corroborates this assertion from her husband. And I believe their daughter when she says the same.

Your officer disturbed public worship when he deliberately detained this family from getting to their church responsibilities and disrupted three phases of teaching and worship services at Gaston Ave. Baptist Church.

Since this harassment of a responsible private Citizen involved more people than just the W. family in that your officer disrupted public worship by detaining innocent people in getting to essential places of service in their church, don't you think this officer should appear at Gaston Avenue Baptist Church and publicly apologize both to the Church and to the W. family.

In the interest of the Dallas Police Department I believe you will agree that any charges against Mr. W. should be dropped immediately as he is a very busy man. But if you do pursue the matter and force it into the courts, there'll be plenty of people pulling for him and urging him on, for we are all aware of the corruption even in D.P.D.—witness the Dallas policeman who owns the building to the north of Dallas where prostitutes carry on unhindered by police, as recently reported on T.V. Very truly yours,

/s/ L. D. W.

A third letter (attachment #3) was sent to *the* chief, apparently written by Mr. CLW's neighbor and fellow church member. This one is typed so you can read it without my transcription.

Richard Street
Dallas, Texas 75206
June 23, 1976

Mr. Don Byrd, Chief of Police
Dallas Police Department
Dallas, Texas 75201

Dear Chief Byrd:

Subject: Harrassment of a Private Citizen by a Traffic Patrolman

This letter has to do with the alledged moving traffic violation--running a red light, to be exact--by Mr. C. L   W   at Greenville Avenue and Ross Avenue on Sunday morning, June 13, 1976, and the harrassment of him and his family by one of your traffic patrolmen. The W   were on their way to Sunday School and Worship Services at the Gaston Avenue Baptist Church where each of the three had definite and important responsibilities.

I did not see this incident nor was I present at any of the proceedings after the patrolman stopped Mr. W   for this alledged violation of the law, but neither were you, so it all boils down to whose word you should believe--the private citizen or the patrolman in uniform. Since there were three againts one, there should be no doubt as to whose word you should believe, even though the patrolman is one of your men. In explaining to members of Gaston Avenue Baptist Church the reason for their inability to get to the Church and their responsibilities, the three members of the W   family all told the same story.

Without any hesitation whatsoever, I can testify to the life, character, reputation and integrity of Mr. W   and his family and bear witness to the fact that they are some of the finest people in the whole wide world. I have known this family for many, many years and have never found any one of them to be default in any area of their lives. They are among the most faithful members of Gaston. They were on their way to the House of Worship when the alledged violation of the law occurred. The fact that they were on their way to Church should have spoken loudly to the arresting officer. Instead, the patrolman exercised the authority of his uniform to lecture Mr. W   on what a fine Christian he was in violating the law and then shoving him around. This within itself is enough to condemn the officer. It seems to me he was making every effort to arouse Mr. W   's anger in order to justify his own misbehaviour. Anyone can be provoked to wrath if pushed beyond self-control. I can assure you that Mr. W   is a fine gentleman, a Deacon in the Gaston Avenue Baptist Church and teacher of one of the Men's Bible Classes. Mrs. W   is the Church Organist, has been for over 30 years. Their daughter, L   is a very gifted musician and plays the piano for one of the departmental assembles of the Sunday School. They love the Lord and are faithful in all their responsibilities.

Needless to say, they were very upset when they were detained for 45 minutes or more and refused the right to proceed to the House of the Lord even though Mr. W   repeatedly asked the patrolman to issue a ticket if he felt he was right in his claim. It is my opinion that your patrolman was completely out of line, that he was a big bully, that he was unsure of his own position when he had to summon two additional patrolman to the scene, and that he certainly interfered with public worship in detaining Mr. W   and his family from getting to their places of responsibility in their Church. Interfering with public worship is considered a crime; running a red light is a traffic violation which Mr. W   ; his wife and daughter claim he did not do. I believe they tell the truth and this letter is to testify to this fact--that the W   family is telling the truth. Your traffic officer interrupted public worship in causing a Men's Bible Class to go untaught; in making it impossible for the pianist to get to one of the departmental assembles; and in causing the Church Organist to be late in getting to her organ to start the morning worship service. This poses the question: WHO VIOLATED THE LAW?

Very truly yours,

ATTACHMENT #3

FBR's *Month-At-A-Glance 1976*
Friday, June 25:   Bloom Annual Mtg
                     4:30
                     OBSERVER
                     10:00
(arrow from 6/24 indicates 10:00 appt moved from yesterday at 10:00)

FBR's *Month-At-A-Glance 1976*
Thursday, Blank June date-box: July 1

FBR's *Month-At-A-Glance 1976*
Friday, Blank June date-box: EAR distribution
                     July 2
FBR's *Month-At-A-Glance 1976*
Wednesday, Blank Jul date box: EAR
                     Blueline
                     Touche

FBR's *Month-At-A-Glance 1976*
Thursday, July 1:   Man. Update
                     ↓

FBR's *Month-At-A-Glance 1976*
Friday, July 2:   Robert – Doris
                     Picnic
                     EAR
                     Bob
(Line may indicate vacation starting on 7-2-76)

FBR's *Month-At-A-Glance 1976*
Saturday, July 3:   10:00 Bob

Chapter 16

No Mid-summer's Night's Dream

Tuesday, July 4, 1976
USA Bicentennial

FBR's *Month-At-A-Glance 1976*
Monday, July 5: _____
(Line indicates vacation on 7-4 thru 7-10-76)
FBR's *Month-At-A-Glance 1976*
Tuesday, July 6:   I A B C _ _ _ _ _ _ _ _
(Line indicates vacation on 7-4 thru 7-10-76)

Dallas, Northeast Patrol Division, Beat 245
00:25 am Tuesday, July 6, 1976
Offense Number 55
Prints Found - Comparison Result, Unk

MID-SUMMER'S NIGHT and it was only seventy-five degrees. The temperature had maxed out at eighty-six, seven degrees below the average temperature of ninety-three and far from the July 15th record of one-hundred and five which would occur in 1996; twenty years in the future. Tonight it was mostly cloudy with the wind wafting out of the east at seven miles an hour.

Seventy-five was hot for a ski mask, but that was what the complainant told Reporting Officers: L.T. Page #2710 and M.R. Scoggins #3601, her attacker was wearing.

American Airlines stewardess, *JEC*, a white female twenty-eight, had only lived in apartment 132 at 7745 Willowstream Court in the Willow Creek Apartments for two months.

Whether it was habit or oversight, being in a new apartment, the living room's east-facing window had been left unlocked. The only barrier, a metal table sitting in front of the window, had not worked. The intruder only moved it aside as after he lifted up the window.

Inside he went to the patio door and unlocked the 'slider' and left it partially open. He found *JEC*'s purse, took out her wallet and carried it as he rifled through it and then left it on the dining room table. Armed with a knife from the kitchen he cut the telephone wires and headed to *JEC*'s bedroom.

He was watching her as she stirred in bed. When she woke he reached out for her throat saying in a soft voice, "If you scream, I'll kill you, I'll kill you."

As he placed his hands on *JEC*'s throat she screamed. Her assailant fled the screaming *JEC*'s bedroom and out the living room sliding glass door.

Deja Vu

Dallas, Northeast Patrol Division, Beat 245
9:30 pm Tuesday, July 6, 1976
Offense Number 56
FBR Prints: #1 & #2

OFFICER RHL JACKSON #2694 wrote up his O/I R before he cleared from the scene at 11:35pm. In the 'Time Dispatched" box he wrote 9:22pm and wrote "Meet Complainant" in the Offense/Incident box. The complainant, *BDD* a white female 28, at apartment 1070, 4676 Amesbury, the Willowick Apartments. He wrote:

Reporting officer was on routine patrol (7/7/76) in the rear of 4600 block Amesbury when he was flagged down by B-- L---- of 4687 Amesbury #178 who stated that the lady who lived in Apt #1070 had heard someone and had a screen removed from her window. Reporting officer contacted above Compl who advised that between 9:30pm – 10:00PM 7/6/76 she was sitting in her bedroom studying (&) heard something outside the window, that she got up went to the window, cleared her throat thinking what she had heard might have been a cat. That someone standing in the dark asked if Compl knew where the mail boxes were. Compl replied, there are mailboxes everywhere you will just have to look for them. Compl got up on the morning of 7/7/76 and found a screen had been removed from a living room window and placed on the patio. Compl's roommate KW was raped in the same apartment about a year ago and entry was made through same window.

Inv. Landers of C/A Persons was called and reported to scene, Lt Day of P.E.S. also reported and processed screen and window.

A supplemental report was filed by Inv. Thompson #2185 of P.E.S. regarding the Att. Burglary at apartment 1070, 4676 Amesbury. Thompson's report, dated 7/8/76, stated:

"Dusted a screen removed from north living room window at above location and lifted comparable prints on the inside portion of the screen on the right side looking into the living room. Print <u>does</u> belong to the "Friendly Rapist" and is the right index finger. Entry into the apartment was not gained due to the fact the window was screwed down. No further physical evidence was obtained."

[**NB**: This same address, this same apartment, almost one year ago is the scene of the rape of *KSW* (July 27, 1975), which Tom and I attributed to the FBR as Offense Number 19 (see page 137).]

Author Note: *Did the FBR know he was going back to the scene of a previous rape? Was it a mistake? Was it his plan?*

Painted '50'?

Dallas, Northeast Patrol Division, Beat 213
1:00-6:00 am Thursday, July 8, 1976
Offense Number 57 (R-34)

RAPE NUMBER FIFTY? A woman of twenty-three, who had lived in unit 3268 at 6619 Shadybrook Lane in The Hill Apartments in 'the Village' for only the last nine months since coming to America from Korea, was the Friendly Burglar-Rapist's latest victim.

SYM's husband had been in Japan on business for the past five weeks. She appeared to the recent observer to be a single woman, living alone. She shopped at the Safeway grocery store at Skillman & Northwest Highway, not in her immediate neighborhood. *SYM*, who described herself as five-foot, one-hundred pounds with long black hair, took tennis lessons at the nearby Village courts and at home, painted in her leisure.

It was not until 10:50am that Officers D.K. Lowe #3770 and J.H. Barnett #1397, working Element 211, were dispatched on a Signal 25, Criminal Assault. They encountered the complainant, a Korean national married to an American national, who was unaware of American police procedures and had to be talked into calling police by a friend she had called to tell her what had happened. In spite of complainant's comments such as, "I don't know, too many questions," officers were able to elicit a considerable amount of information. She was able to give an approximate description of a man maybe five-foot-ten to six-foot, one-hundred-seventy-five pounds, she didn't recall any facial hair but never saw his face. She said he wore a short-sleeved T-shirt, and pants with a big belt buckle; this she knew by feel, not from having seen them.

The Reporting Officers learned the complainant's husband leased their apartment a year ago, before they were married. Complainant related that she had taken a sleeping pill (Sleepeze) at 11:00pm and read for about an hour. Before going to bed about midnight, she checked on her new three-month-old puppy that she left tied up in the kitchen and then made sure the front door was locked and the night-chain in place. What the officers could not clarify was when the rape took place; the best they got was a time-window of from 1:00am to 6:00am.

At approximately 3:41am the almost full moon would set, but only the Friendly Burglar-Rapist knew that... the complainant, even with her artistic skill as an observer, wouldn't remember seeing it or that the skies had been scattered with clouds or that the temperature when she went to bed had been seventy-six degrees, or that the light winds would shift from the southeast to the east-southeast during the night and by morning the temperature would have dropped two to three degrees under mostly cloudy skies.

On the upstairs patio balcony the FBR looked into the living room aided by the dim light his victim had left on; all was quiet. He found the sliding glass door unlocked, opened it, and stepped inside. The smell of oil paints and turpentine filled the air. At the front door he slid back the chain and unlocked the door. He located the source of the paint-smells; an oil painting in-progress and gave it a cursory viewing. He was surprised to find a puppy tied up in the kitchen and even more surprised that the young dog did not make a fuss. He cut the various phone wires.

In her bathroom he searched her cabinets and found some lotion under the sink and placed it on the bedroom dresser. He took the purse he'd found in the living room into *SYM*'s bedroom, finished looking through it's contents, removed twenty-two dollars, and dropped it at the foot of her bed. She was sleeping soundly.

He sat on the edge of the bed and his victim didn't move. He gently shook her.

Groggily *SYM* woke to the feeling of a hand on her back, she thought it was her husband; she was still drowsy from the effect of the sleeping pill.

The FBR said quietly, "Be quiet. If you make any noise I will kill you." He held up a knife for her to see.

SYM tried to yell, but he put his hand over her mouth, "I'm not going to hurt you. Just be quiet & don't make any noise."

He took the cord from her telephone and tied her hands behind her and then took a pillowcase off one of *SYM*'s pillows and pulled it down over her head. He helped *SYM* up off the bed turned her around and cut the crotch of her panties as well as her bra strap so he could fondle her. He put *SYM* back on the bed then lay on top of her and tried four or five times to penetrate her completely. He then got up off the bed and grabbed the lubricant from the bedroom dresser and lubricated his erection. He lay back on the bed and had *SYM* straddle him to complete his penetration.

When *SYM* tried to touch his face, he jerked his head back. She could feel that he had not undressed; she could feel his pants bunched on his thighs and felt the FBR's big, hard belt buckle as he made her ride him to orgasm.

Afterwards he got up and left the apartment through the front door, which *SYM* found open after she had showered and gone into the living room.

Later, after the Reporting Officers, Investigator Landers and the Physical Evidence Section guys had left her apartment; *SYM* noticed something very strange and called to report it. She had been straightening up her apartment when she saw something on one of her oil paintings that had not been there before. A tube of red paint had had its contents squeezed out and applied to the surface of one of her in-progress paintings. What she saw was a red "#50"!

[**NB**: What was reported in Inv. Furr's Supplemental O/IR was that the numerals five-zero were painted in red. To indicate it thusly I used quote marks and a number symbol to indicate what the FBR purportedly 'painted' on the in-progress canvas. Tom's contemporaneous note in our FBR Book is: "Red 50 in Red Painting".[58]

I did not see the canvas, however the P.E.S. SR, dated 7-8-76 reads, "Susp had used a red paint tube to squeeze out #50 on one of her oil paintings. Printed & photos of tube & painting neg results on prints on paint tube." (see image above)

Apparently a photograph of the FBR's painting handiwork does or did exist for Service # 238606H as reported by P.E.S. Inv. RA Furr badge #2377. Did the FBR paint just the 'five-oh' (as in 50) or was their also a number symbol before it (as in #50)? This question remains, at this writing, unknown.]

[**NB (2016)**: Looking for the meaning of the "50" ostensibly applied by the FBR from a tube of paint onto the Comp's unfinished canvas is understandable. In July of '76 it was a logical speculation that the FBR was claiming this rape as his fiftieth. However at the time Tom and I had attributed 57 total offense to the FBR with this rape being the 34th attributed to

---

him. If the FBR indeed was keeping count of his rapes and this (on his count) was number 50, then Tom and I were 16 rapes behind the curve. Was 50 the correct number and if so where were those offenses? Again, using the approximate percentage of unreported rapes as 50%, then one could presume that out of those 'other 16' rapes that at least 8 of them might have been reported. Where were they? Tom and I never saw them. Add to this conundrum Marble's statement to Inv. Lander on the morning of his arrest that he (Marble) went into multiple apartments each night out and when asked to quantify that number Marble said "...you wouldn't believe me if I told you." The FBR's statement then begs the questions: 1) do we believe him, 2) if we believe him do we believe he knows how many he went in each night or on any given night, and 3) if we believe him did he keep count of his break-ins and the break-ins that resulting in a rape?]

Chapter 17

Complaint Unfounded - Not Sustained

FBR's *Month-At-A-Glance 1976*
Thursday, July 8:   I A B C
                      ‾ ‾ ‾ ‾ ‾ ‾ ‾ ‾
(Line indicates vacation on 7-4 thru 7-10-76)

Dallas Police Department, Chief's Office
thru: Internal Affairs Division
10:00 am Thursday, July 8, 1976

INTERNAL AFFAIRS INVESTIGATOR Roosevelt Ford #1707 had concluded his investigation. I was now made aware that I had been 'complained on' and that the complaint had *not* been sustained. I was also provided copies of the complaint and DPD responses. (See previous pages: 226-231.)

Inv. Ford sent the letter below through his boss Captain Billy Prince (who would ten years later become Chief of Police) to then chief Don Byrd.

Captain Prince then promulgated (for the Chief) the additional letters that follow Investigator Ford's.:

Memorandum

CITY OF DALLAS

DATE   July 8, 1976

TO   Mr. D. A. Byrd
Chief of Police

SUBJECT   Complaint of Mr. C. L███ W█████

On Sunday morning, June 13, 1976, Officer Robert J. Sadler, #2441, stopped and issued a traffic citation to Mr. C. L██ W████ for running a red light at the intersection of Ross and Greenville Avenues. As a result of Mr. W████'s uncooperativeness, Officer Sadler felt it necessary to call a supervisor and an additional element.

Because of his detainment and subsequent traffic citation, Mr. W████ directed a letter to you outlining his displeasure.

The contents of Mr. W████'s letter indicate that his complaints involve a situation which will have to be resolved through the courts.

In connection with these complaints, letters were received from Mr. Watson's brother, and from a Mrs. J. R. H█████, a member of Mr. W████'s church. Neither of these people witnessed the incident.

A letter has been written to Mr. W████ explaining how to contest the citation in court. An explanation of procedures concerning other allegations in his letter involving the officer's rights was also given to him.

Letters were also written to Mr. W████'s brother and Mrs. J. R. H█████, thanking them for their interest in this matter.

All letters received are attached to this report.

Roosevelt Ford

Roosevelt Ford, #1707
Investigator
Internal Affairs Division

RF/hjs

Attachments

CITY OF DALLAS

July 8, 1976

Mr. C. Lynn Watson
5555 Richard Avenue
Dallas, Texas 75206

Dear Mr. Watson:

In reply to your letter of complaint dated June 22, 1976, addressed
to Chief Byrd, regarding your experience on Sunday, June 13, 1976,
with the officer wearing Badge #2441, I submit the following to you:

1. The Internal Affairs Division does not investigate complaints
   relative to differences of opinion between a police officer
   and a citizen over the issuance of a traffic citation. We are
   not empowered with the authority to determine guilt or innocence. This determination is a function of the courts and
   has to be resolved in the courts.

2. A police officer is not required to have a witness when
   issuing a traffic citation.

3. You did not charge the officer with brutality, but rather
   "highhanded tactics" which is difficult to interpret, and
   does not indicate misconduct according to the guidelines of
   the Dallas Police Department.

4. You were not deprived of your civil liberty when the officer
   stopped you and issued a traffic citation to you. The officer
   was within his rights to stop you because, in his opinion,
   you violated a traffic regulation. You have a right to contest the charge in a court of law.

5. The officer had a right to call other officers to the scene if,
   in his opinion, he felt trouble might develop. Apparently
   that was his opinion.

6. It is unfortunate you were embarrassed because the officer
   stopped you. Certainly it was not his intention to hinder
   you in the Lord's work. However, you were not stopped without
   just cause; the officer believes he observed you commit a
   traffic violation.

Page 2
Mr. C. L███ W████
July 8, 1976

7. You did not explain what you meant when you said, "by provoking me into a situation where he could charge me with
   offenses which had nothing to do with the violation for
   which he stopped me." However, the officer does have a
   valid case against you which has to be resolved in the courts.

8. It is unfortunate you were late for church, however, the officer is bound by written guidelines to check every person
   he stops for a traffic violation on the police radio. Usually
   the procedure does not take very long if the person stopped
   is completely cooperative. It is indeed your constitutional
   right to take time to defend yourself in court.

9. Officer Sadler has served on the Dallas Police Department
   for nine years. His record reflects exceptional maturity
   and professional competence.

   This officer is not required by any written guideline of this
   department to apologize to you. He may do so at his own dis-
   cretion.

   If the charges against you are to be dropped, they must be
   dropped by the court judge.

If you have any further questions regarding this matter, please contact
Investigator Roosevelt Ford at 748-9711, extension 1166.

Sincerely,

D. A. BYRD
CHIEF OF POLICE

By: Billy D. Prince
Captain of Police
Internal Affairs Division

RF/hjs

CITY OF DALLAS

July 8, 1976

Mr. L. D. W█████
█████Moser
Dallas, Texas   75206

Dear Mr. Watson:

This letter is in reply to your letter of June 22, 1976,
addressed to Chief D. A. Byrd. Since you felt this matter
important enough to write a letter to Chief Byrd, it is
felt that a reply to you is in order.

Your belief in your brother is very commendable, however,
since you were not a witness to the incident, your statement cannot be used in support of Mr. W█████.

A letter of complaint was received from your brother and
it was handled in accordance with the regulations of this
department.

Your concern in this matter is greatly appreciated. If
we may be of further assistance to you, please do not hesitate to contact this division.

Sincerely,

D. A. BYRD
CHIEF OF POLICE

By: Billy D. Prince
Captain of Police
Internal Affairs Division

RF/hjs

CITY OF DALLAS

July 8, 1976

Mrs. J. R. H▮▮▮▮
▮▮▮ Richard Street
Dallas, Texas 75206

Dear Mrs. H▮▮▮▮:

This letter is in reply to your letter of June 23, 1976,
addressed to Chief D. A. Byrd.

It is most commendable that you hold Mr. C. Lynn Watson in
such high regard. It is further commendable that you
respect him enough to believe what he says without the
benefit of hearing the other side. Your comments are appreciated; however, since you were not a witness to the
incident, your statements cannot be a factor in the complaint.

Mr. W▮▮▮▮'s complaint has been received and processed in
accordance with our responsibility in the Internal Affairs
Division.

We respect your comments, and hope the Dallas Police
Department will command a fraction of the esteem you hold
for Mr. W▮▮▮▮.

Sincerely,

D. A. BYRD
CHIEF OF POLICE

By: Billy D. Prince
Captain of Police
Internal Affairs Division

RF/hjs

POLICE DEPARTMENT   CITY HALL   DALLAS, TEXAS 75201   TELEPHONE 214 / 748-9711

Dallas, Northeast Patrol Division, Beat 236
7:51 am Friday, July 9, 1976
Offense Number 58

THE UNREPORTED RAPE of RAB, a white female thirty-four, did not go completely unreported. On July 9ᵗʰ *JM*, a social worker, called police. Officers D.A. Reynolds #3542 and R.L. Reid #3560 met her at 4776 Amesbury #1066 to take her report.

JM told officers that she "has a friend who was raped on 7-7-76 but refuses to make a complaint and does not wish to be identified." *JM* talked to Inv. Landers in Crimes Against Persons and gave him information on the rape and advised him "she had the gown worn by the victim, a lotion bottle that had been handled by Susp, and a glass juice bottle believed handled by the Susp. Susp is believed to be a white male, due to voice and brief glimpse, blond hair, about 6 foot tall with a good build." *JM* related that victim told her Suspect "talked in a whisper and assured her she would not be hurt if she did not cry out and said she was not injured but did feel a sharp object at her side as Suspect told her not to scream." *JM* said the victim advised she had her "head covered to obstruct her view of Suspect" and "tied" her "with phone cord." The victim related that Suspect had entered through an unlocked window." Suspect was said to have told victim to "give me your money," and victim replied, "I have a broken foot and can't get out of bed." She said she told him where her money was and that he took money and left.

Officer Reynolds wrote: "Items were released to Lt. J.C. Day #391 in Central ID.

RAB of unit 1068 at 4776 Amesbury in the Willowick Apartments told a neighbor she had been raped. The neighbor called DWAR, Dallas Women Against Rape, and gave the following account to a counselor.

Reportee stated the suspect was Blond, 6 ft. He had cut the phone cord. The suspect put a pillow case over her head and that it had slipped off one time and she saw his silhouette in the mirror. He turned to see if she was looking and the Compl. closed her eyes.

The suspect touched her with a sharp object and compl. thought it was a knife. The suspect cut her cotton gown off her and she later experimented and says she thinks the sharp object was a pair of scissors. The suspect asked her for her money and she told him to go get it. She told him she had a broken foot and couldn't. Suspect went into kitchen and compl. remembers finding a jar of fruit juice on the cabinet she was sure she had put away.

Reportee said compl. states there was an awfully heavy flow of semen. The suspect was a young man. She said that the suspect had gone into the bathroom (prior to the rape) and got an empty bottle of lotion and tried to squirt some on his hands. Compl. still has the lotion bottle and gown.

Dallas, Police & Courts Building
2:00 pm Thursday, July 15, 1976

[NB this date was picked as representative of the date and time for my court assignment which would have been at least three weeks after the issuance of citation on June 13, 1976.]

THE COURTROOM WAS buzzing with the usual conversation of people who were trying to figure out how to proceed in the Municipal Court system. A city attorney sat at a table while people holding traffic tickets discussed their issues. Some pled no-contest or guilty and were directed where to pay their fines. Others wanted to plead not-guilty and wanted to have their case heard by the judge. The officers who shared the same court date all sat on a long bench to the right of the judge's bench (on the Judge's left).

Once the other issues had been dealt with, the Judge entered and called his courtroom to order. Presently the city attorney called the case re: Citation #41833.

I was called to the stand and sworn in. The city attorney asked me the circumstances of writing the ticket. I told the Court the date, time and location, described the vehicle and license number, that I observed the light at the intersection of Greenville Avenue at Ross Avenue turn from amber to red, that I then observed the defendant disregard the traffic control device, enter the intersection making a right turn and proceed southwest on Ross Avenue. I said I stopped the defendant and issued him the citation # 41833. I left the witness stand.

The judge asked if the defendant had any relevant testimony. The man got up and was sworn in. He told his story to the judge.

Since I *saw* the man "run the red light" I knew he was lying, telling a falsehood, and or perjuring himself. He may have convinced himself of his innocence and thus felt he was telling the truth. Fortunately both of us could not be right.

It was my job to be aware of things like the changing of traffic lights and the position of vehicles around the intersection. I saw the light change, I saw him not stop, I saw him drive, enter and drive through the intersection on red. Pure and simple, cut and dried. I also know from experience that drivers often do not pay attention to their surroundings and therefore run red lights, for example, due to inattention. It is my experience that often the inattentive driver may be 'helped' by their passenger-spouse but rarely does the party in the back seat, a youngster lost in their own world, pay attention, or possibly more importantly from the back seat, have the vantage or angle of view to actually see the traffic light.

In this case each of these people, the driver-dad, the passenger-mom in the right front seat, and the passenger-daughter in the back seat each told the judge that they were staring right at the light and it was green when they (I, my husband, my dad) entered the intersection.

Given this man's unwarranted attack on me, behavior he apparently didn't mind demonstrating in front of his wife and daughter, it was now obvious to me they were scared to say a word against him much less do anything but support and facilitate his lie, that he "did not" violate the law.

Just as the church-lady had predicted in her letter, it was "three against one, who are you going to believe." In this case it's not a matter of belief for the judge. He has to deal with the preponderance of the evidence. The fact that three citizens gave identical sworn testimony that contravened my sworn testimony; he had no choice but to dismiss the ticket.

Author Note: *would that we had dash-cams, back in the day.*

They walked out of the court room feeling vindicated, while irritated that they had been forced to come to court to defend themselves and happy that mean ol' officer had gotten his comeuppance. The judge looked over at me an nodded and shook his head saying: "I know what just happened, sorry, I had no choice." He knew the truth, I knew the truth and God knows the truth.

I left the courtroom renewing my vow to never stop another violator without the specific intention to write them up for their violation.

Funny thing is, that as all my partners knew and my supervisors complained, I was not a ticket burn'em up. I didn't generally go out of my way to write as many tickets as some of the guys.

Unless we had a particular traffic enforcement issue on the beat that required paying extra attention to say, speeding in a neighborhood, or running a specific stop sign or red light, you had to bust the law right in front of me to get written up. Writing tickets was third on my list of priorities. Arresting bad-guys and stopping robbers and burglars were interchangeably one and two.

The public had the perception or belief, and often said things like, "you must be on a quota". It was true that the number of traffic tickets we wrote each month generated revenue for the city and state, and we were encouraged to write more tickets, if our individual numbers were low. The belief in the department was that if you are doing your job you are going to see a relatively certain number of traffic violations during your shift and you were supposed to write them. Regarding a perceived ticket writing quota, I heard one Sergeant explain it this way, *no —we definitely do not have a quota, we can write just as many tickets as we want.*

I received, a couple days later, this Memo sent from Investigator Ford & Captain Prince, through Assistant Chief J. M. Souter, to my boss Deputy Chief R. O. Dixon. Captain Prince noted that "this complaint will not be placed in Officer Sadler's file". Then in a handwritten note Chief Souter underlined and reiterated that the "no reference will be made of this incident in officer's field file either. JMS".

These actions indicated, to me, how little stock was placed in the complainer's veracity. The complainer, as God and I knew, was a prevaricator of the first order and guilty of shameful mendacity.

Memorandum

CITY OF DALLAS

DATE   July 13, 1976

TO   Deputy Chief R. O. Dixon   THRU: Ass't. Chief J. M. Souter
      Central Division   Patrol Bureau

SUBJECT   Complaint Made by Mr. C. L███ W█████
       Against Officer Robert J. Sadler, #2441

The attached complaint investigation is forwarded to you
for your review and information. <u>Please note that this
complaint will not be placed in Officer Sadler's file.</u>

Please return to this office by <u>7-20-76</u>.

Billy Prince

Billy D. Prince
Captain of Police
Internal Affairs Division

mb

*Note what I underlined.
No reference will be made
of this incident in officers
field file either
JMS*

All letters received are attached to this report.

Roosevelt Ford

Roosevelt Ford, #1707
Investigator
Internal Affairs Division

RF/hjs

Attachments

Chapter 18

Almost... Act One

Dallas, Northeast Patrol Division, Beat 245
11:25 pm Thursday, July 15, 1976
Offense Number 59

ALMOST CAUGHT, ACT one. The FBR had just removed one of the screens to a second story window as he stood on the seven-foot fence surrounding the patio of the twenty-four year-old secretary that lived in unit 1164. What the FBR did not know was he was not going to make entry into this apartment via the window he was raising or that had he gotten through the window he would have had an eight-foot drop to the floor below, given this was a loft-type apartment.

Off-duty officer, James MacArthur #3623, living at the Woodscape Apartments was making his security rounds of the property when he saw a white male approximately twenty-four, maybe five-foot-ten and one hundred-sixty pounds. He was wearing a tan knit pullover shirt with light blue dress pants. His hair was sandy brown, collar length and wavy, but neatly combed.

Police officer and would-be-burglar saw each other simultaneously. They both made an immediate and knowing assessment of the moment, intent, and distance.

The FBR jumped from the fence into the soft mud of the adjacent flower beds and ran away as the officer was already running toward him. He ran west on the side walk then between the apartment unit and the Clubhouse next to the tennis courts. With Officer MacArthur trying to close the gap, the FBR continued running at full tilt, north around the pool area. His prior planning to prop open the fenced pool's gate with a rock aided his escape. When he punched the gate it sprang open and he dashed through without missing a step, he continued down another sidewalk leading to the parking lot.

The gate slammed shut, and when Officer MacArthur reached it he had to stop to open it and he lost time and distance. His quarry gained what Officer MacArthur had lost. MacArthur last saw the, to him, unknown suspect running west in the apartment complex parking lot.

MacArthur called for a police and canine unit[59]. The experienced K-9 handler and his dog followed the FBR from the fence of apartment 1164 and the footprints in the flowerbed to the northwest corner of the Woodscape Apartment's parking lot and into the adjacent wooded area. Then, like Officer MacArthur, his canine counterpart also lost the fleet-footed suspect.

Back at the apartment #1164, the P.E.S. (physical evidence section) guys were doing their thing: taking two plaster casts of the suspect's shoe prints he left in the mud as well as photographs. They also found two flood lights near the apartment's upstairs window had been unscrewed.

Officer MacArthur interviewed the resident of #1164, the complainant on the attempted burglary MacArthur had observed. The young woman said she had been asleep until she heard Officer MacArthur yelling at some guy to "Halt!"

P.E.S. Inv.'s L.C. Taylor #1430 and J.H. Whiteley #2646 dusted for fingerprints (neg results), took photos and made plaster casts of FBR's shoe impressions.

Dallas, Northeast Patrol Division, Beat 213
1:20 am Friday, July 16, 1976
Offense Number 60

THE JUST WANING moon appeared and disappeared in the partly cloudy skies. It had been seventy-three at midnight and would be seventy-two by 2:00am. None of that made any difference to the outcome of *MSV*'s encounter with the Friendly Burglar-Rapist. She was a white female thirty years of age and currently unemployed. Her apartment, number 1059 was located in the Villa Madrid Apartments at 8249 Southwestern Boulevard.

The CBS Friday Night Late Movie was "House of Dark Shadows". *MSV* told Reporting Officer G.A. Wren #3618 she finished watching TV at approximately 12:30am, got up and

---

[59] For several years Tom and I had urged that a K-9 unit be dispatched to the scene of FBR offenses in the hopes of determining his direction of travel leaving the scene, where perhaps he parked his oft discussed "truck". We were sure that was a ruse, but where might he park his car, if he was using one? If we knew definitively which way he went leaving the complainant's apartment, or where he parked it would make it easier to prospect for witnesses. The need to have a K-9 unit track the suspect had been explained to earlier investigators as well as to John Landers. John, would make it happen. See page 308, Memo to Landers, dated Nov. 17, 1976, Subj: Daily Activity Report for Capt M.

checked to make sure the front door was locked, though she did not 'throw' the dead-bolt. She left the front window open, about a foot, for circulation, it was summer after all and the cool summer night air felt good.

She woke at approximately 1:20 in the morning to find a man standing alongside her bed, one arm outstretched over her and his hand clamped over her mouth. As *MSV* tried to shake her sleep-stupor she realized he was on top of her.

"Don't move," he said, "or scream!"

"Please don't hurt me!"

"I won't, but don't scream."

"Just take my jewels or money..."

"I already know where your money is, it's in your purse. I have a knife and will use it if necessary, just like I used to get in the front door."

Now "turn over and put your head under the pillow."

MSV squirmed under her assailant and managed to slide out from under him and started screaming.

The Friendly Burglar-Rapist ran out of the bedroom.

MSV jumped up, still screaming, and shut the bedroom door behind her attacker. She kept on screaming, ran to her second story bedroom window, smashed it open with her hand, opened the window and crawled down to the ground. She ran to the next building, to her neighbor's, *KD* and *CS*, apartment #203.

KD told officers that she heard *MSV* screaming and looked out her bedroom window to the parking lot below and saw an older model maroon car parked.

When officers arrived they notified CID, P.E.S. and requested a canine unit. The canine unit followed the suspect's trail westbound out to the parking lot and then south about thirty feet to where a set of tire tracks left the area. The area where the dog lost the suspects trail is where *KD* said she saw the maroon vehicle parked.

P.E.S. found the phone cord in *MSV*'s bedroom cut. P.E.S. observed the entry into the Complainant's apartment was accomplished after the suspect removed the screen from the upstairs apartment's open window. *MSV* told officers the suspect was a young man, five-foot-eleven, 160 lbs, broad shoulders, wearing a white short-sleeved shirt, and that he had white, women's hose over his head.

[NB: The RO for this offense G.A. Wren 3618, Service #249668H, reported it as an Attempt Rape, dated 7-16-76, and gave the following account when he made contact with complainant at a neighbor's where he took the complainant's statement: "...COMP THEN SLID OUT FROM UNDER SUSP AND STARTED SCREAMING. SUSP THEN RAN OUT OF BEDROOM AND COMP SHUT BEDROOM DOOR BEHIND SUSP AND KEPT ON SCREAMING. COMP THEN BROKE OUT BEDROOM WINDOW W/HAND CAUSING MINOR CUTS AND THEN CRAWLED DOWN TO THE GROUND."

P.E.S. came the scene and made the following report: "Entry gained by removing screen from upstairs open window. When compl was awakened by suspect she jumped out of second story window & suspect left. Processed point of entry..."

Author Note: *In this case it is unlikely that P.E.S. interviewed the complainant as had the RO whose account is at odds vis-à-vis the: "crawled down to the ground" vs "jumping out of second story window". Obviously jumped is more eye-catching and dramatic than crawled. This SR is likely the genesis for the Jim Henderson's account in his Dallas Times Herald (DTH) article: Tracking the 'friendly rapist', dated 2-20-1977.* (See pages: 461-472. Also see website: robertjsadler.com.)

FBR's *Month-At-A-Glance 1976*
Monday, July 19:   Write OBZ

FBR's *Month-At-A-Glance 1976*
Friday, July 23:   OBZ. Comp.

FBR's *Month-At-A-Glance 1976*
Monday, July 26:   Elder
FBR's *Month-At-A-Glance 1976*
Tuesday, July 27:   Bapt. 2 –on
                          ↓
FBR's *Month-At-A-Glance 1976*
Wednesday, July 28:   10:00 BGCT

The Map of the Stars

WE WERE VERY serious about what we were doing however strange it seemed to others. We didn't claim to be 'detectives', what we did however was never give up on trying to predict his movements and then interdict the FBR. That tenacity on our part seemed to unnerve certain of our fellow officers. Whether it was luck or good deductions on our part, the other thing that bothered our peers was that we were predicting, with some regularity the when and where of the FBR's next hit.

Here are a couple of examples of how seriously our *expertise* was taken within the department... and conversely how seriously we took ourselves.

Our *office* and our *maps* were often the butt of jokes and conversation. At one point we had created a pin map in the office —trying to visually demonstrate the FBR's activity—and wove thread (in chronological order) from one (pin) offense to another. The resulting form looked something like a strange-legged star[60].

One of the so-called detectives from one of the investigative bureaus "happened" by our office, came in and took one look at our strange, to him, maps and said, "I gotta take a picture of this." A few minutes later he came back with a camera and snapped a photo. No doubt he and his bureau buddies were having a good laugh and sharing, once developed, his new-found funny photo with detectives in other bureaus.

We tried every idea we could come up with to look at the FBR offenses from any and every angle. Some of our ideas were screwy, half-baked, far-out and a few pure genius. We looked at tides, moon phases, moon cycles, menses cycles—any kind of cycle that might help us understand his seeming monthly pattern. We rejected nothing in looking at who the FBR was, how he'd been able to do all he had done without getting caught. In fact no idea was too small a bone to be fleshed out or too big of a bone to be gnawed clean.

Little did we know, though we suspected it, we were still not getting all the data; many of his break-ins, went unnoticed by

---

[60] See "Star Map" on page 508-515 [Note FBR offense chronology changed over time as individual offenses were added and thus the actual placement of the pins changed - when the Star Map was first put up the 'hits' that we pinned and threaded together did look more like a star than what appears in the maps created for this book, using all the final numbers in their final order and chronology.]

absent or sleeping tenants while a number of his rape and attempt rapes went unreported.

We did serious work with the data we did have.

Now, for how seriously we took ourselves.

R.O. Dixon – the FBI and Chicken Bones

Sometime early August 1976

Tom, ever the practical joker and a man who enjoys a good story and a good laugh, saved his lunch sack one day (we'd taken some fried chicken back to the office that particular day). Tom saved the sack of gnawed-clean chicken bones. A day or so later Tom demonstrated his chicken-bone-mojo-prediction method to my guffaws.

Always wanting to improve upon our methodology, we picked up some nuts and bolts, some old square nails that had been there for centuries, matches, etc., and with a single chicken bone put them in that same old greasy brown paper lunch sack.

On some pretext we got Dixon up to the office... told him we'd come up with a new deal on how to predict the FBR's crimes. Of course Dixon was all ears. He fell for anything; bless his heart, he fell for us...

Years later, after Dixon had retired from Dallas and had become the Chief of Police for University Park, Tom took a visiting police VIP from Luxembourg to see him. They got to talking about our FBR case and were going through our methodology again, Dixon shook his head and looked at Tom and said, "I'll never understand how you guys did that... your system."

... we got Dixon up to the office... told him we had this new prediction method. I got a map down and laid it flat across one of our desks. Tom shook that sack and dumped its contents out onto a map.

Tom and I are pointing and interpreting and talking and describing what we saw: "the nail points to that apartment complex, and the screws over here, that must be... that's gotta be the street he was on..." then Tom pointed to the bone and said, "and that's where he had chicken for lunch".

Dixon, didn't say a word, he just turned and walked out... We, of course, died laughing, not at our chief, at ourselves.

Not long after our 'demonstration' an FBI agent called on Chief Dixon, no doubt sent down from *the* Chief's office to visit with Dixon.

The demarcation between federal law enforcement and local law enforcement is a bright line. This is primarily because of jurisdiction, statutes, case law and policy (make that political) processes, and other factors such as training and experience.

In the 1970's the most often encountered contact between local law enforcement (now referred to as LEO's, law enforcement officers) by the Fed's, which in particular included the FBI, was when someone at the local level 'screwed up'.

Claims of civil rights abuses by cops was a frequent complaint of the arrested. Some factor above ninety-nine percent of these claims were unfounded (had no factual basis to pursue), but the investigation of these claims required the FBI to question the veracity and integrity of cops. This did not sit well with either the street cop or the administrators of them, each of whom were subjected to the FBI's intense scrutiny.

It was for these reasons that our boss, Deputy Chief Robert O. Dixon, who at one time had been in command of the department's own Internal Affairs' investigators, was not a fan of having any FBI presence in his office.

On this particular day, R.O. was sitting at his desk in his office, wearing his Chief's uniform and smoking his pipe as a suited FBI agent was sitting across from him. The issue at hand does not matter now, but for whatever reason Bob Dixon wanted this guy out of his hair. At some point the subject of the FBR came up and Bob was recounting our efforts to successfully predict when the FBR was going to strike again. Knowing Bob, a light bulb must have gone off on how he could get this Agent out of his office.

Tom remembers picking up the phone and hearing Dixon say, "there's an FBI agent here and he's really wanting to see how you predict this rapist's next hit," course he'd filled him in on the rapist... "show him what you showed me the other day, on the desk." "Gotcha Chief," Tom said with a smile. Tom said later he could almost see Dixon's 'wink-wink' through the phone line. Tom turned to me and said "Dixon's sending up an FBI Agent to see our FBR predictions methodology and wants us to show him the one we showed him the other day, *on the desk*".

Five or six minutes later the FBI Agent was knocking on our door frame. We exchanged names. He looked around the office, saw the maps on the walls with all they 'crime dots' and the map with the strings running back and forth, like a web, between red-headed map pins. He said he was interested in seeing our prediction methodology that the Chief had told him about.

Tom pulled himself up out of his chair with a solemnity, that only those that know him would see as pure straight-faced-Buster Keaton, bordering on Keystone Cop. "Bob," Tom said to me, "Get down the prediction map and spread it on the desk." As if I hadn't a clue as to what was about to happen, I got one of our folding maps of the city, marked off with the seven areas where the FBR was hitting, and spread it out over one of the empty desks.

Tom sauntered over to one of our filing cabinets and opened the appropriate drawer and pulled out a grease-stained brown sandwich sack. As I finished flattening out the map Tom carefully brought the sack over to the table. He had his right hand under the sack and with his left hand he was choking the neck of the sack together. He shook the sack three times, turned the sack over and dumped its contents on the map. Out poured six square and rusty hundred year-old nails, two buttons, three bottle caps, two unshelled peanuts, a nub of a worn pencil, a couple of paper clips and a chicken bone. The items scattered out over the map, just like all the other times.

The eyes of the FBI Agent widened.

Nonplused, Tom said, "Uh huh, yeah, there's the nail pointin' to where he's gonna hit and these two screws... that's the roads he's gonna travel to get there, that bottle cap, that's his car in the parking lot," Tom paused a beat or two then pointed, "and that bone, shows where he had chicken for lunch…"

The highly trained FBI Special Agent was not impressed with our analytical procedures… Without a word the agent turned and left our office, we never saw him again. It's unknown if he heard us, all the way down the hall where he was surely waiting on an elevator, but our laugher did bring in a few of our cohorts to see why we seemed to be the only ones in the cop-shop having any fun. And every time we saw Chief Dixon, he'd get a grin on his face and thanked us for getting the FBI guy out of his hair.

258

FBR's *Month-At-A-Glance 1976*
Friday, August 13:
(date circled)

FBR's *Month-At-A-Glance 1976*
Saturday, August 14: 𝖋 𝖋
(black ink stamp of 2 black feet, toes down)

Chapter 19

Almost... Act Two

Dallas, Northeast Patrol Division, Beat 245
11:55 pm Sunday, August 15, 1976

ALMOST CAUGHT, ACT two. Dallas Police Officer Gregory Michael Virginia lived at the Woodscape Apartments on Miller Road, east of Central Expressway. His roommate, Officer James MacArthur, had only the month before almost caught the man believed to be the Friendly Burglar-Rapist.

These two unmarried officers, like many others at the time, lived in apartments across the city and bartered their off-duty time for free rent. It sounds like a good deal, but you are literally on-call all the time. You come home from your shift thinking you can relax, but the management and hundreds of residents who live in the complex surrounding you have other ideas.

Somebody get's locked out, somebody is playing their music too loudly, etc., you get "the call". So in addition to opening doors for lockouts and reporting to management on a wide range of security issues, like burned-out lights and abandoned vehicles in the parking lot, you are often required to patrol the property on foot, several times a night; usually filling out an activity log in the manager's office. Depending on the season, you might "work" parties… and you generally, tried to "keep the peace".

Tonight off-duty Officer Virginia left the air-conditioned comfort of his apartment and was on his way to lock-up the clubhouse, securing it for the night, when he jumped a rabbit.

If you have ever been bird hunting, in a field, where your primary attention is scanning the skies as you walk, the sound and sight of a jack rabbit or even a small cottontail breaking from its place of concealment, underfoot, through the brush in front of you can be unnerving or startling, for both the rabbit and the hunter.

Officer Virginia had left his apartment on this warm late-summer night on his midnight rounds. The gibbous moon was twenty minutes above the horizon, the skies were clear and the temperature was a balmy eighty-five degrees with an eleven mile a hour breeze out of the south-southwest. He was casually dressed in blue jean cutoff's and a Polo shirt; on his feet, a pair of flip-flops. It was his custom to lock the clubhouse first. It was a few minutes before twelve.

Year's later Virginia recounted the event. "As I rounded the south end of the pool I looked up to the studio apartment just west of the pool and saw a male standing on the patio privacy fence attempting to remove the screen from one of the windows. I hollered 'Hey, what the hell are you doing?' I knew the man did not live there, that apartment was occupied by a young female tenant. The man, who was dressed in sweat pants with a matching hoodie, turned and looked directly at me and jumped from his position on the fence. I got a very good look at his face. When he hit the ground he began to run west, I gave chase. He continued west, soon leaving the apartment house property heading to the Manderville Road area along the north-south railroad tracks and he vanished. I might add, he was a very fast runner. I returned to the club house/office area and called police. The police helicopter was up and searched the area without success; the K9 unit was also sent without any firm results. He was gone, with only his face in my memory."

FBR's *Month-At-A-Glance 1976*
Monday, August 16:   Quality **(indecipherable)**
                           Bapt.
                           Roadway Propo

Dallas, Northeast Patrol Division, Beat 245
11:30 pm Monday, August 16, 1976
Offense Number 61

CRIMINAL TRESPASS (30.05 PC) Reporting Officer J.M. Ingram #2535 submitted the following report regarding apartment 130 in the Willowick Apartments at 7727 Willow Vine. After consulting with the complainant (*JB*) and witnesses (*LC & TT*) he noted the M/O as: "Took screen off front window and raised window and entered." His narrative of the complainant and witnesses statements states:

THIS OFFENSE APPEARS TO BE THE FRIENDLY RAPIST. COMP JB (W/F 38, INV. ANALYST) & TT W/F/ 30 LIVE TOGETHER AT ABOVE LOCATION IN SEPARATE BEDROOMS. TT HAD HER BOYFRIEND LC

SPENDING THE NIGHT WITH HER, WHO WAS ASLEEP IN HER BED. BOYFRIEND'S NAME IS LC W/ M24. COMP STATED SHE WAS THE LAST ONE TO GO TO BED LAST NIGHT AT APPROX 11:30PM AND WAS 1ST ONE TO GET UP THIS MORNING AT 7:00AM. SHE TOOK A BATH, THEN WENT INTO THE KITCHEN TO MAKE SOME COFFEE. AFTER SHE HAD MADE THE COFFEE, SHE NOTICED A BUTCHER KNIFE WAS STICKING UP IN THE SEAT OF A BAR CHAIR. THE CHAIR HAD BEEN MOVED AWAY FROM THE BAR & WAS SITTING IN THE MIDDLE OF THE DEN, APPROX 4FT FROM THE BAR. COMP REMOVED THE KNIFE & THEN WOKE HER ROOMMATE UP, THINKING THAT HER ROOMMATE WAS PLAYING A TRICK. TT GOT UP & WENT INTO THE KITCHEN AT WHICH TIME THEY FOUND THE WALL TELEPHONE CORD HAD BEEN CUT. THEN THEY NOTICED THE BACK WINDOW HAD BEEN SHUT, WHICH THEY NORMALLY KEEP OPEN ABOUT 4 INCHES SO THEIR CAT CAN COME & GO OUT OF THE APT. THEY NOTICED THE REAR SLIDING GLASS DOOR WAS UNLOCKED BUT WAS SHUT. THEY THEN NOTICED THE FRONT WINDOW TO THE LIVING RM WAS RAISED ABOUT 2 INCHES & THE SCREEN HAD BEEN REMOVED. COMP ALSO NOTICED A WINDOW SLIDE STRIP WAS MISSING. THE STEREO HAD BEEN MOVED FROM ITS STATION & THE THERMOSTAT TO THE AC/UNIT HAD BEEN TURNED DOWN. TT ALSO NOTICED THAT HER BEDROOM DOOR, WHICH IS NORMALLY OPEN ABOUT 4 INCHES, WAS STANDING MORE THAN HALFWAY OPEN. COMP THEN CALLED POLICE. COMP STATES THAT NOTHING IS MISSING IN THE APT. NEITHER ONE REMEMBERS HEARING ANYTHING DURING THE NIGHT. COMP STATES THAT LAST SUNDAY NIGHT 8/15/76 AT APPROX 11:30PM SHE RETURNED HOME BY HERSELF & OBSERVED A WM, ABOUT 25-26, 5'10", SLENDER BUILD, LIGHT COLORED MEDIUM LENGTH HAIR (OVER THE EARS) WEARING A STRIPED SHIRT, LIGHT JEANS & HAD LIGHT COMPLEXION, STANDING IN FRONT OF HER APT ON THE SIDEWALK. THIS SUBJECT SAW COMP & SLOWLY

WALKED AWAY. AFTER COMP WENT INTO THER APT, SUBJECT WALKED VERY FAST BACK BY HER APT.

Remarkably, the partial palm and fingerprints lifted from the scene, P.E.S. noted, "...do not match those of "The Friendly Rapist." Were they right?

Though fingerprints, themselves, don't lie. It is possible the FBR never left any prints at this scene and those 'lifted' at the scene belonged to some male visitor of the complainant's.

Tom and I attributed this offense to the FBR, as did Officer Ingram, the Reporting Officer. Note that Ingram's statement is an opinion, not part of the complainant's or witness' statements as opined in Deputy Chief Fannin's, memo (Subject: "Friendly Burglar" Rapes) of November 7, 1975. [See page 159-162.]

FBR's *Month-At-A-Glance 1976*
Wednesday, August 18: Manager Update

FBR's *Month-At-A-Glance 1976*
Thursday, August 19:   9:00 McBride

FBR's *Month-At-A-Glance 1976*
Monday, August 23:   Roadway 8:00 –
10:35-11

CAPERS Investigator John Landers, who had taken over the FBR offenses from Reba Crowder was busy looking for offenses with a similar M/O. John sent the following TeleType message:[61]

21718 TX PD DALLAS 8-23-76
ALL TEXAS LAW ENFORCEMENT STATIONS
W/M 20-40 5'9-6'0 SANDY BROWN HAIR ENTERS THRU UNLOCKED WINDOW OR SLIDING GLASS DOOR, CUTS TELEPHONE CORDS TIES VICTIM WITH TELEPHONE CORD. LUBRICATES HIMSELF WITH VICTIM'S LOTION, RAPES VICTIM AND TAKES HER MONEY FROM PURSE. SUBJECT ALWAYS VERY POLITE SPOKEN, AND HAS NEVER HURT ANY OF HIS VICTIMS. SUSPECT HAS

---

[61] Copy placed in FBR - Patrol Officers Handbook on the FBR page 8

APPROX 60[62] OFFENSES. IF YOUR DEPARTMENT HAS HAD
SIMILAR OFFENSES REPLY TO INVESTIGATOR JOHN
LANDERS DALLAS POLICE DEPARTMENT, CRIMES
AGAINST PERSONS DIVISION.
INV JOHN LANDERS CRIMES AGAINST PERSONS
DIVISION
TX PD DALLAS DJD 231522CDT

Almost immediately John got a response to his APB and
received the following message from the Huntsville PD:[63]

AZUF 6412 18 07   18.07 07/23/76
PD HUNTSVILLE 08-23-76
PD DALLAS   MSG #8-782
REF TO YOU MESSAGE NUMBER 21718
ATTN INVESTIGATOR JOHN LANDERS CRIMES AGAINST
PERSON DIVISION
THIS DEPARTMENT HAS CASE DATING 8-6-73 ON A
DONALD R. LEGGETT INVOLVING SIMILAR
CIRCUMSTANCES IN WHICH SUBJECT ENTERED THE
HOUSE THROUGH A WINDOW. THE SUBJECT ALSO CUT
THE TELEPHONE LINES TO THE HOUSE BUT DID NOT
USE IT TO TIE UP VICTIM. SUBJECT DID USE A KNIFE TO
THREATEN VICTM WITH. SUBJECT IS A WITHE MALE
BROWN HAIR HASZEL EUYES APPROX 5'8" 150 LBS. DOB/
7-22-52. LAST KNOWN ADDRESS WAS BARCELONA APT
#37 HUNTSVILLE TX
NEXT OF KIN LIST IS A JAMES L LEGGETT 3214 BISTINAU
BOSSIER LA. NAVE NO INFORMATION ON DISPOSITION
OF CASE. NO OTHER INFORMATION IS AVAILABLE. CASE
DID HAVE A FEW SIMILARITIES. IF WE CAN BE OF ANY
OTHER HELP PLEASE ADVISE. THANKS
AUTH JUDGE BEELER
PD HUNTSVILLE RCW 231803 CDT

John penned and signed the following note to this incoming
teletype message: "Eliminated by fingerprint comparison - JR
Landers 2445."

---

[62] FBR attributed Offense #60 had occurred July 16, & Offense #61 a month later on
August 16. Obviously, Inv. John Landers was onboard with the total number of offenses
Tom and I had attributed (at this point) to the Friendly Burglar Rapist!

[63] Copy placed in FBR - Patrol Officers Handbook on page 9

FBR's *Month-At-A-Glance 1976*
Wednesday, August 25: 9:00
Sam
Humphries

Dallas
Sunday, August 29, 1976

Though I do not recall that I saw this article (below) in the Sunday, August 29, 1976, edition of *The Dallas Morning News.* Its appearance coincided with John Lander's taking over the FBR rape cases. If, as Captain Memo surmised (in his remarks), 'imitators' were operating in the FBR's stead then the admission of that theory or its probability along with the detailing of some of the FBR's primary MO markers would have been more likely to fuel 'imitators' rather than inhibit them.

If I had seen it then, I would have been even more incensed than when I found it in my research years later.

Police blame lifestyle in some rapes

By RENA PEDERSON

Dallas police say the free-wheeling lifestyle of the 1970s is backfiring on women living in "swinging singles" apartment complexes.

So far this year, 386 women have been raped in Dallas. Two-thirds of the 103 women raped this summer have been apartment residents, primarily in

> A victim of the "friendly rapist"
> tells her story, Page 36A.

the Oak Lawn, Bachman Lake and Greenville Avenue-Northwest Highway areas.

THE INFLUX of young professionals into those areas in recent years has produced a mobile, affluent group of residents in a "do your own thing" atmosphere.

"You get a so-called liberated bunch of people who want to come and go as they please, and they don't care what their neighbors are doing or who lives around them," said Capt. Don Milliken, head of the DPD crimes against persons department.

"That's why they live there — they want that casual lifestyle. But the result is they don't notice any suspicious-looking activity or report it to police," he explained.

In describing the frustrations police have encountered in trying to solve the rapes, Milliken said, "Apparently these people don't have time to get to know their neighbors, or read the paper or watch the news, because they are usually unaware of the situation, or they don't care."

"In some complexes where four or five women have been raped, we have found they didn't know about the other incidents a few doors away, or weren't concerned. Even when they heard about the other rapes, many of the victims had failed to take simple precautions like locking their doors and windows," he said.

MILLIKEN SAID in one-North Dallas complex where seven women had been raped, officers held safety seminars because female residents were supposedly "living in fear." One week later, the officers on patrol found 13 windows unlocked in one hour.

"I've spent a lot of my own time trying to figure out how these guys decide which apartment to hit, so I went out to check some complexes," Milliken said. "I was not in uniform and I was fiddling with screens, climbing around fences and patios. Several people saw me — but no one bothered to call the police or tell the manager."

Milliken said a full-scale effort is being made to curb the assaults and an officer, J.R. Landers, has been assigned to investigate all leads to the identity of the man popularly known as the "friendly rapist" because he has not seriously injured any of his victims.

Milliken said at least 13 victims have been directly linked to the same rapist by sperm tests and 35 others have been involved in similar attacks.

THE RAPIST'S METHOD of operation follows the same pattern: sometime between midnight and dawn, a young man in his late 20s, who is of medium height with modishly cut brown hair, enters an apartment, usually through a window, cuts the phone cord, awakens the victim, ties a pillow case around her head with the phone cord, rapes her, takes a little money or a few belongings then leaves.

The victims have ranged in age from 16 to 60.

Some have lived alone, some have been raped while their roommates were out or asleep. One was raped while a roommate was asleep with her boyfriend in the next bedroom.

According to the police, the rapist threatens his victims with a knife. He implies he is a "macho" person who could have plenty of voluntary sex with women if he wanted to.

IN AN IRONIC, unfortunate development, Milliken said, publicity about the so-called "friendly rapist" has spawned several imitators. The friendly rapist is not believed to have raped a victim in about six weeks, but other rapes have been committed by men who claimed to be the "friendly rapist" and adopted some of his mannerisms.

In one instance, an imitator took credit for 50 rapes and smeared the number on a female artist's paintings. In another, an imitator raped a woman who had previously been assaulted and claimed he had come back to celebrate his 50th rape.

"It bothers me that these rapists have gained a sort of Robin Hood image and that people joke about the 'friendly rapist,' because anyone who is a rapist is not friendly," Milliken protested.

He emphasized, "Rape is a terrible thing even if the rapist does not seriously hurt someone."

"SOME OF these women have gone through a lot of embarrassment, shock and emotional pain," he said.

"Some of them have been cooperating with the police or helping with seminars for other victims," he went on. "But I have been surprised to learn that some of them were not that concerned. We went to interview one girl and she was playing cards and didn't want to be bothered with talking with us.

"Some of them seem offended by the idea when we suggest that they should put locks on their doors and windows and tell them not to undress in front of windows or open the door to strangers, he went on. They just don't think it can happen to them."

"Some of the rapes also have not been reported until several weeks later when a friend let the word get out," Milliken pointed out.

"I CAN see where some of them don't want to be hassled or think that policemen won't be sympathetic, but the amazing thing is that some just didn't care about helping catch the guy," he said.

"I'm not knocking their lifestyle, but I'm sure these rapists have been seen by someone or they've raped somebody that might have a clue and hasn't reported it," Milliken said.

He added, "It's a very frustrating situation and it makes our job a lot more difficult."

IN AN IRONIC, unfortunate development, Milliken said, publicity about the so-called "friendly rapist" has spawned several imitators. The friendly rapist is not believed to have raped a victim in about six weeks, but other rapes have been committed by men who claimed to be the "friendly rapist" and adopted some of his mannerisms.

In one instance, an imitator took credit for 50 rapes and smeared the number on a female artist's paintings. In another, an imitator raped a woman who had previously been assaulted and claimed he had come back to celebrate his 50th rape.

I have left much of my commentary until later in this book However I did not want the ideas in this article to remain, at this point, unchallenged.

Looking today (30+ years later) at our final list of FBR attributed offenses, *as of the Sunday this article appeared*, Tom and I had already attributed sixty-one (61) total offenses to the FBR, thirty-four (34) of which were rapes. Offense #57, Rape #34 (on our list) occurred on July 8, 1976. That would approximate the "six weeks" of no FBR offenses comment ascribed to Captain Don Milliken.

Between the FBR attributed rape on July 8th and the article of 29 August, we had cataloged four (4) FBR attributed offenses:

Off# 58 'Un-reported' Rape on July 7th (later divulged, no report made) *see pg 245*
Off# 59 Attempt Burglary on July 15th *see pg 250*
Off# 60 Attempt Rape July 16th *see pg 251*
Off# 61 Criminal Trespass on August 16th *see pg 260*

I do not know what the Milliken attributed reference to "other rapes have been committed by men who claimed to be the 'friendly rapist' and adopted some of his mannerisms," means. We looked at every criminal assault that came in across the city and specifically those that fell within the seven delineated areas of the FBR's concentration. We found no rapes that had FBR MO Markers or we would have included them in our list, regardless of the type of offense. If CAPERS had other rapes they were attributing as 'imitators' or copycats, they never shared them with me or Tom.

It is also curious that "one instance" cited as an "imitator" had been the most recent rape, occurring on July 8th. The RO had not mentioned in his report of the Complainant's interview of the 'painted fifty.' However P.E.S. investigator R.A. Furr #2377 wrote in his supplement: "Comp called back and had discovered Susp had used a red paint tube to squeeze out #50 on one of her oil paintings. Printed & photos of tube & painting. Neg results on prints on paint tube." Tom's contemporaneous file note:

Red 50
in Red
Painting

Question, how would an 'imitator' know contemporaneously what "number" the FBR was supposedly up to or close to? Particularly when CAPERS did not acknowledge all the rapes *we* had attributed to the FBR, but rather had attributed *some* to the man eventually arrested for the FBR rapes and other's to an unknown number of mysterious imitators. To my knowledge no one was talking about the FBR having committed fifty rapes, especially not CAPERS, until the "fifty" number appeared on an oil painting of one of the FBR rape complainants. So, why would an imitator guess or know to claim that number.

The first occurrence (July 6, 1976) of the FBR going back to the same apartment was reported on July 7, 1976. The instance of the painted "fifty" on the complainant's oil painting occurred a mile and a half north the next day on July 8, 1976.

As for "an imitator raped a woman who had previously been assaulted and claimed he had come back to celebrate his 50th rape," I can find no corroboration of or for such a statement or claim in the 82 offenses we attributed to the FBR.

On July 27, 1975 the complainant *KSW* (Offense #19 R-16 page 115) was raped in apartment #1070 at 4676 Amesbury. Her roommate was *BDD*. Twenty days shy of one year later, on July 7, 1976 Patrolman R Jackson #2594 was flagged down by a man and alerted a woman in a nearby apartment had a problem. The woman was *BDD* in apartment #1070 roommate of the previously assaulted *KSW*. Officer Jackson filed an O/IR "Meet Complainant" (see page 137-8) and took *BDD*'s statement regarding hearing a noise, seeing a man outside her window and finding a window screen removed.

Then approximately two months later (in this chronology) on September 22, 1976 (see page 234) the FBR entered apartment #1070 at 4676 for a third (3rd) time. This time he raped *BDD*!

No complainant appears twice on our list of FBR attributed offenses except *BDD*, once as Complainant on a "Meet Complainant" and once as Complainant on a "Criminal Assault".

As noted this apartment was the location of two rapes (of different complainants) and one "Meet Complainant".

Unless Captain Milliken had a file of offenses I never saw, I cannot explain the comments attributed to him. As I said, our records do not support the newspaper's quote: "an imitator raped a woman who had previously been assaulted and claimed he had come back to celebrate his 50th rape."

Two possibilities. If such a claim was made by "The FBR" or by an imitator/copycat it would only be known: 1) if the Complainant related it to the Reporting Officer, who would have dutifully included it in the narrative of his report. Such a comment would not be something the RO would omit [keeping the secret to himself or telling the investigator in confidence]; or 2) upon being interviewed by the case investigator the Complainant could have related the suspect's claim and this investigator fearing this information, if made public, might be detrimental to the case or the department might have decided to omit the claim from her supplemental report.

In such a case, most likely, a memo would have be written to a commander detailing the suspect's claim as repeated by the Complainant. At the very least a contemporaneously handwritten case note would be placed in the file detailing this claim.

Given that I can find no O/IR with such information, I can rule out number one. I can say that a review of the investigators' supplemental O/IRs do not include this claim.

Thus it falls to an intentional holding back of information on the part of the investigator. Done so either on the investigator's own initiative or as a directive by a commander—and to what end.

Usually if a point of detail in a case is kept from the public it is so that when a suspect is caught or subject of interest is interviewed and they reveal or do not reveal that detail (that only the perpetrator and the victim would know), it provides potential eliminations or connections, i.e.: perpetrator to scene, to victim, to means... etc.

If indeed *the claim* was made, known, and held back... on first blush that could make sense. To this time the media had not made a particularly big deal of the 'friendly rapist' or his rapes, or the fact that the rapist could be a Dallas Police Officer. A point of view Captain Milliken wanted to keep out of the press and an opinion he would later reinforce, not abnegate.

Whether this was due to the cronyism that appeared to exist between some police and some of the press at the time, the lack of sufficient dot-connecting on the part of police beat reporters or that fact that since CAPERS did not themselves acknowledge all the rapes and ancillary offense Tom and I had attributed to the FBR, how would anyone else make those connections.

Critical thinking? If the department felt such a claim (of having fifty victims and going back for seconds to celebrate), should be held back from the public after it's supposed utterance, sometime between the first of July and the end of August, why then would it be revealed to the press by Captain Milliken on August 29th?

Or? Was this some mastermind reverse psychological gambit by the wily Captain Milliken to get the one-and-only FBR to reveal himself or publicly acknowledge that "he's the man"? I don't think that thought occurred to anyone at the time... it was much easier to believe there were multiple suspects than admit one man had eluded us for three years.

Suffice it to say, this article colored the thoughts of many as you have already seen and will see later.

FBR's *Month-At-A-Glance 1976*
Monday, Blank Sept. date-box: GAZETTE
       Write

FBR's *Month-At-A-Glance 1976*
Monday, September 6:
(Labor Day - date circled)

Men, Mustaches & Mexican Food

My Big-Three-Oh arrived with fanfare. That morning, on a whim, when I shaved I did not shave above my upper lip.

Susan had called our favorite Mexican Food restaurant[64], at the time, (Los Vaqueros, in Highland Park Village) and had them cater a backyard Mexican feast... with margaritas, of course. It was a good, if strange mix: a couple of my wife Susan's friends Ted & Judy Wright (our ski buddies), our next door neighbors, our 'across-the-alley' neighbors, my mother, Susan and I, and some of my cop-partners and their wives: Tom & Janie Covington, Jim Bryan and his date, Max and Pat Countryman, Ted and Judy Yarbro, Warren and Tony Biggs, Chip Bulin and his wife. We had wonderful weather for early September, it was a great evening! As I recall the Bi-GatorSmooth crew didn't talk too much about the FBR.

I had been clean-shaven since I started to shave... While I was in Vietnam I grew one mustache, shaved it off when I went on R&R, grew it back and shaved it off the second time when I went on my second R&R. I came home from Vietnam in November 1970, like I left, clean-shaven. But for some reason, possibly influenced by the fact that lots of cops had mustaches, I started a new one that morning. By the time the party was over and the guests were gone no one could really 'see it', but I could feel the unshaved stubble above my lip. Tom and Jim already had mustaches... soon the Three Amigos of the Bi-GatorSmooth squad would all be mustachioed—as was, reportedly, our nemesis the FBR.

---

[64] It would be a month or so later when I discovered the newly opened **Desperados**, which would become and has remains my all-time favorite Mexican Food restaurant.

Author Note: Although I trimmed it regularly, I didn't shave it off until fifteen years later on my forty-fifth birthday. My then wife, Janine, had never seen me without a mustache and had, just the day previous, suggested I might shave it off. So that morning, again on a whim, I shaved it off. As soon as she saw it was gone, she said, "grow it back!"

FBR's *Month-At-A-Glance 1976*
Wednesday, September 8:   9:30 Bob Bloom
                 Cole Ten

FBR's *Month-At-A-Glance 1976*
Thursday, September 9:   s.3. 7:00

Dallas, Texas
Evening Sunday, September 12, 1976

9/1 2	W	27- 7	PHILADELPHI A	49,09 1

THE DALLAS COWBOYS were the after-church activity on Sunday's in Dallas. In our never-ending quest for clues Tom and I tracked the Cowboy games (in and out of town) to see if there could be any correlations with the FBR's activities. How, if at all, did their schedule affect his? Could he be someone affiliated, even in an ancillary way such as food vendor, with the Dallas Cowboy organization or Texas Stadium. In search of the those answers you will see boxed references throughout the remainder of the book showing the Cowboy game by date, whether it was a win (W) or a loss (L), the name of the opponent and the official attendance numbers. A *clear box* for 'home'; a *dark box* for an away game.

Since the FBR's suspect description was of white male, 20's, medium length dark blond or light brown hair, medium build, 160-180 pounds., it was unlikely that the FBR was a Dallas Cowboy player. We never found a correlation.

Dallas, Northeast Patrol Division, Beat 245
2:30 am Monday, September 13, 1976
Offense Number 62 (R-35)

THE SUSPECT, DESCRIBED as an unknown white male, 20's, medium length dark blond or light brown hair, medium build, husky in shoulders, no mustache wearing a short sleeve striped T-shirt type shirt, faded blue jeans and a beige stocking mask entered apartment 1049 around 2:10 in the morning.

LAW, the nineteen year-old white female, about to become a victim of the Friendly Burglar-Rapist was an Airman Apprentice at the U.S. Naval Air Station in Grand Prairie. *LAW*, was five-foot-four, brown-haired, blue-eyed and weighed about a hundred and five pounds. She was staying as a guest in the apartment of her ex-brother-in-law while he was out of town.

She told Reporting Officers, D.K. Lowe #3770 and L.L. Barbee #2945, that the suspect probably got in through an unlocked window; said her ex-brother-in-law puts his stereo in the open window on weekends so everyone will have music at the pool... and forgot to lock the window.

LAW had been sleeping off and on for hours, had even reset her alarm clock three or four times at one hour intervals; noting at 2:00am, as she reset it for 3:00am, that the hall light, bedroom light and TV were all on.

Ten minutes later when the lights and TV went off *LAW* immediately woke up. When she realized the lights were out she fumbled on the nightstand for her glasses, got up and started down the hall, stopping at a three-switch panel and flipped all three turning on the hall, closet, and dining room light.

The Friendly Burglar-Rapist came out of the second bedroom. From beneath his stocking mask, with a hole over his right cheek, he ordered, "Be quiet, and you won't get hurt. I'm only a burglar."

She noted he was wearing a pair of soft black gloves. In his right hand was a knife with a four-inch blade he'd retrieved from her kitchen. She told the R.O.'s later that she didn't think he ever took the gloves off.

Pointing the knife at *LAW* he explained, "If you'll be quiet, I'm not going to hurt you, but I've got a knife!" He took off her glasses and dropped them on the floor as he turned on the light in the living room and then marched her back into the bedroom from the hallway. Standing her next to the bed he tied her hands in front of her with a phone cord he'd cut from the dining room phone, one tightly, one loosely. "Be quiet and don't move."

He went to the bathroom and returned, removed a pillowcase from one of the pillows on her bed and slipped it over her head. He then slipped the knife under her bra strap and sliced upward, cutting it in two. He cut one strap in front, one in the back. After fondling her breasts he led her toward the living room, turning off the bedroom light.

When they got to the couch he sat her down, "Lie on your stomach." When she had done as he asked he pulled the pillowcase off her head. "Keep your eyes closed and lie on your side." He unzipped his pants and knelt down in front of *LAW*, his already erect phallus pointed at her face, "Now, make me feel good."

She fellated the Friendly Burglar-Rapist for several minutes until he told her to get on her stomach and then to get up on her hands and knees. He got on the couch with her and entered her from behind; fondling her breasts as he repeatedly penetrated her vagina.

Not through with testing new positions, he withdrew and told her to, "now lay on your back." When she was where he wanted her he pressed himself into her again and again, till he climaxed. While in this position he told her to put her still tied hands over his head and onto his neck, as he lay on top of her. After his orgasm he had her take her hands away and he got up, pulled up his pants and then put the pillowcase back over her head.

The FBR then went into *LAW*'s kitchen. She could hear him open the refrigerator and take something out and make drinking sounds. He had taken out a pitcher of lemonade and had drunk directly from the pitcher.

Moments later he pulled her up off the couch and led her by the end of the cord tied to her hands. In the bedroom he tied the free end of the cut telephone cord to the handle of the dresser next to her bed.

"Where's your purse?"

"On the table… aah, no, I think I left it in the car, sorry."

"That's ok." He left the room.

She remarked to the R.O.'s how nice her attacker had been the whole time and how he spoke in a deep whispering voice.

When he came back into her bedroom he said, "I'm going to make sure I can leave, when I make sure, I will tell you I'm going." He then cut the cord to the bedroom telephone. "Now, just forget about this... you can do what you want to do, but it will be a lot less hassle if you forget about it."

LAW didn't hear anything for a few minutes, and then heard the front door open and close. Getting out of bed, she called out, "Sir?" and got no answer. *LAW* removed the pillowcase on her head and unfastened the cord tying her to the dresser handle then untied one hand.

She searched the hallway till she found her glasses, then got dressed, grabbed her car keys off the dining room table and drove to the Shell station at Meadow and Central Expressway to call police.

As cops will, they had to ask the question: why were you getting up every hour, setting and re-setting your alarm clock? *LAW* explained her divorce had just been final on July 20th and then two weeks ago she'd been kicked out of her parent's house because they didn't like that she was dating a forty year-old married man. She told the officers her boyfriend was a Navy recruiter and lived close by on Forest Ridge, and he had helped her get a job with the Navy. She had just gotten back from six weeks training in Mississippi where she had attended Navy Aviation Store Keeper School. She said that she was waiting for him to arrive around 5:00am and didn't want to oversleep. She said he had been to the apartment once, the week before, at the same time.

Investigator Landers, also at the scene, was told by *LAW* that perhaps some of her ex-brother-in-law's "weird" friends might be responsible for the rape, but had no one in mind.

Tactical Officer C.M. Dooley #2003 was called to the scene. He and his canine partner trailed the suspect from complainant's "front door north to the parking lot then went east across a large field." We "ran trail and it ended in a parking lot at 8383 Meadow Road (Meadow Green Apartments). Suspect possibly had car at this location. There was a large spot of fluid and a trail leading from parking lot out onto Meadow Road. There were no other cars parked in this part of the lot. It was about two blocks from complainant's apartment."

FBR's *Month-At-A-Glance 1976*
Monday, September 13:   Eddy Entrie
                             R (indecipherable)
                             AM **OBZERVER**
                             9:30 S B.

274

FBR's *Month-At-A-Glance 1976*
Tuesday, September 14:   Bd mtg 4:00
FBR's *Month-At-A-Glance 1976*
Thursday, September 16:   Lunch **(indecipherable)**

FBR's *Month-At-A-Glance 1976*
Friday, September 17:   GaZette
Copy & Layout (date circled)

9/19	W	24-6	@New Orleans	52,417

FBR's *Month-At-A-Glance 1976*
Thursday, September 20:   ~~Waddel~~

For the reader, understanding the density of apartment complexes in North Dallas and the number of units in a given property, which was often 'next door' to another property company's units is not easy to visualize from the written word. Here is a thumbnail 'aerial' sketch of the Willowick Apts which are described on the next page (275) in Offense #63.

Note: The Willowick Apts. is just one (1) of forty-one (41) apartment complexes 'hit' by the FBR.

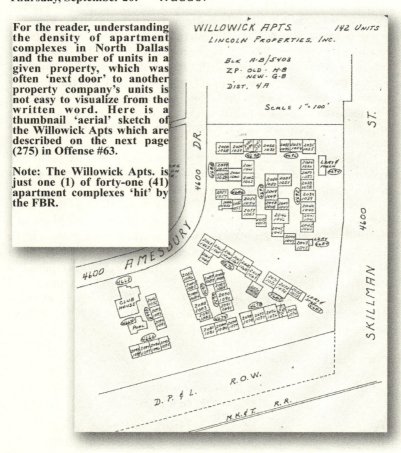

Chapter 20

Woulda, Coulda, Shoulda

**Dallas, Northeast Patrol Division, Beat 245
1:00 am Wednesday, September 22, 1976
Offense Number 63 (R-36)
FBR Palm Print
See Appendix A - Newspaper Article # 29a**

IT WAS DARK in the apartment, all the lights were off, and though it was a calm clear night, with a touch of fall in the air as the temps had dipped into the low sixties, the new moon provided no light.

It was an ordeal she and her roommate had discussed and prepared for; a moment for which they both had stored away an equalizer, since her roommate *KSW* had been raped in this very same apartment in July 27, 1975, and *BDD* had apparently foiled a break-in two days after the Fourth of July this year. Along with their 'other' precautions they had had screws put in the windows so they could not be raised.

BDD, a twenty-eight year-old white female, was a secretary at El Centro College downtown. She worked eight to four-thirty Monday through Friday; tomorrow would be a regular work day; hump day.

When she went to bed Tuesday night, alone in the apartment, her roommate *KSW* was away in Mexico.

The temperature had risen to eighty-four during the day, but before going to bed, with a real taste of fall in the air, she had turned off the AC and took the screws out of a living room window and raised it to let in the cool outside air.

This would be, by our count, the Friendly Burglar-Rapist's third "official" visit to apartment 1070 in the Willowick Apartments at 4676 Amesbury.

He knew the area well, knew the apartment well. He had lost track of how many times he had passed it in the last year trying to decide if tonight would be the night for the other roommate, or maybe he'd go for a second helping of the first roommate. Three months before one of the girls had heard his approach, he'd been too noisy, and he'd had to flee. Tonight would be different.

Apartment 1070 and its upstairs neighbor 2070 were almost a building unto themselves at the end of a row of six upstairs-downstairs units. Their building[65] jutted outward into the facing triangle courtyard formed by the adjacent buildings; as such all four walls of apartment 1070 were visible. On previous nights, since July, he had tested the windows, and found them screwed down. Tonight as he made his way through the courtyard he saw the partially open window of unit 1070.

He took off his shoes as he stood in the flower bed, a moonless night over his shoulder, he donned his dark chocolate brown cotton gloves, pried off the screen and opened the window to 1070 and slipped inside. After doing his usual thing, he headed to the bedrooms, the first was empty. In the second he found two bras hanging on the door knob. He carried them over to the bed and dropped them on the floor, in case he needed them as extra restraints.

BDD was asleep when felt something brush her lips then apply pressure. Startled she woke and knew what it was immediately. A man's gloved hand; she could see it was his left hand on her mouth. In his right hand he held a knife to the left side of her neck.

Oh my God, my God, she thought, *it's him!* She stole a quick glance at her night stand... *too far!* She saw him in silhouette it was too dark to see his face, but she was trying to focus, *he's wearing a mask.*

"Don't scream, don't yell out," said the man with the calm whispered voice her roommate had told her about, "I'm going to do some pleasurizing!"

BDD managed to raise her right hand and touch his hand and realized he was either wearing a glove or a sock on his hands. Trying to maintain control, weighing her options, *BDD* said, "I'm not going to scream, please don't put the knife against my neck, I won't scream."

"Put your right hand at your side." When she complied he laid the knife on the pillow with its tip touching the left side of her neck. "That's just to let you know there is a knife here, put your face in the pillow and close your eyes."

He took hold of her hands and put them together then tied them with phone cord from the phone in the living room. Ok,

---

"get up, out of bed and stand up." Standing next to the bed, her hands tied, wearing sleeping attire consisting of a blue work shirt, sleeping-bra and panties, he added a hood; a pillowcase from her bed. He turned her around and with both hands on her shoulders he pushed, guided her out of the bedroom and down the hallway.

About five paces into the living room he stopped her, stepped away and turned on a lamp. He then grabbed the end of the phone cord tied to her hands and pulled, directing her through the living room, "Don't run into any tables."

From the sound of his soft speaking voice she tried to determine his height, she figured he was approximately six foot tall—she couldn't make out any other physical characteristics.

He led her to the couch, and then dropped the cord. She could hear things that had been on the couch being swept off the couch and onto the floor. He then pulled on the cord and positioned her in front of the couch, "Stand here!"

She felt his hands at her waist, grabbing at the waist band of her panties. He slowly pulled them down to her ankles. "Step out of them," he said. She complied. Next she felt his hands unbuttoning her shirt. Looking down through the opening at the bottom of the pillowcase *BDD* could now see that he had on dark brown cotton gloves, on both hands.

He slipped his hands around her back trying several times to unsnap her bra. "I'll have to cut the straps."

"Please don't," *BDD* said, "it unsnaps in the front."

The Friendly Burglar-Rapist unsnapped *BDD*'s bra and said, "You're being very sensible, you haven't gotten hurt, and if you keep acting this way, you are not going to get hurt." He told her to sit on the couch then redirected her to get on her stomach. Not quite satisfied he said, "Get on your hands and knees and put your forearms on the couch in front of you."

BDD heard the sound of something familiar, the pumping sound from her hand lotion; she knew she kept a bottle on her nightstand. She heard the sound of the pump squishing it out. Later she couldn't remember whether he applied the cold lotion just to himself or to her as well.

Standing behind her he positioned himself and with a forward thrust entered her as she remained kneeling. After a few thrusts he backed out of her, "Lie on your back."

He again penetrated her while she lay on her back, grabbing her left breast with a gloved hand and thrusting to climax after two or three minutes.

BDD felt him lift up off of her and right himself on the floor then heard a zipper sound. She felt a tug on the wire around her hands. He kept pulling till she got up off the couch. Then leading her by the phone cord he pulled her toward the bedrooms.

"Where are we going," *BDD* asked?

"Just come on." He pulled her into her absent roommate's bedroom. "Sit on the floor and be quiet!"

She sat on the floor of *KSW*'s bedroom, next to her nightstand. He took the long end of the phone cord he'd used to tie *BDD*'s hands and tied it to KSW's bedroom doorknob. She heard him in *KSW*'s bathroom, it sounded to her like he had taken off whatever he'd had on this head. He came back into *KSW*'s bedroom and told *BDD*, "I am going to leave in a little bit, but right now, I want to get something to drink, I'll be right back."

After a few minutes of sitting there scared and mad *BDD* thought, *now's my chance*. She opened the drawer of *KSW*'s nightstand and took out *KSW*'s gun.

BDD pulled off the pillowcase and untied herself. She quietly went through the joining bathroom into her bedroom and pulled on a pair of jeans. From her own bedside table she now withdrew her own gun. With a gun in each hand *BDD* searched her apartment only to find her assailant was gone.

The Supplement Report filed on 9.22.76 by RA Pettie #2514 with Bobby Brown #1057 related: Color photos taken of inside of Compl's apt and outside of window where entry gained. Latent print lifted from a cardboard box found in floor next to sofa. Latent palm lifted from inside window sill where entry gained. Compl stated suspect was wearing socks on his hands.[66] Sock feet print in flowerbed outside window. Two partial areas of sock impression dug up & brought to P.E.S. (no plaster kit in car) cast made of cloth weave of foot tracks. Print from cardboard box not "Mr. Friendly's", unknown about palms.

---

[66] An apparent contradiction? The Comp.'s statement as reported by Reporting Officer / R.J. Catona #2942 was that: *Susp. then unbutton comp's shirt (at this time comp was able to see the susp was wearing what appeared to be bro cotton gloves on both hands)*, however, Pettie/Brown reported the *Compl stated susp was wearing socks on his hands*.

On 9.30.76 P.E.S. Bobby Brown's follow-up supplement commented: "A partial left palm lifted from window sill at 5657 Amesbury #1080 was checked against all palms lifted at scene of North Dallas rapes. This palm is the same as one found at BB's rape & robbery at 6059 Village Glen #3208, 23 months ago, 12-18-74. Serv# 401910-F.

FBR's *Month-At-A-Glance 1976*
Thursday, September 23: Waddel ?
        442-2217
        Lunch D P
FBR's *Month-At-A-Glance 1976*
Friday, September 24:   S. A w/Bapts
        11:00 Jim
FBR's *Month-At-A-Glance 1976*
   Saturday, September 25:   Sat 12:00 FB

FBR's *Month-At-A-Glance 1976*
Monday, September 27: Waddel
        San Antonio ?
        D.U. mtg.

Dallas, Northeast Patrol Division, Beat 215
2:00 am Tuesday, September 28, 1976
Offense Number 64 (R-37)

SHE HAD BEEN out most of the day. In the morning she had gone to Nautilus Fitness Center at Skillman and Abrams, then shopping, lunch at Ichabod's, bike riding, and visited her friends upstairs. She had come back down to her apartment and watched TV till about 12:30 or 1:00am then went to bed.

AT 2:54am, Reporting Officers A.R. Cassady #3273 and C.R. Foist #3706 were dispatched to apartment 120C at 5836 E. Lover's Lane, The Citadel Apartments, regarding an aggravated rape. As they arrived it was rainy and sixty-two degrees with just enough of a nine mile an hour wind out of the north-northeast to make it uncomfortable.

They learned that their complainant, *ALB*, formerly of Florida, was a white female twenty-four who worked as a Dallas-based stewardess for Delta Airlines.

In the M/O section of the O/I R (Form 75-1) the R.O. wrote: "SEXUAL INTERCOURSE BY FORCE OF KNIFE"

His narrative was as follows:

THE WEATHER COULD BE DESCRIBED AS COOL & RAINY. COMP WOKE UP SAW GUY STANDING AT END OF HER BED IN DOORWAY & TRIED TO RECOGNIZE WHO HE WAS BUT COULD NOT. COMP SAID TO SUSP "WHO ARE YOU & WHAT DO YOU WANT?" SUSPS SAID, "SHUT UP I WON'T HURT YOU." COMP SAID, "WHAT ARE YOU GOING TO DO?" AND SUSP SAID, "BE QUIET." SUSPS STARTED COMING OVER TO SIDE OF BED & AS HE CAME COMP COULD SEE HE HAD A KNIFE IN HIS HAND. HE CAME OVER TO BED & SAID TO COMP, "TURN OVER, LAY ON YOUR STOMACH, KEEP YOUR EYES SHUT." SUSP THEN WENT OVER TO PHONE WHICH WAS CLOSE TO COMP'S BED AND CUT WIRES. COMP REFUSED TO TURN OVER ON HER STOMACH SO THE SUSP PUSHED COMP ON HER STOMACH & HE PULLED BEDCOVERS DOWN. COMP WAS KIND OF ON HER SIDE & SUSP TOOK A PILLOW & TOOK CASE OFF OF IT & PUT IT OVER HER HEAD & TOLD COMP TO "KEEP HER EYES SHUT & TURN OVER TO WALL. DURING THIS TIME COMP WAS SAYING TO SUSP: "WHO ARE YOU, WHY ARE YOU DOING THIS?" SUSP SAID, "THIS IS THE WAY I MAKE MY LIVING, I'VE BEEN WATCHING YOU." COMP AGAIN SAID TO SUSP, "WHY ARE YOU DOING THIS TO ME? SUSPS SAID, "YOU DESERVE IT." AFTER SUSP HAD PUT PILLOWCASE OVER COMP'S HEAD HE TIED HER HANDS W/TELEPHONE CORD. SUSP ASKED COMP, "WHERE IS YOUR ROOMMATE?" COMP SAID, "SHE IS GONE." SUSPS SAID, "WHEN WILL SHE BE BACK?" COMP SAID, "EARLY IN THE MORNING." SUSP SAID, "I DON'T WANT YOU TO SCREAM, IF YOU DO SCREAM I WON'T HESITATE TO KILL YOU AT ALL." SUSP SAID TO COMP, "COME WITH ME." & HE WALKED HER INTO OTHER BEDRM W/HIM BEHIND HER & W/HIS HANDS ON HER SHOULDER. SUSP PULLED OFF THE COMP'S NIGHT SHIRT, UP TO HER NECK & THEN SUSP PUSHED COMP DOWN ON BED. SUSP TOOK COMP'S UNDERWEAR OFF. SUSP DID NOT TAKE HIS

CLOTHES OFF, JUST PULLED THEM DOWN. COMP SAID TO SUSP, "ARE YOU GOING TO HURT ME?" & SUSP SAID TO COMP "I WON'T HURT YOU IF YOU DO WHAT I WANT & WILL LEAVE AS SOON AS I GET WHAT I WANT." SUSP BEGAN KISSING COMP'S NIPPLES. SUSP GOT ON TOP OF COMP & INSERTED HIS PENIS INTO HER VAGINA & HAD A CLIMAX." SUSP SAID TO COMP, "JUST BE QUIET, YOU ARE DOING JUST FINE. COMP DID NOT HAVE A CLIMAX. SUSP STAYED OFF OF COMP A COUPLE OF MINUTES THEN HE GOT BACK ON HER & INSERTED HIS PENIS IN HER VAGINA & HAD SEXUAL INTERCOURSE & SUSP HAD CLIMAX AND COMP DID NOT. DURING TIME HE WAS HAVING SEXUAL INTERCOURSE THE COMP STATED THAT SUSP HAD TAKEN OFF HIS GOLVES AND KEPT TRYING TO STRAIGHTEN HER LEGS AS SHE WAS ABOUT TO CRY AND WAS SHAKING. SUSPS SAID, "JUST LAY THERE AND SHUT UP." SUSP TRIED TO KISS COMP BUT SHE WOULD NOT LET HIM SO HE FINALLY GAVE UP. SUSP SAID TO COMP AS SHE GOT UP, "COME ON I AM GOING TO TIE YOU UP TO THE CHAIR IN YOUR ROOM." "KEEP YOUR EYES SHUT YOU CAN SEE THROUGH THE PILLOWCASE. SUSP BROUGHT COMP BACK INTO ORIGINAL BEDRM AND TIED HER HANDS TO LEFT ARM OF BAMBOO CHAIR, FOR THERE WAS NO HEADBOARD ON THE BED. SUSP SAID TO COMP, "I AM GOING TO LEAVE. DON'T SAY OR DO ANYTHING." SUSP WALKED OUT OF ROOM AND COMP SAID OUT LOUD, "ARE YOU STILL THERE?" SUSP SAID TO COMP, "SHUT UP, THERE ARE SOME PEOPLE OUTSIDE SO I HAVE GOT TO WAIT A MINUTE OR SO BEFORE I LEAVE." COMP HEARD SUSP IN ICE BOX. SUSP THEN CAME BACK INTO ROOM WHERE COMP WAS & SAID, "I AM GOING TO BE LEAVING SO DON'T DO ANYTHING FOR A FEW MINUTES."

COMP SAT FOR THREE OR FOUR MINUTES AND SHE SAID OUT LOUD AGAIN, "ARE YOU GONE?" COMP DID NOT HEAR HIM SO SHE GOT HER

HANDS UNDONE & THEN SHE TOOK PILLOWCASE OFF OF HER HEAD. COMP WENT TO PHONE & LINES HAD BEEN CUT & WENT TO THE OTHER TWO PHONES IN HOUSE & OTHER TWO LINES HAD BEEN CUT. APPARENTLY THIS IS THE M.O. OF "THE FRIENDLY RAPIST."

Later a partially drunk carton of orange juice that had been in *ALB*'s refrigerator was found to have been left on the chest of drawers in her roommate's bedroom. Also, the Friendly Burglar-Rapist during his "foreplay" had gone through *ALB*'s purse and wallet, removing her driver's license making note of her name. He left them on the bar in the kitchen but took ALB's name to the bedroom where he continually called his victim by her first name throughout the episode. *ALB* told R.O.'s that her assailant smelled like *Jontue* perfume which she had had in her purse, which she learned later, he had spilled.

ALB described the man who raped her as being a "white male, six-foot, 160 lbs., average build, mustache, grey sweatshirt, white men's shoes, dark brown or cotton work clothes. Had Southern accent. Hose over head."

Later in *ALB*'s questionnaire to question 29, [Give your description of suspect: hair (color and length) _____ clothing _____ height _____ weight _____], she provided these answers: "? med. length"; "Gray Jogging Suit"; "6'"; "170".

FBR's *Month-At-A-Glance 1976*
Tuesday, September 28:F.B. 8:30 #6

FBR's *Month-At-A-Glance 1976*
Wednesday, September 29: R.H.
S.B. 9:30

Investigator Landers, trying to leave no stone unturned sent out the following TeleType message:[67]

25338 PD DALLAS 9-29-76 2020CDT

---

[67] Copy placed in FBR - Patrol Officers Handbook on the FBR page 10

AUSTIN DPS
WOULD YOU PLS SEND THIS MESSAGE NATIONWIDE
WANTED BY DALLAS POLICE DEPT

W/M/20-30, 5'9-6'0, BLONDISH BRO HAIR, 150-180LBS, SPEAKS IN SOFT, HIGHER THAN AVERAGE PITCH VOICE SLIGHTLY MUSCULAR BUILD. THIS SUBJECT ENTERS UNLOCKED WINDOWS OR SLIDING GLASS PATIO DOORS IN ADULT APT COMPLEXES. WEARS STOCKING MASK OR SKI MASK, SOMETIMES WEARS BLUE JEANS OR GRAY JOGGING PANTS. WHITE TENNIS SHOES. SUSP ENTERS APT CUTS TELEPHONE CORDS. WAKES VICTIM AND PLACES PILLOW CASE OVER VICTIM'S HEAD. TIES VICTIM TO BED POST WITH TELEPHONE CORD. SUSP THREATENS VICTIM WITH A KNIFE, USUALLY TAKEN FROM VICTIM'S KITCHEN BEFORE SHE IS AWAKENED BY SUSP. SUSP USES VICTIMS LOTION TO LUBRICATE HIMSELF, RAPES VICTIM AND TAKES VICTIM'S MONEY FROM HER PURSE. SUSP USUALLY PLACES PILLOW CASE OVER THE VICTIM'S HEAD BEFORE HE CAN BE SEEN. THIS DEPT HAS FINGERPRINTS ON THE SUBJ AND REQUESTS ANY INFO ON RAPES IN YOUR AREA WITH THE SAME OR SIMILAR M O PLS SEND COPY OF SUPS FINGERPRINTS. SEND TO JOHN R LANDERS, INV. HOMICIDE UNIT, DALLAS POLICE DEPT

INV J R LANDERS
C A PERSONS
PD DALLAS TEX BJS 1928CDT

Author Note: *A number of responses came back, but none of the suspects matched our guy's fingerprints and their MO's would be different enough to be not attributable to the FBR.*

FBR's *Month-At-A-Glance 1976*
End of Month Blank: GaZette Disto

FBR's *Month-At-A-Glance 1976*
Sunday, October 3:   Soc 1:30 Hunt

Dallas, Northeast Patrol Division, Beat 256
Unknown Time Prior to Monday, October 4, 1976
Offense Number 65

IN A MEMORANDUM with the City of Dallas logo:

DATE: October 4, 1976
TO: D.H. Milliken, Captain of Police
SUBJECT: Friendly Rapist Investigation.

Sir:

I received a call from the security officer of the Telephone Company on the morning of October 4, 1976, stating that the telephone cords had been cut in apartment #223 at 5951 Melody Lane. The telephone number at that location is 361-xxxx.

I called this number and was advised by a w/f who identified herself as Mrs. Oxxxs, that she did not have to talk to the police and that we did not have a warrant for her apartment, and that she did not have to say anything to us. She further stated that she had no way of knowing that I was a police officer, and further would not talk to me about the cut telephone cords. She said, "I don't know anything about the cords being cut, they were cut when I got home." In other words, she said she didn't have any way of knowing that I was a policeman and that the telephone cords had been cut while she was away from the apartment and hung up the phone on me.

I then contacted Sgt. Robinson at the Northeast Substation and requested that a uniformed officer go to the location and attempt to talk with Mrs. O. On October 4, 1976 at 7:15pm, I was advised by

Patrolman J.A. Blantom #3702, that he had gone to this location, knocked on the door, and the door was answered by a white female approximately 32 years of age. The female stated, "You're a phony policeman, too!", and slammed the door shut.

Officer's Comment: In my opinion, this could very well be an attempt criminal assault committed by the Friendly Rapist, in that he entered the apartment and cut the telephone cords before checking the bedrooms to see if anyone was home. Upon seeing that no one was inside the apartment, he left the location.

Respectfully submitted,
/s/
John R. Landers #2445
Investigator of Police
Crimes Against Persons Section

[**NB**: Apt. 233, 5951 Melody Lane is in the complex called: The Settlement, the site of two previous FBR related offenses.]

FBR's *Month-At-A-Glance 1976*
Monday, October 4:   S.B. 9:30 #2

FBR's *Month-At-A-Glance 1976*
Tuesday, October 5:   F.B. 7:00
                          3:00 H
FBR's *Month-At-A-Glance 1976*
Wednesday, October 6: IABC
                          Conf.

(arrow indicates IABC Conf. 10-6 thru 10-8-76)

FBR's *Month-At-A-Glance 1976*
Thursday, October 7:   Zeigmann &Burkett
                          S. B. #4 7:00
(arrow indicates IABC Conf. 10-6 thru 10-8-76)

Dallas, Northeast Patrol Division, Beat 214

4:00 am Sunday, October 10, 1976
Offense Number 66

AMERICAN AIRLINES STEWARDESS *CW*, a white female thirty-two, lived at 10824 Steppington #1433 in the Cobblestone Apartments. She had been having a restless night and at that moment was lying in bed, awake.

Minutes earlier, under a full moon, the Friendly Burglar-Rapist had removed a face plate from her sliding glass door to gain entry. In his ski mask and gloves he walked over to the front door and unlocked it, setting up his escape route. Thus far he had not made a sound. He continued down the dark hallway into his victim's bedroom. With the outside temps hovering at fifty-two degrees in the slight five mile an hour north-northeast wind, the apartment's heater fan was humming.

As he appeared in the doorway of *CW*'s bedroom, she saw him and screamed! He turned and ran with *CW* running after him. He first headed for the sliding glass door, then thinking better of it, changed his mind and scooted out the unlocked front door.

CW described her would-be attacker to Reporting Officers, R.A. Spain #3451 and J.N. Stacy 3589, as approximately five-foot-eight, 140 lbs, a white male 20 to 30 wearing blue jeans, a full red ski mask and gloves.

FBR's *Month-At-A-Glance 1976*
Sunday, October 10:   Soc 1:30
                         Civic Center

FBR's *Month-At-A-Glance 1976*
Monday, October 11:   S.B. 9:30 #4

FBR's *Month-At-A-Glance 1976*
Tuesday, October 12:   F.B. 7:15

FBR's *Month-At-A-Glance 1976*
Wednesday, October 13:   B (indecipherable) ?

Chapter 21

A Fighter In Waiting

Dallas, Northeast Patrol Division, Beat 235
12:30 am Thursday, October 14, 1976
Offense Number 67
FBR - Partial Palm Print

ANOTHER VICTIM WAITED at apartment 136 in the First Day Apartments at 5830 Prestonview Boulevard. She did not intend to be a victim and she thought she was waiting on sleep to overtake her, not a rapist.

Outside it was sixty-six degrees under a clear sky; the gibbous moon had risen only an hour before, its light angling in from between the curtain and the edge of the window.

PJ, a white female thirty years old, was snug under her blanket lying on the couch watching TV, the living room lamp competing with the TV to illuminate the room along with slivers of moonlight.

With the room thus lit, the Friendly Burglar-Rapist stood outside *PJ*'s kitchen window looking in and saw his next victim apparently asleep on the couch. He slowly raised the window and methodically moved the five empty old-style glass Coke bottles from the window sill and then climbed in the window.

Watching his victim, who had not moved, and knowing now that some of the sounds of his movements were masked by the TV, he still moved gingerly about the kitchen. He found a knife and cut the phone cord in the kitchen. Moving into the living room he spied *PJ*'s purse and took the wallet out and took it with him to the back of the apartment where he cut the second phone's cord. He went in and out of the bathroom. He found the cash in *PJ*'s wallet and laid it on her bedroom dresser. He opened her bedroom closet, rifled through it, and finding nothing to steal he dumped *PJ*'s wallet on the floor of the closet. Once he had assured himself there was nothing else to steal, he went back into the living room.

PJ was still asleep on the couch. He turned off the living room lamp.

PJ felt a weight settle on her and she woke with a start to see a man sitting astride her.

In his practiced, whispered voice he said, "If you don't do as you're told I will stick this knife in your throat and leave! "Pull your left arm out from under the blanket," he said and when she had done so he bound her wrist with telephone cord. "Now raise your right hand from the covers…"

As he said this he laid the butcher knife on her chest and stood up at the end of the couch. *PJ* grabbed the knife and began stabbing at her assailant.

The Friendly Burglar-Rapist jumped back, yelling obscenities and ran to the kitchen and almost dove out of the kitchen window. *PJ* ran out her front door screaming and yelling for help.

PJ described her assailant to Reporting Officers R. Langran #3337 and R.L. Dorsey #2820 as a white male, thirty, six-foot-one, 200 to 220 pounds, wearing a bulky sweater, jeans and a stocking cap.

P.E.S. B.G. Brown and R.A. Pettie processed the scene and among other "lifts", lifted from the kitchen window sill a partial palm print. They identified the palm as "same as left palm print lifted from 4976 Amesbury #1070, 9-22-76, Serv. #341283H; and 6059 Village Glen #3208, 12-18-74 Serv. # 401910F.

In Investigator John Lander's SR, dated 10-21-76, he noted that the complainant reported finding her wallet in a closet with nothing missing. John also wrote: "This was the "Friendly Burglar-Rapist"-- Prints found at the scene have been identified by P.E.S."

Subsequent to this attack on one of its residents, The First Day apartments issued their monthly news bulletin. It was dated "November 1976." The 8.5 x 14 sheet of goldenrod colored paper listed "Security" as its first topic among the complex's football team news, who won the energy conservation contest, the coming holiday season, the next "Party! Party! Party!", and other useful tidbits. Here is their paragraph on "Security":

Danny, our Security Guard, asks that we remind you to drive slowly, after entering the gate, especially from the gate to the first turn. We have had some slight accidents in that area. Please observe our Security rules. 1.STOP AT THE GATE FOR CLEARANCE. 2. NOTIFY YOUR GUESTS they must stop for clearance each time. 3.Call and notify the guard when you are expecting a guest. No one

will be admitted without clearance…from YOU. If your
line is busy, or you do not answer your phone, an
unexpected guest will not be admitted. 4. Do not go around
another car unless the guard waves you around. Although
we offer the very best in Security, we suggest you use "self-
protection" and be aware that you could be in danger. KEEP
WINDOWS DOWN AND LOCKED AND BE SURE
DRAPES ARE CLOSED AND DOORS LOCKED AT
NIGHT. REPORT TO THE POLICE AND YOUR
MANAGER immediately if you see or hear any suspicious
sounds, activities, automobiles or people. During the night,
call FIRST DAY SECURITY – 233-8XX1. WHEN YOU
RETURN HOME AT NIGHT have your key ready to open
your door. DO NOT OPEN YOUR DOOR TO A
STRANGER. USE YOUR PEEP HOLE! PLEASE report
any salesman or peddlers who knock on your door.

Author's Note: *No mention was made of the dozens of area
rapes or the Friendly Burglar-Rapist, whose terroristic rapes
had been in all the papers, on TV and radio.*

10/17	L	17-21	@St. Louis	64,889

FBR's *Month-At-A-Glance 1976*
Sunday, October 17:   Bye Soc
Rodeo

FBR's *Month-At-A-Glance 1976*
Monday, October 18:   S.B 8:15 #4

FBR's *Month-At-A-Glance 1976*
Tuesday, October 19:   F.B. 7:15

FBR's *Month-At-A-Glance 1976*
Wednesday, October 20:   S.Antonio ?

Dallas, Northeast Patrol Division, Beat 245
3:00 am Sunday, October 24, 1976
Offense Number 68 (R-38)
See Appendix A - Newspaper Article # 29a

AN OFFICE MANAGER for a business in Campbell Center at North Central Expressway and Loop 12, *VAO* had had a full Saturday of errands, arriving home to apartment 103 in the Four Seven's Apartment complex at 7777 Manderville Lane around midnight.

The past Monday had been a black day in Dallas. All week, everywhere she went, the city was abuzz with talk of the Cowboys, how would they do tomorrow after last Sunday's 17-21 lost to the Cardinals?

The city had been riding the Cowboy's out-of-the-starting-gate five game win streak like it was a Porsche on the Autobahn; fast and straight—all the way to the end; the Super Bowl, being the end. The cardiac Cards at home were always going to be tough… but, we had been doing so well.

The city was anxious. Tomorrow The 'Boys played the Bears, but here, here in Texas Stadium. Most everyone agreed Landry would have his team ready to play.

VAO came into her apartment Saturday night, turning on the lights before heading upstairs. Her plan had been to change clothes… She sat on the edge of the bed, and relaxed back.

Two hours later she woke with a start realizing that she had fallen asleep in her clothes. She got up, went downstairs, turned out all the lights, came back up, finished undressing and got ready for bed.

Back in bed and comfy, she was asleep in moments and remained so until the wee-hours of Sunday morning. About 3:00am she woke again, only this time she was awakened by a white male who was standing over her bed holding a knife, with its point to the center of her throat. "Don't open your eyes, lay there still. Don't move, don't talk!" All of this said in a very light whisper.

It had been so easy, here was another window "left open for ventilation;" he loved that phrase. He had easily pried off the screen, fully raised the window and climbed into the living room. Crossing to the front door, he unlocked it. Escape route in place, he went into the kitchen and found the knives and cut the telephone cord. From the fridge he pulled out a Diet Dr. Pepper and began drinking it. He found some magazines (*Apartment Living, Southern Living, Glamour, & Neiman-Marcus Christmas Book 1976*) and took drink and the four magazines into the downstairs bedroom, turned on the light and read while he finished his drink. *Burglary and Rape is a thirsty business.*

VAO held her eyes closed as he sat on the edge of the bed beside her. She felt his weight on the bed shift and heard what she thought was something being cut next to her. She realized it was the phone on the table next to her. "Lift your head and keep your eyes shut." He removed the pillow from under her head and placed it over her face. Now, "put your hands over your head— good. "Keep quiet." She then felt the cord being wrapped and tied around her right wrist and then wrapped around her left hand, binding them together. He stuck the knife to her neck again, to reinforce his words, "keep quiet."

He left her lying on the bed and went into the bathroom, turning on the lights. He discovered her purse on the door knob and rummaged through it, removing the cash he found, her driver's license and some change. He dumped the DL and change on the floor.

He found a bottle of Adios lotion and took it into the bedroom and left it on the night table next to *VAO*'s bed.

He went back to the bathroom and turned off the light. He said, "I'll tell you when I leave, as he walked to her bed and sat on its edge.

"Why are you doing this?"

He scraped the edge of the knife along VAO's neck and said, "Be quiet!" He scraped her neck with the knife several more times. He stood up and reached down and lifted up her nightgown, looking underneath. He then put the knife under her gown's shoulder straps and cut the straps. Next he cut her panties off with the knife. "Spread your legs," he said as he pushed them apart with his hands.

The Friendly Burglar-Rapist unzipped his pants then mounted his victim missionary style. She felt the roughness of his trousers and something sharp jabbing her right side, she thought it might be the knife. Later she realized it was likely his belt buckle. She could tell he did not undress, only had his pants pulled down. She noted with disgust that he climaxed and that his breath was bad; a rancid type odor. She told Reporting Officers, B.L. Anderson #2933 and R.L. Dorsey #3820 that the suspect had a "smooth, calm voice," that he was not wearing gloves, his hands felt smooth to her. During the time he went into the bathroom and had turned the light on she could see a visual outline of suspect and he appeared to be wearing casual clothes, possibly jeans with a long sleeved shirt. *VAO* said he may have also been wearing a stocking cap.

After the rape, he got up and went to her bedroom closet and turned on its light. "Keep quiet, I'll tell you when I'm leaving." She heard him walking across to the bedroom door then across the hall where he snapped on the light in the empty bedroom. She heard him going down the stairs then heard him rummaging around the downstairs portion of the apartment. Next she heard the front door open, but not close.

Lander's SR, dated 10-24-76, stated, in part: "At this time, latent prints found at scene are being compared by Lt. Day of CSS. This offense has most all the elements of those which were committed by the 'Friendly Burglar-Rapist'."

Author Note: *Tom and I had known for some time that John "got it"!*

Unfortunately, with all the time spent in *VAO*'s apartment, all the things he touched, M.R. Jarvis 2913 of P.E.S. reported recovering "poor" latent prints (fingers and palm)

10/2 4	W	31-2 1	CHICAG O	55,00 4

FBR's *Month-At-A-Glance 1976*
Sunday, October 24:   Soc 3:30
                              Hunt
FBR's *Month-At-A-Glance 1976*
Monday, October 25:   S.B. 8:15 #4

FBR's *Month-At-A-Glance 1976*
Tuesday, October 26:   F.B. 8:30

FBR's *Month-At-A-Glance 1976*
Wednesday, October 27:   S.B. 7:00 #4
                          9:00 V.B

FBR's *Month-At-A-Glance 1976*
Thursday, October 28:   S.B. Oct 28
               9:00 #2

10/31	W	20-7	@Washington	65,539

FBR's *Month-At-A-Glance 1976*
Tuesday, November 2:   F.B. 7:15
            # 4 8:15

Chapter 22

Get Out The Vote

Tuesday, November 2, 1976
Election Day

ANOTHER CLOSE ELECTION with far-reaching and lasting consequences. Carter/Mondale defeats Ford/Dole. The electoral vote was tallied 297 to 240, the popular vote was much closer: 40,831,881 to 39,148,634. A difference of 1,683,247 votes.

FBR's *Month-At-A-Glance 1976*
Wednesday, November 3:   Bob ?
Pro. dev. course 4:00
Elder 11:00

FBR's *Month-At-A-Glance 1976*
Thursday, November 4:# 4
7:00 P.C.
4:00 Thurs
1:00 (circled)

FBR's *Month-At-A-Glance 1976*
Sunday, November 7:   **Soc 1:30 MacAr Irving**

11/7	W	9-3	N.Y. GIANTS	60,905

FBR's *Month-At-A-Glance 1976*
Monday, November 8:   Mary S.L. all week

FBR's *Month-At-A-Glance 1976*
Tuesday, November 9:   F.B. 8:30

Dallas, Northeast Patrol Division, Beat 553
1:00 am Wednesday, November 10, 1976
Offense Number 69

REPORTING OFFICERS, M.M. Hay #3651 and D.B. Christian #3432, were using the virtually brand-new Dallas Police Department's revised Offense/Incident Report Form 76-1. The new form forced reporting officers, because of its many sets of givens for each area of a complaint or offense, to gather more information. The idea being that specific M/O data could be collected and the various data searched for by category with the computer; thereby identifying trends and similarities with greater frequency.

They got the Signal 13, prowler call, to 9711 Dalecrest apartment number 133 in the Copenhagen Apartments. They met *DS*, a white male, twenty-seven, at the apartment. The report stated: "No prowler found at loc."

The new O/I R form had only basic information on its single page, as that was discoverable by the public via such things as the Open Records Act and later the Freedom Of Information Act requests. However 'supplemental' reports, the additional pages, as it were, were not part of those open records laws.

On the supplement filled out by Hay the suspect was described in a series of specific blocks: Code, Name, Address, Arrest No., Nickname or Alias, Race, Sex, Age, D.O.B., Wt., Ht, Hair Col., Eye Col. Across this line of blocks Officers Hay wrote: S, unk, w, m, 20, unk, unk, 6', unk, unk. So our suspect was a w/m/20 approximately six-foot-tall.

In the next series of blocks were the highly specific references to the suspect's personal description/s laid out in categories with every imaginable combination of descriptive information including the definitive's 'unknown' and 'other'.

From Hay's circled specifics we know the suspect had long, wavy hair, no facial hair and was wearing a coat which Hay had amended with a parenthetical "green", proving that not every descriptor had indeed been thought of.

After making a search of the complex for the prowler, Hay wrote in the narrative on the final page of his report:

"Officer contacted Comp. again for further details. Comp stated that he first heard prowler by the sound of patio gate latch.

Then Comp heard front door handle being jiggled also. Comp was in bedroom at the time & looked out window. Comp saw Susp walking in walkway of Apts. coming from direction of Comp's patio.

Comp. saw Susp's face as Susp turned toward window. Comp could only see Susp from chest up. Comp said Susp was wearing a green quilted ski jacket. Susp's face was thin & his face was a dark complexion & his hair was thick & parted."

Dallas, Northwest Patrol Division, Beat 554
2:30 am Wednesday, November 10, 1976
Offense Number 70 (R-39)

GLOVED-HANDS CLOSED around her throat. *Cloth gloves?* She thought as her mind and body tried to wake from a dead sleep. With a knife held to her throat, she heard his first words, "If you say a word you are dead!"

In contravention of his own fatal admonition he asked her a question that required to her "say a word…"

"Are you alone?" He asked.

"Yes," came her weak reply.

"Are you married?"

"Yes."

"When will your husband be home?"

"Early this morning."

As if a journalist or a cop, he kept probing, kept asking questions. "Where is he?"

"He is visiting friends."

"Is there anyone else here?"

"No. My brother is coming over to check on me after he gets off work."

"If anyone comes in I'll go out that window." The questions over, for the moment, he said, "Shut your eyes and turn your head toward the window. Remember the knife!"

He tied her hands with the phone cord from the telephone in the living room then pulled a pillowcase over her head. In his low whisper he added, "Don't make a sound!"

Speaking through the opaque flower-covered pillowcase, "Please don't… I have a very bad infection."

"I'm not worried about that, I'm not here for that reason."

The Friendly Burglar-Rapist got up from the bed leaving his victim hooded and tied. He walked around the room. She could hear him opening drawers and rummaging through them opening then closing the closet. Inside she could hear clothes hangers scraping on the rod as he swept them aside. He came out and yelled, "You're lying to me. You're not married." He went to the front door, went outside for a few moments then came back.

He quickly cut off the straps to *MJL*'s pink nightgown with the knife. She felt the knife blade against her thigh, felt it slide up and under her white panties, felt the fabric strain against her as he pulled the knife up and cut through the cloth.

She felt him apply some kind of lotion to her genitals and rub it around. She could hear him apply lotion to himself.

"Move," he said, "to the side of the bed and put your knees up and hands down and don't make a sound. Again, in contravention of his own words, "I'm not here for that reason," he raped his victim, ejaculating inside her.

Moving off the bed he covered her with the bed-sheet and told her he would be leaving now, but would come back and tell her before he left.

When she no longer heard him she untied her hands and went to the landlord's apartment to call police.

Officers Hay and Christian had only just returned to service when they received the Signal 25, rape, at 2889 Clydedale, #220 in the Warren Place Apartments. Their complainant, *MJL*, they learned was a twenty-two year-old white female Loan Clerk whose husband was not home; learned that the suspect had entered through a living room window that the complainant had opened for ventilation before going to bed.

She told officers the suspect had a knife and spoke in a low, soft voice. She related her sister was a speech teacher and *MJL* was very aware of speech patterns. *MJL* said that the suspect's speech sounded as if he had a retainer at one time, as if his tongue stuck to the roof of his mouth when he tried to speak.

They learned that the complainant was robbed of approximately five dollars that had been in her purse.

From their astonished perspective, they learned one other thing that saddened and frustrated them. Crimes Against Persons Investigator John Landers was quickly on scene and found, in plain view, sitting on a shelf in a bookcase at the foot of the complainant's bed, a .25 automatic and a .375 Colt Python!

Complainant told Inv. Landers she could have gotten the pistols while suspect was walking through the apartment, but she said, "he walked so quietly, I couldn't determine where he was in the apartment... so I was afraid to get the pistols."

P.E.S. Officer Ernell Smith #2451, an academy classmate of Investigator Landers and mine, gathered latent prints and other evidence. Tactical Division Officer C.M. Dooley #2003 (Canine Unit) found tennis shoe prints outside the apartment.) Landers reported that Smith stated, "he usually attempts to make a plaster cast of shoe prints." Reports do not indicate that casts were made of the found shoe print impressions.

The suspect was trailed by Officer Dooley's canine partner from the front of complainant's apartment east across the parking lot and through the backyard of the house north of the Pan American Bank. The house is located in 2800 block of Kendale. Dooley said his dog followed the trail into the Bank's parking lot where it appeared the suspect had car parked. Located a pool of oil or fluid where car was parked and a trial of fluid led from the lot onto Kendale and then west on Northwest Highway. A drinking glass was located beside the garage in driveway of house where suspect's trail led. Glass was turned over to P.E.S. Inv. E. Smith #2451 for printing."

Tactical Officer Dooley made two other notes: he had "found tennis shoe prints along the trail similar to other offenses" and that a "trail of fluid was also observed at the scene of the offense at 8215 Meadow, apartment 1049" (occurring Mon. September 13, 1976).

FBR's *Month-At-A-Glance 1976*
Wednesday, November 10:   Bob (indecipherable)
                              7:00-7:30
                              4:00 P C

Dallas, Office of Central Division Analyst
9:00 am Wednesday, November 10, 1976

Today, once again, I was 'taken off the street', per Deputy Chief Dixon's direction, Tom and I started a special assignment working the FBR case, we could work any hours we needed or wanted ... we (I) wouldn't get overtime instead for 1 every hour of O/T I would get 1½ hours of compensatory (comp) time...

This photo was taken sometime in November 1976
Robert Sadler (Billy Bob) on the left & Thomas Covington (Tom Bob) on the right.

Tom is running down a license plate lead & I am charting the data from the latest FBR Offense. In front of my elbow was *the* 'FBR Book'. It contained all offenses attributed to the FBR and depending on when in November this photo was taken, it contained between 69 and 73 offenses. Five things of note: 1) the small bottle of "Liquid Paper" for correcting posting 'mistakes'; 2) the butt of a handle peaking out from my right hip was a 'highly concealable' S&W Model K .357 with 6" barrel & target grips; 3) a mug shot on the wall over my shoulder of a 'hook' we hoped could be our suspect, but was later discounted; 4) on the wall was an oversized copy of my book-logs of all FBR offenses; and 5) there is no computer anywhere in sight —we had no desktop computer, not even a terminal that hooked up to the 'big mother' on the 3rd floor (see below). When this photo was taken it would be 3 months and 8 more offenses before the FBR was caught.

[NB: Liquid Paper was invented by Bette Nesmith Graham (mother of Michael Nesmith of The Monkeys). They lived (at one time) one block over. Mike was a sometimes childhood playmate of mine and a high school classmate of my older sister, Sherry.]

Our name for the 3rd floor computer installation: "big mother".

Chapter 23

Six Steps To Murder

[NB: The FBR Book, mentioned in the photograph on the previous page, was updated daily, if not hourly. I had started it with the second FBR offense in Central Patrol Division (CPD), which prompted me to go back and find the other intervening offenses. "The Book" (a large looseleaf binder - ended up being three books) contained the FBR offenses in chronological order. Each O/IR was accompanied by its various Supplement Reports (CID-investigative report; P.E.S. documenting evidence recovered & processed) any general follow-up SRs, the requests for fingerprint comparisons, results of fingerprint comparisons, suspects 'looked at' and or eliminated, the medical report if the complainant was examined post assault, and the forensic report regarding analysis of fluids: seminal, blood. Additionally, attached to each offense were any notes Tom or I made and copies of the various Complainant Surveys.]

Dallas, Office of Central Division Analyst
5:00 pm Tuesday, November 11, 1976

TODAY, VETERAN'S DAY, Tom interviewed Dr. David Paul, Police Surgeon, from London, England!

Dr. Paul had been on a lecture tour in Dallas, but what Tom garnered from this fabulously experienced Police Surgeon came not as a result of spending and hour in a lecture hall listening to Dr. Paul. No, in typical Tom-fashion, it happened while consuming multiple cups of coffee and three pieces of cherry pie over several hours at a nearby Denny's restaurant.

Between their sips of coffee and bites of pie the two men bonded. Tom played the friendly inquisitor and the good doctor shared his wisdom regarding what he had experientially discovered. The result was Tom learned about the process the criminal proceeds through from rapist to murderer.

Dr. Paul told Tom it was a staged, six-step process and provided the following outline:

Dr. David Paul's Rape to Murder Progression[68]

I. Straight Sex
    A. vaginal intercourse
    B. missionary style
II. Varied Sex (positions)
III. Sodomy
    A.victim
    B. self
IV. Biting
    A. breasts
    B. thighs
V. Sadistic Pain
    A. arm twisting
    B. choking
    C. cutting
VI. Murder

With this 'pathology' in mind we revisited our entire case file and noted the changes in the FBR's crime scene behaviors as the offenses piled up.

We were always mindful that given the proper circumstances the FBR could have jumped from Step I to Step VI – Murder, in a single event.

For the past six months, the FBR had been one misstep from murder.

Dr. Paul's outline was later placed in the Patrol Officer's Handbook we created to educate our officers on the Friendly Burglar-Rapist.

FBR's *Month-At-A-Glance 1976*
Thursday, November 11: <u>Hair</u>

A SIGN THAT the Criminal Investigation Division was getting serious about the FBR was Lt. Roy Westphal's November

---

[68] Copy placed in FBR - Patrol Officers Handbook on the FBR pages 3-4

11, 1976 memo titled: *Criminal Assaults Involving the Friendly Rapist.*[69]

Four steps, which "will be followed" were detailed. But the most interesting paragraph, to Tom and me, was the last and most ominous one for our department's investigative, patrolling, and forensic capabilities. It reads: "Prints are our only form of evidence. Without these, it will be impossible to make a case on the Friendly Rapist."

Memorandum

CITY OF DALLAS

DATE   November 11, 1976

TO   ALL PERSONNEL

SUBJECT Criminal Assaults Involving
         the Friendly Rapist

In the event one of our officers receives a call on a criminal assault where it appears the Friendly Rapist is involved, the below listed steps will be followed in conducting the investigation:

1. The first officer at the scene should seat the complainant and remain with her until the Physical Evidence Section officers arrive. Do not attempt to determine the point of entry or departure as this will be determined by the PES officer. After the point of entry is determined, it should be protected and no one allowed near the point of entry to allow the K-9 Unit to trail the suspect.

2. Protect the scene. If someone must be allowed to enter the apartment, have them be seated and do not allow them to wander freely about the apartment. This includes apartment managers, boy friend, neighbors and officers.

3. After PES has completed their investigation, the reporting officer should conduct his investigation and make his written report.

4. Officers should not ask leading questions and unnecessary questions in an attempt to tie the offense with previous offenses. Investigator John R. Landers, Element #1165 will be at the scene to assist the officers. Inv. Landers and the K-9 Unit are automatically notified by the Dispatcher.

Prints are our only form of evidence. Without these, it will be impossible to make a case on the Friendly Rapist.

Roy W. Westphal
Lieutenant of Police
Acting Division Commander

sj

---

[69] Copy placed in FBR - Patrol Officers Handbook on the FBR page 20

FBR's *Month-At-A-Glance 1976*
Friday, November 12: IABC Banq. 7-9

Dallas, Patrol Division
7:45am Saturday, November 13, 1976
Officer Alvin E. Moore ~ Murdered[70]

FBR's *Month-At-A-Glance 1976*
Sunday, November 14: Soc 1:30
Hunt

Monday Night Football
Dandy Don, Howard Cosell, Frank Gifford

11/15	W	17-10	BUFFALO	57,893

FBR's *Month-At-A-Glance 1976*
Tuesday, November 16: F.B. 7:15

Dallas, Office of Office of Central Division Analyst
5:00 pm Tuesday, November 16, 1976

Finally, the department was moving in the right direction. Investigator John Landers found value in our efforts and expertise. We redoubled our efforts trying to make new progress.

Tom and I had been predicting the next FBR offense for a least a year at this point. We kept refining our picks with each new offense.

Author Note Re: Dr. Paul's Six Stages: *It occurs to me now, and I wish I had thought of it then. Where does a criminal's use of verbal threats of death backed up by the display or the touching of the knife to the victim fall in the six-stage progression... Or does only overt cutting or slicing count as in Stage VI? Is the verbal threat and display a 'rehearsal'?*

---

[70] Officer Alvin E. Moore, badge #3532, who had been an officer for 2 years, 10 months, and his partner answered a early morning disturbance call: juvenile with a gun. After clearing innocents from the scene, Al attempted to talk the juvenile into surrendering. The juvenile shot and killed Al. The juvenile later lunged at Tactical Officers with a knife and was killed. Al was a U.S. Army veteran of the Vietnam War.

Chapter 24

Captain Memo

**Dallas, Office of Central Division Analyst
5:00 pm Tuesday, November 16, 1976**

Bureaucracies run in often strange and complex ways, almost never is that "way" truly efficient.

One of the management tools used within the department was the interdepartmental memo. It facilitated policy, procedures, assignments, ass-chewing, and ass-covering.

Captain Don Milliken, commander of the Crimes Against Persons Section (CAPERS), Criminal Investigations Division (CID) was a master of the memo. He sent them by the hundreds and required them of us. Thus, with us, he became known as Captain Memo.

Author Note: *I had worked with Don over the years in various capacities, even a small undercover narcotics case. I consider him a good cop, a good administrator and friend. In 1989-90 we both worked at LETN - Law Enforcement Television Network.*

CITY OF DALLAS

DATE   November 16, 1976

TO   Investigator John Landers
    Crimes Against Persons

SUBJECT   Anticipated Dates and Locations of
    "Friendly Burglar Rapist"

For the remainder of the period November 14, 1976 through Mid-night
November 20, 1976, the date, day and time pattern should remain consistent as follows:

November 18th, 19th and 20th

Primary Location #1	The Willowick Apartments in the 4600 block of Amesbury Street and the 6000 block of Sandhurst Lane.
Primary Location #2	Village Apartments bounded by Southwestern Boulevard, Northwest Highway and Greenville Avenue.
Second Location	Willow Creek Apartments at Walnut Hill and Central Expressway.

Primary Locations have been defined by date and day of occurrence.

The majority of the offenses have been committed in Primary Location #1
on a by monthly basis with attacks occurring as follows:

Two (2) offenses in March, May, July and September. *Note: Two (2)
offenses each month have occurred on Tuesdays and Fridays, fell on
even numbered days (i.e.: 2, 4, 6, 8, etc.)

Primary Location #2 follows approximately the same pattern as above with
the exception that no attacks have occurred in September, which at this
time the break in the pattern is impossible to explain.

Secondary Location has been defined as the Willow Creek due to the fact
that an offense occurred at 2850 Clydedale (Northwest Area) on Wednesday,
November 10, 1976. Four (4) of five (5) times offenses have occurred in
Northwest, the suspect has followed with an offense in the Willow Creek
Apartments.

There remains the possibility that no offense will follow in the Willow

Memorandum

CITY OF DALLAS

DATE   November 16, 1976

TO   Investigator John Landers
     Crimes Against Persons

SUBJECT   Anticipated Dates and Locations of
          "Friendly Burglar Rapist"
          Page Two

Creek Apartments as High Pressure Sodium Vapor lighting has been in-
stalled in this area and the pattern has altered since its initial use
starting in August, 1976.

T. H. Covington
Crime Analysis Section
Central Division
Patrol Bureau

THC/cmp

Author Note: *I also received the following memo from Landers to Captain Memo which had been attached to Tom's memo above of the same date re: Anticipated Dates and Locations of "Friendly Burglar Rapist" attacks.*

Next Page: *John's memo discusses my ideas to attempt to photograph the FBR's footprints with thermal imaging infrared photography. I had been the one to contact Taylor at TI and review the state of the art re: infrared. LOL: Good to know that my bright idea (that didn't work out) was not really my idea. Perhaps John was protecting me from my own folly.*

Memorandum

CITY OF DALLAS

DATE November 16, 1976

TO D.M. Milliken
Captain of Police
Crimes Against Persons Section

SUBJECT Friendly Burglar Rapist

During the week from November 7-13, 1976, I met with Chief Tuma of the Dallas Fire Department in an effort to determine if any Fire Department personnel are involved in the Friendly Burglar Rapist offenses. I have been assured of full cooperation from Chief Tuma.

I have also arranged with the Tactical Division for a canine element to be dispatched to the scene of all criminal assault offenses believed to be committed by the Friendly Burglar Rapist.

I have met with the Chiefs of both Northeast and Northwest Substations, and also made details at these stations. During the details, the patrol officers were advised that when investigating this type of call, the P.E.S. Section is to conduct the initial investigation allowing them to more accurately determine the point of entry and point of exit of the suspect, and to more easily collect and retain fingerprints left by the suspect. After the investigation by P.E.S. has been conducted, the reporting officer of the Patrol Division will conduct his investigation. This has also been approved by Captain V.C. Campbell in P.E.S. Section.

During this week I also met with Mr. Kirby Taylor who is a photographer at Texas Instruments. He has developed very sophisticated camera equipment that will enable us to take footprints of suspects left at and near the location of these offenses during the night time hours. This will be tested next week for accuracy. I have also arranged for a closed curcuit television camera that will enable us to see the entire apartment complex parking lot of a small apartment complex during the night on a closed curcuit TV screen. This will be put into operation as soon as it has been determined feasible.

Officer T.H. Covington and Officer R.J. Sadler of the Central Patrol Crime Analysis Section have been placed on special assignment to work with me on these projects.

A weekly probability list of suspected locations will be prepared weekly and submitted for your approval. Attached to your memo is a sample of this list which covers the remainder of this week.

Respectfully Submitted,

John R. Landers #2445
Investigator of Police
Crimes Against Persons Section

jw

FBR's *Month-At-A-Glance 1976*
Wednesday, November 17:   8:00 Smith

Dallas, Office of Central Division Analyst
5:00 pm Tuesday, November 17, 1976

MEMORANDUM
Date: Nov 17, 1976
To: Inv J. Landers
Subj: Daily Activity Report for Capt M.

On Nov 16, 1976 I gathered data for updating & completing reports on the FBR problem – these included the updating of the 3yr FBR Offense List by Apt Complex Name & Comp.'s Name. Met w/Landers, Covington & Smoot to discuss yesterday's progress – new leads. Other reports need(ed). Accompanied Landers to Cockrell Hill PD to obtain Susp Ident. Kit[71] & interview (Comp) Daryl Strugell to make up a suspect composite for the prowler call Wednesday, November 10th, Ser# 403452H. Postponed photographic test till 11-17-76. Met w/Landers, Smoot & Covington at 10PM N.E. Substation to brief tactical section. Briefed 'Dogman Dooley'—rest of Tactical not there.
/RJ Sadler/

/RJS/

---

[71] According to various sources the Identikit was the invention of "Hugh C MacDonald of the Los Angeles Police Department who had developed sets of facial features on transparencies to save time sketching descriptions of criminals in 1940 wartime Europe."
*http://www.historybytheyard.co.uk/identikit.htm

Dallas, Office of Central Division Analyst
5:00 pm Wednesday, November 17, 1976

WE KNEW IF we could only identify a way to track the FBR from his victim's location, that could prove vital; we therefore pursued many ideas. For example, canines had already followed him from several crime scenes to (on arrival) empty parking lots.

Having some awareness of infrared photography, and as a long shot, the idea came to me to research the possibility of photographing the FBR's heat signature at the scene or leaving the scene. Knowing how close he kept his transportation would help us in tightening the noose around the locations where we were predicting his next offense.

I had researched the use of publicly available high altitude infrared photography as utilized by the government from geosynchronous orbiting satellites. This led me to a local Texas Instruments' engineer working on infrared imagery. It was evident from the research and conversations that the residual heat signature of a stationary object could be photographed in the infrared range long after the object had left the location. The list of military applications was long and varied.

After returning from my meeting with the Texas Instruments engineer, who I, even as a police officer, had to get special clearance to get in to see, I called professional photographer, Bill Crump.

I had known Bill since my days in DPD's Public Information Office where, as part of my duties, I shot still photography for special events, the department news letter and annual reports, etc. Although DPD had its own photo lab, its resources were limited (primarily black and white) and the man in charge, perpetually busy. Primarily for these reasons we, the PIO, took our photo processing and developing to a local company in near downtown, Kincaid's. It was at Kincaid's I met and developed a friendship with Bill Crump. He had a thriving commercial art business, an industry whose members were not known as staunch police allies. When it came to law enforcement Bill was one-hundred percent "for the cops."

Bill listened to my proposal, said he didn't know if it would work, but he'd be willing to give it a try—he'd supply the infrared film and his expertise.

The sun set at 5:24pm and by ten minutes of six it was dark between the west-end downtown buildings where Crump had his studio.

On the evening of Wednesday, November 17, 1976, from 5:50pm to 6:52pm the weather conditions were: ambient temperature approximately thirty-seven degrees, dew point thirty-four degrees, humidity eighty-nine percent, wind out of the North at eight miles per hour, fog in some areas. We conducted the following photographic research:

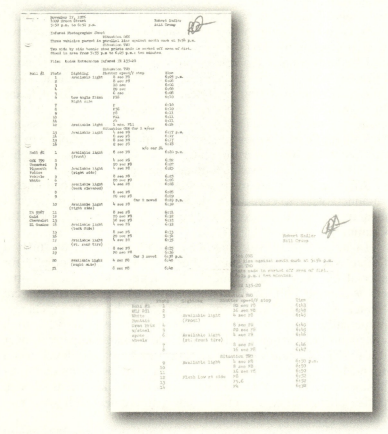

Bill and I staged and shot over sixty frames at various objects with varying heat signatures using bracketed shutter speeds and F-stops using three rolls of Kodak Ektachrome Infrared, IE 135-20 film, which would require special processing.

FBR's *Month-At-A-Glance 1976*
Thursday, November 18:   Press Club
Comp.
600 $15.00

Dallas, Office of Central Division Analyst
5:00 pm Wednesday, November 18, 1976

MEMORANDUM
Date: Nov 18, 1975
To: John Landers
Subj: Daily Activity on FBR Case for Nov 17, 1976

Worked on reports. Contacted Lt. Day in P.E.S. and asked for tape taken as physical evidence in several rape offenses. Tape to be sent to Johnson & Johnson Lab in Sherman Tx for analysis.

Interview(ed) John Catching on his theories about the FBR.

Met with Bill Crump, photographer, and with his assistance, performed infrared photography test to determine its possible use in FBR Case.

Worked from 7:30am to 7:30pm 11/17/75. Worked on reports. / RJ Sadler/

      /RJS/

Chapter 25

Mother & Son: Psychics

INTERVIEWING THE CATCHINGS. From the local media Tom and I were familiar with the stories about Bertie and John Catchings. We had both seen their fictional TV and movie counterparts seemingly and/or demonstrably solve cases of missing persons and homicide. I don't remember which of us had the idea or which of us called to make the appointment. The point was, Tom and I were both keen for the idea. When it came to ideas about catching or how to catch the FBR our motto had become: *let's try it, it might work.*

It was not lost on me, the irony of their last name! We wanted to 'catch' the FBR and were going to talk to the 'Catchings'!

The night had a Halloween kind of feel to it. Tom, John and I were the kids going door to door ostensibly for Tricks and Treats, only wanting the Treats! Going up to the Catching's condo in North Dallas was like going to the haunted house on the hill. We didn't want to go but knew there might be some Treats to be had by going there, we'd best go and get it over with.

Though both mother and son were "genuine" psychics, we were only meeting with John. We sat down in comfortable chairs in the close-feeling living-room. We interviewed each other. We hoped that he might have an intuition, a hunch, a guess or feel for who our FBR might be. If there was something, we'd run it down. Unfortunately he drew a blank, we got nothing. "Of course," he said, "since you are law enforcement, there would be no charge for the reading."

As we were about to leave, Bertie came into the room and her son told her why were there and she says, "You mean the one who drives the brown car?"

Also, escaping my memory, is whether John Landers threat, "If you ever tell anyone about this, I'll kill you," occurred before or after the Catchings interview. (Of course, I'm telling it now.)

I had known John since our Police Academy days together. He possessed a knack for understatement and excellent instincts for catching bad guys. Unfortunately, John Richard Landers, born 11/26/1939, suffered a debilitating stroke several years ago. John passed away October 24, 2015.

THE WORLDS ONLY
MOTHER AND SON PSYCHIC TEAM
BERTIE & JOHN CATCHINGS

HOW TO GET A READING IN PERSON

If you would like to come in for a reading in person from either or both of the Catchings you should call their secretary, for an appointment. The telephone number is (214) 233-5033. A reading lasts for approximately thirty minutes and the fee for the reading is $20.00. You may record the reading if you wish. Their readings consist of a brief handwriting analysis, color-aura analysis, palm analysis, psychometry impressions from any articles or pictures that you may bring and the answer to as many of your questions as possible.

PSYCHIC LINE: Bertie Catchings now offers you her horoscopes. The horoscopes are recorded on a telephone answering machine. For your daily horoscope call (214) 661-1923. For information about advertising on the horoscope lines call (214) 233-5033.

PREDICTIONS: The Catchings now have a list of over 150 predictions for the new year. To order send $1.25 to P. O. Box 12264, Dallas, Texas 75225.

MAILING LIST: If you know someone who you believe would be interested in receiving information about Bertie and John Catchings, please send their name and address to P. O. Box 12264, Dallas, Texas 75225.

PSYCHICS
BERTIE & JOHN CATCHINGS

Bertie & John Catchings constitute the worlds only known mother and son psychic team. They both make their home in Dallas, but spend much of their time traveling throughout the United States. Bertie discovered her psychic gift during her early childhood. John began his psychic career on the 4th of July 1969 when he was struck by lightning. Bertie & John Catchings have both received much acclaim as knowledgable speakers, and accurate predictors of the future. They have hosted their own radio talk show, and have also appeared many times as guests on other radio and television talk shows. Stories about them or their predictions have also appeared in many newspapers and magazines. The following are lists of only a few.

RADIO

KOST   LOS ANGELES, CALIFORNIA
KWKH   SHREVEPORT, LOUISIANA
KROQ   BURBANK, CALIFORNIA
WCBS   NEW YORK, NEW YORK
KBUY   FORT WORTH, TEXAS
KESL   SAN ANTONIO, TEXAS
KFJZ   FORT WORTH, TEXAS
WOAI   SAN ANTONIO, TEXAS
KRMH   SAN MARCOS, TEXAS
KITE   SAN ANTONIO, TEXAS
KAMC   ARLINGTON, TEXAS
WMAQ   CHICAGO, ILLINOIS
WIND   CHICAGO, ILLINOIS
WMBD   PEORIA, ILLINOIS
KTRH   HOUSTON, TEXAS
KPRC   HOUSTON, TEXAS
KILT   HOUSTON, TEXAS
KZEW   DALLAS, TEXAS
WFAA   DALLAS, TEXAS
KNUS   DALLAS, TEXAS
KVET   AUSTIN, TEXAS
WRR   DALLAS, TEXAS

TELEVISION

KENS   SAN ANTONIO, TEXAS
WEEK   PEORIA, ILLINOIS
WEAD   PEORIA, ILLINOIS
KVRL   HOUSTON, TEXAS
KHTV   HOUSTON, TEXAS
KPRC   HOUSTON, TEXAS
WFAA   DALLAS, TEXAS
KDFW   DALLAS, TEXAS
KDTV   DALLAS, TEXAS
KTVV   AUSTIN, TEXAS
KLRN   AUSTIN, TEXAS
KVUE   AUSTIN, TEXAS
KLBJ   AUSTIN, TEXAS

NEWSPAPERS & MAGAZINES

THE JOURNAL STAR, PEORIA ILLINOIS
EXPRESS NEWS, SAN ANTONIO TEXAS
THE RANGER, SAN ANTONIO TEXAS
PARK CITY NEWS, DALLAS TEXAS
AUSTIN AMERICAN STATESMAN
THE DALLAS MORNING NEWS
THE DALLAS TIMES HERALD
LAKE HIGHLANDS HERALD
THE NATIONAL ENQUIRER
RICHARDSON DAILY NEWS
THE NATIONAL TATTLER
THE SAN ANTONIO LIGHT
HOUSTON CHRONICLE
LOS ANGELES TIMES
IRVING DAILY NEWS
OTHER DIMENSIONS
FATE MAGAZINE
SAGA MAGAZINE
PSYCHIC TIMES
HOUSTON POST
NIGHT LIFE

TRAVEL TO YOUR AREA

If you would like to have one or both of the Catchings come to your area for a Lecture/Workshop or to appear as guests on a radio or television talk show or to give readings, please write or call for further information.

HOW TO GET A BY MAIL READING

If you are interested in receiving a by mail reading you should follow one or more of the following procedures. Be sure no matter what procedure you choose to include your birth date, and a self-addressed stamped envelope. Send your mail to P. O. Box 12264, Dallas, Texas 75225. Some readings will be on cassette tapes unless a written answer is requested. You may ask three free questions if your by mail readings total to a minimum of $20.00.

QUESTIONS: The Catchings will answer any questions you wish to ask. Please include a photo, which will be returned to you, and any other helpful information. $2.00 per question is the fee.

PALM ANALYSIS: Send a clear print of your right palm, and be sure that all the lines on both your palm and fingers are visible. The fee is $10.00.

COLOR & AURA ANALYSIS: Send a color photo of the person you wish to have analyzed along with a list of that persons five favorite and five least favorite colors. The fee is $10.00.

PAST LIFE READINGS: Send a photo of yourself, your birth date, a clear print of your right thumb, and a description of any reoccurring dreams that you may have had. The fee is $10.00.

DREAM INTERPRETATION: Send a description of your dream, and please note if your dream was in color. $2.00 per dream is the fee.

PSYCHIC HOROSCOPE: Send your birth date including the time of day, and your place of birth. $5.00 is the fee.

Infrared Photographer

Dallas, Office of Central Division Analyst
5:00 pm Friday, November 19, 1976

MEMORANDUM
Date: Fri 11-19-76
To: Cpt Memo, Thru Inv John Landers
Subj: Daily Activity on FBR Case for 11-18 &
11-19-76

Determined after examination of the color infrared
photographs taken on 11-17-76 that the possible
benefits of this type of photography for use at the
FBR scenes would be negligible. The film could be
used for recording of crime scene physical
evidence where more contrast & definition would
be needed in evidence photos. I further learned in
researching infrared that the residual heat images I
am seeking cannot be recorded on normal or
infrared film emulsion, but may be detected by
electronic instruments such as those I am arranging
to obtain through the services of Kirby Taylor of
Texas Instruments.

Worked Friday night to Saturday morning: 9:30pm
11-19-76 to 3:30am on 11-20-76.

On Monday, will again contact Kirby Taylor, T.I.
and will complete Apt. Name Segment of Same
report.

Long before the current digital heat registers of infrared
imaging there existed technology, that is to say, analog films
capable of registering heat. The black and white image
(white=hot, black=colder) on the next page came from an article
I read from *Photography As A Tool* by the Editors of Time-Life
Books. This is an example, *a police officer kneeling next to the
residual heat left be the human body*, of the infrared capabilities I
am pursuing.

**Infrared image in *Photography As A Tool*
by the Editors of *Time-Life Books***

A PROMISING IDEA, with not wholly unexpected results; either the subject temperature was not hot enough to leave a remarkable residual heat signature, the ambient temperature of air and ground was not cold enough, the equipment/film was not sensitive enough or some combination thereof created the feared negative results. Negative results are not negative results in the sense of 'bad', they are results that do not prove or disprove the hypothesis. In this case, we performed the tests; it could be done; just not with the equipment/film and other field constraints we faced.

What Bill Crump and I needed was either "real" thermal imaging equipment or the ability to task a spy satellite. Neither was going to happen, particularly given what the public understood as state-of-the-art in 1976.

Dallas, Office of Central Division Analyst
One Morning in November, 1976

One morning Tom and I were working over our reports, statistics, maps, and voodoo predictions when Investigator John Landers came into the office. In his laconic manner he pulled up a chair. His sly, almost lopsided grin predicted the unpredictable. John always talked slowly and out of the side of his mouth; not meaning the pejorative phrase used for someone who does not or cannot 'talk straight' or tell the truth. No, it was just John's way. It was as if he was always trying to bring you in on the secret. He walked slowly; he talked slowly and moved slowly. But that was all surface. Underneath John's 'wheels' were always turning at a high RPM.

"You guys aren't gonna believe this," John said, knowing we would. He got up and went over to the maps of FBR hits. He spread his hand over the map like its dots were pips of Braille. He tapped his finger over a dot representing a rape in the "Five-Points" area off Park Lane. "Here, this one! You aren't gonna believe this," he repeated. "I go out to interview the victim…"

John's voice trailed off as he sat back down. John wanted to tell his little story but wanted to be prompted. Tom imitating John's slow delivery said, "And?" like it had five syllables.

Sufficiently prompted John said, "This gal tells me the she's in bed with her boyfriend. She says she kind of remembers him getting up out of bed, which wasn't unusual, an' her droppin' back off to sleep. Next thing she knows is her boyfriend is givin' her the high-hard one and she's screwin' him to beat the band… then, get this, she realizes it ain't her boyfriend. You know the rest, it's in the report, but that's not the funny part."

John paused again and looked up. I looked over at Tom, he looked at me. I looked back at John raised my hands, palms up, curled and uncurled my fingers several times, like a kid's gimme-gimme gesture when it wants something but doesn't yet know how to talk. I added, "Com'on, John, give!"

"So then she tells me, after some more questions, her boyfriend was screwing her downstairs neighbor!

So I interview the boyfriend and sure enough he cops to it. Says he got out of his girlfriends bed, opened the patio door leaving it open onto the balcony, went over the side, climbs down into the girl's apartment below and was screwing her brains out.

Meantime—an' they couldn't 'a' missed each other but by seconds—the FBR sees the open second floor patio door. He climbs up on the first floor patio fence, where inside the boyfriend is screwin' the downstairs neighbor, hoists himself up and over the second floor balcony fence railing and into the vic's apartment through the open door.

After his usual prowlin', he tells her he's "just a burglar", hood's her with a pillowcase and ties her hands—and she's goin' along with it. He starts his rape and this gal is really givin' him the business, thinkin' it's her boyfriend!" Our guy slips out the front door and the boyfriend comes climbin' back up and into the bedroom only to find his girlfriend tied up in bed."

Now this was classic John Landers. It could have been partly true, mostly true or all true but he sold it like he was sitting on a stack of Bibles.

The healthy skepticism of all cops made Tom and I roll our eyes in disbelief as we laughed at the story and its irony. But the facts fit the report even if they weren't 'all' in the written account.

John was just the kind of guy who routinely discovered the strange. He had a way of seeing the deceptions people routinely tried to apply to their statements. This was his edge to getting victims and suspects to tell the truth; which was often embarrassing.

There is no question; we believed John. This investigation had been anything but routine; a friendly rapist? Victims were often complementary of the guy's manner and were embarrassed to have to tell their stories—that they were traumatized by the rape. Some clearly were not traumatized, at least that was what we experienced at the time.

Tom and I both had interviewed victims who did not demonstrate any anger toward the FBR or about being raped. More than one victim told us that they, if not willingly, gave in to the rapist and participated in the sex act with seeming enthusiasm. One young woman even told how Marble, after the rape, "sat on the floor for a long time talking, then raped her again." She said we should stake-out her apartment because the rapist would come back and bragged that "he'll come back for more; I know it… 'cause I really put it on him, I put it on'm good!"

Who knows for sure what the long-term effects were on each of the FBR's victims. Perhaps those that had not thought of themselves as victims were only coping differently than those for whom the rape was the most humiliating, horrifying and sexually degrading event in their lives.

I can only assume that it was the sheer volume of victims we encountered that was revealing what we would have heretofore stereotypically considered as apparent behavioral anomalies.

Certainly these "anomalies" fed the stereotype of women as provocateurs, instigators of sexual receptivity, who say no when they mean yes and despite their puritanical upbringing really do "want it". And having to go to court in the early 1970s as a rape victim (whether the victims were typical or atypical) was an ordeal in which the victim was put on trial by the defense who tried to inculcate doubt in the minds of the jurors as to the veracity of the victim, and portray her, rather than the rapist, as the instigator.

These were just some of the ideas and so-called male-fed fantasies the counselors in the rape-crisis, rape-awareness cause were struggling against and fighting to change.

Rape Is Not Sex

By the mid Seventies, no longer would the community willingly allow victims to be put on trail, particularly rape victims. It was not yet universal, but the meme was in metamorphosis.

The Dallas County Rape Crisis Center was doing an excellent job of counseling and outreach. Janie Covington was one of their counselors, her husband, Tom, just happened to be a Dallas cop who was working on the a multiyear serial rapist case known as the Friendly Burglar-Rapist. It was a natural fit that they should team-up to give educational talks to business and community groups. Tom and Janie developed a presentation on rape which, with questions and answers, usually ran under an hour.

Tom had been working for some time as the police department liaison with the Downtown Building Managers and Security Officers Association providing, among other things, crime analysis and had thus arranged opportunities to inform association members about various crimes, including rape.

The Earle Cabell Federal Building, a beehive of activity, in downtown Dallas was the home of the Federal Courts for the Northern District of Texas, the US Bankruptcy & Magistrate

Courts and the US Attorney's office. Additionally, all manner of federal agencies maintained offices there, such as the FBI, the Secret Service, the U.S. Marshall's Service, and many more. In fact, if you owned outright the vacant lot across the street, home of the closest, non-governmental, parking you'd be a millionaire from its parking fees, in no time.

Through Tom, the security force for the Federal building had arranged for this command performance to be attended by every employee. At that particular moment, as they stood in front of an audience of about a hundred, they would be giving their eighth presentation of the day and would by the end of the day, have spoken to over 1000 people.

Like a well-rehearsed tag-team they played the crowd. Janie stepped up and said, "RAPE is NOT a Dirty Joke. RAPE IS NOT SEX. IT IS VIOLENCE. The dirty joke has often been the frame of reference that society uses to discuss rape—unless you are a victim—you most likely have participated in telling a joke or used conversational innuendo that implied all victims, 'asked for it'."

Tom said that; "was a cheap way for a woman to 'feel safe', the implication was if she wasn't 'asking for it', she was safe from the rapist. And for the man, if he couldn't protect 'his woman', he would just kill the s.o.b. that hurt her... or blame her."

Breaking into his crime statistics, Tom said, "you are safer in a downtown dark alley than in your own bed at home— especially if you don't always lock your doors and windows." When Tom started talking about the FBR, it garnered everyone's attention and each group usually included at least one single female from a North Dallas Apartment complex where the FBR was known to strike. Tom followed that with stories of other rapists, discussed the current penalties for rape and explained current police procedure; ending with, "we try to have a female officer to answer rape calls, whenever possible... to listen and take the victim to Parkland for an exam."

That was Janie's cue. She stepped up and described the procedures at Parkland (the county hospital and emergency care facility). "We have 'faculty', Janie said, "designated to care for a rape victim. She will not see a 'resident' as many of the emergency room patients do, since the residents tend to have moved on in his/her career, even to another town. Parkland's specially designated 'faculty' isn't going anywhere and is thus able to testify on her behalf in court, whenever that might be."

Janie then went over the questions that the doctor's must have answered and how the evidence is collected and boxed and then taken by hand directly to Forensic Science Lab in the next building to maintain the 'chain of evidence'. Looking her audience in the eye, Janie said, "I always carried a box which included the tubes for the blood of the victim, slides for a scraping that might (we hope) include semen from the perpetrator and a comb." She explained that the doctor would comb the victim's pubic hair in order to obtain any of the suspect's hair that might be present.

As Tom interrupted he said, "and when a suspect is in jail... they will definitely comb him in the same way. The fancy microscopes at Forensics can match the two hair samples and help to sway a jury with convincing evidence of 'his' guilt."

Continuing, Janie talked about the victim and The Dallas County Rape Crisis Center's counseling services. Cocking her head just a bit, Janie said, "And she is not necessarily a sexy-looking, pretty, young girl who dresses to show off how she is built. She is not often picked up in a bar—just asking for 'IT'. Rape can happen to anyone, like the overweight middle-aged woman who was simply going to lunch from her job at Sears on Lamar... in broad daylight! She was victimized because she was simply alone in the parking lot when some angry guy was looking for someone to take it out on!"

"Much of my counseling is with dads, husbands, and boyfriends. I can't count the number of times men started out our sessions with the determination to kill. One man was very protective of his little sister and went looking for the guy she named as her assailant. I spent a lot of hours trying to keep him out of jail, trying to convince him to let the police do their job." Janie reminded the crowd, while it has always been society's idea that the "man of the house" should protect "his women", this is unrealistic and no husband should feel or take on that guilt when someone he loves becomes a rape victim.

"Another thing to keep in mind," Janie told the audience, "each victim is different and needs a different type of support. Some want everyone to listen while they try to exorcise the memory by telling it again and again. Some want to keep it absolutely a secret. We, at the crisis center, do not recommend any particular way of dealing with the trauma. However, we do recommend that each victim find a confidant. We are available 24 hours a day by phone. We are available to meet each victim at Parkland and help her deal with that first few hours of shock."

Janie then asked, "how DO YOU treat someone if you believe she is a victim? You let her bring up the subject. Try to treat this violence the same as if someone had burglarized her home. Talk about rape as if it were common because," Janie paused, "IT IS."

"Talk about rape as if she has been 'beat up' and you want to help her feel better. Don't tell her she shouldn't have been 'there'—wherever 'there is', she should have a right to be there. Personally, I spent many a night in the park across from our home when I was growing up. I would go over and sit alone in the swing under the stars because my brother and two sisters made too much noise and I wanted to be alone." Making up a name Janie said, "why couldn't Linda, do the same thing? Her mother tried several ways to blame her when she was the victim of three boys who accosted her in Reverchon Park."

Various members of the audience shook there heads, some understanding vicariously, others because they had been there in the judgement seat.

Tom changed the pace again as he talked about Dr. David Paul's theory about the progression of violence a rapist goes through. From theory Tom took them back to the real world explaining "the FBR was in stage two, but close to stage three."

Winding up, Tom and Janie talked about self-defense. Using Tom, Janie demonstrated the most vulnerable places to hit a man. She talked about, "how to carry your keys." For a little levity she said, "swing your purse, how heavy is that thing... at his head" and; "you can run faster with your dress up than he can with his pants down." Then in a more serious tone, "Run. Run toward light and people. Yell 'FIRE'! People simply seem to respond faster than if you yell, "HELP", so yell 'FIRE'!"

"Remember, most of all...BE AWARE of where you are and follow your instincts. If you don't feel like you should go alone to your car, DON'T. If you feel safe, walk with your head up, your keys ready to immediately unlock the car, get in, lock the door and drive away."

During the Q&A the subject invariably turned to weapons. "My preference," Janie said, "is not to carry a gun. Tom taught me how to use one. I carried it for a while. Then I began to examine myself. Would I kill someone? No, I probably would just be furnishing a weapon for him to use on me, so it is now up in the closet. I can find it to defend my children. I might feel differently if I were out somewhere. But each person must answer for themselves the legality and the emotional aftermath of using a weapon."

They closed as they started, in unison, Janie and Tom said: "RAPE is NOT a Dirty Joke.

RAPE IS NOT SEX. IT IS VIOLENCE."

Dallas, Northwest Patrol Division, Beat 554
2:30 am Sunday, November 21, 1976
Offense Number 71 (R-40)

OFFICER M.M. HAY #3651 again caught a Signal 25 along with his partner for that shift, Officer J.W. Przywara #3643. Hay wondered, *is this another "Friendly Rapist" offense,* as they drove to meet their complainant at her apartment, number 2112 at 9861 Harwell, the Lofts Apartments.

It was a cold morning—raw. The eight mile an hour wind out of the north was pushing a wet forty-four degree fog. It surrounded you like a scene out of a black and white Lon Chaney werewolf movie.

KLP, w/f/22, was a Flight Attendant for Braniff, flying out of DFW International Airport. She had spent a normal Saturday, making a run out to DFW, shopping at Valley View Mall and visiting with friends at nearby Chapel Creek Apartments before coming home and doing a load of wash in the apartment complex laundry room and finally going to bed around midnight.

KLP woke with a hand on her head and a knee on her arm! A man was holding a pair of scissors to her throat. "Keep you eyes closed and don't move, and don't say a word or you're going to die!" He tied her hands with a telephone cord and then tied the other end to the door knob of the bedside closet. "Keep your eyes closed," he took a case off one of her pillows and put it over her head, "and you'll be all right."

"What do you want?"

"I just want to find your purse and take any money you have, so just stay quiet." He left her on the bed and went into the bathroom.

When he returned, he pulled back the covers. Using the scissors he cut the length of her floor-length gown and pulled it away from her body.

She asked him why he was doing this to her and he replied, "I owe this to you."

He cut off her panties then used the scissors to trim her pubic hair. She heard him unzip his pants and felt his weight shift. He was kneeling over her. "In a second there is going to be something right here to put in your mouth and I want you to do a good job."

He untied her hands from door knob and raised the pillow case to the top of her nose, leaving her eyes covered. As he positioned his penis near her mouth she detected a faint soap aroma. Though she could not see his face, she was able to see that he was wearing a light blue sweater with a white yoke, a pair of faded blue jeans and a pair of black gloves. He reminder her of the scissors and to "Keep quiet and you'll be all right," as he forced his victim to take his penis in her mouth.

When he was ready he pulled out and moved down her body and penetrated her vagina continuing his forced sexual assault. He had not yet climaxed when he withdrew and made *KLP* take him in her mouth again. Withdrawing again he made her straddle him and take his penis vaginally as he sat on the edge of the bed. Tiring of this position he made her stand up and turn around with her knees on the edge of the bed and told her to put her weight on her elbows and forearms. Standing on the floor behind her he said, "Remember the scissors and be a good girl." He entered her from behind and continued to thrust to orgasm.

After he retied her hands to the door knob and said, "I'm going to go out of the room, but I'm not leaving."

She heard the refrigerator open and close, then nothing.

KLP got out of bed, pulled off the pillow case and turned on the closet light. She thought the suspect was gone and used a pair of her scissors from the shelf near the closet to cut the phone cord from her hands. She picked up the bedroom phone, but it was not working. She went to the living room to the front door and found it locked and bolted. *KLP* left her apartment and went to her neighbors to phone police.

When Officers Hay and Przywara arrived they found the complainant's patio door unlocked and found that the cord used to bind the complainant's hands had been cut off the phone in her roommate's bedroom with scissors from her room. Her roommate had gone out of town the day before and was due back today. They also found an empty Pepsi-Cola bottle, that complainant said had been in the refrigerator.

Since the complainant never saw the suspect, other than complainant's description of the suspect's clothing, his 'faint soap aroma' and the sound of his 'soft/polite' voice, no information was included as to suspect's age, height, weight, or general build.

Latent prints were lifted from the Pepsi bottle and the telephones.

In Investigator John Landers' report of the next day he wrote: "These prints, according to H.O. Ford of P.E.S., did not compare with those of the "Friendly Burglar-Rapist"."

He then wrote, "Suspect cut complainant's pubic hair with the scissors then forced complainant to commit oral sodomy on him. In Officer's opinion, the suspect was not the "Friendly Burglar-Rapist," but was one of the impostors who is capitalizing on the MO of the "Friendly Burglar-Rapist."

Author Note *1: Re: Offense #71, Tom and I were so focused on FBR, we definitely attributed this offense to the FBR, even though (again) latent prints found at the scene did not compare with those already collected and ID'd as the FBR's. What had been in the papers, to that time, as to 'exactly' what the FBR had 'done' during the rapes could have been 'copied'. One question of significance would be <u>who would you conclude committed this rape if the FBR was caught and all "FBR-style" rapes stopped</u>? That is a question you can ponder at the conclusion of this book.*

FBR's *Month-At-A-Glance 1976*
Sunday, November 21:   Soc 1:30
                 Civic Center

FBR's *Month-At-A-Glance 1976*
Monday, November 22: 8:30 Bob
                 9:00 DAV wm

Dallas
November 22, 1976

Thirteen years ago, John F. Kennedy was killed on the streets of Dallas. Notwithstanding the grief of his family and the nation, it is never a happy memory for the city. But those of us who live here, who call Dallas home, remember.

Dallas, Northeast Patrol Division, Beat 256
4:00 am Tuesday, November 23, 1976
Offense Number 72

LEVITZ FURNITURE STORE clerk, *TS*, a twenty-one year-old white female had arrived home to her apartment, number 1197 in the Lofts Apartments located at 7140 Fair Oaks, around 9:30 pm on Monday night. She was in bed asleep when it happened sometime around 4:00am the next morning, Tuesday, November 23rd.

TS and her boyfriend were awakened by noises downstairs. *TS* said, "What was that?" She and her boyfriend had a several minute conversation in bed about the noise... that it was probably nothing.

At 4:00am it was forty-eight degrees, overcast and blustery; who wants to get up out of a warm bed and investigate things that go bump in the night.

It was not until they got up later Tuesday morning that they realized what the noises must have been. They found the kitchen had been ransacked and the cord to the telephone had been cut, a window that they had left unlocked was missing its screen and a five dollar flower pot tray was gone.

TS called her mother, then the police. The complainant told Reporting Officer D.J. Coker #2536 that she thought it was probably her conversation with her boyfriend that must have scared off the intruder.

The screen was thirty paces north of complainant's apartment... the screen had apparently been sailed like a Frisbee into an open field. The area where the screen landed was soaking wet from a nearby natural spring. Anyone who went near the location would get knee deep in mud. The screen was printed, with negative results.

Officer Coker called Investigator Landers and advised, "This might be (the) Friendly Burglar-Rapist."

Chapter 26

Charts & Graphs

**Dallas, Office of Central Division Analyst
5:00 pm Wednesday, November 24, 1976**

MEMORANDUM

Date: Wed 11-24-76
To: John Landers
Subj: Daily Activity on FBR Case for 11/22-24/76

Made on-site investigation of many of the
apartment complexes in the FBR case to determine
proximity of complexes to all neighborhood
facilities and nearest vacant fields. All of the
approximately 34 complexes either border a vacant
field or wooded area or are within two blocks of a
comparable area. I have listed the 34 complexes in
chronological order to show the concentration of
offenses in each Apt Complex. As yet I am unable
to determine a sequence or pattern from a listing of
this information.

On 11-23-76 accompanied Landers & Covington to
interview the roommate and friends of *KP* (offense)
#46715H.

On 11-24-76 interviewed *AB* & *JM*. The correlative
factor between these women is each one had done
their laundry the day before the morning of their
attacks. This may or may not be significant at this
point.

Contacted Kirby Taylor, Tex. Inst., who is referring
me to Night Vision Lab—US Navy for possible use
of electronic heat-sensing devices. /RJS/

Author Note: *Replicas of the aforementioned lists are shown in
Appendix B Charts 1 & 2 - see pages 564 & 566*

MEMORANDUM

Date: Wed 11-24-76
To: J Landers
Subj: D. A. O. FBR Case

Re-contacted Lt. Day P.E.S.. 4:50pm 11-24-76 concerning ordering info on following service #:

237110F; 237116F; 344796G; 354830G; & 358213G.

Lt. Day had misplaced list after assigning this to a subordinate who made no report back to Lt. Day. We are trying to locate adhesive tape used on above offenses by FBR.
/RJS/

Author Note: *I later crossed out the first service number when I initialed my copy of the memo.*

MEMORANDUM

Date: Wed 11-24-76
To: J Landers
Subj: Rudolph Valentino Shaw

Ck'd w/DSO obtained pix & fingerprint card—this man & his associate mentioned in offense # 213754E need to be investigated concerning the FBR case.
  Rudolph Valentino Shaw wm
   DSO ID# 202150 DOB 10-26-41
/RJS/

[NB: Determined later – not involved in FBR]

Dallas, Office of Central Division Analyst
5:00 am Thursday, November 25, 1976

MEMORANDUM

Date: 11-25-76
To: JL
Subj: Line Graph— FBR Offenses – By Apt Complex

Completed line graph listing the apartment complexes where FBR offenses have occurred. The apartment complexes are arranged in chronological order and noting the offenses in sequence order. As of this report 34 different Apt. complexes have been hit.

This line graph indicates the FBR will strike next in an apartment complex he has not previously hit.

Chart to be up-dated as offenses occur
/RJS/

[**NB**: the total number of different complexes where we attributed FBR offenses became 36... *there would be five more to add to that number*.]

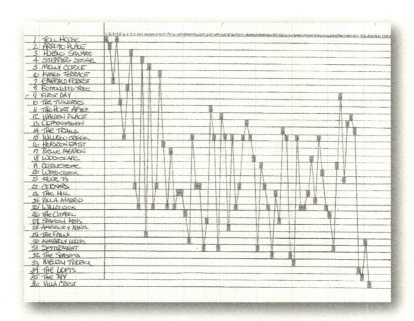

[Here is the same information on a computer generated spreadsheet... I could only dream of having word processing, computerized document search and retrieval, and spreadsheet graphic and computational capabilities.

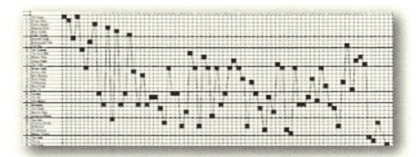

In November of 1976 Steve Jobs, 21, had already made this dream come true. He had formed Apple Computers in his garage with Steve Wozniak. Their *Apple 1* went on sale three months earlier in July. However the ubiquity of desktop & laptop computers would be almost two decades in the future.]

	FBR Attributed Offenses	Chronological Order:		Offense by Apt Complex
#	Apt Complex Name	Area	# of Offenses	Offense in Numeric Order
1	Toll House	VII	2	1, 5
2	Arroyo Place	VII	1	2
3	Hill Top House	OOA	1	3
4	Emerald Forest	VI	1	4
5	The Tuileries	V	1	6
6	Willow Creek	II	10	7, 26, 32, 35, 37,40, 42, 52, 55, 61
7	Buttonwood Tree	VI	1	8
8	Pueblo Square	VII	1	9
9	Corners & Corners E.	III	6	10, 16, 27, 28, 39, 46
10	Willowick	I	9	11, 15, 19, 21, 38, 47, 56, 58, 63
11	Stepping Stone	VII	1	12
12	The Falls	IV	2	13, 81
13	Molly Coddle	VII	1	14
14	Kings Terrace	VII	1	17
15	Horizon East	II	1	18
16	Belle Meadow	II	1	20
17	The Hill	III	4	22, 23, 49, 57
18	The Citadel	I	2	24, 64
19	Kimberly Woods	IV	2	25, 74
20	The Settlement	IV	4	29, 33, 44, 65
21	Spanish Keys	I	2	30, 50
22	The Point After	V	1	31
23	Waldan Place	V	2	34, 70
24	Amesbury Manor	I	1	36
25	Copenhagen	V	2	41, 69
26	Woodscape	II	2	43, 59
27	Cobblestone	II	2	45, 66
28	The Seasons	IV	2	48, 53 (83X captured)
29	The Trails	V	2	51, 71
30	Melody Terrace	IV	1	54
31	Villa Madrid	III	1	60
32	Woodcreek	II	1	62
33	First Day	VI	1	67
34	Four 7's	II	1	68
35	The Lofts	IV	1	72
36	The Ivy	IV	1	73
37	Villa Crest	IV	3	75, 77, 79
38	Claridge Park *	IV	1	76
39	Melody Park	IV	1	78
40	Bluffs	III	1	80
41	The Brookshir	OOA	1	82
			82	

Dallas
Thursday, November 25, 1976

I did manage to spend time with family, eat turkey, dressing and pecan pie and watch the annual Thanksgiving Day Cowboy game. This year the dreaded St. Louis Cardinals came into Texas Stadium and left with a loss. It was a typical game against the Cardiac Cards: Dallas 19, St. Louis 14.

Fortunately for me, Tom, John, our families and the women of North Dallas, the FBR apparently stayed home. I gave thanks he did not ruin anyone's Thanksgiving.

Chapter 27

No Cowboy Game Today

Dallas, Southwest Patrol Division
12:40 am Sunday, November 28, 1976
Officer Robert W. Wood, ~ Murdered[72]

Dallas, Northeast Patrol Division, Beat 245
3:00 am Sunday, November 28, 1976
Offense Number 73

AN IRONIC CALL! Scared and frightened *CH*, a twenty year-old white female called *MJH*. *CH* was the daughter of *MJH* who had been raped by the Friendly Burglar-Rapist in her 5961 Melody Lane apartment, number 210 in The Settlement at 2:00am on Monday morning May 10, 1976[73].

Reporting Officer R.C. Osgerist #3668 answered *CH's* call for help. He found his complainant, *CH*, in her apartment, number 1002 at 7225 Fair Oaks, The Ivy Apartments.

CH told Officer Osgerist that she heard someone trying to get into her bedroom window, but he did not get in. The complainant related that her mother had been a victim of the FBR. Osgerist searched the area of the complainant's apartment and did find that the screen had been removed from her window. Complainant told the Officer she did not get a look at the suspect or hear him leave.

---

[72] Officer Robert William Wood badge #3641 and his partner, Teressa Turko, stopped a vehicle on Hampton Road for driving without headlights; only its parking lights on. Whether there was a driver and a passenger in the car or not… is in dispute. Whether it was Adams and or Harris in the car is likewise in dispute. Woods, in his second year with the DPD and a veteran of the Vietnam War, was murdered by one of them in the early minutes of Sunday, November 28, 1976.

Randall Dale Adams was arrested and convicted of Officer Wood's murder, sentenced to death. Adams had maintained his innocence and said David Ray Harris shot Robert.

Years later Harris, on death row for the murder made of Mark Mays, was interviewed in 1988 by Erroll Morris's documentary (The Thin Blue Line). Harris's dramatic on-camera replay of Harris taped audio statement was accorded the status of a confession to his murder of Wood.

In part due to the documentary, Harris' conviction was overturned in 1989 and he released from prison. Adams had maintained his innocence and said David Ray Harris shot Robert. Harris was executed on June 30, 2004. Adams died in 2010.

[73] See Offense Number 44 (R30) page 195

The rape of *MJH* by the FBR occurred at The Settlement Apartments, less than a half a mile northeast, as the crow flies, and less than a two minute drive by car.

FBR's *Month-At-A-Glance 1976*
Sunday, November 28:   Soc. 1:30
                                 Hunt

FBR's *Month-At-A-Glance 1976*
Monday, November 29: Noble
                                 Butler

Dallas, Office of Central Division Analyst
9:00 am Tuesday, November 30, 1976

Tom and I were working long, but not horrific hours. In the twenty days since beginning our *new* FBR special assignment I had taken two and a half weekends off as well as Thanksgiving Day (though I still managed to get in some office time, work through my charts and kick out a memo or two). I had worked (not counting today) only thirteen days but managed to racked up forty-one (41) comp-time hours.

MEMORANDUM

Date: 11-30-76
To: JL
Subj: Cut Phone Cord Re: Sexton 358-4xxx

Rcvd info from John Black of Bell Tele, via Landers that Rxxx Sxxxxn, Phone # 358-4xxx reported his phone cords cut in a burglary. Cole's Directory shows phone number listed to Rxxx Sxxxxn at 2525 Community. Pho. Co. records list Sxxxxn at 9855 Webbs Chapel. Called 358-4xxx— Secretary said Sxxxxn out. Left call back message for 'Joe' Sxxxxn.
/RJS/

[NB: The X-d out letters in the above memo are inserted to protect the individual's identity.]

FBR's *Month-At-A-Glance 1976*
Tuesday, November 30: 4:30 Bd mtg

FBR Weather Forecast
Dallas, Office of Central Division Analyst
5:00 pm Wednesday, December 1, 1976

MEMORANDUM

Date: Dec 1, 1976
To: US
Subj: FBR Weather Forecast
Of the last six offenses, FBR has hit on:
    SUN 10-10-76
    THU 10-14-76
    SUN 10-24-76
    WED 11-10-76
    SUN 11-21-76
    TUE 11-23-76
If this is a pattern it is reasonable to assume his next two target dates will be a Sunday followed by a Monday. We are forecasting: SUN Dec 5th & Monday Dec 6th or 13th.

/RJS/ /THC/

[**NB:** A later notation on this memo read: Update (12-2-76) FBR is believed to have struck SUN 11-28-76. Monday Dec 6 & Dec 13 are prime dates.]

FBR's *Month-At-A-Glance 1976*
Thursday, December 2: Call Roy Butler

North Dallas
3:00 pm Thursday, December 2, 1976

MJH WAS RAPED by the FBR around 2:00 am on Monday, May 10, 1976. Then, six months later, at 3:00 am Sunday, November 28, 1976, *MJH*'s daughter, *CH*, called her mother to say someone tried to break in. (See Offense Number 73 page

331) We wanted to talk to *MJH* to see if there could be a connection, something more that sheer coincidence.

The following interview occurred at 3:00pm on December 2, 1976, at the residence of Complainant *MJH*. Present were *MJH*, Officer T. H. Covington and Investigator John Landers. The following questions were asked of *MJH* to which she responded (*MJH*'s answers in bold):

1. When did your daughter move into her present address? **"About two months ago."**

2. Do you think anyone has ever been in your apartment without you knowing about it? What I mean, about not knowing about it, is that old eerie feeling you get when something seems out of place or not right? **"No."**

3. How long do you think the suspect was in your apartment before the attack? "I went to bed about 12 and the first time I looked at the clock after he work me up it was 2:15AM. He left right after he talked to me last and I heard the front door slam or close and I immediately went to the front door. He left the front door slightly ajar and I found that he had either untied my hands or some type knot was used that came loose when I pulled on it. He used two different cords to tie me with."

4. Have you had, or did you have before the attack, any obscene phone calls, wrong numbers or telephone surveys before the attack? **"NO, other than what I call normal."** How about after the attack? **"No."**

5. Were you ever stopped by the Police for any reason before the attack? **"No, other than being in an accident about 4 years ago."**

6. Have you ever seen or suspected anyone you met before the attack? "No." How about after the attack? **"Only the package boy at the Tom Thumb, he seems a bit weird."**

7. Do you have pictures of your daughter which would have been accessible to a person entering your apartment? **"No, he would probably have seen her if he had been watching the apartment, she comes over often."**

8. Do you recall the suspect saying he would be back or say anything that would lead you to believe he would attack your daughter? "None."

9. Do you and your daughter see one another often or go shopping together? "Yes." Whose car do you usually go out in? **"Mine."**

10. Where do you have your prescriptions filled and where do you buy patent medicine such as aspirin, etc." **"Skillern's."** Do you pay for them by cash or check? **"Both."**

11. Do you still have the same car you had when you were attacked: "No." What kind do you have now? **"A 1976 red Camaro."** What

kind of car did you have when the attack occurred? **"A blue 1973 Mercury."**

12. Who carries the insurance on your car? "St. Paul Fire, through Chuck Insurance Agency." Have you ever had any damage estimates such as hail damage done on your car? "No."

13. How and when did you move into your present address? "I moved about June 1st and used a moving company and they were Firemen."

14. How did your daughter move into her present address? **"Her father moved her in."**

15. Who or what kind of person do you think committed this offense against you and your daughter? "I really don't know, I think he is rich and doesn't have to work and that way he can spend his days watching women and the night raping them."

16. When you went to the door, did you hear anyone running or a car start up and leave? "No, but my roommate saw **a man standing in the breezeway with a plastic bag** and she almost fell down the stairs."

17. When and where do you do your laundry? "There at the complex, the laundry was right outside my front door." Do you launder in the daytime or nighttime? "Both."

18. Where did you live before you moved here? **"The Settlement III."**

19. You mentioned your sister, where does she live? **"At Buckner and Ferguson"** An apartment or house? **"Apartment."** Is she married? **"No."** What is her name? **"JG."**

20. Is there anything else you think may be of importance? **"No."**

21. Was there anything he did that you noticed as different or unusual? **"Only that he turned off the TV at the back."** This big set here in the living room? **"No, the small Panasonic I kept in the bedroom."** You mean the regular controls such as volume or vertical hold? **"No, he used one in the back of the set. I didn't notice that until the next day or so when I tried to turn it on. I couldn't get a picture."** Have you had to have that TV repaired before or after the offense? "No." How long have you had the small set? **"About 4 years."**

SUMMARY:

There seems to be no significant difference between this offense and the other victims I have interviewed. There are only several possible factors to dwell on at this time.

1. Again we have **Skillern's** being used as the Pharmacy.

2. This is about the second or third time a package boy or someone connected with **Tom Thumb** has been mentioned

3. Why and how did he know how to tune out the picture or sound on the back of the small TV set when all of the normal control are not on the back where the fine tuning adjustments are? I asked her where the regular controls were and she said, "**The side**," indicating with her hand an up and down motion.

Dallas, Office of Central Division Analyst
5:00 pm Thursday, December 2, 1976

MEMORANDUM

Date: 12-2-76
To: JL
Subj: FBR Weather Forecast & Apt Complex Line Graph

Since 11-25-76 FBR has added is 35th different complex to his list. This offense in the Ivy Apt. Complex is at 7225 Fair Oaks. This offense occurred on SUNDAY 11-28-76 to the daughter of a previous FBR offense.
This further solidifies the pattern of New Area and sets up (Refer to 12-1-76 forecast) MONDAY Dec 6th or 13th as prime hit dates.

[**NB**: Later notation to Memo: "hit 12-6-76 12:35am"]

Dallas, Office of Central Division Analyst
5:30 pm Thursday, December 2, 1976
A Problem Defined & Solved
Area Location Maps & Area Definition

Initially law enforcement for the city was served from the downtown Police and Courts Building at 106 South Harwood. As the city grew the need for establishing police outposts grew along with it.

For years the city had been segmented into five geographic areas of police responsibility. The Police and Courts Building still served as the location for all administrative and investigative functions and the headquarters for the "Central" Patrol Division, then each of the other four quadrants of the city had their own patrol division substation: Northeast, Northwest, Southeast and Southwest.

Each of these divisions had (usually) four sectors which were further geographically divided into (usually) eight 'beats'. The 'beat' (e.g.: Beat 121) remained the geographical term for the area an individual 'beat officer' would be responsible for patrolling. In the early seventies in the DPD the term 'element' came into vogue.

As the squelch broke on the squad car's radio, the patrol officer would hear the dispatcher say, "Element 121, Signal 25, followed by the address of the call, then perhaps, "handle Code 2!" (if there were a 'lights' or Code 3 if a 'light's and siren' priority was assigned to the call).

As this growth took place, the divisional maps remained fairly consistent. Now, in the computer age, instead of programmers following the geographic hierarchy, they preferred to break down the city into even smaller 'reporting areas.'

So over time while 'beat configurations' might change, or so the idea went, the reporting areas would remain the same. This of course was one of the problems in trying to utilize computers for crime analysis in the City of Dallas. We were looking at Divisions, Sectors, Beats, streets and actual addresses. The computers were looking at Reporting Areas. You could know the other designations, even the street addresses, but if you did not know the Reporting Area, you might not get an effective or inclusive report.

This was the problem that Tom and I encountered in late November of 1976. The beat configurations were going to change and thus all of our 'beat' oriented analysis was going to be skewed; some offense that occurred two years ago on beat 214 at 1245 A Street would now be beat 243. So to eliminate these analysis issues, Tom and I devised our own concomitant areas of FBR Offense concentration. We looked at the clusters of offenses and defined seven different areas.

We plotted the FBR's offense by Area as well as the other keys.

MEMORANDUM

Date: Dec 2, 1976
To: JL
Subj: Area Location Maps & Area Definition[74]

Completed seven maps of the geographical areas of concentration for the FBR.
Each Map has an area of concentration visually outlined and written out. The areas are numbered in Roman numerals: I – VII.

/RJS/

Author Note: *The original seven (7) maps we created, outlined and numbered (with Roman numerals) one through seven, were to help Tom and I further refine our targeting. By defining the areas of concentration (which had not been done before) we were better able to see developing area patterns. Heretofore the offenses had only been tracked by 'beat' and 'reporting area'. (see 7 maps on page 339)*

I had been working on these for several days. I did not have access to wall-sized 'city' maps like the ones in Planning & Research or those I had created for my little office when I was first appointed as Division Crime Analyst. In fact, I wasn't supposed to have them. Not that they were prohibited but it was a

---

[74] Copies placed in FBR - Patrol Officers Handbook on the FBR pages: 32, 35, 37, 39, 41, 43, & 45

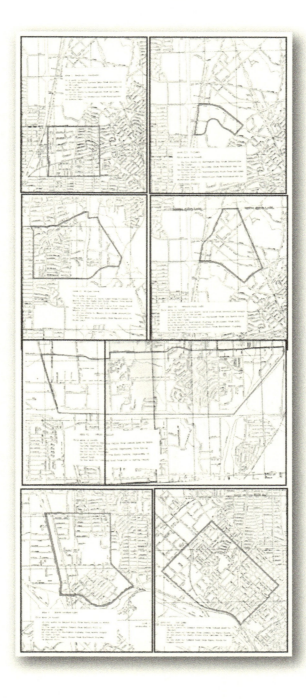

continued from Author Note: *The original seven (page 338)*

touchy subject that Tom and I were working citywide on the FBR instead of staying in our bailiwick (Central Patrol Division) Various noses had been out of joint for some time.

I looked at the 73 citywide offenses, to date, that Tom and I had attributed to the FBR. I determined a geographical area which contained various concentrations of FBR offenses. I then created a boundary around that area using street names for boundary lines. I had to locate a city map and find a way to get each area to fit on a single sheet of 8.5x11 copy paper. Area VI was so large I had to use two sheets of paper which I 'taped' together.

When completed on Dec. 2, I made copies so Tom and I could start using them immediately. A copy was also attached to the Dec 2nd (above memo) to John Landers re: Area Location Maps & Area Definition. I kept the originals, which I still have, so we could continued to make copies for our various plotting and planning. Amazingly the scotch-tape I used is still holding to the individual maps the little cutouts of text I used to type up and denote the boundaries.

Subsequently, the seven maps were included in the forty-nine page Patrol Officer's Handbook that Tom and I put together for officers in the field. It is probable that Planning & Research (P&R) was given a copy as well. Apparently, (I didn't know it at the time) these maps were duplicated using my geographical areas of concentration and my area definitions on one of their wall-sized city maps in Planning & Research's crime analysis room. Except P&R used Arabic numerals instead of Roman numerals and this map shows they were pin-pointing rapes only. That would be the genesis of the picture accompanying The Dallas Times Herald article Sunday **Morning, February 20, 1977 on page one.**[75] **(see next page)**

---

[75] Appendix A - Newspaper Article #14b1 "Tracking the 'friendly rapist' [see website: robertjsadler.com]

Author's Note:

Planning & Research Wall Map

Blow-up of photo by
Phillip Gould appearing
Appendix A - Newspaper
Article #14b1 or website

MORNING, FEBRUARY 20, 1977   Circulation, 744-6101   14 $
                              Classified, 748-1414
                              Other Depts., 744-6111

ndly rapist'

POLICE kept map pinpointing offenses attributed to the 'friendly rapist' and
divided them into areas — from Oak Lawn (7) north to LBJ Freeway (6).
— Staff Photo by Philip Gould

Interesting to me is the fact that P&R used my boundaries and numbering system, albeit they used Arabic numerals. Looking at the maps and those demarcated boundaries in 2016 I'm wondering why I didn't just number them in a clockwise fashion, i.e., starting with the northern-most area being one (1) in stead of roman numeral VI.

I know that when I set those boundaries they were determined by two factors: 1) a boundary that would encompass the concentration of offenses in each area and 2) the initial movement by location between one offense and the next. When the map was created the FBRs offense were patterning: from area I to II to III to IV to V to VI to VII. This meant the FBR was crisscrossing North Dallas to commit his offenses.

Still, if P&R had come up with the boundaries my question would be why wouldn't they have followed a more normal clockwise number of the area, regardless of the volume of offenses within the boundary instead of coming up with the same boundaries and boundary numbering as I had, which would mean they were following my rationale. Following my rationale seems illogical because P&R was not in agreement with my and Tom's count of FBR offenses.

Chapter 28

Nine Fingers

THE HEROES OF the Physical Evidence Section (P.E.S.) had lifted various prints from the FBR crime scenes.

When a person is arrested or submits to be fingerprinted for a job, their 'prints' are put on what is known as a ten-card. There is a rectangle designated for each of the ten finger (tips) as well as a place to lay down the four fingers of each hand. These cards are done, in the old days, by hand and done three times. One card would remain with the agency creating the card, one would be forwarded to the state (TCIC) for its database and one sent to Washington D.C. to be included in the NCIC (National Crime Information Center) which was started in 1967.

The Standard & Ubiquitous
TEN CARD

The 10 finger positions are:

1] *R Thumb*; 2] *R Index*; 3] *R Middle*; 4] *R Ring*; 5] *R Little*;

6] *L Thumb*; 7] *L Index*; 8] *L Middle*; 9] *L Ring*; 10] *L Little*.

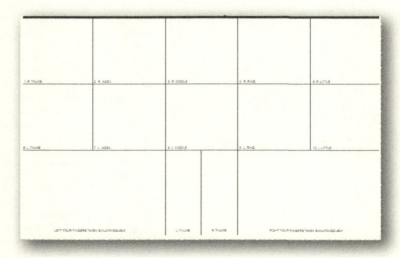

Below is the composite of eight of the FBR suspect's prints. This flash card or comparison card was carried by many of us, just in case and many more saw it in the FBR: POH[76]. Lt. Day was the night supervisor of P.E.S. or as it used to be called, the Identification Bureau. Lt. Day was the fingerprint genius who (was the first one to 'put the FBR's fingerprints in the correct order) was scheduled to retire about halfway through this thirty-nine month investigation, but decided to stay, and did, until the FBR was captured. In fact one of the latents Lt. Day lifted turned some heads. After other staff had processed one of the FBR scenes and struck out, Lt. Day decided to 'lend a hand'. Tom read Lt. Day's supplement indicating he'd found 'comparables', so Tom went downstairs to ask him about it. The explanation sounded all mater-of-fact coming from Lt. Day. The FBR's point of entry had been a window; glass, frame, and screen had all been processed with negative results. Lt. Day then did something no one else had thought to do. Lt. Day printed the underside of the window's sill and found latents later ID'd as the FBR's.

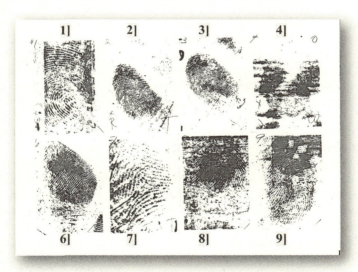

AT THIS POINT in time we had, in fact, nine (8 shown here) of the FBR suspect's ten fingers identified from latent prints lifted at the scene of his numerous offenses. Note the thumbprint #6] in the lower left corner above. This thumbprint contains an

---

[76] Copy placed in FBR - Patrol Officers Handbook on the FBR page 47

unusual elliptical feature with a tail, that came to be known to us as 'the tadpole'. (see blowup on page: 421)

Given the fingerprint evidence residing in the Physical Evidence Section under the quiet and intense eyes of Lt. Day, there was never a question of could we convict this guy, it was only a matter of when we caught him! We knew that even if we had somehow made a technical mistake during his arrest and thereby nullifying that individual case, the simple act of his arrest would net us the positive identification of The Friendly Burglar-Rapist. This positive ID, by fingerprint, would link him to scores of offenses.

Forensic Evidence - Blood Typing the FBR & Questions

In the mid 1970s the DPD did not have it's own crime lab, like you see on TV for cities like New York, Miami, Las Vegas or Los Angeles. Any laboratory work done for the DPD was through the Southwestern Institute of Forensic Sciences.

Not many cops knew the exact science behind blood typing, but most investigators and street cops knew that a chemical analysis could be done on blood to determine its 'type', i.e.: the blood groups designated as A, B, AB & O. The general public, at the time, was most familiar with blood types for reasons of donating blood, receiving a transfusion, or getting a marriage license, when a 'blood test' was regularly required to determine if two individuals had compatible Rh factors. These 'incompatibilities' could negatively affect the couple's potential progeny.

As just mentioned, as cops, we knew each of these groups could be further discriminated as to their Rh factor either positive or negative. Thus you if you turned in a blood sample from a crime scene for typing you could get one of ten possible outcomes: A, A+, A-; B, B+, B-: O, O+, O- & AB. One additional important factor could also be determined: secretion. Blood from an individual could be said to be from a 'secretor' or a 'non-secretor'. It is generally accepted that 80% of the human populace are 'secretors'. This means certain antigens, proteins, and enzyme properties in the blood of the secretor can also be found in a secretor's other fluids and tissues such as: saliva, teardrops, skin, urine and semen.

Although scientific analysis could be applied in many ways[77] in the mid Seventies, it was generally too time-consuming and too expensive to be employed in the general course of, what were considered, routine investigations. The standard protocol was, if it was collected, to test blood, in general, for such cases as criminal assault and homicide and semen in specific for criminal assaults. And if your suspect was determined to be a 'secretor' then certainly a cigarette collected at the scene might lend, if tested, additional forensic evidence against the suspect. However, in the mid 70's that type of evidence was either not generally collected or not specifically tested in that way. Our P.E.S. guys might have collected, say, a pop can[78] left at the scene and presumably drunk from by a suspect and test it for fingerprints. But a swab of the rim for saliva was not, at the time, routine.

All this to say that we did collect some forensic evidence from various of the FBR crime scenes. This most often meant fingerprints and possible semen, if a 'rape kit' was done when a complainant went voluntarily to the hospital to be 'checked-out' or 'examined' post assault. From the blood analysis done at the Southwestern Institute of Forensic Sciences laboratory (the county funded lab staffed by the Med School) we learned that our suspect was a secretor and had at least two different blood types: A and O.

How can that be? Well, it cannot be unless you have two different and distinct or multiple suspects. Thus, the "real investigators" *knew* our theory, that the criminal assaults Tom and I had attributed to the one (still anonymous) FBR suspect based on our pattern/MO recognition, were wrong!

For this reason alone, many in the DPD felt compelled to discount our theories and data; felt compelled to invent or "see" what might be anomalous MO's, in certain offenses, as being committed by "copycats" or "impostures". Investigator Crowder,

[77] For example if, when we approached them, Johnson&Johnson had not agreed (*pro bono*) to analyze our athletic tape evidence it is doubtful that a) our county forensic lab would analyze it, b) had the comparative database from which to conclude anything beyond perhaps fiber content or adhesive chemical properties, c) the lab had the budget for doing the testing and d) the DPD would have afforded the bill if the county wanted the PD to pay for the test. See rjs MEMO 12-8-76, Subj: FBR Daily Activity and Johnson&Johnson letter: [see website: robertjsadler.com], also see page 368.

[78] See FBR Offense #81 (see pg 399), P.E.S. Brown comment (inset dated 2-1-77) pg 407

for example, kept trying to hang her hat on the fact that there were different blood types, so she'd say, "Oh, it's got to be a different guy!" And Captain Milliken told the press back in August: "publicity about the so-called "friendly rapist" has spawned several imitators." [See page 264-268]

As Tom put it, "We were saying, okay, but look at the MOs, there aren't any copycats out there," (doing this), as far as we could tell. Tom did admit, "I did worry about it."

We acknowledged that the general MO of the FBR offenses was in the papers, on the news, but the actions of the rapes we attributed to "our" FBR suspect were too similar to be real copycats and "his" MO did evolve over time.[79] In other words he didn't do "everything" the same way "every time"!

It could not be said that even this was factually true. It could be that he did do everything the same way every time, but since each complainant and, generally, the reporting officers were different so that each individual O/IR might have similarities and dissimilarities.

This is one of the reasons why we pressed for a new O/IR form that forced the reporting officer to ask a specific field of questions, thus individual complainants could be consistently queried about specifics making repeated MO recognition more accurate.

Additionally, Tom and I wanted to know exactly how "the lab" (Southwestern Institute of Forensic Sciences/SIFS) was handling our FBR evidence. To that end Tom arranged and got us an appointment to get a briefing at SIFS toward the middle of December 1976.

FBR's *Month-At-A-Glance* 1976
Friday, December 3:   Nobel ?

---

[79] For example, in the months before Guy Marble was caught, the FBR had not been reported to have been talking about his "truck'. Last mentioned: Offense #41 4/11/76. The next reported mentioning of "truck" would be in Offense #75 12/8/76.

Dallas, Office of Central Division Analyst
5:00 pm Friday, December 3, 1976

MEMORANDUM

Date: 12-3-76
To: JL
Subj: Cut Pho. Cord, Re: Rxxxe Joe Sxxxxn

Joe Sxxxxn called back 12-3-76 11:30p. Sxxxxn related vandals had broken into his residence at 9855 Webbs Chapel and "tore-up his apartment & beat up his roommate." In the process, Sxxxxn's phone was ripped from the wall. Neighbor's believed this incident to be drug related.

This incident has no connection w/FBR

/RJS/

MEMORANDUM

Date: 12-3-76
To: JL
Subj: Subject Elimination

Sent names of 9 Skillern's employees to ID for records ck. For possible elimination as FBR

/RJS/

MEMORANDUM

Date: 12-3-76
To: JL
Subj: FBR Victim's Age Chart

Charted the ages of the Victims from the 72 FBR offenses to date.

Of these 72 offenses:
    39 were 25 yrs old or older
    39 were 25 yrs old or younger

Of the 5 most frequently 'hit' age groups, ranked 1- 5:

1	10	Victims were 23 years old
2	7	Victims were 24 years old
	7	Victims were 28 years old
3	6	Victims were 25 years old
4	5	Victims were 21 years old
	5	Victims were 22 years old
	5	Victims were 26 years old
5	4	Victims were 30 years old

No other significant data at this time

/RJS/

12/ 5	W	26- 7	@Philadelphia	61,09 1

Dallas, Office of Central Division Analyst
11:00 pm Sunday, December 5, 1976

MEMORANDUM

Date: 12-5-76
To: JL
Subj: FBR Subject/Suspect Elimination: Skillern's

DPD ID check returned. Only one subject had a Dallas record. Subject: Txxxx Wayne Kxxx, wm 1-14-53. Info placed in Covington's 'Suspect File'.

For Re: See Memo 12-3-76
Subject Elimination – list attached.

Author Note: *The FBR victim survey, that Tom had devised, had been sent out to every one the FBR complainants. We garnered a lot of information which we plumbed for leads. The ubiquity of Skillerns was noted on numerous returned surveys.*

At that time in Dallas in addition to several independent pharmacies, there were several "five and dime" chain stores that had in-house pharmacies: Rexall, Woolworth's, Walgreens, and Skillern's[80]. Although Skillerns had several locations in North Dallas, they were not on every street corner as their modern-day counterparts seem to be. It was therefore not alarming that many of the FBR's North Dallas rape complainants would trade with the same Skillerns either for there prescriptions or for their over-the-counter drugs and sundries. However, this link made us think!

Pharmacists get to see their individual customers up close, they know generally, if not specifically, the state of their medical or health condition, they have access to their address and phone numbers. A pharmacists, or one of their assistants, would be in a perfect place to encounter women to target for burglary and or rape.

---

[80] James Skillern, was in Lewisville by 1880, where he established a drug store in 1885. By 1910 the company was known as Skillern and Sons Drugs and had numerous stores throughout north Texas, with headquarters in Dallas. re: Steve Fulsom http://www.dallaspioneer.org/stories/historical.php?ID=395

With this "bright idea" in mind, Tom and I went to see the head of security for the Dallas Skillerns stores. He was very cooperative and gave us a list of all their Dallas locations as well as a list of their employees including the pharmacists. The most interesting or unusual person on the list raised our eyebrows. He was an individual who refused to work a regular shift at the same store, which was the custom. He insisted that he be the fill-in pharmacist whenever and wherever there was an absence which would require a substitute. He worked all the different locations that served North Dallas, for example.

Armed with "the list" Tom and I devised a plan to obtain fingerprints for comparison with those collected at FBR crime scenes. We did not want to accuse anyone falsely or prematurely and we did not want to damage the reputation of individual pharmacists or the Skillern's chain by having our "idea" of "taking a look" at Skillerns employees being leaked or exposed to the media.

We honed our list down to nine men of interest. Then very quietly we compiled an array of mug shots and placed them in several plastic document covers. Without telling anyone what we were doing we went to the locations and met the nine during their on-duty hours. Over the next week, plus, we gathered fingerprints.

Call it a ruse, or a pretext, Tom and I told the pharmacists we were looking for an individual (whose photo was ostensibly part of the photo array) involved in forging prescriptions. Gingerly we handed off the glossy, unblemished, clear plastic document covered array to the pharmacist. We asked if he recognized any of the persons in the array. Since, the crime was spurious and the mugs shots unrelated we did not expect any identifications. However we did get comparable prints from all nine of our persons of interest.

We always thought it would have been ironic, if not funny, if one of the pharmacists we fingerprinted had turned out to be wanted for some crime or if one of our mug shots had been identified for some other reason. Neither happened.

We took our document covers filled with latent prints (referred to as "names") to the Identification Section. The document covers were dusted and the prints compared with those of the FBR. None were a match. We crossed another bunch of names off our list and searched for the next "bright idea".

Chapter 29

Silver Linings

**Dallas, Northeast Patrol Division, Beat 213
12:45 am Monday, December 6, 1976
Offense Number 74**

ATTEMPT CRIMINAL ASSAULT was the call to which Reporting Officers W.L. Russell #3803 and L.L. Barbee #2945 were dispatched.

Shift change had been at 11:00 and 11:30pm. The split shifts came in on a thirty minute stagger unless they were currently on a call. They came off duty and their relief came on. Russell and Barbee had not been on the street more than an hour when the call came.

They met complainant *VEH*, a w/f/23 at her apartment, number 2098 at 6466 Ridgecrest, The Kimberly Woods Apartments.

At midnight the temperature was hovering at fifty-one degrees. Rain and fog was luffing in the ESE winds, which meant the full moon could not be seen. Although it was a dismal night for patrol, as Russell wrote it was "cold and raining", there was to be a silver lining.

Once again the Friendly Burglar-Rapist entered through an unlocked sliding glass door. The following is Officer Russell's narrative after interviewing *VEH*:

> At approximately 12:45am the comp was awakened by a man standing next to her bed. The suspect had the comp's head resting in both his hands. As comp (woke) suspect told her "Be quiet, don't say anything." Suspect then told comp to put her hands straight down at her side. Suspect blocked the comp's near arm with his body and with one arm held her left arm. The suspect then used his free arm to reach across and shake the pillow case free from the extra pillow on the comp's bed. Suspect then placed pillowcase over comp's head. Suspect then wrapped excess telephone cord around his hand. Comp then said the suspect attempted to put the telephone cord around her neck. The comp became

frightened and began to scream loudly. Comp said suspect got up and ran out the front door. Comp described suspect as a w/m/20-30 wearing a gray cotton sweatsuit. The top was hooded and had a pouch front for the hands. Comp said suspect had the hood up when he fled. Comp said the suspect's voice was monotone and firm. Comp also stated that at 10:30pm 5 Dec 76 while walking her dog she passed a man wearing an identical sweatsuit as the suspect. Comp described this man as a w/m/20-30 with blond mustache. The man at 10:30pm spoke to comp. He said that it was a nasty night to walk the dog. Comp said this man had on Adidas-style running shoes (white in color & later picked out a picture of the "Adidas Runner" from a book of running shoes.). Suspect entered comp's apartment through sliding glass door which is located on the second floor. Suspect used a cinder block to aid in climbing to the comp's patio. Suspect placed cinder block on the top of the first floor privacy patio fence which enabled him to elevate himself enough to pull himself up to the comp's balcony. Comp had not used her sliding glass door in a long time and could not tell R.O.'s if it had been locked or not. Crime Scene Search, Inv. Landers, 2340 and K-9 unit were dispatched to the scene.

Investigator John Landers #2445 was notified of the offense and hurried to the scene. In his report he wrote:

I contacted comp just minutes after this offense occurred. Comp stated that she was walking her dog outside her apt at 11:30pm (just 1½ hours before this offense occurred) and observed a w/m/22-28, 5'9", 150-160 lbs, blond hair, walking near her apt. The comp stated that the suspect was "nice looking" and was dressed in tennis shoes, gray jogging pants and gray jogging sweater which had a zipper in front and also had a hood. The suspect was startled by the comp and held his head down and stated (as he passed her) "nasty night isn't it?" (It was raining slightly) The comp stated, "Yeah, it's a nasty night for jogging." The suspect then replied, "I do this every night." While the suspect talked to comp he held his head down and never stopped walking. Comp went inside her apt and went to bed. Approximately 1½ hours later, the comp was waked by a suspect who was dressed exactly like the above suspect. The suspect stated, "Put your arms down by your side and do as I tell you and you won't be hurt." The comp complied and the suspect placed a pillowcase over comp's head. It is believed that comp's dog was in the kitchen at this time. The suspect did not go into the kitchen to get a knife, and tried to tie comp's hands with the telephone cord while it was still attached to the telephone. The comp became frightened and jerked the pillowcase from her head and began screaming. The suspect then stood up by the bed and when comp continued to scream, suspect ran to the living room and exited through the front door which he had apparently unlocked before waking comp. P.E.S. (B.G. Brown #1027) was at scene and determined that entry was made through unlocked sliding glass patio door (I concur). No prints were found at scene. (Comp stated suspect wore soft cotton gloves). Canine element was also at scene, but due to the rain was unable to track suspect.

Reporting officer believes the suspect to be the "Friendly Burglar-Rapist." This offense follows the pattern this suspect has established over the past few days. Comp will be re-contacted for further info.

Dallas, Office of Central Division Analyst
5:00 pm Monday, December 6, 1976

MEMORANDUM

Date: 12-6-76
To: JL
Subj: FBR Offense "74" Ref. #66

FBR struck 1:10am Mon. Dec 6th in Area IV, *as predicted*. Was at the scene to interview Comp/Wit. 1:30am to 5:30am. Came back to work 8:00am. Contacted 5 North Dallas High Schools & obtained yearbooks from 4 schools for the years 1964 thru 1972. All principals, except Mr. Kelly of Thomas Jefferson, were very cooperative. After explaining the urgent necessity of having his school's books Mr. Kelly remained uncooperative and displayed an attitude of 'my problems are worse than yours.'

/RJS/

Charted the ages of the Victims from the 72 FBR offenses to date.

FBR's *Month-At-A-Glance 1976*
Monday, December 6:   Call Sheila
Roach Noon

Dallas, Office of Central Division Analyst
11:00 pm Monday, December 6, 1976

MEMORANDUM

Date: Dec 6, 1976
To: JL
Subj: FBR Suspect Identification

Spent from 6:00pm to 10:00pm, 12-6-76, with victim on FBR offense #73, Ref. #66. Used artist Linda Robertson to make a rendering of suspect she (victim) saw.

Reviewed student yearbooks from area high schools w/neg. results. More yearbooks will be reviewed w/Comp-Wit on 12-7-76.

Request CCM's (Citizen Certificate of Merit) for Linda Robertson and JH (Complainant/Witness) 2/18/76

/RJS/

MEMORANDUM

Date: 12-6-76
To: JL
Subj: FBR Weather Forecast

According to analysis of FBR offense distribution charts, the following 5 Apt. Complexes are prime targets and are ranked 1-4 in order of probability:

1*) The Citadel 5836 E Lover's Lane   Area I
2) The Willowick 4676 Amesbury   Area I
3) The Settlement 5952 Melody Lane   Area IV
4) The Seasons 6257 Melody Lane   Area IV
5) Melody Terrace 6131 Melody Lane   Area IV

According to date probability, *Sunday Dec 12th should be the next FBR Strike. (*my personal pick.)

/RJS/

Author Note: *The FBR didn't hold to his probability, he would 'hit' next in Area IV, but would choose a different date and complex*

Author Note: *Part one of the silver lining was that VEH [FBR Offense #74 page 329] was not raped and she saw her attacker prior to the attack. On December 6th, although DPD did not have an in-house sketch artist, like those always seen in movies, Tom and I knew we needed one.*

IdentiKit Generated Image of Possible FBR Suspect

This IdentiKit picture, created on November 16, 1976 (see pages 308) by assembling a composite from overlaying separate pages of noses, eyes, lips, hair etc., was that of a Prowler suspect, a possible FBR suspect. Although Tom and I believed this Prowler was the FBR, the composite never seemed close enough to reality.

When *VEH*'s sighting occurred we set out to get a sketch artist. We found Linda Robertson, and along with Landers, Linda, Tom and I met at *VEH's* apartment.

VEH and the artist (who had never done a 'police sketch' before) worked together to produce what *VEH* said was very close to what the suspect, that attacked her and with whom she had talked before the attack, looked like.

Part two of the silver lining was that we now had not only a physical description of The Friendly Burglar-Rapist but also a virtual photograph of him as well.

"FRIENDLY BURGLAR-RAPIST"
(AS SEE BY EYE WITNESS)
FORWARD ANY INFORMATION
TO INV. JOHN R. LANDERS, EXT. 551

Chapter 30

The Big Break

TALK ABOUT "OLD-SCHOOL"! We had no iPhones with cameras, no hand-held digital cameras, no scanners, no desktop or laptop computers on which to "cut & paste" photographs and documents together and send them to a desk-top digital printer.

By late afternoon on December 7th, *Pearl Harbor Remembrance Day*, I had taken a photograph of the artwork done by the sketch artist, had the film developed and printed. I then taped the smaller photograph to a spot I'd left blank in a Patrol Division Analyst Information Bulletin I had typed up. Put both of them face-down on a Xerox machine and made copies.[81]

They went into immediate distribution throughout the police department.

---

[81] Copy placed in FBR - Patrol Officers Handbook on the FBR page 2

This subject is believed to be:
WM 22 - 28 years old
5'9" tall, 150 - 160 lbs
Light to medium build
Firm muscles
Faint blond mustache

This subject has been seen
wearing a gray cotton sweat
suit with pouch type pocket
in front, possibly a zipper
down the front, and a full
hood with draw string. White
socks and white Addidas type
running shoes with dark blue
or green stripes on the side.

This information bulletin is strickly for law enforcement use only.
This rendering is not to be made public. This rendering is not to
be shown to any complainant by anyone other than Inv. John Landers,
Crimes Against Persons.

Remember this is only an artist's conception, not an actual photograph!

Dallas, Northeast Patrol Division, AREA IV
7:00 pm Monday, December 7, 1976

On Monday night, December 7, 1976, between 7pm and
10pm, (the evening after I had reduced the FBR's sketch made
by Linda Robertson to a photograph), Tom did what any good
investigator would do, he put shoe leather on the street. On his
own initiative (with Lander's imprimatur) Tom, taking a couple
of uniformed beat officers with him, made sixteen contacts that
night, showing the FBR's picture in the neighborhood of the
"Five-Points" intersection.

Two and a half hours after Tom's foray through the FBR's (Area IV) turf the FBR struck a half-mile away at 12:30am on December 8th. Tom's memo[82], dated 12.8.76, subject: "Persons contacted for viewing photo of "FBR"" detailed his efforts to Landers:

On December 7 1976, the following persons were contacted and shown the photo of the "FBR" and gave the following responses.

1. Brad Collins w/m 23 was observed running in the 6100 block of Melody Ln. and was stopped by this reporting officer and responded as follows. Subject Collins lives at 8350 Park Lane #156 and does not fit the description of our suspect. He runs on Monday, Tuesday and Thursday nights. Generally runs from 7 to 8PM and never recalls seeing the person in the photo.

2. The King Neptune, a fast food establishment, at 8446 Park Lane was contacted at 8PM and the owners and operators, Bill and Mary Little did not recognize the person in the photo. They close at 11PM and can be reached at the place of business by phone at 368-9793.

3. 7-11 Store at 8440 Park Lane was contacted at 8:05PM and the two employees, Tres Musselman, a w/m and Cindy Wheeler, a w/f who get off the evening shift at 11PM stated they did not recognize the person in the photo. They can be contacted at work on phone number 368-9695.

4. Ed and Linda Phillips who own and operate The Texas Chicken Company at 8424 Park Lane, phone 692-7981 were contacted at 8:10PM and did not recognize the person in the photo as anyone they knew or as any of their customers. Texas Chicken Company closes at 11PM.

5. Mr. Stan Donnell, w/m, owner and operator of The Medicine Cabinet Pharmacy at 8440 Park Lane, phone 363-6266 did not recognize the person in the photo as any customer he knew. Mr. Donnell closes

---

[82] Copy placed in FBR - Patrol Officers Handbook on the FBR pages 13-15

his business at 8PM and was contacted by this reporting officer at 8:12PM.

6. At 8:15PM, employees and owner of The Grand Junctions, a pizza parlor, were contacted at 8420 Park Lane. Mr. Don Yost, the owner, who can usually be contacted at the following two telephone numbers, 363-4495 or 661-1867 related the following: He recalls the subject in the photo "being in his place of business with another w/m sometime between 8PM and 9:15PM on Sunday December 5, 1976." "He was in the company of another w/m who was dressed in a red sweat suit." The subject, in the photo, had on a great sweat suit and thinks it had the hood and a front pocket or pouch. He does not remember what they purchased but remembers they left together in a car but does not remember the color or make. The main difference in the photo and the subject that was in the store is "the eyebrows seemed heavier and straighter and the eyes were sunk in further, hair was long but had some slight curl to it and it was light brown." The person who came into his store generally fits the height and weight of the subject in the photo. Another employee, Gabe Jagger, w/m, who can be reached by phone at 363-4495, also remembers these two being in the store. The main reason they remember the subject is, he has a definite likeness to Mr. Yost and when seen at a distance, could be mistaken for Mr. Yost except Mr. Yost has a medium beard and very heavy sideburns. The Grand Junctions closes at 2AM on weekends.

7. At 8:30PM, Jean Young who works for Red Colemans #24 at 8405 Park Lane was contacted and does not recognize the person in the photo. She can be contacted by phone at 363-1624. Red Colemans closes at midnight.

8. Mr. E.H. Farley, w/m and Mr. E.H. Ueckert w/m who work at at Green Park Liquor Store, 6867 Greenville Ave. were contacted at 8:35PM and stated they do not recall seeing the person in the photo in the store at any time. They can both usually be contacted by phone at the store number. Phone 361-2482.

9. Jim Rider and Keith Sparks, both w/m's were contacted at The Pleasure Shop, 6852 Greenville Ave. at 8:40PM. They both stated they did not know the person in the photo and do not recall ever seeing him in the store. They can be reached at the store by phoning 368-9409.

10. At 8:45PM Bill York and David Vick, w/m's 19 and 18, were contacted at the Beer Barn, 6886 Twin Hills. They both recall seeing this subject at the Apartment complex, Acacia Village, about 3AM the morning it was pouring down rain. They saw him pass about 6 or 8 times and had the jacket pulled up over his head to keep the rain off him. They recall he had a coat pulled over his head and thought it had a fur collar on it. Both Bill and David live at 8317 Park Lane apt. 253 and can be reached by phone at 692-6109.

11. At 8:55PM, Mr. Al Cascio was contacted at Al's Food Store at 8209 Park Lane. Mr. Cascio recalls seeing the person in the photo come into the store occasionally in the company of a w/f and as he recalls drives a van. Unknown color. Mr. Cascio remembers that the man he speaks of wears a robe of some sort and lives on Fair Oaks or Holly Hill. Mr. Cascio can be contacted by phone at 363-3778.

12. At 9:05PM, Sharaline Bruce w/f, was contacted at the 7-11 Store, 6760 Shady Brook. She, Miss Bruce, states the subject in the photo looks identical to one of the night employees that comes to work at this store at 11:30PM. He has worked for 7-11 only six weeks and told her that he formerly worked for the Brookhaven Country Club and was fired from that job for an unknown reason. Subjects name is William H. Clark and he rides a Honda motorcycle to work. He works the 11PM to 7AM shift. Miss Bruce works the 3PM to 11PM shift and can be contacted by phone at the store number, 368-9431. Subject. work schedule has been as follows,

Nov. 27--28--29--30-- Dec. 1--2--3--4--5--6--7
       Off 8 8 8   Off 8 8 8 8 8
     Sat Sun Mon Tue   Thur Fr Sa Su Mo Tu

13. Officer checked with Mr. Al Perales, w/m who is a part time clerk at the Quick Way Food Mart, 8106 Southwestern Blvd. He does not recall ever seeing the person in the photo come into this store. He is only at the store about three evenings a week and they close at midnight. Mr. Perales work phone number is 361-4972.

14. Mr. M Food Store at 5740 E. Lovers Lane was contacted at 9:40PM. Officer talked with Mr. Cecil Freeman, work phone 368-9432, and he states he does not recall ever seeing the person in the photo come into the store while he has been there. He further related that if Officers would check back next Thursday evening the regular evening clerk would be there and he may be of some help. The regular clerk's name is Robert (last name unk.)

15. At 9:55PM Mr. Pete Todora was contacted at the Parket Market, 4724 Greenville Ave. He related that the person in the photo did ring a bell with him but he was not sure if he had been into the store or not. A Xerox copy of the suspect was left with him and he would call if he could remember when or where he had seen this suspect. Mr. Todora can be reached by phone, 363-4907.

16. Last stop of the evening was 6119 Greenville Ave to talk with Ken Fallis, evening clerk at the Stop and Go Market. Mr. Fallis was contacted at 10PM and states he does not recall seeing this suspect come into the store. Mr. Fallis can be contacted at his work by phone no. 369-8656. Mr. Fallis also stated that Officers should come back and see the regular night clerk who comes to work at midnight. He could not remember her name but knows most of the regular night customers that come in.

/s/ Thomas H. Covington Police Officer #2273
Central Patrol Division

Author Note: *we know now how similar the sketched likeness of the FBR suspect really was... it is any wonder some folks might have recognized or thought they recognized him?*

Map of 16 Locations A-M
Where FBR Photo Was Shown
by Tom on 12-7-1976

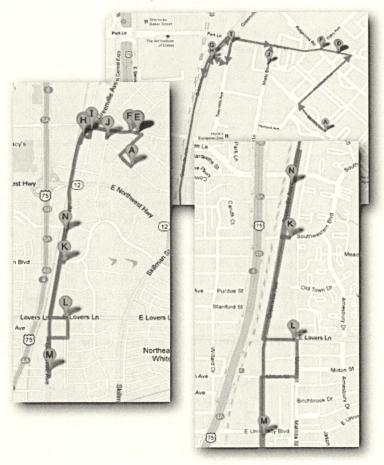

Dallas, Northeast Patrol Division, Beat 213
12:30 am Wednesday, December 8, 1976
Offense Number 75 (R-41)

REMOVING THE SCREEN only took a few seconds; he
walked with it toward, then flung it into, the parking lot, where it

skidded under a parked car. Lifting the window only a few more inches; he was inside and out of the thirty-six degree temperature; the slight 4.6 mile per hour breeze out of the south did nothing to exacerbate the cold. Clear and cold, the two things he had going for him were that it was not raining and the full moon would not rise till after the sun came up; no complication. The blueprint had been drawn; he had followed it for years. Tonight would be no exception.

AAA had been lying in bed, nearly asleep. She had a wet washcloth over her eyes. She was distraught over the death of her French Poodle and had been crying. She thought she heard a noise but dismissed it as probably having come from the radio.

The next thing she remembered was a man on top of her commanding her, "Don't move, don't talk and you won't get hurt. I have a knife and I really will kill you." He pricked her several times with the point of the knife. He took the pillow from behind her head and unsheathed it of its pillowcase which he then pulled over her head and pulled down over her face. He reminded her, even though she had the pillowcase over her head, "Keep your eyes closed."

Now, "give me your left hand first," which he tied, now "your right hand." He put her hands together and bound her with the cord from the roll-up bamboo shade on her sliding glass door.

After he had *AAA* tied up, he got off the bed turning on the bedside lamp and then wandering through the apartment, turning on lights and searching cabinets and drawers. He had told her to lie still, which she did.

He cut the phone line in the kitchen, found her purse and purloined two twenty dollar bills. She heard him open her refrigerator. At one point he picked up a plant from the living room coffee table and took it out on *AAA*'s patio and left it

She could hear him cutting the cord to her phone in the bedroom after he came back into her bedroom. Next he grabbed the hem of the maroon turtleneck sweater she was wearing and lifted it over her face. He cut *AAA*'s bra off, then her panties and began to fondle her.

He forced himself between her legs, entering her and telling her as he thrusted in and out, "You better make it good." He kept moving till he climaxed. After he withdrew he told her, "Give me a minute, I'm going to see if it is safe to go to my truck."

AAA waited until she felt safe then got up and went to a male neighbor's, who called the police. When the R.O.'s arrived she told them she had already taken a shower and thus she was not taken to PMH to be examined. *AAA* said that she would go to her own doctor tomorrow.

Complainant stated that the suspect was a w/m/22-30, 190 lbs, 5-9 to 5-11, long light brown hair, unknown eye color and was wearing a cotton sweatsuit of unknown color, with a toboggan or hood. She said he smelled clean, no cologne or sweat and that he sounded educated and spoke with a soft/polite voice.

Investigator Landers added the following:

> I contacted this comp just minutes after the offense occurred. Comp's French Poodle had died earlier this evening and comp had been crying after returning to her apt at 11:30pm this date. Comp was in bed with a wet wash cloth over her eyes when suspect laid on top of her and told her not to make any noise. Suspect stated, **"I have a knife and if it's you or me, it's going to be you."** At this time, the telephone cord in kitchen had been cut. The telephone in comp's bedroom was the old type which was stationary in the wall (cord) and was hidden behind an end table. Suspect cut drawstring from bamboo curtain which covered the glass patio door next to comp's bed and tied comp's hands together with this cord. After comp was tied, suspect found the bedroom phone and cut the cord and placed pillow case over comp's head. Suspect then wandered through apt and opened refrigerator. Comp did not have any type of beverages in the refrigerator. Suspect then returned to comp's bedroom and took a bottle of lotion from comp's dressing table, then sat on comp's bed. Comp was dressed in a turtleneck sweater, bra and panties. Suspect then pulled comp's panties off, raised comp's sweater over her head (covering the pillowcase) then cut comp's bra straps with the knife. As suspect started to enter comp, he stated "You'd better make this good," After the act, suspect stated "Give me a minute to get to my truck," NOTE: Comp told me this was the

"Friendly Rapist." She stated that she knew his M.O. and that he (suspect) had "done all the things that he'd done in the past," including mentioning his truck[83]. She also stated that suspect was "well-educated" but could not tell me exactly why she thought so. Comp went to friend's apt nearby & had taken a bath before officers arrived at the scene. During the act, comp was wearing approx $3,000.00 worth of diamonds. Suspect did not mention this jewelry at all. Suspect got Comp's driver's license & $56.00 from comp's purse but only took $40.00 and threw $16.00 on the bedroom floor. Suspect was wearing jogging pants and dark knit cap (which could have been a ski mask) but it was not covering his face. Comp cannot make ID of suspect because she could not see through the pillowcase which covered her face.

12/7: *AAA*, w/f/27 Villa Crest Apartments number 107, 6514 Ridgecrest. clear cold, RO M.J. Harrison #3317 and R.L. Newell #3476... took two 20's 40 bucks

FBR's *Month-At-A-Glance 1976*
Wednesday, December 8:   Noble ?
                        Noon Sheraton
                        IABC

Dallas, Office of Central Division Analyst
Dep. Chief Dixon's Office
9:00 am Tuesday, December 8, 1976

Having received Chief Dixon's 'okay' back on November 17th and now having 'the tape' in our possession, we reminded the Chief of our conversation. He gave us authorization to sign-out a smooth car and take it 'out of the city limits'.

That morning Tom and I drove up to Sherman to the Johnson & Johnson plant. We met with two great guys; Leonard Winter,

---

[83] Last reported mentioning of "truck" was on Offense #41 4/11/76, eight months ago.

Director, Quality Assurance & John Jackson, Technical Assurance & Services. We gave them some of the tape used by the FBR. We asked them, "What can you tell us about this tape?" They looked at one another and one of them (I believe it was Leonard) said, "I can tell you a hell of a lot about it—why?"

We told him all about the FBR case.

His head nodded and he said, "Give me a few days..."

Dallas, Office of Central Division Analyst
5:00 pm Tuesday, December 8, 1976

MEMORANDUM

Date: Dec 8, 1976
To: JL
Subj: FBR Daily Activity

Went to Dallas Morning News to get names of contractors[84] in Area: 1, 2, 3 & 4. In order to locate carrier who is supposed to favor the FBR artist conception.

Collected tape used to bind FBR victims on Offenses: 237116F, 344796G, 354830G & 358213G. Tape given to Leonard Winter, Dir. Quality Assurance & John Jackson, Technical Assurance & Services – Johnson & Johnson in Sherman Tex. Tape to be sent to East Coast lab for analysis. Update report 12-20-76. /RJS/

Updated charts. Planned for night surveillance. Carried out night surveillance

Author's Note: There were too many individuals, companies and organizations to count who quietly provided lists of individuals for us to look at and eliminate as persons of interest. So please allow me, here, to thank them all for their cooperation. Many were certain none of their 'company' could be "the one." Still others felt anxiety in sharing information. All wanted the

---

[84] newspaper carriers / deliverymen

FBR caught and hoped they were right about their people. Again, Tom and I thank you for your cooperation and help.

FBR's *Month-At-A-Glance 1976*
Thursday, December 9: Noble ~ Ardmore
                  Noon Thurs   CoZ.
FBR's *Month-At-A-Glance 1976*
Friday, December 10:   (date circled)

Dallas, Office of Central Division Analyst
5:00 pm Friday, December 10, 1976

MEMORANDUM

Date: Dec 9 &10, 1976
To: JL
Subj: Daily Activity

Updated charts. Planned for night surveillance. Carried out night surveillance w/negative results in terms of catching the FBR. Did contact a number of suspects[85] who were ID'd, fingerprinted, then eliminated as FBR suspects.

More night surveillance is planned. /RJS/

12/12	L	14-27	WASHINGTON	37,279

Dallas, Office of Central Division Analyst
5:00 pm Sunday, December 12, 1976

On December 12th, VEH picked out the type shoe suspect was wearing from a catalog of running shoes: Adidas Runner (*The Runner*) as seen in a running magazine dated October 1076.

---

[85] today we would probably would have used the term 'subject' here rather than suspect...

(See author's website for image: robertjsadler.com)

FBR's *Month-At-A-Glance 1976*
Monday, December 13: Joint mgt.
4:00 IABC

**Dallas, Office of Central Division Analyst
5:00 pm Tuesday, December 14, 1976**

MEMORANDUM

**Date: Dec 13 & 14, 1976
To: JL
Subj: Daily Activity**

Reviewed yearbooks with Complainant/Witness. Worked on elimination of suspects so far gathered.

Attended instructional briefing by Sally Williams at Southwestern Institute of Forensic Sciences. We were briefed on her blood typing testing & analysis of the evidence gathered in FBR cases.

Made up new master chart w/addition of fingerprint info., suspect blood type, & offense sequence numbering. /RJS/
Dallas, Office of Central Division Analyst
5:00 pm Tuesday, December 14, 1976

RECEIVED FROM SALLY Williams her latest blood grouping & enzyme testing[86] of the FBR rape evidence. Only trouble was... well, you will see later.

---

[86] Copy placed in FBR - Patrol Officers Handbook on the FBR page 21

SOUTHWESTERN
INSTITUTE OF FORENSIC SCIENCES
AT DALLAS
5230 Medical Center Drive
Dallas, Texas 75235

TELEPHONE 638-1131
AREA CODE 214
REPLY TO:
P.O. BOX 35728

Criminal Investigation Laboratory

December 14, 1976

Investigator John R. Landers   RE: Blood typing on
Dallas Police Department   "Friendly Burglar Rapes"
Crimes Against Persons Section
Main and Harwood
Dallas, Texas 75201

From blood grouping and enzyme testing on seminal fluid from
twenty seven criminal assaults, encompassing the time period from
July 1974 to the present, it has been determined that the assailant
has the following blood group and frequency distribution:

BLOOD GROUP	FREQUENCY %
A	40
Secretor	80
PGM 2-1	37.3
Pep-A 1-1	99.8

11.9% Total Frequency

Sarah (Sally) B. Williams

SBW:mj

✓cc: Officer Tom Covington
Central Div., DPD

Dallas, Office of Central Division Analyst
5:00 pm Tuesday, December 14, 1976

Memo re:
Summary of *Money & Property Taken in FBR Offenses* [87]

Memorandum

CITY OF DALLAS

DATE   December 14, 1976

TO   Investigator John Landers
       Crimes Against Persons

SUBJECT   Summary of Money and Property Taken from
          Victims by Subject Known as the "Friendly Burglar-Rapist".

This summary is gathered from the seventy-five (75) offenses attributed to
the "FBR" over the past three (3) years.

As of December 9, 1976:

	FBR RAPES				FBR RELATED OFFENSES	
1973	1	INCREASE	PERCENT	0	INCREASE	PERCENT INCREASE
1974	9	+8	INCREASE	0		
1975	14	+5	55.5%	10	+10	
1976	18	+4	28.57%	23	+13	130%
TOTAL:	42			33		

42 Rapes
33 Related Offenses
75 TOTAL FBR Offenses

DAY of WEEK	NUMBER of OFFENSES OCCURRING
SUNDAY	8
MONDAY	10
TUESDAY	15
WEDNESDAY	12
THURSDAY	12
FRIDAY	13
SATURDAY	5
	75

25.5 Days - Average days between rapes in 1976
14.472 Days - Average days between all FBR offenses
11.767 Days - Average days between FBR dates 7/30/74 and 12/9/76
27.173 Years Old - Average victims age in 75 offenses
26.39 Years Old - Average age (Remove extrm. age groups)
$75.00 - Most money taken in FBR offense
$1.00 - Lease money taken in FBR offense

---

[87] Copy placed in FBR - Patrol Officers Handbook on the FBR pages 17-19

December 14, 1976
Page Two

Total property and cash money loss to date involving thirty-three (33)
offenses are averaged as follows:

Total cash loss $603.15
Average cash loss   20.10
Total property loss   1233.00
Average property loss   205.50   six (6) offenses
Total cash and property loss   1836.15
Average loss (cash and property)   55.64

Offense loss summary

Number offenses with cash only loss   27
Number offenses with cash and property loss   3
Number offenses with property only loss   _3_
TOTAL OFFENSES   33

Only three (3) offenses have had cash _and_ property taken and these are
#284374-G, 342302-G and 382248-H and are listed accordingly.

File Number	Chart Number	Offense Number	Type Offense	Amount Taken	Property Value
#2	4	248973-F	R	17.00	
#3	5	283127-F	R	14.00	
#6	7	342398-F	R	8.00	
#9	11	83737-G	R	20.00	
#10	12	103880-G	R	6.00	
#11	14	139028-G	R	8.00	
#12	15	150346-G	R	1.00	
#13	16	172369-G	R		Ring $100.00
#13-A	17	173655-G	Robb	4.15	
#16	20	284374-G	R	60.00	Silverservice&pot plant 115.00
#17	21	299194-G	R	15.00	
#18	22	314712-G	B	50.00	
#18-A	23	314966-G	B	20.00	
#19	26	342302-G	B	20.00	
#20	27	344796-G	R	15.00	
#23	30	365250-G	R	18.00	
#24	31	382904-G	R	40.00	
#25	32	385719-G	R	72.00	
#27	34	424821-G	R	2.00	
#28	35	56459-H	R	15.00	
#29	36	76996-H	R	5.00	
#30	37	84982-H	Robb	16.00	
#33	40	115516-H	R	10.00	
#34-B	43	154185-H	CT		Diamond Ring 1,000.00

December 14, 1976
Page Three

File Number	Chart Number	Offense Number	Type Offense	Amount Taken	Property Value
#37	47	167907-H	B	10.00	
#38	48	169092-H	B	15.00	
#39	49	169071-H	B	35.00	
#41	51	190124-H	Robb	20.00	
#41-A	52	195460-H	B		Swim Suit 2.00
#43	54	214548-H	R	20.00	
#47	58	238606-H	R	22.00	
#60	68	382248-H	R	5.00	Silver knife 10.00
#67	75	436799-H	R	40.00	

T. H. Covington #2273
Police Officer
Crime Prevention Officer
Central Division
Patrol Bureau

R. J. Sadler #2441
Police Officer
Central Division
Patrol Bureau

cmp

Dallas, Office of Central Division Analyst
5:00 pm Wednesday, December 15, 1976

MEMORANDUM

Date: Dec 15, 1976
To: JL
Subj: Daily Activity

Returned High School yearbooks to:
    Hillcrest, Prin. John M. Marshall
    W.T.White, Prin.
    Bryan Adams, Prin., Asst.
    Highland Park, Prin., Asst.

These gentlemen were most cooperative and helpful to the FBR investigation. Recommend a letter of appreciation be sent to the school board & these men

Worked on eliminating suspects. /RJS/

MEMORANDUM

Date: Dec 15, 1976
To: JL
Subj: Daily Activity

Contacted Principal Kelly of Thomas Jefferson HS for the second time. This time we secured the schools yearbook for our investigation. Due to Mr. Kelly's initial attitude the review of possible suspects, who had attended TJ was hampered for one week. Mr. Kelly did not call officers the day after our first visit, as he said he would.

Worked suspects. /RJS/

Chapter 31

Tom's Three-year Comparison

Also on December 15, 1976, Tom completed the draft, summarizing our efforts to date, and published a four page memo with five attachments to Inv. John Landers, Crimes Against Persons, subject: *Three Year Comparison and Summary of Offense Attributed to the "Friendly Burglar-Rapist"*.[88]

The first part of the memo is transcribed here. The rest of the memo detailed the stats as shown in the charts that were attached.

Memorandum   City Of Dallas

Date: December 15, 1976
To: Investigator John Landers
         Crimes Agains Persons

Subj: Three Year Comparison and summary of Offenses
         Attributed to the "Friendly Burglar-Rapist".

The first recognition of offenses by the "Friendly Burglar-Rapist", hereafter referred to as the "FBR", was detected by Police Officer R. J. Sadler #2441, while working as Central Division Crime Analyst in November 1973 (Offense #340698-E) and at that time noted only as "an unusual M.O.". In July, 1974, the "FBR" committed another offense (#237116-F) and the similarity in the M.O. was noted and compared.

Several offenses were noted between November 1973 and July 1974 and were compared, but the "FBR"'s M.O. was not established and was therefore discounted.

The first person Officer Sadler spoke to regarding the similarity in the offenses was police Officer T.H. Covington #2273, this reporting officer, who, at the time was working closely with Apartment Mangers and Apartment Residents. Other information was being disseminated to field officers as his pattern became clearer and the M.O. began to follow an almost exact pattern each time.

About the time offense #5 (#307548-F) occurred, units of Planning and Research and Crimes Against Persons became aware of, or were made aware of, the M.O. and information began to flow on an irregular basis between units.

Officers Sadler and Covington continued to monitor these offenses continually and started filing them in two categories: Possible and Probable.

Possible offenses are those which do not contain all elements of the M.O. and have no conclusive evidence such as fingerprints or blood type to confirm they were committed by the same person.

Probable offenses are those which contain all or several elements of the M.O. and have fingerprints or blood type to confirm they were committed by the same person.

Categorizing the Probable offenses into yearly surveys gives the following results. (See attachment #1)

---

[88] Copy (with graphs) placed in FBR - Patrol Officers Handbook on the FBR pages 22-30

Author Note: *the original graphs were filled-in by hand on graph paper. The graphs were copied and placed in the Patrol Officers Handbook. Recently computer generated replicas (with all offenses included) can be found on pages 518-522.*

Tom recalls he and I had long conversations about the validity and usefulness of the odd and even day metrics. We did not place any particular significance in the basic coin-flip of odd-even days, but decided to always include that factor in all our predictions: FBR weather forecasts. At the time, it seemed "even" days were winning the day.

With the completion of Tom's 3-year comparison memo we were ready to put together our compilation of FBR information for the troops. We called it the Patrol Officers's Handbook. The forty-nine page 'handbook', in a top-bound, metal fastener, report binder, was restricted and intended for the use of our hardworking patrol officers doing their best to apprehend the FBR in their areas of patrol responsibility.

As I recall we made about 25-26 copies: 7 copies each were sent to the Patrol Divisions: Central, NW & NE; Tom and I kept copies (my copy was #23); 1 copy went to Chief Dixon; 1 copy to John Landers; 1 copy to Planning & Research (probably).

PATROL OFFICER'S HANDBOOK - CONTENTS

FBR's *Month-At-A-Glance 1976*
Thursday, December 16:   Lunch 12:30
C.H.

Dallas, Office of Central Division Analyst
9:00 am Thursday, December 16, 1976

Tom and I received the invitation below from Captain Memo. Finally, we thought, *some* organization; maybe we can get some cooperation?

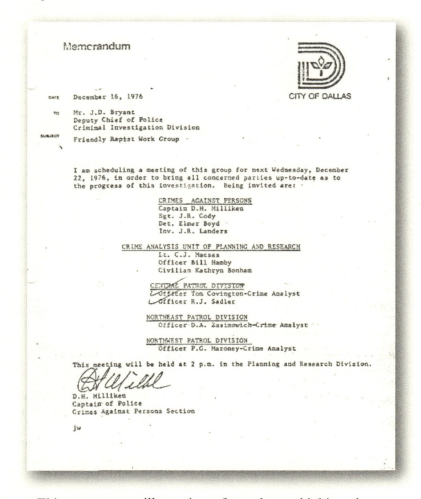

Memorandum

CITY OF DALLAS

DATE   December 16, 1976

TO   Mr. J.D. Bryant
        Deputy Chief of Police
        Criminal Investigation Division

SUBJECT Friendly Rapist Work Group

I am scheduling a meeting of this group for next Wednesday, December 22, 1976, in order to bring all concerned parties up-to-date as to the progress of this investigation. Being invited are:

CRIMES AGAINST PERSONS
Captain D.H. Milliken
Sgt. J.R. Cody
Det. Elmer Boyd
Inv. J.R. Landers

CRIME ANALYSIS UNIT OF PLANNING AND RESEARCH
Lt. C.J. Macsas
Officer Bill Hamby
Civilian Kathryn Bonham

CENTRAL PATROL DIVISION
Officer Tom Covington-Crime Analyst
Officer R.J. Sadler

NORTHEAST PATROL DIVISION
Officer D.A. Zasimowich-Crime Analyst

NORTHWEST PATROL DIVISION
Officer P.G. Maroney-Crime Analyst

This meeting will be held at 2 p.m. in the Planning and Research Division.

D.H. Milliken
Captain of Police
Crimes Against Persons Section

jw

This memo was illustrative of top-down thinking that was institutionalized throughout the police department and certainly not organizationally unusual for the times. The meeting was scheduled arbitrarily, without consultation (with us or anyone else as far as we knew). The memo's subject: "Friendly Rapist Work Group" was suggestive of some cooperative effort about to occur, however the first paragraph seemed to negate that effort. There was no agenda attached to this memo or subsequently provided. We were just supposed to show up in six days to be "brought up to date as to the progress of this investigation."

Who was going to be doing the bringing up to date? Neither Tom nor I were asked for our input before the meeting. We were not asked to supply, for example, a position paper describing our analysis. No suggestion was made for anyone 'to be prepared to discuss your knowledge of the case'.

At least, Tom and I thought, we got invited!

I never sought, nor did Tom, any control over this investigation. We only wanted to participate by sharing the understanding and expertise we had amassed over the last three years.

Perhaps it was unintentional, but yes, it was annoying not to be accorded the title Crime Analyst next to my name.[89] Particularly since I was *the* Central Patrol Division Crime Analyst. (Tom received that designation after I went back to patrol.) I had discovered and linked various offenses to an MO: that of a friendly burglar who was a rapist, that these various offenses were being committed by the same suspect, the FBR. An observation I had long ago brought to everyone's attention who would listen.

FBR's *Month-At-A-Glance 1976*
Friday, December 17:   RT xmas Party

Dallas, Office of Central Division Analyst
5:00 pm Friday, December 17, 1976

We now have all but one of the FBR's finger prints... we can even arrest him for spittin' on the sidewalk and let him go... as long as we got his prints on a jail house ten-card, we'd have the

---

[89] Sour grapes, on my part? Perhaps, at least in the sense of still not being taken seriously for the work we had done and expertise we brought to the table.

bastard. In point of fact, all we really needed to take was one print—the tadpole! That was all we were looking for!

Dallas, Northeast Patrol Division, Beat 213
3:00 am Sunday, December 19, 1976
Offense Number 76

MEET COMPLAINANT AT 8350 Park Lane #336. [FBR Offense Area IV] Reporting Officers, W.L. Russell #3803 and L.L. Barbee #2945 met with *DMK* a white female, thirty. (Cold and clear - Maybe the women of Dallas were becoming more cautious. Perhaps the word was getting around. The FBR had struck in this 'area' 13 times.) *DMK* told R.O.'s that she had heard noises on her patio and called police. She didn't need to tell the officers she was scared. Officers Russell and Barbee checked complainant's apartment inside and out and found no signs of an attempted forced entry. In conclusion Russell wrote: "Comp. did not see anyone and could give no suspect info."

Our file copy was marked: "Just a good Possible." Even so, I felt this Meet Complainant call warranted inclusion as an attempted offense of the FBR.

1976 Divisional Playoff				
12/19	L	12-14	LOS ANGELES	48,341

Dallas, Office of Central Division Analyst
8:00 am Monday, December 20, 1976

MEMORANDUM

Date: Dec 16 thru 20, 1976
To: JL
Subj: Daily Activity

Worked on elimination of suspects.

Planned for & executed night surveillance in Northeast area. Secured from Dallas Metro two ambient light gathering devices to aid our surveillance. Night activity was extremely slow. Numerous vehicle licenses gathered, also contacted many suspects who were fingerprinted for FBR elimination. The FBR did not strike during our surveillance.

/RJS

Dallas, Office of Central Division Analyst
9:00 am Tuesday, December 21, 1976

Sent Memo to JL, Subject: Johnson & Johnson Tape Analysis. Telephoned Sherman office w/negative results. Will try to contact again 12-22.76
/s/ RJS

Dallas, Office of Central Division Analyst
9:00 am Wednesday, December 21, 1976

Telephoned Sherman office w/negative results. Pertinent parties on Xmas vacation.

Chapter 32

The Big Deal-e-Oh FBR Working Group

Dallas, Planning and Research Section
2:00 pm Wednesday, December 22, 1976

WE ALL ASSEMBLED around Lt. Macsas' Crime Analysis Unit table in their 'map room'. On both sides of the room were floor-to-ceiling maps of the city, outlined with the different patrol division sector, beat and reporting area configurations. The maps were so large that they had to slide on tracks. Their maps, like my smaller versions, were nubby with colored round-headed pins.

The eleven of us from Captain Milliken's memo were present.

Author Note: *Looking back, I do not recall anyone distributing a meeting agenda, much less handouts of pertinent facts to be discussed by Capt. Memo's "Friendly Rapist Work Group".*

THE ELEPHANT IN the room. In preparation I had provided Tom, John Landers, and Bobby Buck Smoot with a copy of my assessment re: FBR SUSPECT ELIMINATION. I had compiled my analysis of the "Situation," the "Problem," and the "Solution."

At the time of this meeting, Tom and I had spent the longest time with this case, given that I was the first one to recognize and begin tracking the suspect, and Tom was less than a 'half-a-step' behind...

From the first FBR attributed offense, a police officer had been suspected of possibly being the FBR, and later not only *a police officer*, but *a Dallas Police Officer*. This fact had been a story in the press, although not an ongoing one. The suspect *could* be a cop and yet we, the department, had done nothing to eliminate a single Dallas officer.

[NB: with the exception that the Dallas PD & Houston PD link had been explored by Inv. Linda Fulghum #2937 as related in her Supplement Report, dated 4-9-75: "Suspect stated he 'was a Dallas Police officer and had trained in Houston'. A check of personnel records revealed that we have no officers with this Department at the present time who have worked for the Houston Police Department prior to coming to DPD."][90]

Fulghum's follow-up does not really cover all the permutations of the FBR's statement. So, however unlikely it might seem, the question remained, is the FBR a Dallas cop?

Whereas we had worked to eliminate scores, if not hundreds, of other suspects and groups, such as Dallas Firemen who work often enough with and are close enough to a lot of officers to know police jargon and police procedures.

When it seemed *we* had been "brought up to date", though not 'given' the floor, I spoke up and, passing out my info sheet, proposed the following:

---

[90] See page 113, 122, 383 re Investigator Fulghum's report.

FBR SUSPECT ELIMINATION

SITUATION:
1. FBR has used police-type jargon
2. FBR has called himself a Dallas Policeman
3. FBR fingerprints are on file
4. No complete file on DPD police prints
5. All male DPD officers should be positively eliminated as FBR suspects

PROBLEM:
How to obtain DPD fingerprints for elimination

SOLUTION:
1. Memo from Chief Byrd to all Divisions
2. Set up 3 day operation
3. Have each Div. Commander appoint one supervisor familiar w/fingerprinting be responsible to:
   a. Gather on 3x5 cards prints of every male officer in that Division's left thumb, right index finger, name & badge number
   b. Fill out 3x5 cards w/name & badge number for officers not available for printing
   c. Hand-carry cards to Lt. Day, P.E.S.
4. Lt. Day's men eliminate Officers by comparison to FBR prints
   a. Notify Inv. Landers, who will be responsible for obtaining prints not forwarded
   b. After review, forward all cards to Off. Covington for permanent filing.

The above was rejected out of hand by Captain Milliken as "not good, might cause too much media reaction unfavorable to the department."

Of course no one had intended on informing the media and if the media did find out they could hardly say it was a 'witch hunt'. It would have simply been the right thing to do. If the media asked, we could acknowledge the FBR's claim to be a cop and that though were sure the claim was bogus the public deserved for DPD to affirmatively take action. We did already have the fingerprints of most every officer, they were taken early in the hiring procedure—but the taking of some officers prints had, somehow, fallen through the cracks.

This would have been a relatively simple in-house method to quickly gather the prints and eliminate everyone. And, I didn't bring up John Lander's memo, dated November 16, 1976, in which John informs Captain Memo that he had "met with Chief Tuma of the Dallas Fire Department in an effort to determine if any Fire Department personnel are involved in the Friendly Burglar-Rapist offenses" and Chief Tuma promised his "full cooperation."

The "working group" meeting was adjourned never to be reconvened; at least to my knowledge.

FBR's *Month-At-A-Glance 1976*
Thursday, December 23: Frank Ott

Dallas, Office of Central Division Analyst
9:00 am Thursday, December 23, 1976

BUSINESS AS USUAL. I received a Routing Slip from Special Investigator John Gee, Criminal District Attorney's Office for Dallas County re: "Request your appearance for a trial set in County Criminal Court 5 on the 6th floor of the Dallas County Court House; Date: 1-12-1977 at 9am; John B. L. for DWI; Arrest # 76-100091; Docket # 76-1776-F.

The sins of someone else's past were catching up to me; a prior arrest I made was finally coming to court. The arrest number indicated it was in 1976, but for the life of me I couldn't remember who or when; I'd have to find my notes before trial. Just one more thing to do that takes time away from the FBR case.

FBR's *Month-At-A-Glance 1976*
Friday, December 24: Holiday

Dallas, Office of Central Division Analyst
9:00 am Wednesday, December 29, 1976

GIVEN THE FBR's past pattern of laying off in January and February we made the following predictions for the "First Hit of 1977": Tom Covington picked "Middle of February: 8th, 10th, 12th;

Bob Smoot: "Last of January: 24th or February 1st"; and I suggested: "the FBR's first 1977 hit would be: 3rd, 5th, 15th of February".

AS A GUIDE for ourselves, we developed a "FBR Offense Fact Sheet". The primary use was to note the individual key M/O markers (etc.) to achieve 50 points of comparison

These were some of the usual analysis points we filtered regarding each of the offenses:

1. Offense number _____
2. Book [ ], File # [ ], Chart # [ ]
3. Type of Offense _____
4. Number of days since last FBR offense: _____
5. Number of days since last FBR Rape: _____
6. Date of Offense: ____
7. Hours of occurrence: _____
8. Average time of Offense: _____ /TGR____ /TC6____
9. Day of week:
10. Apartment number of victim:
11. Plotting Area:
12. Reporting area: _____ /Patrol Div. _____
13. Investigator assigned:
14. Victim's parents:
    a. address: _____
    b. phone: _____
15. Victim's Race: _____ Sex _____ Age _____
16. Suspect's Point of Entry (POE): _____
    a. if window, where was screen _____
17. Sets up escape route: yes/no // where: _____
18. Weapon used: _____
19. Weapon belongs to: Victim / Suspect / Unknown
20. Where does victim keep weapon used: _____
21. Mentions knife: yes / no
22. Victim: Did/did not see/feel: weapon
    a. knife
    b. scissors
    c. unk sharp object
23. Suspect wears mask: yes/no; if yes type:
    a. ski mask

  b. stocking/women's hose w/wo eye cutouts
24. Suspect: did/did not: cut telephone cord / other cord
25. Ties victim: yes/no with what:_____ to what _____
26. Victims clothes
     cuts / rearranges / unbuttons / pulls up – down /
     removes: bedclothes/ clothes
          i.   nightgown
          ii. bra
          iii. panties
          iv. other
27. Turns on/off lights
28. Searches apartment: yes/no
29. Suspect uses Victim's/Roommates Name, name ___
30. Mentions: Roommate/husband/boyfriend/guest/child
31. Victim: does/does not have:
     a. husband/roommate/boyfriend/guest/child/dog
32. Suspect seems to have/have not 'done' his homework
33. Suspect uses/doesn't use lubricant: victim's/suspect's
34. Type Sex Act: vaginal / oral / anal / masturbation /
fondles / repeats coitus / other act
35. Suspect tells victim: she deserves it/this, etc, yes/no
36. Tells victim to:
     a. be quiet
     b. I'll slit your throat
     c. threatens to kill
     d. does/doesn't mention truck
     e. says/doesn't say: I'm just a burglar
37. Mentions parking lot: yes/no Can pkg lot be see from
victims Apt: yes/no
38. Tells victim: I'll let you know when I'm leaving: yes/no
39. Other statements _____
40. Lifted fingerprints yes/no: from what& where _____
41. FBR prints match yes/no
42. FBR prints lifted: #: 1/2/3/4/5/6/7/8/9/10
43. Suspect's blood type: _____
44. Stolen property & value: ___
45. Suspects drinks/eats during offense // what _____
46. Carries out trash or other object yes/no: what _____
47. Point of Exit (POEx) _____
48. Is POEx same as: POE/Escape Route // yes/no
49. Dog tracking: yes/no // where: _____
50. Suspect description: _____

Author Note: *As previously mentioned these FBR Offense Fact Sheets (surveys) were either hand-delivered, mailed out to complainants for their voluntary input, or filled in by Tom, me or Bobby Smoot, based on the O/IR for each offense.*

Chapter 33

Fair-Haired Golden Boys?

Dallas, Office of Central Division Analyst
9:00 am Thursday, December 30, 1976

GOLDEN BOYS? NO. If anyone is thinking that what I was doing was being well received by anyone other than Chief Dixon, and my partner Tom, guess again. To those who even gave it some thought, we were of the opinion, Investigator's in CAPERS thought Tom and I were pains-in-the-ass.

Those that worked closest with us, John Landers and Truly Holmes appreciated the case-knowledge, perspective and insights we possessed. Chief Souter (I suspected) and Captain Memo (I was assured) would rather that I was back in patrol 'where I belonged.' Investigations was not a place for Patrolmen.

That sentiment was not dissimilar with that of the officers and supervisors in the field. My own field supervisor Sergeant Fred Rich, who was also a friend, felt much the same way. His was a more pragmatic view. I was one of his men, I was assigned to him.

My not being there reduced his manpower resources and made scheduling and 'doing his job' a little more difficult. He wrote: *"Officer Sadler meets or exceeds standards in all categories. This evaluation is nowhere near his potential due to the fact he does not have a great deal of interest in the patrol function. I believe his work efforts should be directed toward the patrol function as long as he is assigned to patrol."*

Fred would have preferred that I was assigned to CAPERS as an Investigator, and he be given an everyday on-the-job street cop to fill his roster. I can't blame Fred either for his evaluation (which was fair) or his desire to have a 'full team roster'.

Admittedly, Fred's worries never crossed my mind. I had started this hunt for the FBR and I wanted to finish it. During the rating period of July 1 through December 31, 1976, I was assigned to Fred, but for the most part I had been on Special Assignment (more than the two months Fred mentions) per Chief Dixon.

And Fred was correct, during the time, when I was in the field, the FBR was something I continued working on. In my mind (besides Tom) somebody had to be working on it! Of course 'others' *were*, but not in coordination with me or Tom.

DALLAS POLICE DEPARTMENT
Performance Evaluation Report
PATROL BUREAU

Employee Name	(Last)	(First)	(Initial)	I. D. Number	Rank or Title
	Sadler,	Robert	J.	2441	Police Officer

Rating Period	Assignment(s)		Division
From 7-1-76 To 12-31-76	Second Watch	110's Relief	Central

IF CATEGORY DOES NOT APPLY—MARK BOX

DO NOT LEAVE BLANK

Rater Mark With Check Mark (✓)

Reviewer Mark With (X)

If Not In Agreement.

Second Reviewer Mark With (O)

If Not In Agreement With Originator.

INITIATIVE — Initiation of Action By an Employee
1. Offers suggestions and constructive criticism.
2. Develops and utilizes methods to solve crime and crime trends.
3. Works without close supervision.

PUBLIC CONTACT — Officer's Contacts With the Public
1. Exercises patience in citizen contacts
2. Treats each citizen contact with interest and concern

COOPERATION — Ability to Work With Others
1. Willingness to share information.
2. Willingness to share recognition for work jointly done.
3. Completes his share of group work assignments.
4. Fellow officers and other divisions, bureaus, and agencies.

SAFETY PRACTICES — Awareness and Concern For the Safety of Herself/Himself and Others in:
1. Operation and care of vehicles.
2. Handling of firearms.
3. Handling of prisoners.
4. Potentially hazardous situations.
5. Others — Specify

DEPENDABILITY — Accepts and Fulfills Responsibilities
1. Observes rules regarding duty hours.
2. Proper use of sick and/or injury time.
3. Remains on assigned beat.
4. Observes rules regarding markouts.
5. Makes all assignments
6. Keeps supervisor informed.

VOLUME OF ACCEPTABLE WORK
1. Arrest activity in relation to offenses.
2. Traffic enforcement in relation to motor vehicle accidents and traffic problems.
3. Calls for service answered.
4. Felony in-the-act arrests.
5. Offenses cleared by arrest.
6. Stolen property recovered.

WORK ATTITUDE — Interest and Enthusiasm for the Job.
1. Willingly adapts to new procedures and surroundings.
2. Accepts direction (training, supervision, instruction).

APPEARANCE AND DEMEANOR
1. Correctness and condition of uniform and personal equipment.
2. Physical appearance (weight, posture, hair trimmed and combed, etc.)
3. Presents an alert and professional manner while performing his duties or dealing with the public.

FIELD PROFICIENCY AND EFFECTIVENESS — Quality of Work
1. Interrogation and interviews.
2. Written reports (makes proper reports in a correct manner).
3. Knowledge and proper utilization of procedures, policies, and regulations.
4. Radio procedures.
5. Oral communication.
6. Development of information sources.
7. Field notebook.
8. Practices aggressive patrol techniques.
9. Ability to improve through field experience.

JUDGMENT — Evaluate situations, Consider Alternatives, and Arrive at Effective Solution
1. Reliability under stress.
2. Consistency.
3. Unbiased and impartial.
4. Ability to control emotions.

SUPERVISORY EFFECTIVENESS — For those who supervise others.
1. Training
2. Leadership
3. Evaluation of Subordinates
4. Scheduling and Coordinating
5. Decision Making
6. Maintains Discipline

DALLAS POLICE DEPARTMENT

Rater Interview Summary

PATROL BUREAU

Officer _____ Sadler, Robert J. _____ I. D. # 2441 _____ Rating Period From 7-1-76 to 12-31-76

1. STRENGTHS (Define—Do Not List—Use Extra Sheet if Necessary)
Officer Sadler excells at public relations and presents a very "professional police" image while carrying out his duties. During this period he spent about 2 months on special assignment outside his patrol assignment. Officer Sadler was charged with 33 preventable offenses, cleared 21 offenses and 10 arrests for preventable offenses. He issued 38 citations, made 11 jail traffic arrests and was charged with 3 injury accidents. He distributed 11 CID pamphlets and turned in 1 target hardening supplement.

2. IMPROVEMENTS NEEDED to meet or exceed standards—(Outline Specific Steps For Ratee to Follow)
Officer Sadler meets or exceeds standards in all categories. This evaluation is no where near his potential due to the fact he does not have a great deal of interest in the patrol function. I believe his work efforts should be directed toward the patrol function as long as he is assigned to patrol.

3. IMPROVEMENTS ACCOMPLISHED Since Last Rating Period.
Officer Sadler spent a great deal of time and effort attempting to solve the Friendly Burglar Rapist cases.

4. OVERALL RATING for This Period. ☐ Exceeds Standards ☒ Meets Standards
☐ Improvement Needed ☐ Not Satisfactory

RATER: I certify this report represents my best judgment.
Rater's Signature _J.E. Rich_
Title _Sergeant_ _____ Date 12-31-76

REVIEWER: (If None, So Indicate)
Reviewer's Signature _____
Title _Lieutenant_ _____ Date 12-31-76
Reviewer's Signature _____
Title _____ Date _____

EMPLOYEE: I certify that this report has been discussed with me. I understand my signature does not necessarily indicate agreement.

☐ I wish to discuss this report with the reviewer.

Comment _____

Employee's Signature _Robert J. Sadler_
Date _12-31-76_

Author Note: *Since November 10th when 'this latest' Special Assignment began, I had worked thirty-six days. I had taken three days (24 comp-time hours) off, and, still, had amassed over 142 hours of comp-time (17.75 days).*
To police administrators, that is a nightmare to justify.

FBR's *Month-At-A-Glance 1976*
Friday, December 31:   ~~Carl Geiger~~
                            ~~Parkland IABC~~
                            -Holiday
                              1977

Chapter 34

Hibernus Interruptus?

Dallas, Northeast Patrol Division, Beat 212
Between 12:12 & 7:00 am Monday, January 3, 1977
Offense Number 77

OFFICERS W.L. Russell 3803 and L.L. Barbee #2945 had once again been called to the Villa Crest Apartments. This time for a prowler call. It was just after midnight. They met the complainant at his apartment, number 212 at 6514 Ridgecrest.

Barbee and Russell knew they patrolled the hunting ground of the Friendly Burglar-Rapist and thus took all such calls seriously. Apparently an un-described suspect was seen, and complainant felt his lock had been tampered with. Given the activity on the night I felt it was likely enough that this prowler was the FBR, I attributed this O/IR to the FBR.

Offense Number 78

UP THE STREET at 6416 Ridgecrest in apartment 1004 in the Melody Park Apartments a loud television disguised the sound of her intruder's movements as *MLG* sat in her bedroom watching TV with the door closed.

Sunday night had turned into Monday morning before the twenty-three year-old white female, whose job was as a draftsman, was ready for bed.

MLG got up and went to the TV to turn it off. When *MLG* turned around, as she explained to Reporting Officer D.K. Lowe #3770, she saw "the bedroom door wide open." *MLG* said she "heard someone in the apartment." She called out her roommate's name several times and got no answer as she "heard the front door close." *MLG* said realizing the noise was not caused by her roommate she went out the apartment's back door. At a friend's, next door, *MLG* called police.

On Officer Lowe's arrival she found that both complainants' phones had had their cords cut. *MLG* told Lowe "a w/m/30's has been peeping in her front window the last few weeks a couple of times."

Offense Number 79[91]

AT SOME POINT, tangent to the investigation into the other two calls on Ridgecrest, the need arose for *GMcA* to call police. Officer's R.A. Spain # 3451 and M.J. Harrison 3317 were sent to the Villa Crest Apartment at 6514 Ridgecrest.

Their complainant who lived in apartment 218 was a twenty-five year-old black female insurance writer. She told reporting officers that she had gone to bed around 12:30 and woke this morning feeling cold. Said when she got up to turn up the heater she noticed the front window had been raised up and the screen was missing. She confirmed that the window had been closed when she went to bed but did not indicate if it was also locked; however it did not appear to have been forced. R.O. listed M/O as "Removed screen & opened unlocked window."

GMcA reported that she had not heard anything during the night nor found anything missing.

The R.O. wrote: "The M.O. of Susp. fits that of Friendly Rapist. P.E.S. called to location.

Dallas, Northeast Patrol Division, Beat 213
5:00 am Wednesday, January 4, 1977
Offense Number 80

THE NEW YEAR'S inactivity of the FBR's prior year's patterns seemed to have been broken. *JMR* a white female twenty-five, a Cytotechnologist at the Swiss Avenue Medical Building near downtown was accosted in her apartment at 8831 Southwestern. *JMR* had been asleep. A man was in apartment 1238 with her. He was man about five-foot-ten to six-foot, muscular, wearing a black ski mask and ski jacket.

---

[91] Offenses # 77, 78 & 79 tend to corroborate or validate Marble's later admission of going in multiple dwellings on a given night.

The man had jumped on her while she lay in bed asleep and put a knife to her throat.

"Shut up and don't move. I won't hurt you."

JMR frantically tried to make sense of what was happening.

"Don't look at me and calm down." He got hold of her left arm and tied her left hand with cord he'd cut from one of her phones. He removed a case from one of her pillows and was in the process of slipping it over her head.

JMR objected saying, "No… I'll scream—"

"I'll have to hurt you if you do."

"I don't care!"

"Don't worry I won't hurt you, I do this for a living and I am only going to steal from you." He continued, "I have been here for several minutes quietly but I stumbled and woke you up so I had to jump you."

She was listening to his voice for clues, it was a "medium tone and void of accent."

"Be quiet and I won't hurt you."

"Why are you tying me up?"

"So you won't follow me."

"Why don't your tear the phone out of the wall?"

"That's what you are tied with."

"I'll be quiet, just don't cover my head."

Disregarding her wishes, he slipped the pillowcase over her head and then tied her right hand, keeping the knife at her back. "I'm going to steal from you then leave."

The Friendly Burglar-Rapist got up off the bed, went into the bathroom and turned on the light.

JMR heard her attacker open and closing different drawers and cabinets.

He came back into the bedroom saying, "Don't turn around and be quiet." He sat down on the edge of the bed. "Now you know why I'm here, it's for you."

JMR saw cord wrapped around her attacker's wrists as if to strangler her and he placed this cord against her throat.

He then tore her nightgown's shoulder straps.

"You don't have to do that," *JMR* said.

"I have to, your hands are tied."

He slowly pulled *JMR*'s nightgown down and off and then removed her panties. She felt something wet. She later stated she thought he was using some kind of lubricant. He fondled her breast and penetrated her vagina with his fingers. When he got on top of her, *JMR* realized he must have taken his clothes off.

She told Reporting Officer C.E. Maxwell #2768 that her assailant failed at penile penetration. She said she felt his weight shift and he told her to get on her hands and knees. Getting behind her he again tried to penetrate his victim and again he failed.

"Ah shit!" A moment later he said, "I'm going outside now and I'll come back and tell you when I'm leaving" and then left through front door. *JMR* reached the backyard door and ran to a neighbors and called police.

JMR recounted to Officer Maxwell that the entire ordeal lasted approximately twenty minutes.

Canine Officer J.M. Beene #3191 reported: "I was called out at 5:40am this date to respond to above address on Criminal Assault. On arrival K-9 Thor picked up trail of (suspect at) comp's front door leading down a sidewalk, leading south where K-9 turned east still staying on the sidewalk where we followed the trail approximately one block to a large parking lot of The Bluff Apartments adjacent to Skillman St. At this point K-9 lost trail in parking lot. Unable to find any unusual oil spots or anything out of place in parking lot."

Crimes Against Persons Investigator John Landers was also called to the scene and made the following report which added a few more clues:

> I contacted the Comp just minutes after this offense occurred. P.O.E.[92] was apparently thru unlocked sliding glass patio door. Comp was awakened by suspect who had cut her telephone cord before waking her. Suspect tied Comp to headboard with cord and threatened comp with a knife of unknown description. Suspect took Comp's purse to bathroom and apparently looked at driver's license (it was left in wallet on bathroom sink). Suspect then opened several dresser drawers throughout the apt and returned to Comp's bedroom where he began putting a pillowcase over Comp's head. Comp stated she

---

[92] P.O.E. - point of entry

asked him not to use the pillowcase because it would make her panic. Suspect then instructed Comp to remain laying on her stomach and he put a pillow on top of her head. Suspect then raised Comp up on her knees and removed her Tampax and lubricated himself with some unknown tube lotion. Suspect then attempted to enter Comp vaginally but was unsuccessful. Comp stated she was tense and was physically small "in that area". Suspect then became frustrated and got off the bed and told Comp he was leaving. Suspect then placed a small length (20") of rope around Comp's neck and stated, "You know I could kill you very easily, you've been dealing with a psychotic crazy person." Suspect then left the apt thru the front door.

When suspect removed Comp's gown he tore the shoulder straps (rather than cutting them) and pulled Comp's gown downward.

Comp is moving to her parent's home in Beaumont, Texas located at....

JR Landers #2445

Below is the completed "Fact Sheet" for this offense. Note the "1-4-76" date, *a new-year writing mistake we often make the first few days of a new year*, should read 1-4-77:

[NB: Once again, below, though it may be for the reader to determine their actual significance, these (*Week-At-A-Glance*) entries are included so as to provide insight into the 'notated' days of FBR's work calendar for 1977. The entries will appear throughout the book in chronological order as brief inclusions. The 'script' font is not indicative of his writing, only to set the notations apart.

Also, the activities and notes fall within a time slot; therefore unless specified, times will be included as "(1:30-slot)" showing where activity was 'slotted' in the book.]

FBR's *Week-At-A-Glance 1977*
Monday, January 10:   **Hansen mtg (1:30-slot)**

FBR's *Week-At-A-Glance 1977*
Tuesday, January 11:   IABC (4:00-slot)

Dallas, Office of Central Division Analyst
9:00 am Wednesday, January 12, 1977

In Court: Give Testimony
re: a DWI arrest I made in 1976

FBR's *Week-At-A-Glance 1977*
Thursday, January 13:   **Wayne I Bob (2:00-slot)**

FBR's *Week-At-A-Glance 1977*
Friday, January 14:   Exchange (3:00-slot)

FBR's *Week-At-A-Glance 1977*
Tuesday, January 18:   Selwyn (9:00-slot)
          IABC (4:00-slot)

FBR's *Week-At-A-Glance 1977*
Wednesday, January 19:   T.A.C.T. (2:00-slot)–

FBR's *Week-At-A-Glance 1977*
Monday, January 24:   **Oken-Loury (10:00-slot)**

January 24, 1977
***Helter Skelter*, Part 1 Re-Airs**
[see * April 1, 1976 page 164]

January 25, 1977
***Helter Skelter*, Part 2 Re-Airs**

Dallas, Northeast Patrol Division, Beat 256
11:30 pm Tuesday, January 25, 1977
Offense Number 81 (R-42)

THREE QUIET WEEKS, what Tom and I had come to expect in January, were interrupted when the Friendly Burglar-Rapist hit again. On our list of O/I R's we had attributed to the FBR, it was his eighty-first.

Reporting Officers S.C. Mallon #3789 and M.R. Scoggins # 3601 arrived at 6537 Melody Lane, The Falls Apartments, and met their complainant *DES*, a white twenty-four year-old teacher at Skyline High School. *DES* told officers she had been in her apartment (number 256) where the assault took place. The officers noted that the suspect had gained entry by prying off front lower window's screen and prying open window with an unknown tool.

The following is Mallon and Scoggins' narrative account of their interview with *DES*.

> COMP STATED THAT AT APPROXIMATELY 11:10 PM SHE WAS LAYING IN BED ASLEEP WHEN AN UNK SUSP PUT HIS RIGHT HAND TO HER THROAT AND SAID "JUST BE QUIET AND YOU WON'T GET HURT." COMPL COULD NOT SEE SUSP BECAUSE LIGHTS WERE OFF. SUSP THEN PUT PILLOW CASE OVER COMP'S HEAD AND THEN A PILLOW ON TOP OF THE PILLOW CASE. SUSP TOLD COMP TO REMAIN STILL AND THEN LEFT THE BEDROOM FOR A FEW MINUTES. SUSP RETURNED TO ROOM AND TOLD COMP "STICK YOUR HAND HERE," SUSP THEN

GRABBED COM'S LEFT HAND AND TIED AN
END OF A TELEPHONE CORD TO IT.
TELEPHONE CORD WAS PASSED AROUND
HEADBOARD RAIL AND THEN TIED COMP'S
OTHER HAND. DURING THIS TIME SUSP
TOLD COMP "YOU DON'T WANT TO SEE
WHAT I LOOK LIKE OR YOU'LL GET HURT."
TELEPHONE CORD HAD BEEN CUT FROM
KITCHEN WITH "KITCHEN SIZZORS [*sip*]."
SUSP THEN CUT GOWN FROM COMP AND
THEN HER PANTIES. SUSP STRADDLED
VICTIM AROUND HER WAIST AND BEGAN
FONDLING HER BREASTS. COMP ADVISED
THAT SUP WAS A W/M/20'S,
APPROXIMATELY 160 LBS, 5'8" T0 5'10", A
SOFT SPOKEN VOICE AND HAD A "NON-
TEXAN" ACCENT. BELIEVE SUSP WAS
WEARING BLUE JEANS AND POSSIBLY A
STOCKING CAP. SUSP WAS CLEAN SHAVEN,
NO FACIAL HAIR, AND WAS WEARING A
LIGHTLY SCENTED AFTER-SHAVE LOTION.
WHILE STRADDLING COMP, THE SUSP
FORCED COMP TO PERFORM ORAL SEX ON
HIM. AFTER A SHORT PERIOD OF TIME THE
SUSP WITHDREW HIS MEMBER AND
BEGAN MASTURBATING WHILE SITTING
ON COMP. SUSP TURNED VICTIM OVER ON
HER STOMACH, LUBRICATED HER WITH
HAND LOTION THAT WAS SITTING ON
NIGHT STAND, AND THEN ATTEMPTED TO
PENETRATE COMP ANALY. FAILING THIS,
THE SUSP TURNED COMP ON HER BACK
AND PERFORMED SEXUAL INTERCOURSE.
SUSP CLIMAXED WHILE INSIDE COMP.
SUSP THEN TOLD COMP "I AM GOING OUT
ON THE BALCONY AND SEE IF IT IS CLEAR.
I AM GOING TO GET IN MY TRUCK NOW.
DON'T MAKE A SOUND FOR 5 MINUTES OR
I AM GOING TO COME BACK AND HURT
YOU. SUSP THEN FLED APARTMENT. COMP
WAITED FOR FIVE MINUTES, UNITED HER
WRISTS, AND WENT DOWNSTAIRS TO

NEIGHBORS AND PHONED POLICE. FRONT
DOOR WAS AJAR WHERE SUSP FLED FROM
APARTMENT. OFFICERS BELIEVE ENTRY
WAS GAINED THROUGH FRONT LOWER
WINDOW OF APARTMENT. COMP ALSO
STATED THAT WHILE SUSP WAS TALKING
TO HER HE WOULD PERIODICALLY PUT A
SHARP OBJECT TO HER THROAT. OBJECT IS
BELIEVED TO BE HEAVY SHEARS. INV. T.M.
HOLMES #2521 FROM C.A.P. QUESTIONED
COMP. ELEMENTS 44, 46, AND 47 FROM
P.E.S. CAME TO LOCATION. TELEPHONE
CORD, AND PRINTS FROM VARIOUS
OBJECTS TAKEN BY P.E.S. AND PLACED IN
PROPERTY ROOM. COMP TRANSFERRED TO
PARKLAND HOSPITAL FOR EXAMINATION.

ELEMENT 897, CANINE OFFICERS, WAS AT
SCENE WITH REPORTING OFFICERS.

WHAT WERE WE to make of this seeming break in pattern?
Where had he been in years past and why was he not there now?

[**NB**: Sometime between John Lander's last appearance at the
FBR crime scene on 1-4-77 and the appearance of Truly Holmes
on the 1-25-77 FBR crime scene, Landers was re-assigned and
Holmes took over the FBR investigation for CAPERS, Crimes
Against Persons Section.
Neither Tom nor I had been informed or made aware that this
change was to take place.]

Dallas, Office of Central Division Analyst
9:00 am Wednesday, January 26, 1977

TODAY TOM RECEIVED the long awaited letter from
Johnson & Johnson regarding the tape The Friendly Burglar
Rapist had used in four offenses (237116F, 344796G, 354830G

& 358213G). We had hand-carried our FBR evidence samples to their Sherman, Texas offices on December 8, 1976. It is obvious from the letter [dated 1/5/77] and attached lab report [dated 1/2/77] that Johnson & Johnson took our request for assistance seriously.

WE WERE HOPING for a clue, any kind of clue; another lead to follow from Johnson & Johnson. Unfortunately the samples tested and analyzed came from two widely distributed types of athletic tape:

1) Kendall's BIKE PRO-ZONE Trainer Tape
2) J&J's ZONAS Athletic Tape.

Tom and I had been vindicated, again. The tape, according to J&J's analysis was 'athletic tape' not 'medical tape'. It was athletic tape that you could buy in any store that handled athletic supplies. And yet some, Kathryn Bonham, for example, (a very good crime analyst in Lt. Macsas' shop at Planning and Research), still insisted it was surgical tape even after we got the letter from Johnson & Johnson.

Our ideas (guesses, other than medical uses) as to what kind of job he had, or the hobbies and life-style, our suspect had known no bounds. We now focused on not just 'users of adhesive tape' but now included possibly a 'trainer', 'coach', or 'athlete'.

> *The entries in the* FBR's *Month-At-A-Glance 1976 show notations for "Soc" on various Sunday afternoons. That note could mean "social" but it is believed it had meant "soccer[93]", if so this might be how and where he used or obtained this type of tape. Example see 1976: 10/3, 10/10, 10/17, 10/24/, 11/14, 11/21, 11/28.*

FINALLY IT HAPPENED! The department agreed to commit tactical resources to the field, to be deployed at our direction. We'd 'hit' enough of our FBR predictions that the Chief had decided 'it was worth a shot'. Dixon had told Tom, "this started with us, I want it to end with us!"

---

[93] See pages 489-490 re: *Guy William Marble: Soccer Player - Sprinter - Jogger*

*Our many many thanks are not enough for our
Division Commander, Dep. Chief Robert O. Dixon who
allowed us to spend so much time working on this
crime spree. He continually wanted briefings and
eventually recommended our prediction system be used
to deploy twenty-two officers for sixty days. Chief
Dixon took us to the Patrol Bureau Commander, Chief
Jim Souter, who gave us the men and time to carry out
the capture.*

Again, other chiefs and commanders were dubious of our
predictive capabilities and more than one of them told us, "your
jobs are on the line"! In fact as we left Chief Souter's office he
caught Tom's eye. Tom said later, "Chief Souter had a grin on his
face when he motioned for me to come back in his office and
was smiling when he said, "If this doesn't work, you two will
hunt another job, won't you!"

*We used less than one week of that two months. I say
"we", but... I was somewhere else.*

FBR's *Week-At-A-Glance 1977*
Thursday, January 27:   **Tommy Lout (10:00-
slot)**

FBR's *Week-At-A-Glance 1977*
Friday, January 28:   BGCT (2:00-slot)

FBR's *Week-At-A-Glance 1977*
Monday, January 31:   **ZALE P.R. Conf.
(10:00-slot)**
        KERA At Bloom (2:00-slot)

**Dallas, Northeast Patrol Division, Beat 255
2:35 am Tuesday, February 1, 1977
Offense Number 82**

ATTEMPT AGGRAVATED RAPE. Dallas was in the full
throws of winter. It was now 42 days since the winter solstice on

December 21ˢᵗ and still 47 days till the Vernal equinox on March 20ᵗʰ. At Dallas Love Field the weather conditions had been recorded at 2:00am as being 28.9 degrees, humidity was sixty-one percent, the barometric pressure (at 3:00am) was 30.29 inches with a south wind, steady at 5.8 mph. The skies continued to be clear. At first glance, if you could see the moon you would say it was full; it wouldn't rise for another hour and a half.

SB a white female 26 was an accountant at a downtown Dallas firm located in the Republic Bank Tower, the tallest building in Dallas when it was built in 1954 surpassing the previous record holders, The Mercantile Building with it's clock-tower, and the Magnolia Building with it's Flying Red Horse.

When *SB* had gone to bed, the night before it, had been Monday, January 31ˢᵗ; end of the month accounting issues have their own set of pressures as does the first of the month. *SB* had gone to bed at a reasonable hour. Her apartment, number 232 was on the second floor. If asked she wouldn't remember the number of times she had heard that second floor apartments were safer.

Reporting Officer L.T. Page #2710 noted on his O/I R that the weather condition was "clear & cold — Temp Low 20's" He wrote:

> COMP. WAS ASLEEP IN BED WHEN SUSP CRAWLED UP ON TOP OF HER. SUSPECT TOLD COMP. TO NOT MAKE A SOUND AND INDICATED THAT HE HAD A KNIFE. SUPS. MADE COMP. FEEL THE KNIFE WHICH APPEARED TO BE A SMALL THIN STEAK KNIFE. COMP. WAS THEN TOLD TO TURN OVER. COMP STARTED SCREAMING AND SUSP. FLED OUT THE FRONT DOOR.
>
> SUSP. APPARENTLY ENTERED THROUGH OPEN SLIDING GLASS DOOR ON BALCONY. TELEPHONES IN BOTH THE BEDROOM AND KITCHEN HAD BEEN CUT. COMP'S PURSE WHCH WAS HANGING FROM BEDROOM DOOR KNOB WAS TAKEN TO KITCHEN WHERE SUSP WENT THROUGH CONTENTS AND TOOK A SET OF KEYS TO COMP'S APT AND OFFICE. THE CORD FROM THE

KITCHEN TELEPHONE WAS FOUND LAYING
BY COMP'S BED. A QUART BOTTLE OF DR.
PEPPER WAS TAKEN FROM ICE BOX AND
PLACED ON KITCHEN COUNTER TOP.

COMP. DESCRIBES SUSPECT AS A WM LATE
20'S TO 30's 5'9 TO 6'0 – 180LBS, AVG BUILD,
WEARING A NYLON STOCKING OVER HIS
FACE, DARK SHIRT, BLUE JEANS, DARK
WAIST LENGTH JACKET, AND WHITE
TENNIS SHOES. SUSP'S SPEECH WAS DEEP.
SUSPECT WAS CARRYING A SMALL, THIN
STEAK KNIFE COMP. STATES THAT
SUPECT'S MANNER WAS AGGRESSIVE AND
THAT SHE WOULD BE HURT IF SHE DID
NOT COOPERATE, HOWEVER HE DID NOT
USE VULGAR LANGUAGE OR FORCIBLY
HIT HER. WHEN COMP. SCREAMED AT
SUSPECT SHE LUNGED TO GET AWAY AND
SUSTAINED A MINOR LACERATION ON
RIGHT HAND WHICH DOES NOT REQUIRE
MEDICAL ATTENTION. IT IS UNK IF SUSP.
MAY HAVE INJURED HIMSELF.

COMP. STATES THAT SHE HAS DATED A DH
WM28, PHONE XXX-3501 WHO HAS
SIMILAR PHYSICAL CHARACTERISTICS AS
THE SUSPECT. COMP. STATS THAT DH'S
VOICE IS SIMILAR TO SUSPECT'S. DH ALSO
HAS A UNUSUAL BODY ODOR, BAD
BREATH AND ACCORDING TO COMP. DOES
NOT GET ALONG VERY WELL WITH
FEMALES. DH LIVES IN UNIVERSITY PARK,
BUS. PHO # XXX-3501.

FOLLOWING ELEMENTS AT SCENE TO
ASSIST IN THE INVESTIGATION: CRIMES
AGAINST PERSONS – T.M. HOLMES
ELEMENT 1126, P.E.S. ELEMENT 46 AND
CANINE ELEMENT 898.

Crimes Against Persons Investigator Truly M. Holmes #2521 filed the following report:

Inv. Officer was notified by dispatcher's office by telephone at 2:50am on date of offense. Inv. Officer arrived at scene of offense a few minutes later and assisted in processing the Crime Scene and personally interviewed the Compl.

Compl. stated she leaves her upstairs sliding glass balcony door partially open to allow her house cats to go outside; this door was determined to be the point of entry. The suspect had removed a quart bottle of Dr. Pepper from the refrigerator, drank some, and left the bottle sitting on the kitchen cabinet. The suspect had also taken Compl's purse from her bedroom, emptied the contents out onto the kitchen cabinet, and took Compl.'s driver's license out of her wallet. The suspect then cut the cord of the kitchen telephone and carried it into the bedroom, where Officers found it on the floor, beside the bed. The suspect also cut the cord of the bedroom telephone, then awakened Compl. by lying on top of her and ordering her to turn over, (Compl. was lying on her stomach.). The suspect held a knife to Compl.'s throat and stated, "Don't scream lady, Just turn over." Suspect touched Compl's hand with the knife to make her more aware of it. The Compl. immediately screamed several times and began pushing the Susp. off. Compl. received a very minor laceration on the back of her right hand. The suspect immediately fled out the front door of the apartment. Compl's next door neighbor – Ms. LB w/f/45, 9790 Audelia Rd. #231, xxx-4115 – stated she heard Comp.'s screams and heard someone run along the stairway landing, but by the time she got to the window to look out, the suspect was gone.

Compl. described the suspect as a w/m/late 20's, 5'9"-6'0", medium build, wearing white tennis shoes, waist length brown-? jacket, and possibly blue jeans. Susp. also wore a stocking mask.

This general physical description and M.O. are similar to the friendly burglar rapist. Recommend this offense be classified as suspended, pending development of workable leads.

TM. Holmes #2521

Later, after Brown made his comparisons, Tom penned a 'red ink' note across the front page of this offense's O/I R (below). Thirty-two years later the faded note is hard to make out, but (see inset) it reads:

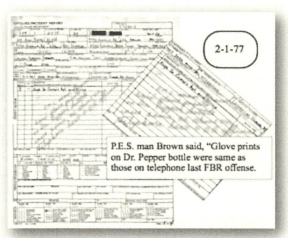

P.E.S. man Brown said, "Glove prints on Dr. Pepper bottle were same as those on telephone last FBR offense.

[NB: DNA sequencing and identification was in its most embryonic state in the early Seventies. It would not be until after 1976-77 that the technology would begin to spread widely, and years before costs were lowered and speed of result enhanced. Had the sophisticated and rapid gene-sequencing and recognition hardware and software been available during the time of the FBR investigation, it would have been easy enough to have identified our suspect from his semen or hair, or his saliva on the Dr. Pepper bottle from the above crime scene, for example.]

FBR's *Week-At-A-Glance 1977*
Tuesday, February 1:   **T.A.C.T.   DMV (10:00-slot)**

AMALIE   (3:30-slot)

FBR's *Week-At-A-Glance 1977*
Thursday, February 3:   TACT DMV (11:00-slot)

FBR's *Week-At-A-Glance 1977*
Tuesday, February 8:   **IABC 3:45 (3:30-slot)**

WHILE TOM CONTINUED working on the FBR case from the office, I was once again, back in harness, but I remained in contact with Tom; doing what I could to stay involved.

Even cop-work has its politics. I think Sgt. Rich's comment on my year-end evaluation that: *I believe his work efforts should be directed toward the patrol function as long as he is assigned to patrol*, had its desired affect.

All the comp-time I was building up was not going to cost the City money out-of-pocket, but in order to 'pay' me my compensatory time, I would have to be off from work and therefor not on-duty. This actually cost the City money, twice: I was still being paid while taking off on comp-time and they had to put someone in my place. In my opinion, paying me overtime and being done with it was the cheaper route. As it was, when I took my comp-time, I would essentially be taking one-hundred-forty-two hours of paid vacation.

I think Dixon was in a catch-22; he wanted 'us' to stop the FBR, but he didn't want to short his patrol ranks (as no doubt had been explained by Sgt. Rich, my sector sergeant and Lt. Posey, the watch commander), and Dixon didn't want to have to justify paying me comp-time on the special assignment. And since I was assigned to the Patrol Division and Tom was assigned to Community Service Division, it was easiest to send me back to Patrol.

And with my reassignment to the streets, the Chief told me to take my comp-time ASAP or risk losing it.

With both reluctance and relish, I went back to the streets. I was reluctant because I desperately wanted to continue my investigation, my involvement in the FBR case. I relished the reassignment because it allowed me more time at home. My wife and I would plan to take a long ski vacation, using up a lot of my comp-time.

What was my only question? Faced with having to take my 'comp-time' I picked the time when the FBR had not hit… early February in any of the previous four years.

Several ironies were in play. I planned for us to take our trip between the dates of my last two picks. I wanted to be back in Dallas, ironically, late Sunday night February 13th-early morning February 14th to spend Valentines with my wife, at home.

In our December 29th FBR Strikes Next after his hiatus 'pick'm' contest:

> FBR Offense 78 occurred on 1/03
> FBR Offense 79 occurred on 1/04
>
> Bob Smoot picked "Jan. 24th or Feb. 1st"
>
> FBR Offense 80 occurred on 1/25
> FBR Offense 81 occurred on 2/1
>
> Tom picked three dates in Feb. 8th, 10th, 12th
>
> I suggested "the FBR's first 1977 hit would be: 3rd, 5th, 15th of February".

WE WERE ALL on target with Bobby Buck coming closest to the bullseye. It was ironic that the FBR had seemingly laid low in January and February, but we predicted his 'hits' then anyway. However, none of us predicted that one of those dates would be the last we would have to predict and would end in the FBR's capture.

During this week, days before my 'vacation', my partner, Tim Yarbro, and I received a DB call.

Summertime is the usually the worst time to receive a signal 27, a dead person, or more vernacularly a dead body, DB. In the summertime a decomposing body in a closed room can get ripe very quickly… and there is no smell that compares to the decomposing body. It is a smell with substance.

All "scents" that the human nose can sense or 'pick up' are due to there being molecules of that 'scent' in the air which receptors in our noses detect. The molecules that make up a decomposing body are particularly pernicious. They attach and permeate seemingly everything, your clothes your hair, your skin.

Clothes can be burned, your skin scrubbed raw, but those molecules that permeate your hair 'stay for a while' and the molecules you breathe into your lungs, become part of you. That sometimes is a very unpleasant thought as well as reality.

On this particular February morning, it was cold and had been cold for sometime. The idea of a stinking dead body did not occur to anyone until we got to the scene. The reason for the call: neighbors, a house away, could smell 'something' coming for the garage apartment behind their house. No one had seen the resident for days—maybe longer.

It was our call, but my partner and I were not the first on the scene. We approached the steps of the over-the-garage apartment in time to see two officers beating a fast retreat down the rickety wooden stairs.

"You can have it." They said.

"You got here first!" I offered.

Pointing to their hand-held radios the senior partner said, "We didn't Code 6, it's yours."

"Thanks," my partner and I said.

It is an unfortunate story, someone living alone and dying alone. That's why we get the call.

To make a long story short, I was the only one who could stand to make the trip up the stairs and 'discover' the body. I had the fortune at the time of having a severe sinus cold. I literally couldn't smell a thing. I was more worried about whether my sinus condition was going to keep me from going on or enjoying the ski vacation my wife had planned with friends in the next few days.

The Chief had forced me to start taking the comp time I'd piled up. Tom and I had already decided the upcoming week and a half had historically been the FBR's hiatus.

So off we went to Crested Butte Colorado, Susan, I, Ted and Judy Wright.

Our second day on the mountain a disgustingly awful discovery was made. The dead body that I could not smell had permeated my sinus cavities, which were already filled with 'you-know-what'. And now, all that you-know-what was permeated with the smell of you-know-what!

The altitude and the low humidity of the mountains had my sinus' drying out and draining. For four foul days instead of the pine-fresh crystalline mountain air surrounding me I smelled and tasted what I had not smelled in that tiny apartment back in Dallas.

But I did not have things as bad as Investigator John Landers who, unbeknownst to me at the time, was also in Colorado, at the same ski resort, Crested Butte and had been involved in a skiing accident. I found out later he'd taken a flying ski in his crotch, which he said had swollen up like....

FBR's *Week-At-A-Glance 1977*
Wednesday, February 9: **G A I L M O O R E (9 : 0 0 - slot)**

> **D.V. Austin (10:30-slot)**
> **Mary – (2:00-slot) v**

More Preparation & Preparedness
meets:
"Be Prepared"

Dallas, Office of Central Division Analyst
Thursday - Sunday, February 10-13, 1977

FOR THE MOST part of the past three years Tom and I had worked together on a daily basis. It was strange and I felt a bit despondent that I was not there at what would become the critical moment in our mission to stop the FBR. Of course, given the FBR's habit of not hitting in February, I thought I would be back in time to renew my participation on February 15th, the date I had picked for his first hit of 1977. Of course the FBR had already hit in January (twice on the 3rd, once on the 4th and 25th) And, damned if he didn't hit for the first time ever in February—on February 1, 1977.

For the past four days Tom had been orchestrating our general plan to deploy Tact if they ever gave us the chance. A plan Tom refined to a fare-the-well while I was still in Colorado. Tom was undaunted with my absence; Tom was an excellent police tactician. Not that my presence would have changed things, it just might have spread out the load. Tom had everything under control. Tom had given the plan he created for a tactical deployment in three areas to Chief Souter, a plan that could last as long as sixty days. Chief Dixon was in high spirits.

Three days before deployment Tom met with the tactical officers to, as Tom said, "explain the deployment and have a run through to see if any cracks in our deployment ideas or system" appeared.

Two days before deployment the tactical run-through went off without a hitch. Tom was still coordinating with Special Operations to get all twenty men together. It was a matter of some of them clearing days off and other scheduling issues. Tom said later he "wondered if Chief Souter was serious when he asked if we could find another job if this failed." "After all," Tom added, "twenty men in twenty cars is a big investment." That night's deployment went off without a hitch - we were ready for the real thing!

On "Day 1", the first night of 100% deployment, Tom scurried around the PD. He doubled checked his analysis, called Chief Dixon midday to report that tonight would be the first full night with 100% manpower. Tom went to the Intelligence Division to check out one of their night-vision devices for the duration of the operation. Next he stopped by Central Patrol Division and spoke briefly to Chief Dixon, then headed to the Crime Analysis Office to triple check the *date, time, day survey* to see if his prediction was correct.

It was as close as anyone could get to perfect without having all the factors, the puzzle pieces, with which to see the complete picture.

Tom walked over to the City's garage to double check that they had the twenty-one (21) unmarked cars set aside and ready to go for the night's deployment; they were ready!

Tom told me what he was thinking at that moment: *God I'm hungry. A giant greasy burger sounded good*, but *settled* he said, *for Chinese... need some sleep too!*

Tom said he thought about me too, that I was still in Colorado, and wondered, *wouldn't it be ironic if Bob missed the big one like he did on the J.C. Shannon deal.*

In a note, Tom wrote:

"Made a 2nd stop at Special Operations to confirm the full list of patrol officers for the deployment. They were giving us two sergeants for those necessary decisions needing to be made by a supervisor. Time to go home and get supper and some sleep. Only 6 hrs before deployment starts at 10pm. This leaves only 4 hours to sleep before deployment. Supper, shower, and travel time ate up 2 hours of this. Well, I had managed with this much sleep before; working that 2nd job Police Officers always have.

10pm—off to work on our deployment, tomorrow is Valentines Day, will have to get card & maybe flowers for Janie."

Chapter 35

Bingo, Jack! Two

FBR's *Week-At-A-Glance 1977*
Tuesday, February 14:   PERSONNEL ASSOC.
↓ **6:30**

Dallas, Northeast Patrol Division, Beat 255
1:10 am Monday, February 14, 1977

VALENTINE'S DAY WAS was an hour and ten minutes old.

While I had been enjoying, for the past week, skiing down the slopes of Crested Butte in Colorado as part of my forced-taking of the comp-time I had amassed, Tom had been hard at work. Using our well-honed, at this point, plotting methods to track the FBR's activities. Tom was predicting the next "FBR Weather Forecast" and directing the Tactical Unit on it's deployment.

As Tom recalls, "Souter (Chief Souter) gave us twenty-two (22) guys for sixty (60) days, and told us, 'if this don't work you'll have to find another job.' When we got those guys, and it took two days to get everybody in "sync, days off, at the range time, and etc., the first night didn't go like we wanted it to. It was actually the second night of operations when we had it like we wanted it."

Per Tom's instructions the officers would trade off, going into the FBR target area one at a time, spending no more than thirty minutes walking the area to limit their visibility. Once again, preparation and preparedness meets with a little luck; or, is that opportunity?

Dallas Police Tactical Officer Barry Whitfield #3055 told Tom later, "In all honesty you were lucky..."

In fact, ironically, unluckily, at the very moment Barry Whitfield was encountering our Friendly Burglar-Rapist suspect, Susan and I had just gotten home and were heading to bed after a 23-hour drive from Colorado.

Per Officer Whitfield's arrest report, on beat 243 at 1:10am on 2-14-77 he arrested a man he described as a wm, six-foot, 175lbs, medium length brown hair, mustache, blue eyes, in the 6200 block of Ridgecrest Drive, Dallas, Texas. The man was arrested for Failure to I.D. as a Witness, Sec 38.02, a class C Misdemeanor and Inv. of Burglary, Sec 30.02, a second degree felony.

On his person the arrested man had "two golf gloves" and "one nylon panty hose".

The arrestee was ten days from turning 30 years of age. He gave his residence address as 10749 Sandpiper, Dallas, Texas and his employment as: Vice President of Public Relations Advisors, Inc. of 3000 Diamond Park in Dallas. The following is the narrative of Barry Whitfield's arrest report:

> Officer Whitfield observed above defendant walking west on the sidewalk behind 6220 Ridgecrest Drive. Def was peering toward the second story. Def stopped, walked east on the same sidewalk, while again peering into the windows. Subj. fit the description of the FBR. Officer approached Def and displayed his badge. Officer told Def that he was a police officer and asked Def what he was doing in the complex. Def stated that

he lived there. Officer asked Def for his ID. Subj said that he did not have his ID with him but would take officer to his apt and retrieve his I.D. Officer asked Def where he lived and Def stated Apt 2011. As officer and Def proceeded to the alleged apt, Def ran from Officer Whitfield and was arrested as he fell to the ground.

Officer Whitfield placed Def's gloves and nylon stocking in Central Prop Rm on tag No 210949.

The rest of the story, Barry told Tom about being lucky, was: "In all honesty you were lucky. I was out there walking—we changed guys every thirty minutes so we wouldn't be too conspicuous. I was sittin' in my car, I was already tired when I got to work and thought *I'm gonna skip my first turn.* " Then," he told Tom, "the next thing I thought was, if he hits my name's gonna be mud!" Barry said, "I got out of my car, started walking, turned the first corner and there ol' Guy was, had his sweat shirt on, everything was perfect" (matched the picture) "and he was lookin' up at some second floor stuff—"

Tom interjected, "We'd told the guys that 'he' was gonna hit a second floor, he was gonna hit between one and two...and Barry got him at 1:10am. Barry was in plain clothes... Barry got him, an' he didn't even have any handcuffs with him." Later, Barry would receive the "Golden Handcuffs Award".[94]

Barry told Tom, he "approached Marble, identified myself and asked him 'what are you doing here?' 'I live here,' the guy said. I asked, 'what apartment do you live in and Marble spouted off some number. I then asked him, 'Do you have some kind of identification.'" Barry related to Tom, "Marble reached for his rear pocket, like he was gonna get some ID out, and he took off running."

Barry chased him down, said he had "quite a little run to get him down."

Marble told us later; "when he rolled me over that ol' boy had that gun right in my face..." "I was just shakin'," Marble said, "I just knew I was gonna die."

---

[94] Appendix A - Newspaper Article #16 DMN 2.23.77 "Police officer receives award" [see website: robertjsalder.com]

Tom smiled and said, "Barry came on his radio and said, 'I got'm but I'm gonna need some handcuffs'—"an' I mean it rained PO-leece."

Officer Ron Riggs read Marble his 'rights'.

> **Author Note**: *If you are wondering about the differences in what Barry wrote in his arrest report and what he related of "his story" to Tom, remember certain elements of legality need to be in an arrest report and don't necessarily have to be detailed in a conversation recalled at a later time.*

On February 14th, Bob Smoot was there. I don't remember if he was still with Community Relations or was the Northeast Division Special Projects Officer at that time. Smoot had a PR personality; he'd be somewhere talking to the "nobs" or who ever the head-guy might be. Though he may have had no specific reason to be there on the stake-out, they were not his forte, he made the effort to be in the field that night.

Like Tom, who was there to watch the deployment of Tactical forces per his 'Weather Report, Bob heard Barry say, "I got'm!", and was part of the 'rain', more like the downpour of police closing ranks on Barry's position.

We'd had two important things going for us, besides Tom's predictive deployment of Tactical. One, we had a sketch, a likeness of our suspect and two, everyone knew we had nine of the FBR's ten fingerprints, we just didn't know those nine fingers belonged to Guy William Marble Jr.

Tom had a contact in St. Louis where a massive military database of fingerprints resides. Tom had them run FBR's nine prints. "We had their classification codes and he ran them for me —and zip, nada, he hadn't been in the service.

> Author Note: *That raises an interesting question of how had a man 18 years old in 1965 not been picked for the draft? A college deferment for four years (66-69)? But what about after he graduated?*

Everyone had been schooled per our *Patrol Officers Handbook on the FBR*. [Remember our suspect had the one finger (left thumb) that in the very center of it was a tadpole-like mark, or ridge detail.] Tom said, "Smoot 'ironed' him right there.

I saw Smoot drag out his little personal ink pad and fingerprint our captured suspect. After lifting Marble's thumb up off the piece of paper, Smoot says, 'Look here guys, here's the tadpole!'"

Smoot and crime analysts NW (Maroney) & NE (Zasimowich) were under the gun. As Tom put it, "we had taken the lead on this thing and were pushing it so hard they were feeling our heat. The interesting thing was, whatever we asked'm to do, they jumped in there and did!"

Dallas (University Park)
1:30 am Monday, February 14, 1977

ON THE EDGE of the bed, about to swing my feet up and under the covers, the phone on my nightstand rang. I said, "Hello?"

The unmistakeable and delighted voice of Thomas Harvey Covington Jr., sang out, "BINGO JACK! We got'm! Meet us at Crimes Against Persons."

"Be there in fifteen minutes," I said.

I turned to Susan and said, "We got'm, the FBR is in custody, I'm going in! They're taking him downtown now. I'll be back as soon as I can."

I redressed, grabbed my gun, badge, and handcuffs, jumped in my car and headed downtown. I *was* there just fifteen minutes later.

And perhaps a last personal irony, I once again had not been in on the BINGO JACK! Two of the longest and most interesting cases I had worked, worked so many hours on, and I missed both the J.C. Shannon, Jr., and the Guy William Marble Jr., arrests!

DURING THE THREE-PLUS years the FBR (Guy William Marble Jr.) terrorized North Dallas, his victims rarely got more than a brief glimpse of him in a darkened room, or perhaps caught a flash of his clothing.

They described seeing blue jeans and different colored slacks, red ski masks, stocking-masks fashioned from women's white or tan or black stockings or panty hose, brown cloth gloves, rubber gloves, black leather gloves, occasionally the generic 'tennis shoes' or running shoes. Others were only able to describe his clothing as feeling rough, like jeans or corduroy, or describe gloves that felt like cotton socks on his hands.

We were truly lucky that the one witness who could actually describe the FBR was able to help an artist draw his likeness, in this case, in the 'hood' the witness saw him wearing. Given the number of times someone had given us a subject description, in this case, it's interesting that he was described wearing something no one else had described before.

It was Guy William Marble Jr.'s misfortune that he decided, three months later, to wear the same thing our witness had seen him wearing on December 6, 1976. If he had been wearing slacks and dress shirt, like he had done many times, would Barry have had the immediate reaction he did when he saw Marble in he hooded sweatshirt?

This photo of Guy William Marble Jr., was taken in the offices of the Dallas Police Department, Crimes Against Persons in the early morning hours of February 14, 1977. This was a color picture taken by a DPD photographer of Guy William Marble Jr., shortly after he was brought, still in handcuffs, into the Crimes Against Persons, CID offices on the 3rd floor of the DPD, then located at 106 South Harwood. This is a grayscale scan of that color photograph. The color photograph, over-rich in the hue of red, showed Marble to have reddish brown hair, eyebrows and mustache and blue eyes. Marble is wearing what became known as his 'trademark' gray hooded sweatshirt. Beside the picture I added a scan of his business card (with hole punch added by rjs). I wonder if he ever considered what a public relations nightmare he created for his company? (see color photo on website)

FBR's *Week-At-A-Glance 1977*
Monday, February 14:   PERSONNEL ASSOC.
                    ↓ 6:30

(The above notation in Marble's personal calendar was slotted for the evening of Monday, February 14th with an arrow drawn through to the day below of Tuesday, February 15th and the time 6:30 appeared in the "Evening" 'slot' for 2-15-1976.)

He missed this meeting, sitting in his jail cell.

Dallas
Crimes Against Persons Section: CID
Physical Evidence Section
Wee Hours of Monday, February 14, 1977

Within minutes of his arrival at CAPERS, our suspect, who had identified himself as Guy William Marble Jr., was virtually fingerprinted by Bobby Brown, P.E.S. master fingerprint analyst. Brown took hold of Marble's hands, turned them, gave them the once-over, and proclaimed, "This is our man; this is the Friendly-Rapist."

All it took was Brown's quick-eyed scan of Marble's thumb to see the unique tadpole feature in the middle of his left thumb. This feature identified Guy William Marble Jr., as the Friendly Burglar-Rapist and (along with the rest of his digits) linked him to scores of offenses on which some of his latent fingerprints had been lifted.

Remember this CARD from page 343?

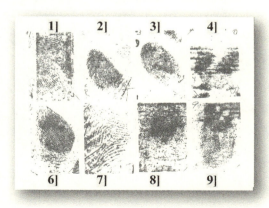

DPD Physical Evidence Section
Fingerprint Lifts from FBR Burglary-Rape Scenes:
The 'Famous' left thumb 'tad-pole'!

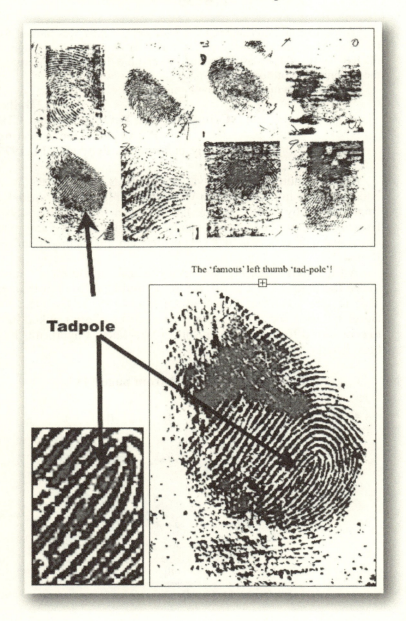

The 'famous' left thumb 'tad-pole'!

Tadpole

Dallas
Crimes Against Persons Section: CID
Approx. 2:00am Monday, February 14, 1977

RETRIBUTION AND REVENGE can sometimes blind the reasonable. In the early hours of Valentine's Day 1977, I was not the only person called to come 'put hands' on the arrestee.

Although "Billy Bob Buck" Smoot had already ID'd Marble in the field, Det. Bobby Brown came up from P.E.S. to help ID our arrestee. Other's had also been called and were filtering into the cop shop to get a glimpse of the infamous Friendly Burglar-Rapist or Friendly Rapist as some called him.

The media was gathering.

Also responding to the notification that the FBR had been caught was Dallas Police Sargent, *HB*. Avoiding the slow as molasses elevators, he got up a head of steam taking the stairs, two-at-a-time. Fire was in his eyes and his belly. No one knew his plan—whether it was to exact his pound of flesh from a man whose name he did not yet know or carry out his own arrest, trial, conviction and execution.

The story is, that night as John Landers was going through 'the book' with Marble someone called Landers and said *HB* was there and comin' up! Landers sent somebody to intercept him—so he never did get up there on the 3rd floor...

When Jim Bryan, (who had left the department in December '75) heard the story he said in later years, "*HB* woulda blown him away in a minute! I used to work with *HB* out at Northwest, an' I know he would have..."

Tom also said... "I truly believe, in my own heart, if we hadn't intercepted him, he'd a walked right in, not say howdy-do, nothing, an' woulda blew ol' Guy Marble away..."

Why did we think *HB* was capable of such audacious action?

Many of us knew *HB*, had heard of his exploits as a gunner on a destroyer during *WWII*. We all knew him as a hard, tough, but fair man. But the idea of fairness can fly out the window when it comes to protecting one's country, one's family, particularly one's own daughter.

Fortunately Sgt. *HB*, heading up the stairs toward CAPERS, where Marble was being 'interviewed', was shortstopped just as he entered the office by a quick thinking detective.

Why would we think Sargent *HB* might do this? If you haven't figured it out; about this time of the morning, eighteen months earlier, the FBR, now ID'd as Guy William Marble Jr., raped the nineteen year-old daughter of Sargent. *HB*. She had been the FBR's prey in, by our count, Marble's 29th offense, Marble's 20th criminal sexual assault. (see pages 153-154)

The Media Frenzy

Dallas - Across the country
Tuesday, February 15, 1977

The news of the FBR's capture had gone out on the news wire services almost immediately to cities large and small. The media scrambled to report on the capture of the infamous FBR— reporting what they *knew* or rather what was reported—thus they did not always get it right.

Based on what you have read thus far, see if you can pick out at least 7 inaccuracies in this UPI 'story', printed in the *Simpson's Leader-Times*, from Kittanning, PA on Tues. Feb. 15, 1977 and transcribed below. If you do not find them, you can see them on my website @ robertjsadler.com.

"DALLAS (UPI) -- The first report came in October 1974: A young, single woman was raped by a man wearing a pillow case over his head. He held a knife at her throat, tied her to her bed and attacked her.

Then, before leaving, he apologized.

In the 18 months since there have been 50 more attacks, each rape similar to the first. But police hope with the arrest of a public relations executive Monday, the case of the"friendly rapist" is closed.

"He was kind of polite about the rapes," a police spokesman said. "he told his victims he didn't want to hurt them and never has hurt one of them, other than raping them.

"He hasn't beat or killed them."

Police identified the suspect as Guy William Marble Jr., the 29-year-old vice president-business manger of Public Relations Advisors, Inc. Fellow workers said he most recently had been an adviser on the statewide media campaign of the Baptist General Convention of Texas.

By late Monday Marble had been charged with five rapes with bonds of $250,000 on each count.

Officials said his fingerprints matched those taken from the apartments of at least 20 victims of the "friendly rapist."

For several months police said they had been analyzing the crimes, trying to predict where the assailant would strike next. They said for several weeks they had been staking out various apartment complexes.

Sunday night and on into Monday morning they staked out The Season's, a complex of about three hundred apartments. A plainclothes officer said at about 1:10 a.m. Monday he noticed a man in a jogging sweatshirt and jeans walking in front of the apartment complex, looking into windows from the street.

The officer said he approached the man and asked him for identification. The man fled, but the officer ran him down after a brief chase.

Police said Marble is married and has one child.

At one time Marble was a police reporter with a Lubbock newspaper and police said what he may have learned of police tactics as a reporter may have helped him evade officers for the past several months.

Persons at the newspaper who remembered Marble said he had worked there for about six months in 1971.

They described him as "friendly and good at his work."

'Friendly Rapist' Suspect Arrested

DALLAS (UPI) — The first report came in October of 1974: A young, single woman was raped by a man wearing a pillow case over his head. He held a knife at her throat, tied her to her bed and attacked her.

Then, before leaving, he apologized.

In the 18 months since there have been 50 more attacks, each rape similar to the first. But police hope with the arrest of a public relations executive Monday, the case of the "friendly rapist" is closed.

"He was kind of polite about the rapes," a police spokesman said. "He told his victims he didn't want to hurt them and never has hurt one of them, other than raping them.

"He hasn't beat or killed them."

Police identified the suspect as Guy William Marble Jr., the 29-year-old vice president-business manager of Public Relations Advisers, Inc. Fellow workers said he most recently had been an adviser on the statewide media campaign of the Baptist General Convention of Texas.

By late Monday Marble had

been charged with five rapes with bonds of $250,000 on each count.

Officials said his fingerprints matched those taken from the apartments of at least 20 victims of the "friendly rapist."

For several months police said they had been analyzing the crimes, trying to predict where the assailant would strike next. They said for several weeks they had been staking out various apartment complexes.

Sunday night and on into Monday morning they staked out The Season's, a complex of about three hundred apartments. A plainclothes officer said at about 1:10 a.m. Monday he noticed a man in a jogging sweatshirt and jeans walking in front of the apartment complex, looking into windows from the street.

The officer said he approached the man and asked him for identification. The man fled, but the officer ran him down after a brief chase.

Police said Marble is married and has one child.

At one time Marble was a police reporter with a Lubbock newspaper and police said what he may have learned of police tactics as a reporter may have helped him evade officers for the past several months.

Persons at the newspaper who remembered Marble said he had worked there for about six months in 1971.

They described him as "friendly and good at his work."

---

2 Continued From Page One

said the gunman shouted at him: "Get out of here. Go home and tell my mother not to work."

Chapter 36

Attention To Detail!

Dallas, Central Patrol Division
7:00 am Wednesday, March 8, 1977

"ATTENTION TO DETAIL!" Those three words were what we all heard, if we were listening, as the sector sergeants and the watch commander prepared us for our daily roll call briefing.

Our names were called, and our element assignments were confirmed.

With few exceptions, once getting 'picked up' on a regular detail, you worked the same watch and beat (element) every day. The various special assignments, if there were any, were read out, as well as any BOLO's, new Special Orders and the always crowd favorite, Memos from the Chief.

Memos go up the chain of command as requests, memos come down the chain of command as demands. Memo's addressed to Bureau Commanders and then later annotated by 'a bureau commander' with addenda such as: WC FYI, (Watch Commanders, For Your Information) would usually be kept in the WC's files. Very few of the later directives found their way to the bulletin board and some few got read out in detail.

Watch Commander, Lt. Wayne Posey, apparently felt this one important enough for us to hear. He read the following out loud in detail:

"There are 254 officers in the Department on which fingerprint cards are not available. These officers will be contacted in the near future for fingerprints."

As you will note (page 425) this memo has two sets of initials below the signature and signature block of Executive Chief Dahman. The initials are JMS and ROD. JMS was for Assistant Chief James M. Souter and ROD was for Robert O. Dixon, Deputy Chief, Central Patrol. This memo had rolled all the way down hill.

Under their initials I penned: Central Patrol Div; Read In Detail 3-8-77; Lt. Posey, quoting him: "You will comply."

This memo was written on March 3, 1977. Since Chiefs, ostensibly, work 8-5 Monday-Friday, Dahman's memo was written approximately thirteen business days after the capture of the Friendly Burglar-Rapist and seventy-two days after I had suggested this fingerprinting be done in Captain Memo's "Friendly Rapist Work Group" meeting in Planning & Research at 2pm on Wednesday, December 22, 1976. Coincidence?

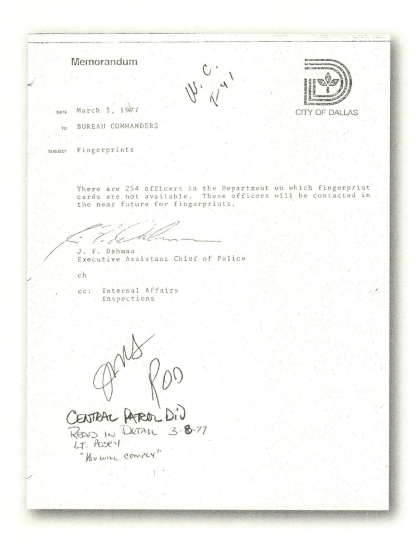

And of course this *non-related event* did not "cause too much media reaction unfavorable to the department," even when pointed out later by the media.[95]

That *cat* had been out of the bag for some time. In fact the media reaction had always been muted, perhaps because they never got their facts straight. Note the February 20, 1977, Dallas Morning News article titled: "Rapes' probe theories told". In the article, reporter Kathy Hast said, "The rapist apparently knew about police investigative methods and used terminology that led investigators to believe he had some connections with a police department. Hast interviewed DPD Investigator Evelyn (Reba) Crowder who was quoted as saying: "There was a lot of concern about that... (W)e didn't necessarily think it was a Dallas police officer, but somebody with (police department) connections. We checked people that worked in the courts building, security officers, and checked all ex-officers with any kind of problem. We checked out police officers, as distasteful as it was."[96]

First, we *didn't* think he might be a police officer because he used police jargon and might know investigative techniques! Second, no, we thought he might be a police officer because *he said* he was one! Although Ms. Crowder said, "we didn't necessarily think he was a Dallas officer," well Tom and I sure thought he could be or could have been! Why? That's right, because *he said* he was! In the twelfth (12th) offense I attributed to the FBR, which was committed on or after about 1:30 am on April 1, 1975, *he said* (quoting from Officer Max Countryman's report of the Complainant's statement to him):

> "Advised her not to be afraid because he was just a Burglar.
> Suspect also advised he was a Dallas Police Officer for about
> one year..."

It does not get more definitive than that! So yes, we had to consider that this suspect could have been (until all were eliminated) a Dallas police officer, perhaps an exceedingly daft one to make such a statement. Nonetheless, he could be or could have been a cop, a Dallas cop! He could have been related to a Dallas cop, etc. Reba either never read FBR Offense Number Twelve, gave it no weight or forgot. Tom and I did not.

---

[95] See Appendix A Article #31 See website: robertjsadler.com

[96] See Appendix A - Newspaper Article # 13 See website: robertjsadler.com

Bottom line, we could not check out our guys because we did not have the means to get it done. And, *maybe* Reba did not want to (or had been told not to) admit the truth to the reporter.

Some Questions Answered:

As stated in my "**Author Note**: Re Offense #72" Tom and I were both definitely laser-focused on the FBR. Anytime someone floated their own theory of who it was, whether there were multiple FBR's, imitators or copycats, we had the data to back up our theories and opinions.

The idea of an FBR imitator copycat or copycats was held by a number of people, among them Captain Milliken (see pages 265-269). And certainly when quirks or seeming anomalies in the purported FBR's MO cropped up, the claim copycat and imitator was made. And yes Tom and I had to and did consider the idea of a copycat, (Offense #40, page 194), but the FBR MO Markers continued to point in only one direction; a single perpetrator.

Investigator Reba Crowder held to the imitator/copycat belief, even going so far as to dub one of these 'anomalies' "The Tongue Twister". Even Investigator Landers (on Offense #72) wrote in his report: "In Officer's opinion, the suspect was not the "Friendly Burglar-Rapist," but was one of the impostors which is capitalizing on the MO of the "Friendly Burglar-Rapist.""

Here is my note after Offense #71 on November 21, 1976.

Author Note 1: *Re: Offense #71, Tom and I were so focused on FBR, we definitely attributed this offense to the FBR, even though (again) latent prints found at the scene did not compare with those already collected and ID'd as the FBR's. What had been in the papers, to that time, as to 'exactly' what the FBR had 'done' during the rapes could have been 'copied'. One question of significance would be who would you conclude committed this rape if the FBR was caught and all "FBR-style" rapes stopped? That is a question you can ponder at the conclusion of this book.*

Here is my answer. With the arrest of Guy William Marble Jr. as the Friendly Burglar-Rapist, there were no more "FBR-style" rapes continuing to occur.

Sure, one could posit that 'all' the FBR copycats and imitators decided to cool it or quit imitating the FBR's MO or they decided to change their MO or they simply decided that the arrest of the FBR was their signal to get out of the burglary and rape business altogether.

Recall our interview with the psychic John Catchings back in November of 1976? How he drew a blank, but his psychic mom, Bertie, came in and said, "You mean the one who drives the brown car?" [97]

Question Answered! Turns out that Guy William Marble Jr., drove a brown Chevy Nova. His get-to and getaway vehicle was parked close by on the night of his arrest. This vehicle was impounded, but lo and behold, it had no leaking transmission.

But it provided other clues. According to Pound Ticket #9180 filled out on 2/14/1977 at 6:30am the vehicle impounded for protective custody (from a parking lot in the 6200 block of Ridgecrest) was 1976 Chevrolet 2dr., Texas license number JBE 466 with VIN:1Q87D5N642296. A record of the property in the vehicle was noted as:

1 Motorola AM-FM radio
1 set of golf shoes
1 set of golf clubs
1 basket ball
2 pair sunglasses
5 cassette tapes (no titles listed)

Question Answered! Marble was an athlete of some degree. He apparently played golf and basketball and we later learned during his post-arrest interview that he was a runner. All of these sports could explain the need for or use of athletic tape of the kind used in several offenses and tested for DPD by Johnson & Johnson laboratories.[98]

Also, remember, back on November 10, 1967, for Offense #70 a canine unit was called out and the O/IR stated: The suspect

[97] See page 312

[98] See pages 368, 382, 402

was trailed by Officer Dooley's canine partner from the front of complainant's apartment east across the parking lot and through the backyard of the house north of the Pan American Bank. The house is located in 2800 block of Kendale. Dooley said his dog followed the trail into the Bank's parking lot where it appeared the suspect had his car parked. Located *a pool of oil or fluid where car was parked* and a *trail of fluid* led from the lot onto Kendale and then west on Northwest Highway. A drinking glass was located beside the garage in driveway of house where suspect's trail led. Glass was turned over to P.E.S. Inv. E. Smith #2451 for printing."

Tactical Officer Dooley made two other notes: he had "found tennis shoe prints along the trail similar to other offenses" and that a *"trail of fluid was also observed at the scene of the offense at 8215 Meadow, apartment 1049"* (occurring Mon. September 13, 1976).

Question Answered. Also during his post-arrest interview with Investigator John Landers where Marble admitted being a runner, frequently running late at night, he gave up much more.

In what I am sure, even given the stress of the moment, seemed an innocent question posed by the disarmingly laconic Landers, Marble gave up that he did have a car with a leaky transmission. Marble was asked, "What'd you have to do to get your leaky transmission fixed?" Marble replied without hesitating, "Had to put in a seal in..."

Landers said later Marble got a queer look on his face as if to think, *how did he know my car used to have a transmission leak?* Then Marble seemed to nod, knowing he had just been caught at something even if he didn't know exactly what it was.

Though Truly Holmes was the CAPERS investigator who 'had the FBR cases' and succeeded John Landers as lead investigator as Landers had succeeded Reba Crowder, it was Landers who conducted the Marble post-arrest interview at Truly's request.

I am aware that Landers showed Marble the offense book containing all the cases Tom and I had attributed to him and Marble took credit for them all, a story John recounted to me and Tom on numerous occasions. So I am unsure why DMN reporter Bill Kenyon (see Attachment A - Newspaper Article #4) wrote: "Sources said (DPD Investigator Truly) Holmes showed Marble 81 Offense reports and that Marble indicated involvement in all but one—and **revealed he had raped 12 other women** who apparently had not reported the attacks to police."

It is possible that Truly did as was reported and it is also possible that Kenyon or his 'sources' got the investigator's name wrong.

The point is, Marble 'copped' to offenses we attributed to him and possibly committed more. Landers also asked Marble, "Just how many places do you go in a night?" Marble replied, **"You wouldn't believe me if I told you, but it's a lot."** And remember what Marble told Virginia Huston on December 6th when she happened upon him in the rain as she was walking her dog: "Yeah," Marble said, "it's a nasty night for jogging... I do this every night." [99]

Whether it was braggadocio or fact, he raped nearly forty-five women in Dallas and maybe as many as seventy-five. And— there could be more. He did travel.

Question Answered. There were no copycats... In his own words, Guy William Marble Jr., did 'em all. And though Kenyon 'reported' Marble admitted his "involvement in all but one..." I was never apprised of which "one" that was and no one could tell me if it was a rape, attempted rape, burglary, prowler, etc. So that claim was never verified or verifiable. Likewise, to our knowledge no one ever followed up on the twelve other rapes Marble 'revealed' he committed—that were not contained in our FBR book.

Then of course, there was the forensic evidence!

Forensic Evidence
Blood Typing the FBR & Answers

AS PREVIOUSLY STATED we were convinced there was only one man out there committing the FBR crimes. Tom and I couldn't explain away the different results with blood evidence, but we knew something wasn't right—and here's why!

It was not until after the capture of Guy William Marble Jr., that something quite disheartening came to light. After Marble's arrest, his blood was drawn, sent to and typed by 'the lab'. The result was different from every other test of blood and semen collected from various of the FBR crime scenes.

---

[99] See page 351 Offense Number 74 *VEH* - Virginia Huston [O/IR #434478H 12-6-76]

Tom said, "I was stunned to find the discrepancies..." and said he thought, "good God, every offense report we had, since day-one, that we'd been sending out there, not only Guy Marble's, but all the others, were incorrect..." Tom scratched his head and to follow up arranged a personal meeting with the Chairman of all pathology of the Southwestern Medical School, Vernon Stembridge. He was responsible for the Southwestern Institute of Forensic Sciences lab. Tom said, "Here's the lab tech's memos for various crime scene samples and here's the one from Marble's actual blood draw testing." (containing all the memos for the 'lab tech' who had typed both the FBR crime scene blood and semen samples)

This is just another example of Tom's acuity on display along with his 'never give up' attitude. If it had not been for Tom asking the question, seeking the answer, it was apparent that no one would have looked at this situation until, perhaps, at trial. Then, if the defense attorney was smart enough to have looked at the various pathology reports and then brought up or questioned the differences in blood typing, it would have been easy enough for the defense to say, 'must have been someone else, not my client, see the blood doesn't match!'

Much to Dr. Stembridge's credit he looked at Tom's letter and attachments and told Tom, "There is something wrong here." Stembridge started an internal review. Tom said, "here's what happened. He (Stembridge) found that it all came back to one particular step in the test...it had to be done under certain controls and they had not instituted those controls. Because they were not in place, their results were skewed. Apparently the lab did not know that the test had to be done under certain controls (for example: testing in a non-contaminated area or some such common sense thing). As soon as they put the proper controls in place, bingo, everything lined out. But prior to that every test was wrong, not only ours but everybody's!

"We didn't have one correct test on GWM Jr., until after he was arrested and Tom got the mess ironed out. Tom furnished Dr. Stembridge the names and all the offenses we attributed to Marble. Dr. Stembridge had the lab go back and test them including the previously omitted step, under controlled conditions and we got a letter back from the Doctor, or Dixon got a letter back from him, saying they (the lab) had confirmed the blood type—**all the evidence was retested and it was confirmed they matched Marble's blood type**."

The GUN Anomaly
Copycat or FBR? A Retrospective

**Dallas, Northeast Patrol Division, Beat 236 4:17 pm
Wednesday, February 6, 1974 Offense Number R-1?
NOT ORIGINALLY ATTRIBUTED to FBR[100]**

No Prints Lifted
(see page 41-55)

*...pulled a gun on Comp and told her not to scream that he
was a Burg. that just got caught...*

AS PREVIOUSLY STATED, I always questioned whether I
or we (Tom and I) caught/found *every* FBR offense.

Perhaps not so *obviously* I knew that not all rape offenses are
reported. Was there a possibility that the FBR committed rapes
that went unreported? Given the statistics for non-reporting
versus reporting, why would I (or you) think otherwise.
However, all I could work on were the reported offenses.

What gave us perhaps a false feeling of confidence was that
the FBR admitted to all but (supposedly) one of the offenses we
had *attributed* to him. That confidence was shaken when during
his interrogation by Inv. John Landers, the FBR (Guy William
Marble, Jr) said he went into multiple locations every time out!

One must postulate that if a rape, committed on a given night,
were reported you could not preclude the possibility that he had
already been in several apartments (committing a *burglary of a
habitat at night* each time). This thought also begs the question
of would he continue to burglarize other apartments even after
having committing one rape or could he possible commit two or
more rapes in a single night?

Further if more burglaries (and or rapes) were occurring as
Marble claimed, why were there not more reported offenses?
While it is plausible that one or even many victims of the
burglaries committed by the FBR may not have missed any
property or noticed a spurious unlocked window or door, and
didn't know they had been burglarized. It is not plausible that an

---

[100] This offense was brought to my attention in 2014 by Mr. J Patrick Rick. Now, in
January 2016, I am considering that this offense may have been committed by the FBR.
Regardless, the information is illuminating.

assaulted woman would not know she was raped. That she would decide not to report her assault would be her choice. And following the statistics that puts the number of unreported rapes at percentages of fifty percent (or more) then Marble's number of actual rape victims could have been perhaps eighty or more.

For these reasons, I always worried that I could have missed something unreported and thus worked hard with the reports we did have to ensure we caught every potential FBR offense.

We read and reviewed thousands of Offense/Incident Reports (O/IR) from 1973 (and before) until the FBR's capture in February 1977. We looked for ways to include or exclude each offense we reviewed as having or not having FBR M/O Markers.

We catalogued over fifty (50) individual FBR M/O Markers, nineteen (19) of which were the most often encountered.

Each offense was objectively read and reviewed (two separate operations). When read, the offense would be placed in one of two categories: 1) *probably not* and 2) *possible*. When reviewed the *probably not's* were either downgraded to *not* and discarded or upgraded to *possible*.

When the possibles were reviewed they either remained *possibles* or were upgraded to *probable*. In the last review the *probables* were then either downgraded back to *possibles* or became the offenses we *attributed* to the FBR.

The FBR M/O Marker for "weapon": *mentioned, displayed, or used* (physically felt by Comp.) occurred in 81% of all rapes attributed to the FBR. However the weapon was usually a knife or a sharp object the FBR said was a knife or the Comp. thought was a knife.

In 39 months I do not remember any rape offense listing a weapon, to wit: a GUN! Tom, in 2016, likewise does not remember our ever encountering a *gun* being used by the FBR.

As we honed and refined our FBR M/O Markers based on each additional rape case reviewed, a gun was something we did not see. More importantly, had we seen a gun connected to a rape offense, we would likely have discarded that offense as *not possibly* an FBR offense.

Why am I considering including this rape offense from February 6, 1974 as a possible/probable? In 2014 I was contacted by a man who was arrested for rape and was later pursued by Reba Crowder and other investigators as potentially either *the* Friendly Burglar Rapist or one of his copycat/

imitators. Telling, Mr. Rick's wife: "Just because he was No Billed, doesn't mean he's not guilty."

Mr. J. Patrick (Pat) Rick was the man arrested. During our initial contacts in 2014 he wanted to draw information from me without divulging his reasons. By the time he told me about his brush with the law, which had resulted in his being No Billed for the offense resulting from his arrest, examining trial and Grand Jury appearance, I was at best, very dubious of his purpose.

Mr. Rick particularly wanted to know if the offense he was arrested for could have been committed by the FBR. Was I aware of the offense? Was it ever considered as an FBR offense? He noted that it was not in my book. [*It is now been included on page 41-55.*]

Mr. Rick supplied me with a copy of the O/IR for the offense and when I read the report in 2014 I shook my head. I immediately thought, "No way. This is not an FBR offense. A) it occurred in the afternoon and B) the suspect used a gun."

The O/IR narrative is supposed to be a telling of what happened, demonstrating the elements of the offense. The report is not supposed to be 'cop jargon' or written in the Reporting Officer's (RO) own words. Ostensibly it is a relating of the Complainant's words, using direct quotes whenever possible. As the reader you depend on the ability of the RO to accurately capture the Comp's words.

After reading the Arrest Report (AR) and the transcript of the Examining Trail (ET) which was followed by the Grand Jury hearing and a "No Bill", reflected on the police department's Prosecution Report (PR), I was convinced that indeed Mr. Rick had been too hurriedly presumed the suspect, too hurriedly arrested and too hurriedly proffered for prosecution... with little investigation of the Suspect's: means, motive and opportunity.

Not only did I believe Mr. Rick did not commit the offense he was arrested for, in my opinion, he should never have been arrested.

That said, in January of 2016 I agreed to meet with Mr. Rick in Dallas to discuss his circumstantial nexus with or to the FBR. In preparation for this meeting. I once again poured over the O/IR, AR, PR and ET. It was when I finally put this February 6, 1974 rape offense in context with the FBR chronology of offenses that I said to myself: *Whoa!*

The first offense I became aware of and later attributed to the FBR occurred on November 15, 1973 and became R-1 (Rape 1).

In my chronology of FBR offenses, R-2 occurred on July 30, 1974. It is easy to see the wide gap in time between these offenses and why I intuited there had to be others in between.

Now, in 2016, I required myself to re-look (with 1974 eyes) at this offense, given what I knew about the M/O of the suspect who would be come known as the FBR. I owed it to this offense (and Mr. Rick) to reassess this offense as I would have assessed it in February 1974, five months before I would become aware of R-2. (see pages 57-58).

I had no recollection of seeing this offense. First, as it had occurred on the Northeast Patrol Division, it would not have crossed my desk as the Central Patrol Division Crime Analyst in February 1974. If I remember correctly, the other four patrol divisions had not yet pulled one of their patrol officers inside to be their division's analyst.

Regardless, it would be several months before I ordered copies of all rape and attempted rape offenses (city-wide) from 1970 through 1975. Offense #38546-F, Agg. Rape occurring on Wednesday 2/6/1974 should have been in 'the pile'. Could I, or later Tom, have missed it. Yes, that is a possibility.

In my "whoa" ah-ha moment, I told myself that I had to look at this offense with only the knowledge of one previous offense.

Comparing R-1 (11.15.73) with the 2/6/74 rape offense I now call the 2/6/74 rape "R-1?" (R-1 Question Mark). There are 14 similarities. Among the dissimilarities is that in R-1 no weapon is *mentioned, displayed* or *used* (which does not preclude the possibility that the attacker had a gun) while in R-1? a weapon, to wit: a gun was used. With only two offenses to review or consider I would have to say I would have marked down *gun* as an M/O Marker and noted that this was dissimilar to R-1.

Whether that difference was anomalous or not would not be known until more data was available for comparison. All things being equal, given the multiple similar FBR M/O Markers in R-1 and R-1?, it might very well have been catalogued as attributed to the FBR, even though that M/O Marker (gun) was never again encountered.

Perhaps for the FBR, he considered it a 'lesson learned': that carrying or having a gun was possibly too cumbersome or dangerous, when every victim's kitchen was equipped with multiple knives and other sharp objects. These knives, most often those of the Comp., became the FBR's go-to weapons of choice whether or not *mentioned, displayed* or *used*.

Review the two graphics at end of book (pages 574 &575)
for comparison of "Offense # R1?" with others & MOs

~

A Demonstration of Relative Size
Hard to Confuse?

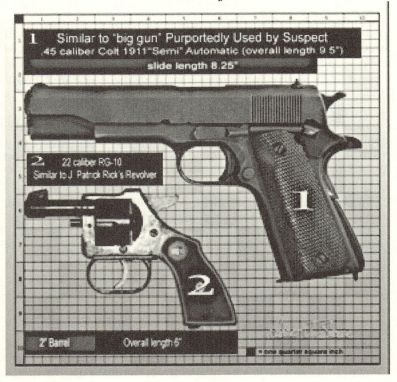

Graphic shows actual relative size of [1] a ".45 Automatic" as described (with help) by DGSB and reported in O/IR Service #38546-F and [2] the type of .22 caliber revolver found in a sack, under the spare tire in the trunk of J. Patrick Rick's car.

I HAVE CONCLUDED, based on the information at hand, re the other FBR M/O Markers, that R-1? would have to be considered a *probable* and pending exclusionary evidence I would now include this offense as one *attributed* to the FBR.

But Wait!

If you go back and reread the February 6, 1974 O/IR, the AR, and the PR a number of dots are never connected (I'll leave that for Mr. Rick's book) but more than that the officer's report is woeful at best and at worst it led to the arrest of the wrong man much to the relief, I'm sure, of the actual rapist. This inadequate O/IR and AR leads me to conclude that the statements of the Comp., the Comp.'s husband/witness and those of the neighbor/witness are problematic in themselves.

Such inadequacies lead to speculations.

What was actually said? When and by whom? For example the Comp was supposed to have told her husband that her attacker had a gun... a large gun. It is apparent that the RO and or his partner had to explain the difference between a revolver (a wheel-gun) which has a cylinder to hold rounds and a semiautomatic, which in contrast, has basically smooth sides. All of which leads the RO to indicate that the Comp identified her attacker's weapon as a .45 caliber automatic (such as a Colt 1911 which of course is a semi-automatic). Now compare this back and forth to get the Comp to describe her attacker's gun with the report saying she was supposed to be holding her husband's .22 revolver. The Comp obviously knew where she and or her husband kept that gun. Where was it when she was attacked by a man with a much bigger gun? And... how does she consider it prudent that she is going to be able to go after or repel this attacker by getting her little gun to go up against his big gun? Of course, perhaps, she was in shock and those thoughts never occurred to her.

Again, according to my reading of the RO's report, the husband comes home, enters his apartment door to find his wife naked moving toward him and holding his gun. After numerous reads I am still unable to determine who (Comp or Comp's husband) is giving suspect's description to the RO.

The RO writes about the actions of the attacker and then a response by the Comp.: "...He pulled phone out of wall and left apt. She stated she grabbed her husband's gun and ran down hall to catch him when her husband walked into apt." There is no time frame to indicate how long after her attacker left that Comp, found/got her gun and pursued her attacker. Did the attacker leave, being immediately pursued by the Comp with a gun. Only to be seen by Comp's husband/witness seconds later in front of his apt door.[101] Then nonchalantly[102] passes by the Comp's husband on the stairs, thus becoming a/the suspect?

You can make your own speculations. We'll never know exactly what took place. The report is too inadequate to draw accurate conclusions. That said, here is my speculation.

What if there never was a gun, big or otherwise "pulled" on the Comp.? What if her attacker physically man-handled, overpowered her or used an unreported knife, taped her up and assaulted her? What if the initial interaction between attacker and victim happened some other way than was 'explained' to the RO... and there never was a gun?[103]

What if the Comp was embarrassed that she was assaulted, was overpowered by a man, taped up and raped? What if she was embarrassed or mad/angry at herself that she did not or could not defend herself. What if she was scared to get her/her husband's gun from wherever it was and use or try to use it?

What if because of her embarrassment she made up that her attacker had a "big gun" in order to make her attack seem less like her fault in her or her husband's eyes. What if her husband was the kind of guy that expected his wife to handle herself, that 'his' gun was there to protect her. A wife of such a man might want to have an excuse for being raped and it not being her fault (leaving the front door open/unlocked) or possibly perceived it as her fault. Such a wife might say something on the order of "He had a big gun, Honey, what could I do?"

Of course this is wild speculation for which I have no solid ground to stand on... And, I am not speculating to cast aspersions. But, suppose this speculation were correct and the

---

[101] The examining trail testimony of Comp and her husband further muddy this possibility.

[102] The only words that come to my mind to describe the man in the hallway (more appropriately the area would be called a breezeway or landing leading to and from the stairway) in lieu of descriptors of him exhibiting aberrant behavior such as: unhurried, purposeful, unconcerned, to wit: nonchalant. How many criminals are able to so well control themselves in that situation. My opinion is many would break and run—to get as far away as possible, as quickly as possible. Apparently the Comp's husband saw no fight-or-flight response from the man he encountered on the second floor landing.

[103] Having read literally thousands of rape, attempt rape, day & nighttime residence burglary offenses during the FBR's reign of terror (11.15.73-2.14.77), I do not recall ever seeing a report where the suspect *mentioned, displayed* or *used* a .45 caliber "automatic" other than this one.

attacker never had a gun. In that case this offense would certainly not have been discarded and excluded in February 1974 or later as not being committed by the Friendly Burglar Rapist.

Gun equals anomaly, a one off? Without the "big gun", I would have attributed this offense to Guy William Marble Jr. With the gun, as I look at it today in 2016, I would not exclude this offense. I would categorize it as a *possible* on the low side and a *probable* on the high side.

Since the Comp did go to the hospital where a rape kit procedure could have been conducted, that forensic material could have been compared to Marble and positively included or excluded him or Mr. Rick.

Again, I make these speculations based on intelligence guided by experience. I intend no harm to the reputation and memory of the Comp.

We will never know all the answers. It is my understanding that the Comp.'s husband/witness and the neighbor/witness have no desire to be interviewed. Further, *GDSB*, who later divorced her then husband/witness, has recently passed away. May she rest in peace. I am sorry that we did not identify her rapist and provide her with some measure of justice and perhaps closure.

Making the Case for Mr. Rick to be the Comp.'s attacker?

In order for Mr. Rick to have been a viable suspect a number of facts and presumptions would have to be manipulated.

Fact: Rick in presence of patient and others in PMH Burn Unit for some period of time administering a life-saving treatment which concluded at approximately 3:45p

Fact: Comp. states rape occurred between 3:50 and 4:15pm

Fact: Witness places Rick at PMH at 4:05pm

Fact: Husband comes home approx 4:10pm, sees man on landing

Fact: There are discrepancies between Comp's and Husband's 'suspect' description

Fact: Husband at 4:20p? runs next door, gives Wardell description of man he saw

Fact: Wardell says he drove around apartment complex

Fact: Rick arrives at apt complex in his car at approx 4:30pm

Fact: Rick sees man in car watching him as Rick arrives at apt complex

Fact: Witness Wardell sees Rick in car, follows from entrance, watches him park, etc. (this fact not reported by RO)

Fact: "Big Gun" (.45 automatic) and remainder of surgical tape not found

Fact: Stocking's ROs found were not IDd by Comp as hers nor IDd as item/s used by her assailant.

Given a PMH to the Noel Road apartments drive-time window of 15-30 minutes, in order for Mr. Rick to be GDSB's rapist he would have had to have left PMH by at least 3:15-3:30pm. Negating Rick's alibi witnesses' testimony.

Then allowing an additional 5 minutes (minimum) for Rick to have parked his car near but not in the complex and then walk to Comp.'s apartment, arriving (just after she unloaded her first load of shopping and left her door open and went back down to her car) at approximately 3:50pm.

After the assault Rick would have had to leave Comp's apartment at approximately 4:10-4:15p in time to be seen by Husband. Then Rick would have, in the next few minutes, had walk to a dumpster in the complex, deposit Comp's stockings, then walk out of the complex to his car, also disposing of, along the way, the "big gun" and the roll of surgical tape he had brought with him. Next, get in his car and drive to the entrance of their apartment complex at approximately 4:25-4:30pm to be seen and then followed by Witness Wardell.

Of course in this hypothetical, Rick could have kept the gun and tape on his person, brought it home and secreted it in his apartment, which was never searched. All this also presumes that it would have been Mr. Rick's intent to at least burglarize Comp's apartment, so he went to her apartment believing neither she nor her husband would be at home. Or, his intent was to rape her in which case he would want to make sure Comp. was at home and waited for the moment when he could walk through her unlocked (even open) front door to lay in wait.

One question that bothers me. How did anyone just happen to arrive at Comp's apartment at the propitious moment she left her door open to go down and retrieve her second load of shopping... then slip inside only to jump out from the bathroom after she returns, puts down her shopping and then walks into her bedroom?

Comp states that she had made an earlier shopping trip, put up her groceries and gone out shopping again. She stated she locked the door and that it was locked when she returned home the second time.

The idea seems implausible that a man lurking in plain sight (or not) was close enough to watch Comp leave her door unlocked and or decided to, on happenstance, give her doorknob a jiggle and finding the door unlocked, slipped inside to burgle the apt. and or lay in wait for the GSDB to return so he could assault her. The simultaneity of such outlandish consecutive coincidences does not make logical sense.

I submit it is more plausible that she left the door unlocked the first time, that the burglar/assailant was already in the apt when she returned the second time, with an arm load of shopping, put her key in the lock and turned it thinking she was unlocking her unlocked door, went inside dropped some things and went back to the car. The surprised assailant, caught between being discovered and or escaping, waited to see if Comp. was coming back or not, before leaving. She comes back, he subdues her and rapes her.

Whether using the facts or an outlandish set of circumstances, I am unable to make a logical case that J. Patrick Rick perpetrated the criminal assault on GSDB.

Targeted vs Random Victims / Broken Patterns

First offenses, I have now realized, are the most difficult to link to a serial offender given the immense variables of difference! You have different locations, different victims, different reporting officers, different investigators, different crime scene and lab techs. All you have to go on as an analyst/ investigator are the elements that end up in reports, evidence or interviews with witnesses that specifically link one case to another.

For example, if the perpetrator wears in every offense a white-face clown mask with a red whiskey nose you are going to have a pretty easy time of linking offenses. But sometimes all you get is "the suspect wore a mask" or "looked like he had a bulbous nose". Or consider, if the responding/reporting officer asks the Comp, "What did he look like?" and the Comp says: "I never saw his face". While that is true, what if the Comp isn't asked and doesn't mention she didn't see his face because he was wearing a clown mask with a red nose? So perhaps that linking information goes unreported or undiscovered.

Thus having multiple linking data, what I called M/O Markers, makes the task of connecting a serial offender's offenses more likely. Particularly when rarely if ever does a given offense contain all the known M/O Markers of the serial suspect.

For all the 'different variables' listed above finding common denominators in the initial review of potentially similar offenses is problematic.

When looking for victim or complainant zero or number one and then two and three, it is easy to understand that limited linking data can easily lead an analyst/investigator to potentially exclude an early offense from those later linked to a serial offender by multiple M/O Markers.

The first offense (in November 1973) attributed to the FBR was also the first offense noticed and none were found to precede it. The offense against *PJT* (R-1) [104]occurred in the afternoon: Comp left apartment door open to go downstairs to the laundry room and returned to her apartment to be confronted and then raped by an assailant using 'cop jargon'. The second offense (if we now include it) against *GDSB* (R-1?) [105]occurred in the afternoon, Comp left her apartment door open to retrieve groceries/shopping from car downstairs and returned to her apartment had her hands 'taped up' and raped by an assailant using 'cop jargon'.

Finally the third offense, against *JP* (R-2) [106]occurred in the wee hours of the morning (4:30am). The suspect gained entrance with a key obtained in a previous daytime burglary and had her hands 'taped together' and raped by an assailant using 'cop jargon'.

Obviously, the use of 'cop jargon' links these three offenses., while using 'tape' in R-1? & R-2 link those two. However, the time of occurrence moves from afternoon to morning and breaks the pattern, or does it. I could speculate that had *JP* been home during 'the burglary' when the suspect took her spare key, she would have been raped in the afternoon.

But in retrospect the most intriguing thought for me is that these women appear to have been targeted! It is possible that suspect used a second floor sliding glass door to gain entrance (his most often used point of ingress) unaware that his victims

---

[104] see pages 8 & 11

[105] see pages 41-55

[106] see pages 57-58

had left their apartment doors open and was 'surprised' when the Comp/s came home and decided to act on the opportunity to rape the Comp/s. It is also possible that the suspect saw the Comp leave their second floor apartment to go to (R-1, the laundry room & R-1?, get groceries/shopping items from her car), liked what he saw, entered their apartment through their open door and waited on their return to commit his assault.

In the third offense (*JP* R-2), though the reason is unknown, the suspect intentionally returned to rape *JP*; i.e., she *was* targeted.

From that point forward it does not appear that the FBR's victims were targeted, but rather were random victims of opportunity, owing to his proclivity for going into multiple apartments each night he prowled. Perhaps these future victims were targeted by the suspect in one sense, in that he used tale-tell signs of a female presence such as: plants in the window, etc. and he looked for easy access such as open doors and windows.

However, it does not appear from a review of all our files that he knew or had seen his victims prior to his entry into their apartment and his attack, with one bright exception.

The FBR made the career-ending mistake of chatting-up a woman on a rainy night and then later entering her apartment where she foiled his assault. She became his Achilles Heel. She recognized and described him to an artist.

It was the FBR's clothing description from that night and that likeness she helped create with the artist that put him on Tactical Officer Barry Whitfield's radar and facilitated the FBR's capture.

See: *Postscript 3c* at the end of the book.

Fast forward to the fall of 2016...

Chapter 37

One Step from Murder: The Friendly Burglar Rapist

AS VETERAN POLICE officers, Tom and I were aware that criminal behavior can and does evolve over time. We thought this and were concerned about the potential for Guy William Marble Jr.'s physical contact with his prey to escalate from sexual assault to include battery and/or murder.

Remember, as early as August 8, 1974, his 4th attributed offense, he had threatened his victims with death. The FBR was quoted as saying: "Don't' say anything, I will kill you."

As a result of Tom's discussion with Dr. David Paul, a London Police Surgeon, in November 1976, we were heartened and yet concerned by the quantification of our experiential thesis.

One more way we kept track of the FBR's offenses was to plot his movement on Dr. Paul's Six Step - Rape to Murder Progression. Dr. Paul called them steps, six in all. Somehow we started referring to the 'steps' as stages.

Tom did a post-arrest assessment of all the FBR's offenses. Based on the information reported by the Complainants or learned during follow-up investigation, Tom noted that Guy William Marble Jr., remained in Stage One (straight sex: vaginal intercourse, missionary style) from the first offense through offense number thirty-three.

As of Offense number 33b and continuing through number 46 Marble began to experiment with varied sexual positions constituting his being in Stage Two.

With offense #47a Marble moved to Stage Three (Sodomy: a. victim, b. self) by performing cunnilingus on his victim and then in subsequent offenses requiring his victims to perform fellatio on him. But maybe he should have been at Stage three since Offense Number 3 on Saturday, August 3, 1974, when he had performed oral sex on his victim.

Stage Three was where we agreed his progression slowed. On several subsequent offenses the FBR did demonstrate a focus on his victim's breasts that had moved from 'mere' fondling to kissing, licking and sucking. This focus was a clear departure from his previous behaviors. Significantly there were no reports of his 'biting' his victim's breasts or thighs as would be indicative of Dr. Paul's, Stage Four. Perhaps the case can be made that Marble had moved into Stage Four, but that his 'new' focus had not yet manifested itself in physical pain. I submit that a woman being forcibly assaulted by a man would find his licking, kissing, and or sucking of her breasts to be as psychologically painful as the physical pain of actually being bitten.

Recently reviewing the files again for this book, I found other incidents of note. May 30th (our #50) is the first reported incidence of assaultive bodily injury. The Complainant sustained a 'busted lip' as she struggled with her assailant. Though the Complainant's injury was likely inadvertently obtained, (her struggling with the FBR being the proximate cause), since he did not (apparently) overtly act to injure the Complainant. Nevertheless the resultant injury was in the commission of another act of forced aggression against the Complainant by the FBR and as such is the direct fault of the FBR however 'inadvertent' his action might have been. Thus this injury, in my opinion should be considered as behavior caused by the FBR. However due the lack of apparent intent or the inadvertent nature of the injury it does not rise to the level of Dr. Paul's Stage Five: Sadistic Pain.

We all understand the meaning of 'pain'. Sadistic Pain would be a degree of pain inflected by a 'sadist', typical of Freud's anal stage of development; *sadistic-masochistic*. The Oxford English Dictionary defines 'sadism' as:

"a form of sexual perversion marked by a love of cruelty. Now understood as cruelty that evidences a subconscious craving and is apparently satisfied, sexually or otherwise, by the infliction of pain on another by means of aggressive or destructive behavior or the assertion of power over that person; also *loosely*, deliberate or excessive cruelty morbidly enjoyed."

It appeared to me that GWM Jr. was pushing the outer boundaries of sadism in offenses 74, 79 & 82 respectively. In 74 Ms. Huston had seen her attacker! She foiled Marble's attempt to rape her after he "wrapped excess telephone cord around his hand" and then got scared when he "attempted to put the telephone cord around her neck." This fear for her life, her screaming and fighting back, scared off Marble and saved her from rape and possible saved her life. Had she not screamed, had she not resisted, would this have been the moment Marble crossed the line to murder the only woman who had ever gotten a good look at him? In 79 the FBR put a rope around his victim's neck and said, "You know how easy it would be to kill you?". This mock-chocking might be considered subliminal or subconscious role-play. Or rehearsal for Stage Six behavior he felt justified in acting out.

Next in Offense 82 he repeats the behavior of 'sticking' or 'pricking' his victim with the point of the knife to remind them it is there. In the ensuing struggle the Complaint was 'inadvertently' cut by the FBR's knife, causing him to flee. The injury sustained was a minor 'defensive' wound to the right hand. Again the Complainant's resistance was the 'proximate cause' of the injury, but again any proximate injury sustained during the commission of a criminal act would legally be the fault or responsibility of the perpetrator.

In retrospect, given the above definitions, actions and the three incidents on May 30, 1976; January 4, 1977; and February 1, 1977, I believe Guy William Marble Jr., moved past Stage Four and we should have placed Marble Jr.'s 'progress' toward murder, if not nominally, in Stage Five, a supernumerary of the same and on the edge of Stage Six.

Remember Marble's own words about rehearsal and acting out from the epigraph at the beginning of this book:

Dallas Morning News 5-24-1998 [107]
Quotes from article: Rapist to leave prison...

"Sexual abnormalities and obsessions are hidden in a dark corner of the mind, an emotional cancer that sprouts in childhood and seldom gets treated in our society," he wrote. "The rehearsals for my crimes began in grade school, and nobody ever took enough interest to notice, to help me understand. Acting out those fantasies as a young adult was inevitable."

These comments were ostensibly couched as pertaining to his juvenile 'abnormalities and obsessions', but they could very well have applied to his actions during the commission of a number of his crimes, most notably when 'he put a rope around his victim's neck and said, "You know how easy it would be to kill you?"' Was this a rehearsal, a preparation, for his next step on Dr. Paul's offender arc, that being murder?

Over the last several months of his reported attacks Marble was 'foiled' more times than he was successful. Marble experienced instances of erectile dysfunction. It is reasonable to

---

[107] Appendix A- Newspaper Article #34 DMN 05.24.98 (text) "Friendly Rapist to leave..." [See website: robertjsadler.com]

posit Marble was frustrated & ready to act out more aggressively. The difference between rape and murder was only a matter of time and circumstance; specifically one misstep on the part of either Marble or one of his victims.

Tom and I agree, Marble was ***one step from murder***.

Irony of Ironies

Perhaps the most ironic element of Guy William Marble Jr.'s arrest for the FBR rapes is that he was, at the time of capture by Officer Whitfield, wearing the same clothes as those worn three months earlier (12/6/1976) when the one and only witness (Virginia Huston) who had seen, really seen, our suspect described him to Tom, John Landers, me and artist Linda Robertson.

Compare Ms. Robertson's sketch, as described to her by Ms. Huston, of the FBR on the left and Marble's 'tired' book-in photo (taken hours after his arrest) on the right with his face recently superimposed (using PhotoShop) over the Robertson sketch in the lower right-hand corner. An amazing likeness.

Chapter 38

Kudos, Well Deserved

Below is the text of the commendation letter I wrote for Ms. Huston and Ms. Robertson.

February 22, 1977
Mr. D. A. Byrd
Chief of Police

SUBJECT: Recommendation For Citizen's Certificate of Merit to be Awarded to Miss Virginia Huston and Miss Linda Robertson.

Sir:

We recommend that Miss Virginia Huston of 6466 Ridgecrest #2096, Dallas, Texas, and Miss Linda Robertson of 5545 Alpha Road #2053, Dallas Texas, be awarded the Citizen's Certificates of Merit for their assistance in the investigation and subsequent arrest of the Friendly Burglar Rapist. Without the aid of the two (2) women, the visual identification and recognition of this suspect would have been impossible.

On December 6, 1976, at 1:10 A.M., Miss Huston became a victim of the Friendly Burglar Rapist. Fortunately, her struggle with her attacker frightened him away. Luckily for our Department, Miss Huston recognized her attacker as the same man she had seen only a couple of hours earlier while she was walking her dog in the apartment complex. Though shaken by her experience, she was able to give to investigators a complete and accurate description of her attacker.

Some months earlier, Miss Linda Robertson had a prowler at her residence. Northeast Division Special Projects Officer B.B. Smoot screened this report for any possible connection with the Friendly Burglar

Rapist's case. While Officer Smoot interviewed Miss Robertson, she offered to draw a sketch of her prowler. The sketch was done and a remarkable likeness was rendered, but there was no connection with the Friendly Burglar Rapist.

After assuring us that she could identify the Friendly Burglar Rapist, Miss Huston agreed to put her recollections on paper with the help of an artist. Since the Department does not have a sketch artists available, Officer Smoot remembered Miss Robertson's sketch and contacted her about helping us with an artist's conception of Miss Huston's suspect. Miss Robertson readily agreed to give her time and talent to help.

At 6:00 P.M., the same day, only seventeen (17) hours after the attempted assault, we met in Miss Huston's apartment with artist Linda Roberson. After several hours of sketching, erasing, questioning and redrawing, Miss Robertson had rendered to Miss Huston's satisfaction a nearly perfect drawing of her attacker, the Friendly Burglar Rapist.

(page two)

In additional to cooperating with the making of the artist's conception, Miss Huston agreed to look through area high school yearbooks in an attempt to identify her attacker. At that time we had no idea who the Friendly Burglar Rapist was and Miss Huston was the first and only victim to have seen the suspect. Officer Sadler provided yearbooks from five (5) North Dallas high schools for each of the last eight (8) years. In all, Miss Huston viewed approximately 120,000 photographs. A Herculean task at best, but one she took gladly and accomplished quickly. Though no suspect was identified, we were able to add one fact to our store of knowledge: "Very low probability Friendly Burglar Rapist is a local Dallas boy." Future contact with suspects with out of town background could be given more scrupulous attention.

When Officer B. Whitfield observed Guy W. Marble, Jr., prowling The Seasons Apartment Complex on February 14, 1977, he related later that the composite drawing kept flashing in his mind when he looked at Marble and he said to himself several times, "They match, it's him"; so the Friendly Burglar Rapist was arrested.

It is clear that without the help and time so unselfishly given by these two (2) citizens, the Friendly Burglar Rapist would still be on the streets at this moment. We would like to express our personal thanks for their help by requesting that the Department promptly present a Citizen's Certificate of Merit to Miss Virginia Huston and Miss Linda Roberson for their invaluable assistance in the Friendly Burglar Rapist's case.

Respectfully submitted

/s/ Robert J. Sadler
/s/ Thomas H. Covington

Both Ms. Huston and Ms. Roberson were each presented with the Dallas Police Department's Citizen's Certificate of Merit. Perhaps, they should have also been awarded the 'golden handcuffs'.

Recognition

IN THE COMING months Tom and I did learn that we would receive some departmental recognition. Instead of the Police Commendation Bar, the third highest departmental award, the 'board' recommended that we receive, for our efforts, The Meritorious Achievement Award, a step down from the PCB.

I had returned to patrol, working the third-watch 3-11pm. I received my MAA certificate and bar one afternoon before detail, after a matter-of-fact reading of the award letter.

Although I was pleased to have the 'board' find that the actions and dedication of Tom and I had 'some' value, it was a somewhat hollow victory for me.

Shortly after the capture of the FBR, I had a conversation with Captain of Police Don Milliken, then head of Crimes Against Persons and boss of Inv.'s Landers and Holmes. I broached the subject of recognition for my partner as well as Investigators John Landers and Truly Holmes.

Don's offhand comment about our getting "our share of the lion's roar," delivered as we parted in the hall and meant with no ill-will or ill-intent, always struck me as endemic of the institutional 'heart' of many agencies. They often are not aware of the talents and skills of their employees and if they are aware, take them for granted or worse fail to make use of those talents and skills, as well as often fail to recognize and reward their troop's extraordinary efforts.

Author Note: *Of course we were "only doing our jobs" and were not seeking sycophantic pats on the back. It was simply an unfortunate fact of the 1970s that ordinary as well as extraordinary efforts often went unheralded, thus not encouraged. If this was not the result of some institutional blindness, what would you call it when the good works of its 'troops' went unpublicized. The department did not recognize the opportunity to create 'good PR' with our work and award. There was no mention of us, our work or our award by any of the local media or even in our own The Dallas Police News, of which I had been a part when I worked in PIO.*

The main reason Officer Whitfield's "Golden Handcuffs" award was publicized was that the awarding entity (Greater Dallas Crime Commission), aware of its own PR profile, was desirous of the attention their award brought to their organization. Most likely someone at the GDCC called the paper and arranged for the event to be covered.

This was my experience in the 1970s. If this sounds, in the least, like sour-grapes or that I have disdain for the Dallas Police Department, let me disabuse you of those notions. I have the highest regard for the Dallas Police Department and it's officers past and present; as for the future, that is to be determined.

However a recent issue (April 2012) of the Dallas Police Association's newsletter, The SHIELD, published

a VIEWPOINT article: Does the Department Appreciate Its Most Valuable Resource? by David M. Sullivan #5979, DPD retired [108]who wrote in his last paragraph: "...I am amazed that senior police leaders mostly ignore the extremely dedicated, talented, and knowledgeable police officers so eager to contribute."
Apparently the institutional blindness I observed in the 1960s and 70s has continued.

It was my opinion then and now, in terms of public relations, our supervisors [Deputy Chief R.O. Dixon, excepted!!] should have been falling all over themselves to recognize Tom, John Landers, Truly Holmes and me. But they didn't.

Capt. Don Milliken said, "You'll get your share of the lion's roar." Meaning, I presumed, if we wanted to puff up our chests and roar in the streets, about what we'd all done, we were welcomed to do it.

Though I decided to accept my ephemeral 'share of the lions roar' I was not willing to accept that for my friend and partner Thomas H. Covington Jr.

Although it was my job, as the Division Crime Analyst to have noticed and analyzed the M/O of what became the FBR, it was not Tom's. But to Tom's credit he jumped in with both feet and made his 'job' (Special Projects Officer) conform to my need to make heads and tails out of the enigma that became the three-plus-year saga you have just read.

Of course neither Tom nor I were responsible for any crime analysis outside our Central Patrol Division; we saw a larger need and filled it.

And even though I made the initial identification of the FBR and his M/O, it was not my job to continue to follow up, to investigate and plan his capture. That was something I had to do and could not let go of. Tom took, or had, the same attitude.

We believed that what we saw continuing to happen to Dallas citizens needed to stop. Thanks to Tom and the hours we spent working the FBR case, and the "go-get-'em" nod we received

---

[108] Appendix A Item #10 see roberjsadler.com http://www.dallaspa.org/html/April2012.htm Dallas Police Association The SHIELD, Volume XXXI, No 4, April 2012, page 12 & 13, VIEWPOINT: Does the Department Appreciate Its Most Valuable Resource? by David M. Sullivan #5979, DPD retired.

from Chief Dixon, what we did, that we "weren't supposed to do," much less be able to do, was pretty remarkable.

Tom was a true partner. To say who-did-what is, at this point, almost impossible to separate. At the time, I knew Tom's efforts were indispensable, particularly when I was back in harness. I wanted to ensure that Tom was recognized.

I talked with my friend, one-time patrol partner, and Investigator Truly Holmes and asked him to put in a recommendation for Tom. Truly told me he "wouldn't know how to write it up, but that if I wrote the letter for Tom and included myself, he would sign it and forward it to the Chief," (Chief of Police).

I had spent time in the Army where the art of commendation and award writing was an historic and accomplished skill. Using that experience, I reviewed the requisite parameters for the awarding of the departmental Police Commendation Bar, which, truthfully, our accomplishment fit to a 'T'. I then penned a commendation recommendation for Tom and myself and gave it Truly.

The rest is history.

"Chief Dixon was proud of us," Tom remembered, "we were kind of heroes to him and he was glad we got the 'glory'... that the 'solution' had come out of Central Division, that we did something none of the other guys could do! But, if it had not been for Dixon, we'd have been sunk!"

And if Dixon had learned that I had been the one to pen our commendation letter, he probably would have said three things, perhaps not in this order, *you guys...*, *I should have thought of it myself...* and, *regardless, you guys deserved it!*

Unfortunately Chief Dixon passed away before the first edition of *One Step from Murder: The Friendly Burglar RAPIST* was published. A copy was presented to his widow, Dorothy.

Author Note: *A "Dear Chief" letter usually goes directly to the Chief and does not usually get shortstopped on its way to the Chief's desk. It is also possible (and I would be remiss to not mention) that Truly may have handed off this commendation recommendation for concurrence to his commander, Captain Milliken. Don may have signed-off on this Dear Chief if he was aware of it and or let it proceed without comment. Thus, for my "share of the lion's roar", we may also have Don to thank. So, thanks, Don! Oh, and thanks, Chief Don Byrd.*

Here is that letter:

February 24, 1977

Donald A. Byrd
Chief of Police

SUBJECT: Recommend the Police Commendation Bar be awarded to:
Officers Robert J. Sadler, #2441, and Thomas H. Covington, #2273

Sir:

During a long investigation on downtown BMV's, the Central Patrol Division Crime Analyst Robert J. Sadler and the Special Projects Officer Thomas H. Covington developed a unique M.O. plotting technique which resulted in the arrest and subsequent conviction of J.C. Shannon in October, 1974, an arrest which cleared ninety-six BMV offenses involving nearly a half million dollars in property loss to the victims. In addition to the Shannon case, these officers had been working on the Friendly Burglar Rapes since the first offense on November 15, 1973. As the Friendly Burglar Rapist (FBR) began to increase his activity in the late summer of 1974, Officers Sadler and Covington continued to record and catalogue the movements of the FBR, applying the successful techniques used in the Shannon case.

From the beginning of their investigation of the Friendly Burglar Rapes, Officers Sadler and Covington encouraged and supplied detailed information on the FBR to anyone in the Department who would listen. It became apparent to me that these officers were more knowledgeable about the FBR than any other source in the Department. Their expertise in assembling and analyzing the information they amassed resulted in their accurately predicting the movements of the FBR, and, on numerous occasions, they were able to pinpoint precisely the date, time, and place of his next attack.

This was the situation when their long-standing suggestion to form a large, covert-tactics team came to life the second week of February, 1977. The twenty-two man team was deployed on the specific information produced by Officer Covington from the M.O. plotting techniques developed by Officers Sadler and Covington. Shortly, the FBR suspect (Guy William Marble, Jr.) was caught at 1:10 a.m. on February 14, 1977. This arrest cleared 79 offenses, the majority of which are felonies.

Officers Covington and Sadler have been invaluable to me in this investigation. Clearly, without their knowledgeable assistance the investigative supplements on the collection of offenses referred to as the Friendly Burglar Rapes quite likely would still read, "recommend these offenses remain suspended, pending new leads". Therefore, I heartily recommend these officers be awarded the Police Commendation Bar for their diligent efforts which showed great skill, imagination and devotion to their duty, the Dallas Police Department and the citizens of Dallas.

Respectfully submitted,

Truly M. Holmes

Truly M. Holmes #2521
Investigator
Crimes Against Persons

ftd

Chapter 39

From A Different Perspective

THE FOLLOWING UNSIGNED-undated open-letter/flyer was produced after the arrest of Guy William Marble Jr. Though there are inaccuracies (see note below), the flyer does relate the angst & anger held by some women at the time, particularly "The Kitty Genovese Womens Project" of New York City. Below the scanned copy is a typed portion of the document.

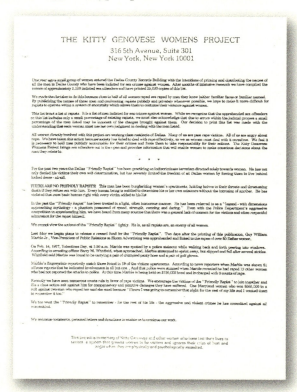

For the past two years the Dallas "Friendly Rapist" has been practicing an indiscriminate terrorism directed solely towards women. He has not only denied his victims their own self-determination, but has severely limited the freedom of all Dallas women by forcing them to live behind locked doors – afraid.

THERE ARE NO FRIENDLY RAPISTS! This man has been burglarizing women's apartments, holding knives to their throats and threatening death if they refuse sex with him. Every human being is entitled to determine his or her own existence without the intrusion of another. He has violated that most basic human right with every victim added to his list.

In the past the "Friendly Rapist" has been treated in a light, often humorous manner. He has been referred to as a "legend- with dimensions approaching mythology – a phantom possessed of speed, strength, cunning and daring." Even with the Police Department's aggressive competition in apprehending him, we have heard from many sources that there was general lack of concern for the victims and often respectful admiration for the rapist himself.

We cannot view the actions of the "Friendly Rapist" lightly. He is, all rapists are, an enemy of all women.

Last May we began plans to release a reward fund for the "Friendly Rapist". Two days after the printing of this publication, Guy William Marble Jr., Vice-President of Public Relations at Bloom Advertising was apprehended and linked to the rapes of over 50 Dallas women.

On Feb. 14, 1977, Valentines Day, at 1:50 a.m. Marble was spotted by a police stake-out while walking back and forth peering into windows. According to arresting officer Barry M. Whitfield, when approached Marble attempted to sprint away, but slipped and fell after several strides. Whitfield said Marble was found to be carrying a pair of crumpled panty hose and a pair of golf gloves.

Marble's fingerprints reportedly match those found in 19 of the victims apartments. According to news reporters when Marble was shown 81 offense reports that he indicated involvement in all but one. And that police were stunned when Marble revealed he had raped 12 other women who had not reported the attacks to police. At this time Marble is being held on $750,000 bond and is charged with 3 counts of rape.

Recently we have seen numerous courts rule in favor of rape victims. We encourage the victims of the "Friendly Rapist" to join together and file a class action suit against him for compensatory and punitive damages they have suffered. One Maryland woman who won $385,000 in a suit against two men who raped her said she sued because "I knew I was going to remember that night for the rest of my life and I wanted them to remember it too."

We too want the "Friendly Rapist" to remember – for the rest of his life – the aggressive and violent crimes he has committed against all womankind.

In addition to the open letter the "WOMENS PROJECT" offered a reward for the FBR. The ad refers to International Womens Day—March 8, 1977. The source of the publication is unknown as the date published. (see below)

The text (on page 459) of the Project's reward notice: The bold letter emphasis is mine and is explained in "Inaccuracies..."

$1,000 REWARD
FRIENDLY RAPIST

The "Friendly Rapist" as he has been referred to by the Dallas Police Department and the local media has been **credited with the rapes of at least fifty [50] women** in the north Dallas area.

He is called "friendly" because his victims report that he speaks in a gentle, friendly manner, despite his threats--and at times he is apologetic about his actions.

He operates in apartment complexes, late at night and in the early morning hours, much like a cat burglar. While burglary is not his primary motive, he does rob his victims.

After gaining entrance through unlocked windows he frequently places a pillow case over the woman's head, ties her to the bed, and threatens to slash her throat if she does not cooperate with him.

On Jul 30, 1976 at 3:30 a.m., he returned to one woman's apartment a second time, arrogantly proclaiming: "Since this is my 50th time, I decided you are going to be twice."

THERE ARE NO FRIENDLY RAPISTS! This man is burglarizing women's apartments, holding knives to their throats and threatening death if they refuse sex with him. He is practicing an indiscriminate terrorism that not only denies h is victims their own self determination, but severely limits the freedom of all women. Every human being is entitled to determine his or her own existence without the intrusion of another. He is violating that most basic human right with every victim added to his list.

Women do not enjoy rape, nor do women enjoy living in fear. The "Friendly Rapist" is, as all rapists are, an enemy to all women. It is for these reasons that we have joined together to offer this $1,000 reward for information leading to his arrest and conviction.

We do not see the prison system as a solution to rape--prisons have evolved into breeding grounds for crime that reinforce the hostile and aggressive behavior in men that is inherent in rape. However we are left with no alternatives--we want his continual violence against women stopped immediately and... [unreadable] ...will accomplish this.

Any person having information concerning him is asked to contact us at our mailing address. For additional information please see REWARD INFORMATION on Page 3.

Inaccuracies re:
Genovese Project Letter
$1,000 Reward Flyer

1) This article/flyer came out after the capture of the FBR. Marble was not "credited", offenses were attributed to him by Tom and me. But more importantly, Marble took credit for the offenses attributed to him, except one... then said he had raped at least a dozen more than the 43 rapes we had attributed to him.

2) He gave himself 'the name' in initial offenses when he said, *"...I'm just a friendly burglar."* His manner was 'friendly' as opposed to the oft-times 'aggressive' behavior of the usual burglar or rapist encountering a resident at home, and some of his victims referred to him as 'friendly'. I had also identified his M.O. at both burglaries and rapes, thus he became: The Friendly Burglar-Rapist. This *nom de guerre* was never, to my knowledge, 'given' to the media—they picked it up from 'cop shop scuttle butt'.

3) There was no reported rape on 7/30/76 that was attributed to the FBR.

4) He did target one location three times and did victimize occupants twice - different victims.

5) On one occasion he did 'print' the number '50' in paint on a canvas a victim was painting... and that victim was actually his fifty-seventh (57th) victim according to our chart and that offense occurred July 8, 1976 and was the FBR's 34th reported and attributed rape.

6) To my knowledge, (then and certainly not contained in any documents I have subsequently reviewed), the FBR never "proclaimed"," arrogantly" or otherwise that "Since this is my 50th time, I decided you are going to be twice," nor anything even close. It is reported (see page 264-5) in a August 29, 1976 interview with Captain Milliken that an FBR 'imitator' made a similar such claim—I have no other reference to confirm the actual claim.

7) At first the flyer gets it right re threats and cooperation, but FBR was never *"threatening death if they refuse sex with him"* he used a knife/sharp object along with these and other life threatening words to intimidate and gain control of is prey.

[**Author's Note:** RE: *DTH "Tracking the 'friendly rapist' The hunters…"*

As a writer I understand 'literary license', which extends its umbrella to cover opinion and fiction but not to the relating of facts or accurate unbiased observation which I was given to understand is the definition of 'reporting'.

However well intended Mr. Henderson's efforts were or how 'informed' his sources, printing or providing incorrect facts does not come with that licensure. The article (the reported story) below has too many inaccuracies, based on my knowledge, to let stand as is. In fact there are more inaccuracies in the DTH article below than I have space to correct, so I have footnoted some of the inconsistent statements with a brief comment and/or refer you to a page elsewhere in the book for clarification.]

The Dallas Times Herald
Sunday Morning, February 20, 1977

Tracking the 'friendly rapist'

<u>The hunters</u>

How unraveling the mystery became obsession for police

By Jim Henderson
Staff Writer

Text of article follows:
(NB.: an exposé with many misinterpretations [rjs]):

To some of the cops who stalked him, he was merely a nuisance, causing them to spend long, idle hours sitting in parked cars or pacing about darkened neighborhoods waiting for a rendezvous that seemed more and more remote as the months passed.

To others he became a preoccupation, if not an obsession, responsible for a mystery whose solution could surely be found in the mounds of paper that had accumulated in his wake.

In the minds of a few, his feats had given him dimensions approaching mythology — a phantom possessed of speed, strength, cunning and daring.

Excerpt: *The Dallas Times Herald*

They knew him only as the "friendly rapist" [109] and while they pursued him without pause for more than two years, he raped, burglarized and assaulted dozens of victims, prowling freely through the labyrinthine complexes of so-called "singles apartments" that spill across large areas of North Dallas.

He may have been responsible when the count is final, for more than 80 crimes, leaving few clues, making few mistakes. Legends have been made of smaller stuff.

---

[109] The suspect, in the series of rapes attributed to Guy William Marble Jr., was variously referred to as "The Friendly Burglar", "Friendly Burglar", "The Friendly Burglar-Rapist" and by the acronym: "FBR".

"Sometimes it would seem that we were after a fictitious person," one police officer would later recall, "someone who was bigger than life"

But to his victims he was real. One jumped through a glass window [110] trying to escape him; another tried to stab him; another accepted the coat he offered after taking her from her apartment into a winter night.[111]

Victim after victim gasped for breath through the pillowcases [112]that covered their faces while he raped them and when he had gone, struggled to free themselves from the lengths of telephone cord that bound their hands.

His string of crimes probably began on a Thursday afternoon in mid-November of 1973. At 2:12p.m. that day, a 23 year-old woman who lived in the Toll House apartments on the northwest of Downtown Dallas off the Dallas North Tollway reported that she had been raped.

From a police standpoint, there was nothing remarkable about the incident. The rapist had not been overly abusive, the woman could provide little information about him and, as the weeks passed, the complainant was pushed aside for pressing matters.

It was pulled back out of the files 212 days later when a 33-year-old legal secretary was sexually assaulted in her Arroyo Place apartment in the same vicinity. That rape bore vague similarities to the previous one. [113]

It took place in the afternoon (4:30)[114], the apartment was entered through a window, possibly one that had been left unlocked, and the assailant politely introduced himself as a burglar. As he left the apartment, he mentioned driving a pickup truck.

---

[110] One complainant (Offense Number 60) did "break out her bedroom window w/ hand causing minor cuts then *crawled down to ground*." Though, the P.E.S. did use the word "jumped" see page 251-253.

[111]rjs: I'm not saying those three things did not happen, that they could not have happened or that someone did not say they happened... however in all the materials I reviewed, over 3.33 years, I never saw or heard anything to corroborate those three events.

[112] Several complainants reportedly "gasped" when they were awakened by their attacker. Exactly two (2) complainants reported at some point during their attack: "I couldn't breathe." or "I can't breathe." See Offense Number 10/R-10 page 95 & Offense Number 15/R14) pages 124-126.

[113] There was nothing vague about the similarities, several FBR MO markers were present in both, in specific "cop jargon". See Pages 8 and 11.

[114] The criminal assault occurred at **4:30 am**... not p.m. (per O/IR 237116-F) See Offense Number 2, Page 57.

See OPEN-DOOR on DTH Page 20
Open-door lifestyle of N. Dallas singles helped rapist
Continued from Page One

Again, the woman could provide little information.

The clues to date: The rapist was about six feet tall, weighed about 160 pounds, spoke with no discernible accent, possibly drove a truck and had type A blood—the latter fact determined from semen tests[115]

And for a rapist, he demonstrated an unusual concern for the welfare of his victims.

"You should be more careful," he told the second one as he bound her hands with tape. "This could happen again."[116]

Within 10 days, two more rapes occurred, but the location had shifted to Northeast Dallas. And for the first time, one occurred in the early morning hours. But the similarities were stronger than the variations.

Again, the intruder, before committing rape, identified himself as a burglar and casually mentioned his pickup truck.

Now the police had two new clues. His fourth victim, at the Emerald Forest Apartments, said she could identify his voice, although he spoke with a neutral kind of "disc Jockey" accent.[117]

Before the end of 1974, six other rapes of similar nature were reported, most of them in North Dallas. [118] After his last assault on Dec. 18 of that year, the rapist took a rest.

The police, at the time, were moving toward a more systematic approach to the case. Rather than assign the cases to various investigators. Capt. Jack Davis, who was in charge of the police division that investigates crimes against persons, decided early in January of 1975 to put one investigator on the rapes full-time.

The job went to Evelyn Crowder, a former airline stewardess who had married a policeman and joined the force herself nine years ago, after her third child was out of infancy. She went from the dispatch office to personnel to the tactical division. Within five years, she was a detective.

---

[115] Unfortunately, these blood/semen tests were faulty and would be faulty for 3.33 years. See Page 432 & 433 *Forensic Evidence - Blood Typing the FBR & Answers*

[116] Actual statement made during the rape, after the victim's hands were bound: "you should be more careful, this could happen to you again." See Offense Number 2, page 57

[117] Nothing in the O/IR, Supplements, or FBR Fact sheet mentions a "disc jockey" reference. In fact the complainant on the fourth FBR case (at Emerald Forest Apts.) gives no description at all of the suspect's voice. Offense Number 4, page 59.

[118] Through the end of 1974 there had ten (10) rapes attributed to the FBR and all of them were be in "North" Dallas. Note: "North" was ubiquitous and expansive term & its definition generally depended on to whom you were speaking and where 'they' lived.

By this time, the label "friendly" was routinely being applied to the rapist by the press and the police, but Mrs. Crowder was not given many clues.[119]

"There was almost nothing to go on," she says. "We had no fingerprints [120] and none of the victims could describe him."

In the weeks before the "friendly rapist" turned up again on March 15, Mrs. Crowder went through the police department's list of former sex offenders and known burglars and questioned dozens of them. Nothing.

She went through names of employees at apartment buildings where rapes had occurred, looking for a common denominator. Nothing.

She held group meetings with victims, probing their backgrounds for any point, however minute, where their paths might have crossed. Nothing.

She checked companies that did business with the apartment complex —carpet cleaners, gardeners, telephone installers, maid services, security patrols -- looking for a name to appear more than once. Nothing.

With the rapist still lying low, she[121] asked that a psychological profile of the man described by many of the victims be compiled by the city's psychological testing service.

Dr. S.S. Somodevilla and investigator Charles Baker[122] interviewed the previous victims individually and held a group session with several of them.

Some of their conclusions: the rapist was middle-class, had some college education, an I.Q. of about 120, was methodical (indicating, some investigators thought, he might be associated with the medical profession), had orthodox sexual tastes and sought out victims from his own social and economic class.

Running counter to that theory were certain other clues the police had collected. Frequently the rapist mentioned owning a pickup truck and at least once was disdainful of "you rich North Dallas girls."[123] But the psychological evaluators saw these as parts of a disguise.

"We were pretty sure that he wanted them to think that he was a poor redneck from a poor part of town," Dr. Somodevilla says "We never did buy that."

---

[119] Tom and I met with Inv. Crowder and immediately offered our 13 months of knowledge on the 10 rapes we had already attributed to the FBR. She eschewed our ideas and never deigned to accept our help for the duration of her assignment to the FBR cases.

[120] First prints lifted were at the scene of Offense Number 3 & 6 see page 58 & 75

[121] Tom initiated the request to Dr. Somodevilla and hand-carried the baseline documents to him for his use.

[122] S.A. Somodevilla, PhD. (not S.S.) & Officer Charles F. Baker, MA See pgs 104-110.

[123] I have been unable to corroborate this statement anywhere in the documents reviewed for this case. However, in Offense Number 10, page 95 the FBR did make this statement to his 30-year-old female victim: "I thought you're one of those rich kids from SMU."

The rapes began again at 5:30a.m. on Saturday, March 15, 1975, at the Willowick Apartments in North Dallas. Two weeks later, he moved back to the Live Oak area in East Dallas near downtown.[124]

Wearing his usual hooded sweatshirt and sneakers, the rapist found an unlocked sliding patio door and surprised the sleeping 25-year-old occupant. This time his manner was less than friendly.

"Don't move," he warned her, "or I'll shoot you. I'm a Dallas police officer." [125]

That possibility sent jitters though the police station and drew other divisions deeper into the investigation. Crime analysts began [126]putting into statistical form details supplied by the research division. The patrol and tactical divisions began making stake-out plans.

Initially, the work produced no new information, but did help eliminate false clues.

The pickup truck was a sham, they concluded after the rapist told one victim, "I'm going to take your stereo and television and put them in my truck," then left without them.

The theory that he was a jogger also was dropped when each new victim confirmed that her assailant, despite wearing a sweatshirt, neither felt nor smelled of perspiration.[127]

Throughout the spring of 1975, the investigation went nowhere.

"Then we got a fingerprint," says Mrs. Crowder, who was beginning to weary of the chase. "I thought we had him for sure."

She fed the print through computers from the courthouse to the FBI office in Washington and waited for the name of a suspect to land on her desk. Nothing.

Based on the rapist's sketchy pattern of attacks, a decision was made to stake-out the Willowick Apartments on Amesbury Avenue, since the rapist had hit there three times previously.

For several nights in July, tactical division officers cruised the area in unmarked cars and occasionally walked through the complex in blue jeans and tennis shoes. Nothing.

---

[124] The referenced offense (Offense Number 12) occurred 2800 Douglas Avenue in the Oak Lawn area of near North Dallas - see Pages 116-123 [Live Oak in East Dallas (at its nearest point) is some 3 miles or 30 blocks away.]

[125] Neither in Offense Number 12 (see Page 116-123) or subsequently; the FBR suspect was never reported to have said: "I'll shoot you."

[126] I had been working on the FBR for 17 months, building graphs, analyzing, cataloging and plotting his moves along with Tom Covington - but no doubt, this case changed everything for everyone, the FBR finally got other people's attention.

[127] FBR's being a jogger was never abandoned by Tom or me. The fact that he spent so much time in a specific area and inside numerous apartments throughout the night only meant it was not likely that he was walking and out jogging for miles, stopping and committing a rape then possibly jogging home... depending on how close he was too his neighborhood. The fact that the FBR neither smelled of sweat or was sweaty only meant that was his condition when with his victims and does not negate his being a jogger or jogging. Also see pages 108, 466, and especially pages 489-490.

Three weeks later the rapist surfaced in another area of North Dallas.

Until August of 1975, 19 of the 21 offenses credited to the "friendly rapist" had been rapes. The other two were attempted rape and criminal trespass. What puzzled the police most at that point was that they had been unable to learn more about him.

That month, Davis was promoted to deputy police chief and transferred out of the crimes against persons division. His successor was Capt. Don Milliken, who had been with the department for 16 years. He didn't like what he had inherited.

He wondered: What kind of man enters third-floor windows with the nearest balcony six or eight feet away? What kind of man rapes women and then lounges around their apartment drinking orange juice and leafing through magazines? What kind of man can rape a woman, linger in her apartment, come face to face with her minutes later and be lucky enough to have picked a victim nearly blind without glasses?

"He was like someone we had known all our lives," Milliken says, "yet we knew nothing about him."

Milliken spent a warm autumn evening strolling through some of the apartment complexes where the crimes had been reported. He wanted to see what the rapist saw while looking for victims, feel what the rapist might have felt.

He discovered that Dallas was not exactly a town that dreaded sundown. He found dozens of windows and patio doors unlocked or partially open; curtains parted to admit the glow of yard lighting. He roamed those areas until nearly dawn and no one thought his presence suspicious.

Answering a call at one of those apartments some time later, a patrolman parked his car a half-block from his destination. In that short distance, he spotted eight unlocked windows.

"The lifestyles in those areas helped him," Milliken says. "Someone had to have seen him prowling around but didn't think that much about it."

The architecture of the apartment buildings helped him, too. They are designed for the illusion of privacy: Narrow breezeways, trees and shrubbery, walls of rock and wrought-iron, rough wood privacy screens around the small patios, paths that circle and wind between the high wall buildings.

Some nights the "friendly rapist" would enter as many as a dozen apartment before selecting a victim. [128] He planned his escapes well often making sure that all exits from an apartment were unlocked before awaking the occupant.

Once, on his way out, he stole a container of trash as a precaution against someone questioning his presence outside the apartment.

---

[128] "Dozen" is speculation. The fact is when asked "just how many places do you go in a night," the FBR replied: "You wouldn't believe me if I told you, but it's a lot." See Page 238, 431 & 526. On page 431 reporter Bill Kenyon says Holmes told him Marble took credit for twelve (12) rapes on in our books. Marble told that to Inv. Landers, but Holmes could have also learned this information later. As far as I know the word "dozen" was not uttered by Holmes, Landers or Marble re: the number of places he entered per night.

On Thursday, Dec. 11, 1975, the "friendly rapist" confronted a 26-year-old woman at Walden Place. In the fashion that rarely varied, he carried out his 24th rape. By then he was also credited with 10 lesser offenses.[129]

It was nearing Christmas and the nights were cold.

He took a 68-day vacation.

In January 1976, investigator Crowder said she wanted off the case. She felt she was growing stale and new ideas were needed.

Also, she needed sleep. Over the months, investigators had called her whenever a rape was reported, which meant a ringing telephone at all hours.

"It's driving me crazy," she told Milliken, who replied:

"The only way you're going to get off of it is if you catch him or if you die." But she didn't catch him and she didn't die. Last July she turned the case over to investigator John Landers, who spent several days reading the files, sent teletypes nationwide in search of similar "MOs" (methods of operation). More fingerprints had been collected. They were rechecked. Nothing.

As Milliken had done, Landers walked through each apartment complex that had been the scene of a rape. No new leads.

But some important changes were beginning in the "friendly rapist's" own behavior

He was being credited with more related offenses than rapes and he had almost abandoned his pattern of occasionally leaving his North and Northeast Dallas turf to strike in Northwest or downtown. He was working almost exclusively in the early mornings and was appearing at the same apartment on several consecutive outings.[130]

At 11:15 pm on July 15, a patrolman on stake-out spotted a man fitting the rapist's description trying to enter a window at the Woodscape Apartments on Meadow Road.[131]

The man jumped to the ground and outran the officer. But he left a tennis shoe print in the moist dirt.

---

[129] The December 11, 1975 rape was the FBR's 34th attributed offense, 24th attributed rape, and on that night/morning at 2am it was a warm 60 degrees with a gulf breeze blowing out of the south. See Offense Number 34, Page 168

[130] 1) Whether the FBR was credited with more related offenses than rapes was always problematic. Tom and I knew early on that he was going into apartments and committing different crimes depending on what or who he found or didn't find. 2) The FBR never abandoned any of his target areas (we still do not know the total of apartments he entered and 'burgled' or where he raped). 3) The FBR had been striking between midnight and 6am for a long time. 4) The only time he 'hit' the same apartment complex consecutively was Offense Number 56 (a meet Complainant - screen removed) on July 6-7 see page 234 and Offense Number 58 (an 'unreported' rape) on July 9, 1976 page 245.

[131] Officer MacArthur was off duty, working as 'security' for his apartment complex and encountered the FBR on his 'security rounds'... there was no stake-out. See page 250.

Two hours later, he attempted to rob an apartment about a mile away.[132]

Throughout the investigation patrolmen Tom Covington and Robert Smoot, working as crime analysts at the central substation [133], started to expand their collection of graphs showing the days, times, and areas in the order of frequency that the rapist had favored.

They met with Landers and tried to refine their method of predicting where the rapist might appear next. The stake-outs still produced no suspects. They did, however result in the capture of other burglars, prowlers and hubcap thieves.

The system was imprecise, mostly because the rapist had avoided any predictable pattern. Covington's system was patterned after one that had been used in October 1975 to catch a man who was operating an auto burglary ring. [134]

Throughout last summer, the "friendly rapist" continued to elude the police and, in the fall, continued to narrow his territory, enabling the crime analysts to refine their predictions. [135]

The police continued their stakeouts. The "friendly rapist" continued to elude them.

Then on Dec. 6, 1976 Landers got his first major break.

A 25-year-old woman at the Kimberly Woods apartments, in the 6400 block of Ridgecrest Avenue, was walking her dog at about 10p.m. when

---

[132] I don't know what offense the reporter is referring to. The next FBR offense occurred contemporaneously with July 7th, but the offense went unreported to police until the Complainant went to DWAR for counseling on July 9, 1976. see page 245. There was no offense 'two hours later" after Offense Number 56.

[133] Special Projects Officer Thomas H. Covington Jr. and Central Division Crime Analyst, Officer Robert J. Sadler, worked out of the Central Patrol Division (Central [downtown Police & Courts Bldg.). It was never considered a 'substation' as were NE, NW, SE, & SW). Officer B.B. Smooth (Bobby Buck Smoot) worked as a Community Relations and Special Projects Officer at Northeast Patrol Division. Nothing 'started' to expand, I started and we maintained and augmented our charts and graphs everyday.

[134] 1) The "system" Tom and I developed, which we simply called our *date, time and day survey* was never based on the FBR's "predictable pattern" or lack thereof, rather we analyzed his offenses to look for patterns then we predicted where we believed he would strike next... and we did. 2) Yes the "system" was developed during our work on the J.C.Shannon case, who was a motor vehicle burglar, committing 90 offenses we tagged him with... but it was never determined to be a "ring", just one burglar plying his nefarious trade.

[135] Based on my review of documents, the FBR neither narrowed nor "continued to narrow" his territory in the summer of 1976. What enabled Tom and I to refine our predictions was that the FBR continued to commit offenses giving us more data with which to work.

she encountered a man wearing a hooded sweatshirts. They exchanged a few words. He seemed nervous and evasive.[136]

At 1:10 a.m., he entered her apartment and raped her.[137]

Although she didn't see his face during the attack, she was able to provide the police with a detailed description of her attacker from having seen him earlier in the evening.

Two nights later, at almost the same hour, the rapist struck again a block away at the Villa Crest apartments. It was the beginning of a pattern, it seemed, that might lead to his capture.[138]

Instead he took his usual Christmas break.[139]

Landers, as Crowder had done, was tiring of the case and its endless disappointments. Once, his stake-out crew spotted an open window that had obviously been forcibly entered. A backup squad was summoned. Inside, they found a drunk who had lost his key.

There were other disappointments. The legend of the "Friendly Rapist" had grown to the point where other rapists tried to imitate his technique. Women reporting rapes sometimes insisted it was "friendly" and when blood test or other data disproved their convictions they were outraged.[140]

Landers was preparing to turn the case over to investigator Truly Holmes when their prey surfaced again after a 26-day layoff.[141]

Oddly he reappeared where he had...

See "WE ONLY' on Page 21
'We only have to trick you once,' suspect told
Continued from Page 20

...last been reported -- in a stretch of apartments along Ridgecrest. Three nights in a row, a man entered women's apartments within a block of each other. The fourth night, the intruder moved less than a mile away

---

[136] Virginia Huston was walking her dog about 10:30pm when she encountered the FBR, he was "startled by the comp and held his head down..." not "nervous or evasive". see Pages 352.

[137] The attempt criminal assault of Virginia Huston occurred at 12:25am and Ms. Huston fended off her attacker. **She WAS NOT RAPED!**

[138] This was a continuation of past behavior not a "beginning of a pattern". It did not "seem" to be to be a "pattern" that "might lead to his capture."

[139] There was no "instead". Tom and I expected him to take his December-January hiatus, he had done it in 1973-74, 1974-75, 1975-76 and now again in 1976-77.

[140] To my or Tom's knowledge not one copycat FBR rape was ever substantiated. See pages: 147, 164, 266, 267, 346, 347, 429. As for "...when blood test or other data disproved their convictions..." the blood/semen test results were wrong! see pgs 431-432.

[141] The FBR's last attributed offense of 1976 was on Dec 19th and his next was Jan 3rd - that time period is 15 days not 26.

but returned to the Ridgecrest neighborhood three weeks later to commit one rape and attempt another.[142]

By the time Holmes took charge of the investigation, the tactical squad had tried various methods of flushing the rapist into an area where they could trap him, of sealing off large areas and patrolling them inconspicuously. None had worked.

By Feb. 7, an area of large apartment complexes bounded by Hemlock Drive on the Northwest, Eastridge on the East, Melody Lane on the South and Ridgecrest on the North was picked for another stake-out.

The plan was to station officers at all exits and, at hourly[145] intervals, have one drive in, park and walk through the area.

Covington was convinced that, if they were to catch the "friendly rapist," it would result from a report of a burglary or a prowler. Rapes took too long in being reported to be of value on a stake-out.

On Feb. 9, three days after the nightly stakeouts began, tactical officer Barry Whitfield, a 28-year-old expert marksman, returned from Florida where he had spent six days competing in a regional pistol match.

Like many others, he had been stalking the rapist for nearly a year and spent a fitful week off the case.

"I kept thinking that if they caught him while I was gone, I would die a slow death," Whitfield recalls.

He was one of those to whom the "friendly rapist" had seemed larger than life.

Whitfield finished second in the expert pistol competitions and immediately rejoined the surveillance team.

On Feb. 12, he was on one of his missions inside the stake-out area when he heard a loud noise, perhaps a howl, coming from the balcony of a nearby apartment. He drew his pistol and jumped to take a vantage point.

The noise had come from two fighting cats.

At 1 a.m., two days later [144]Whitfield left his position on the perimeter of the apartment complexes and drove inside, taking his turn at foot duty. He parked his unmarked car near the leasing office of the

---

[142] Once again Mr. Henderson is unfortunately incorrect on his chronology of events:

Crim.Tresp	Park Lane	Sun	3:00 AM	12.19.76
Prowler	Ridgecrest	Mon	12:12 AM	1.3.77
Crim.Tresp	Ridgecrest	Mon	12:45 AM	1.3.77
Crim.Tresp	Ridgecrest	Mon	3:00 AM	1.3.77
Att.Rape	Southwestern	Tue	5:00 AM	1.4.77
Rape	Melody Lane	Tue	11:30 PM	1.25.77
Att.Rape	Aurelia	Tue	2:35 AM	2.1.77
Apprehended	Ridgecrest	Mon	1:10 AM	2.14.77

[143] Whitfield told Tom: "we changed guys every thirty minutes..." See Page 414-5. You can also read Barry's personal account of that night on page the next page - 473.

[144] Close... it was the second night, first night of 100% deployment - See Page 416.

Seasons, the largest of the complexes in that area. With more than 600 units sitting like a maze on the sloping terrain, it seemed a bad place for a footrace with an athletic rapist.

Ten minutes after getting out of his car, Whitfield saw a mustachioed man in a hooded sweatshirt and blue jeans.

Whitfield yelled to him and the man turned and started to spring away but fell to the ground after a few strides. The officer held him down with one hand, pointing a gun at his head with the other. [145]

"Don't move or I'll blow your head off," he said. [146]

The man on the ground turned his head slowly, looked into the barrel of the pistol and lay quietly. [147]

At last, the police had a suspect: Guy Marble Jr., a public relations executive and a former police reporter.

Two years of tedious, unglamorous and frustrating investigation, forty separate stakeouts, hundreds of hours of interviewing victims had led to this night. [148]

The hunters hoped the chase was at last over.

After questioning the suspect at length, Capt. Milliken expressed it to him this way:

"You can trick us a thousand times, but we only have trick you once."

---

[145] See Pages 473-480.

[146] Officer Whitfield could have said that, but it is not reported in any documents I have, nor was it told as scuttlebutt around the cop-shop that I ever heard. However, in my 6.7.12 interview (page 473-480) with retired Sgt. Whitfield he confirmed he had said something similar, if not those exact words.

[147] The FBR, Guy William Marble Jr.'s own words: "when he rolled me over that ol' boy had that gun right in my face..." "I was just shakin'," Marble said, "I just knew I was gonna die."

[148] Tom and I were not privy to all the actions of various individuals and groups within the DPD. It is possible that various beat officers were assigned 'stakeouts' in their respective areas: Central, NE, & NW, but I was never made aware of them. It is possible that various tactical units were assigned to specific FBR related 'stakeouts' during his 39 month reign of terror, but I was not aware of them, other than the ones Tom organized in February of 1977. I assume Reba Crowder, and I know Landers and Holmes, conducted their own FBR related 'stakeouts', but we were not specifically informed. The ones we do know about are the ones Tom and I conducted together and separately. So, is it possible that '40 separate stakeouts' occurred over those 39 months? More than possible, I would say it was a lot more than 40. And, yes, it would not be an exaggeration to say that there were 'hundreds (over a thousand) of hours of interviews with victims; even more if you count family members, witnesses and potential persons of interest who were also interviewed.

Barry Whitfield's Memories

Tom, Janie Covington and I sat down with
retired DPD Sgt. Barry Whitfield at his home
on the night of June 7, 2012
and asked him to relate his recollections
of the events surrounding his arrest on 2.14.1977
of
Guy William Marble Jr.
aka
The Friendly Burglar Rapist

DAYS BEFORE THE capture of the Friendly Burglar Rapist, Officer Barry M. Whitfield had traveled to Pompano Beach, Florida with the Dallas Police Department pistol team to participate in an NRA sponsored Regional Police Combat Pistol Competition. The team traveled in a motorhome, and the long drive provided no opportunity for the physical fitness regimen that required all Tactical Division officers to routinely jog for miles and perform strength training at a local health club on a regular basis.

Barry told us he was happy to be there, competing for DPD and himself, but one thing concerned him while he was over a thousand miles away from Dallas. He often thought about the Friendly Burglar Rapist. Barry said, "I did not readily advertise it at that time but I was a religious man. I prayed regularly and I prayed for the capture of the FBR." He said, "While in Florida, I remember praying that the FBR would be caught, but if he had not been caught by the time I got back, I prayed that God would give me the strength, the courage and wisdom to catch him..."

"I won second place in the Expert Class. It was my third competition and I fired a Master's level score with my on-duty revolver (the handgun I carried while in uniform). I had chosen not to purchase a custom made 'police combat' pistol and holster, and that made the competition much more difficult." It posed a serious handicap, and I was likely the only competitor who didn't have a competition pistol and holster in the Expert Class. I wanted to be proficient with the tools of my trade, so that's why I elected to compete with my duty weapon. I was very proficient and confident of my skills with a handgun."

"Throughout the time we were gone, and in particular the time we spent on the road in the motorhome, I didn't stretch my legs. For a runner, which I had become since joining the Tactical unit, your body gets used to workouts and "I needed a run." When I got back to Dallas, I picked up my soon to be fiancée, Deborah Hafer, and drove to Spring, Texas to visit my older brother, Jim. During my visit, Jim and I decided to go for a run. So, off we go. At the end of our 3-mile run, my brother decides he's going to beat me home. I wasn't going to let that happen, and I got there first but pulled both calf muscles in the process. I should have stretched".

"Upon our return to Dallas, I had difficulty walking and considered calling in sick, but Deb urged me to go in. Something else spurred me forward. I wanted to apprehend the FBR. By the time I got to work, I found walking tolerable but somewhat painful. The idea of getting out and walking those vast acres of apartment complexes was not appealing. But, I had the feeling that I had to get out, that if I didn't and he did hit, I'd be very upset with myself... so I got out of my unmarked car and entered the apartment complex".

"I was working alone the night of FBR's arrest, since my partner was on vacation leave. The target area that I selected to patrol was several miles square, and the Shadybrook Apts., were within this area. It was like looking for a needle in a haystack, and I had chosen the exact spot where Marble was stalking his next victim. I choose to believe that God had a hand in that".

"I walked gingerly into the interior of the apartment complex. I knew it was time for FBR to hit. Tom Covington had said it was "time for him to hit", in this area and during this time of night. I really wanted to catch this guy. Every officer wanted to catch him and everybody was 'pissed off' about the problem".

"I found a dark shadow next to some shrubs and stood listening and watching, because I could hear about as much as I could see. I typically walked the complexes, but tonight I decided to walk, stop and listen and then move on slowly. Almost immediately, I see a man step into view and walk up the sidewalk—across the plaza from where I stood—looking up at the apartment windows of the upper floors. He walked past me on his way to the end of the building complex, then came back and went to the other end again; each time looking in all directions through the passageways between the buildings. As he walked back and forth, he specifically looked up at the window of a particular apartment".

"At the far end of this line of apartment buildings, and across the plaza from where I stood in deep shadows, he turned a corner and disappeared from view. The man was definitely suspicious, and I thought his clothes fit the general description of the FBR, so I wasn't about to let him get away. I knew if I lost sight of him, I might not catch him in a footrace. Sounds travel strangely among apartment buildings—echoing off the apartment complex walls at night. I had learned this by chasing two vehicle burglars a few weeks earlier. I could hear them running but couldn't tell in which direction. Those suspects escaped and that was very much on my mind".

"I cut across the plaza and started running down the sidewalk on that side and in the direction I had seen him disappear. The entire plaza was illuminated by several domed lights on metal poles adjacent to the sidewalk and on that side a large weeping willow tree stood. The tree cast a dark shadow on the sidewalk and it was from this shadow that I saw the man I thought to be the FBR reappear. I immediately stopped running, and the man walked toward me. I stood quietly under the boughs of the willow, completely concealed in darkness. I wanted to let him get as close as possible before I revealed myself".

Of course like many officers, Barry had seen the FBR likeness in the Patrol Division Analyst Information bulletin and had burned that image into his mind. From the conversations with Tom during his briefings to Tactical and reading the Patrol Officers Handbook on the FBR, Barry said, "I knew our suspect was in good shape, was reputed to be muscular and a runner". It was well known that several officers had gotten in a foot chase with a man they supposed was the FBR and lost the race handily. Barry knew that at one time we thought he might be a professional athlete. Barry also knew that he was known to use a knife, and might have one in his possession. It had never been reported, but it was always possible that he had a gun. So approaching a suspect like that, at night, alone, one who might rabbit, or turn and face you with a weapon were all thoughts racing through his mind as he watched the suspicious man walk toward him. The closer the man got the more he realized this guy fit the general description of the FBR suspect.

Barry said he waited as long as he could.

"The man couldn't see me in the shadows as he walked toward me. I stepped out of the shadows and managed to get a yard or so closer. He was about 7 or 8 yards away. It startled him as he suddenly realized my presence. He turned and quickly began to walk away. I said in as friendly a voice as I could muster, 'Sir, may I ask you a question?' The man, soon to be identified as Guy William Marble, stopped, turned and said, "Sure".

"I stepped toward the man, and while I was watching his hands, I saw he had on blue jeans and a grey hooded sweatshirt (as in the Robinson/Huston drawing and accompanying description)... in my mind I said 'Man, this looks like him'. "Another step closer, and a few feet away I noticed the three stripes on his running shoes (Adidas), and thought, "Man, this really looks like him!" Then, at arm's length, I looked into the face of the Friendly Burglar Rapist. I saw the almond shaped eyes I had seen in the drawing and I thought, "This is the Son of a Bitch!" I knew I had him. He had light brown hair and was the right size and weight. He was wearing the exact same clothing as described. I was wearing plain clothes, jeans, a beer-logo'd T-shirt and a zip-up sweatshirt. I displayed my badge as I stepped closer and announced that I was a Dallas Police Officer. I asked him, 'Can I see your ID'. He said he didn't have identification. I asked, "Do you live here?" 'Yes', he said".

Not at that exact moment, but earlier, many thoughts had occurred to Barry... "I thought about all his rapes, the burglaries, the victims he'd hurt, the families he had affected, the embarrassment to the police department, the FBR's continuing to offend was a slap in the face to the DPD, it was like he was flaunting his crimes in our face... I, like a lot of other officers, took that personally... I wanted to stop him then and there; I did not want to let him get away. At the time of the arrest, Barry said he thought, "I could have reached out and laid hands on him, but I hesitated. I was scared, I was alone, and I didn't know how this guy would react, if he was armed. I tried the radio, to get back-up, but the handie-talkies we had were almost useless, no one knew where I was, nor could they understand where I said I was."

Barry said, "I had been in Tactical for about 4 years, and we took our training seriously and I was in good shape and bigger than the guy in front of me and I figured I could take him one on one... if the foot chase didn't last too long and the guy wasn't as fast as the myth seemed to indicate. What kept alarming me was that we were alone and I didn't want to take the chance that I could be bested one-on-one and thus give him a chance to get away. I tried again to get back-up, but was getting no response on the radio."

I asked him, "What apartment do you live in?" The FBR said, "2011," and offered to take me there to retrieve his ID. The next flash of thought I had was "remembering Tom telling us that it was possible that the FBR had taken trophies or mementos from his various crime scenes, so I thought, if this guy really lives here and takes me to his apartment that would be great, might find evidence to link him to his crimes."

"When the guy turned to lead me to 'his apartment', I noticed a piece of pantyhose protruding from his rear pants pocket." The internal alarm bells that were already ringing just got louder. "I thought, this is him and there is no way I'm going to let him get away!" At that moment the FBR took flight and Barry was prepared to shoot him if necessary.

There is the old bromide about the body's decision in a crisis moment requiring *flight or fight* and that in such moments the brain floods the blood with adrenalin. The flight response had already kicked in for Guy William Marble Jr., he was fleeing for his life. The man running a few steps ahead of Barry was fleeing his impending arrest, the man had failed to ID. That is a misdemeanor and in Barry's mind the man was under arrest from that moment he had failed to produce identification and sought to evade Barry by running. Barry Whitfield was experiencing something unique to police officers, that of the momentary and virtual brain embolism... like the bursting of a blood vessel in the head at the prospect of a suspect or a prisoner escaping arrest or your custody... and the immediate even more dire thought, that the suspect or prisoner might get away!

To counter this, Barry's *fight and flight* response instantly kicked in and he gave chase. The funny and amazing thing about adrenaline; it seems to both block pain and add strength to the big muscles in the body. Barry's calves, that were moments ago, burning and aching causing him to almost hobble along rather than walk naturally, now were powering him forward painlessly.

The two men were racing through the darkened sidewalks and breezeways. Barry said, "I was close enough to tackle him, but didn't because I didn't want to miss! If I missed him, he might get away!" After they had run some hundred yards, the fleeing man was just steps ahead. Barry said his main thought was, "He is NOT gonna escape!"

Barry continued, "We ran some distance and descended a short flight of stairs. While descending the stairs, I pulled my pistol (a Walther .380 caliber semiautomatic) and yelled, "Stop or I'll shoot!" The FBR was about 5-yards away at this point and running at top speed. I lined my sights on center of his back. He heard my command and turned his head to see what I was doing. He hit a small a pile of dirt and stumbled over it. It was at that very moment I was about to pull the trigger. He went down hard enough for the dirt to fly "like a cartoon character bitin' the dust". It saved his life. I can still remember my sight picture between his shoulder blades". I wouldn't have missed."

"He was lying on his belly," Barry said. "I ran over and put my foot on his back. He was reaching into the pouch pocket of his sweatshirt. I commanded him, in no uncertain terms, 'put your hands where can see'm!' But he didn't, instead he stuck his hand under him and into the pouch of his sweatshirt."

Untold things go through your mind as a police officer making arrest. Is it legal, do all the elements of the crime or offense exist, what is happening around you, is the suspect alone, are there accomplices, and if it's an undercover arrest will some citizen think I'm the bad guy, does he have a gun... "I don't know if he had a gun, no one's ever said he did, but he could! Could he have a knife, he's known to use one. Armed is armed... knife or gun. What does he have in that pouch? Why won't he do as what he's been told, why is he sticking his hands in his the sweatshirt's pouch pocket?"

Barry continued, "I pressed my foot down on his back, making certain I didn't lose my balance. I was pointing my gun at my potentially armed suspect's head... and again said, 'Get your hands where I can see'm'. The man continued to squirm, I don't know why or what he was doing or why he wouldn't show his hands? My gun was a double action semi- automatic, I didn't need to cock the hammer, but I did... for effect... I pointed the muzzle of the gun at the back of Marble's head and cocked the hammer back and shouted for the last time for the man to show his hands. This time Marble turned his head and looked back over his shoulder to see the gun pointed at his head. when he saw me cock the hammer he shot his arms out straight in front of him..."

Barry told me, "Marble doesn't understand how close to dying he came that night. I didn't know if he was armed or not, he wouldn't obey my commands to show his hands... I came very close to pulling the trigger." Marble had the golf gloves he used on a number of offenses in his pouch pocket. He was trying to dispose of evidence. He was not armed.

Later Marble said, about Barry, to one of the officers standing around, "I knew he was scared, I felt his foot shaking on my back. Barry later responded, "If he had any idea how scared I was, he would have laid there like a stone!"

Given the circumstances, it was close, but Barry would have been justified. If Barry had seen anything that looked like a weapon in Marble's hands, or Marble had made any additional threatening moves he would have most likely died...

The main reason I didn't shoot him Barry said, "I didn't *want* to kill him. I had no desire to kill anyone, but I would have killed him if necessary. Moreover, he had a kind of mystical quality. I wanted to know why we couldn't catch him, how he had done what he had done, that he'd gone so long without getting caught, had done so much to hurt so many and we all wanted to know why and how."

As Barry explained his mental questions, I realized Barry was where I was in that moment next to the body of The Creeper in October 1973... wanting answers to questions I knew being in patrol was not going to provide. Wanting answers to those questions patrolmen don't usually get, was one motivation that stayed Barry's hand.

After Barry's fellow Tactical Officers arrived at the scene of the arrest, Investigator Truly Holmes responded, and they transported Marble to 2014 Main Street for processing. Barry described the event as follows, "Shortly after the arrest, we were walking from the basement of 2014 Main St. to the Crimes Against Persons (CAPERS) office, Marble looked at Barry's T-shirt and said, "I can't believe an officer wearing a Shiner Beer T-shirt arrested me. 'You could have a least had the decency to wear a Coors T-shirt!' I thought at the time, this guy came close to meeting his Maker and now he's quipping about my T-shirt. What an arrogant bastard."

[Note: To commemorate this moment, when Tom attended the dinner hosted by Police Community Awards Committee, via the Underwriters Association at the Fairmont Hotel as part of Barry's Officer of The Month recognition, Tom brought a special gift. From Tom, Barry received, in pillow case tied with a length of telephone cord, and containing a six pack of Coors beer.]

As Investigator Truly Homes and Barry were writing Marble's arrest report in the CAPERS office, Marble sat handcuffed next to Barry. Barry looked up to see a DPD Sergeant he knew, standing in the doorway. The Sergeant said, "Is that him?" Barry said, "Yeah, that's the Friendly Burglar Rapist."

Truly Holmes looked up, quickly got Barry's attention and said, "Why don't you take him into the interview room. I need to talk to... (Sgt. HB)." Barry escorted Marble to the interview room, and it wasn't until years later that Barry found out that Sgt. HB's daughter had been one of Marble's rape victims.

Det. Holmes talked to HB for some length of time that evening, and it is not known what was said, but what is clear, HB was there for a reason, a reason only he can explain."

I want to reiterate the first words Barry spoke when he began his recollection of this arrest and to finish the conclusion of Barry's comment that I left dangling by an ellipsis.

Barry began: "I did not readily advertise it at that time but I was a religious man. I prayed regularly and I prayed for the capture of the FBR." He said, "While in Florida, I remember praying that the FBR would be caught, but if he had not been caught by the time I got back, I prayed that God would give me the strength, the courage and wisdom to catch him, and I believe that prayer was answered."

In my opinion, Barry was right. God answered a lot of prayers that St. Valentines' Day morning!

Finding A Reason For Charges
Burglary of Habitat W Intent to Rape vs Aggravated Rape

As much as I knew then and know now (in 2016) about the investigation, crime analysis, arrest and prosecution of Guy William Marble Jr for the Friendly Burglar Rapist crimes, there are and have been holes in my knowledge.

For example there are (in my mind) unresolved issues about how Marble was charged, how the charges were changed, to what Marble pled guilty and exactly what his sentence was.

From newspaper reports, Dallas County records, court records and those of the Texas Department of Corrections there is little consistency. Rather than re-state these 'discrepancies' (some mentioned in Chapter 40 below), which will only muddy the water (now in 2016), let me state the relevant facts.

Marble was arrested on February 14, 1977. He was jailed and subsequently pled guilty to multiple charges of *Burglary of a Habitation at Night with the Intent to commit a Felony, to wit: rape.* Marble went to prison and was released on May 26th 1998.

In previous internet searches for relevant articles on Marble I apparently missed this one published in Texas Monthly magazine in May of 1977. This article establishes, assuming the writer's facts are correct, the most cogent reasoning for the changes in the FBR's charges that I have heard/read.

TEXAS MONTHLY Article May 1977

Friendly Burglar?

It looks as though the suspect police believe to be Dallas' "friendly rapist" won't be tried for rape after all. Instead he will go on trial for burglary—yet another example of the flexibility (some would say "vagaries") of the new Texas Penal Code.

Guy William Marble, Jr., 29-year-old public relations executive reputed to be responsible for some forty rapes in the North Dallas area during the past three years, was initially charged with three counts of aggravated rape after his arrest in mid-February. When the case went to the grand jury, prosecutors asked that the indictments be switched to burglary of a habitation with intent to commit a felony.

Their reasoning was this: the Penal Code delineates two kinds of rape—aggravated rape, which involves a direct threat of death or serious bodily injury with a deadly weapon, and simple rape, which does not. Aggravated rape carries a maximum sentence of life; simple rape, just twenty years. Prosecutors were worried that they might not be able to make a charge of aggravated rape stand up in court. For one thing, the nickname "friendly rapist," though something of an anomaly, might lead a jury to question whether Marble threatened his victims with a deadly weapon. And even though Marble is alleged to have displayed a knife during some of the rapes with which he is charged, it might be difficult to prove that he presented it in a threatening manner.

Rather than run the risk of having the crime reduced by a jury, prosecutors elected to change the indictment to burglary of a habitation with intent to commit another felony—which, like aggravated rape, also carries a maximum sentence of life. But prosecutors have an easier burden of proof to meet: whether Marble used a weapon in a threatening manner is no longer at issue. All they have to show is that he illegally entered a residence with intent to commit another felony (in this case, rape).

J.A.

"Friendly" label won't help Marble in burglary trials.

Dallas Times Herald

Chapter 40

Marble Pre-release Article: May 25, 1998

Though there were a number of factual discrepancies, an Associated Press article appeared in the Monday, May 25, 1998 *Lubbock On Line State, A Service of The Lubbock Avalanche-Journal.*

NB: Discrepancy: According to Dallas County court records: Guy William Marble Jr., was initially charged with one count of Aggravated Rape and three counts of Burglary of a Habitat; in fact, in each of the cases, for which he was charged, the offense committed was aggravated rape. After almost nine months of legal maneuvering by his court-appointed defense team, Marble, Jr., pled guilty before the court on four counts of Burglary of a Habitat on November 29, 1977 and was sentenced that day on each count to 60 months (5 years) imprisonment in a State Penitentiary.[149] It would appear (I don't have the answer) that the Aggravated Rape charge was changed to Burglary of a Habitat to induce Marble to plead out. These four sentences began as of his arrest on February 14, 1977. If these sentences had run (or been served) concurrently (at the same time), which often happens, he would have been eligible for release in approximately five years from 2/14/77 or February 1982. If these four, five year sentences ran consecutively (one after the other) and he served them out, his release date would be sometime after 1997. However, records obtained from the Texas Conviction Database reports Marble (State ID: 02306027) as being convicted of burglary: "BURG-HAB-WITH INT TO RAPE 7 CTS" with court order confinement "60 YEARS", court provision literal: "CONC EACH COUNT".[150] [CONC is taken to mean concurrently] In order for Marble's release to occur twenty years after his arrest/conviction (approximately February 1998) one of two scenarios must have occurred. One, he served an aggregate of twenty years for his four, five your sentences and did his full time. Or two, he did twenty years, one-third of his sixty 60 year sentence for the seven counts he served concurrently, which the AP article states as the case. Along with an "unconditional release". The fact remains Marble was released Tuesday, May 26, 1998.

---

[149] Appendix A Item #9 Search Results for GWM Dallas Co. Criminal Background Search Dallas County, Dallas Texas 2009 (See page 560)

[150] Appendix A Item #2 (See page 541)

Here is that Associated Press article (dateline Dallas):

Last modified at 12:48 a.m. on Monday, May 25, 1998

`Friendly rapist' to be released after 20 years behind bars

DALLAS (AP) - Guy Marble, who was dubbed the "Friendly Rapist" in Dallas in the 1970s because of his habit of chatting with his victims, becomes a free man again this week.

The 51-year-old former Dallas advertising executive by day and sexual predator by night will be handed $100 walking money and an unconditional release from prison on Tuesday. He says he's a new man and that no one has anything to fear from him.

"I'm just an old man with a bad back who is looking for a few years of peace and contentment," he responded to written questions by The Dallas Morning News.

"I stopped being a threat to anyone a long, long time ago," Marble wrote from a pre-release center in Overton, 18 miles east of Tyler.

"There's nothing `friendly' about it when you're tied up, blindfolded, with a knife in your throat, and raped," one victim, now 51, said of Marble's attack on her in 1976. "He's still a hated person as far as I'm concerned."

"The fact that I am very sorry for the hurt I inflicted on those people is probably not of any consequence to them and their families. That's understandable," Marble said.

A stake-out arrest in early 1977 ended a two-year hunt for the "Friendly Rapist," who was blamed for about 50 attacks, mostly at apartments in the Greenville Avenue area about five miles northeast of downtown Dallas.

When the crimes occurred, Marble was an athletic, 29-year-old family man and a vice president with the Bloom Advertising Agency, with accounts including the Southern Baptist Convention. He was also an alumnus and poker-playing buddy of the local press corps, having worked at a variety of small newspapers.

At the time, rape carried a lesser sentence than burglary, so prosecutors picked the seven strongest cases and **charged Marble with burglary with intent to commit rape**.

According to police lore, a detective linked Marble to the rapes based upon a look at the suspect's hands: an unusual fingerprint loop matched the crime scene evidence. Marble accepted a prosecution offer to plead guilty and take a **60-year prison sentence.**

Having served a third of the sentence, he's eligible for release.

For 12 of his 20 years behind bars, Marble edited and largely wrote The Echo, the 160,000-circulation monthly newspaper of the Texas prison system.

Prison life began with a variety of menial assignments, including chopping wood.

In 1979, a Houston court granted the uncontested divorce petition filed by his wife of nine years, who, since remarried, declined to comment.

In 1985, Mr. Marble was transferred to The Walls, the Huntsville prison unit where he was named editor of The Echo. As such, he was one of the few prisoners with his own office, which he outfitted with donated computers and software.

From his cell and office, Marble culled articles from outside newspapers and reported on criminal justice and prison issues. Under a pen name, he started "Dear Darby," an advice column for prisoners. He wrote fiction and stayed in contact with various literary journals and publications.

In a letter to *Texas Lawyer*, Marble criticized a state Supreme Court justice this way: "As Gustav Flaubert wrote, `Our ignorance of history causes us to slander our own times.' "

While that sort of elevated discourse may have preserved Marble's self-esteem, it did nothing to endear him to wardens and guards, prison spokesman David Nunnelee said.

"They thought he was kind of uppity. He thought he was better than other prisoners," said Nunnelee, who worked with Marble because the prison public affairs office oversees production of The Echo.

The native of Galena Park near Houston said years of voluntary counseling showed him **he could blame the rapes, in part, on people who failed to identify and address his youthful deviance**.

Nunnelee expressed surprise at Marble's claim that he had undergone "hundreds" of hours of counseling. He said Marble was not involved in any group or individual sessions during the last dozen years, when they worked together.

Marble was married twice while in prison.

In September 1987, records show, Marble married a Houston church worker in a ceremony during which he was represented by a stand-in, or proxy, before a Harris County justice of the peace.

The marriage was annulled with Marble's consent in December 1989. Marble, the woman and the proxy all declined to discuss the circumstances.

Marble married again in **January 1996**, using a Huntsville courthouse bailiff—since elected sheriff —as proxy. **His bride** was **Dominique Malon**, a **French journalist** who met Marble during a tour of the prison by Amnesty International. She's said she'll be in East Texas on Tuesday for his release.

Like all married couples under prison rules, they have been allowed only non-conjugal visits, with physical contact limited to hand holding and public embraces.

In his recent letter to the newspaper, Marble was guarded about his plans.

"Self-employment is the most likely scenario. When it's time, I can support myself with computer skills and writing. Exactly where I will settle is uncertain right now, **but far away from Texas is a safe bet,"** he wrote.

Author Note: *The sad thing about Marble's prosecution and changing charges from Aggravated Rape to Burglary of a Habitation at Night with Intent to commit a Felony, i.e. Rape is not that the case was now easier to prosecute with the same range of punishment. It is not even that they let him pled to only a handful of offense netting him a 60 years sentence for each. No what is sad is that he should have gotten life and failing that his plea deal should have been for these sentence to run consecutively (one after the other) instead of concurrently (served at the same time). Running concurrently as they did meant, with good-time, he would be out of the penitentiary after 20 years unless he managed to be granted a parole.*

Other Dallas Serial Rapists

'Named' serial rapists were not new to Dallas. As mentioned on page 82 there was *the Phantom Rapist* in the 1940s and Jim Bryan remembered hunting for *The Oaklawn Rapist* in the sixties. Lester T. Page recalled that after Marble, *The Friendly Burglar Rapist,* other 'named' serial rapists emerged (though for shorter periods and with fewer victims than the FBR) such as: *the Potbellied Rapist, the Polaroid Rapist, the Mountain Man Rapist, the North Dallas Preacher Rapist, the Ski Mask Rapist* and *the Village Rapist.*

I don't know if this rapist ever achieved named status, but Scotty Holt related: "We had a serial rapist in the 120's back in the day. We noticed after each rape a man fitting the suspect's description was seen circling the area on a bike watching the cops. He'd flee from sight before anyone found him. About the 5th or 6th rape I spotted him at Gilbert & Oaklawn. The whole sector showed up and had a nice talk with him. He wasn't wanted, so we gave him a good chewing out. I pointed out it was illegal to ride a bike at night without lights & reflectors. He was shaking in his boots, I think from some kind words from Boland & Maselli. So he started pushing his bike in the street. I put him in jail for 'pedestrian in the roadway' and put his bike in the pound. We checked the bike later and it had been taken in a burglary. He pled out to all the rapes and got life."

The FBR & The Internet

I FOUND A good bit of 'old' information about the FBR/ GWM Jr and a smattering of info on his wife (as of his 1998 release) Dominique Malon. Here are just three links. The first two have to do with 'thin' public records:

http://home.comcast.net/~lmarble77/unlinked/ps63/ps63_049.htm

http://home.comcast.net/~lmarble77/unlinked/wc43/wc43_124.htm

The third link:

A&E website
http://community.aetv.com/service/displayDiscussionThreads.kickAction?
as=119137&w=278284&d=662052

The above A&E website link replays word-for-word the previous link-cited May 25, 1998 pre-release article. Since this article was posted "on the web", readers often can and will post their own comments in response on "discussion boards" providing some insight into the feelings of readers of the article. Below are their responses:

Discussion

> Mr. Friendly Rapist - Part 1/3, Part 2/3, Part 3/3
> In *SUDDEN TERROR*, Mr. Crompton wrote about some other rapists that were also active during Mr. EAR's reign... he made a reference to a rapist in Texas known as *THE FRIENDLY RAPIST*, who was caught back in 1977.... and then released from prison in May of 1998...

here's the article about his release: `Friendly rapist' to be released after 20 years behind bars*

Author Note: *I have deleted the redundant article which appeared as: Part 1/3, Part 2/3, Part 3/3*

Recent Replies

THERE ARE NO FRIENDLY RAPISTS
Stupid for him to ever be called that.

The Friendly Rapist/STEP FATHER?
What kind of a stupid woman would marry that guy and what kind of a horrible mother would subject her children to him. Disgusting!

Re: Mr. Friendly Rapist - Part 1/3
"The native of Galena Park near Houston said years of voluntary counseling showed him he could blame the rapes, in part, on people who failed to identify and address his youthful deviance." *That's nice. Why is it always someone else's fault? Chances are......he'll offend again.*

Makes you wonder if it will ever change...
The laws have to be made so that these criminals remain behind bars. I suppose that will only happen when the legislators, senators etc. all are victims of rape. Sounds harsh but what is the saying. Nothing changes until it happens to one of them.

Guy William Marble Jr
Soccer Player - Sprinter - Jogger

I RECENTLY FOUND an online posting from "Find's Treasure Forums" posted on December 31, 2006 at 12:00AM. I am unable to contact the 'poster' so I will not use his name and only paraphrase his posting.

The gist of this gentleman's post is that he was 20-something in the late 1970s and liked to play softball and soccer after work and weekends on various city leagues. He talked about having a team member from Houston named Guy Marble. One of the other team members was a 30-something who had been 9.4 college sprinter with whom they tried to keep up with during after practice wind-sprints. He indicated that Marble was a close second to the real-deal sprinter.

The man also related that **Marble would ask** one of his friends on the team, before practice ended, to cover for him should his wife call to find out if he was there or perhaps on his way home, that he **(Marble) had** some **business to take care of.** The takeaway was that they thought perhaps 'Marble was cheating on his attractive wife'.

The poster said he was aware of the news stories about a rapist in the area where he had his apartment, that man was being called the friendly rapist. He also related that he had heard that police or an apartment resident[151] had almost caught the guy a couple of times, but he was **"too fleet afoot"** and **he wore a hooded sweatshirt.**

One night the poster's soccer buddy called to tell him to watch the 10 o'clock news that **the friendly rapist had been captured and it was their soccer teammate Guy Marble Jr.**

This anecdotal story supports the facts we believed were true: that Marble was a runner and a soccer player. My guess is that the poster was also familiar with Marble's wearing of a hooded sweatshirt. What we had never heard was that Marble used others to shield his extra-extra curricular activities from his wife, it is unknown that these cover-story requests to friends included times when Marble was also committing crimes. The question then is… how many others did he use to cover for his time away from home?

These cover-stories might suffice for 2-3 hours after practice. For example if the team practiced from say 6pm to 8pm then Marble might logically be 'covered' from 8pm to perhaps 11pm. But, obviously, those type of alibis won't cover his middle of the night forays into north Dallas apartments to commit burglary and rape. What, then, were his excuses for being out almost all night?

---

[151] see "Almost...Act One" page 250, & "Almost... Act Two", Mike Virginia's story of chasing the FBR, page 259.

Author's Note: Given the number of details herein, of which the general public were not aware, I believe this post is true.

America's Most Prolific
Serial Rapists

Guy William Marble Jr. wm 30 [3+year spree] 1973-1977
82 Offense/Incidents Attributed to the FBR:

42 Rapes (*plus one unreported was 'reported' = 43*)
12 Rapes (Marble "copped" to 12 not attributed in our 82)
6 Attempt Rapes
5 Robberies
9 Burglaries
2 Attempt Burglaries
7 Criminal Trespasses
7 Criminal Mischief's
3 Prowlers
1 Meet Complainant

Marble's total (*82 attributed + 1 unreported + 12 additional rapes*) = **95**

1) **Jon Barry Simonis** wm 31 [3yr spree]
Gadsden Times – Jan 15, 1982 [received 21 life sentences on rape convictions] reportedly completed 55 rapes along with 30-35 other sexual assaults in 12 different states.

2) **Dr. Edward Franklin Jackson, Jr**. bm 38 [4yr spree] 1975-1978 faces: 36 counts rape, 46 agg burglary (other charges total of 94 counts) Sarasota Herald-Tribune Sep 23, 1982 Columbus, Ohio (AP)

3) **Sacramento Rapist** (see **Ex-Cop Arrested*** – claimed to be linked with 72 rapes before he was linked to an attempted murder)

Rape, Rapists & Murder

The **East Area Rapist*** (EAR) is unofficially linked to approximately fifty (50) assault offenses which include rapes in the Sacramento and Contra Costa Counties during the period from June 1976 to July 1979.

An additional ten (10) offenses are supposedly linked to the EAR through DNA, that occurred in southern California during the period of 1979 through 1986. These ten southern California murder cases (which included four rapes) had a suspect who was named The Original Night Stalker (ONS).

Some of the EAR fifty attributed cases were not completed rapes. From the newspaper accounts and internet information I have been able to review it would be reasonable to put the number of actual rapes attributed to EAR/ONS at forty-eight (48) completed rapes.

If one individual is responsible for the EAR and the ONS offenses his MO evolved significantly from one-on-one rapes (at the scene of his adjunct burglaries) to intentionally encountering couples (disabling the man and raping the woman) to full-on murder.

In an April 4, 2001 article in the San Francisco Chronicle, Staff Writers: Erin Hallissy and Charlie Goodyear, say that in January the Orange County Crime Lab matched the DNA profile of the East Area Rapist with that of the still unidentified murderer known as the Original Night Stalker.

2018 UPDATE: Ex-Cop Arrested

*Joseph James DeAngelo Jr. wm 72 - [12 year spree 1974-86] said to be responsible for 12 Murders and 51 rapes (possibly more) when he would have been between 28-40 years old.

Ex-police officer, **Joseph James DeAngelo Jr., was arrested Wednesday, April 25, 2018** at his Citrus Heights home. He is accused of being a burglar, rapist and murderer. DeAngelo was a police officer from 1973 to 1976 in Exeter (near Visalia, in the lower central valley between but closer to Fresno and than Bakersfield). Then from 1976 to 1979 he was an police officer with the town of Auburn, 30 miles northeast of Sacramento.

The Sacramento Bee reported, April 25, 2018, "The East Area Rapist is believed to have raped 37 people in the Sacramento area and Central Valley between 1976 and 1978."

Via DNA evidence, from decades old crimes, matched familial DNA in public databases that linked and led to the arrest of DeAngelo, 72, of Citrus Heights, California. DNA links DeAngelo to serial crimes attributed to the "East Area Rapist," southern California's "Golden State Killer," the "Original Night Stalker," and the "Visalia Ransacker".

[Coincidentally, from 1992-95 I lived in Citrus Heights, not far from DeAngelo's home.]

Chapter 41

Unsung Heroes

OF THEIR DAY-to-day efforts to capture the FBR, the work that many unsung heroes did within their own divisions, I am not personally familiar. I am sure that they contributed in many and similar ways that Tom and I did and got virtually no recognition for those efforts.

Let me publicly acknowledge and thank Northeast Division Crime Analyst, Officer D.A. Zasimowich and Northwest Division Analyst, Officer P.G. Maroney. I do know that they cooperated with Tom and me at every turn.

I am much more familiar with the contributions of Officer Bobby Buck Smoot. Though working as a Community Relations Officer & Northeast Division Special Projects Officer, he was always about solving crimes and catching hooks. He worked hand and glove with Tom and me. More particularly, working with Tom as I was returned to the field in early 1977.

To these three gentlemen (more unsung heroes) go my and Tom's heartfelt thanks.

The Author's Partner:
Thomas Harvey Covington, Jr.

ALTHOUGH I FIRST tumbled to the MO of the FBR and began tracking him, I must again emphasize, it was not long before Tom joined me in our investigative and analytical odyssey... **And most importantly,** after I was shunted back to patrol in January 1977, leaving Tom alone to carry forward with what had been our day-to-day mission, **Tom kept the fire burning. He created the opportunity to finally close the loop around the FBR's activities. I may have 'started this' but it was Tom who 'finished it'!**

Even after Marble's arrest Tom solved the enigma & fiasco with the blood tests (see pages 431 & 432). There should have been front page newspaper headlines:

COVINGTON SAVES D.A.'S & DPD'S ASS
IN FBR CASE UNCOVERING COUNTY BLOOD LAB BLUNDERS

About my partner Tom, *I* can't say enough. However there was and is much more to Tom than our three-plus-year partnership, trying to catch the FBR. Here is just a sample:

As Scoutmaster, he was given the Silver Beaver award which is the highest award for an adult. Tom joined Cub Scouts in 1945 and remains today as Scouting Coordinator for Kirkwood United Methodist Church in Irving, TX. While Tom was Scoutmaster (and a DPD officer), the Scout Troop earned 29 Fifty Miler Awards, 23 Historic Trails Awards and produced ten Eagle Scouts.

While serving on the DPD as a Crime Analyst, he was awarded Outstanding Officer of the Year by the Dallas Police Community Awards Committee.

He was awarded the Runner-up to Officer of the year by the Friends of Dallas Police.[152]

The Wynnewood Lions Club awarded him a Melvin Jones Award for service above reproach. According to the Lions Club website: "The Melvin Jones Fellow Award is the highest Award of the Lions Clubs International Foundation (LCIF)."

The Dalcliff Wynnewood Lions Club recently awarded him the Jack Wiech Award, making Tom a Life Member of the Texas Children's Camp in Kerrville, TX.

For 34 years, Tom portrayed one of the disciples in a Last Supper Tableau called "Master, Is It I?" Tom first was Andrew, then took the part of Judas for the last seven years. He never missed a performance as the group traveled across Texas and Oklahoma, doing a minimum of five performances each year (that's over 170 performances).

A Personal Special Thanks To

---

[152] See Appendix A Item #8 for full text of Tom's recommendation letter from Sgt. Abney see page 555-559.

The twenty-one investigators who were assigned to individual FBR and related cases, chief among these being CID investigators: Crowder, Landers, and Holmes.[153]

The efforts of the two P.E.S. shift commanders: Lieutenant's Knight and Day, aided by their Physical Evidence Section Investigators, nineteen (19) of whom are documented on various Supplement Reports regarding the fingerprints and other physical evidence gathered at FBR crime scenes are to be lauded for their inestimable and important role in capturing the FBR.[154]

Without question, many in the Dallas Police Department (sworn & non-sworn) had dedicated hours to the capture of the FBR. It is all the patrol officers who worked to catch the FBR I wish to laud unquestioningly. And thank you so much to the seventy-one officers (71) who actually responded to calls from FBR complainants, taking their statements, and forwarding their observations to investigators & analysts for our consideration.[155]

Other unsung heroes were Officers Beene with his K9, Thor and Officer Dooley who, with his K9 partner, provided invaluably to the end result; nailing down the confession of Guy William Marble Jr.[156]

Lastly, though not unsung, witness Virginia Huston, artist Robinson and Officer Whitfield were so integral to the FBR's capture that their efforts and action require our continued thanks.

Kennedy Assassination - Watergate
Operation Analysis Section of Planning & Research
Public Information Office (PIO)

I am somewhat baffled, even looking back after all these years, at how disconnected we were; P&R's Operation Analysis Section and the five Division Crime Analysts. Let me take you back.

In 1971-72 I was one of a six-person team known as the PIO, the Public Information Office. Our staff consisted of three

---

153 See Appendix C, page 566

154 See Appendix C, page 567-

155 See Appendix C, page 568-

156 See Appendix C, page 571-

civilian positions: **Director Bobby Gene Shaw[157],** Assistant Director **Ed B. Spencer,** our Administrative Assistant **Kay Tate** and three sworn personnel: Officer **John T. Waterson,** Officer **David N. Beidelman** and myself. I had known Bob from years before in Tulsa. David and I had worked the streets together and had been roommates before I went into the Army. Tim became a fast-friend and brought me into the game of golf. And Ed Spencer[158] and I had gone to high school together.

Together, under Bob Shaw's stalwart direction, and answering only to the Chief of Police, we coordinated the public interface with the police department. We credentialed the media, set media contact guidelines, liaised with local, state and national media, arranged and coordinated press conferences, put out the weekly house-organ the DPN (The Dallas Police News - Ed was Editor); were the staff photographers and reporters for the DPN as well as producing the department's annual report brochure; produced and hosted a weekly television program, and shot film for various uses. Our primary purpose was to get out the Chief's message to the public and field all calls for public information whether from the public or from the media, and be the spokesperson/s for major police related or involved events.

Bob was privy to all manner of police related events during his tenure... even The Kennedy Assassination and Watergate. No, he was not in Dallas in 1963, he was in Tulsa working at KVOO TV. But ten years later in 1973 his name was woven into one conspiracist's theory.[159]

During the majority of this time we worked out of the same suite of offices as the Chief of Police. Our office common area passed through to another common area that housed the Planning & Research Division, where Lt. Macsas' Operation Analysis Section maintained its offices.

---

[157] In the 1960s Bob Shaw had been the Sports Director at KVOO TV in Tulsa, Oklahoma, His boss had been my father, Bill Sadler, who was then the station's Executive Producer. Now Bob was *my* boss! Sadly, my friend Bobby Gene Shaw passed away at the age of 85 on Father's Day, Sunday, June 21, 2015.

[158] Following Bob Shaw's retirement from DPD, Ed became the PIO's Director. Ed retired after 20 years with the DPD and took the PIO job for the Dallas County Sheriff's Office following the retirement of our our good friend and former DMN reporter Jim Ewell who had been the PIO for Sheriff Don Byrd (former DPD Chief of Police).

[159] http://ajweberman.com/noduleX24-THE%20TRAMP%20SHOTS.htm

As one of the department's PIOs I often had to obtain information from the Operation Analysis Section (OAS). As mentioned earlier I took the in-office photos for the DPD Annual Report in which the Analysis Section[160] was featured. So, given the many occasions I had to interact with their staff, I developed what I thought were good, solid, and friendly relations with them all.

Over time I watched and learned what they did and how they did it. I found them all to be dedicated and extremely interested in detecting crime trends and interdicting those crimes. In 1973 when I was appointed the first Division Analyst I spent a couple of weeks as one of their team, doing their day-to-day work creating, I thought, even deeper ties.

I took my position as the Central Patrol Division Crime Analyst (CPDCA) in October 1973 and it was not until three years later, on December 22, 1976, that we had a joint meeting per Capt. Memo's "Friendly Rapist Work Group" memo.[161]

Other than that meeting Captain Memo called, held in their office, I cannot remember any other formal or informal joint meetings between P&R OAS and the CPDCA. I don't remember making regular trips up to the third floor from my basement office to confer with them on crime trends or vice-versa. Additionally, even after the Patrol Division Analysts had been appointed to the other four patrol division I don't believe we ever had a joint or combined meeting. If we did these meetings were, as a consequence, unremarkable.

Of course, at the time, P&R had no obligation to keep Tom or me "in the loop", or the other Division Analysts. Macsas' group did not apprise us of their actions or work they might have been doing with various investigators, patrol or tactical units.

It is a shame that there was no coordination among us. No telling what could have been gained or what may have been lost by the lack of constant sharing (the same idea).

It is my memory that at different points we tried to make our information available to P&R OAS and in fact never sequestered our information or knowledge from anyone.

Tom and I both remember Kathryn Bonham, longtime civilian analyst with the P&R OAS, had her own 'book' on the FBR

---

[160] See photograph page 31

[161] See pages 379-380, 383 & 426

(containing only the rapes *she* attributed) which did not match our book of *all* the FBR offenses *we* had attributed. It was our understanding that she did not believe we were on the right track. For example she was, at one point, adamant that the suspect or suspects in the FBR criminal assaults were recently released sex offenders as did Inv. Crowder. Looking back it may have been that Inv. Reba Crowder was plugged into Kathryn's ideas (or vice versa) on the FBR and this may have made it easier for Crowder to dismiss my and Tom's perspective....

After our 12.22.76 meeting with Captain Memo, in the P&R map room, Kathryn was dubious of our methodology, our conclusions and predictions, saying her's was better. In the elevator going back to our office Tom said, "I know what Kathryn's methodology is..." letting his voice drop. Ever the straight man to Tom, I said, "What?" Tom brightened, "She uses the SWAG method: Scientific Wild Ass Guess!" I just shook my head and laughed.

Of course, if you've read this far, one could easily say there was a considerable amount of SWAG in our methodology.

We held no animosity for Kathryn or Reba, we just wanted the 'powers' to take Tom and I seriously and work with us to catch that son-of-bitch FBR.

That we and Kathryn did not agree on the FBR was not something for which I fault Kathryn, she was a fine analyst and had produced lots of actionable insights (city-wide) long before my tenure as the Division Analyst for Central Patrol Division.

We simply disagreed. As to how Lt. Macsas and the rest of his group felt about our conclusions, I have no recollection. Ironically, P&R OAS was using Tom and my FBR *area designations* on *their* maps[162] at least since December '76. As that information had been provided in our December 2, 1976 memo to John Landers and we included those area designations and maps in our *Patrol Officer's Handbook* re the FBR.

Believe me, Kathryn Bonham and Reba Crowder were not the only ones in the department who questioned Tom and my methods, our analysis, our conclusions... and probably, at times, our sanity.

---

[162] Appendix A - Newspaper Article #14b1 See page 343 & website: robertjsadler.com

Perhaps (in a generous nod to their hopefully honorable intentions) the naysayers held to their belief in multiple suspects so strongly because of the spurious results of the blood tests.

Again, with all those who questioned us we simply disagreed. In the end Tom and I were proven correct in our assessment, analysis, and predictions.

Chapter 42

After-Action Analysis

GOING THROUGH OUR FBR Books again, was emotional, enlightening and cathartic. Once the FBR was caught and in the hands of CID, where he would be interviewed and the case would be prepped for presentation to the District Attorney, Tom and I knew that would be that. We would no longer be involved... my and Tom's analysis would end.

I always longed for the opportunity to review and reanalyze the totality of the information we had amassed and see what we might have done differently or what things, unimagined at the time, we might have been able to do with today's technology and tools. (See *2017 Postscript 3b page 577*)

Of course the first thing that would likely have occurred was that the blood, semen and other trace evidence would have been handled (by the lab) much differently. A routine DNA examination of the suspect's fluids would have given us the "dead-bang" comparison for any next or succeeding rape. There would have been no question about his biological identity even if we had not yet identified him by name. Fingerprint evidence and witness statements, which in this case primarily consisted of complainant narratives, would be ancillary to the biological evidence. If there were copycats, that fact would be known immediately. The importance of M/O, for the purpose of identifying a crime as being committed by the same suspect, would be diminished.

However if our suspect was in no database, as was the case in 1977, modern technology could not simply pull the culprit's name out of the air. In the end, the first-hand knowledge of the crime would have been what put the suspect in our hands today, just as it did in 1977.

But here are some facts, numbers and analytical suppositions relative to closing out the FBR case as it existed in 1977.

There were a total of eighty-two (82[163]) offenses that Tom and I "booked" or attributed to the FBR, Guy William Marble Jr. Of these eighty-two offenses there were: 42 rapes, 6 attempt rapes, 1 unreported rape, 5 robberies, 11 burglaries, 7 criminal mischiefs, 7 criminal trespasses, and 3 prowlers.

#	Types Of Offenses Attributed to FBR
42	Rape
6	Attempt Rape
1	Unreported Rape (referred)
5	Robbery
11	Burglary (Including Attempt Burglaries)
7	Criminal Mischief
7	Criminal Trespass
3	Prowler

We cataloged over fifty individual FBR traits, things he did during the commission of his crimes, that made up his M/O, method of operation. It is unlikely that he did or would do everything the same, each time he entered a victim's residence. He did however, have a routine. That routine or general M/O consisted of a number of specific, identifiable actions, what I call M/O Markers, that appeared, if not in each, in many reported and attributed offenses. The other variable is that we were depending on a) the complainant accurately describing what took place to the reporting officer or investigator and b) the RO or investigator accurately reporting what the complainant described.

How did the FBR chose his victims? The case files tend to indicate he may have seen a few of his victims elsewhere before the attacks and followed them home and thus specifically targeted some of his victims. His choices of apartments were on both first and second floors. Perhaps not remarkable, second-story apartments residents falsely believed that they could leave

---

[163] Eighty-three (83) with the inclusion of the rape (R1?) on 2/6/1974

their upstairs windows and doors unlocked, or worse, open and be safe. He apparently looked for two things: an open window/door or unlocked window/door as his main targets of opportunity. Secondarily, it appeared that he favored apartments with potted plants either in or by a window/door, as a sign or indicator that the apartment was probably occupied by a woman rather than a man.

Overall, the FBR entered a victim's residence by an unlocked window or door; the door was usually a sliding glass patio/balcony door. Once inside, the FBR went about establishing his escape route, which might involve unlocking/unlatching a front door, raising another window, or unlocking or leaving unlocked the sliding glass door. These exits were often in different parts of the apartment so as to minimize his being trapped. Next he searched for a knife, usually in the kitchen, then he set about cutting telephone cords to both disable the phones and provide himself with a means of control over his victims. He would then stealthily continue prowling the apartment, looking for money, driver's licenses of the residents to determine who was living there: age, sex, & ID photo. Purses and wallets contained those items as well as cash, which he would take. If he didn't like what he saw or got spooked, he would leave and go to his next target of opportunity. He had plenty of targets and plenty of opportunity. He implied that he went into multiple apartments each night he prowled. I never got a handle on how many nights a week he prowled, but when he did, it was not just one hit or miss attempt.

Once he decided he liked what he saw, he continued rummaging and perusing through the victim's personal items. By doing this he could usually ascertain the marital or dating status of his victim as well as their general health. The presence, or lack thereof, of multiple toothbrushes or men's toiletries, were strong indicators as were the types of over-the-counter and prescription drugs found in the victim's bathroom.

These activities apparently turned him on; were his foreplay. By the time he approached his victim, except when he had clumsily or inadvertently awakened them—in which case he would spring, he would put his hand over his victim's mouth to stifle their first instinct to scream and to gain immediate control.

He kept his voice low, a whisper, to avoid discovery by others who might be present in the apartment, and perhaps to disguise the characteristics of his voice. His manner of speech was deliberate as he communicated to his victim a variety of opening lines to keep them docile and compliant. His threats of bodily harm were backed up by either the threatened use of a weapon (usually a knife) or the actual display or touch of the weapon.

He then proceeded with two consistent steps. In no specific order he would hood the victim with one of there own pillowcases, put a pillow over their face, pull their gown over their face, etc., and then bind their hands together or to a bedpost, for example. The bonds could be any manner of things from bras to the rubber hose from a douche bag. His most often used restraints were cords from the telephones he had already disabled.

Once his victim was secured and intimidated he would engage in more foreplay, moving about the apartment, touching, moving things. If he had not already, he would retrieve something to utilize for lubrication. Unless she was already naked, he would undress his victims. This usually entailed cutting with a knife or shears through gowns and bra straps, or cutting through the crotch of the victim's panties. If he seemed particularly enamored with a particular victim he might have them stand up so he could "see" them better and would often pull off their panties slowly[164] and have them step out of them.

He was generally gentle, but only as a means to elicit cooperation. When faced with verbal obstinacy he would threaten greater immediate bodily harm; often using the threat of death.

The rapes themselves, the intercourse itself, was usually proceeded by fondling of the victim's breasts. On occasion, requiring his victim to perform fellatio on him or his performing cunnilingus on his victim as an immediate precursor to vaginal penetration. Generally he didn't last very long. Anal penetration (or attempting) was only reported twice. Likewise the act of kissing of the victim by the FBR was usually confined to a report of his kissing the breasts. It is possible that any number of his victims may have had to submit to his kisses. Those who did mention it usually did so in the context of preventing or trying to prevent his kissing them. On a couple of occasions his victims remarked on his rather insistent French Kissing causing the

---

[164] Numerous victims were reported to have specifically used the word "slowly." Perhaps Marble practiced this behavior for his own arousal or it was done to further demonstrate his control or to humiliate his victim—perhaps all three.

investigator at the time to think this M/O Marker meant it was not the FBR and thus she tried to dub him the "Tongue Twister", but it was actually the FBR.

Again, we, in trying to analyze and then predict the FBR's offenses, had to deal with what we were told.

So M/O Markers came and went. Complainants reported the FBR referring to himself as a cop only twice. When he committed rape he referred to himself as "just a burglar", or something similar, approximately 40% of the time.

After he completed the rape, he might throw the covers over his victim, might tell them he would be back and never return; sometimes he mentioned he would tell them before he left (sometimes he did, mostly he just left); sometimes he mentioned seeing people in the parking lot and was therefor unable to leave, only to leave the victim wondering. Before leaving he might help himself to something from the refrigerator, if he had not already. Or he might take the victim's trash with him to help disguise his leaving the victim's apartment.

In the describing of his general M/O here, if you have been a close reader, you will have realized I have left out many of his specific traits. However, now you can see how we could have catalogued over fifty individual actions that became part of the FBR's M/O.

Recently, in reviewing all 82 of the FBR O/IRs, I picked out nineteen of his actions (somewhat randomly-not *the* "top 19") . I tracked these 19 FBR M/O Markers through all 82 offenses Tom and I attributed to the FBR. Here are a couple of graphical illustrations of those markers, starting with his entering through an unlocked window or door 100% of the time for *rapes*.

19 FBR M/O MARKER TRAITS

The following chart shows the same nineteen (19) M/O Markers as they related to the total number of offenses (82) we attributed to the FBR as both a raw number and a percentage. This was also done for the total number of rapes (42) we attributed to the FBR as both a raw number and a percentage.

As you can see it was not always a given that any one M/O Marker was the give-away or the reason we attributed an individual offense to the FBR. Likewise we did not have a set number of markers that determined that an offense was or was not the FBR's. In fact, we never had a full list of markers that we had catalogued. However, in most every case there were multiples of the FBR's M/O Markers present that allowed Tom and I to definitively say this was an FBR offense.

19 FBR M/O Marker Trait Charts

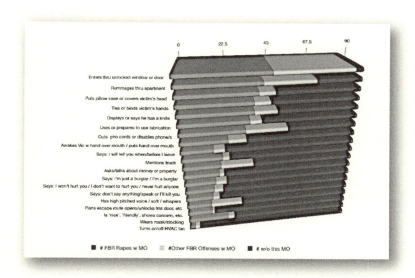

Offenses This # have M/O Marker		Offenses This % have M/O Marker	19 FBR M/O Markers	Rape Offenses This # have M/O Marker		Rape Offenses This % have M/O Marker
78 of 82	or	95%	Enters thru unlocked window or door	42 of 42	or	100%
61 of 82	or	74%	Rummages thru apartment	38 of 42	or	90%
43 of 82	or	52%	Puts pillow case over or covers victim's head	36 of 42	or	86%
41 of 82	or	50%	Ties or binds victim's hands	34 of 42	or	81%
44 of 82	or	54%	Displays or says he has a knife	34 of 42	or	81%
37 of 82	or	45%	Uses lubrication	32 of 42	or	76%
49 of 82	or	60%	Cuts pho cords or disables phone/s	30 of 42	or	71%
30 of 82	or	37%	Awakes Vic w hand over mouth / puts hand over mouth	22 of 42	or	52%
23 of 82	or	28%	Says: I will tell you when/before I leave	20 of 42	or	48%
22 of 82	or	27%	Mentions truck	19 of 42	or	45%
23 of 82	or	28%	Asks/talks about money or property	18 of 42	or	43%
19 of 82	or	23%	Says: I'm just a burglar / I'm a burglar	17 of 42	or	40%
20 of 82	or	24%	Says: I won't hurt you / I don't want to hurt you	15 of 42	or	36%
18 of 82	or	22%	Says: don't say anything/speak or I'll kill you	14 of 42	or	33%
16 of 82	or	20%	Has high pitched voice / soft / whispers	13 of 42	or	31%
27 of 82	or	33%	Plans escape route opens/unlocks front door, etc	12 of 42	or	29%
13 of 82	or	16%	Is 'nice', 'friendly', shows concern, etc.	12 of 42	or	29%
16 of 82	or	20%	Wears mask/stocking	11 of 42	or	26%
5 of 82	or	6.1%	Turns on/off HVAC fan	3 of 42	or	7.1%

The Friendly Burglar-Rapist (Guy William Marble Jr.) lived at 10749 Sandpiper, Dallas, Texas 75230 within four (4) miles of 79% of his offenses and lived within three (3) miles of 70% of his offenses. As Tom and I plotted each new incoming offense we always wondered where the nexus was... where did he live, where did he work and what impact did that have on the choosing his predatory turf.

Two thoughts have obvious weight when considering how not to establish a psychological arrow pointing to your criminal lair. The first is that you do not commit crimes close to home, or in your immediate living-zone, which can leave a hole in your offense density that points back to you. The second is that you do 'hit' close to or in your living-zone in order to throw off the criminalist.

Modern-day TV programs such as "NUMB3RS" use intricate formulas and algorithms to massage statistics into revealing the motivations and movements of criminals. Tom and I would have loved to have had a whiz-kid to assist us. In fact I would love to have some real-life whiz-kid take our data now and see if they could tell us where to have looked before we figured it out.

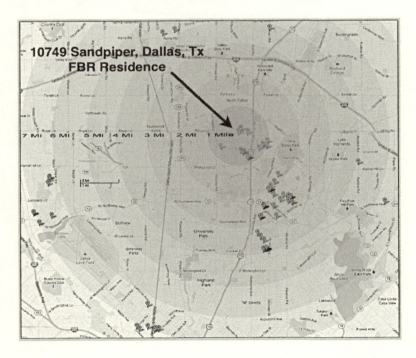

The apparent limitations of all our calculations and predictions were, a) did we have all the reported offenses? and b) what would the pattern or prediction be if we also knew the total universe of attempts, entries, and unreported crimes/offenses?

Our wall map [separate from my six big crime maps] started as a folding Dallas street map on which I dotted the locations of the first twelve rapes, which of course did not begin with the first offense I noted but rather after the second FBR rape in CPD. Once I went back and found the "real first" and the intervening offenses, analyzing and plotting them city-wide seemed the natural thing to do. Thus the chronology of offenses on our maps and charts changed as I found and inserted intervening O/IRs.

As time went by the offenses marked on the map began to show some clustering. There seemed to be an obvious directionality to the FBRs movements from one side of town to the other: south to north, east to west and/or the reverse.

In the midst of our trying to make sense of the directionality of the FBR's movements, the department decided to reconfigure the beats. Now the historical FBR data we had been tracking "by beat" would be impossibly skewed by the reshaping, reconfiguring and renumbering of the individual patrol beats. That prompted our defining the FBR's target areas with boundaries rather than beat configurations. Thus defined by *our* geographical boundaries, the clusters of FBR hits allowed us to more effectively narrow down our prediction targeting.

About this time the "Star Map" came into existence. We put a new map up on the wall and pinned it with the offenses, by Area, thus far attributed to the FBR. We then strung thread from pin to pin in the chronological order of their occurrence. Also when we created the "Areas" and defined them we, for some reason, did not put Area I at the chronological beginning and it became by default the last: Area VII. The most probable explanation as to why the areas were given their individual Roman numerals was that at that moment in time the FBR was going from what we designated as Area I, to Area II, to Area III and so on.

Thus, before the Star Map, we did not have the benefit of "seeing" these "movement's" initially "strung together" or the areas he frequented as we later defined them. We also did not know the whereabouts of the FBR's residence as we do now: 10749 Sandpiper, which is marked with an "X".

This map shows the first ten offenses, all rapes. The transition arrows between each offense for the first ten are white with a black out line and an arrowhead at the end point. (Not visible below) The FBR's 1st attributed offense occurred at 4315 Brown Street (Area VII), for number 2 he went north a couple of blocks to 2600 Arroyo Avenue, the next (#3) he went east across town to 10454 E. Northwest Highway to a location to which he would never return and which was never included in one of our seven defined areas. From there he went north for #4 to 13626 Maham Road (Area VI), then back south to Area VII for #5. He went back northwest to 9633 Starlight Road (Area V) for #6, then back east to Area II for #7 at the Willow Creek Apartments. (Note: The Willow Creek Apartments no longer exist. It was a large complex with all of the internal street names having or beginning with the word "Willow". For the purposes of these maps all nine (9) of the FBR's offenses with Willow Creek addresses will be represented by one dot.) For offense number 8 he went from Area II northwest to Area VI, then back south to Area VII for #9. For #10 he moved back northeast to strike in Area III.

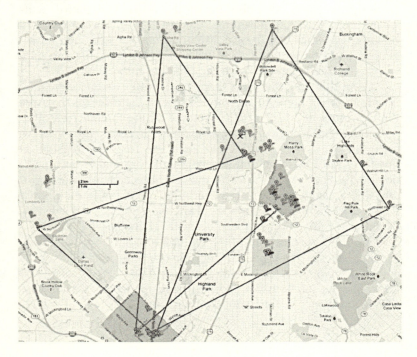

Those first ten offenses show his widest dispersion between offense locations, north to south and east to west. His general movement was south to east to north to south to west to east to north to south then back to east again. Was this a conscious or unconscious patterning. Was he trying to deliberately position his movements or was it simple "randomnicity". At this point the map resembles triangles more than a star. Also, don't loose sight of the fact that these ten offenses occurred over a 13 month period from November 15, 1973 to December 18, 1974.

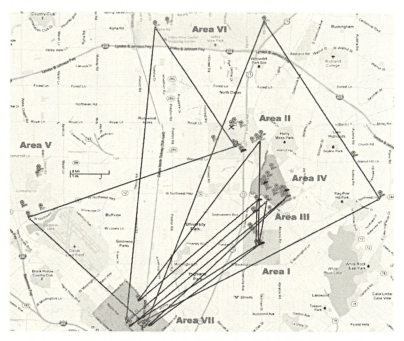

As you can see the next ten show a marked south to northwest to south (actually southwest) pattern. At this time I began to encounter FBR attributed offenses besides rape. Of the next ten FBR offenses six (6) were rapes, one (1) attempt rape, one (1) criminal trespass and one (1) robbery.

From #10 in Area II he goes due south to for #11 at 4620 Amesbury Drive in Area I. Then in order: SW for #12 Area VII, NE for #13 Area IV, SW to Area VII was #14, NE to Area 1 for #15, due north to Area III for #16, SW to Area VII for #17, back NNE to Area Area II for #18, then on back due south to Area 1 for #19, then NW to Area II for #20. The second ten (10) offenses of the FBR cover the nine month period from 12-18-74 to 8-20-1975 Do we really have a pattern?

Next ten (offenses 21-30) show a very pronounced alternating north to south to north to south proclivity utilizing Areas I, II, III & IV. It only took two months for the next ten (10) FBR offense to hit my desk; covering the period 8-20-75 through 10-23-75 during which time the FBR had abandoned Areas V, VI & VII.

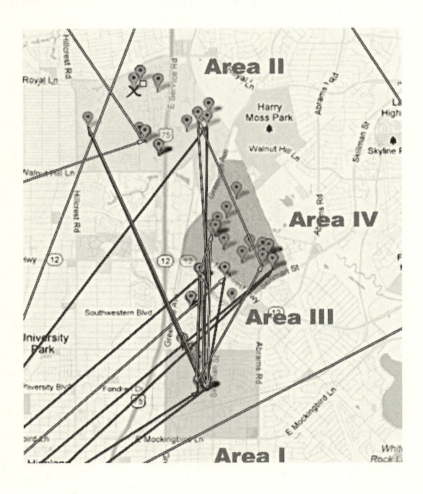

Offenses 21 through 30 involved four (4) rapes, three (3) burglaries, one (1) attempt burglary and one (1) criminal trespass.

The next thirty-nine (39) offenses (31-68) bring us up to the point where Tom and I began a "new" special assignment, November 10, 1976, re: the FBR and subsequently started pinning the map to the wall and decided to string some thread between the dots to see what we came up with. These thirty-nine (39) offenses occurred over the year between 10-23-1975 and 10-24-1976. *At one point there was what appeared to be a star pattern*. The FBR is now averaging 3 to 4 "reported" offenses a month. The map below shows how his north-south axis has become even more pronounced, particularly given the size of the map. As we analyzed the totality of offenses to this point, we felt more and more comfortable in being able to predict (ok, guess) whether he was likely to go north or south from his last reported offense. We had already been "right" a number of times.

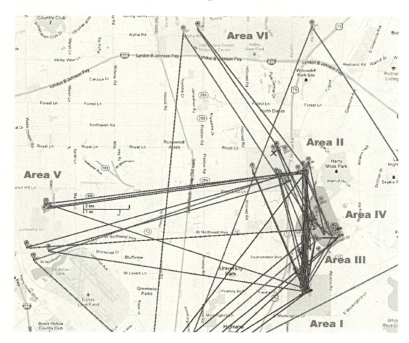

The next six (6) offenses, broke pattern. For offenses 69, 70, and 71 he hit each time in Area V, then the next three, 72, 73, and

74 were all in Area IV. And this (Offense #74) is where the FBR had his first (as far as we knew) bad luck. He tried to attack someone he had just seen earlier... who then remembered him and was able to provide her uncannily accurate recall to an artist who then interpreted the witness' detailed description into a remarkable likeness of The Friendly Burglar-Rapist.

Then, with the exception of one "hit" in Area III the remainder of the FBR's offenses, until he was captured, were concentrated in Area IV.

As if there was some karmic system at work, the FBR broke his pattern to go out of the area (OOA) for his 82nd and last reported offense, an attempted rape in the 9700 block of Audelia, west of Area IV. Number 82 occurred at 2:35am on Tuesday, February 1, 1977. In two weeks, on February 14, 1977, he would head back to Area IV for the 19th and final time.

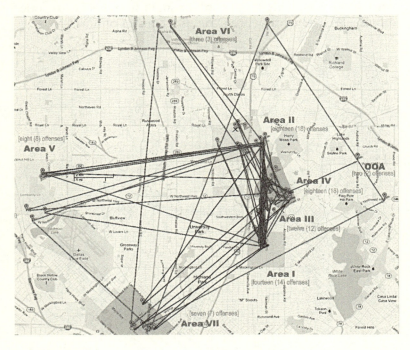

For three years and three months (11/15/1974—2/14/1977) Guy William Marble Jr. went where he wanted night after night entering domiciles where he did not belong and violating the mental and physical peace and tranquility of the domiciles' occupant/s with only his depraved conscience as a guide.

It should be noted, of the pin maps represented on these pages, that the smaller the map the more dense and definitive the patterns sometimes seem to be. On the other hand, 'back in the day' it was practically impossible to 'see' or demonstrate these offenses (city-wide) on a large enough scale (large enough map) to look for other definitive patterns that a larger scale might provide.

Perhaps we could have made use of the large maps in Planning & Research, but we (Tom and I) were not on the same theoretical or practical page with Lt. Macsas' group. [See photo on page 31]

By area, here are the number of offenses Marble committed in each:

Area & No. of Offenses	
Area I	14
Area II	18
Area III	12
Area IV	18
Area V	8
Area VI	3
Area VII	7
OOA	2
Total	82

Friendly-Burglar Rapist
Attributed Rapes & All Offenses
by
Apt Complex Name - Area - Number of Offenses
& Offense Numeric Order

The chart below and the map on the next page details the location of the forty-two (42) rapes Tom and I attributed to Guy William Marble Jr.

				FBR Attributed Rapes & All Offenses by Area / # of Offenses / Offense Numeric Order			
#	Apt Complex Name	Area	# of All Offenses	Total All Offenses	# of Rape Offenses	Total All Rapes	Offense in Numeric Order
1	Amesbury Manor	I	1		1		36
2	The Citadel		2	14	1	8	24, 64
3	Spanish Keys		2		1		30, 50
4	Willowick		9		5		11, 15, 19, 21, 38, 47, 56, 58, 63
5	Belle Meadow	II	1		1		20
6	Cobblestone		2		1		45, 66
7	Four 7's		1		1		68
8	Horizon East		1	18		8	18
9	Willow Creek		10		4		7, 26, 32, 35, 37, 40, 42, 52, 55, 61
10	Woodcreek		1		1		62
11	Woodscape		2				43, 59
12	Bluffs	III	1				80
13	Corners & Corners East		6	12	3	5	10, 16, 27, 28, 39, 46
14	The Hill		4		2		22, 23, 49, 57
15	Villa Madrid		1				60
16	Claridge Park *	IV	1				76
17	The Falls		2		1		13, 81
18	Kimberly Woods		2				25, 74
19	Melody Park		1				78
20	Melody Terrace		1	18	1	6	54
21	The Seasons		2		1		48, 53 (83X captured)
22	The Settlement		4		2		29, 33, 44, 65
23	The Lofts		1				72
24	The Ivy		1				73
25	Villa Crest		3		1		75, 77, 79
26	Copenhagen	V	2		1		41, 69
27	The Point After		1		1		31
28	The Trails		2	8	1	6	51, 71
29	The Tuileries		1		1		6
30	Walden Place		2		2		34, 70
31	Buttonwood Tree	VI	1		1		8
32	Emerald Forest		1	3	1	2	4
33	First Day		1				67
34	Arroyo Place	VII	1		1		2
35	Kings Terrace		1				17
36	Molly Coddle		1	7	1	6	14
37	Pueblo Square		1		1		9
38	Stepping Stone		1		1		12
39	Toll House		2		2		1, 5
40	Hill Top House	OOA	1	2		1	3
41	The Brookshir		1		1		82
				82		42	

An Exclusive Crime Perspective

CAPERS (Crimes Against Persons), the investigative division responsible for rape (criminal assault) cases, did not look at the entirety of offenses Tom and I attributed to the FBR. They were charged with investigating and clearing only the FBR's rapes.

If Tom and I had only been looking at this number of rapes, the final picture would have looked like the one below.

Forty-two rapes is its own high number, but 42 over 39 months it is statistically just over one (1) rape per month—initially assigned to different investigators.

Given that perspective and the idea within CAPERS, for most of the FBR's 39 months of activity, that not all these offenses were committed by the same person perhaps it was reasonable that one rape per month was not statistically spectacular or noteworthy.

Area Map Showing Only FBR Attributed Rapes

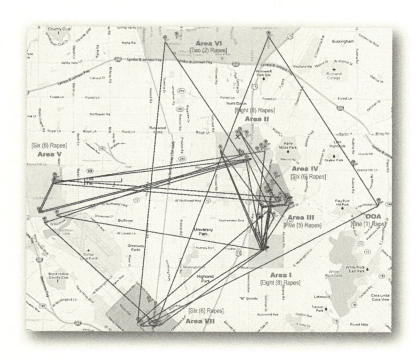

An Inclusive Crime Perspective

From Tom and my perspective, what made the FBR unique and what was beneficial to this investigation, was that fact that he was also a burglar or used burglary techniques (entering a habitat at night for the purpose of committing a crime) to facilitate his criminal assaults.

If the FBR had been scouting his victims, in a bar for example, following them home and then accosting them as they opened their apartment door, we would have been factoring into our investigation all those correlative offenses.

For these reasons Tom and I had, from the beginning, focused on *any* O/IR with FBR M/O Markers that could be ancillary to rape or burglary included in the category of offenses below.

#	Types Of Offenses Attributed to FBR
42	Rape
6	Attempt Rape
1	Unreported Rape (referred)
5	Robbery
11	Burglary (Including Attempt Burglaries)
7	Criminal Mischief
7	Criminal Trespass
3	Prowler

Data Point Articulation - Charting & Tracking

It would be easier to say what we did not chart than what we did. We charted and plotted every data point we could think of. Here are just a few.

Date of offense
> Day of the month, day of the week

Time of offense
> time between onset of offense and call to police
> duration of offense, time report began, time report ended

Time of call dispatch
Beat of offense
Sector of offense
Service number of offense
Type of offense
Complainant's name, gender, age, DOB
Address of offense
> Apartment number, ground floor, 2nd, 3rd
> > Name of Apartment Complex
> > > Number of times
> > hit, dates of, dates between,
> > > what complex he hit just prior & next

Area of offense (one of seven designated areas)
Days since last offense
Days between rapes
Dates of Cowboy games
Dates of moon phases
Dates of full moons
Tide charts relative to time of offense
50 plus M/O Markers
Evidence recovered
> fingerprint, blood

Holidays relative to last hit, before next hit
Historical and local events (entertainment, sporting, social)
Weather relative to each offense (before, during, after)
> Temperature, precipitation,
> > wind strength & direction, cloudy/not cloudy

Occupations that might put a suspect in all areas

Date, Time, & Day Surveys

Tom and I 'conjured' many, many, many, more... some humorous, some outrageous, most just good common sense.

However, in the end, nothing significant correlated to the FBR's actual offenses as we became aware of them. There were matches here and there.

What became apparent (see charts on pages 518-522) was that the FBR offenses were occurring all times of the year except January and February; he had hit on 23 of the 31 days of the month, usually between the 4th and 24th, on both odd and even days; had hit on every day of the week, although Thursdays and Saturdays had the least hits; and he had hit between the hours of 9pm and 7am with the most prevalent hour being 2am.

These surveys, as we called them, (date, time, and day survey) became our most reliable guide to predicting the FBR's movements. They allowed us to predict or guess correctly with a reasonable degree of accuracy the area and date of his next offense. Whether this was true predicability or just the elimination of other possibilities, we were able to narrow "date, time, and location" often enough to demonstrate the reliability of our method.

With no other real options to proactively attack the FBR problem (i.e. and patrol officers not being able to see through buildings and observe and attack "on-view"), the department had to rely on calls from victims after the fact which meant his identification had to rely primarily on forensics and, at the time, that generally meant latent fingerprint evidence.

Once others were convinced and we could pinpoint the likely target area/s of the FBR's next hit and we had a reasonable, witness-aided, facsimile of his likeness, the wheels of the FBR capture machine began to roll.

Here are the updated charts referred to on previous pages, except these include all offenses attributed to the FBR and each "box" has the designated Offense Number. Something relatively easy to do on a modern-day spreadsheet such as this. Below, in the modern-day example, the colors in each block of the box are color-coded, although in this book they will likely appear in shades of grey... but wow, wouldn't this have made visualizing each set of data points so much easier! [165]

SHOWS ALL OFFENSES [Trends Are Internal]

DAY OF WEEK

	1	2	3	4	5	6	7	8	9	10	11	12	13	14	15	16	#	%
SUNDAY	19	21	41	50	66	68	71	72	73	76							10	12.1
MONDAY	16	25	27	40	44	45	46	61	62	65	74	77	78	79	X		14	17
TUESDAY	12	14	17	28	35	47	52	53	54	55	56	58	64	80	81	82	16	19.5
WEDNESDAY	10	13	20	33	39	42	48	49	63	69	70	75					12	14.6
THURSDAY	1	4	5	9	18	30	31	34	57	59	67						11	13
FRIDAY	6	15	22	23	24	29	36	37	38	43	51	60					12	14.6
SATURDAY	2	3	7	8	11	26	32										7	8.5
																	82	

It is very easy to see, looking back at these totals, that there was not a great difference between what days of the week he hit. Again, these are reported cases and does not and cannot take into account the unknown number of other apartments he entered each night he prowled. However, as we went, there did appear to be trends. We followed those when we could.

---

[165] To see these charts (and more) in color go to my website: robertjsadler.com

Similarly the chart below changed with time. You can see why we wondered what he was doing in January and February for three years. He hit once in February (Offense #35 2.17.76) and did not hit in January until Offense #77 in 1977. We then attributed four more offenses in January!

What triggered this change... or had he always done this and his offenses went unreported? I don't think that was the case, but we never found out why we got no reported FBR offenses in January and February. Then, of course, Offense # 82 occurred on February 1, 1977 and we captured him thirteen days later before he could commit another February offense!

MONTH	OFFENSES ORDERED BY MONTH										
JANUARY	77	78	79	80	81	82					
FEBRUARY	35	X									
MARCH	11	36	37	38	39						
APRIL	12	13	14	40	41	42					
MAY	15	16	17	43	44	45	46	47	48	49	50
JUNE	18	51	52	53	54						
JULY	2	19	55	56	57	58	59	60			
AUGUST	3	4	20	21	61						
SEPTEMBER	5	6	7	21	23	24	25	62	63	64	
OCTOBER	8	26	27	28	29	30	65	66	67	68	
NOVEMBER	1	9	31	32	33	69	70	71	72	73	
DECEMBER	10	34	74	75	76						

Looking for any kind of statistical clue, I kept track of the times that the FBR offenses encompassed. In my original charts the times were charted with both the time the offense commenced and when it concluded. This provided a larger bell curve of data but essentially the mean was made up of the three middle hours of the night/morning, from 1am to 4am. Just over half (42) of the offense occurred during this time period. In my recently updated Time of Day chart I use the *offense began* time.

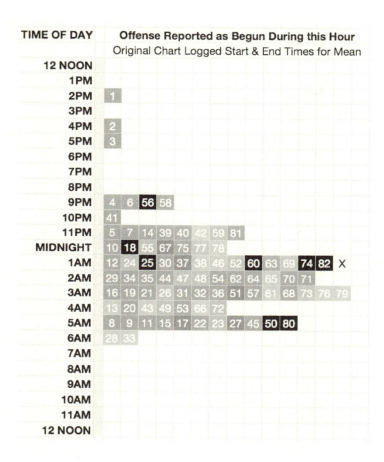

TIME OF DAY	Offense Reported as Begun During this Hour Original Chart Logged Start & End Times for Mean
12 NOON	
1PM	
2PM	1
3PM	
4PM	2
5PM	3
6PM	
7PM	
8PM	
9PM	4 6 56 58
10PM	41
11PM	5 7 14 39 40 42 59 81
MIDNIGHT	10 18 55 67 75 77 78
1AM	12 24 25 30 37 38 46 52 60 63 69 74 82 X
2AM	29 34 35 44 47 48 54 62 64 65 70 71
3AM	16 19 21 26 31 32 36 51 57 61 68 73 76 79
4AM	13 20 43 49 53 66 72
5AM	8 9 11 15 17 22 23 27 45 50 80
6AM	28 33
7AM	
8AM	
9AM	
10AM	
11AM	
12 NOON	

I had charted the offenses by the days of the week, but also wanted to know if there were any trends as to days of the month. For a long time his trend was to hit the middle fourteen days of a month.

520

	S	MON	TUE	WED	THUR	FRIDAY	S	
DATE OF THE MONTH - SORTED BY DAY OF THE WEEK								
1			12 82					2
2								
3		77 78 79					3	4
4		65	80			51	26	4
5		40			5	36		3
6		27 74	55 56 58		31			6
7					9	43		2
8			52 53	75	4 57		32	6
9						15		1
10	66	44		69 70				4
11	41				34			2
12						22 23 24 37 38		5
13		62						1
14		45 X	28		67			3
15					1 59		11	3
16		61				60		2
17		46	35			29		3
18			47	10				2
19	76			48 49				3
20				20			6	2
21	71			42				2
22		25	54	63				3
23	72				13 30			3
24	68			39				2
25			81				8	2
26		16		33	18		7	4
27	19		17					2
28	73		64					2
29		14						1
30	50						2	2
31	21							1
	S	MON	TUE	WED	THUR	FRIDAY	S	
	10	15	15	11	12	11	8	82

At the conclusion we can see that the only day of the month the FBR missed having a reported offense was the 2nd. Thirty-nine (39) months in a row the women of Dallas were safe on the second day of the month. That certainly was merely coincidence.

All along there were trends that appeared to develop—though skewed from time to time, the "Odd/Even" days of the month evened out.

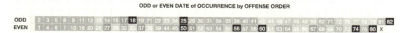

I can see patterns within patterns, but I have no mathematical equation to make statistical sense of what we saw at the time, or now. Once again, it became apparent that he was favoring Area II, III, & IV between the hours of 1am and 4am virtually any day of the week or month. However, there were tendencies to go to certain areas after hitting in another. Then of course there were the anomalies, where multiple offenses were reported on the same day, time and location. Seemingly the closer we got to him, his frequency of reported offenses increased.

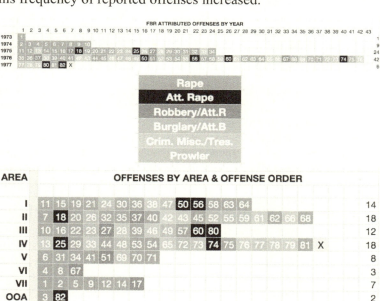

That is why all the ancillary offenses to facilitate his rapes were so important to us. In fact it was the myriad of other offenses (criminal mischief, criminal trespass, prowler calls, attempt burglaries and attempt rapes) that helped us develop a way to not only track his movements, not only allow us to predict his movements, but additionally added some of the most valuable evidence against the FBR. In particular it was a burglary at night (an attempt criminal assault) that provided and literally put a face on the FBR suspect and facilitated his capture when that information was coupled with the prediction Tom provided (for the stakeout of 2-14-77) via all the ancillary and rape cases we reviewed, analyzed, and plotted.

As mentioned early on in this book, capturing bad guys is usually about first-hand information and secondarily about physical evidence. The physical evidence in this case primarily consisted of latent fingerprints lifted at the scene. You have read where the fingerprint evidence was found, but let's discuss when it was found and how that timeline might have impacted the investigation of this case.

According to my records, we did not get our first "print" in the FBR case until Offense Number 10 (12-18-74) and the last was obtained at Offense Number 67 (10-14-76). A total of nineteen (19) of the eighty-two (82) attributed FBR offenses had been identified as belonging to the FBR (Guy Marble Jr.) by comparison of fingerprints or palm prints. That's less than 25% having fingerprint evidence. Of these nineteen, twelve (12) were reported as rapes; two (2) were robberies; two (2) were burglaries; one (1) each was an attempt burglary, criminal mischief, and a criminal trespass offense.

What is even more disconcerting, if those numbers disconcert you given today's CSI mania, is the dispersion of time between the collection of viable fingerprint evidence and the fact that for the last four (4) months of the FBR's activity NO fingerprint evidence was collected from his last fifteen (15) offenses.

Where the ancillary offenses were of not much additional 'help' was with biological trace evidence. With the exception of one (1) "robbery" no biologics were collected. However on twenty-five (25) of the FBR's 42 attributed rapes, where either suspected semen was collected at the scene or as the result of a medical personnel preparing a 'rape kit', the blood type of the FBR suspect was determined. We learned later how unreliable these lab test were[166]. What a difference today's DNA processing would have made. There would have been no room for interdepartmental bickering about multiple FBR suspects!

---

[166] see page 431-432: Forensic Evidence - Blood Typing the FBR & Answers

FBR Offenses Where Latent Print Evidence was Obtained					
Offense Number	Rape Number Sequence	Type Offense	Area	Date	Latent Print Evidence
1	*1*	*Rape*	*VII*	*11.15.73*	*NONE*
10	10	Rape	II	12.18.74	Palm
15	14	Rape	I	5.9.75	7
20	17	Rape	II	8.20.75	2,3,4,9
21	18	Rape	I	8.31.75	1,8
25		Attempt Burglary	IV	9.22.75	6
27		Robbery	III	10.6.75	2,3,6
28		Criminal Trespass	III	10.14.75	6,8
29	20	Rape	IV	10.17.75	1
31	22	Rape	V	11.6.75	6,8,9
32	23	Rape	II	11.8.75	6,5,8,9
34	24	Rape	V	12.11.75	2,8
44	30	Rape	IV	5.10.76	7
45	31	Rape	II	5.14.76	7,8
47		Burglary	I	5.18.76	1,2,3
48		Burglary	IV	5.19.76	Palm & 2,3
53	32	Rape	IV	6.8.76	2,3,3,6
56		Criminal Mischief	I	7.6.76	1 & 2
63	36	Rape	I	9.22.76	Palm
67		Robbery	VI	10.14.76	Palm
74	*Witness ID's FBR - a sketch rendered*		*IV*	*12.6.76*	
83x	*FBR captured*		*IV*	*2.14.77*	

Remember, we attributed these offenses to the FBR (by virtue of his M/O Markers) when no one believed us and our opinions, theories. Our predictions were never vindicated (even with his capture) until late on that Valentine's Day morning by the FBR himself. It was the words from Guy William Marble Jr.'s own mouth that proved the work Tom and I did as reliable and right on track. All the thousands of hours we spent were proven worthwhile for the police department, the city and for Tom and me. The millions of thoughts we conjured over 39 months as to who he was, what his occupation was, where he went, who his friends were, what were his hobbies, where did he hang out, what kind of car did he drive, was he married, divorced, have children, a steady job, was he intelligent or just lucky, was he a sociopath doomed to graduate to murder? All these scenarios of criminality we pondered. All these questions and so many more were all validated by Marble's taking credit for the offenses in "the book", *our book* of attributed FBR offenses!

In my opinion, our looking at the total of his offenses, rather than "just the rapes" is what facilitated his capture and prevented his committing additional offenses, in particular more rapes.

In the end it was the mass of information we had collected, the analysis we had done and our passion to continue to press for action (by those who would and would not listen) that helped put all the chess pieces in place to checkmate Guy William Marble Jr. before he murdered.

You have to ask yourself, when you hear a woman who has just been assaulted recount the statement below, as she did to Investigator Landers, whether this statement by the FBR is acting, bravado, or an underlying thought in the criminal's mind, and a precursor of action, waiting to be played out.

Marble told his seventy-ninth victim as he "placed a small length (20") of rope around Comp's neck, 'You know I could kill you very easily, you've been dealing with a psychotic crazy person.'"

Author's End Note:

Tom Covington and I attributed a total of eighty-two offenses to The Friendly Burglar-Rapist. These O/IRs (offense/incident reports) consisted of rape, attempt rape, robbery, burglary, criminal trespass, criminal mischief and prowler calls.

Given that the rapist Guy William Marble Jr., (who pled guilty to multiple burglaries connected to the rapes and was subsequently convicted), acknowledged and alluded to having committed the reported rapes attributed to him plus reportedly another twelve (12) not on our list; given that the number of unreported rapes are thought to be between 30% on the low side to as much as 80% unreported on the high side, the actual number of Dallas women raped by The Friendly Burglar-Rapist could range from 57 to150.

In spite of all our diligent efforts, we spent many a sleepless night wrestling with the knowledge that Guy William Marble Jr. continued operating unchecked by law enforcement for, as it turned out, over three years. As only bit players on society's stage it is not our place to apologize for the acts of others. However, to this day Tom and I are saddened and chagrined that we were unable to do more to stop him before we did.

Several unknowns have always bothered me: 1) the FBR seemed to stop committing rapes in December, January, February of some years—we could never get a handle on that—if he wasn't committing rapes here, was he committing them elsewhere? 2) some evidence indicated he may have traveled to different cities within Texas, even possibly to other states during his three-year crime spree. I've always found it curious—did GWM Jr. commit similar crimes in other cities and states? 3) why did I only find offenses in Dallas[167] that were attributable to Marble starting in 1973 when he was 25-years-old? In his own words he said: "The rehearsals for my crimes began in grade school, and nobody ever took enough interest to notice... Acting out those fantasies as a young adult was inevitable." [168]

A good case could be made for the fact that Marble was addicted to this behavior. Why then wouldn't "the rehearsals" for his "crimes" and the "acting out" of "those fantasies as a young adult" have continued unabated until caught?

Likewise, in terms of trying to discern the pattern of his addiction, it was a matter of frequency. His frequency gave us more clues, more puzzle pieces toward his capture. For Marble, what kind of frequency did he require to feed his addiction? I always felt it was more than we were seeing, more than what was reported. He told John Landers as much when asked, "how many places did you actually go into each night, three, four, five... or more?" Guy William Marble Jr, The FBR, nodded and told Investigator John Landers:

"You wouldn't believe me if I told you, but it's a lot!"

Again, the rapes detailed herein were based on what we knew; actual reported rapes... plus one that went 'unreported'.

We do not know the actual ratio of unreported to reported rapes, but all indicators point to the unreported number being higher than we thought then, and probably higher than we think is occurring now.

---

[167] When did Marble come to Dallas? Until he was caught in 1977 we had no 'person' to focus on much less investigate his history. The focus of this book was telling the story of the FBR hunt and capture. Perhaps now I can focus some time on life of Guy Marble before FBR.

[168] Appendix A - Newspaper Article # 34 See website: robertjsadler.com

You have just read about the exact number of rapes, attempt rapes and burglaries, etc., we attributed to the FBR. At this point you know exactly what the FBR said regarding his "frequency" and you can judge for yourself how many rapes this man actually committed. We didn't know what decisions he made to or not to assault a particular resident. We don't know if he did or did not have a limit of burglaries per 'outing' he would commit without choosing someone to assault. We don't know if once he had raped someone if went home or would continue breaking into a further series of apartments and finding a second or third suitable victim, rape more than once a night. We do have multiple offenses we attributed to Marble on the same night, but never more than one rape.

Finally, one last time, the appellation or *nom de guerre,* as I called it, of "friendly" in Guy William Marble Jr.'s infamous moniker, *The Friendly Burglar-Rapist,* was given him by himself and reported by his victim... when **Marble said:**

"Don't make a sound... or I will kill you. Shhh, shh, I'm a friendly burglar, I'm just a friendly burglar; I won't hurt you, if you keep quiet."

That phrase, uttered by Marble, was noted by me in the rape offense reported as occurring at 5:00am on Thursday, November 7, 1974. I catalogued that offense as Offense Number 9 (see page 94) - as it was the ninth offense I had attributed to this suspect who, thenceforth, I called "The Friendly Burglar-Rapist" or "FBR" for short. I added the "hyphen Rapist" to the "Friendly Burglar" because that was what he was often there to do... it completed his ritual!

Remember, the first offense I attributed to the suspect, later termed the FBR, occurred on 11-15-1973 on a Central Patrol Division beat. It was not until 10 months later, on 9-5-1974 after a second rape offense occurring on a CPD beat and attributed to the FBR, that I began to wonder if he had 'hit' in other parts of the city. I then went through the intervening months' rape offenses, from all sectors of the city, and found the other eight FBR rapes that had occurred between "my" two CPD offenses.

No one in the city had put these rapes together. To CAPERS and Planning & Research they were just ten unfortunate random acts of rape committed by different rapists.

At this point I had accounted for approximately ten (10) citywide cases having FBR markers instead of only the two (2) in the CPD. It was then that the FBR's moniker was solidified.

I did not go back through the intervening months' O/IRs looking for burglaries, attempt burglaries, and etc. that might have had the signature methods of operation of the FBR. Had I done so, there might have been even more offenses attributed to the FBR.

I know none of the Bi-GatorSmooth crew (Jim, Tom and I) ever mentioned the FBR name to the media. The moniker was then picked up, propagated and prolonged in continued use by the media, police and the public. It was always understood by Tom and me that not one of these forced criminal assaults was 'friendly'! Each was committed by fear, intimidation, the use of restraints and the threat of bodily harm and/or death.

It is hoped that over the years the women assaulted by Marble have found a way to get past those moments of terror, to have had worry-free, productive lives. However, remember, readers, we all have memories. Now that you know their stories, you can understand and imagine those terrifying moments occurring over thirty-plus years ago have not been totally expunged, they will have been relived time and time again.

For those moments of mental replay, in my opinion, Guy William Marble Jr. can never be forgiven and though he can "say" he has paid his "debt to society" for the crimes he pled guilty to—can he ever be free of the earthly penance for each moment even one of his victims has replayed the memory of his actions?

Marble can never be excused of all of his crimes against society by paying part of the bill, and having "paid that debt", in part, be allowed to luxuriate in his old age fantasizing and replaying for his own 'pleasure' (as he no doubt did in prison) the hooding, binding and raping of his prey.

This book is dedicated to the peace of those he assaulted and the constant reminder that Guy William Marble Jr. should never rest easy with his thoughts.

Afterword

Where's Waldo?

Where *Is* Guy William Marble Jr.
or whatever name he uses today?

As you know by now, Marble did get out of prison in May 1998. It has been my and Tom's desire to locate GWM Jr. and confront him with the prospect of giving us the definitive interview on The Friendly Burglar-Rapist, and if he would not grant an interview, then possibly in the asking, he might make some revelatory statement. Neither is expected.

But it might be enough to know exactly where the FBR is today and what he has been doing since his release from prison. Has he truly "…stopped being a threat to anyone a long, long time ago,"[169] as he claimed prior to his release? I don't want to guess anymore, I want to know, don't you?

Since 2006, through the normal public data avenues and various contacts with local, state and federal agencies, I have been unable to establish the past or current whereabouts of Guy William Marble Jr.

For example, in 2009 a source told me that Marble was or had been living in San Antonio, Texas. I subsequently found a reference [170] that GWM Jr. had a San Antonio address.

I contacted the SAPD in October 2009[171]. In December I received a quick response[172] to my 2nd request (once it got to the right person) letting me know that Marble was not and had not been a registered Sex Offender in San Antonio and the address I had located was not at this time related to Marble; the current residents had been there since 2006 and they had no information about the prior owner/s. However, there was one bit of enlightening information. Sergeant Fulcher wrote: *"The Texas Department of Corrections had information that Marble was*

---

169 Appendix A - Newspaper Article # 34 See pgs 546-552 & website: robertjsadler.com

170 Appendix A - Item # 2 See page 541

171 Appendix A - Item # 5 See page 543

172 Appendix A - Item # 6 See page 545

paroled to Beaumont, Texas in 1998 according to our intelligence unit."

This is the first instance of my hearing that Marble was "paroled" rather than "released, for time served" in 1998. If he was "paroled" what were his restrictions? Where are the records? The statute indicates he should have been required to register as a sex offender. Did he? When did or does his parole expire? Where is Marble?

Remember in January 1996, while still in prison, GWM Jr. married French journalist, lawyer and anti-death-penalty advocate Dominique G. Malon in Walker County Texas[173]. Statements at the time by Marble[174] and Malon[175] indicate they were contemplating living abroad. France would be likely. Additionally, he may have changed his name either by assuming an identity or by changing it legally.

> "Twenty years ago, Mr. Marble told a reporter that he hoped to win release, change his name and disappear. Texas state law does not allow a former inmate to change his name until two years after his release." [176]

If Marble legally changed his name after 2000 there should be a court record, a county court record; but what county? It's the proverbial needle in the haystack; there are over 170 million acres in Texas divided into 254 counties.

Did Marble also "disappear" as he told the reporter he "hoped" to do?

To that end, if you know of the past or current whereabouts of one Guy William Marble Jr., his current *nom de plume*, or any name he goes by (legal or not) let us know.

If you have a personal anecdote or a personal experience with GWM from anytime in the past to the present, let us know.

GWM Jr., Tom and I know you are out there. We know others know where you are and what you have been doing. We have no doubt we will be hearing from many of them. When we find out, we will let the public know.

---

[173] Appendix A - Item # 4 See page 542

[174] Appendix A - Newspaper Article # 34 See pgs 546-552 & website: robertjsadler.com

[175] Ibid.

[176] Ibid.

As of December 2011 when I completed this manuscript the question still remained: **Where *is* Guy William Marble Jr.?**

Then in February 2012 Jim Bryan put me in contact with a detective now with the DPD Sex Crimes Unit. They had both worked in patrol at Central. I called and acquainted the detective with the now 35 year-old conviction of Guy William Marble Jr. and that I had been unable to either locate him or determine whether he ever registered[177] as a Sex Offender. Given my understanding of the Texas statute[178] I related that Marble may be in violation of the requirement to report.[179]

On March 29, 2012 this detective provided a welcome tidbit of news. Being circumspect about what could be revealed, the detective indicated that GWM Jr was alive and was currently of some interest. The detective reiterated that since Marble had not returned through Dallas, after his release from prison, Dallas did not have jurisdiction and thus the detective was waiting on information from DPS & possible federal agency action.

I inferred, if indeed Marble did not report, it might be possible Guy William Marble Jr. could be subject to arrest.

Three months later, on Monday July 2nd the detective, revealed that **"we know where he is, but he is (Marble) out of the country," "I don't now how/why they let him out..."**

I was apprised on Wednesday, July 11th that the detective had discussed providing me with the whereabouts of Marble with one of the unit's supervisors and told me, "I talked with our sergeant..." and the sergeant "...will not allow the info to be released".

I can understand if the DPD or some other agency has something 'working' and may not want to reveal means or methods, however, the record of a convict, is not private. The

---

[177] Marble still does not appear in the Texas Sex Offender Registry as of April 23, 2012.

[178] On September 1, 1997, the **registration requirement was made retroactively applicable to any person whose "reportable conviction or adjudication" occurred on or after September 1, 1970 if the person was still in the Texas criminal justice system for that offense on or after September 1, 1997.** Marble was still "in the system" on 9.1.1997 and remained "in the system" for eight (8) more months. His release date was May 26, 1998. See Appendix A Item # 11. See page 562.

[179] Texas Sex Offender Registration Program - first sex offender laws in Texas went into effect on 09/01/1991. These laws have been amended every legislative session since. FAQ #37 see http://www.txdps.state.tx.us/administration/crime_records/pages/faq.htm

whereabouts of a convicted sex offender is not protected information from the public, quite the contrary.

I was advised that perhaps the Houston Police Department Sex Offender Unit had information. Or I could file an open records request. I contacted the HPD's sex crimes unit and thus far have not found an interested ear. Messages left for contact have thus far gone unanswered. On Thursday, July 26th I filled an Open Records Request with the DPD. The senior police official that recommended this action told me "they have 10 days to respond." We will see...

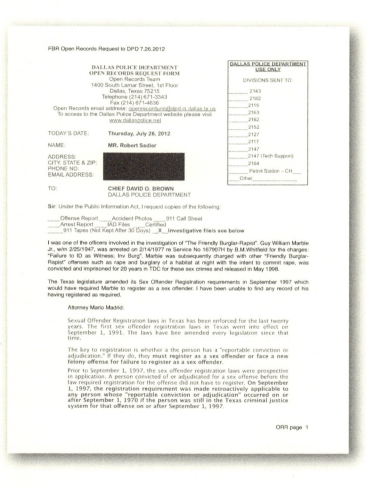

FBR Open Records Request to DPD 7.26.2012

Texas Code of Criminal Procedure Article 62.001(5) is the controlling statute and defines "reportable conviction or adjudication" as follows:

5) "Reportable conviction or adjudication" means a conviction or adjudication, including an adjudication of delinquent conduct or a deferred adjudication that, regardless of the pendency of an appeal, is a conviction for or an adjudication for or based on:

(A) a violation of Section 21.11 (Indecency with a child), 22.011 (Sexual assault), 22.021 (Aggravated sexual assault), or 25.02 (Prohibited sexual conduct), Penal Code;

(D) a violation of Section 30.02 (Burglary), Penal Code, if the offense or conduct is punishable under Subsection (d) of that section and the actor committed the offense or engaged in the conduct with intent to commit a felony listed in Paragraph (A) or (C);

Given the statute cited, Marble may thus be guilty of committing a felony, I requested Dallas Police Department Sex Crimes Unit to look into the whereabouts of Guy William Marble, Jr. and determine his sex offender status.

Earlier this month I was told that information does exist regarding Marble's whereabouts, that he is out of the country. When asked to be provided with details of this information, a supervisor with DPD Sex Crimes Unit declinec to allow the information to be released.

Please provide any investigative record or note regarding and detailing the current whereabouts of Guy William Marble Jr and his status, vis a vis the Sex Offender Registration requirements of the State of Texas. Additionally, please provide where and or what agency/s currently have information in their database regarding the record of Guy William Marble Jr. DOD 2/25/1947; SID 02306027; TDC 274515.

Sincerely,

REQUEST RECEIVED BY: _____

ADDITIONAL TIME LETTER GIVEN YES or NO _____

ORR page 2

I received two follow-up letters from the DPD on August 6th and 9th (both postmarked "AUG 10 2012") regarding my ORR. The first explained that my request had been received, but that the information I had requested "will require additional time to retrieve." The August 9th letter informed me that the information requested "has been collected and is ready for release." Unfortunately, I had not been to the mailbox for about ten days. When I found those letters on Monday, August 20th; I headed downtown.

Returning from the Jack Evans Police Headquarters building, I reviewed the information acquired by Detectives Tittle and Dilbeck of the Dallas Police Department Sex Crimes Unit. I cannot thank Detectives Lori Long Tittle and Reed Dilbeck enough for their diligence in finding the information for which I had been searching. What they found was quite illuminating.

The first document of interest is titled: "ADULT SEX OFFENDER REGISTRATION PRE-RELEASE NOTIFICATION FORM" (ASORP-RNF)[180]. It's second bold face title explains: "THIS IS NOT THE REGISTRATION FORM". Directly under this title are the instructions to: "Mail Original to: Texas Department of Public Safety, Special-crimes service, Sex offender registration Program, P.O. Box 4087, Austin, Texas 78773-0426". The date of the notification is typed as 05/26/98. This document answers the question, was Marble supposed to register and if so, when and for how long?

According to this ASORP-RNF, which was initialed and signed by Guy Marble Jr. on 5/26/98, Marble was informed that his "DUTY TO REGISTER EXPIRES (check applicable time): X Lifetime". Additionally, Marble had a "VERIFICATION REQUIREMENT (check applicable time): X Every 90 Days". Marble was informed and directed by this document thusly: "You are covered by this law and required as of the date, 06/03/98, to register with the law enforcement authority (chief of police or sheriff) in the city or county where you live or intend to live for more than seven days." "You must contact this law enforcement agency in person not later than the 7th day following your arrival in the city or the county and complete the verification or registration process." This document bears a date stamp which indicates it was received by Texas DPS (Department of Public Safety), Crime Records Service on June 4, 1998; a week after Marble's release and one day after Marble was supposed to have reported to the Chief of Police of Beaumont, Texas or the Sheriff of Jefferson County, Texas in which the city of Beaumont is located.

This ASORP-RNF lists Marble's "PROPOSED RELEASE ADDRESS" as "4650 Collier St., Beaumont, Texas" in Jefferson County, zip code "77006".

Let me make it perfectly clear, according to the ASORP-RNF, Marble was required to register as a sex offender and verify his residence every ninety days, for life! (my emphasis)

The second document of note was a very poor copy of the state's "APPLICATION FOR TEXAS DRIVERS LICENSE OR

---

[180] See scan of document & comments on website: robertjsadler.com

IDENTIFICATION CARD"[181]. This document is stamped, twice, "NOT A DRIVING PERMIT", which means the ID Card was for identification purposes only. This document appears to have been filled in by hand by Marble and contains his "usual written signature", "Guy Marble" and is dated "5/28/98".

In the pre-release notification of Marble's sex-offender-status to DPS the ASORP-RNF was dated May 26, 1998, (the day of his release from prison), and it further shows that Marble gave his "proposed release address" as within the city of Beaumont, Texas, Jefferson County. Two days later (5/28/98) Marble is filling out another state document, which he also certifies with his signature, listing his "RESIDENCE ADDRESS" as what appears to be: "331? Carnab..." in the city of "San Antonio".

As you may recall, in August 2009, I had found one database[182] search which listed Marble with an address of "3318 Carnaby, San Antonio, Texas 79247". With addition of the "8", this appears to be the same address Marble inked-in on the his application for a DPS, Texas ID Card. In a response to my inquiry of October 23, 2009, San Antonio detectives went to this

address, found no Guy William Marble, Jr., nor any link with Marble to this property, past or present. Further SAPD Sex Crimes Sgt. Tom Fulcher stated: "In reference to Guy Marble, he is not now, nor has he ever been a registered Sex Offender in the City of San Antonio."

Generally, if you do not have a driver's license, you must present yourself in person along with appropriate identification at a local DPS Driver's License office in order to obtain a Texas

181 See scan of document & comments on website: robertjsadler.com

182 Texas Criminal Database 8/16/2009 Tx. Sex Offender 08/24/2009, State ID 02306027

Driver's Licenses or DPS (state-issued) Texas Identification Card. If I was going to be living in Beaumont, I'd get my driver's license or state ID card in that city. However if I knew I was going to be living in San Antonio I would go there to apply from my ID card. It would be unusual not go to the city within which you intended to live, in order to obtain this ID; particularly when you move "[y]ou are required to make that change of address with the Texas Department of Public Safety (DPS) within 30 days." I find it very curious then, that two days after getting out of prison and having informed authorities he proposed to live in Beaumont, Marble is applying for a state ID card with a residence address, 280 miles or five hours west of Beaumont, in San Antonio, Texas. Where did Marble actually reside immediately after his release from prison? Beaumont? San Antonio? Somewhere else? I don't know... and as far as I can tell neither did the State of Texas.

Several presumptions now exist; *one*, once issued Marble would be required to change the address of his state issued Identity Card within thirty (30) days if there was a change in his residence address and *two*; Marble was required to register as a sex offender in person within seven (7) days of his release; *three*, he was required to notify police in person within seven (7) days if he changed his address; and *four*, he was required to reverify his sex offender registration every ninety (90) days, for life! It would appear that Marble did none of these things. The failure to make a proper change of address to your state ID may be an administrative infraction with only minor consequences, however, the failure to register and maintain your sex offender registration, is a felony!

Where did Marble reside after his release from prison? And where is he living now? As to the first question, I currently have no information regarding the location or locations of Marble residential domicile/s between May 26, 1998 and September 22, 2010. As to where Guy William Marble, Jr is today, I now know!

Marble left the State of Texas and the United States of America, holding a U.S. Passport, almost two years ago. He left on Continental flight 32[183] from Houston Intercontinental on Wednesday, September 22, 2010 bound for Charles De Gaulle airport, Paris, France.

The shame of it is, given the information I received today (August 20, 2012), Marble's 'leaving the state' was just nine months after my October 23, 2009 request to the SAPD to check out Marble's San Antonio address. Had any number of the people and agencies I had asked to help locate Marble in 2008, 2009 done so, perhaps he could have been arrested for his apparently on-going felonious failure to register and maintain his sex offender registration.

In 2008 was Marble already in possession of his passport? Regardless, when did he apply for and receive his passport? It apparently is not prohibited for a convicted felon to be issued a U.S. Passport. Given the ten-year life of currently issued passports he could have had one since 2000. Did he have one pre or post-911? When does Marble's current passport expire? Did Marble have to admit to his sex offender status or his convictions for sex offenses on his passport application? Did he make any material misrepresentation (lie) on his passport application?

The current "Application For A U.S. Passport" does not indicate a prohibition against convicted felons except if: 1) their conviction is for a "drug offense", 2) for "'sex tourism' crimes statue", and 3) "not the subject of an outstanding federal, state or local warrant of arrest for a felony...". None of those three situations applied to Marble, as far as I know. However the fact that, according to my reading of the statue and his ASORP-RNF, Marble was required to register as a sex offender (for life) and apparently did not, which is a felony, would subject Marble to arrest for his failure to register and maintain his registration.

Given Marble's signed ASORP-RNF and the receipt of same by DPS, why would his records not be flagged? Was Marble ever listed as "noncompliant" for not registering as a sex offender as he was required to do? He should have been on a watch list for failure to register/maintain registration and a warrant for his arrest should have been issued culminating in his name being put on a State Department no-fly list.

---

[183] Using August 2012 schedules as an example, Continental 32 departed Houston Bush Int'ctl (KIAH) at 3:30pm CDT with a scheduled arrival Charles De Gaulle/Roissy (LFGB/CDG) at 7:34AM CEST. The flight duration is approximately 8 hours 42 minutes.

On September 22, 2010 Guy William Marble, Jr. arrived in France. And according to a source Marble claimed his destination to be in Blunoy, France and listed his "contact information in the destination country," as Dominique Gislaine Rejane Malon. In the 1998 pre-release article we were told, "Ms. Malon would not say whether her husband plans to join her and her two daughters at their home in a Paris suburb near Orly Airport, where she works for a French magazine about Africa." Various websites searched revealed that Malon lives or had lived in Blunoy, France.

That same Marble pre-release article revealed: "**Laurent Melier, a French Consulate spokesman in Houston, said Ms. Malon visited that office in 1996 and spoke of her efforts to have Mr. Marble join her in France. He said she took steps to ensure her marriage was recognized by France, a prerequisite for Mr. Marble to earn citizenship based on marriage.**

But, another consular official said, **French law would not allow Mr. Marble to become a citizen or even get an extended visa because of his criminal record. A tourist visit of up to 90 days would require no background check or visa, but it would be illegal for him to stay any longer**. Ms. Malon said the couple planned to comply with all laws."

Since I have no information that Marble returned in the interim to the U.S., it would appear that Marble may have been living in France since September 2010. If that is the case has he complied with or is he complying with French law? Has the law changed in France since 1998? Has Marble applied for French citizenship? Has he revoked his American citizenship?

Bottom line, I know where Guy William Marble, Jr., the Friendly Burglar Rapist, indicated his destination would be as of his arrival in France in 2010. I have the address! I could publish this address, but it has already been almost three years... is Marble still there today? I want to be able to confirm his address.

Do *you* know where the convicted rapist Guy William Marble, Jr lives today? If you do, let me know!

And no, it's not enough *just* to know where he *probably* is.

The End... for now

Post Script 1:

As sometimes happens with true crime books, the revelations in its pages often lead to new revelations by persons with information not available to the author. It may be that a second book or sequel to *One Step from Murder: the friendly burglar RAPIST* could occur if such additional stories or information come to light. In particular: 1) the whereabouts and resolution of Marble's circumstances; and 2) if any of the women whose stories are revealed in this book (or their family, friends or acquaintances) would like to get in touch with me to tell me how Marble, the FBR, affected their lives, I am here to listen and or tell there story, if that is their intent.

Appendices

Note: Due to size constraints, though various items are footnoted as being in the appendix only a few could be included.

I have devoted a new section of my website robertjsadler.com to accommodate these documents for viewing, research and comment. These and other documents and materials will be available for your review and study.

I encourage you to visit
robertjsadler.com
& click the FBR tab
to see information not included in
One Step from Murder: the friendly burglar
RAPIST.

Appendix A Item #1

Identification, Records & Location Information
Guy William Marble Jr. w/m DOB: February 25, 1947

Name. . . . : **MARBLE,GUY WILLIAM JR**
Address . . : **3318 CARNABY**
City, St Zip: **SAN ANTONIO , TX** 78247
Physical Characteristics:
Sex . : Unknown
Eyes: Unknown
Race. : Unknown
Hair: N/A
Height: UnKnown
Weight: UnKnown

D/L Number. : [TX] 15516371
Class...... : **ID CARD**
Birthdate: **02/25/1947**
Phone...... :
Validated: 05/05/2007
OptOut...: Yes
Last Transaction: 05/05/2007 :   DELETED RECORD
Restrictions / Endorsements

Appendix A Item #2

```
DCS Information Systems    | © 1994-2009 v4.1.6
Time: 10:53, 10/23/2009 |        TX Judicial
Report          | DCSI UFD: 08/16/2009
-------------------------|
DPPA:03
|---------------------------------------------
```

The information provided is obtained from the Texas Conviction Database and contains all CONVICTIONS and FELONY DEFERRED ADJUDICATIONS that are contained within the Computerized Criminal History system maintained by the Texas DPS. This file only contains information reported to the DPS by the various Texas reporting courts and may not be complete. This file does not contain arrest records. The database is replaced monthly from updated information received from the Texas DPS. The information is provided for tip and lead purposes only and DCS recommends the user independently verify any information obtained from this database prior to use of the data!

Tx Criminal DataBase 08/16/2009 Tx Sex Offender 08/25/2008

State ID: 02306027   Sex: M   Race: White
Name: **MARBLE,GUY WILLIAM JR**   Height: 6-00 Eyes: BLU
Date of Birth: **02/25/1947**   Weight: 177 Hair: BRO

- - Known Alias - -   - - Known Alias D O B's - -
MARBLE,GUY   **01/15/1947**
MARBLE,GUY JR
MARBLE,GUY WILLIAM

- - Summary of Offenses - -
CD_Date___ Disposition_____
Offense_____
      CONVICTED   BURGL

Record: 1   StateID: 02306027 Name: MARBLE, GUY WILLIAM JR

Offense Description. . . . . : BURGL
Court Disposition. . . . . . : CONVICTED
Court Offense (Free Text) . : **BURGL -HAB-WITH INT TO RAPE 7 CTS**
Court Confinement. . . . . . : **60 YEARS**
Court Provision Literal. . . : **CONC EACH COUNT**

Author's Note: The above circled area in Appendix A Item #2 indicates the DCS Info. System has GWM Jr as a "Tx Sex Offender 08/25/2008", however, then as now, Marble is no where to be found in an Sex Offender data base, local, state or national.

Appendix A - Item # 3

email sent 3.2.2010
Records: Guy William Marble, Jr. (SID 02306027)

...
Tue, March 2, 2010 5:05:12 PM
Robert Sadler <robert-sadler@sbcglobal.net>
From: ...
View Contact

To: exec.services@tdcj.state.tx.us

TDCJ – Executive Services
P.O. Box 99
Huntsville, TX 77342-0099
E-mail: exec.services@tdcj.state.tx.us
Facsimile: 936.437.2125

Re: **Guy William Marble, Jr. DOB: 02/25/1947; SID: 02306027**
        Open Records Request
        General: File of former inmate
        Specific: Hearing/s Record for Guy William Marble,
Jr.
during the period 1977 through May 1998

I desire to obtain the record/s for Guy William Marble, Jr. during the period between 1977 and 1998. Pursuant to Open Records statues and Texas Administrative Code, Title 37, Part 5, Chapter 147, Subchapter A, Rule § 147.6 would you please inform me as to the number of records/ pages in the Guy William Marble, Jr. file, the cost to obtain these records and your guidance on the most efficient way of obtaining said records.

Respectfully,

Robert Sadler

Appendix A - Item #4						
Marriage / Divorce Search						
Event Type	Mar Date Div Date	Mar/Div County	Husband Name Wife Name	Year of Birth	Age at Event	# of Child
Mar	Aug 31, 1968	Harris	MARBLE Guy William Jr SCARBORO Marylyn Sue	1947 1947	21 21	
Div	08/31/1968 06/12/1979	Harris	MARBLE Guy William Jr SCARBORO Marylyn Sue	1947 1948	32 32	1
Mar	Sep 23, 1987	Harris	MARBLE Guy William Jr WALKER, Linda	1947 1948	40 39	
Div	09/23/1987 12/08/1989	Harris	MARBLE Guy William Jr WALKER, Linda		42 41	
Mar	Jan 22, 1996	Walker	MARBLE Guy William Jr MALON, Dominique G	1948 1952	48 44	

Note: The above information is publicly available on the internet, the year of birth discrepancies are not the author's.

Appendix A Item #5
10.23.09 email to SAPD

----- Forwarded Message ----
From: Robert Sadler <robert-sadler@sbcglobal.net>
To: sexcrimes@sanantonio.gov
Sent: Fri, October 23, 2009 7 PM
Subject: Request for Verification of SO Resident

Dear Sir or Madame:

I am one of the Dallas officer's responsible for the arrest of Guy William Marble, Jr. (The "Friendly Rapist) in February 1977. He was released from TDC in May of 1998. It is my understanding that he was required to register as a sex offender and would have to maintain his registration. It is my understanding that he is or was in your jurisdiction. His name does not appear on the State Sex Offender List nor on the National database.

I would appreciate your checking on this individual and informing me of his current status.

Sincerely,

Robert J. Sadler

Here is the information I have:

According to various public records the last known address of **Guy William Marble Jr., w/m DOB: 02/25/1947** (Tx Criminal DataBase 8/16/2009 Tx Sex Offender 08/24/2008, State ID 02306027) was 3318 Carnaby, San Antonio , Texas 78247 .

> State ID: 02306027
> Name: MARBLE, GUY WILLIAM JR
> Offense Description: BURGL
> Court Disp   CONVICTED
> Court Disposition (Free Text): BURGL – HAB-WITH INT TO RAPE 7 CTS

Marble served 20 years in TDC and was released in May of 1998.

A check of the Texas Sex Offender List shows no result for Marble. The result was also negative for Marble on the National database.

Can you confirm that:
>   A. Marble is a currently registered Sex Offender residing in the City of San Antonio ?
>   B. That his current SO registered address is 3318 Carnaby, San Antonio , TX
>   C. If he is not now a currently registered SO residing in San Antonio , has he ever been a registered SO in San Antonio.
>   D. If he was a registered SO in San Antonio
>   a. what was his last known address
>   b. when was his address last verified
>   c. did he make notification or notify SAPD of his intent to move
>   d. has he informed SAPD that he has indeed moved to another jurisdiction
>   i. what forwarding address did he give.
>   ii. when did he register in that jurisdiction

Appendix A Item #6
12.02.09 SAPD response to 2nd

⊞

From: Robert Sadler [mailto:robert-sadler@sbcglobal.net]
Sent: Tuesday, December 01, 2009 2:03 PM
To: PD Sex Crimes Unit
Subject: 2nd Request for Info: Fw: Request for Verification of SO Resident

Dear Sir or Madame: As you can see I am forwarding my email to you on Fri, October 23, 2009 4:22:19 PM, to which I have yet to receive a response. Please verify the below information and respond.

Thank you
rjs

RE: 2nd Request for Info: Fw: Request for Verification of SO Resident

...

Wed, December 2, 2009 12:42:48 PM

From: Thomas Fulcher <Thomas.Fulcher@sanantonio.gov>

To: robert-sadler@sbcglobal.net

Cc: Andrew Carian <Andrew.Carian@sanantonio.gov>

Mr. Sadler,

In reference to Guy Marble, he is not now, nor has he ever been a registered Sex Offender in the City of San Antonio. Base on the information you provided I sent detectives to the Carnaby address and contacted the residence at that location. They have lived there several years and are not familiar with Marble. The Texas Department of Corrections had information that Marble was paroled to Beaumont, Texas in 1998 according to our intelligence unit. Should you develop any information on his whereabouts either drop us an e-mail or contact the local Law Enforcement agency in that jurisdiction.

Thanks for bring this information to our attention.

Sgt. Tom Fulcher #3269
San Antonio Police Department
Sex Crimes
214 W. Nueva, San Antonio, Texas 78207
Phone: (210) 207-7476
Fax: (210) 207-2821
Email: tfulcher@sanantonio.gov

From: PD Sex Crimes Unit
Sent: Tuesday, December 01, 2009 2:39 PM
To: Jesse Mckinney; Thomas Fulcher
Subject: FW: 2nd Request for Info: Fw: Request for Varification of SO Resident

---

Appendix A - Newspaper Article # 34

Appendix A - Newspaper Article # 33

Text of DMN 12.19.1986 FBR Parole Denied 3rd time

PAROLE DENIED MAN SUSPECTED IN DALLAS RAPES.

The Dallas Morning News - Friday, December 19, 1986
Author: Austin Bureau of The News: The Dallas Morning News (DAL) + _____

AUSTIN -- Guy Marble Jr., linked to as many as 75 rapes in Dallas in the mid-1970s, has been **denied parole** from state prison **for the third time**.

Marble's bid for release was rejected by a three-member review panel, said Glenn Heckmann, deputy director of the State Board of Pardons and Paroles. The vote was 2-1 against his release. He will be eligible for review again in February, 1988.

Marble, nicknamed "the **friendly rapist**,' was arrested on Valentine's Day, 1977, and later sentenced to 60 years in prison on a charge of burglary of a residence with intent to commit rape.

Police said he may have been responsible for as many as 75 rapes over three years. He began serving his sentence in February, 1977.

Marble was denied parole in February 1985 and again in July of that year, Heckmann said.

He said that the parole board had received letters opposing Marble's release, but the source and content of that correspondence is confidential by law.

Edition: HOME FINAL Section: NEWS Page: 34A Dateline: AUSTIN
Record Number: DAL272727
Copyright 1986 The Dallas Morning News Company

'Friendly Rapist' to leave prison

Dallas serial predator in '70s says he's no longer a threat; victim still haunted

By Pete Slover
Staff Writer of The Dallas Morning News

After two decades in prison, the "Friendly Rapist" will walk free Tuesday, newly married, looking for a fresh start — perhaps in France — and promising the world there's nothing to worry about.

Dallas was unnerved in 1977 by the Jekyll-and-Hyde unmasking of Guy Marble, by day a charismatic ad executive, by night a serial predator with victims in the dozens.

"There's nothing 'friendly' about it when you're tied up, blindfolded, with a knife in your throat, and raped," one victim, now 51, said of Mr. Marble's 1976 attack. "He's still a hated person as far as I'm concerned."

About to be handed $100 walking money and an unconditional release, Mr. Marble, 51, professes his own rehabilitation.

"I'm just an old man with a bad back who is looking for a few years of peace and contentment," he wrote in response to written questions by The Dallas Morning News.

"I stopped being a threat to anyone a long, long time ago."

Mr. Marble penned his contrition from a prerelease center in Overton, saying he has conquered sexual obsessions rooted in childhood.

I have looked into those dark corners of my mind confronted my demons, he wrote. Exposed to the light of day, our secrets lose their power over us eventually.

Mr. Marble has married twice since entering prison in 1978, most recently to a French anti-death-penalty activist who waxes romantic about their future together.

For 12 years behind bars, Mr. Marble edited and largely wrote The Echo, the 160,000-circulation monthly newspaper of the Texas prison system.

Mr. Marble, a native of Galena Park near Houston, said years of voluntary counseling showed him that the rapes

Please see MAN on Page 24A

'Friendly Rapist' to leave prison - Dallas serial predator in '70s says he's no longer a threat; victim still haunted

The Dallas Morning News - Sunday, May 24, 1998
Author: Pete Slover, Staff Writer of *The Dallas Morning News*

[Note: Bold Text - Emphasis added - mine - rjs]

After two decades in prison, the "Friendly Rapist" will walk free Tuesday, newly married, looking for a fresh start— perhaps in France—and promising the world there's nothing to worry about.

Dallas was unnerved in 1977 by the Jekyll-and-Hyde unmasking of Guy Marble, by day a charismatic ad executive, by night a serial predator with victims in the dozens.

"There's nothing "friendly' about it when you're tied up, blindfolded, with a knife in your throat, and raped," one victim, now 51, said of Mr. Marble's 1976 attack. "He's still a hated person as far as I'm concerned."

About to be handed $100 walking money and an unconditional release, Mr. Marble, 51, professes his own rehabilitation.

"I'm just an old man with a bad back who is looking for a few years of peace and contentment," he wrote in response to written questions by The Dallas Morning News.

"I stopped being a threat to anyone a long, long time ago."

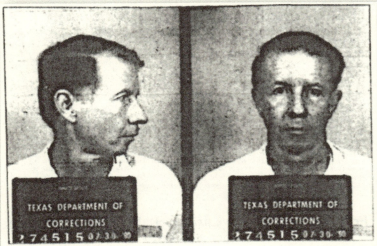

"I'm just an old man with a bad back who is looking for a few years of peace and contentment," Guy Marble, known as the "Friendly Rapist," wrote in response to written questions by *The News*. At right is a photo of Mr. Marble in 1977 after he received a 60-year sentence.

Mr. Marble penned his contrition from a pre-release center in Overton, saying he has conquered sexual obsessions rooted in childhood.

"I have looked into those dark corners of my mind, confronted my demons," he wrote. "Exposed to the light of day, our secrets lose their power over us eventually."

Mr. Marble has married twice since entering prison in 1978, most recently to a French anti-death-penalty activist who waxes romantic about their future together.

For 12 years behind bars, Mr. Marble edited and largely wrote The Echo, the 160,000-circulation monthly newspaper of the Texas prison system.

Mr. Marble, a native of Galena Park near Houston, said years of voluntary counseling showed him that the rapes were, in part, blamable on those who failed to identify and address his youthful deviance.

"Sexual abnormalities and obsessions are hidden in a dark corner of the mind, an emotional cancer that sprouts in childhood and seldom gets treated in our society," he wrote. **"The rehearsals for my crimes began in grade school, and nobody ever took enough interest to notice, to help me understand.**

"Acting out those fantasies as a young adult was inevitable."

In early 1977, Mr. Marble's stake-out arrest ended a two-year hunt for a man Dallas police had dubbed the **"Friendly Rapist"** and had blamed for about 50 attacks, mostly at Greenville Avenue-area apartments.

The label, derived from the attacker's habit of chatting with his victims, was a product of the times.

In those days, Dallas police gave media-ready nicknames to most serial criminals: The late 1970s also saw the "Greasy Rapist," the "Jumper Cable Rapist" and the ".45-Caliber Rapist."

The oxymoronic label "friendly," unimaginable as applied to a rapist today, caused little stir then. It was borne of an era when police, without criticism, pronounced that victims had put themselves at risk through a "swinging-singles" apartment lifestyle.

Police lore has it that a detective immediately linked Mr. Marble to the rapes based on a look at the suspect's hands: An unusual fingerprint loop matched the crime-scene evidence. The media devoured the story.

Mr. Marble was an athletic, 29-year-old family man and a vice president with the Bloom Advertising Agency, with accounts including the Southern Baptist Convention. He was also an alumnus and poker-playing buddy of the local press corps, having worked at a variety of small newspapers.

In Mr. Marble's own recently written **words: "Surprise and fear were the main factors,"** he wrote. "People had to ask themselves, if the college-educated professional in the nice North Dallas family home is also this dangerous night predator, are we safe from anyone, anywhere?"

At the time, detectives said Mr. Marble admitted to as many as 40 attacks. Police never publicly cataloged those offenses, and defense attorneys would later claim the numbers were unfounded.

Unlike today, rape carried a lesser sentence than burglary, so **prosecutors picked the seven strongest cases and charged Mr. Marble with burglary with intent to commit rape**.

Confronted with fingerprint evidence, he accepted a prosecution offer to plead guilty and take a 60-year sentence.

Prison life began with a variety of menial assignments, including chopping wood. In 1979, a Houston court granted the uncontested divorce petition filed by his wife of nine years, who, since remarried, declined to comment.

His daughter, now 28, did not respond to an interview request. Prison records show she was among a number of Mr. Marble's relatives, including his siblings, who visited him over the years.

In 1985, Mr. Marble was transferred to The Walls, the Huntsville prison unit where he won the editor job. As such, he was one of the few prisoners with his own office, which he outfitted with donated computers and software.

"Receiving the work assignment as Echo editor in 1985 turned out to be both an emotional and intellectual life saver," he wrote. "The challenges of prison journalism, walking the tightrope of a censored publication, saved me from the mind-numbing lethargy of this environment."

From his cell and office, Mr. Marble culled articles from outside newspapers and reported on criminal justice and prison issues.

Under a pen name, he started "Dear Darby," an advice column for prisoners. He wrote fiction and stayed in contact with various literary journals and publications.

In a letter to Texas Lawyer, Mr. Marble criticized a state Supreme Court justice this way: "As Gustav Flaubert wrote, "Our ignorance of history causes us to slander our own times.' "

While that sort of elevated discourse may have preserved Mr. Marble's self-esteem, it did nothing to endear him to wardens and guards, said **prison spokesman David Nunnelee**.

"They thought he was kind of uppity. He thought he was better than other prisoners," said Mr. Nunnelee, who worked with Mr. Marble because the prison public affairs office oversees production of The Echo.

Mr. Nunnelee **expressed surprise that Mr. Marble said he had undergone "hundreds" of hours of counseling. He said Mr. Marble was not involved in any group or individual sessions during the last dozen years, when they worked together.**

In September 1987, records show, Mr. Marble married a Houston church worker in a ceremony during which he was represented by a stand-in, or proxy, before a Harris County justice of the peace. The marriage was annulled with Mr. Marble's consent in December 1989. Mr. Marble, the woman and the proxy all declined to discuss the circumstances.

He married again in January 1996, using a Huntsville courthouse bailiff—since elected sheriff—as proxy. His bride was Dominique Malon, a French journalist who met Mr. Marble during a tour of the prison by Amnesty International.

Trained as a lawyer, Ms. Malon, 47, had made a special cause of death row inmate Samuel Christopher Hawkins, a former Amarillo butcher known as the "Traveling Rapist."

Mr. Hawkins, who said God directed him to his victims, was linked to at least 30 rapes, including the rape-slayings of a 12-year-old girl and a 19-year-old pregnant woman, who was stabbed more than 20 times and nearly decapitated.

"He is not an animal: Read his case," she told reporters on the eve of his 1995 execution. "Back in France, I would bring you into my home and show you all the crafts he has made—clocks, jewelry, drawings, for everyone in the family."

Ms. Malon spoke Tuesday from Huntsville, where she stopped to be a witness at a prisoner's execution before going to East Texas for her husband's release.

"Whatever happens, our intention is to live together one day at a time," she said. "No ocean will separate us."

Ms. Malon would not say whether her husband plans to join her and her two daughters at their home in a Paris suburb near Orly Airport, where she works for a French magazine about Africa.

In a 1996 article about her death row activism, Ms. Malon told the French newspaper Le Figaro that **Mr. Marble "will be able to start a new life abroad with his French wife, far away from bad memories."** She spoke under a pseudonym "to protect her privacy and facilitate his transition," but the reporter who **wrote the article recently confirmed her identity.**

Laurent Melier, a French Consulate spokesman in Houston, said Ms. Malon visited that office in 1996 and spoke of her efforts to have Mr. Marble join her in France. He said she took steps to ensure her marriage was recognized by France, a prerequisite for Mr. Marble to earn citizenship based on marriage.

But, another consular official said, **French law would not allow Mr. Marble to become a citizen or even get an extended visa because of his criminal record. A tourist visit of up to 90**

days would require no background check or visa, but it
would be illegal for him to stay any longer.** Ms. Malon said the
couple planned to comply with all laws.

"I can only say good things about my husband. I love him,"
Ms. Malon said, adding that Mr. Marble had been open about his
past and his therapy. "It's not difficult for me to understand the
things that he did, so it's not difficult for me to accept them."

**Twenty years ago, Mr. Marble told a reporter that he
hoped to win release, change his name and disappear. Texas
state law does not allow a former inmate to change his name
until two years after his release.**

In his recent letter, Mr. Marble was guarded about his plans.

**"Self-employment is the most likely scenario. When it's
time, I can support myself with computer skills and writing,"
he wrote. "Exactly "where' I will settle is uncertain right
now, but far away from Texas is a safe bet."**

Like all married couples under prison rules, they have been
allowed only non-conjugal visits, with physical contact limited
to hand holding and public embraces.

Experts who have studied such relationships say women are
often attracted to the safety and control offered them in a prison
romance. In Ms. Malon's case, those restraints will disappear as
she joins a husband whose crimes were characterized by his total
domination of others. Given one adjective to describe Mr.
Marble, Mr. Nunnelee, the prison spokesman, said he would
choose "manipulative."

Recent letters discussing a possible interview with The News
show Mr. Marble's efforts to steer the process. First, he
suggested he wouldn't talk but needed a qualified reporter to help
on an autobiography. When that proposition went unanswered,
Mr. Marble agreed to an interview—on his terms. He wrote:

"If we talk, it will not be a traditional interview where you
record or write down answers... No notes, no voice-activated
recorder in your pocket... Any discussion of my family, close
friends, or personal life after release will be off limits."

The News did not accept the offer.

More than 20 years after his attack on her, his 1976 victim is
still haunted by the thought of Mr. Marble's domination.

"Little things you realize are a result of what he did—fear of
being controlled, for instance," she said. "For years I couldn't
drive on the inside lane of the freeway. I felt too hemmed in."

Mr. Marble said he doesn't expect forgiveness and, given the chance, couldn't venture what he would say to his victims.

"A thousand attempts at finding words would be hollow rhetoric in the face of their emotional pain. There are no answers, no explanations that can ease the tragedy I brought into those lives," he wrote.

"I can only hope that those victims and their families eventually found a way to relieve the anger, either through their Faith or other sources of strength and healing.

"The fact that I am very sorry for the hurt I inflicted on those people is probably not of any consequence to them and their families. That's understandable."

Caption: PHOTO(S): 1&2. "I'm just an old man with a bad back who is looking for a few years of peace and contentment," Guy Marble, known as the **"Friendly Rapist,"** wrote in response to written questions by The News. The above photos are from 1990. At right is Mr. Marble in 1977 after he received a 60-year sentence.[184]

Edition: HOME FINAL
Section: NEWS
Page: 1A
Record Number: 1021170
Copyright 1998 The Dallas Morning News

---

[184] *The DMN* article's mugshot photos (top) are Texas Department of Corrections in-custody inmate photos with (it is assumed) Marble's TCD Inmate # 274515 dated 07-30-90. The bottom photograph is a post-arrest, pre-book-in photograph taken on the morning of Marble's arrest shortly after his arrival at CID for questioning, approximately 1:30am on 2.14.77. On other records Marble has a "State ID" or SID # of 02306027. It is unknown what the difference/s is/are in these two numbers. Marble also shows to have had a Department of Public Safety ID Card #1551637.

Appendix A - Newspaper Article # 35
DMN 1.3.1990 ID man retires
[excerpted by rjs]

Detective dusts off retirement plans - Hailed by peers, fingerprint expert ends police career

The Dallas Morning News - Wednesday, January 3, 1990
Author: Lee Zethraus, Staff Writer of The Dallas Morning News:

On Valentine's Day 12 years ago, **Guy William Marble Jr.** was arrested by Dallas police after he was caught peering into some windows outside a North Dallas apartment.

When the suspect arrived at the police station, a sharp-eyed detective named Bobby Brown took the man's hands, turned them over and said, "This is our man. This is the "Friendly Rapist.' '

The story of how Lt. Brown was able to look at the man's fingers and identify the prints with the naked eye was just one of many told by Dallas and University Park police as they recalled the lieutenant's 35 years of police work.

Lt. Brown said identifying the "Friendly Rapist' was one of the highlights in his career. He played a major role in matching Mr. Marble 's fingerprints in 25 other cases— through more usual methods—which resulted in a 60-year prison sentence for Mr. Marble, who was linked to as many as 75 rapes during the mid-1970s.

The Oklahoma native said his law enforcement career began after two years of service in the Navy and one year in Korea. He said he returned home to work in the oil and natural gas businesses but had a change of heart and came to Dallas to join the Police Department in 1954.

"I just wanted to do something different,' he said.

After about five years as a patrol officer in South Dallas, Lt. Brown was promoted to detective. And it was his attention to detail that prompted his interest in fingerprint identification. In 1963, he took a fingerprint course from the Texas Department of Public Safety in Austin.

Later that year, he was called to assist in one of the biggest crime scene searches in U.S. history -- on the sixth floor of the Texas School Book Depository.

Lt. Brown and another Dallas officer were assigned to make detailed scale drawings of the sixth floor, where Lee Harvey Oswald allegedly leaned out the window and shot President John F. Kennedy.

Lt. Brown said they did recover fingerprint evidence that Mr. Oswald had been in the room near the window.

"His palm prints were on the boxes that were stacked at the window,' Lt. Brown said. "And they were on the rifle and there were spent cartridges on the floor.'

Lt. Brown said that after Mr. Oswald was arrested, he was asked to get some hair samples from the suspect.

"I asked could I clip some of his hair, and he just said, "Sure,' and started pulling out handfuls of his hair,' Lt. Brown said. "He was a smart aleck.'

Terry Hayes, identification supervisor for the Plano Police Department, remarked on Lt. Brown's photographic memory.

"He's one of the best in the United States,' Mr. Hayes said. "He can just remember fingerprints.'

Besides working on the Marble rape case together, Mr. Hayes said he and Lt. Brown handled many other Dallas investigations. He said he was always amazed to watch Lt. Brown get a "chaw of tobacco' and begin studying portions of fingerprints lifted from a crime scene.

"He would never really say anything, but walk over to a file cabinet stuffed with fingerprint cards and thumb through them and pull the card to match,' Mr. Hayes said. "He's the one to go to if you need a second opinion.'

The department sometimes uses computers at Dallas police headquarters to assist in fingerprint identification, but technology hasn't taken over this investigative art.

Lt. Brown plans to retire Jan. 16 after 35 years of police work.

see full article:

Edition: HOME FINAL
Section: PARK CITIES Page: 1J
Record Number: DAL1111003

Appendix A Item # 8
Feb. 25, 1985 Recommendation Letter for THC
Officer of the Month (pages 1-5)
Note: Tom was Awarded Officer of the Month
which automatically put forward this letter for Officer of the year
Tom received the Runner-Up Officer of the Year Award
from
Friends of Police
and
Officer of the Year
from
Dallas Community Police Awards Committee

Memorandum

CITY OF DALLAS

DATE   February 25, 1985

TO   Lieutenant Terry R. Hauck
Community Services Division

SUBJECT   Recommendation that Corporal Thomas H. Covington, #2273,
be Awarded the Officer of the Month Award

Corporal Thomas H. Covington has been a member of the Dallas Police
Department since September 19, 1966. For over two years, Corporal
Covington has been assigned to the Crime Analysis Unit of the
Planning and Research Division and under my direct supervision. His
overall performance during the entire period has been outstanding.
For example, he was instrumental in identifying a burglary ring
operating in the Dallas area over the past year. The burglary
operation was responsible for the theft of video and computer
equipment valued at over three and one-half million dollars. As a
result of his efforts, a task force was formed from area law
enforcement agencies and various divisions within the Dallas Police
Department. Twelve subjects were eventually arrested and over two
hundred offenses cleared. On another occasion, Corporal Covington
connected, by M. O., approximately forty safe burglaries in the
Northeast Division. He contacted the Northeast Division, briefing
division personnel on possible future targets, including dates and
times. Based on information, two officers were assigned to the
problem. As a result, a suspect was arrested and twenty-three
offenses were cleared.

Corporal Covington's efforts in Crime Analysis are not limited to
the apprehension of criminals and the recovery of property. He is
very adept at using all of the resources available within the Police
Department to impact crime. On many occasions, he has identified
crime trends that could be reduced through crime prevention
techniques. For example, Covington observed a rise in cigarette
thefts from gas stations during the past year. Noticing that the
suspects and M.O.'s were many and varied, Corporal Covington felt
that the thefts were crimes of opportunity. He requested that the
Crime Prevention Officers assigned to the Community Services
Division contact the oil companies involved. Sergeant L. E.
Beilharz later notified me that numerous companies had been
contacted and many of their suggestions had been adopted. Almost
immediately, the cigarette theft offenses were dramatically reduced.

Recommendation for Officer of the Month Award
Corporal Thomas H. Covington, #2273
February 25, 1985
Page 2

Corporal Covington's duties also include the coordinating of all
activities for visitors from other police agenices. During the past
year, the Planning and Research Division hosted approximately
twenty-four guests whose visits ranged from one day to three
months. In all cases, Corporal Covington performed in an exemplary
manner, assisting the visitors with transportation, housing, and
tours of the Department. One such visitor was Sergeant Nobuo
Hamaguchi of the Osaka, Japan Police Department. Sergeant
Hamaguchi's visit lasted three months. His mission was not only to
observe all facets of the Dallas Police Department's operation, but
also to observe our cultural and social habits. Corporal Covington
coordinated Sergeant Hamaguchi's entire itinerary with the Police
Department as well as housing and transportation. He spent a great
deal of his off duty time with Sergeant Hamaguchi, including a
weekend trip to the Japanese Consulate in Houston, Texas.

At no time did Corporal Covington allow this to distract him from
his normal duties. In fact, during one of his more hectic days, an
area businessman came into the Crime Analysis Unit complaining about
the number of times his business had been burglarized. Instead of
referring the man to the Patrol Bureau, he discussed the problem
with the man. Corporal Covington, who was familiar with the
problem, explained to the man what the Police Department was doing
about the problem and certain crime prevention techniques that he
could employ. When the businessman left our office, he was no
longer an angry and frustrated critic of the Police Department.

During Corporal Covington's nineteen years with the Dallas Police
Department, he has received forty-one personal commendations,
including the Certificate of Merit and a nomination for the Civic
Achievement Award.

The commendations have been distributed evenly over his career, and
noted, not only the usual assistance to motorist and courtesy on
call, but also his self restraint and professional demeanor. For
example, in 1970, Corporal Covington was commended when he and three
other officers diffused a disturbance involving approximately fifty
subjects, the majority of whom were intoxicated. The letter stated,
"Had this situation not been handled in a gentlemanly, business-like
and diplomatic manner, there very easily could have been a riot with
some people hurt. These four officers took an awful lot of verbal
abuse . . ." On another occasion, Corporal Covington and his
partner were commended when they pursued, on foot, and apprehended a
purse-snatch suspect.

Recommendation for Officer of the Month Award
Corporal Thomas H. Covington, #2273
February 25, 1985
Page 3

The commendation stated, "When the officers came back, they had
scratches and marks all over them like they had been in a fight with
a wildcat but they got him. Even then, they still treated the boy
very courteously, and were very kind to the lady victim . . ."

More recently, Corporal Covington was commended in 1979 when he
identified a warehouse theft trend at the 2001 Bryan Tower
Warehouse. Corporal Covington, using crime analysis techniques, had
predicted when the next offense would occur. Armed with this
information, the 2001 Bryan Company Security staked-out the
warehouse and apprehended the suspect. As a result, approximately
200 offenses were cleared.

In 1977, Corporal Covington was awarded the Certificate of Merit.
Covington received the award for his efforts in the arrest of Guy
William Marble, Jr. - the "Friendly Burglar-Rapist." Covington had
been analyzing the "Friendly Burglar-Rapist" offenses over a period
of several years and was able to "predict" the rapists activity.
Based on Covington's projection of when and where the rapist would
strike again, Marble was arrested in February of 1977. Seventy-nine
offenses were then cleared.

Later that same year, using the same method of analysis, Covington
personally arrested a subject. The subject had been breaking into
vehicles parked in the Holiday Inn parking lot at 1015 Elm Street.
Based on his analysis, Covington and another officer reported to
work on their day off at 4:00 a.m. On the second day of the
stake-out, a subject was arrested clearing ninety-six offenses.

Corporal Covington is constantly looking for new ways of analyzing
the offense reports and transmitting that data to the officers in a
timely manner. During the past year, he designed a computer
printout that would indicate the total value of property stolen in
specified offenses. This printout allowed him to target and connect
burglaries occurring across division boundaries involving unusual
volumes of merchandise usually associated with organized crime.
Corporal Covington also assisted in the design of the Flagged
Offense System which is scheduled to be implemented in the near
future. This system will enable officers calling in an offense
report to disseminate suspect information to all necessary divisions
immediately. This same data will be available for instant review by
computer terminal, thus enabling valuable suspect information to be
passed on to subsequent watches.

Recommendation for Officer of the Month Award
Corporal Thomas H. Covington, #2273
February 25, 1985
Page 4

Corporal Covington's involvement in special projects has not been
limited to this past year. In 1975, he participated in a task force
regarding off-duty employment of police officers. As a result of
the task force recommendations, procedures were established
requiring off-duty officers employed as security to complete all
paperwork connected with any offense or arrest initiated by that
officer. Obviously, this resulted in the savings of many on-duty
worker hours. In 1978, Corporal Covington served on a committee to
recommend proposals for future legislative considerations and to
identify communication problems within the Police Department.

In 1980, Corporal Covington organized the Downtown Security Officers
Association. This organization is still active with one hundred and
two members. In 1982, he re-organized the Dallas Hotel-Motel
Security Officers Association which had been inactive for several
years.

Corporal Covington's activities are not limited to the Police
Department. He has been a member of the Kirkwood United Methodist
Church for sixteen years. He has served on the Administrative Board
for the past ten years and on the Education and Youth Committee for
the past year.

Corporal Covington is also active in the Boy Scouts of America. He
has been the Scoutmaster of Boy Scout Troop 771 for the past fifteen
years. The troop's activities include a yearly excursion, at
Covington's expense, to various areas of interest throughout the
Southeast. The trips usually last a week and have taken him as far
as Ashville, North Carolina. Corporal Covington's most recent trip
with the scouts covered over 3200 miles in 8 days, visiting over 12
historical sites.

For his work with the Boy Scouts, he was awarded the District Award
of Merit in 1974. In 1975, he was awarded the Silver Beaver Award,
which is the highest award an adult can receive from the Boy Scouts
of America.

Corporal Covington is also the Post Advisor for Explorer Post 181,
sponsored by the Central Patrol Division. He is also the Second
Vice President of the Wynnewood Lions Club. His duties include
chairing the Boy Scout Committee for the Lions' Club District 2X1
(Dallas/Ft. Worth Area).

Recommendation for Officer of the Month Award
Corporal Thomas H. Covington, #2273
February 25, 1985
Page 5

Corporal Covington's attendance record during the past year was
excellent. He did not take any sick leave and, in many cases,
worked past his normal duty hours. For example, during the weekend
prior to Christmas, a large number of items were donated to the
Police Department's Operation Santa Cop Program. The items had been
delivered to the various patrol substations and had to be
transported to the Property Division for sorting and delivery.
Corporal Covington and his wife reported to the Property Division on
both Saturday and Sunday, working for over eight hours on each day.

It has become apparent to me that Corporal Covington's exceptional
performance over the past year is merely indicative of his
performance throughout his entire career. Obviously, Corporal
Covington's dedication to duty and devotion to excellence are those
qualities we must encourage and reward in order to establish an
exemplary role needed for both our younger and more mature
officers. Therefore, I recommend Corporal Covington be considered
for the Officer of the Month Award.

Larry J. Abney
Sergeant of Police
Planning and Research Division

dh

1092A

I concur DXH

I concur

i concur

Appendix A Item # 9
Search Results for GWM Jr
Dallas Co. Criminal Background Search
Dallas County, Dallas Texas 2009

Guy William Marble, Jr. Dallas County Court Records

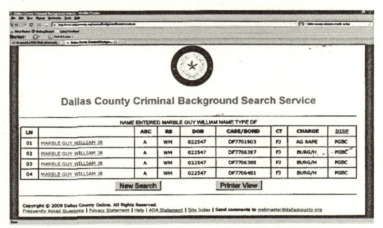

NAME ENTERED MARBLE GUY WILLIAM NAME TYPE DF

LN		ARC	RS	DOB	CASE/BOND	CT	CHARGE	DISP
01	MARBLE GUY WILLIAM JR	A	WM	022547	DF7701903	FJ	AG RAPE	PGBC 11/29/77 Burg/H 60 Mos (5 yrs)
02	MARBLE GUY WILLIAM JR	A	WM	022547	DF7706387	FJ	BURG/H	PGBC 11/29/77 Burg/H 60 Mos (5 yrs)
03	MARBLE GUY WILLIAM JR	A	WM	022547	DF7706388	FJ	BURG/H	PGBC 11/29/77 Burg/H 60 Mos (5 yrs)
04	MARBLE GUY WILLIAM JR	A	WM	022547	DF7706481	FJ	BURG/H	PGBC 11/29/77 Burg/H 60 Mos (5 yrs)

If sentences run CC (Concurrently) – he would serve 5 years total beginning 2/14/77 making his release date: approx 2/14/82.
If sentences run Consecutively (one after the other) he would 5x4 = 20 years total beginning 2/13/77 making his release date: approx 2/14/1997.

FJ Criminal District Court 3
PGBC Agreed plea of guilty before the court.

Appendix A Item # 11
Texas Sex Offender Registration
article posted 2.23.2012 by Mario Madrid
in *Houston criminal Law Journal.com*
http://www.houstoncriminallawjournal.com/

POSTED ON FEBRUARY 12, 2012 BY MARIO MADRID

Texas Sex Offender Registration

Sexual Offender Registration laws in Texas has been enforced for the last twenty years. The first sex offender registration laws in Texas went into effect on September 1, 1991. The laws have bee amended every legislation since that time.

The key to registration is whether a the person has a "reportable conviction or adjudication." If they do, they must register as a sex offender or face a new felony offense for failure to register as a sex offender.

Prior to September 1, 1997, the sex offender registration laws were prospective in application. A person convicted of or adjudicated for a sex offense before the law required registration for the offense did not have to register. On September 1, 1997, the registration requirement was made retroactively applicable to any person whose "reportable conviction or adjudication" occurred on or after September 1, 1970 if the person was still in the Texas criminal justice system for that offense on or after September 1, 1997.

Texas Code of Criminal Procedure Article 62.001(5) is the controlling statute and defines "reportable conviction or adjudication" as follows:

(5) "Reportable conviction or adjudication" means a conviction or adjudication, including an adjudication of delinquent conduct or a deferred adjudication that, regardless of the pendency of an appeal, is a conviction for or an adjudication for or based on:

(A) a violation of Section 21.11 (Indecency with a child), 22.011 (Sexual assault), 22.021 (Aggravated sexual assault), or 25.02 (Prohibited sexual conduct), Penal Code;

(B) a violation of Section 43.05 (Compelling prostitution), 43.25 (Sexual performance by a child), or 43.26 (Possession or promotion of child pornography), Penal Code;

(C) a violation of Section 20.04(a)(4) (Aggravated kidnapping), Penal Code, if the defendant committed the offense with intent to violate or abuse the victim sexually;

(D) a violation of Section 30.02 (Burglary), Penal Code, if the offense or conduct is punishable under Subsection (d) of that section and the actor committed the offense or engaged in the conduct with intent to commit a felony listed in Paragraph (A) or (C);

(E) a violation of Section 20.02 (Unlawful restraint), 20.03 (Kidnapping), or 20.04 (Aggravated kidnapping), Penal Code, if, as applicable:

(i) the judgment in the case contains an affirmative finding under Article 42.015; or

(ii) the order in the hearing or the papers in the case contain an affirmative finding that the victim ~~r~~ ~~s~~ ended victim was younger than 17 years of age.

(F) the second violation of Section 21.08 (Indecent exposure), Penal Code, but not if ~~~~ ~~~~nd violation results in a deferred adjudication;

(G) an attempt, conspiracy, or solicitation, as defined by Chapter 15. ~~~~ ~~~~de, to commit an offense or engage in conduct listed in Paragraph (A), (B), (C), (D), or (E);

(H) a violation of the laws of another state, federal law, the laws of a foreign country, or the Uniform Code of Military Justice for or based on the violation of an offense containing elements that are substantially similar to the elements of an offense listed under Paragraph (A), (B), (C), (D), (E), (G), but not if the violation results in a deferred adjudication;

(I) the second violation of the laws of another state, federal law, the laws of a foreign country, or the Uniform Code of Military Justice for or based on the violation of an offense containing elements that are substantially similar to the elements of the offense of indecent exposure, but not if the second violation results in a deferred adjudication.

Again, if a sex offender fails to follow the rules of registration, they will be charged with a felony.

If you or someone you know is in need of a Sexual Assault Attorney in Houston call Houston Sexual Assault Lawyer Mario Madrid at 713-877-9400.

Appendix A Item 12
Website: HoustonSafetyNet.org
re: Sex Offender Registration
EXCERPTS
http://www.houstontx.gov/police/hsn/sor.htm

Sex Offender Registration - Adult

The Adult Sex Crimes Unit registers offenders that have been convicted of sex offenses committed against adult victims.

The U. S. Congress passed the Sexually Violent Offender Registration Act (1994), and all fifty states have enacted laws requiring convicted sex offender registration.

The Texas Sex Offender Registration Law became effective on September 1, 1991, and was amended by the 1993, 1995, 1997, and 1999, Regular Sessions of the Texas Legislature. **The 1997, regular session changed the beginning date for sex offender convictions,** requiring registration from September 1, 1991, to **September 1, 1970.** This was an addition of (20) twenty years of "convicted" sex offenders who must register." The latest amendments have also mandated that **offenders must re-register annually for lifetime if convicted of** the following offenses under Texas Penal Code Sections:

22.011 Sexual Assault

30.02 Burglary with intent to commit sexual assault

An offender that has been convicted more than (1) one time for a sexually violent offense must register every (90) ninety days. Additionally, all offenders must keep the registering agency informed within (7) seven days upon the offender changing his/her address.

CHANGES IN LAW

The September 1, 1999, Texas Legislation changed the penalty for non-compliance of the registration law from a "state jail" felony for the above offenses to the following:

> Convictions for Attempted Sexual Assault and Indecent Exposure remained a State Jail Felony.

> **Convictions for "Sexually Violent Offenses" listed in the above Penal Codes were enhanced from a "State Jail Felony" to a "Third Degree Felony."** The offenders

requiring ninety- (90) day registration was enhanced from a "State Jail Felony" to a "Second Degree Felony."

PUBLIC INFORMATION

The 1999 legislature amended the release of public information of registered sex offenders to "include" the following:

Offenders numeric address

Offenders photograph

Offenders date of birth

Offenders social security number

Offenders drivers license number

For additional information regarding information of registered sex offenders refer to the Department of Public Safety website:

http://records.txdps.state.tx.us

http://www.crime-stoppers.org/houston_sex_offenders.php

Texas VINE (Statewide automated crime victim information and notification system)
Toll Free: 1-877-TX-4-VINE
Information on Texas VINE from Attorney General

For information on the complete sex offender registration law, refer to the Texas Code of Criminal Procedure, Chapter 62.

SUMMARY

Research and experience has shown that sex offenders have a very high rate of recidivism, which means that they pose a very high risk of committing additional violent sex crimes after being released from custody. It is imperative that they comply with the registration law and the terms of their conditions of parole/probation. It is believed that the closer monitoring of the offender will curtail the opportunity for repeated offenses and increase the apprehension of offenders, thus giving additional protection to the community.

APPENDIX B Chart 1

Note: Only twice did the FBR 'hit' the same Apartment Complex twice in a row: Offenses #22 & #23; #27 & #28. Offense #74 is where we got his 'likeness'! And would-be Offense #83X was where he was captured.

#	Apt Complex Name	Area	# of Offenses	Offense in Numeric Order
	FBR Attributed Offenses Chronological Order: Offense by Apt Complex			
1	Toll House	VII	2	1, 5
2	Arroyo Place	VII	1	2
3	Hill Top House	OOA	1	3
4	Emerald Forest	VI	1	4
5	The Tuileries	V	1	6
6	Willow Creek	II	10	7, 26, 32, 35, 37, 40, 42, 52, 55, 61
7	Buttonwood Tree	VI	1	8
8	Pueblo Square	VII	1	9
9	Corners & Corners E.	III	6	10, 16, **27, 28**, 39, 46
10	Willowick	I	9	11, 15, 19, 21, 38, 47, 56, 58, 63
11	Stepping Stone	VII	1	12
12	The Falls	IV	2	13, 81
13	Molly Coddle	VII	1	14
14	Kings Terrace	VII	1	17
15	Horizon East	II	1	18
16	Belle Meadow	II	1	20
17	The Hill	III	4	**22, 23**, 49, 57
18	The Citadel	I	2	24, 64
19	Kimberly Woods	IV	2	25, 74
20	The Settlement	IV	4	29, 33, 44, 65
21	Spanish Keys	I	2	30, 50
22	The Point After	V	1	31
23	Walden Place	V	2	34, 70
24	Amesbury Manor	I	1	36
25	Copenhagen	V	2	41, 69
26	Woodscape	II	2	43, 59
27	Cobblestone	II	2	45, 66
28	The Seasons	IV	2	48, 53 (83X captured)
29	The Trails	V	2	51, 71
30	Melody Terrace	IV	1	54
31	Villa Madrid	III	1	60
32	Woodcreek	II	1	62
33	First Day	VI	1	67
34	Four 7's	II	1	68
35	The Lofts	IV	1	72
36	The Ivy	IV	1	73
37	Villa Crest	IV	3	75, 77, 79
38	Claridge Park *	IV	1	76
39	Melody Park	IV	1	78
40	Bluffs	III	1	80
41	The Brookshir	OOA	1	82

82

Note: **Bold = back-to-back offenses**; Red = Rape; *Bold/blue/italic = Witness ID*

APPENDIX B Chart 2

#	Apt Complex Name	Area	# of All Offenses	Total All Offenses	# of Rape Offenses	Total All Rapes	Offense in Numeric Order
				FBR Attributed Rapes & All Offenses by Area / # of Offenses / Offense Numeric Order			
1	Amesbury Manor	I	1		1		36
2	The Citadel		2	14	1	8	24, 64
3	Spanish Keys		2		1		30, 50
4	Willowick		9		5		11, 15, 19, 21, 38, 47, 56, 58, 63
5	Belle Meadow	II	1		1		20
6	Cobblestone		2		1		45, 66
7	Four 7's		1				68
8	Horizon East		1	18		8	18
9	Willow Creek		10		4		7, 26, 32, 35, 37,40, 42, 52, 55, 61
10	Woodcreek		1		1		62
11	Woodscape		2				43, 59
12	Bluffs	III	1				80
13	Corners & Corners East		6	12	3	5	10, 16, 27, 28, 39, 46
14	The Hill		4		2		22, 23, 49, 57
15	Villa Madrid		1				60
16	Claridge Park *	IV	1				76
17	The Falls		2		1		13, 81
18	Kimberly Woods		2				25, 74
19	Melody Park		1				78
20	Melody Terrace		1	18	1	6	54
21	The Seasons		2		1		48, 53 (83X captured)
22	The Settlement		4		2		29, 33, 44, 65
23	The Lofts		1				72
24	The Ivy		1				73
25	Villa Crest		3		1		75, 77, 79
26	Copenhagen	V	2		1		41, 69
27	The Point After		1		1		31
28	The Trails		2	8	1	6	51, 71
29	The Tuileries		1		1		6
30	Walden Place		2		2		34, 70
31	Buttonwood Tree	VI	1		1		8
32	Emerald Forest		1	3	1	2	4
33	First Day		1				67
34	Arroyo Place	VII	1		1		2
35	Kings Terrace		1				17
36	Molly Coddle		1	7	1	6	14
37	Pueblo Square		1		1		9
38	Stepping Stone		1		1		12
39	Toll House		2		2		1, 5
40	Hill Top House	OOA	1		1		3
41	The Brookshir		1	2		1	82
			82		42		

APPENDIX C

A Personal Special Thanks

To All The Investigators on the FBR & FBR-Related Cases (in order of seniority)

R. M Wagoner #709

J.W. Murdock #1534

Eugene Stansell #1689

J.E. Ozment #1818

G.E. Luther #2354

John R. Landers #2445

N.W. Crawford #2456

K.W. Harris #2465

Truly M. Holmes #2521

C.W. Hudson #2533

N.W. Agee #2553

T. Falgout #2608

C.F. Royal #2692

Evelyn Reba Crowder #2894

L.T. Fulghum #2937

D.H. Fitzgerald #2978

J.R. Raef #3080

M.L. Kidd 3094

R.D. Lewis #3104

J.E. Smith #3123

D.A. Gardiner #3321

To Lieutenants Knight and Day...
**and DPD's Modern-Day Crime Scene Investigators of the 1970's
who provided the linking evidence & insured the guilty pleas
of the FBR - Guy William Marble Jr.**

P.E.S
Physical Evidence Section
Investigators

Lt. Knight
Lt. J.C. Day
Det. B.G. Brown 1057
Det. Dale Hankins 1171
LC Taylor 1430
BT Beddingfield 1513
BE Barnes 1552
Inv. FM Jenkins 1970
Sgt. WL Bradon 2025
HO Ford 2052
GE Thompson 2185
RA Furr 2377
Ernell Smith 2451
RA Pettie 2514
ER Rhodes 2584
JH Whiteley 2646
MR Jarvis 2913
JM Mabery 3123
JE Smith 3123
JJ Shubzda 3357
HF Brown 3448

And
To *All* The DPD Officers Who Investigated & Answered FBR & FBR-Related Calls for Service & Who Searched For Him Night & Day

[My apologies to those in every area of DPD who were involved and not listed below by name & badge number. God bless you all!]

71 DPD Officers Who Answered 82 FBR Service Calls

T Hopson 1224	EJ Kittle 2906	WM Manson 3506
LR Lamont 1272	RV Brigance 2911	SG Ricamore 3514
DP Winterbauer 1356	BL Anderson 2933	DA Reynolds 3542
JH Barnett 1397	RJ Catona 2942	MI Miller 3554
HC Reidling 1610	LL Barbee 2945	RL Reid 3560
DW Brown 1977	RL Townsend 2989	MD Richards 3574
JE DeVore 2077	RR Horan 3041	BJ Wapner 3577
RB Bounds 2184	JL Austin 3045	MR Scoggins 3601
J Prelow 2194	EW Smith 3086	GA Wren 3618
SR Bell 2298	JE Smith 3123	JA MacArthur 3623
MW Angell 2318	PJ Hernandez 3195	JW Przywara 3643
JT Carey 2448	JF Martin 3236	PA Crawford 3644
JM House 2495	GJ Fernandez 3282	MM Hay 3651
RK Rickerd 2526	AR Casady 3272	GN Hendley 3673
JM Ingram 2535	Jess Lucio Jr. 3301	RC Osgerby 3668
DJ Coker 2536	MJ Harrison 3317	JA Blantom 3702
PR Hughes 2551	BJ Morris 3318	CR Foist 3706
RG Hale 2614	R Langran 3337	DD Melancon 3760
RHL Jackson 2694	JM McPherson 3370	DK Lowe 3770
LT Page 2710	DB Christian 3432	SC Mallon 3789
CE Maxwell 2768	WR Bricker 3445	WL Russell 3803
GD Payne 2798	Rodney Spain 3451	RL Dorsey 3820
ML Countryman 2816	P Bunge 3452	JT Thompson
JM Hunter 2874	RL Newell 3476	

Tactical Division Officers
To *all* of you who worked so many hours trying to find, stop or capture the FBR please accept my most sincere thanks!

To Man and His Dog
Tactical Division Officers - K9 Unit

J.M. Beene #3191[185]
and his K9 Thor

C.M. Dooley #2003[186]
and his canine companion

who provided valuable support and a key
piece of ancillary evidence
that helped secure
Guy William Marble Jr.'s confession
to Investigator John Landers
in the early morning hours of February 14, 1977,
in which Marble admitted
being the man we called the Friendly Burglar-Rapist
and was so convinced,
because of Dooley's 'tidbit', that Landers knew
more than he was letting on - and
'copped' to all but one of the offenses in our 'Book'
and admitted to several more
not previously known

And a Very Special Thank You to
Tactical Officer Barry M. Whitfield #3055[187] (our hero)
who saved our bacon, who proved our theories,
who made use of *Linda Robinson's* image of the FBR
provided by our intrepid witness *Virginia Huston*
putting an end to the nightmare called
the Friendly Burglar-Rapist
by
recognizing and arresting
Guy William Marble Jr.,
while he was still
only
one step from murder

---

[185] see page 395, 495

[186] see pages 273, 298, 308, 430-1, 495

[187] In addition to the "Golden Handcuffs" awarded by the Greater Dallas Crime Commission, Barry was also chosen as May 1977 Officer of the Month by the Police Community Awards Committee, via the Underwriters Association. Barry retired from DPD with the rank of Sargent.

Never Ending Thanks

To My Dallas Police Department Partners:
(with whom I shared a treasured part of my life)

David Noel Beidelman †
Warren T. Biggs
Chip G. Bulin
James (Jim) Bryan
Max L. Countryman †
Thomas (Tom) H. Covington Jr †
Ed Herbst

Truly M. Holmes †
Fred M. Jenkins
Robert C. Martin *
Billy L. Powell *
Freddy Smith
John Timothy (Tim) Waterson
Tim Yarbro

Other Officers with whom I had the pleasure of working the Dallas streets (*thanks for always having my back*):

B. [Ben] J. Adamcik
L.J. Abney
M.H. Abney
W.J. Barber
Harvey R. Barham †
J.W. Barnwell
B.D. Bateman
B.R. Bean
Paul M. Bacerra
Ted H. Bedsole
Jim M. Beene
M.H. Bell
W. Lowell Cannaday
Ben F. Caperton
J.T. Carey *
Roger D. Carney
Dan L. Carpenter
Andy M. Cargile
J.A. Castelman
R. W. Cawthon
Larry N. Clark
David Clark
D.J. Coker
G.D. Collier
R.D. Collins
J.D. Compton
R.L. Cormier ††
W.A. Craven
Bobby Joe Dale ★†
Terry A. Donovan
J.P. Doyal
D.F. Duram
J.B. Eastis
Raymond T. Epting*

Greg W. Evans
Don Flusche, Sr.
Don Flusche, Jr †
Roosevelt Ford
Jerry Wayne Foster
R.S. Gage
Robert Garza
Roy R. George
C.D. Gerloff
J.E. Gibson
V.E. Gomez
Doug L. Grantham
S.W. Greer
B.J. Hamby
Kim Hammond †
Dolan K. Hargrove*
R.H. Hawkins
Roy E. Hodgens
Frank L. Hearron [*]
Gill Henson
Dick Hickman *
J.D. Holt
R.S. [Scotty] Holt
K.R. Johnson
M.E. Jones
R.H. Kirks
J.L. Kirksey
D.W. Knight
David M. Kunkle [**]
Larry H. Lamountain
John R. Landers*†
Leslie G. Lane††
B.S. Lovejoy

E.E. Mackey
J.E. Martindale
R. N. Mason
K. M. Mayfield
I. J. McKee
Levi Mc Quietor ††
A Medrano
C.D. Mendenhall
Richard Millward
D.L. Montgomery
R.L. Morris
A.H. Mullins
Frank C. Muscato
E.E. Newsom
S.R. Norris
Fred R. Overstreet
A.L. Owen
D.M. Parton
E.W. Patterson
J.C. Petty
K.D. Petty
Carroll O. Prewitt
J.P. Pruitt
John R. Raef
Robert A. Rowe
W.P. Saunders
S.M. Short
Ernell. Smith *
B.B. Smoot
D. A. Sorenson
Chuck A. Still
R.R. Stotz
Lonnie G. Strudy
Joe A. Stugill

Jack T. Swafford	Ron D. Weldon	R.M. Yager
M.K. Swofford	B.D. Williams	Gene Yee
S.B. Tanner	C.J. Williams	
Jim R. Theis *	D.P. Williams	
Greg E. Thompson	R.B. Wilson	* Same Academy Class
J.T. Thompson	W.G. Wilson	† Deceased
J.G. Tilley	W.B. Wilson	†† Killed In Line of Duty
R.N. Trussel *	Frank P. Winton	★ Motorcycle Officer, introduced me to DPD
G.M. (Mike) Virginia	W.W. Woodward	
E.R. Walt	R.J. Worth	★ Field Training Officer

Sgt. W. Lowell Cannaday (Later Asst. Chief)
[*] Frank L. Hearron (Later Deputy Chief)
[**] David M. Kunkle (Later Chief of Police)

And Thank you to My Supervisors
(Who are blameless in all I did)

Sgt. Thomas R. Gregory
Sgt. James D. Mercer [Say-dad/Hey-dad]
Sgt. Charles R. Orsburn [Big O] †
Sgt. Fred E. Rich
Lt. Wayne Posey
Lt. M.P. Southard

Deputy Chief Robert O. Dixon †
Assistant Chief Paul McCaghren

Chiefs of Police

Charles H. Bachelor †
Frank W. Dyson
W. A. Byrd †
Billy Prince

And an enormous thanks to the following
Non-Sworn Personnel
Bob Shaw †: Director Public Information Office
Ed Spencer: Dir. Public Information Office
Kay Tate: Admin. PIO
Kathryn Bonham: Analyst, Planning & Research

Thank you very much to proofreaders:[188]
Jim Evans
Tom & Jane Covington & especially Jim Bryan

---

[188] I believe they caught everything... so if you find an error or typo now it is likely because I added *new content* after they completed their work; *this is 8th Edition.*

Lest We Forget

For the most part the story of the FBR was essentially concluded with Marble's guilty plea and his incarceration. The stories of his victims have gone on. And though the actions of the FBR brought more attention to the crime of rape within the DPD, and the Dallas community as a whole, the crime of rape or criminal assault rages on in Dallas as it does elsewhere.

As sexual assault and abuse of women has not abated these crime victims should never be forgotten and their attackers pursued with the same diligence as that shown the murderer. It is often repeated, perhaps as a deterrent warning, that the statue of limitations never runs out on murder. Many do not realize the same condition exists for sexual or criminal assault.

Texas
CODE OF CRIMINAL PROCEDURE
TITLE 1. CODE OF CRIMINAL PROCEDURE
CHAPTER 12. LIMITATION

Art. 12.01. FELONIES. Except as provided in Article 12.03,
felony indictments may be presented within these limits,
and not afterward:
    (1) no limitation:
        (A) murder and manslaughter;
        (B) sexual assault under Section 22.011(a)(2), Penal Code,
           or aggravated sexual assault under
           Section 22.021 (a)(1)(B), Penal Code

With no statute of limitation on rape **the cases that go 'cold' need on-going pursuit by both the police and community.**

Case in point: Following the Dallas Mavericks winning the NBA Championship on the evening of June 13, 2011 a young woman who had been enjoying the game with friends left the restaurant to walk to her car and drive home. Instead of going home, she was brutally beaten, robbed and raped. One year later her attacker remains at large. Ashley Green recently released her name publicly in a June 23, 2012 article in the Dallas Morning News. Her aim was to re-energize the public regarding that night, the location, and the facts of her attack in the hopes of uncovering clues that police could use to arrest and prosecute her attacker.

Perhaps someone has information and was unable to provide it to police at the time, or did not realize they had helpful information. Maybe someone has had contact with her attacker and knows of his guilt or actions and realizes now is the time to come forward and will do so.

Most citizens come forward without remuneration, however sometimes the 'witness' has reason to be afraid to come forward. A reward is often a necessary incentive. In this case this reward notice was printed in the DMN article:

> "REWARD: A $50,000 reward is being offered for information leading to an arrest and indictment in the case. Anyone with information can call police at 214-671-3584 or Crime Stoppers[189] at 214-373-8477. Tipsters can remain anonymous."

Lest we forget the prey, the victims, the complainants of the rapist known as Guy William Marble Jr., they, like Ashly Green, have had to live with their memories. Quoted in the DMN article regarding her memory Ms. Green said, "Now it's just a part of me, and I don't really know if there will be a day where somehow this doesn't cross my mind."

Fifty-thousand dollar reward[190]

or not, we should never forget Ms Green nor stop looking for her attacker. However, as they did in the 1970's era of the FBR, the numbers still favor the attacker. According to Scott Goldstein's article:

> *428 Sexual assaults were reported in Dallas in 2011*
> *200 Approximate number of sexual assaults unsolved*
> *in Dallas in 2011*

> *Breaking it down - Research by the Rape, Abuse and Incest National Network shows that 46 of every 100 rapes in the U.S. are report to police. Of those, 12 lead to an arrest, nine are prosecuted, five lead to a felony conviction and three rapist spend at least one day in prison.*

Even with all our cultural advances there are still those among us who prey on women; abuse them and rape them. Help stop the cycle of abuse. Help law enforcement to pursue and prosecute these predators.

---

[189] The Dallas Crime Stoppers program was initiated and modeled after my father's "Secret Witness" program.

[190] I cannot help but imagine what the impact would have been of the 70s equivalent of a $50,000.00 reward for the arrest & conviction of the Friendly Burglar RAPIST.

Feb 6 1974 Rape Suspect Demonstrates 42% (8 of 19) of Most Often Encountered FBR M/O Markers

Of 82 FBR Attributed Offenses This # have M/O Marker		Of 82 FBR Attributed Offenses This % have M/O Marker	19 FBR M/O Markers	Of 42 FBR Attributed Rape Offenses This # have M/O Marker		Of 42 FBR Attributed Rape Offenses This % have M/O Marker	O/IR 38546-F Un Attributed Rape Offense 4pm Feb 6 1974 M/O Marker
78 of 82	or	95%	Enters thru unlocked window or door	42 of 42	or	100%	x
61 of 82	or	74%	Rummages thru apartment	38 of 42	or	90%	x
43 of 82	or	52%	Puts pillow case over or covers victim's head	36 of 42	or	86%	x
41 of 82	or	50%	Ties or binds victim's hands	34 of 42	or	81%	x
44 of 82	or	54%	Displays or says he has a knife	34 of 42	or	81%	
37 of 82	or	45%	Uses lubrication	32 of 42	or	76%	
49 of 82	or	60%	Cuts pho cords or disables phone/s	30 of 42	or	71%	x
30 of 82	or	37%	Awakes Vic w hand over mouth / puts hand over mouth	22 of 42	or	52%	
23 of 82	or	28%	Says: I will tell you when/before I leave	20 of 42	or	48%	
22 of 82	or	27%	Mentions truck	19 of 42	or	45%	
23 of 82	or	28%	Asks/talks about money or property	18 of 42	or	43%	
19 of 82	or	23%	Says: I'm just a burglar / I'm a burglar	17 of 42	or	40%	x
20 of 82	or	24%	Says: I won't hurt you / I don't want to hurt you	15 of 42	or	36%	
18 of 82	or	22%	Says: don't say anything/speak or I'll kill you	14 of 42	or	33%	
16 of 82	or	20%	Has high pitched voice / soft / whispers	13 of 42	or	31%	
27 of 82	or	33%	Plans escape route opens/unlocks front door, etc	12 of 42	or	29%	x
13 of 82	or	16%	Is 'nice', 'friendly', shows concern, etc.	12 of 42	or	29%	
16 of 82	or	20%	Wears mask/stocking	11 of 42	or	26%	x
5 of 82	or	6.10%	Turns on/off HVAC fan	3 of 42	or	7.10%	

WAS IT OR WASN'T IT THE FBR?

Date	11/15/73	2/6/74	7/30/74
Offense	1st Rape Attributed to FBR	Rape (Not Previously Attributed to FBR)	2nd Rape Attributed to FBR
Time	(afternoon) 2:30 - 3:00 pm	(afternoon) 3:50 - 4:10p	(night) 4:30am

Similarities

Susp Discription	white male	white male	white male
	24-26	25	unk (per voice, possibly late 20s early 30s
	5'11	5'8" to 5'10"	5'8'
	185-190 lbs	155-160 lbs	unk wt. (muscular)
	gloves	gloves	gloves

Similarities

MO Markers	door left open	door left open	used key for front door obtained in previous burglary
	man fully clothed	man fully dressed	man fully dressed
	red sky mask	stocking over his head	dark, asleep, hooded before did not see Susp
	Comp screamed, put hand over mouth, take to bedroom	Comp screamed he put her in closet	could not scream
	You just caught a burglar in the act.	"He was a burglar that just got caught"	Don't move, I'm a burglar
	tied her wrist w belt and bra	bound wrists with surgical tape	I have to tape your hands and mouth... and feet
	put pillow case over her head	put pillow case over her head	put a pillow case over her head
	rummaged around apt.	rummaged around apt	rummaged around apt
	leaves through open door	leaves through open door	leaves through front door

Disimilarities

	no weapon displayed or mentioned	• hand gun displayed •	puts knife to Comp's neck
	gloves, brown	gloves, black	gloves, rubber
	does not mention truck	does not mention! truck	mentions truck
	use of lubricant not mentioned by Comp	use of lubricant not mentioned by Comp	uses lubricant
	entered front door	entered front door	entered through window

Postscript 2: 2016

Final Word (for now) on Where's Waldo?
Where *Is* Guy William Marble Jr.

In May of 1998 on the day of his release Marble was notified and acknowledged, with his signature, his requirement to register (for life) as a Sex Offender. Marble's willful disregard of the law continues to this day, exacerbated by his fleeing the state and the country.

Though Marble has served time for four of his offenses, there are over seventy-five[191] for which he never answered. Even if he may be no longer physically capable (at 69 as of 2/27/2016) of scaling second floor balconies or committing sexual assaults as he once did, **there remains, over his head, a felony to answer for; to wit:**
> **failure to register (for life) as a Sex Offender.**

When speaking about Marble Jr. having fled the United States back in 2010 for Europe, I was recently told (February 2016) by a well-placed law enforcement source:

"France knows he's there.
They won't give him back."

ॐॐ

Postscript 3: 2017

Truly M. Holmes

~

Geoprofiling of the FBR Offenses

~

43 Years After the Rape Arrest of Pat Rick

---

[191] including the 40+ rapes for which their is no statute of limitation. (page 572)

P.S. 3a:
The Passing of Truly Holmes

It is with heavy heart that I report that Truly M. Holmes passed away on May 5, 2017. Truly was a excellent patrol officer, partner and investigator. He was the finest of Dallas' Finest! He was a man you admired, a man you could trust, a man you would be happy to follow and a man who recognized the contributions of others. He was a man who invested in others.

Among his many qualities, Tom and I appreciated his dedication, friendship, and especially his confidence in our information and methods vis-à-vis the FBR.

Our prayers for Truly's family and all those who loved him.

Here is the obituary published in the Dallas Morning News:

Truly Marion Holmes 1946-2017

HOLMES, Truly Marion ~ Truly Marion Holmes lost his two-year fight with cancer on May 5, 2017. Truly was born in Graham, Texas on July 20, 1946. He served in the U.S. Army as Drill Instructor, before beginning his career with the Dallas Police Department. He worked his way up (to) the rank of Investigator in Narcotics Enforcement, Sexual Assault, Homicide, and Dignitary Protection with the U.S. Secret Service, where he was assigned the protection of presidents, local, and foreign dignitaries. He was also accredited as a U.S. Marshall for the U.S. State Department before being attached to the Dallas FBI Field Office on a Joint Terrorism Task Force for seven years. Truly was directly involved in the identity of the terrorists who attacked our country on 9/11/2001. He retired in 2005 where Truly and his wife, Lou, moved to the Hill Country, built their retirement home, and eventually began working in the private sector with local attorney's. Truly is survived by his *wife,* Lou Cano-Holmes, *Son*: Damon Matthew Holmes, *Daughters*: Stephanie Holmes-Mills, Candice Holmes-Thornton, April Clair-Haag, Gina Clair-Burrage, *Grandchildren*: Hailey Rae Holmes, Hayden Lee Holmes, Brittany Nicole Hudspeth, Crista Rene Hudspeth, Lindsey Kay Hudspeth, Colin David Burrage and Rachel Clair Burrage. *Sister*: Patricia Patterson and *Brother*: Doug Holmes. Private memorial services will be held at a later date. In lieu of flowers, donations may be made to your local cancer research facility.

P.S. 3b:
2017 Geoprofiling of the FBR Offenses

About 2012 I became aware of software being utilized to analyze crime data. I had even contacted DPD's Mark Stallo (now retired) to set up a meeting regarding his use of 'this' software, which I did not know was Rigel™. I even independently researched Rigel™ and ECRI. I put references to ECRI and Mark Stallo's books, on crime analysis, on my website. I was unable to positively connect with Mark and felt uncomfortable in asking him to use DPD resources to run 'my data' even though the case was an 'old' DPD serial rape case.

In late March of 2017 I was reacquainted with the idea of geographic profiling. I began researching and found that a Canadian criminologist, Kim Rossmo, had found a way to turn crime data into a geographic profile that identified the location or area of highest probability were a suspect, committing crimes under investigation, would live.

As I am given to understand, starting as a non-sworn employee of the Vancouver Police Department in 1978, Kim became a sworn officer in 1980. He took a degree in criminology in 1988. Continuing his studies he obtained a PhD in Criminology from Simon Fraser University in 1995. His doctoral thesis explained a formula he developed to infuse then current investigative methods with computer aided analysis technology that became known as 'geographic profiling'.

Dr. Kim Rossmo co-founded Environmental Criminology Research, Inc.: ECRI, the entity responsible for developing his **analysis software called, "Rigel™"**. As I mentioned above, I had not remembered, now in 2017, I had added information on ECRI to my website some five years ago.

I found that Dr. Rossmo is now the Endowed Chair in Criminology and is Director of the Center for Geospatial Intelligence and Investigation in the Department of Criminal Justice at Texas State University. I sent Dr. Rossmo an email to his university address asking if he would be interested in running my data points on the FBR through his software program. I heard back from him almost immediately with an offer to work with me to define the data parameters that he would need to 'run' my case.

Kim asked me if I knew Mark Stallo, I related the above. It was not until then that I realized Kim and ECRI were the people Stallo had been working with.

In addition to working with Dr. Rossmo, he introduced me to the President of ECRI, Ian Laverty, so that Mr. Laverty could also work with me to refine my "MO Marker" data (in particular the **FBR's 19 Most Prevalent MO Markers**) into what they call "Linkage Factors".

The genius of Rigel™ (first introduced in 1997, 20 years after Marble was caught) is that it determines the highest probability of where a perpetrator of (serial crimes, for example) would live. In situations were a suspect pool may exist, if one of the suspects, or the suspect, lives within the boundary of the area Rigel™ identifies or pinpoints as the perpetrator's probable home/residence, other suspects (outside of these boundaries) can be set aside while investigators focus their time on the (in bounds) suspect/s.

The FBR offenses/crimes provided an interesting case study for Kim and Ian, in that there was a known/arrested/convicted suspect/perpetrator. His residence location was known. And there were hundreds of data points Tom and I had collected as "MO Markers" for Rigel™ to review.

With all the data-mining and refining completed it was a simple matter to let the computer do it's job. ECRI's proprietary analysis software combed through the data, making millions of calculations. The visual results are in the images that follow on the next few pages.

This graphic (***Image A***) shows a current map of the north Dallas area with red dots indicating all the FBR's 1973-1977 offenses. The north-most blue square is Marble's residence and the south-most blue square is the location of Marble's arrest on Valentine's Day, February 15, 1977.

[Note: some dots cover over others
so not all 83 offenses appear to be counted]

Image A

[**Author's Note**: The image designations, text inserts, arrows and explanations are the authors' not ECRI's]

This graphic (***Image 1***) is a the color map produced by the Rigel™ geographic profiling software. The color scale represents percentages, dark orange being the highest. The colors make it easy to visualize the areas of highest probability of where a suspect lives. In this case it showed the FBR 'suspect's' residence well inside the highest probability colors. It also dramatically shows the 'hot' area, 'crime base' or 'hunting area' of the FBR.

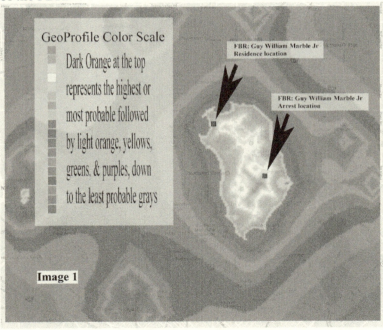

Image 1

In this graphic, Dr. Rossmo used only the top 10% of the data from the Rigel™ run of all crimes and his refined analysis to produced *Image 2*. It clearly places the FBR's place of arrest (the lower blue square) in epicenter of his hunting ground.

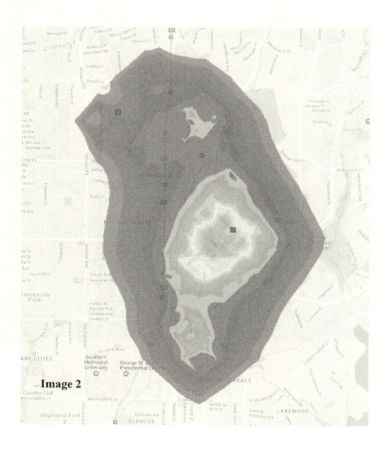

Image 2

Next are *Images 1* & *2* side by side.

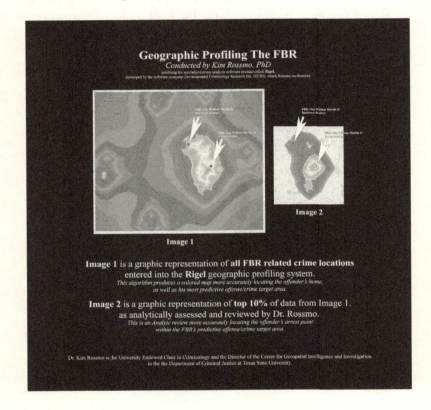

Note:

To see *Images: A, 1, & 2* in greater detail and in color please view them on my website: robertjsadler.com. Click on the "FBR" tab and scroll down... way down.

Here (in reduced opacity) *Image 1* overlays *Image A*. This allows the 'crime dots' from the *Image 1* to demonstrate their relativity to the color mapping of the FBR's geographic profiling produced by the Rigel™ software.

Notwithstanding we caught the FBR (Guy William Marble Jr) utilizing our 1970s non-computer aided methods, if we had had Rigel™ (back in the day) it would have also pinpointed the FBR's prime hunting area as the place to focus targeted surveillance.

Just as our methodology did not identify as single suspect, much less '*the* suspect' neither would Rigel™. However what Rigel™ does positively quantify is that the analysis that Tom and I undertook was accurately predictive, that is to say: right on the money.

Thus when our plan for targeted surveillance was put in place, based on our predictive analysis, the FBR was quickly caught.

But it was not just that we had targeted surveillance in place, based on thirty-nine months of analysis. We were graced by three additional factors: 1) a sketch and description of the suspect provided by an almost-victim, *Virginia Huston*, and a very good artist, *Linda Robinson*; 2) the suspect came to his hunting ground wearing the same or similar clothing to that in the suspect sketch and matching the suspect description; and 3) a highly motivated and observant officer, *Barry Whitfield*, performing the stealthy targeted surveillance to observe and arrest the suspect/ perpetrator: Guy William Marble Jr.

I want to thank **Dr. Kim Rossmo** co-founder of **ECRI** and **Ian Laverty, president of ECRI,** for their gracious investment of time and expertise to enhance my knowledge of geographic profiling and for applying their knowledge and computer software to my FBR data. Thanks also for sharing the graphic results of the Rigel™ program with me and giving me permission to share the results with my readers.

Everyone wants to know who the perpetrator is. They want the easy identification obtained when the fingerprints or DNA of an individual are 'in the system' and a match is generated to latent prints or biologics (DNA) collected from a crime scene. Unfortunately not every crime is committed by someone already 'in the system'. And certainly the suspect is unknown in many cases. It is in these type cases were Rigel™ can be of most help identifying the area of highest probability for a suspect's residence or hunting ground. Different tactics are required for each, but both give the investigator a narrower geographic footprint to search and narrows down a potential suspect pool.

Note: Time is of the essence…

November 15 1973 through February 14 1977, 39 months, approximately 273 seven-day weeks, or 1,170 days was a long time to collect data points to compare. With 83[192] total offenses attributed to the FBR he was committing an offense, on average,

---

[192] The original list of offenses Tom and I attributed to the FBR was 82. "Offense #R1?" on page 41 was not included in previous editions of OSfM. The rape offense dated February 6, 1974 was brought to my attention in 2014 by Mr. J Patrick Rick. In January 2016, I considered that this offense may have been committed by the FBR. After further review I have concluded that this rape was very likely the nascent work of the FBR. I have now (2017) attributed it to the FBR, thus the total of attributed FBR offenses now totals 83.

every 83 days. Of course, in reality, there were offenses closer together and longer spans between them here and there. The point is that in the beginning only bits of the FBR's MO was observable, not a pattern. With each new offense we went into analyst mode, cataloguing each specific crime behavior (sequentially reported, first spoken about by the complainant and then written down by the Reporting Officer) we could quantify and waited to see if it would repeat. Behaviors such as: "I'm just a burglar," "I'm just a friendly burglar," or "mentions his truck." These behaviors were part of his overall *Modus Operandi*. I called them "MO Markers" and later data points or "Linkage Factors" as Rigel™ terms them.

For Tom and I each new case, (back then) whether occurring today and tomorrow or yesterday and three weeks from now, was analyzed one at a time. As the crimes piled up other comparative analysis was attempted. Thus it took time to acquire all the subsets of information... to have enough to compare and still more from which to make predictions. Each iteration of our analysis took... exponential factors of time.

And perhaps the truly facile genius of Rigel™ is it's speed. Once the data is fed into the Rigel™ software program and it's algorithms run through it's zeros and ones, its answers only take seconds.

Given our analysis then and that of Rigel™ now the result appears the very similar. Ours took studied time. Our result was our analytical guess. The guesses of Rigel™, on the other hand, are based on a proven predictive algorithm, which of course took a good deal of study and application to perfect.

Though the Rigel™ result, in the beginning of a serial case, may be just as difficult for investigators and administrators to put stock in (as ours was), the underlying scholarship behind Rigel™ (and history of success) heightens its credibility over that of two guys with pencils, a first generation Texas Instrument's hand-calculator, hand-drawn graphs, and spending hours and hours of 'chair-time' reading and reviewing offense reports and looking for MO Markers, trends, and patterns.

With the worldwide successes by agencies utilizing ECRI and its store of products, they have no need for my recommendation. But, they have it.

I wholeheartedly recommend the problem solving expertise of ECRI, in particular Dr. Russmo and Mr. Laverty.

P.S. 3c:
43 Years After the Rape Arrest of Pat Rick

In the fall of 2016 Mr. Rick found out that his decades old arrest record (with it's single and only 1974 arrest) qualified for expungement or expunction. This is a process by which a Mr. Rick would petition the court to have all record of his arrest, etc., erased. If granted, all reference to his 1974 arrest[193] for aggravated rape, a charge which was 'No Billed' by a Dallas County Grand Jury, would be wiped from the record.

In November of 2016 Mr. Rick's case *was* expunged! Unfortunately his attorney never notified him.

In early 2017 Mr. Rick traveled to Dallas to get certified copies of all the court documents relative to his charge, held by the Dallas County Clerk. That's when Mr. Rick found out, indeed, his case had been expunged.

I was happy to hear, after all these years (43), that Rick's ill-advised (in my opinion) arrest, the accusation that he was a rapist, his night in jail, the examining trial, the eventual **No Bill** handed down by the grand jury, his subsequent scrutiny by another investigator as a possible FBR suspect, and the issues arising from having a felony arrest record was at an end.

There is much more to Pat Rick's life, before and after that, now expunged, 'arrest' that he explains in his fascinating upcoming book.

At last these modern day law enforcement and court repositories, etc., of old paper, microfiche and now digital records have all been told to remove the name of James Patrick Rick from all such repositories.

I could not help but think of the 1956 Cecile B. DeMille movie: *The Ten Commandments*, when Moses is brought, chained, before Sethi and Rameses reveals Moses' Jewish heritage and faith in God.

With heavy and yet unyielding heart Sethi decrees:

> *Let the name of Moses be stricken from every book and tablet, stricken from all pylons and obelisks, stricken from every monument of Egypt... So let be written, so let it be done!*

And thus it was when the Dallas County District Court Judge signed Pat Ricks's *Order of Expunction*, regarding all modern manner and methods of records documentation and records keeping, this was the modern-day equivalent of his saying:
"So let be written, so let it be done!"

---

[193] See pages 41-45 & 433-442.

The Story Behind the Picture
previously on the back cover

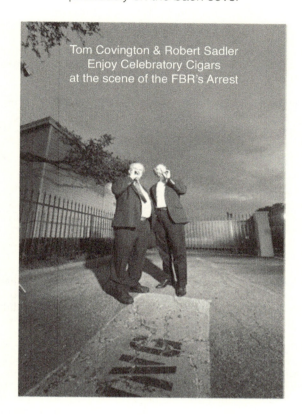

In 2012, thirty-five years after our three-plus-year endeavor resulted in the arrest of the FBR, ridding Dallas and its citizens of an urban terrorist, my friend and photographer, Bill Crump, heard that I had completed the manuscript for this book. Bill wanted to take a picture of Tom and me at the scene of the FBR's February 14, 1977 arrest. For us it was a moment of celebration for having completed the manuscript and of reflection on what we had been fortunate to accomplish for the citizens of Dallas all those years ago and in remembrance of the honorable women who had been the prey of the serial rapist Guy William Marble Jr.

Final Post Script

DPD Badge #2273
Senior Corporal Thomas Harvey Covington Jr (Ret.)
9/13/1936 - 12/14/2017

It is with profound sadness I announce the passing of my dear friend and partner. Tom Covington was already on the police department when I joined in 1967. We've been friends these last fifty years.

I met Tom when we worked in patrol. Then in 1973 we became forever linked 'as partners' as we worked together daily for the next 39 months to help capture the FBR on the Valentine's Day in 1977. (Well, you know that now, if you've read the book!) That friendship and partnership never ended until his passing on Thursday, December 14th. The memories, thank the Lord, will continue!

As I said earlier in this book, Tom's contribution to our collaboration was intrepid and indefatigable! Though I had maintained some of my notes and papers, if Tom had not secured the remainder of our notes and papers much of the detail in this book would be greatly lacking. Thank you, my friend, for all your hard work and support.

Tom was a gregarious, affable, quick-witted, inventive, intelligent, brave man and decorated officer. He was someone everyone considered a friend. He was fun to work with, always wore a smile and offered his infectious laughter at the drop of a hat... sometimes you didn't even need to take off your hat.

Unfortunately a couple of months ago Tom, who was dealing with diabetes, was diagnosed with inoperable liver cancer. Although he was told he might survive a year or two... it would not be without it's pain and hardship for him... and Janie. Perhaps the Lord's Will was to take him home sooner rather than later. Tom took a bad fall at home on Wednesday and was rushed to hospital with head trauma; he was unresponsive and gone the next day. Though we wanted Tom's presence among us to continue, I am thankful and have to count his passing as a blessing that he did not have to endure the pain and cruelty of his cancer. May the Lord bless Janie and their family.

Rest In Peace, ol' friend and partner. You were the best!
You will be greatly missed and fondly remembered!

rjs

Obituary*

Thomas Harvey Covington Jr., 81, went to be with our Lord on December 14, 2017, at Parkland Hospital where he was being treated for a fall. He passed away of multiple causes that included cancer and diabetes.

He leaves behind a wife of 61 wonderful years, Janie. *Children*: Thomas and wife Alison Covington, James "Rusty" Covington, Jeannine and husband Mark Beegle, a sister Elaine and Jack Holmes. He had eight *grandchildren*; Misti and Mark Tankavich, Cory Davis, Cari Davis, LaTisha and Bryan Shafer, Sean Davis, Amanda and Terry Self, James Boone and Tara and Colton Garrett. *Great Grandchildren*; Aaron, Morgan, Dalton, Kyleigh, Kyle, Kamryn, Colby, Christian, Brantley, Masynn, Jordan, Lane, Shane, Aaragon, Legend, Jason, Elizabeth and Little Terry, and Great Granddaughter Ellie., also many nieces and nephews.

Tom was a well-loved man that participated in many activities throughout his life. He served 9 years in the National Guard achieving the rank of E-5. He was in the recon and assault weapons platoon as well as the combat support company 1st Brigade, 142 Infantry Regiment. He began his career as a Police Officer with the Borger Police Department. After 3 years with Borger PD he joined the Dallas Police Department in 1966, retiring as a Senior Corporal with 21 years of service. He received the department's Meritorious Achievement Award in 1977 for his part in the capture of the FBR. In '85 he was nominated and received The Officer of The Month Award from the Dallas Community Police Awards Committee and was 1985 Runner-up Officer of The Year, awarded by Friends of Dallas Police.

After retiring from the Dallas PD he and his partner, Robert Sadler collaborated on *One Step From Murder: The Friendly Burglar Rapist*. This true-crime story chronicles an illusive serial rapist (FBR) that Tom and his partner helped capture after 39 months of diligent analysis.

Tom was an United Methodist Certified Lay Speaker for 20 years. A member of DALCLIFF WYNNEWOOD LIONS CLUB for over 30 years, becoming a Melvin Jones Fellow, a Life Member of the Texas Children's Camp, and a Life Member for the "Sports Extravaganza." For 34 years he played St. Andrew and Judas Iscariot in the tableau, never missing a performance. He also drove for Meals on Wheels for 34 years. He was a member of Kirkwood United Methodist Church for 47 years. And during his over 50 years of Boy Scouting he received the Silver Beaver Award for Distinguished Service from the BSofA National Honor Council.

* Edited for clarity and space.

One More Final Post Script

DPD Badge #3055
Sergeant Barry Madsen Whitfield (Ret.)
11/11/1948 - 8/6/2023

It is with profound sadness I announce the passing of my dear friend and the man who put hands on the elusive Friendly Burglar Rapist of the mid to late 1970s and effected his arrest! Bringing to an end my, Tom Covinton's, Inv.'s Reba Crowder, John Landers, Truly Holmes and the rest of the Dallas Police Department's thrity-seven month search to catch the rapist and send him to prison. [See page 473: "Barry Whitfield's Memories" of that night, in his own words.]

Barry was a great friend, an outstanind officer, and was loved and admired by many. Barry's life impacted mine in major ways. He was the 'tip of the spear' for Tom Covington's final prognosticaion of when and where the next FBR 'hit' would occur. With the artist's skectch in hand of the suspect, Barry enecountered a man wearing the same outfit as in the artist's skectch who also looked like the image in the sketch and stopped him. Obviously on the prowl for a victim, the suspect did not have any identification and told Barry it was in his appartment, and then ran from Barry. Officer Whitfield gave chase overcame, subdued and arrested the man. The man this book was written about,was now in custody; the man who was responsible for over 80 offenses, over 40 of which were criminal assaults, rapes. Tom, I and the women of the City of Dallas slept alot easier after Barry's arrest of the suspect in the early morning hours of Valenties Day, February 14, 1977. So thank you, Barry—Rest In Peace, brother. And yes, *you* were *our* Hero.

From his obituary:

Barry Madsen Whitfield passed away on August 6, 2023. He was born to Travis and Mary Joyce Whitfield on November 11, 1948. Barry was a beloved husband to Deborah Whitfield for 45 years. His memory will be cherished by all who knew him.

Barry was a dedicated and experienced Dallas police officer for 35 years. He served his community with honor and bravery, always putting the safety of others before his own. Barry's commitment to his job was unwavering, and he worked tirelessly to keep his city safe. Over the course of his career, Barry faced many challenges and dangers, but he never wavered in his determination to serve and protect. He will always be remembered as a true hero for his service to the Dallas Police Department.

He was always there for Andrea, Woody, Mike, Missy, Randy Smith, Terry McKnight, Tom Wafer, and Ronnie Hale. His loyalty knew no bounds, and he was a true friend to each and every one of them. Whether they needed a shoulder to cry on or just someone to talk to, he was always willing to lend an ear.

Barry is survived by his children, Barry W. and wife, Sara, Travis Whitfield and wife, Ivy; grandchildren, Nova, Travis and Victoria; sister in law: Nita Whitfield; his brother in law whom he considered a brother, Don Hafer and wife, Myra; and father-in-law, Don Hafer, Sr. He was preceded in death by his parents and brother, Jim Whitfield.

Note From The Author:

Thank you for being a reader of my novels, poetry and this True-Crime book. I hope that you found value in reading *One Step from Murder: The Friendly Burglar RAPIST* and that you'll consider leaving a review or rating on Amazon, Barnes & Nobel, Goodreads, or wherever you like to share information about books.

I invite you to peruse my website

robertjsadler.com

where you will find the **"FBR" tab**
with **documents, charts, photos and commentary**.

About The Author:

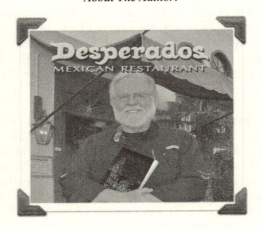

(Author in front of his favorite Mexican restaurant
holding one of his novels)
Photo by: Bill Crump - Bill Crump Photography

Robert J. Sadler: Private Investigator, Security Consultant, Vietnam Veteran, former Dallas Cop—is the author of the amazing True-Crime story of the FBR and a riveting series of novels chronicling the life and investigations of Michael Grant: Ex Dallas Police Homicide Lieutenant, Private Investigator and sometime government spook.

As a Private Investigator and Security Consultant, Robert has worked with a diverse group of clients including attorneys, individuals, and mom-and-pop businesses as well as multinational corporations and government agencies.

As a novelist, Robert is currently working on book 28 in his series of novels subtitled "*from the Black Book Investigations of Michael Grant & Associates.*" His latest novel is *Innocent*

Afternoon (#27).   Next in the series: *Hearts On A Crocheted Doily is* due out in fall of 2023.

As a poet, Robert has penned over 4300 poems. He has four large volumes of poetry: *Poetic License #4121964 Opus I, Opus II, Opus III, Opus IV & Opus V.* Each of the volumes contain 900 to 1000 poems. His award-winning poetry has been published regionally and internationally.

As an artist and photographer Robert has shown and sold his work in a variety of locales. He currently has some 1000 images available for viewing and purchase through FineArtAmerica.com as well as through his website robertjsadler.com.

Robert is a Rotary past-president and Paul Harris Fellow. He was once recognized in *D MAGAZINE* as one of Dallas' top-ten PIs.

Robert fulfilled his long-held goal to tell his and
Tom's real-life True-Crime story
about a Dallas serial rapist.

New York Times bestselling author of *Black Dahlia Avenger;*

Black Dahlia Avenger II; Most Evil; & Most Evil II
Steve Hodel, LAPD Det. III (ret.) says:

"Robert J. Sadler's book comes highly recommended. Sadler is a former Dallas Police Officer and veteran novelist of 28 (as of 2023) previously published mysteries.

**His True-Crime book
*One Step from Murder: the friendly burglar
RAPIST*
is a good one!"**

I hope there will only be one more update… when Marble is finally arrested for failure to register (for life) as a Sex Offender as required after his 1998 release!

As of 8.8.2023:
I have no update on Marble, born 2/25/1947.
He would now be 76, if he is still alive.

Also By Robert J Sadler

Next from the Black Book Investigations Series of
Michael Grant And Associates
LATIN FOR ELSEWHERE

Book #28 **Hearts On A Crocheted Doily**

Book #27 **Innocent Afternoon**

Book #26 **Clown of Karakoram**

Book #25 **Red Sky**

Book #24 **Cat With One White Socking**

Book #23. **Milk & Cookies**

Book #22 **No Expectation of Privacy**

Book #21 **The Pritzker Problem**

Book #20 **Penguins & Black Swans**

Book #19 **Almost Evening**

Book #18 **Ten Boxes**

Book #17 **No... It's raining**

Book #16 **Just before...**

Book #15 **Murder at Betty Sue's Café**

Book #14 **Baladine's... Alive?**

Book #13 **The Good Alibi**

Book #12 **The Bad Alibi**

Book #11 **We Were Once Knights**

Book #10 **Buttermilk Skies**

Book #9   **Thirty Seconds From Midnight**

Book #8   **The Sun Never Sets**

Book #7   **BOXMAN**

Book #6   **The Murder Fever**

Book #5   **Cry... Walk, Run!**

Book #4   **Innocent And Guilty**

Book #3   **And... Never Again**

Book #2   **Judas Oracle**

Book #1   **Jamaica Moon**

Short Stories

Flying Car Angst
Cold Coffee
Rare Books Rare Blood
The End
Dallas
On The Road To RedVille
The Moon & The Magpie Fairy - Tale Part 1
The Moon & The Magpie Fairy - Tale Part 2
Sea Sick? Not Me!
GG64
Why The Caged Rabbit Runs
A Roll In The Clover
Beenie Weenies
Empty Carton
The Podiatrist's Assistant
Homicide Hooligans
DarkSpeed
39 Circles
The Butterfly Affect

True Crime

One Step from Murder:
The Friendly Burglar RAPIST

Poetry

Poetic License #4121964 Opus I
Poetic License #4121964 Opus II
Poetic License #4121964 Opus III
Poetic License #4121964 Opus IV
Poetic License #4121964 Opus V

Visit the Author's Website:
robertjsadler.com

Made in the USA
Coppell, TX
03 May 2025

48958888R00350